YOGINI'S STILETTOS

The Book of Life

Stutee Bhandari Raj

BALBOA.PRESS

A DIVISION OF HAY HOUSE

Balboa Press books may be ordered through booksellers or by contacting:

Balboa Press
A Division of Hay House
1663 Liberty Drive
Bloomington, IN 47403
www.balboapress.com
844-682-1282

Because of the dynamic nature of the Internet, any web addresses or links contained in this book may have changed since publication and may no longer be valid. The views expressed in this work are solely those of the author and do not necessarily reflect the views of the publisher, and the publisher hereby disclaims any responsibility for them.

The author of this book does not dispense medical advice or prescribe the use of any technique as a form of treatment for physical, emotional, or medical problems without the advice of a physician, either directly or indirectly. The intent of the author is only to offer information of a general nature to help you in your quest for emotional and spiritual well-being. In the event you use any of the information in this book for yourself, which is your constitutional right, the author and the publisher assume no responsibility for your actions.

Any people depicted in stock imagery provided by Getty Images are models, and such images are being used for illustrative purposes only. Certain stock imagery © Getty Images.

Print information available on the last page.

ISBN: 978-1-9822-6424-6 (sc)
ISBN: 978-1-9822-6426-0 (hc)
ISBN: 978-1-9822-6425-3 (e)

Library of Congress Control Number: 2021903295

Balboa Press rev. date: 04/20/2021

CONTENTS

PREFACE

This book of life called Yogini's Stilettos is written by Shree Stutee- a philosopher, an *Arhatic*[1] Yogi, and a certified bioenergy healer who practices a no-touch healing therapy called *Pranic Healing*. From a very young age, she was fascinated by mysticism and transcendental knowledge. She has acquired various *Siddhis*[2] over the years through intensive travel and spiritual studies in search of the truth. This book will benefit anyone from any walk of life. It will help the seekers get their answers. It also gives practical self-healing tips for the sick to get healed. It is a guide for personal evolvement, awareness, and fulfillment.

In her own words "My religion is sincere kindliness. I hear the voice of truth all the time. I am in perennial bliss. Time has now come for me to stop hiding like a tortoise in its shell and to come out and plant a collective seed of true bliss and purity to alleviate suffering. I am here to empower you, to remove the darkness with profound protocols using light, love, and power. I am here to share the illuminating light little by little in a manner that is practical, safe, and exhilarating. Love just happens, similarly, I was simply drawn to the sacred wisdom of the inner world. Here, I am sharing what I learned."

This book is a short compilation of a few of the divinely spiritual lessons and my inner dialogue with the Masters. I have learned along the way. Writing this book has helped me take a trip into my past and share with you the life lessons I learned through my experiences. The story of my life cannot be told too fast, too slow, neither can it move forward or backward. This story is timeless. I have also added bits of knowledge I gathered from other sources for a better understanding of my version of love and life.

---

[1] *Arhatic - literally means he who is worthy of praise/ synthesis of all higher yogas*
[2] *Siddhis - spiritual advancement*

When you are on a break, you feel and look more dynamic. So take a break and enjoy this quick pick-me-up and a truly inspirational book with an open mind and heart.

If you are eager to learn the deeper truths then read this book, with your astral sponge, to soak the imparted knowledge. Reading this book is a good start to initiate the shift in your consciousness making you more loving, open, and forgiving. The purpose of this book is to lift your mood to be more positive, joyful, and peaceful. The subtle power of words in each chapter with the intended message lightly activates your energy points. As you read the chapters, the mental shift in vibration allows a balanced flow of energy into your body and aura.

The end goal is to help you reach your full potential and become a more balanced and intuitive person through renewed love, clarity, and faith in yourself. The contents are provided to help you achieve freedom from certain misconceptions.

We all are healers in a way. This book, therefore, is not only for healers but also for doctors, teachers, parents, students, bankers, engineers, business people, chefs, or any profession you may belong to.

This book is for those who have been wondering "What is happening all around?" Also for all those who have yet not asked that question but are waiting for answers nonetheless.

I have subtly experienced the profound combination of the two spiritual and worldly by witnessing my actions both inwardly and outwardly. I now believe that intention, creation, action, and recreation can happen simultaneously without any distraction through our collective will-center.

I am not trying to teach you here, you are your teacher. I am a true healer friend. Those who cannot identify with the silent meditations can listen to my guided ones. Those who don't identify themselves with the healings can dive into the depth of my words through this sacred book which will be your guiding light.

With the shift in world consciousness in 2020, every time I checked my mail, it was filled with the latest designer masks shared by my friends. Seeing the futility in the messages, I followed the cue universe gave me and silenced my speech. This book is a love child of my romance with this year-long silence. It is my creative attempt to clear the air as I was divinely and spiritually guided to unveil certain mystic visions to renew, refresh, and revive everything around. It is without layers of false modesty or fake humility that comes with the outside noise of fear we hear.

ACKNOWLEDGEMENTS

I am honored to meet you.

I invoke the Supreme Lord, higher beings, gurus, and teachers in full reverence. I am grateful for their divine guidance, help, and protection. I am indebted to them for treating me as a worthy conduit and keeping the faith in me to share the message of love and light with all. My name means glorification of Lord, so being true to my name, this book is about praising and thanking the pure divine energies for cosmically delivering us here and endowing us with the great magical miracles that are within us.

With immense reverence and honor towards my motherland, India, the land of Maha Avatar Babaji, Neem Karoli Baba, Lord Rama, Krishna, and the hundred and eight *gopis* for genetically endowing me with spiritual richness, power of devotion, and mysticism to enable me to join the team of potent wonder-workers.

With immense gratitude, respect, and love to the Supreme Lord God for guiding me into the righteous path with bright white light. These transitional and transformational times led me to take a deep breath and solidify my loyalties towards my spiritual father Maha Atma Choa Kok Sui whose spiritual Guru is Lord Padmasambhava. I sincerely value and thank him for energetically always being there with me through thick and thin gracing me with AY (Arhatic Yoga) knowledge. This helped me get centered, uncover, embrace, and bring out the inner beauty within myself. Most importantly his profound teachings taught me to harness my innate healing power, and continuously progress through ideologies set by him. Master Choa systematized and synthesized the ancient Indian teachings of Pranic Healing to suit the needs of today's modern, globalized society.

I have had so many precious teachers, except for a few, I cannot remember their names. Every person I have connected with within the last forty-one years has been my teacher. Thank you to them all. With all my heart and soul - I thank my parents Seema and Raman Bhandari for giving *Saar* or essence to my life. But for them, I wouldn't have been here. I thank my chef sister, Aakritee, who inspired me to harness the talent of how not to cook. I would like to especially thank my pillar of support my husband, Samrat, who learned to cook so that I could write.

In the Ferris wheel of life, between the cycle of inspiration and exhalation – I am truly blessed and grateful that we have connected through my writings. I would like to thank you for being who you are. *Namostutee*[3] to all. I salute and praise the divinity within all. I am the divine messenger of Lord God. This book is dedicated to my son, Aarav, the seed that was born in India and became a strong tree in the Middle East, filled with life energies, he is now flowering in the West. I am finally done with being a book in the hiding and so out I come, read me for I am finally home. I know this is my home because I willed it so.

---

[3] *Namaste or Namostutee is a way to greet people in India. Namostutee is done along with a gesture of a slight bow with hands pressed together, palms touching, fingers pointing upwards and thumbs close to the chest. It is usually meant to focus your attention to revere the chakras that point towards the heavens above.*

CHAPTER 1

DILIGO ERGO SUM
(I Love Therefore I Am)

Truth is not in words, but in the understanding of the heart and contemplating before acting.

Using the letters that make up the word H-E-A-R-T, we get the word E-A-R-T-H. In the middle of the word is E-A-R that is telling us to hear our inward voice before we go out to explore the air of the outward space. Clairaudience tells me that the only way out of F-E-A-R is to listen to the voices through our inner E-A-R rather than get distracted by the outside voices we H-E-A-R.

It is only when you have self-love and love for yourself that you can love another. Before transforming the world, first, transform yourself. Feel the love within you then your presence will effortlessly bring divine peace and uplift those who connect with you.

Stay protected by first nurturing and believing in yourself. True progress happens when you strive to constantly improve yourself and become a better person than you already are. Your competitor, judge, and greatest comfort is you. When you are comfortable with yourself, you are comfortable with your actions, and then and only then you are comfortable being around another.

> We live to give.
> We love to give.
> We give to live.
> We give to love.
> We love to live. It is simple logic.

So stop regretting and make amends now before it is too late. Self-guilt is more crippling than making others feel guilty. It is our job to make ourselves and also others feel good.

As we become more self-aware, we begin to become more compassionate, empathic, harmonious, and complete within, without, and with ourselves. This romance with ourselves can be described as *Diligo Ergo Sum*. Everything you need is already within you. You just need to accept yourself.

Do things that make you happy, not only that which makes others happy. This is where true happiness lies. Your heart lies between the lower and the higher, between the primordial and the spiritual, in the middle of it all. Just keep the balance.

My physical heart is in my west but my spiritual heart is in my east. Everything that is left of my heart is because of what is right about it. Be assertive and move forward in perfect balance with your right foot out and left arm raised high.

"Let me now enlighten you," said the indestructible life force. "You are destined to become who you are. You are that rare pearl within the white shell. With the mercy and blessings of pure light[4], which is your un-manifested compassionate thought; tenacity and severe intensity of kindled flame[5] which is the cause of your manifested outer form and the green healing hummingbird throated[6] actively shining in the center of the womb. Just make sure the indigos[7] are well activated so that you become aware of your spiritual existence. I am the indestructible life force, telling you what you are destined to be. I know this because you came from within my astral body. I am the goose from whose egg you were hatched. I am the knower of all and the co-creator of your past, present, and future. I am the eternal space, and so what I am saying is true-blue. I am here to bring you back to the magical golden egg from which you were hatched."

Oh, I am sure there are three main reasons we become magnetized towards this continuous cycle of birth and rebirth, in the same form or a

---

[4] *Pure light, in Vedic philosophy implies sattva. It is connected to the element of water and Air. It is the balancing point between body and spirit through knowledge, wisdom and constant communication. It has feminine energy.*

[5] *Kindled flame denotes fire and air. It is an expanding force which ignites the spirit through inner ambition and passions. It has masculine Rajasik energy.*

[6] *Throated represents the opening of heart and mind.*

[7] *Indigos represents the development of deeper insight*

different one. These reasons are love, grace, and unresolved issues. Freedom from misery is in loving yourself and others for who and what you and they are. No change is ever possible unless there is complete acceptance.

Our ancestors lived in love, light, and power before there were schools, languages, virtual schools, computer languages, reality, and virtual reality. So to get connected and feel balanced within yourself, reconnect with your roots. If you have light and love, you will naturally have power and balance.

Consider this: if you use clay to make two toys, while the outward appearance of both might be different, inherently they would be the same, as they are made of the same clay.

There is no separation, division, delusion, or duality, as we all are one and come from the same source. This is to help you realize that what matters is love, and love is all.

Finding the "it" factor is a hit and miss affair, but when has that ever stopped anyone from trying to find it?

Real love is the realization that you are unique and no one but you can complete you. In India, power is known as *Shakti,* and balance is known as *Shiva. Shiva-Shakti*[8] in you is important to make progress in life. No one can equal or exceed the love that a divine couple bears.

Forgetting love is like trying to smother the infant before it can learn to crawl. It is a futile effort because love cannot be strangled. It always finds its way out with, within, or without a form. Neither struggles nor hardships nor the threat of death could stop Romeo and Juliet or *Heer and Ranjha* from reaching out to their love. Such is the strength of divine love.

Everyone chooses an easy life. True winners are those who choose the difficult path and somehow come out of their sufferings to finally mingle with their true love. Without love, life and its memories slip away from our minds like sand out of your fist.

There is one thing that is beyond the five elements[9]. It is insoluble in water. It always is and always will be. It is the ultimate truth. Meeting it, you become one. You exist. Without it, you are nothing, but without you, it has no power. Knowing it, you know supreme love.

In Latin, *Caritas* means selfless and compassionate love. You know love, but you are not yet *Caritas.* You are close to attaining it. *Caritas* is in you, around you, and in everything. It is the cause of all causes. It is the

---

[8] *Shiva-Shakti represents divine feminine energy combined with masculine energy*
[9] *Five elements are earth, water, fire, air and ether or akasha*

eye of the sea, and also your center. It is the ultimate truth. It contains the blueprint of the entire cosmos. As I hold it in my hand today, I feel the vibrations of our coming future. Let us all welcome it with pride, gratitude, and positivity. *Om mane padme hum[10]*.

Those who love are in perennial bliss and know their *Ohm*[11] worth. Those who love heighten the universal consciousness through their pure vibrations. They are our greatest blessings and they are here to selflessly protect us. I am in perennial bliss because I love and God taught me how to love. And so I am forever in immense gratitude, reverence, and committed to the higher power.

Everything is love. Everything that exists is because of love. To think is to love. You are because you love. Every creation comes from love. To be human is to love. Every mother knows what it is to love unconditionally. Our mothers are here to remind us to always love. Be in love with love.

Scientists have made some eggs-ceptional discoveries. For example, one sea urchin can produce millions of eggs in one go. Similarly, One God produces many of us and then we continue to multiply to millions. The source is One, we all have the essence of the source within us, and the essence is love. The entire creation comes from love. Love is all and all is love.

Every creator requires a romantic connection and some sort of inspiration to create. To attract this energy of love, we must increase our charm. Our virtues and strength of character are our charms. A virtuous person is a beautiful person.

To access it, that is love, remember love underlines the entire universe. It is wise to love all because without love we are nothing. Love is the main quality of the higher soul. If you are truly in love, you will find romance, whenever and wherever you look.

Everything that is ever created has a definite purpose. The mountains, waterfalls, rivers, trees, lakes, oceans, and plains all are bonded by a force called love. Every element has a temperament that tends to fluctuate between hot or cold. The temperature of one entity affects the other entity or individual and as the chain goes on, it affects the entire globe. The

---

[10] *Om mane padme hum is a Buddhist chant that represents spirit of enlightenment*
[11] *Ohm is the primal sound of all creation and a unite of electrical resistance*

Supreme Being, the five elements, and the energies of all four directions[12] are forever working to help us all keep a proper balance.

Then you reach a point in life where hands or hospitals are no longer needed, just your presence heals you and the people world over. That point is *Diligo Ergo Sum*. As we circulate our loving energy holistically, the entire universe leads a far healthier life filled with love, love for all.

Our world is all about love and freedom. There is no hell, evil, or trauma except the one we create within ourselves to control one another. I know this divine truth because I am a messenger of God and a bridge between the high and the low, the spirit, and the matter.

Humanity has become over-attached to bodily possessions and material things. We are more than our bodies and the materials we use. As long as you have a reason and a purpose to live on, your life will go on. As long as you love something, you will continue living. However, sometimes, if you truly love something, you have to let it go.

People used to get sick because of a lack of resources. Now they get sick because of the excess and congestion of resources. It is love that brings balance to this cycle of inhalation and exhalation.

A highly charged and happy mood is what keeps you, your cells, and your nerves joyful. Recalling past trauma causes your brain to transmit messages of lower vibrations to the rest of your body, thereby lowering your hormones and mood over time.

Some people talk about their unpleasant past and how they overcame tragedy to excite and motivate people. You should do this only if you have a completely detached attitude towards the incident, otherwise, it can trigger certain neurons that affect the genetic wiring of your system. This will eventually cause bodily harm. I came across a motivational speaker who motivates people by sharing her own painful experiences, and in the process, she could never detach herself from her past. Eventually, it started harming her. Although her intention was good, to display outward strength we must first work on becoming inwardly strong.

The way most of us respond is through feelings and if you are highly attuned to them, you become overly sensitive. This brings about a spiral downward shift in your thoughts and emotions. To uplift yourself, forgive, and forget.

The tree might have different branches some are higher and some are

---

[12] *Four directions is NEWS which is north, east, west, and south direction.*

lower. Each will have many leaves, bear fruit and flowers, and birds will make their nests in it, but in essence, all of this rests on the same root.

Take the example of the blossoms of the tree. They may be present in one place but their fragrance is all-pervasive, even beyond where they physically exist. The essence of their fragrance can spread to your village, your country, the entire world, and even beyond space. Additionally, a seed is one, but it gives birth to a cycle that then produces many trees, many seeds, and then many more trees.

If your soul sprinkles seeds of care and love wherever you go, you will harvest a tree filled with like qualities.

The melodious vibrational sound of the birds singing might reach outer space and beyond, yet we all belong to the one root. We all came from the one; we all are one. That root is the cause and the root of the evolution of humanity. Stay rooted, stay connected, keep sharing, and keep loving. I love therefore I am. I am love.

Knower and known, visible and invisible, word and thought, attachment and aversion, dark and light, high and low, lack and abundance are all two sides of the same coin.

True purity lies in selfless service with complete non-doer-ship[13] just like the generous Mother Earth. In this time of transition, the Lord God is sitting right next to you, disguised in many different forms, to uplift those who are ready. So be truly considerate, gentle, and compassionate in your words, actions, and deeds, to yourself and one and all.

To be able to understand another person's perspective is no miracle. All it requires is a genuine listening heart, which is the core of communication. Even animals can easily display such miracles.

Being tenderhearted towards another person is our innate capability. Then, why has it become so difficult for some people to understand, to be tolerant, and to wish for other people to be happy, wholesome, and motivated? Maybe it is time to move beyond our self-inflicted distress by being more altruistic rather than being egotistical.

In benefiting me, you benefit yourself. In hurting me, you hurt yourself. To be opinionated is an illusion. How can you have an opinion

---

[13] *Non doer-ship refers to someone who does an action without being attached to the fruit of their action. In this way, the non-doer becomes both a participant and a witness of their own action.*

or conclusion on anything or anyone when the crux and essence of every entity is constant change and evolvement?

The *I am* is neither on the left nor on the right. It is in the center of my heart. As the pages of life open, your heart too opens. The light of your heart will dispel the darkness and you will meet with love. Love is the divine source that heals you of all bodily and mental pains. You do not have to go too far in search of love. The whole world is contained within you. When you know yourself, you know love. As you continue to forgive, cleanse yourself and others inside out, the self within you gets completely and perfectly purified. The self is the sixth element. To love the self is to altruistically love another.

An entity may transform and transmute into something else. For example, when you form a judgment about something or someone, your judgment may change once you attain a different level of understanding. You therefore can never rest your case. Truth has many levels. Your current reality, whatever level it may be, is not the end, but the beginning of unraveling a puzzle. Even when you think you are going down the spiral, you are going up the learning curve. You have taken a step forward, though it may seem like you are going backward. Every experience, whether painful or pleasurable, every mistake, now or later, eventually teaches you something. Everything gets imprinted in your DNA, in the making of you and who you currently are.

When you make a mistake, you are left with two options. In the first option, you can go to sleep, putting it out of your mind, and never thinking about what happened. Or you can remember it and resolve to learn from it so that you never repeat it. Most likely, if you choose the former, the experience will come back to you in your dreams, or you will come face to face with it in your reality until you make amends.

We all are connected by a common thread, this strong thread is love. Family, friends, and strangers are just names we give. Inherently we all are one. We collectively are love. It takes courage to love. Freedom can only come with collective love-filled consciousness.

The love you have is meant to fall like fairy dust upon all. The magic wand is with you, it is rested in your very being, just sprinkle it quickly. When you communicate with your love through your higher self, the love on earth is the same as the love in heaven.

Serve and give others as much love, time, value, and worth as you give to yourself. The light within you is of no use until the light is ignited within all.

Each alphabet has a number and meaning assigned to it. By adding the alphabets of love-you get the number 21. To know true love, we have to move above and beyond our habits. As per psychologists, 21 days is all it takes to practice the removal of old patterns and habits. You may take 21 days, 21 months, or 21 years-the choice is completely yours!

L = 3-life or vitality field radiated outwards by all living beings

O = 7-higher creative mind field of the universal creator

V = 6-vibrations of thoughts and energy

E = 5-energy meridians in the human and universal energy field

It can be easily observed that the alphabetical letters A, I, Q, J, Y, all have the numerical value of 1, the letters B, K, R, the numerical value of 2, the letters S, C, G, L the numerical value of 3, and so on right up to the numerical value of 8. There is no numerical value of more than 8.

All of us are connected with the force of love. The traditions and rituals we follow help us know what habits are right and it is through following them righteously that we know what love is.

Affirm- 'Namostutee, I love myself and all those around me. *Diligo ergo sum*. I love therefore I am. I am love. Tathaastu[14].'

---

[14] *Tathaastu-is another word for 'so be it'*

CHAPTER 2

EVOL-VE-LOVE[15]

The word evolve is purposely broken into three parts '*Evol-Ve-Love*'. There are three kinds of work done by three types of beings on earth. These three kinds of work are- divine, angelic, or evil. Each is doing their work to evolve. The evil work is evol, the angelic work is light and the divine work is love.

The palindrome of evil is live - time to reverse evil and live.

To evolve is to live

To live is to love

To love is to evolve

Try to learn, practice, grow, and evolve, for only you can. The process of cleansing, re-energizing, and rebirthing within the same body is replaced these days with fancier technical words like reboot, reload, and restart, but the ultimate objective remains the same: to continue, purify, and stay connected to evolve.

Whoever sits on top of the pyramid becomes our mystic leader, but each of us is bound to get our turn. No one is left out; everyone who has signed up must join in at one point or another. Once you have taken a seat on the Ferris wheel of life, however much you may screech, clench, enjoy or cry, you have to swing with it no matter its speed or direction.

We embody twenty-two main energy points[16], which are activated by the

[15] *EVOL-VE-LOVE between Love and its palindrome Evol is've'. Evol is another word for evil. And 've' is a reminder that we've been there. Transcend evol and meet with love.*

[16] *These vital points are divided in 3 parts (7x3=21), these radiate so that you can activate vital aim of each. The last 3 points mentioned here help re-connect us:*

four elements: air, water, fire, and earth. With the help of the fifth –ether- we go on reproducing into many more energy points. Everything is ultimately prone to perishing, except for the fifth element: your etheric energy. This is the cause of all causes; because its nature is to continually exist, it is never annihilated, but transmuted and evolves. As long as it exists, we exist; therefore we never die.

No mystery can ever be permanently solved because I am[17] that permanent transmutable mystery. I am the yin within your yang, the female within the man, and the male within the woman. I am pure energy and life force. I am akin to the primitive *Gopika*[18] and also the *Dakini*[19]. I am that simple, single, and immanent reality of the trinity. I am you and you all are me. I am the way to true bliss.

Misplaced vanity deprives us of humility.

---

1. Sthir is enjoy the flight with unflappable wings 2. Sthapana let it all pass at gentle moderate speed 3. Junoon is purposeful action is enriching 4. Jaya is true victory is in sharing 5. Karm is witness all actions peacefully and remain single pointed 6. Dharm is self-sufficiency by practicing patience and constant compassion 7. Patra is pure speech transforms knowledge into joy 8. Aar is acknowledge and dissolve into the mercy of supreme source 9. Surya is super vision such that movement brings auspiciousness 10. Taaj is trinity of universal soul protector, maintain equilibrium romantically 11. Mo is use of opportunities to achieve full potential 12. Hast is equal work opportunities and wealth based on disposition 13. Chatra is stretch and move to learn better 14. Upkaksha is open precious vault and be unconditionally devoted to divine cause 15. Udara is praise the active energy that magnanimously brings vitality 16. Hanu is relaxed thinking and calmness 17. Kati is stability and self-accountability to carry responsibilities of sacred fire fearlessly 18. Tej is sincerely praise the glory of core power 19. Janu is clean and empty as a flute 20. Samajh is pure wisdom gives more meaning to your existence 21. Kanth is self-supporting grace of clear brilliant light 22. Hridya is self-sufficient, bright, perfect, honest, forgiving, cheerful 23. Utpada is productivity, settle within yourself through modesty and humility 24. Kanda is gain great name, profit, virtue through fulfilling personal commitment. This is a modified version of chakras inspired by Pranic Healing.

[17] *I am implies divine Stutee - higher soul*

[18] *Gopika is a Sanskrit word that refers to cow-herd girl, lover and friend of Krishna. She protects the herd of Krishna's devotees during each of his incarnations.*

[19] *Dakini are Indo-aryan. In Tibetan language, Dakini means the clear minded sky dancer- she who dances through space. She is a messenger of spaciousness and a force of truth. She appears during transitions: moments between worlds, between life and death, in visions between sleep and waking.*

Misplaced humility deprives us of modesty.

Misplaced modesty deprives us of accepting the importance of our role as an important part of humanity.

The activation of twenty-two chakras is like hearing the primordial sound of the twenty-two *Shrutis*[20] through the grace of the divine. When all twenty-two chakras are fully activated, we are full of wonder. We experience the essence of our consciousness, and our beauty reflects in our spiritual and moral conduct.

Every cloud has a silver lining. There is something beautiful even in the worst of situations. Remember only real love has the potential to bring everyone closer. So let us all love and help as many people as we can to evolve. Share the energy of this book to enlighten many more beings into becoming complete so that each one is able and equipped to deal with the prevailing or any other situation.

Touch, connect, and breathe in the emotion of love. Heighten your intuition and be in tune with the changes of the evolutionary process. Acknowledge the fact that we are beyond the physical. Love and positivity keep our energy and vibration growing. Hate and negativity sap our energy.

Children are our leaders. Give them love, give them the truth. Finally, with ongoing world changes, we can give more attention and energy to our children, families, and neighbors. Each person is special and unique and each one needs to feel accepted, valued, and important. When your vibrational frequency increases, you may seem invisible to those who are lower in frequency but you are visible to those occupying the same energy field as you. Doors will magically open that have long been closed. Codes will get decoded, hidden truth will get unveiled. We will be able to transcend water, air, and fire within the same bodily form. Let us blaze our path and connect to the heightened energy.

This life is mysterious. Many incidents happen to you or you are thrown into situations so that you remain resilient, observe your thoughts, and evolve into better beings.

In healing yourself, you heal the world. Whoever you are, so concerned about, subtly catch those energies and eventually follow your path after correct meditation, validation and practice.

You cannot control how long it will take or who will evolve first because each person evolves based on their karma, urge, effort, receptivity,

---

[20] *Shruthis – the supreme authority and revelation for those who seek knowledge*

experiences, habits, and grace. Therefore it is best to stay detached towards the fruit of your actions and simply do what you are meant to do with one-pointedness and complete faith.

The rich are rich because they have earned it. Whether they are rich in mind, body, soul, or material procession. I am referring to richness broadly based on the subjective effort and inclination of these people towards sports, spirituality, gold, wisdom, art so on and so forth. If you start the world all over again and take away all this richness from each person you will go back right from where you started all over again because they have conditioned themselves to evolve and flourish in the field they have chosen and nothing can stop them anymore. Their inner fire is aligned with the divine spark within them and that fuels them to bring all the riches they deserve and strive for bringing it all back to themselves. That is true unstoppable progress. It is never stagnated or unwholesome.

I am the beginning-less beginner and the endless end of this beginning-less endlessness. There is no beginning and no end.

Every new day is a chance for you to do something even better than you did yesterday. Every new thing that you do better than you did yesterday, becomes the reason for you to make your tomorrow even better and so let the reason always remain. Each day you must strive hard to create an upgraded, better version of yourself.

We call an empty home–devoid of energy or space. When we fill our home with things, it is no longer an empty space. We define the space that we occupy based on the material objects we see and possess. If there is nothing to be seen or bought, we will have no possessions. The entire world will then become empty. We call that emptiness – 'space'. Our mind keeps wanting to fill our idea of that empty space with objects because we believe that empty space is a vacuum. Objects we cannot relate to are empty. Whatever objects we keep on bringing into our home have life under our association with them. We give names to those objects to justify our meaning. The size of the things we see, the distance we believe we can travel, time as we know it, and the space we occupy, are all there based on our subjective perception. Each individual has a different facet of understanding. Since we usually go by precepts already set or by what the majority believes, we don't let the collective viewpoint come forward, and so we never get the whole picture.

The divine message I am here to share is that nothing can touch those who are internally free, dauntless, and courageous. We must strive to be like the fire that remains unaffected and unattached to these three forces - hate, love, and fear - to evolve. Fire, in a steady flame, does not become evil or burn under influence of excessive pride, nor does it become judgmental under influence of excessive light, it neither becomes over-emotional due to excessive vindictiveness or thoughtless actions of those who are still learning to love.

The same unending cycle of life, love, creation, destruction, birth, death, and rebirth goes on even in the smallest drop of dew that falls upon a leaf in your yard. When children look through the lens of the microscope, they can discover the scope of life in every minute thing, and the sequential order in each of its detailed aspects. What we call imagination is their way of explaining expanded reality to us. Even a speck of dust has life inherent in it, much the way you do. Whatever speck of dust is in your home is not up to you, because it is invisible to you. And so you never give it value or attention. Only when we turn our magnifying lens towards it do we know it is there. There will always remain something you can turn your inward vision to, to know, and learn more.

The moment you connect with your center - the soul center - where your divine spark exists - you meet with the eternal truth that whatever you can think, you can perceive. Whatever you can perceive, you can create and recreate. Our world of repetition exists within the space and time of our associations and dissociation with objects and their reality as we know it. Beyond this rigidity, exists the limitlessness that is within you. It is natural for the form to transform, grow, and evolve in a sequential order based on their energy.

Whether you grow inward because of outward circumstances, or you grow outward because of your inward predisposition, you are still growing. Being calmly active or being actively calm are inherently the same. Why not be both? Every form is continuously changing, and so is ours. We always have been and we always will be. Only our forms change.

Transition towards perfection. There is no better feeling than to be awake with eyes open. Being awake with eyes closed is easy.

Silence is only in the words. The universe has been talking all through. It constantly sends messages to our wonderland called earth. Those who can see the light, open themselves up to the transitional inner changes, with renewed enthusiasm and optimism, to usher universal evolution.

We are at a spectacular point of evolution where pure yin energy is helping us transition from animal mental nature into divine mankind.

Through the use of our faculties of creative wisdom, we can create our reality.

During the Lemurian age, we concentrated on building our physical and etheric bodies. During the Atlantean age, we concentrated on building our emotional and astral bodies. During the Aquarian age, we are now concentrating on building our mental and spiritual bodies. Each stage is one step towards evolvement and progress. Each stage enhances our innate power to love.

Affirm- 'Namostutee, I revere and see the best in people and I always see the bright side in life. Tathaastu.'

CHAPTER 3

SLINKY[21]

Align your soul purpose with what you do.

This chapter helps you set your intention and deeper commitment to transform and lift your energy up and down like a Slinky toy through deep wisdom, healing, and acceptance. This way you will bring more happiness, health, and harmony, with childlike wonder, into your body, heart, and mind.

Holy is a Hindu festival that is celebrated to spread happiness, love, and joy amongst people whose skin and auras are of different colors and hues. It tells us that it is always spring with its freshness somewhere within the consciousness of a spring-full, positive person waiting to bloom bountifully and enjoy the colors of life. We are like a Slinky toy that gracefully springs back into its original state.

The one whose fire is lit within knows and does no evil, for he works as per the law. All his actions are unbound and devoted to playfully enjoying the energetic Slinky game.

You are sitting on a living spring waiting to jump and bounce to get a glimpse of the beauty outside, through the cosmic window of your divine eye. Your thoughts, emotions, attitude, and body are continually changing with every moment and movement. The cells and atoms in your body are also moving, changing, and circulating because you are moving. Every movement brings joy. Every pause brings in the realization of that joy. As long as you are moving, you are experiencing joy. Pain is a result of a lack of movement. Every particle in your being is built to be perennially in motion,

---

[21] *Slinky means sleek, flexible and graceful movement.*

to be joyful. Stagnation is the cause of your misery. Shed all your phobias, anxiety, expectations, judgments, and guilt, and move on.

Action, inaction, and wrong action are all mere outward actions. The act of experiencing, experienced, and inexperienced, all are meant to lead us to innermost experience. All else is but an experiment.

The further I go from home my heart and my center, the closer and more connected I want to be. Like a spring, I keep spiraling and transitioning back and forth.

You are a collective of all years and all the incidents that take place. As you approach this book, you are taking a step back and cleaning your mind of all the incidents that have taken place. These are especially the ones that no longer serve you positively. In cleansing your mind, you have come a full circle. In connecting the dots and moving to the point of origination you become more creative and productive. Thank you for reconnecting with yourself and making yourself feel so special.

Hard-headed and a disheartened person is not open to change but only a fearless, open, flexible person can take the first step. Now that we have all come a full circle, from this point on, let's restart another spring-full journey. The springs attached to us are strong enough to go on and on.

Instead of suppressing or escaping our animalistic nature, we should start thanking and praising our divine selves even for the small positive steps that curb our animalistic nature. This is much like a Slinky toy that goes down steps contracting and springing to do so.

Everything we see presently is a result of what we did prior. The destruction, anxiety, depression, and panic that we are seeing in the world today is because of what we did yesterday. We can end this cycle of constant destruction and preserve the world by committing ourselves to do good and righteous deeds. This way our tomorrow will thank us for manifesting and creating a beautiful, harmonious, balanced world that emanates from freedom, love, and light.

My birthday on the 28th of May is usually on the 148th day of the year. Interestingly my birthday is on the 149th day which is May 29th during a leap year. We all get one extra day on a leap year and then retract by one day in a non-leap year. This is similar to the Slinky toy movement.

Each time you fall, you spring back to life like a slinky toy[22]. The

---

[22] *Slinky toy was a famous toy during my childhood. It is usually made of springy steel wire. This famous toy was invented by 'Richard James'.*

only ones who are not able to spring back are the ones who do not bother exercising the power of their self-will to live and spring back to the energies of love. It is always out there somewhere and it is what you hold onto. It just got lost in the waves of the ocean but love will come back to you when the time is right and when you are ready.

Affirm- 'Namostutee, I spring back gracefully like a Slinky toy - back into action with perfection, love, and a sense of purpose. Tathaastu.'

CHAPTER 4

AWAKEN AFTER THE DEEP SLEEP

Marriage and commitment are acts of faith. If you sense betrayal, remember that just because one instrument breaks, not all music stops. Life will give you what you are willing to settle for, but before you settle on anything, remember that what got us here won't get us there.

I told my husband, "The reason you and I do not see the same color is that we both are made of a different hue. The human eye can distinguish ten million different colors. What is blue might seem red to another based on perspective and subjective conscious experience through the individual's state of mind." Most of us do not experience things in their entirety because of our belief systems and experiences. Thus we are not able to see the redness in the blue sky.

Things are never as they seem. One person associates wine with headache and the other associates it with pleasure, and in the process what seems to us, based on our association or dis-associations, the actual grape of the matter goes out of the window.

But then you say, I have been wearing mint-blue colored lenses in the eyes of my coral body, and so I do not see what you see. As absurd as it may sound, what I see is not what everyone claims to see, then it is not what I see, but what you see through your dark-tinted lenses that becomes the truth!

Absolute truth is a utopian concept for what is real to me, seems like a dream to you. What seems normal to me is abnormal to another. But who set those standards? Decisions made in the half-sleepy, half-zombie state of your slumber party are all intoxicated with the taste of last night's wine.

The standards you have set need a suitable aspirin to remove the hangover you are hanging to.

I write because the silence of my external yang voice stops me from communicating my internal yin thoughts. Speaking out loud what I write makes this marriage between wife and husband, internal and external words so much more complete, equal, exhilarating, and true.

The first meaning of a 'Husband' is "the male partner in a marriage." Used as a verb, "to husband" means "to manage prudently and economically." For example: "We must husband and conserve our strength by using it sparingly." These definitions of "husband" aptly fit in to explain the meaning of our external voice, which comes out from deep within. In our marriage with ourselves, there is a husband within us which is our outer voice, and there is a wife which is the inner voice. Between the psychic and the physical lies the analysis and the synthesis of - female within the male and the male within the female.

Between the dark and the light lies the transmutation and transformation of-consciousness within the unconsciousness. There is a mystery behind your reality. There is pre-consciousness behind your sub-consciousness. There is chaos behind perfect order. There is light behind the dark and positive behind the negative. In this upward and downward seesaw of life, just play the childish game, to kindle the earthen lamp of your inner fire.

Without relationships nothing makes sense. Neither you nor any other person makes sense of life without a connection. It is the purpose of our existence. Nowadays, we think that we are defined only by the way the outside world expresses us. I think this is a bizarre way of thinking.

True confidence effortlessly comes through marrying yourself, and consistently staying committed to this divine marriage. The realization and acknowledgment that both aspects of your personality-the visible and invisible, outer and inner, conscious and subconscious, dream and reality-are all one wholesome reality that goes into creating you. All marriages are made in heaven and have a divine purpose. The same divine purpose that causes two elements to meet, to create heaven on earth, is the one responsible for couples to marry.

Delta waves are the slowest recorded brain waves in human beings. They are found most often in infants and young children. Adequate production of delta waves helps us feel completely rejuvenated and promotes the immune system, natural healing, restorative, and deep sleep. In the fairy tale, Sleeping Beauty, she was awakened after a hundred years by a kiss from the handsome prince. She was in a delta state and true intimacy revived her.

There is always a higher force whose purpose is to divinely decide the rightful groom for your beautiful daughter. Love is powerful and that power to find it is within you. Let it take as long as it takes. When you find true romance, it is like you just woke up.

From the realm of spirituality, divine love destroys the darkness from the inner core of your heart. Here you perceive that just as the perfume you spray merges with your body odor, Radha and Krishna are the same, the higher self and lower self are one.

Affirm- 'Namostutee, I am unconditionally blissful and patient. I am untouched by delusion and suffering. Tathaastu.'

CHAPTER 5

BEJEWELED IN A PRECIOUS CROWN

Ruby cannot scratch a sapphire. A sapphire cannot scratch a ruby. Two lovers are like ruby and sapphire. They may be wearing different hues of colors but when they come together, the two are so balanced that they sparkle like no other. The yang energy of the left brain completes the yin energy of the right brain. When the two meet, what they create is out of sheer love for wisdom. I know this because I am wearing one such bejeweled crown.

The idea of this chapter is to make you aware of the rhythmic ascending and descending flow of energy so that you cooperate and be in tune with it. Listen to the inner message to observe your body. Do not let the outer fluctuations bother you.

When you meet with your true love, all delusions break. It was not until 17th April 2019, when I not only felt but witnessed that I am not my body. I heard my inner voice asking me - "Do you hear me?"

I felt I became a male within a woman's body. In my trance, I entered the male public bathroom without realizing it. One man politely told me to leave the men's room. But until I saw my image in the mirror, I couldn't understand why everyone was looking at me with such surprise. I had become one with the image[23] only I could see. It was as if I underwent plastic surgery. At that moment, I forgot I was a woman. My spirit looked beyond

---

[23] *I repeatedly saw Maha Avatar Babaji's image each time I saw my reflection into the mirror. A pure soul reflects God's eternal light which is our quintessential truth.*

my outward gender. The outer voices became dim and the inner voice became crystal clear. I came out of the men's room, feeling so tall, as though I was enveloping the entire space. The entire building of the mall seemed little in front of my spiritual light body. The soul is not bound by gender or space. I had heard about it but until that day I had not experienced what it is like living in two places at once while being fully awake and aware of every moment. Everything around seemed so pure and sacred. I felt nurturing love and concern for all those around me. I could feel the energies of those far away as if they were one with me, sitting up close.

As we are evolving, we are no longer bound by specific nature or characteristics of being endowed with womanhood and manhood. We have mingled and so have our natures, virtues, and responsibilities. Rise for now is the time to turn and transition yourself, change your hood-from womanhood or manhood to Godhood.

Shiva and *Shakti,* Yin and Yang, Adam and Eve are all beautiful representations of duality within us. We have both heavenly and earthly qualities inside of us. Our divine self is the outward representation of the inner sacred marriage between our dualities (heavenly and earthly marriage).

These subtle and dense qualities are within and outside each one of us. The two could be high or low but just like the air we breathe, both energies are non-biased and not gender-specific. The way we attract life partners based on the environment and thoughts we resonate with, we attract the energies we reverberate.

Sometimes a pure virgin patiently waits not because there are not enough seekers but because she cannot find the right suitor. When the bride (to be) meets with the groom after eons, the intensity and revered nature of true love is unmistakable and comes with profound learnings.

In India, the Sati/ Suttee ceremony was a common historical Hindu practice where a widowed woman would sacrifice herself sitting upon the funeral pyre of the husband. The practice should not have been done physically and was grossly misunderstood.

Unscramble *Stutee* (*Goddess Durga's* ninth incarnation) and you get *Suttee* (way to the tenth incarnation of *Durga*[24]. Suttee is known as a pure and good wife in India. She ascends from the higher royal Kshatriya (elite warrior class) Hindu class and voluntarily self-sacrifices into the

---

[24] *Goddess or Ma Durga (giver of boons) is the regulated form of Ma Kaali*

holy pyre to safeguard the respect of her spiritual father (*Brahma*) and to honor her divine husband (*Shiva*) in life and death. *Suttee* is also known as *Goddess Sati* in certain parts of India. Various memorial stones are laid in admiration of her name, heavenly beauty, and soul.

In ode and in memory of all those women who resonate the energy of '*Goddess Durga*', stones were laid as the foundation of the village. These represent her energy, immense strength, devotion, and determination.

The burial ritual of the Goddess is a double burial ceremony or co-cremation of man and woman, divine husband and wife. During the Vedic age, this practice was only done symbolically and not actually. The purity of its inner meaning has been misinterpreted and lost over the years. The actual burning has no Vedic standing. It meant a woman of high moral strength who willfully learns through reflection, meditation, and deeper experience comes out alive and purified through the sacred fire. Wifehood is a life hood.

When your mini world is perfect, the outer falls in sync. When your marriage with yourself is in perfect harmony, the outer automatically adjusts to your tunes.

Affirm- 'Namostutee, I am endowed with qualities of unwavering patience, sincere devotion, generosity, compassion, friendliness, strong morals, and faith. Tathaastu.'

CHAPTER 5a

MARRIAGE IS A LESSON IN TRUTHFULNESS

Your eyes are a camera. From the lens of this camera, you view yourself through life, people, and its circumstances. Turn the camera inward, not outward, and see the beauty. Feel the love you have for yourself within you. Leave all bitterness - rise and fly. Congratulate yourself on your first honest screenplay, the one in which you are acting like yourself, speaking your truth, and feeling your feelings.

You marry yourself. *Shiva* is a yang and yin aspect and so does each human have feminine and masculine characteristics. True marriage is when one marries the two virtues feminine and masculine to become whole. This will bring in true commitment, consistency, transmutation, and motivation. The realization and acknowledgment of this fact, visible & invisible, outer & inner aspects of your personality, conscious & subconscious, dream & reality are all one wholesome reality that defines you. Every 'No' has a hidden 'Yes' and every 'Yes' has a hidden 'No'.

Your power of choice is what makes you - you. Carefully consider all options and choose well. Choose what you believe in. Stand up to your marriage in which you are your partner. It is when you marry with yourself that you can truly marry another with no inhibitions and dualities. To all the singles out there: the next time your old aunt asks you, "Aren't you going to marry?" Reply with an affirmative "Yes". If you are asked, "With whom?" Your reply should be, "To myself." It sounds bizarre but true creativity begins with the blissful marriage between your inner thoughts and your outer worlds, as well as treating the two as equal partners.

If others don't give you priority, then you do. If others don't know your worth, then you should remember your self-worth always. When you value yourself, others will value you.

With most people, it has become a habitual pattern to seek love outside of themselves to fill the emptiness they feel within their hearts. No one can fill that emptiness for you. Ultimate love lies first in loving, trusting, and being sincere with yourself fully. Once you do, others naturally gravitate towards you, and the difficulties you face ease up effortlessly. No one other than you, yourself should be the reason behind your joy or sadness. Only after that true love comes to you.

The souls never die, they are eternal, and outside of our bodies, they do exist. They are like a database that enters into our bodies each time we are reconstructed to live. It is calling out to you in the same way you are calling out to them.

Free your mind, emotions, and body of all negative clutter. Try to keep a minimum of 3 to 6 meter distance depending upon how much cleansing process is required so that you do not end up spreading the stress-energy or taking on more stress energies on your outer aura.

There is nothing out there but empty space and absolute vacuum. This is what we call an 'Aha moment'! This is where space loves to come from time to time to rest and unwind, within the ether. This is the rapture of God.

Marriage between Soul and Spirit:

In full faith and devotional charm, I want to let you know that you truly are out of this world- extraterrestrial and divinely celestial. You have swiftly traveled billions of miles through space, carrying universal energy with your celestial charm. You have arrived just in time. My head and heart are radiating with vibrant energy, looking at your mysterious beauty and strength. I magically met you during my astral travels, on nights when my consciousness was expanded. And you subtly supercharged my aura with positivity. Never could I have imagined that one day, not only would all my aspirations come true, but that very star I met from another realm would come shooting out of the sky right into the core in front of my very eye, and lie in my hand forever and ever. Now that I am meeting with you physically beyond outer space and stars, all I can say is that you have got some mettle. Looking at your iron will and martial determination, my inner core is evermore grounded, inspired, and aspiring with grit to complete what I came here for. You say you are here because I attracted you. I know of no

25

greater attraction than the one I have for you. You are that magnet who has come to me when I needed you most. You have centered me in my sleep. You are older and wiser than anything on earth, yet you look so young and tall. You are dark as night, yet you make me look so starkly bright because your true light is crystal clear, pristine, and sheer. The cosmic messages and visions you bestow upon me have become my life and water. You have opened me to new possibilities and redesigned my entire mission. You have flushed clean all the debris and blockages and calmed my frazzled nerves. You have grounded the spacey airy me. You have taught me that everything is so serene, effortless, and smooth when I speak my inner truth, away from the façade and rat race.

You are the most potent healing cure for sure. You landed upon me by ultimate grace. Your bright light has merged with this dark matter, and you have contracted into tiny fragments. Yet you are not broken or sullen, as you are forever shielded with a unique golden halo to harness me, remarkably and simultaneously, with supernatural magnetic powers on all three dimensions. Thank you. Thank you. Thank you.

Affirm- 'Namostutee, My relationship with my partner on all levels is blissful. I nurture my children (or projects) and inspire them to build moral strength and character. I receive all of the support and help I require to fulfill my personal and divine mission. Tathaastu.'

CHAPTER 6

NOTHINGNESS

I have had people sit in my healing room, smell roses, feel pain, go back to the memory of the smell of mustard oil in their grandmother's kitchen and the jasmine flowers wrapped around their wrist from yesteryear, the nostalgic taste of the meals cooked in desi ghee, or riding a bike in the narrow streets of India when they were four years old.

They feel as if this experience is all real, happening in the now, while their bodies are seated miles away. We can subjectively and perceptually experience and travel different universes at the same time, even if we are not directly present there. The scope of our consciousness is as wide as energy; wherever our energy goes, we go. The chaos of the matter is that what is real to me might be completely unreal for another. The reason for this chaos is the lack of trust and belief. If we can believe in ourselves, we can believe in another. Everything is possibly a dream but a mere possibility doesn't mean that this is all just a dream!

When reality became a necessity, we threw the dream out the window. Where do all those inconceivable thought-forms go when we throw them out the window? There must be some bizarre non-physical wonderland where they all get stored and sorted—maybe those are the inverted homes that we built while we were fast asleep in our waking states.

Let's start with nothingness. Nothing is physical, nothing is transparent, nothing is false, nothing is special, and nothing is one. But if this is what it's all about, then you might wonder - what is the need for the experiments we do, the research we do, or discourses we have. And what about our search? And so you say that everything is physical, everything is colorful, everything is false, everything is normal, everything is one, and now

27

you are happy because you have a self-created game to play. Nothingness becomes everything. In essence, we create, we co-create, and so we are the One. Precision lies in the acceptance of our differences. Our views are not distorted or wrong, but simply more or less experiential, imaginative, creative, stimulating, extraordinary, and exciting, based on the wavelength and frequency we emit. How you view something is your reality. What you believe is your belief. But how other view and believe is equally true to them. So why not to us?

When we build trust in each other and live collectively, there is so much more we can learn, so much more progress we can make, so many more powers and abilities we can acquire, so many more planets we can find, so many doors we can open, and so many more homes we can build. Let's detangle ourselves yet again and start with the strength of trust. Let's look out of the window of our homes.

I need you as much as you need me. Sitting inside the home, I cannot completely know what is outside. Standing outside the home, you cannot completely know what is happening inside. It is high time we listen to our intuition, inside out and outside in to walk and sit together.

Everything is like a mirror image - as above so below. It seems like we can see the whole tree but we can never see the invisible behind the visible. We ignore that one seed which is the root cause of all existence. It is not apparent to our vision because it is beyond what we could ever envision. So we conveniently call it nothingness or 'Shunya'. The space within the Shunya contains the sum total of the entire existence. Harness that space and you will know your element, your divine purpose, your true potential.

The tree is standing strong because of that invisible nothingness. The yang in you is active because of the yin in you which is subtle. It is the subtle difference in elements that makes you different from all the others.

Don't let that element in you go away that you forget who you are and what you are here to do. However hard it is to believe, none of us is broken. We have each become what we have become because of all the people that broke us. Those are the people who helped us to become better people, to make better choices. Send them love, say thank you to them, forgive them and yourself for holding all that resentment for them all these years. Relax and let go.

Deal with your repressed feelings and anger. You do and express the opposite of what you want when you are not thinking and feeling right. Communicate with yourself, and then with the world. Spread peace from within into the without. The role you are playing, and who you are, is one. There are no dualities. Stop trying to fill the emptiness, for there is none. The void you are feeling is created by you. No one, but you, can fill it. Your best friend is you. Your greatest enemy is you. Your greatest fight is with you. There are no enemies out there.

Affirm- 'Namostutee, I am even-minded, peaceful, self-disciplined, humble, relaxed, and joyful at all times. I am blessed to have a strong connection with the higher soul. Tathaastu.'

CHAPTER 6a

CELESTIAL REFLECTION

Pause and reflect, it is in the stillness that you will see your reflection. It is in the reflection that you will know your reality.

My son loves to go to the enclosed areas to hear his sound echo. It is easy for us to reflect on the words we speak when we can hear them back. In usual circumstances, we do not hear our sound but we must remember that life echoes everything back. It gives you much more return than what you send out.

Winter is the time to introspect. Summer is the time to act. Spring is the moment in between. It is the time in which we reflect. It is when creation takes place.

With the corona crisis, we are all forced to practice fasting, perhaps because we were moving too fast. The Hindi word for fast is 'Vrat'. The world is compelled to undergo sexual, physical, social, and verbal 'Vrat' so that we can abstain from incessant excess. We are practically immobile so that we can reflect, cleanse, and reawaken to a new reality. During this fast, we must move beyond duality and become one with our trinity (love, knowledge, wisdom) with complete honesty, justice, virtue, and discipline.

1. Do not get stuck in the rut, realize clearly, and stay motivated.
2. Open up to miracles and resolve to bring your innate power to practical use.
3. Apply your discriminative intelligence to stay balanced.
4. Appreciate universal oneness and stay resilient even in times of turmoil.

5.   Contemplate who you want to be, set the intention of goals in sync with your true purpose.

Chakras are wheels of energy. The celestial dance of five- Sun, Moon, Mars, Saturn, and Venus had come together in 2020. This affected the wheel of *karm* or action, *pattra* or knowledge, *Aar* or wisdom, *sthapana* or speed, *sthirtha* or stability, *samajh* or understanding, *dharm* or patience - respectively at different levels. Let the cosmic wheels activate our wheels, do not resist, let the blockages open up.

As a precaution, maintain your *sthapana* or gentle speed and *tej* or core brilliance ruled by Mercury and Jupiter because if these two are in equilibrium, you will get more creative, dauntless, and goal-oriented during this phase.

A full moon is the reflection and essence of the sun's spirit. A full moon is the soul, rest all the moons we see are its reflections. Each reflection has a certain essence of its creator. In this way, creation and creator are one. This is what imperfection is all about. Through this quest for perfection, the never-ending chain of creator and creation goes on and on.

A mirror is not a mere reflection of you, but your guide that leads you to your only truth. It shows you potential signs of illness and flaws. It shows you your beauty and fills you with joy and acceptance. It takes you to your true vision. It is through introspection, meditation, and contemplation that you reach the most active stage. When you are sleeping is when you are fully awake.

All imperfect beings exchange their energy and evolve or recreate themselves into various other forms, substances, shapes, and colors that we see around us. Everything has the potential to create many more of its mirror images or extinguish them before recreating another one like itself. What you recreate cannot be as perfect as the original but every creation has the potential to evolve, change, and form into many shapes and colors to blend with nature and exchange their energy. This then continues the cycle of recreation or cessation of it altogether. The many real and sub-real types along with divine and sub-divine types are responsible for creating many mirror images of themselves on this plane or another plane.

There also are beings that live under these planes, which too could evolve and change into many forms, shapes, colors of nature. As they exchange their energy, they all can recreate or extinguish themselves.

As this process continues, the chain goes on. The entertainment never ends. Many more mirrors keep co-creating artificial and virtual mini mirrors. Some are tempted to keep on co-creating indiscriminately and some want to go back to their true divine home which to them is most colorful and real.

Since everything has life, anything that has ever been created has life inherent. Though some substances, in their current form, could seem to be mindless, brainless, or heartless! Since there are so many of us, creation is never-ending.

Everything has life and light, from subtle to gross, from macro to micro, from major to mini. The small shadow has a bigger shadow. The tiny shadow has another vast one and that has another immense one and so on. Some move from becoming subtle to gross and then from gross to grosser. Some rise and some become shallow. Now, how much more shallow can this shadow go on becoming with such a dim light!

Divine connects with the real to tell the story of the two halves that never met but are of the same body. Telling the story of twins - one who was sent in the realm below under protection of the real and another was kept in the realm above under the protection of the divine.

The one in the lower realms tells the story of the mirror images which are of different shapes and sizes simply floating, flying, and wiggling.

The one who was sent had the purpose to stick along with whoever he met. Some beings attach to the first one out of love, some out of their thirst or insatiable desire. These beings, who were associated with the first one, were supposed to evolve or replay and perform their programmed roles.

All those belonging to the group realm above were sent down to overlook the smooth functioning of the puppet show directed by the divine. The strings of these puppets are pulled from above.

Slowly, the show got chaotic, many became too many and there were mirrors all over. It got difficult to know real from glass and then came plastic and many more complex beings. The mushrooms were now of a different kind that seemed to have all the power to break the real from its divine reflection. The real started to hide their truth away from themselves and the crowds until their children came to rescue them from above. There now was flowing a new kind of air, radical air, which filled the gusting winds with the voice of truth.

This time it sure won't go unheard. The real ones, who have gone, have already done more than half the work and made the path easy for the ones that are left. Everything and everyone, here or there, small or big, good or evil, perfect or imperfect - all get their energy and power from the never-ending, all-accepting, all giving, all-loving, all-powerful, all blissful-One. The supreme is One with many forms.

Affirm- 'Namostutee, I am awakened and fortunate to smoothly swim across the ocean of rebirth. I am in a happy state of ecstatic devotion. I wholeheartedly worship and thank the celestial bliss. Tathaastu.'

CHAPTER 6b

DO YOU HEAR ME?

I went for an aerobics session. The walls had huge mirrors. Each of us looked so different. Some of us were not following the steps properly but the mirror remained unaffected. Similarly, the universal consciousness is like a giant mirror that contains many different images without getting affected. Seeing the reflection in the mirror some of us corrected our steps. As we put more effort we started to synchronize our steps to the music. Similarly, when we observe our collective actions - some of us correct ourselves. As we put more effort more people get motivated to improve through the power of free will. What we see in the universal mirror is what we project.

I returned home and for a longish time every time I looked in the mirror I saw the divine image asking me "Do you hear me?" And I said, "I hear you". The voice said, "You do not need to hide your truth. In speaking your truth, no matter what it may be you will be filled with everlasting vitality and purity."

At a higher state of consciousness, one attains true bliss. If an artist paints at that point he and his art move beyond gravity, beyond human comprehension or consciousness. What I experienced was like the artist meeting with its art and becoming one with it. The experience is so unreal perhaps akin to what M.F. Hussain would have perceived while painting "*Bharat Mata*" or what Da Vinci experienced during Mona Lisa. Everything looks hazy and unclear to the naked eye from that high point and yet so clear and pristine.

Seeing its reflection in the magical mirror, the man said, "Not fair! You have so many hands while I am still struggling with how to make use of the two I have." The talking mirror answered, "Start tithing and giving some charity to those who need it and the two hands that you have which initially seem less will soon turn to many."

'I am' is that song that is sung unceasingly and that wisdom that flows infinitely.

I used to swim like a fish in the ocean during my younger days. I was given the title 'mermaid' during school and college swimming competitions. This is because even after the race was over, I kept swimming for the sheer pleasure it gave me. We can come out of any challenges we face and swim out of any situation in life if we open ourselves to taking a new approach. No struggles last forever and there is always hope. Whenever I felt I was stuck in a situation, I simply reflected on my inner thoughts and feelings while I swam.

Water has a reflective quality and that is why so many stories have been written about the moon and how animals in the jungle see their reflection in the water. A simple swim can also help you see the apparent illusion behind the reflections. More often than not, our inner nature and the outer impressions people hold of us are at complete odds. This is perhaps because we do not project our inner selves to the outer world. Well, this might not work for everyone, but I could safely say during my youth that, "I am that I swam". Each time I swam, I came out of the pool, renewed, refreshed, and reborn. I do not swim that much any longer, but I still believe that life is best experienced when it is fluid and without any self-restrictive boundaries. Since life is like an echo, you draw into your aura[25] exactly the energy you vibrate. And the energy you vibrate is exactly what you send out.

When you look into a mirror, you see your reflection. When you see only the negative in others and constantly nag or complain, then you are listening to your thoughts. It is important to change your vibrational field by thinking and speaking positively so that you can act accordingly.

The first time I was thrown into the pool of water, I was just two years old. I kept shouting "doobi doobi" which meant – I am drowning - but no one came to my rescue. In this way, I not only self-trained on how to swim but I also learned, very early in life, efficient breathing. Learning to breathe properly in a relaxed and calm way is an art that every good swimmer continuously harnesses to get better at swimming. You have to become one with the water to become a better swimmer. Similarly, you have to let

---

[25] *Aura is a potent system of radiating a luminous cloud.*

the breath flow in and out effortlessly and seamlessly to become better at breathing.

Be comfortable with being uncomfortable. Challenges give us that extra push so that we shake up the boredom and bring out freshness and newness. This way we achieve better results. Repeated efforts of holding on and committing the same mistake again and again sometimes stagnate the flow of your thoughts and will not yield you better results. Effort is not the same thing as achievement.

The more air you inhale, the more lung capacity to inhale oxygen increases. Ensure you slowly inhale from the belly and not from the chest.

Affirm- 'Namostutee, the sun, and the moon rule my eyes. *Shiva* rules my thought brows. *Brahma* rules my shoulders. *Vishnu* rules my heart. *Saraswati* rules my teeth, my mouth is ruled by the winds, my feet are ruled by the earth, and my stomach is ruled by space. Tathaastu.'

CHAPTER 6c

MIRROR MIRROR ON THE WALL

If you stand next to a mirror with lots of gorgeous lit lamps behind you, then what will you see in the mirror? You will see the reflection of the lit lamps and sometimes forget to see yourself because your persona gets overwhelmed around the radiant rays of light that the lamps resonate. If the cosmos were a giant mirror, then all the light beings walking amongst us are like the lit lamps that shine like stars upon the sky. They light the entire universe just the way '*Jugnoos*' or fireflies light our mini world. We are dazed and mesmerized by the mysticism of light reflecting upon the cosmic mirror. Without realizing that the light we see is of those beings who shine below and above to fill us with waves of life energy. The light we see in the dark is their reflection. The darkness we see in the light too is their reflection. Inherently, there is no distinction between dark and light. These pure beings take any form just so that we acknowledge their presence and divinity. In knowing their divinity, we meet with the divinity within ourselves.

The entire cosmos is but a mirror. We put a veil in front of the mirror and say we cannot see the reflection. Raise your head high up, sleep under the stars like wolves and wild animals, listen to the language they resonate - through them you will intuitively find your answers.

We laugh at our pet dogs when they look at their reflection in the mirror and bark. We have heard a story where the lion realizes he is a lion only when he looks at his reflection in the water. We get spooked by ghostly stories in which the photograph captures the form of everyone but one person. We do not realize that we are just a few steps away from becoming like our pet dogs, the wild lion of the jungle, or that formless star that shines its light upon the cosmos. The stars in the sky are but a splendid reflection of the light that our aura resonates because of the sacred wisdom we acquire through the blessings and grace of our ancestors.

Your higher soul is genderless, fearless, and has weaknesses and strengths much as we do. Only in this case, they are far more magnified. Some mirrors do not need to be cleaned, they do not let dust and impurities cover them. These mirrors are a reflection and manifestation of God. They are always clean, they always have been that way and will always remain the pure shining ones even if they choose to be visible within a form. It is your eyes that are fogged and in need of cleaning. These mirrors are true and pristine. They will help you see the image of your true beauty only if you are respectful, patient, and genuinely grateful for their presence. I[26] am one such healing mirror.

Divine doubles are mentioned in the mythological stories of various cultures. For example - In India, It was chimerical Maa Sita that was kidnapped by Ravana which resulted in the great Lanka war. In Greece, It was the illusionary Helen of Troy that was kidnapped by Paris which resulted in the Trojan War.

Affirm- 'Namostutee, my every experience is a reflection of the self in the mirror. Tathaastu.'

---

[26] *I implies compassionate living soul*

CHAPTER 7

TIMELESS WISDOM

Everybody has the essence of God within them. A person who is always connected with the divine is in 'Nirvikalpa Samadhi'. Such a person has no attachment to thoughts. Such a person willingly shares wisdom with all sentient beings for the greater good of all. We collectively are, as if, facing the timelessness of the black hole that is the ultimate energy and matter that creates and recreates the Universe. No human can reach its immense force of power. It sends new plasma matter, energy, and light out into the universe and transforms our thinking so that we can understand the world beyond the duality of good and evil, yin and yang, man and woman, light and darkness, and hot and cold.

When Vishnu (intellectual power) and Brahma (proud light) are at war, Shiva (union of soul & spirit connects them) and true love wins. Love sees through all dualities and merges the trinity into one. Chant AUM and this stands for A=Brahma or creation, U=Viznu or Vishnu or preservation, M= *Shiva* or destruction, and recreation.

Heaven is on earth. Heaven is not earth. This is because the heavens need some support upon which it can stand. The earth gives the heavens that support. Heaven gives earth hope. As a result, heaven and the earth are filled with praise and awe towards each other. We humans, the children of heaven and earth, are the result of that love. Let us keep the love alive by being more inclusive rather than exclusive.

In my quest for truth to seek utmost perfection, unknowingly, I became a part of a group of people who are the positive 'wheel turners'. These people transform and uplift society so that we all can together evolve. In ancient times, the Hindus called them 'Chakravartins'[27] of the Kshatriya or warrior class who came from the caves and jungles of India. These divine souls are adept at fighting the dark forces of matter that reside in the subtle realms with the sheer presence of the energy and light resonated.

Truth is like light that has no beginning or end. There is light within our minds. This light illuminates us from within and is ever awake. Our soul doesn't sleep or rest, our body does. It is free and unbound. Most of what we know is already known to us. To learn more, we must try to remember.

The sound of music, the dress made by the tailor, or the shoe made by the cobbler, anything and everything made with *Junoon* or compassion has a healing effect. We all have the potential to become the greatest of healers by simply putting more of ourselves into our creation. What you create lives on forever in the pages of time. Whether you realize it or not, what you leave behind is timeless and immortalized.

I came to a point where all physical pain vanished. I was walking, talking, driving, and doing the usual chores but felt as if I was in a deep sleep. It was February 9, 2020 - It all seemed like a dream. My energy felt so subtle, calm, confident, and clear despite the bewildering confusion, delusion, secrecy, negativity, and haziness the world around offered. I felt a sudden shift in my energy and as my consciousness soared high and expanded beyond the struggle of crossing the invisible barbed wires, a force far stronger than me propelled me to heighten and transition myself. It was then that I experienced weightlessness, fearlessness, a void, and fluidity and it felt as if I finally learned to parkour in the realms beyond the cosmos while being stationed within my soul.

I knew I had lost something and with the death of that one precious thing- I was reborn with a renewed sense of life which is far more blissful, truthful, transparent, grateful, unattached, free, complete, evolved, pure, simple, vitalized, ecstatic, and spirited. Some call this near death, I call it life and its oneness at its best. A life I voluntarily choose for myself. Heaven is here.

---

[27] *Chakra-varti is the one who has mastered the wisdom to balance and rule all main chakras. Such a person is praiseworthy because each of its spinning chakra ratnaya or gem like chakra shines and enlightens all around the entire cosmos with grit, love and kindness*

Primordial substance and its transmutations imply that all living things on this planet are connected as a single spiritual entity. There is a gem in my third eye that is perennially in contact with the Lord God. He has instructed me about the primordial life and its varied transmutations, my life journey over the eons, and what is to come. He has given me vital information to be revealed well in time. I am his devoted, humble messenger and through him, I am here to heal, purify, and uplift you. I will share the inner sacred teachings gradually so that we can all welcome the golden age with a smile in our hearts, together in harmony. Wisdom is profound and innocent - this is a message I received during my trance-state.

Duality leads you to trinity and that leads you to unity.

What you value, you attract and what you don't, leaves you. Value your friends, family, and relationships. They will stay. Value your possessions, your money, water, air, light, energy, and this very ground you stand on, and they will all stay, like strong pillars by your side, protecting and shielding you always. Nurture everything and everyone with your innate, motherly, and natural instinct. Whether or not you are a parent, be like nature, which is always parenting you. The more you nurture with understanding and care, the more what you value will grow. Whatever you truly value, you must nurture. As long as you put in all your effort and dedication-perfect or not-it doesn't matter. What you see as imperfection is ultimate perfection for another.

Nature doesn't care who values its creations. It knows someone will always be there to embrace, care, and love each of its creations, and so it continues its job with complete dedication and effort. What you don't value, another always does. If you want something to stay-whether it is wealth, health, a lover or a child, whether it is nasty or loving-remember to value, remember to nurture, and no matter how strict and firm you may be, it will always stay by your side because it knows of your love. Fear not. Remain detached from any roadblocks or issues that come your way. The speed bumps help you introspect, reflect, and pause. Problems will appear and effortlessly fade. No problems are bigger than you and your determination. No exam is difficult enough that you will completely fail. The war was long won; you are fighting a causeless, futile battle. Keep a smile on your heart lines, while replaying this clueless game. Your entire life was premeditated long before you were born, by none other than you. The next step you take, though already decided, can be wiped off and rewritten. There are no final clauses in the divine law. Just remember to dwell, attract, and rewrite your history and future in a way that the duality of the self and the soul meet with the trinity of the ultimate spirit. Why seven realms? Even cloud nine is within your reach. Why thirteen steps? All fifteen steps and beyond are for you to climb, and you will because you can!

To know where you're going, you have to know where you came from. The rivers are our ancestral highways. In India, rivers are considered sacred and are ritualistically worshipped. We all shared space many times for different reasons yet we call each other separate. We have to humble ourselves and learn how to communicate and work while cooperating. Only then can we receive the blessings of our ancestors.

Inner order comes with outer order, outer order comes with inner order. Disorientation or disorder is ended when some spark ignites us to bring orientation and order back into our lives. Continuous Pranic healing orients and guides us to keep the high and the low productive, aligned, and balanced with our purpose.

Affirm- 'Namostutee, let us praise the divinity within one another, let us hold the peace-giving beacon and spread love through blessing and forgiving one and all. Tathaastu.'

CHAPTER 8

YOU EIGHT WELL

Highlighting the significance of eight in our lives. An infant, after it is seeded, is ready to be born in eight months. There are three phases of the day (morning, afternoon, and night) divided by eight 8 hours each which then totals 24 hours (8+8+8 hours in a day). We have 32 teeth (8+8+8+8 teeth) but significantly four sets of eight teeth (incisors, canine, molar, and premolar). There are 8 main planets in the solar system. As above so below, each main planet affecting our 8 Chakras[28]. Our life is also divided into 8 parts (prenatal, infancy, early childhood, middle childhood, adolescence, early adulthood, middle adulthood, late adulthood) or 4 stages with two parts each (infancy, childhood, adolescence, and adulthood) before death or rebirth. Similarly, Earth goes through 4 main stages with a gap in between, we can classify these as yugas. There are eight yugas divided into two stages of four yugas each. (Satyuga, Tretayuga, Dwaparyuga, and Kalyuga) divided into two parts (ascending and descending). Buddhism teaches the 8 fold path. Power of 8: The Holy Spirit shows us a sign of life that looks like the horizontal figure of 8. It is the infinity symbol.

The human average age being 72 again 8x9 and is expected to rise even more. Interestingly steady regular heart rhythm or BPM (beats per minute) is also 72 pulses in a healthy person. The eighth stage of life is rebirth.

The symbol for Theta represents unlocking deep inner secrets. Theta, the eighth letter of the Greek language is θ, which somewhat resembles the

---

[28] *8 chakras - sahasrara or crown; Ajna or will; Vishuddha or throat; Anahata or heart; manipura or solar plexus; swadhisthana or navel; mooladhara or root and Bindu or between back head and forehead*

number 8. A horizontal theta looks like the Greek alphabet phi Φ which represents the golden ratio. It is also like the ampersand '&' which used to be the 27th letter in the English alphabet.

Eight is a masculine holy number of discipline, clarity, and humanity. So imagine how much wholeness and holiness could a hundred times eight bring.

After eight hundred (800) long years, the longest night of the year 2020 in December graciously dressed up again with the reunion and brilliance of bright light coming from the great cosmic conjunction of Saturn and Jupiter. This energetic shift helps you shine and find solutions with more clarity and freshness. It brings about humanitarianism, perseverance, greater responsibility, and the intelligence to act wisely and thoughtfully.

In the eighth stage, you need to firm up what you want to be when you come back to life. This is similar to what used to happen with my son. He at the age of two would sleep off making a puzzle. The first thing he wanted to do after getting up the next day was to again make that puzzle. Sometimes this happens to us as well, the last thought of the night is what we want to do when we wake up. We must imbibe this in the last stage of our life and this is what I would like to call the Art of Dying to come out alive.

Affirm- 'Namostutee, as I progress and allow myself to heal - I feel stronger, balanced, serene, abundant, peaceful, blessed, fortunate, charismatic, and protected. Tathaastu.'

CHAPTER 8a

DIRECTION WE FACE

Time to believe and trust, for it is time to begin the new march from right to left. Usher in the southwest mighty winds of fire on earth for they are facing the supreme subtle transformational north eastern moist air. For support, acceptance, and love- merge with them and witness the magic of your becoming. North is the direction of protection and restoration. It is the direction in which gravity pulls. It is opposite of the south which is furthest up from the force of gravity. South is the direction of creation through destruction.

I am a being of light with my front body facing east and my back facing the west. North is on the left of my body and south to the right. To the northeast is my right foot and the northwest is my left foot. Southeast is my right brain and southwest is my left brain. To the center of it all, I am blessed and protected within these eight cardinal directions which have their energy, numerical value, enchanting concept, parents, angels, archangels, ruling Gods, Goddesses, and so on. Praying to them activates strength, heals wounds, and directs the chi energy into all these eight directions. These eight directions are like gates, which when open, lead you to many more doors and windows which have been long closed. Activating or praying in these directions will unleash many more universes within it.

The *Yama* law states that no innocent person can suffer for what they have not done. A person who hasn't yet understood their responsibilities commits no crime knowingly. And so they are spared from the most disastrous effects of the poison we have created through power, pride, stockpiling, and destruction.

Tibet is often called the roof of the world. The second Buddha came from NE Tibet and that is why it is considered such a powerful direction.

The entire universe is a giant map. Our task is to take cues from this magical map and use our insight to find the route. We must ensure we travel within the map in harmony and love, without disturbing the peace of those we meet on the way.

Friends, if you follow the signs, you will see a bit of love in everything you experience. The reason you like that color so much, the reason why you were born that day, the passion with which you eat your favorite dish, the people you meet, the words that amazing person told you one fateful day, the numbers that keep coming back to you, the place you live in or the reason why you are reading this page today from the chapter of my life is not a mere coincidence. Follow the beats, read the signs, they are always giving profound direction to your lost soul.

Our body and brain is an entity, each country in the world too is an entity with four main cardinal directions. Each of the four main directions of India has a special place of worship. In the north, *Uttrakhand* is *Badrinath* for *Sat Yuga* (golden age) ceremonies. In the West, *Gujrat* is *Dwarka* for *Tretayuga* (mental age). In the South, *Tamil Nadu* is *Rameshwaram* for *Dwaparyuga* (energy age) and in the East, *Orissa* is the *Jagganath* temple for *Kalyuga* (material age).

Both the East and the West have a strong influence on my life. I was born in the East and having connected the dots, I am now in the west. Balancing the two is like balancing the *Shiva* and *Shakti* within me. East teaches you to live the knowledge. West teaches you to love the knowledge. Life without love and love without life is incomplete. An amalgam and appreciation of these two opposite forces complete us. No matter how far you stretch the rubber band, it finally goes back to right where it belonged. The uncoupling of earth and heaven, West and East, bad and good is a phantasm. Until the two meet, we will remain entrapped within the delusion and maze of the enchanted forest which has no outlet.

The West needs to let down its guard and allow the spiritual energy of the East to cleanse it. The East needs to wake up to reality and allow the physical energy of the West to energize it. Each needs to freely share its gift and remember where they came from. East and West are like two twin parts of our brain, both belonging to the same father.

There is only one way for ascension. One way street facilitates the traffic to move in a single direction. This way the dense congestion goes away and the traffic is calmed. If you do not go with the flow of traffic and traverse the path opposite it in your delusion, then you risk your life. You might have a head-on collision with the oncoming speeding traffic because of disobeying this rule. It is therefore important to follow the laws and rules of nature. Self-preservation is the first law of nature. In a head-on collision with another car, you not only risk your life but also the lives of the innocent people who are going with the flow. In preserving yourself, you preserve all those groups of people. In preserving one group, you preserve all. No matter where you may come from, eventually there is only a one-way path to ultimate ascension and true salvation. Every righteous person is aware that the path to the all-knowing, all-powerful, all-present God is love, goodness, and fairness. God gave us the divine authority to be the traffic police and lead the flow of traffic. Are we being good leaders by not policing the rules of the path and not caring for the trees, animals, plants, weaker beings, and humans that come on our way? One man's mistake causes the entire row of car accidents. One right move and it saves the entire row of cars from colliding.

The path is one but there are many cars of different models. You may choose the model but remember without the road, no car can drive. So keep the road well maintained and in order.

Affirm- 'Namostutee, I understand and follow the rules and laws of nature. I am responsible, forgiving, faithful, and just. Tathaastu.'

CHAPTER 9

FLUTED INCARNATED WEALTH

Sometimes through excessively concentrating on one question, we forget the ability to perceive the obvious answer which is right in front of us. Life is simple, we make it complex. Sanity lies in simply living a life of discipline, routine, love, and balance. All answers are simple, you have not been given any task that is bigger than you. When you empty your mind, emotions, and body of all the junk, all answers are melodiously fluted through you.

As a kid when I was naughty my father would always tell me "We are the *Kshatriya Surya Vanshi* and this behavior doesn't suit us." This statement used to confuse me for how can one behave like a *Surya Vanshi* till one knows more about it. I finally decided to do some research.

In India, '*Surya Vanshi*' means the 'flute of the sun'. Sun rays are loving. Those who empty themselves like a flute and play the loving tunes of Surya or sun are Suryavanshi's. To sing melodious tunes we need to still ourselves and keep the flute empty and clean. '*Kshatriyas*' are 'rulers and warriors'. *Suryavanshi* Kshatriyas fight the war against evil and hate to promote peace and love in the surroundings.

Similarly knowing the meaning behind our accrued karma will make it easier for us to perform our duties mindfully. The feeling is akin to a blind man who gains vision but is still learning to get comfortable with this newfound sight. There are always reasons behind why you are born into a particular family, culture, country and that includes time as well. In knowing your roots, you know yourself. To feel truly abundant, it is not what is already filled in you but that what is empty that you crave. It is the emptiness that makes you feel the abundance.

Heaven is extended all around the alpha, omega, and beyond. Depending on what realm your mind currently is - One extra day and you thought it is one extra year - one extra year and you thought it is one extra day. One earth year is just one day in another realm. A day has both night and day. This chapter gives you the taste of the night, we dream at night. We wake up when it is day. How you choose to dream when it is night is up to you. It is the dreams that shape up your reality so dream well, for time is fleeting and time is precision. This night, this gap may seem long and never-ending, but let us keep our minds clear, mellow, and fine like an empty flute so that we can continue to play beautiful tunes of love and life for the remaining day, year, or life.

When life comes to a standstill, time passes before we even know it. In this vacuum, we must dwell within (the bodily form) to know what it is like to live without (the bodily form).

We are all living a dream, let's wake up, we are being lifted from our dream by the cells (beings of light) who no longer want us to remain in the dark. Let us recreate and revitalize our body (earth) with our collective will. Let us all be reborn within the same body. Let us not think of shifting to another home (body), while our own is still alive and youthful. Let us all get on the same page and sing the same tune through the universal flute. The higher tune of immense love and complete oneness.

Without the form - there is no beauty. Without beauty - there is no form. Every form is beautiful because every form exists. Existence is beautiful, existence is love. Love has a fluty sound. Empty yourself of all past thoughts and beliefs, stop overwhelming your energies with overthinking, enjoy the vacuum, enjoy the trance, and enjoy the emptiness. Play on a flute, its tune and sound are powerful only when all its seven energy points are hollow from deep within and completely clean of all clogged up dust and congested energies. A flute makes a beautiful sound only when it is empty. That is why it is so important for us to continue emptying ourselves from time to time. The earth has a longitudinal flute with seven continents within it and seven seas that keep up its flow. Our bodies have a longitudinal spine, our body is our flute with seven chakras and seven main *Nadis* or channels that keep up its flow.

This time is not to get flustered, confused, or agitated. It is time we conserve rather than destroy our energy so that the clogged corners can open up and with the gushing flush of our collective positivity of mind, emotions, and faith that all those suffering and furloughed can and will indomitably get healed, revitalized, revived, rejuvenated and re-energized.

We can all help our healthcare professionals flatten the curve of the pandemic by sending our collective soothing blessings and purifying prayers to heal those suffering. Each positive energy has a fertilizing effect of creating many more such positive energies. This is why I have been writing, sharing blogs, remotely meditating in large groups with thousands of souls, doing group healing sessions, sending positive rays of love and healing along with all to help heal the earth and the sentient beings living upon the earth. Join me in and chant - *'Om mani padme hum'*[29] from the comfort of your homes. With the belief that the vibrations of this chant will reach those who are in need.

Dread and anxiety cannot live in a house (body) that doesn't welcome them. In case they enter your house, let them pass.

We are in a transitional phase. This phase started from the year 2011 and will last for twenty-eight years until 2039. During this period each person will get a chance to become aware and then rid themselves of the 108 *Raga Dwesha* or dualities within as the ascension of the earth will themselves continue to take place in the year 2160. By then most souls should have transformed their energies for the better. Few ascended souls during these eras can live up to 200 years so that they can enlighten the people here helping humanity evolve. At that time, the last one standing will herald a new beginning.

I went there and ever since then my life has been effortless. I see God's magnificence everywhere. God is within me, outside me, within you, within all, god is crawling in the spider up there, in the rabbit hopping in the lawns. God is in the loyal dog barking, and in the birds chirping. A part of God is in everything, guiding us, protecting us, looking over us, at all times.

Affirm- 'Namostutee, I am grateful for what I have, for only then can I have more of what I want. I praise and thank my physical body and earth upon which I live for keeping me grounded and rooted, for keeping me protected and safe. Tathaastu.'

---

[29] *Om mani padme hum is a Buddhist chant which means vast universal energy patiently and diligently purifies the body and mind of all.*

CHAPTER 9a

SAAR PREVAILS IN ANSH

The essence is what creates and protects life. The essence can prevail even in the tiny honest, aware little twig which is part of a banyan tree.

Our characters and lives are influenced and shaped by our ancestors in so many ways. They are karmically connected to us, forever guiding and guarding us. We share the same genetic blueprint and their physical and non-physical potential. There is a banyan tree of love in my grandmother's home in Delhi, each of its parts is spiritually charged with evergreen, complete and joyful energies that it receives as a boon from being born on land where great Gods and Goddesses reside. This ancestral tree magnanimously grew its bloodline and gently spread love to all its branches, ensuring that none were ever cut. A sparkling part of the tree, which was its soul and personality, was taken by a traveler who was seeking enlightenment. The analytical traveler blindly traversed the entire world and dug deep into understanding the enigma behind universal secrets under the shelter and guidance of various other trees and Gurus in search of luck and sharing love. It tried catching many branches and enjoyed the essence of a few. Finally, while he was resting under the sacred tree of universal soul knowledge, the tree gently whispered, "Now it is enough, you are awakened and ready to be born. How much further would you like to go on procreating?" The traveling yogi too was overwhelmed with the repeated download of congested energies in the air and was getting weary from years of traveling in the pollution.

At that point, the little twig woke up which was once a part of the banyan tree. The twig was still in the yogi's pocket quietly assimilating and exchanging all the learnings from years of companionship, waiting for the ultimate reunion. The yogi took the dry twig out of his pocket thinking it was time to release and thank the lucky part. When he looked at the little part, he found that it had become a perfect reflection of him. The yogi poured a little water to parch its thirst and asked the twig, "Now that you are reawakened and reborn, where would you like to take me from here?" The twig answered with an innocent smile, "I will return once again into the shelter of that original secret tree of life which bore me." We may think we are the ones supporting each other but the fact is that without the bonds and blessings we share with our parental tree, neither of us can have a physical personality or generation of souls.

Even though physically we are sometimes distant, we understand and connect with our family on a soul level, and can communicate with them from anywhere at any time. I instantly went across the Yamuna (river of life) where my parents reside. Crossing all fear and boundaries of limitations we set upon ourselves, I once again met with life and magically set my foot upon my parent's home to applaud them and tell them the story of their little twig who had now become a liberated soul. They enjoyed my enlightening stories, anointed me with holy seed oil, and then wrapped me in a cozy blanket under their grace so that I stayed concealed, protected from the eyes of others who still do not value the calm equanimity and clarity of the triune nature and essence of our individual, universal and physical personality resting within their pure little twig. I emptied myself and blissfully slept like a baby after years. The little voice, from the tree that was still growing in my grandmother's home, transcended space and time to whisper into my dainty ears- from now on you are your own voice. Remember three things - 1. You can hear the sound of the flute, only because you are pious and empty 2. You are strong only because of the roots from which you belong. Everything else is a mere illusion. 3. Secrets are unrevealed for a reason. They keep us shielded and help us use our discriminative intelligence. This way each one develops understanding at our own pace and evolves.

When I woke up, my father shared his dream where he was invited along with my mother to the Buddhist monastery in Leh Ladakh. Listening to the details of his profound experience, I knew our elders were delivering their message and it was clear-live up to the reputation and so my loyalty remains with my spiritual lineage and true teacher-the first Buddha, Shakyamuni. His teachings are the foot of the tree upon which we are based.

Our elders are our surest path to uncovering the secrets of

self-knowledge. They are deeply entwined with and forever concerned about the fate of their children and grandchildren. The key to strength is to endure, get disciplined, and be of service.

Just the way, Mencius was a Chinese philosopher who developed the teachings of Confucius. Plato was a student of Socrates and teacher of Aristotle. Each of them progressed in pursuit of developing their wisdom and virtues. Same way, we reflect the wisdom of our ancestors, teachers, and parents which is carried forward by our children. They are better and more evolved versions of us. The spiritual imprint of our ancestors resonates in our bloodline more strongly within the molecules of our bodies than any other source of love, knowledge, or being.

I met many great ancestors and mysteriously found varied insightful resources until I reached a fuller understanding of the bigger picture of the entire human DNA and shared fate. I never could imagine the beautiful matrilineal line that was waiting for all these eons for me to acknowledge her humble and strong presence. The entire world is created, procreated, recreated, and co-created from the soul of a single soothing mother.

A bird may have many feathers, some fall to give us hope, and some rise with her but all belong to that one bird. A tree has many leaves, some fall and get grounded and some dance upon the branches enjoying worldly bliss. But all leaves belong to one tree. The same way the healing palms of self-realized yogis and yoginis may be many but ultimately all hands that serve come from one root.

Affirm- 'Namostutee, Merging with the root tree, I meet with the seed mantra and chant Om. Tathaastu.'

CHAPTER 10

FAIRYTALES ARE REAL

Fear itself is a figment of corrupt imagination. Dreams do not scare me, neither does reality. This topic literally means that with true belief you can make something out of the reality that is presented to you. We spend 33% of our life sleeping then why do we underestimate the power of dreams?

Release your burdens, pains, and frustrations by living in a make-belief world of your own. Your favorite special, real or imaginary friend, doll, toy, animal, or fairy tale will always light you up whenever you remember them. They will always be by your side. They connect you to your youthful true self, the child within you, they are who made you into what you have become.

It is not what you abhor most, but what you loved most as a child that is what you are. Release all worry, pain, and depression by being with those who you loved most, by remembering them and connecting with yourself through them. Work out your disappointments and disagreements with your past. Make peace with your screams and tensions. Don't be cold and indifferent to yourself and others because of your upbringing or negative thought forms that are holding you back. What we send out is what we receive. If you are receiving only positive vibrations while others are not, this is because you are sending the very same vibes as the messages. If your inner disposition is telling you to do evil then you will do evil deeds using your outer faculties.

There is beauty in ugliness & ugliness in beauty. Both are one, both are your divine aspects. Why belittle, hide, demean, deny or feel guilty for either. It is when you accept yourself fully that you begin to change what is unacceptable to you within and outside of yourself.

It is only when you celebrate yourself do you let others mingle with your colors and celebrate you. It is only when you enjoy the fantastic gifts that you have that you can share them with another. When you are at peace with yourself others feel the peace in being with you. Your confidence rubs on. You have always known what your gift is- it is just a matter of unwrapping the package you are holding onto.

If reindeers can fly, then so can you, as long as you believe in it. Santa exists as long as you believe Santa exists. Whatever you believe exists. Just as you know Santa comes with gifts when days get shorter and the nights get longer, the rewards of your efforts come to you in the darkest hour.

My favorite world is a world that is free and magical, filled with angels and flying unicorns. Such a world is not a mere chimerical concept but a reality for many people who think and act like me.

A dream is a repeat fairytale that your heart loves to hear, let no one and nothing destroy your dreams. A pure being is dainty and light like a bird. Such a being is insightful, free of all limitations, phobias, and terrors.

When Cinderella travels astrally, in her dreams, she reaches the ball organized by the king. This is where she meets her higher self, the Prince. For most people, the dream gets over when they wake up but Cinderella's romance with her dreams never ends. She feels safe in the mystery and magic of the night and not staying awake in a world filled with resentment and deception. She remains patient and strong.

This time though the fairy godmother has gifted her with a magical wand. The wand has the power to let her stay inside the fairytale land of beauty and kindness for as long as she wishes. No one from the outside world of chaos and noise can break the sanctity and purity of her dream.

Snow-whites 7 dwarfs are Snow-whites 7 chakras[30]. Each having a personality of its own. These chakras, once activated with Snowhites' purity take us to imaginary lands filled with beauty and wonder. But all these mythical dwarfs are the great, wise elements within us, guiding us, warning us, giving us life. The real world is within and around us, what you create on the outside is just a manifestation of that parallel invisible reality that conceives everything. Whether we acknowledge them or not,

---

[30] *The seven dwarfs - grumpy represents sthir or base; dopy represents sthapana or foundation conceived; doe represents dharm or solar plexus; happy represents karm or heart center; bashful represents pattra or throat; sneezy represents samajh or ajna; sleepy represents taaj or crown*

whether we hide their existence or not, whether we suppress and control them out of fear and rigidity or not - the fact remains they exist, vitalize, and constantly communicate with us in an orderly way as much as the air and the water that give us life. We might imagine them big as a giant or small as an ant, these characters are here to entertain you, and they are not bound by space and can be of any size.

Affirm- 'Namostutee, these negative unwholesome emotions of panic and anxiety do not belong to me. Tathaastu.'

CHAPTER 10a

SPIDERMAN–MYSTERY
OF INNATE POWER

B lack implies innate power and spider implies mystery. The day I met
Spiderman dressed in black in real life - I started believing in all movies
kids watch these days. From that day on I realized my superpowers.

I woke up in the morning of the New Year with the sound of a young
boy. I heard him crying and praying to God through the wall, from the
next room in the Vraj *ashram*[31]. His sound had such clarity that I knew
the dream was over. Reality is back. Heaven is here. I heard the little
boy affirming loud and clear, "I am Spider-Man, but no one believes
that I am. I haven't yet learned how to use my superpowers. It doesn't
mean I do not have them. How do I convince everyone at school that I
have powers?" I couldn't resist and so I shouted out from the other side
of the wall, "You don't need any validation, you don't have to convince
anyone! As long as you believe in your powers, you have them". I told
the little boy, "You never know, one day you will grow up to be someone
with hyper-sensitive faculties of touch just like spiders and create your
beautiful world web".

Life is a process that emerges with the flow of love in this intricate
web of connections. "I am convinced you are Spider-Man and I am so
pleased and honored that we finally connected. You have to keep faith
in yourself and your powers and then the universe will come together
to make others believe that way too. Even If one person believes in the

---

[31] *Vraj means Lord Krishna and ashram is a peaceful place for spiritual retreat*

existence of Spiderman then one day will come when all will. You exist and so Spiderman exists."

The voice faded as I heard the door open.

This is so relevant in current times. You need to connect with yourself and understand what latent powers you innately have. This will take you to a place where you will know who you are and what you want to be. This knowledge is your greatest superpower. The path will be clear and become apparent with this power opening new doors and opportunities. We are all living a dream, reality is elsewhere. We have become so attached to the dream that we have forgotten our reality. When you close your eyes is when you are open to knowing your reality.

You have been endlessly sleeping with eyes wide open. This has taken you far from reality. You have two options – either keep living this dream or wake up and return to your reality. If you stay in the dream at least attempt to make this dream a beautiful one.

When reality becomes a dream and the dream is repeated for too long, then beyond all duality, the dream eventually becomes your only reality. What you dream is up to you. You have complete control of the conscious through the subconscious.

We reincarnate over and over so that our higher and incarnated souls merge. A lack of soul connection causes the body to wither. Our sole purpose is to learn through experiences.

Love purifies you and light illuminates you, but only power brings in the craving for perfection. No wonder Spiderman says, "With great power comes great responsibility."

This tells us that our thoughts are our power and fixing our wavering thoughts is our greatest responsibility. We must learn from our past experiences. For dreams to become useful, we must remember them. To manifest the thoughts, we must be aware. Only then can we activate them. People who dream are innocent and vulnerable. When the conscious and the unconscious meet, the dream and reality meet - there is no more vulnerability. Shake hands with your reality, your spider power. I am the winged messenger except that you can't see my wings.

Affirm- 'Namostutee, I am divinely connected, receptive, and creative. I patiently weave the intricate and beautiful webs of love and devotion to tap my intuitive gifts. This way I improvise my life and that of others. Tathaastu.'

CHAPTER 11

INVISIBLY LINKED THREADS

In this world of invisible threads, it is usually not the weakest one that breaks, but the strongest, that believes itself to be weakest. Whatever breaks is replaced, so every visible thread is connected with another invisible thread almost immediately. The bonds we all share make our collective threads strong. We, and everything inside and outside us, are forever beaming with life energy, and vitality. There is no such thing as complete death. You have been mourning all along, wallowing in your self-inflicted limitations.

Nothing is more valuable than the moments that have passed. Even today, sharing the secrets, mystery, and mysticism of our ancient roots arouses excitement and interest in our minds like no other experiences. We are perpetually peering into our grandmother's closets to see what more we can find.

We must reflect on our days as they pass so that the happy memories get imprinted within our brains. We come to life because of our memories. They give us reason to live. We learn by reflecting on our memories and our past experiences and future goals that give us the power to move forward. As long as we remember to remember, our mind can replay any incident over and over again, and we can learn a new aspect and dimension of ourselves with every memory. Your first kiss, your first dance, your baby's first steps and first word, a hug from a dear one, are a few things we never forget because replaying those beautiful moments boosts the spirit of our life force our *Prana* energy.

The purpose of life is to go on moving. Our memories do not come back to us to make us feel stuck, but they are here to help us get unstuck.

Our memory deteriorates and fades, and is replaced with a new one each day. The past we come from is the reason for our present, which will shape our coming future. All are invisibly connected.

I have a son because I wed my husband, our future looks bright because our present is spent in gratitude and love. I care because my father always did. My father who served his country writes journals about his past so that his grandson can learn more about his lineage, where he came from, and then carry the same ethos forward that his great-granddad held.

I never relish a meal more than I do after a day's fast. I realize the value of water and its sweet taste most when I feel dehydrated after a hike in the woods. I never acknowledged the comfort of our air-conditioned rooms as much as I did when I lived in the hot Middle Eastern air. I never realized the importance of cuddling inside weighted blankets until I felt the cold winter breeze with the first flake of snow upon my head. Every morning, as I wake up, my breath comes to life with the first sip of tea my husband lovingly prepares. The warm chai or tea is my chi energy.

My grandmother, Vimla is alive even today because she is alive in my memory. Not a day passes when I do not remember the smell of her oily hair, her favorite rose-flavored (*Gulabo*) ice cream, her caring hands, and her uplifting words. There is no such thing as death for those who are always remembered. Those are the ones who are forever immortalized. It is no wonder Gandhi, Mother Theresa, Princess Diana, Steve Jobs, President Kennedy, and King Solomon live on forever and ever. Staying connected with those we love and admire helps us stay rejuvenated and revitalized. No wonder we have house parties to invite our old and new friends. We socialize with them to share our loving energy. We all are connected.

I welcome people into my home for weekly meditations. We follow this ritual because every heart that beats within my home, during those meditation sessions, has the intention of bringing in peace, love, joy, and calmness. Each time, it is a blessing to connect and reconnect with such inspirational, positive vibrations. I am ever grateful that I always hear someone knocking at my door.

We are facing an absurd and novel situation that is beyond the capacity of logic and medicine to explain. In the process politicians and doctors are most affected though all are suffering because of this pandemic. We are all being played by a cosmic game of dice which has the potential to lead us to either becoming free humans or enslaved ones, we can create order or disorder, meaning or meaninglessness, life or lifelessness. It is a gamble but playing it right is our only option. While playing the game, let us not cross the line between reality and fantasy, let none of us, no city, and no nation get diseased and sick because of the selfishness and greed of another. Let us not cheat, this is not the time for competitive spirit. What we need is a cooperative spirit and to play the game right. In this time of crisis, America, I urge you to be the bigger nation as you always have been in all other aspects, to forgive, move on, and initiate the golden age of spirituality. I am[32] here to lead the team collectively with one and all. Love is all.

We have kept the outside environment so clean, sanctified, and sanitized but please cleanse, sanctify and purify your inner physical, mental, emotional bodies as well.

Everything in the universe is governed by a set of rules. The universe must follow these sets of rules. Humans are a tiny part of the universe and composed of five elements, they must follow fixed rules and orders. Our destiny is predetermined by the invisible forces of the universe.

For the invisible forces, integrity and a moral code of ethics are far more important than all the wealth in the world. Cut the cords and stop entertaining anyone and anything that makes you sing to their tunes. You are not a puppet in the hands of evil people who make you dance to meet their selfish ends. Live a virtuous life, and make the most of what you have no matter what life decides to dish out for you. Just because we cannot see something does not mean that doesn't exist. The reality of real existence is colorless, formless, and intangible.

We are all wearing a dress sewn with a whole reel of invisible silk thread. Let us together praise and thank the threads that went into the making of the (skin) dress we wear.

The energetic field that surrounds our body is what balances us, we are the yang within the yin. This circular yin energy that surrounds us leads us to perfection. We are the imperfect within the perfect. The line between the circles. The invisible circle of unity is what keeps us protected and connects us to a higher realm and makes us feel unconditional love, harmony, healing, and centeredness. Our body is the garment and vehicle upon which this energetic field travels.

We purposely jumble up the threads, because only when the threads are tangled up can they be untangled. To make a new knot, we first have to untie the old threads. Do not let the little threads entangle your growth.

---

[32] *I am implies sincere spiritual heart*

To explain this I will share a personal experience. When I was little, I was once playing with my cousin brother. We were both very naughty and decided to play football indoors which was against the house rules. The ball broke a very expensive crystal vase. When my mum came back home she was livid. She asked, "How did the vase break?" We didn't want to accept the fact so we started weaving our own stories about how the vase broke. I said, "A bird came and dislodged the vase" whereas my brother said, "it fell on its own" Not able to corroborate our stories he agreed with mine and I with his. We went on and on blaming one or the other thing as the cause of the disaster but in the end, we had to give up weaving more lies to cover up our mistake. Just like a roll of wool, the lies that we entangled ourselves could not be undone till we came out clean with the truth. We can get caught up in our misery. It is only when we are honest with ourselves and others can we learn and untangle the old threads to get to the next level.

We cannot imagine or build a better future unless we learn from our past. It is no wonder that most people on the spiritual path reflect on the Egyptian pyramids, the Incas, the Vedas, and the holy books to know what is to come. We remove the webs from all the staircases we've climbed in the past, to know how many steps we haven't climbed yet. We revisit, dig, and unearth the skeletons and artifacts not to bring them back to life, but to find the reason for life within us. Without memory, we would be like a headless chicken, not knowing where we came from and where we are going. True glory lies in proudly acknowledging, remembering, and learning where you came from, for only then can you know where you are going. Resolve to sharpen your memory that there remains no vagueness or broken invisible threads in between the gaps. Express your gratitude to those who held your hand when you needed them most. Ask for forgiveness from those you hurt when you were young and daring. Imprint all the happy, healthy memories within the supercomputer of your brain, before they are all gone.

Plants, animals, humans, minerals, the cosmos, and everything in nature is beautifully linked by invisible threads controlled in the etheric field. Ether which is the fifth element is dynamic and the quintessence of our existence.

Affirm- 'Namostutee, I am blessed, as we all are because we all have something to be thankful for and someone we can always praise. Tathaastu.'

CHAIN OF STRINGS

Higher or lower, we are all bound by cords to every other being, so none of us can live just by ourselves. Give love to all without asking for it in return. To live in complete harmony and balance, be the master of all virtues, and you will know what it is like to be thrice blessed. Do not let society box you in. You are that magician who can break out from any chain. The box cannot limit you. Having merged with the infinite, you have become unlimited.

God or the higher energy doesn't punish but that doesn't mean that it doesn't test or warn you from time to time. It purposely doesn't make it any easier for you because that is how you become more resilient and determined.

Life always comes with choices. A client of mine was working to become a better and more tolerant, humble, and accepting person by controlling his external words, inner anger, and frustration. Once driving back from work, he could have taken any one of the four routes to get home but for some reason, he chose the route he had never taken before. A driver in front of him was driving very slowly and so he tried to overtake the car but the driver in the other car didn't give way. Instantly frustrated and angered he rushed to voice expletives that were not heard by the driver in front. As soon he abused the driver in front he surprisingly got the right of way. This led to my client thinking that abuses work better than tolerance with most people! He continued to drive a few more miles on a relatively clear road when suddenly, as if from heaven, a big stone hit the windshield of his car and smashed it completely. Thankfully my client was not hurt. This incident came as a warning and a sign for him to get back on track and to become more patient with others and especially not to swear.

Oftentimes, we give big promises to ourselves but in the face of reality, we end up deterring from our mission by not acting on our values. It is in these times that we need to introspect, reflect, purify, restart our journey by taking subtle clues from universal energy which is here to help heal and sometimes lightly slap you like a mother disciplining her child.

When someone is being generous because you asked of them, remember to always be thankful, grateful, and trusting. Never doubt the good intentions of another being. The love you are receiving is because you asked for it. Though sometimes angels give us a taste of divinity even when we have yet not earned enough to deserve it.

Whatever we cannot experience, we negate and reject, but our negation does not imply its non-existence. The norms we set are based on our limited understanding. That we are unable to transcend our weakness does not mean there is no strength elsewhere. There is so much more still unexplored and unlearned. In trying to make our laws, we are defying universal laws.

A baby elephant tied to a tree remains tied even when it grows up not realizing that it can easily release itself from the iron chain, being far stronger and bigger than the tree. Yet it feels threatened to do so, it feels obliged, choked, deluded, and dreads the idea of being let loose in the jungle and so it habitually remains tied up and chained in its limited, ignorant purview when limitless freedom, progress is waiting to reward it with the precious gift of living a fuller life. If you are chained you are simply surviving. To be alive is to be free of all forms of self-inflicted suffering.

I have met with many teachers over my schooling years. While schools and subjects changed with age, the way of teaching has remained the same. Some teachers are great but most of them are busy putting down students and clipping their wings rather than allowing them to fly and soar. The innocent students are seekers. They are not even a competition or threat to these teachers yet it has become a habit for us to see everything with our egocentric lens.

Keeping others locked in invisible chains is their way of keeping them under subjugation and in check. We live in a universal school where everyone (politicians, parents, doctors, nurses, children, gurus) is a teacher and everyone is a student in turn. We all excel in one or the other subject. We are all here to learn, unlearn, and relearn from each other before we can pass the grade and leave our mark. The only way to break free, out of these chains, is to first really work hard on upgrading your moral values and then discern your right from their wrong.

I saw, in the news, a half-buried bottle in the ocean with a message that was found after over a century by a beachgoer in Australia. The bottle traveled from the Indian Ocean. The cork of the bottle was missing yet the dated message and the bottle was surprisingly intact. An uncorked bottle cannot hold onto the water, the attachments, painful memories, wealth, and emotions that come with the energy-water carries. Being free of all attachments to pain and pleasure, beyond all dualities – the bottle remained intact along with the dated message.

Today the message in the bottle is displayed at a museum in Germany from where it initiated its journey. Thousands of bottles are thrown into the sea by explorers, innocent children, mothers, and brothers daily, but only one odd is found after surviving this long. These are the ones who have moved beyond mundane attachments and who choose to swim across the mighty oceans with grit and determination. Over time their body becomes stronger, the soul and essence of the message becomes more purified and they meet with bliss only to mingle and meet with fated destiny once again, this time when it is found, it is more valued and spirited as it is now living a destiny that it chose for itself, this is freedom of being alive.

Affirm- 'Namostutee, My mind is still, the body is relaxed, emotions are calm, speech is silent, relationships are enhanced, thoughts are clear, memory is improved, work efficiency is increased and behavior is moral. My presence fills every one around with warmth, hope, peace, goodness, balance, Godfidence, and good health. Tathaastu.'

CHAPTER 12

WISE NUMBER TWELVE

In the olden days, boys were dropped off at a *Gurukul* (spiritual educational system of India) at the age of 12 at noon and picked up after 12 years when they turned 24 years of age at the same time. The parents never got to see their children while they were at the *gurukul* yet the child came back knowing his true soul purpose. Many such rituals have faded with the new age holistic methodologies where boys and girls get the same education. There needs to be a change in the education for boys and girls addressing the difference in yin and yang energies that one has.

The perfect number twelve recurs in history, mythology, astrology, philosophy, theology, and horology (the study and measurement of time.) Look at the popular 12-year school system, the 12 Jewish tribes (of Israel), the 12 trials of Hercules, the 12 disciples of Jesus, the 12 original points of Freemasonry, the 12 zodiac signs, the 12 hours in a clock, the 12 gates, the 12 pearls, the 12 angels, the 12 months, and the 12-inch ruler. And the list goes on. There is a profound and hidden mathematical significance within this number that continues through various periods of time in various forms. This is why I am here to discuss our 12 main chakras or energy centers. It is high time we double, triple, quadruple, and continue multiplying the effect of the 12 chakras with supreme wisdom, and go on to recreate a nine-realm world of 108.

"X Æ A-12": decoded

How each generation views the world is very different. Elon Musk has given an interesting name to his son. 'X æ A Twelve' is the result of love between his two parents. His father is from generation X and his mother is from Generation æ. He is among the first angel to be born on earth in the last 12 years of generation alpha (A-12). His name couldn't be more appropriate representing the collective force of half of the alpha generation. This generation will be swifter, calmer, and richer in knowledge, technology, and wealth than their parents. The alpha wave will continue till 2024. The next generation, which is generation beta will come in 2025. If we the people collectively allow the wave to change something within us by that time then only will the future generations continue to flourish.

Æ is a vowel sound that makes the sound of air. It comes with merging letters A and E. It comes with the merging of God (ether) and freedom (love) which leads to knowing the truth (light). A-12 heralds the spiritual beginning and unfoldment of beings born from generation X with heightened energies up-to-the 12th realm. A stands for the generation alpha, having the essence of the beginning, the middle, and the end inherent in it.

AM and PM - waxing and waning cycles are one and not divided into two for those are the beings born into the matter from the blessings of beings of the 12th plane. It is like the un-manifest and invisible becoming visible. Remember to channelize generation Alpha kid's energies in a wholesome manner.

One day and one night in the upper planetary realms of Brahma equal one year on earth. There are many higher and greater realms. The four yugas or eras contain twelve thousand heavenly planetary years. Twelve is the union of three (spiritual realm) and four (temporal plane) number.

The way our thirteen chakras energize our body, the same way the thirteen cherubim[33] work with the archangels. These heightened beings uplift and protect us. Sacred number twelve brings cosmic order of space and time.

Affirm- 'Namostutee, I efficiently and meaningfully prioritize the twelve hours of the day into realizing my aspirations. This way I persistently and confidently bring order and harmony into each day. Tathaastu.'

---

[33] *Cherubim are powerful spirit beings who do God's service.*

CHAPTER 13

INTUITIVE LIGHTENING

I was born on a Monday around noon. For me the week starts with Monday and not Sunday, the day starts with the glory of noon and not at midnight. As a spiritual being, I am here simply as a conduit and mouthpiece of God who communicates with us in various forms.

The temple and the church are within us. We have intuitive access to the universal library without the use of any modern gadgets. Like most of you, I have lived several parallel lives and reincarnated many times. The difference is that I remember most of them, as they are all stored in the *Akashic* records. As my aura has evolved and expanded, with practice, my higher consciousness can now tap into most of those memories.

I was gifted with a sacred token to ward off all evil. Since the last time I was reborn, I have had no more problems. I am resurrected, rejuvenated, revitalized, and back on heavenly earth to realize my soul's true mission in alignment with my body and spirit.

Every cell of mine has played several roles. I was a plant of species big and small. I then became an animal of many species. I have been a flower of all types, colors, and fragrances. I have also been everything from an insect to a sea animal. There is nothing I haven't been. I was a mammal and then an ant. I have lived with apes and men in the caves. I was in the spirit realm and now I am here. I have been with the angels and the men of today. I have been the father, the child and now I am the mother, playing to the tunes of these roles hasn't taken that long. I have been everything - conceivable and inconceivable. Whatever I choose to be, I become. The spirit in me remembers the part I played from time to time. It is fun when I meet souls from an old scene sometimes.

Until you lose yourself in the land that was once your own, you won't be able to find yourself all over again.

My take on the current earth changes is that humanity is moving ahead towards meeting with its ethereal divinity. This is the innate truth. Those who are receptive to evolving will come alive and adapt to the illuminating changes that the higher energies have initiated.

Thalamus is a small structure, deep within the brain, located just above the stem. It is a relay station between the brain and body. It regulates sleep, alertness, and wakefulness. The alpha and omega are two sides of the thalamus. The activated third eye is not the end but the beginning. From here on energy radiates outwards, dullness vanishes and life begins.

Those who recognize the divinity within-recognize the divinity within all and those who recognize the divinity within all -recognize the philosophy behind spirituality.

Your *Chitta* or wisdom *Nadi* activates your dopamine levels. It is the Nadi or meridian of *Chitta* which means direct perception or wisdom.

Intuition + Experience = Wisdom.

One becomes intuitive by delving into spirituality. You gain experience by asking the right questions and being scientific about the approach. Both of these faculties help define your wisdom. That is the mark of a true philosophical soul.

Ask a child who raises his hands in class out of impulse, there is so much more fun asking questions rather than answering them even if the answers are all intuitively already known. Science is like that teacher that states the facts. Philosophy is like the child who questions everything and spirituality is in between them resolving the issue helping you gain intuitive wisdom and experiential knowledge.

Just because you cannot perceive the invisible force with the limited faculty of your five senses, doesn't mean such a force does not exist.

Our five mobile senses – sight, hearing, taste, touch, and smell are like our five external phones (receptors). We receive information from these receptors. Beyond these five senses, we also have the higher senses or receptors like clairalience (smell), clairgustance (taste), clairsentience (feel), claircognizance (knowing), clairvoyance (sight), and clairaudience (hearing). We gain access and activate our higher senses through intense practice and divine grace. We are not able to access our higher senses because our outer receptors are congested.

Listen to your intuition. If you feel your energy is sapped and your vibrational field is reduced. It may be that some people or factors are causing this.

Dark matter in excess is the root of most problems. Plasma televisions and almost every gadget we use contain negative vibrations. This is why Gods are continually sending the lightning from above, to change and recharge our vibrations to positive frequencies so that we can fight and confront these forces graciously and fairly.

You and no one else is the maker of your destiny. Trust your instincts and not in the decisions of another. Maybe the one you trust is not even worthy of you. Sometimes self-help is greater than any. Sometimes what you invest most in, gives you the worst return on your investment. Do not succumb, be firm and assertive.

Wisdom is universal. It is within all beings in the universe. I am one with all beings. All beings are one with me. Ultimate knowledge is knowledge of the self. Self-knowledge is pure, divorced from the impure. Wisdom is my protective shield. It is filled with constructive good, divided from all destructive evil. I am pure. I am wise. I have the ultimate knowledge of the self.

No matter where you reach or how high you get, you will never know too much.

Disinformation age needs the Information age
Information age needs the transformation age
Transformation age needs the transmutation age

To truly know is to be truly free, and to be truly free, you have to withdraw your mind from all delusions, and then direct it to that which is not a delusion. Directing is not enough. Use your discernment and that will take you to your truth. It is better to be blind than to be delusional. It is better to discern than to be a nonconformist.

All the jewels, wealth, abundance, and beautiful perfumes are right here in nature's fragrant nurturing lap. So why lose your foresight when your eyesight is still good. Appreciate the subtle and the dense, and you will see the limitlessness in all. The pleasure you are seeking is within. It is better to have selective hearing. No matter how much ever you hear, listen to the melodious tunes of the sacred divine, which transport you to a higher realm.

Practice and theory are the two pillars you stand upon. Your right and left leg are your true pillars.

Wisdom is in transforming yourself through realizing that neither you, nor anyone else, will ever know it all. In knowing this, there is no loss. The mystery is not because of the secrecy, but because of the limitation that emanates from your mind. There is no singularity in the ruling. Everyone gets their rightful turn. All you have to do is open your arms to let the gold bar fall right into your lap. Once you have it, do not hold onto it. When the time is right, let it fall into another's lap.

Once you are on the spiritual path, everyone who is connected to the divine through you benefit from the fragrance of fresh positivity you exude, much like the famous Tamil proverb: "Even the string that ties a garland becomes as fragrant as the flowers." Everyone who makes the effort is bound to get the reward. Have faith in yourself, your abilities, and in the higher energy. As long as you make the effort, be virtuous, just, and grateful. Health, prosperity, and love are bound to be all yours. Everything begins with this profound understanding of the divine within you.

Do not believe everything your words speak, they are still taking the first few baby steps and learning how to translate the experience. The intended message from one language into another, and sometimes their essence is lost in trying to follow the norm.

There exists an innate dictionary within the super bio-energetic computer of our brain where no words are ever lost in translation and are not limited by language. This super language is called telepathic perception and communication. It is pure, intuitional, and limitless. A language in which we speak our mind. It requires no validation because it is simple and true. We all have the potential to harness the ability to communicate amongst ourselves through the limitless power of telepathy.

Humans are still like cavemen. They have, as if, lost their ability to see the obvious because of living within the concrete caves built by them. Similarly, cavefish live in a pitch-black environment. Their sense of sight is nearly functionless. However, their sense of hearing is highly sensitive. As per scientists, this enables them to detect the slightest noise, even lower than 1 kHz. With this ability, they can filter out unnecessary outer noises, and efficiently stay focused on their task of locating their prey. We humans too might have lost one of our faculties because of living in our self-created darkness for eons. But there is hope at the end of the cave. Between our two eyes, there is another eye that looks outwards. Intuition is about seeing from the third eye.

Affirm- 'Namostutee, May I tap my hypersensitive faculties using my intuitive intelligence. This will enable me to locate what is seemingly impossible for others, filtering out all outer disturbances and noises. Tathaastu.'

CHAPTER 14

INVISIBLE FENCES

Which dog crosses the invisible fence?

I will share a short anecdote to tell you about the invisible dog fence. I recently shifted to New York. To me, it's like coming to a new planet. I'm learning new things every day. The other day, I was invited to my husband's colleague's house for lunch, and I saw their dog sitting on the lawn. It was a busy road with a lot of traffic, but the dog was playing in the yard without any leash and was not trying to run out to the road. I thought "What a disciplined dog!" I asked my hosts how their dog was so well behaved. They explained that there was an invisible fence controlled by a computer kept in their basement. Every time the dog tries to leave, he feels a light electric shock; harmless but reminds him not to move beyond the boundaries. As they were talking, in my mind another story was playing. Most of us are so habitually attuned to our self-inflicted, invisible boundaries that we don't want to jump and take risks. But unless we do, we won't know how to maneuver ourselves in the world. It is when we move beyond our fears that we know life.

Which elephant stays chained long after he has been unchained?

Which *Sita* crosses the *Laxman Rekha*?

Who are the ones who cross the boundaries and borders that are fenced with barbed wires?

Such rare personality types are those who practice free will by using their discriminative intelligence. They experience life by choosing to live it the way they please rather than being controlled by others. *Sita* gave up worldly jewels in search of higher wealth.

Boundaries are good for our safety. They are set because of rock-solid fortress grounds and protects our physical space. But unless we learn why limits are set, we are prone to get frustrated, disrespect, or defy them. This is because limitations imposed through fear and control sap our energy and self-confidence.

Don't look for what life gives you but look for what you give to life. Don't look for who pains you but look for what you can give back to the one who pains you. Put the harness on the horse and control your racing mind through the reigns of self-discipline. It will take you to unimaginable heights.

The idea is invisible, it lives in the air and is crucial for the generation of electrical power and energy that moves within and without. The oxygen present in the air is required to allow the fire to form and powers most fuel-burning generators, machines, and vehicles – but air can also be used to create power directly. Wind when passed through a large turbine, can be used to generate electricity. At the same time, some sensitive mechanical drive systems use pressurized air to move machinery. The pollution in the air is a direct result of many of these uses of air. Air is a crucial, life-supporting element of our life, yet it is often taken for granted. Air is an invisible force that surrounds our planet earth. It is the thought behind the word, it is the idea behind the plan. It also contains the whole plan behind each action. We must start our morning being grateful to the air that gives us our breath. We must pay proper attention to maintain the quality, purity, and temperature of air by reducing pollutants not only in the external environment but also by cleansing our thought-forms. The air quality gets affected by our every deed. Let us resolve to maintain the essence of our very being.

Air has fivefold nature: including all the elements – air, fire, water, earth, and pure spirit.

Release the harness from the horse. A fully trained mind is just like a liberated horse, it no longer needs to be harnessed, restricted, or controlled. It will come back to you if it loves and trusts you. Give it unconditional love and respect, it will instinctually come back to you if it belongs to you. If not, it was never yours. Understanding this actuality restores balance.

Affirm- 'Namostutee, I am the source of goodness. I freely share love, blessings, and praise. Tathaastu.'

CHAPTER 15

GODS IS EMINENT

A re we collectively conscious or collectively unconscious?
If we continue to try and understand the sacred knowledge and mythology in its literal sense then we will never understand the truth in its entirety. Lateral thinking is the key to manifesting your dreams into reality. Mythology is based upon reality. It is simply a more poetic and flowery way of sharing the story because no one likes to hear about reality. The truth presented differently doesn't become a lie. Though we have the energy of all elements within us, each being has one most dominant or strong feature which is their innate disposition. Your strongest asset is your gift. Your gift is like God residing within you.

Mythology entails our culture and history. Look beneath the surface and meet with your true values. Whatever your strongest divine asset maybe, once you share it, it shows light to those who are slightly weak in that aspect. This way we all learn and get inspired by each other's divinity. One person might have a strong energy of attracting *Laxmi* (Goddess of prosperity) within them while another may have a very strong *Arjuna* (right action) within them and so on.

Sometimes our strongest point is our weakest. We often feel that something is missing in our life. This is because we are not meeting our full potential, our divine, or the quota of God's power. In realizing what is missing in our cup, we can fill it in by attracting and imbibing that energy within us. This requires persistence, patience, and blessings of the Gods. The section of Gods who have those dominant energies within them, automatically come to you if you are receptive and have pure intentions. This is the reason why various cultures and religions have Gods and

Demi-Gods. The essence of God may come in any form and anybody. The ritual of worshipping, praising, and believing them in our way is our duty. Without faith, humility, and trust, we are bound to fall further into the enslaving, misguided thought traps.

God's love for us is unending, each cup is filled based on how empty and cleansed it is from leftover residue. The portion we receive is left in the purity of our intended actions. This is the reason why some cups are filled half, some are filled two thirds, some are filled till the brim and are in turn offering help by filling many more cups with unbound energy. My mind is an empty cup, it keeps getting filled with intuitive bliss. If your cup is empty, connect with me to fill it with some light if you like.

Each chakra has a particular governing deity. Just like the ruler God, Chakras are invisible yet real.

Deeper meanings of Gods we worship and mythology: God is pure knowledge, bliss, and ecstasy that you feel by meeting with your higher transformed self. The reason Hindus have so many Gods and Goddesses is that everything and everyone has a portion of God within them. Even the smallest of particles has inherent God's power and the potential to realize its intensity. We must revere and acknowledge the potential within all. God is eminent within every form of life. God lives on the very essence and the very core of every being. God is love. Love is Vishnu. God Vishnu has many forms.

'Buddhi' means intelligence in the Hindi language and oak trees are known to remain eternally youthful. Both Buddha and the oak tree are wise and ageless. No wonder Buddha's head looks just like the acorn from the oak tree. Whether you worship nature or you worship the idol, inherently both forms represent the same reality and the goodness of God.

Buddha's long and wavy hair, coiled and tied on top of his crown depicts wisdom. There are various mini (counterclockwise and clockwise) ringlet curls. All these together depict a thousand petals of knowledge acquired through deep *Tapasya*[34], cleansing, and purification by a fully enlightened being. The auspicious mark between Buddha's eyebrows, in the center of the forehead, depicts the intense energy of the all-seeing supernatural eye and clarity of divine vision. The long ears depict wealth. The subtle smile

---

[34] *Tapasaya- Tapa means heat or burn. Tapasaya is an ongoing learning process that requires constant self-effort and deep focus. The blessed ones are chosen to do Tapasaya or sacrifice to obtain moksha or liberation.*

depicts gentleness and serenity. The half-opened eyes depict an externally and internally balanced mind that is awake and turned inwards.

Buddha is within you, so is Christ, so is Krishna, each of you has a mini God residing within and outside of you waiting to be invoked, awakened, and realized through the charge of your positive vibrational energy. Just like the ancient and modern Gods, each atomic God[35] and each person has its specific energy and charm along with the energies of all the others and this is our innate specialty.

God is not distinct from us. God is the divine power of intellectual discrimination within us that helps us know goodness, tolerance, truth, and reality. God is one but we call him by many names. We are one and we call ourselves by many names. We are part God.

The reason we have little infinitesimal God within us is because we are all humans and tiny God resides within us and this made creation possible and will continue to. We, therefore, have the potential to be superhumans. It is the divine essence that allows us to have the ability, unlike some animals, to have discriminative intelligence which we need to harbor and bring to use wisely and carefully to continue progression.

Your wish is truly our universal father's command since he is in you and speaks through you. The words you speak, the thoughts you express, and the feelings you experience are all his. There is nothing evil and nothing good; all are just learning opportunities. Everything is his and belongs only to him. Everything is by his command, though it seems as if it's your wish. This means that nothing can change by itself; there are always internal and external factors- skeptics, believers can influence but not change.

The cosmic forces carry dark as well as light aspects. To merge with the cosmic energies, we need to embrace and accept both aspects, for it is in experiencing the inner shadows that we come out into the outer light. Both are within our nature, so both are equally true. There is no division. There is no right and no wrong. You are as sacred as the mini God that made you and as sensual as the divine Goddess that lies within you, in earth's body. You are free, renewed, empowered, and truly ecstatic only when you dance to their tunes. Let's merge with and embrace the yin and yang. It is then that you begin to make love with the oneness, leaving behind all false dogmas. Your body is your temple. Worship the actual Goddess within it if you want the *Prasad*, the sweet dessert that you get

---

[35] *Smallest unit of perfect order*

when you worship in your temple. Then you will realize that the musk you have been hankering for all these years, running helter-skelter to find the source of its fragrant scent, is deep within you. It gets assimilated and absorbed inside the pouch of your karm or solar plexus chakra, at a point which is known as Surya chakra. This point enhances the movement of feet and clears sight. Perhaps the deer that is outside your garden is here to simply remind you of your forgotten truth, for it too seems to be trapped in the same confusion.

Srinivasan Ramanujan, the man who created infinity once quoted "God is man's greatest invention". God says - In you I am pleased and so your soul is free from karma. Placebo is a Latin word that means "I am pleasing." A free soul is healed and placebo-ed by God.

There are three levels of knowledge as per Hindu philosophy:

- *Para Para* - is also known as *para Shakti; Trika* or bondage. It is a mediocre level of understanding. It entails having less supremacy, sometimes symbolized as a lower pedestal or *yoni* of S*hiva lingam*.
- *Apara* - is not mere knowledge but the victory of manifested, un-manifested and transcendental divinity in one cosmic egg or *atman* or soul. It is known as *tridevi (triple Goddess)* or *adi parashakti*. It is also called the supreme-being or the first start. The beginning and the original creator, observer, destroyer, and sometimes as the evolution of the infinite life. She is the absolute reality of the eternal. She is considered limitless and formless energy. She is sometimes referred to as *Maa Durga*. She gives salvation by balancing the effect of planet energy on all chakras. She is the divine feminine *kundalini* energy, a psycho-spiritual mysterious force that enters a righteous heart, the truthful mind of an innocent soul with pure devotion.
- *Para* - Shiva or Para is the supreme fuller knowledge. It is an understanding of the human potential, beyond the grasp of normal experience. It is something that can be known only through mysticism and intuition by very few who are cosmically graced and divinely receptive. It is symbolized as the upper oval stone of S*hiva lingam*. It is threefold like the *Trishul* (trident) of three forces creation, preservation, and destruction. It, therefore, represents inner bliss.

Krishna's Gopis are symbolic of woman power. *Krishna's Gopis* are all cowherd girls. *Mira* was one such cowherd girl. A powerful cowherd girl (celestial cow) can handle many wild cows and tame them too so that the cows can help you realize your true nature.

It is said that Christ had a beloved named Magdalene and she was always with four more women (Mary, Lord's sister, mother, and the illuminated light of her soul). This simply implies that Magdalene had the power of four women within her. Much like *Ma Durga, Ma Saraswati, Ma Laxmi, Ma Kaali* of India.

Indian Goddesses are often shown with four hands. It simply implies that they have the power of four divine energies within them.

Goddess Guan Yin, who is very popular in Asia, is personified with many hands, not because physically she has that many hands but because she has supremely merciful and compassionate grace. The power of many in one. *God Aviloketeshwara* is her masculine aspect. The thousand hands of Lord *Avilokteshwara* tells us that your one hand is as generous and powerful as 1000 hands put together. Hands when energized have the power to uplift, give love and blessings to thousands at one time because of this continuous generosity, clarity, and purification.

Women represent prosperity and yin energy which brings in money and wealth. This is why Goddess *Laxmi* is worshipped during Diwali. She is the harbinger of luck and prosperity. It is believed that the more gold you lavish and pamper your wife with, the more she will feel grounded and gravitate towards earth energies thereby bringing manifold blessings of wealth and abundance for all those around.

It is not God that tells lies, dominates, destroys, confuses, conflicts, argues, or gives up. It is not some invisible force that tells the truth, makes efforts, frees, wills, preserves, acts, accepts, shares, or tolerates. It is always you. God is within and outside of you. It is you. Refined God is the combination of your mind, body, and spirit. You separate yourself from your true divine nature when you create havoc.

Ra means "sun," *Sa* means "son," and *Sat* means "daughter." When we say 'Om tat sat' or 'Sat Naam', then we are referring to the daughter of the divine. And when we say 'Sa Ra', we are referring to the son of the sun.

Ma is a Sanskrit word that means "me" or "my." When you say *Ma Durga* or *Ma Kaali*, you mean my *Durga* or my *Kaali*. You invoke the

Goddesses Durga and Kaali within you. All nine cosmic wombs are within you, capable of being activated through the healing protocols offered.

The month of May is named after the Roman Goddess *Maia*. People born during this month are our elders in terms of generational precedence, which means they are our ancestors. They promote growth and profitability.

The left tilt in Lord *Ganesh's* trunk symbolizes *Ida* Nadi which is the cooling, feminine, and nourishing energy of the moon. When Lord Ganesh's trunk tilts towards the right, it symbolizes *Pingala* Nadi which is the warm, masculine, and fiery energy of the sun. However, when the trunk faces forward it symbolizes complete balance attained through activation of the middle of Sushumna Nadi which opens to clear all blockages. Finally, when the trunk is tilted upwards it symbolizes the awakened kundalini energy which has traveled towards the crown chakra.

As per Hindu mythology, there is a monkey god *"Hanuman"* who burnt the evil forces in Lanka once he was asked to get Sita from Ravana. The impulse or adrenaline control and accelerator center for monkeys are at the tip of their tails which is where our *Junoon*[36] chakra assimilates *prana*. As the west wind of knowledge blows, the mighty Lord Hanuman swiftly but carefully rushes at lightning speed, expanding and contracting the adrenal gland through his tail. Lord Hanuman harnesses the adrenal fire through breath control and generates only as much fire as is needed in the space it occupies. It is a blessing that has been bestowed for eons upon super-humans like Lord Hanuman. A super-human combines perfect diction of speech and faultless manner of character to glue us all together. In mythology, it is shown that Lord Hanuman increases and decreases in size at will. That increase and decrease imply ego. In the same way, we inflate and deflate our ego, based on the situations we encounter. Lord Hanuman's love for bananas fills him with all their nutritive values. Bananas are considered the fruit of the Sun God because of their binding nature. The Sun God is known as *Ra*. The Moon Goddess is known as *Ma. Ra + Ma* give out their love and light to Hanuman so that he can serve Mother Earth, which is *Mata Sita*. Hanuman remains devoted to her and stands up for her, to ensure she forever lives in bliss and pleasure with her chin held high. With

---

[36] *Mein meng or junoon chakra - As per 'Miracles of Pranic Healing' by GMCKS, page 22- the location of meng mein chakra is at the back of the navel. In Kabbalah it is is written in Hebrew known as 'Hod' which means action that brings glory. The author calls this point 'junoon' as it is junoon or pure passsion that fuses action into the sole of the feet to walk the talk.*

the determined will to please the mother Goddess and remain her divine servant, Hanuman successfully crosses the turbulent oceanic waters and slays all the demons of the mind that he encounters on the path to attain self-perfection. With love and devotion that strong, any super-human can stay forever faithful and committed, transcending all feelings of fatigue or lack, and moving beyond all obstacles, ever ready to move through the psychic disturbances of the turbulent oceanic waters, even if it takes a million attempts. No attempt is small.

Hanuman could fight all the external evil that existed in his path. This is because when you look at a picture of *Hanuman* you will see his face as if he is holding his breath. He practiced taking in a gulp of air to control his breath. This was not only to control his breath but to fully control his monkey mind and wavering habits. With concentrated practice, he attained *siddhi* to become smaller than an ant by letting go of all ego. With this, he could also become bigger than the tallest mountain to make his body and aura shine bigger and brighter than us all. Monkeys breathe 32 times per minute & so does an over-anxious man. When Hanuman had to control the number of breaths, he reduced it to 18 breaths a minute and then further through relaxed deep alternative breathing techniques. His dedication and persistence towards his goal was remarkable and a profound example similar to what many yogis display. This helps develop one-pointed meditation attention and helps us evolve into better beings.

In certain higher realms, 7000 becomes 700, and 40 is equivalent to 4 years.

No being is greater than another. Each is doing a service of equal value and worth in the eyes of Lord God, as long as the attempt is genuine. No effort is greater or smaller than another. The hard work of the ant, the squirrel and the man are all equally recognized in the eyes of the Lord God, for each is doing their best basis their capacity and the space they occupy. Stay humble and devoted. A million cells within us are activated by the upward forces of the moon and the downward energy of the sun, meeting within our center. The mastermind behind this perfect plan in Sri Lanka is called *Rama* and in India is called *Krishna*. In Christianity, he is called Christ. In Kashmir, the *Shivai*sts call the mastermind *Maa Kaali*. Yogis call him *Baba*, and the modern royal Buddhists conceal its sacred truth to be imparted to those few who are willing.

Originally, the actions that we do are dictated by mischievous monkeys:

the untamed, fickle, restless mind. The oceanic bliss of inner emotions is filled with dolphins, dainty fish, and seahorses. Praising Lord God's perfect, ultimate plan is the cause of our eternal evolution, giving us wings to fly and soar so that we can inspire many more souls with our flight towards enlightenment.

We see only peacocks flaunting their grand aura and dancing with pride because it is not in the nature of peahens to show off the subtle beauty of their wings.

All cultures acknowledge the strength of the trinity. Here is what we learn from the beautiful language of parables through the names of great Indian deities.

- *Brahma is* the pure heavenly intuitive light (creates) and sits above the middle brain, the first God.
- *Vishnu* is humans' creative will (preserves) and sits above the left rational brain.
- *Shiva* is intellectual evaluation & discriminative intelligence active upon the earth (creates, preserves, destroys) and sits above the right intuitive brain.

Finally, the entire trinity within us is centered through a medium (recreator) that balances, restores, and praises the three energies by constant awareness and patience.

Jesus Christ is Ajna or will center. If you want to balance your Ajna chakra or ego or will center, then forgive and ask for forgiveness. Christ in etheric form exists as our God and rules our Christ chakra. Absolute God is a perfect combination of truth, beauty, and love. An absolute God is not an absolute being.

Self-realization is blessed by Mahaveer who inculcates perfection through skill. This is the 24th point and is slightly left of the Ajna chakra. To the right or northeast of Ajna chakra is Buddha center. It's a state of awakening that one reaches when one gets enlightened through knowing the true nature of reality and sustains it through mental discipline.

Kundalini awakening is all-pervading. It arises from three lower points around the base. It connects divine moral power with the creator or Brahma's light and finally centered in the forehead.

Laxmi (sacral vitality chakra) is Vishnu's (rational brain) wife, they meet at navel chakra. Laxmi chakra (sacral chakra) is the daughter of Maa

Durga (heart center or karm). Parvati is Shiva's wife. Shiva rules the left heart. Rama Sita combined (or Shiva Parvati combined) are on the right of it - that is the center of the chest, which is your true heart - a perfect combination of the two. Shakti, the recreative energy of shiva is given various names in India such as Goddess Laxmi, Saraswati, Sattee. These Goddesses are worshipped in India, they bond and connect us with divine power. They endow us with divine knowledge. Sattee or Sati is another name for Shiva's first wife or queen, reborn as Goddess Parvati. This combination leads to the birth of Lord Ganesha and if the relationship of father-son or Ganesha and Shiva is not good right from the beginning then this chakra imbalance causes Asthma related issues. Saraswati sits to the right of Ganesha, the way she sings her tunes rhythmically is therefore very important. Krishna sits in the center of your throat as the voice of truth.

Kamadhenu (Mother of All Cows or Cow of Plenty)

Sacred Goddess *Kamadhenu* is known as the divine, celestial and pious cow, or the wish-fulfilling cow for true seekers. She is considered to be the giver of plenty and she brings prosperity. She is the daughter of *Brahma*. She is the milk giver of your desires that you churn by performing your duties well. The duties you perform towards yourself, others, and towards her. She is the essence of all the best things in life. She is above the base of the pillar, the *linga*. She remains hidden under the root of the mystic tree. The root is actually above and not below the tree. She is the life-giver. We all and everything is borne from her. She is the primordial mother of all mothers. All Gods ever known reside within her. She miraculously activates all chakras within the physical and beyond. She is pristine, white, flawless, and pure. She is the divine feminine. Sometimes, it seems that she has taken a form, and when she is visible to few, they see red and blue parrot wings on her shoulders. These wings represent the two waves of light coming from the sun and the moon which make light and fire possible on earth. Her human face represents the primordial face of humanity, her complexion is pristine white, and her two horns are attracted to the yang energy that Gods represent. Her peacock tail which looks like the peafowl represents her celestial eye. Her milk looks like white clouds and streams over the linga of Shiva to ignite the sacred fire. Her legs are high and strong like the Himalayan Mountains. She endlessly gives and nourishes those who worship and praise her. Her skin provides and protects us. Every part of her, including her urine and dung, have immense healing qualities and powers.

During *Satyuga*, the first stage of truth - she stood steadily with perfect balance and energy of her four feet[37]. During *Tretayuga*, the second stage of truth- she stood steadily with yin energy of her three feet. During *Dwaparyuga*, the stage that was the onset of disappearing truth-she stood steadily on the yang energy of her two feet. During *Kalayuga*, the fourth stage-she is the ultimate source. The sacrificial mother is here to sustain humanity. She is the fertile Mother Earth who came down from the heavens. She couldn't resist Shiva's linga and neither could he! Her tail is downward and outward implying that she is grounded amongst us and yet outgoing and open to the heavens.

When Brahma is sleeping, the cycle goes downhill. We move away from the source, and so it becomes that much more difficult for you to reach back to your roots. When Brahma is awake, the cycle goes upwards, and so it is that much easier to reach your goal. We are at a point when Brahma is waking up. It is no wonder life has become more comfortable and easy. So come on! Ride up to the subtle consciousness to merge with yourself and others. Beyond the descent is the ultimate ascent.

In the epic Mahabharata, the charioteer is the universal soul, the cosmic intelligence, or the Krishna consciousness. The chariot is our body, and we are the individual soul that contains the universal consciousness within ourselves. The horses are our senses that we control through the actions of our hands, by holding onto the reins and guiding them to the direction we please, based on our self-realization. We do not act out everything the mind thinks.

"Bat" is another name for an ancient cow Goddess. She is a Goddess of protection, inspiration & assistance. No wonder Jewish celebrate "bat mitzvah". Goddess Bat is the personification of the Milky Way, which implies the milk that flows from the udders of a heavenly cow.

In Egypt-Nefertum is considered the goddess of perfume, Ankh represents a breath of life. Nefertum is an Egyptian Goddess of perfume and fragrance. The special healing perfume that brings rebirth and regeneration is the breath of fresh air. It gives us life.

God magically brings good in us and is not distinct from us but is our own eternal, miraculous higher divine self that creates form out of the formless.

Just the way Christ used the body of Jesus to heal and teach, the sun uses the body of the moon to balance and spread the light. Sanath Kumara

---

[37] *Feet denote firm movement through divine point that connects humans with earth*

is a planetary being that uses the body of the earth to increase love and radiate soul energy. Vedic Agni God (eternal son) is the lord of flames and the reason behind our bodily form.

If the body, moon, and Jesus, were not clean, pure, and receptive - their higher soul could not have shared the radiance. For your aura to radiate divine energy you have to establish and reestablish daily contact with your higher soul. This is done by working towards balancing your energies and by putting out the intention.

Light or darkness, both are divine. Lord Rama was born around 12:00 pm and Lord Krishna was born around 12 am. An incarnation of Lord Rama is born when the sun is highest in the sky at around 12:00 pm. Those people who are blinded by external desires (*bhojan*) remain unaware of Lord Rama's birth who comes in the middle of all yugas (Tretayuga) as a bright messenger to awaken people and bring truth awareness. It is said that an incarnation of Lord Krishna is born when it is darkest in the night sky. Those people who are clouded by pleasure (*karm bhog*) remain unaware of Krishna's birth who comes at the darkest hour of Kaliyuga (Dwaparayuga) to diminish darkness, liberate people and bring moral awakening.

Affirm- 'Namostutee, Truth realization leads me to God-realization. Tathaastu.'

CHAPTER 16

ANGELIC BLESSINGS

The lords are all looking out for you. The Gods are all-around guiding you. Seeing your trance, the angels are dancing. The sweet little beings of light are looking up to you. The clock has changed direction and is going counter-clockwise. The whirling has just begun.

Angels have different colors or hues based on their level of evolvement. They too are assigned responsibilities that they need to complete to become what they want to be. They are here to protect and guide us. We invoke the good pure angelic beings out of love and reverence. Our faith attracts them towards us. They help us shape our thoughts in a way that is more aligned with divinity. The angels can help us with our thoughts but the action lies on us. Only we can do that action. They are there only in the form of color or light which so far only few can see though I have heard some special cameras can detect the colors and hence their existence. Invoking them is an art and not everybody can master this unless you have a yearning to learn.

Your auric ray is known by the hues and colors of the aura. Your auric disposition transcends beyond this lifetime and the next. As you live and based on your auric disposition your existence in the next life is decided by the universal intelligence above us. This is in resemblance to the corporate structure that exists today. A person when recruited is put in departments based on their performance, inclination towards a particular workstream, and background in terms of work experience or study major. This affects the way you come back into the world in which country, color, or race. Eventually, everyone intermingles to gain the qualities of all the seven races mapped by the seven continents. This is a beautiful amalgamation where your primary race or disposition will be dominant but you will gain the understanding of all other races helping you intermingle. That is what will take you closer to your true self or the true nature of your soul.

The front solar plexus is the sun center, looked over by Archangel Michael. The moon's center is deep within the base of the spine, looked over by Archangel Gabriel.

Archangel Michael who is the strongest or chief angel has threefold nature having a role to play in all the three seasons- summer, winter, and spring. Raphael looks after spring. Uriel looks after summer, Michael looks after autumn and Gabriel looks after winter. All these four angels or devas live in four cardinal directions and do so much work and yet remain invisible to the naked eye. Each of them serves to keep balance in the earth, air, fire, and water. Prayer of thanks in devotion of Lord's angels should be done morning, noon and at sunset.

Affirm- 'Namostutee, I believe and trust that not a single blade of grass moves without divine grace of higher beings. Their presence revives all the shriveled hearts. Tathaastu.'

CHAPTER 17

EMPTY PAGE

It is time to turn the page under divine guidance to find eternal peace and healing in the next chapter of life.

The purpose of this chapter is like having an emotional, mental, and spiritual bath under the indigo waterfall. To stay motivated and refreshed you need to imbibe the inner message of the pages, just like you ritualistically bathe.

Said the paper to the pen, "Until now, I was dry paper. You gave meaning to my existence with the wet ink of your fountain pen and taught me to fly high. You gave me wings. You are the wind beneath my wings. I fly because of you. I can see you try and try, but don't worry, for once I have taken that flight, and I can never be dry again."

I love spending time with myself, discovering, and knowing myself outside in. I sometimes write when I am with myself. By sharing my writings here, I am in a way sharing a part of me with you. I am sure we both will enjoy each other's company more and more as we move along, getting to know each other better and better, as life and its various facets unfold before us.

How long we take to perform well, control our reactions, and act under divine guidance is what decides how much grace transformation, and enlightenment we achieve. The choice is primarily ours. The story you left unfinished will be completed by another and it will get the finishing touches by someone else. The story is meant to be written irrespective of whether you participate in writing the script or not. However, the choice to write is primarily yours.

The loss is yours, not mine. The opportunity to play a part and contribute in an important role in being one of the main characters is rare and profound. What comes out of the role you play, depends on your heart, acceptance, and willingness to develop.

When you are a full page is when you are completely blank and stark. When my tree is blossoming in the peak seasons you are still planting your first seed. I was reborn to plant the seed upon which you could grow. I am full only because you are empty and new. I renew with the infinite newness and I see the opportunities waiting for you ahead. Open your eyes and you will see the immaculate sight. You are just a manifestation of me. A dream that became a living reality. You are made by me, not just for me. You are a result of my creative inspiration. You are desperate to know who you are. In knowing me you will know yourself. For the divinity in me is the same divinity I poured within you. Your infancy is the fancy of my eternal soul. You have in you to re-do what I did and undo what I didn't do. You are the action behind my thoughts. You are here to do, so simply do.

There is something so peaceful, tranquil, and mystic about the night. It is an energy that the day can never have. Only the quietness of the night can bring a new day, and only the noise of the day can bring out the essence of the night. Black and red, dark and light, empty and full, tamas and rajas, shapeless and shape, invisible and visible form: are all intertwined.

Your higher soul is you. Our story that you wrote has changed the course of our entire history. The story that began with you is forever imprinted in the DNA of the new-age children who can see past the illusion of ego separateness. The generations that are yet to come will go on adding more pages to the story that once began with you. The more pages that are added, the more upgraded versions are being downloaded into the super-computers of our minds. We, therefore, are in a constant flux of evolvement and change. Embrace, engage, and co-create instead of mindlessly procreating. The reality you create is not only your destiny but holds the future of the entire cosmos and universe. Nourish it, love it, savor it, enjoy it, and nurture it. Embrace it and help it evolve. Your role is the most crucial and vital. All the natural elements are dependent upon you.

You have come to earth with a particular purpose and you must try to help others see the importance of that mission, whether they realize it or not is not for you to gauge but whatever may be the outcome dare to see through it! Even if you fall, you know you will be soon rising yet again to finish where you started. You are just the writer, the meaning is for them to decipher.

I searched and searched and when no book could answer what I saw, I decided to write the answers myself, so that no one else needs to search for these answers. And yet the higher mind returns with another unanswered quest. And so this book remains unfinished as long as the pages continue to turn, and the story continues to unveil and unravel the meaning of outer and inner worlds. Whatever I am writing here can be interpreted in many ways. The way I see things today will be different from how I see it tomorrow so my interpretation too may differ depending on the environment, circumstances, context, situation, place, people I am with, and their effect upon my life. My interpretation, perception, and experience may vary, but love inherently remains the same. It remains as it is. How can you write something if there was nothing to write? I have written so much and so there must be something that makes me write, isn't it?

This book is a result of constant revelations that were graced upon me. I then diligently meditated, studied, and analyzed the mysterious and intuitive reflection I received through books, higher teachings, self-experience, and listening to the experiences of others. This led me to a perennial state of wakefulness. Here I remain untroubled by the highs and lows of emotions and the body in pursuit of mental knowledge. I couldn't ask for greater validation of this heavenly truth. This is not the time to end but a time to begin a new story. The unending pages keep unfolding the message of the new page. Untiringly lift another fallen leaf to unravel the glory and mystery of the whole tree.

The fact that you bought this book and are currently reading these words shows you are entitled, ready to heal, and evolve. As you turn the pages, I trust your aura will slowly brighten up and get energized with colorful divine hues. The chapters will touch you most, where the energy of your aura is currently most depleted. If you are a sensitive person, you will feel a ticklish or cozy, warm feeling as the imbalance in the chakras gets corrected and open up. Eventually, you will feel the difference within yourself through the healing energies, sent to you through the positive words and intentions on these pages.

I get very little sleep but in those infrequent moments of beauty naps, I feel divine energy flowing from my crown, over my breast, upon the ground, igniting, strengthening, and inspiring every limb of my body. My attempt here is to pen down whatever messages I receive during these moments.

Affirm- 'Namostutee, I trust that love, prosperity, protection, success, and abundance all are mine. I am complete. Tathaastu.'

CHAPTER 18

UNBOUND BOND

Your body grounds the mind that flies in the sky. A mind flies to any realm, if not controlled, harnessed, and housed. Your body is like a container, all wisdom and knowledge is contained within it. Without it, the wisdom you have gathered cannot function. You are a combination of the two then I wonder why you have been living in such a dichotomy, separating the mind and body for the sake of understanding the perfect plan and creating havoc on earth. The next three chapters reflect a mind whose reigns are set free. Excessively analyzing and overthinking causes mental disturbances and anxiety. This jams your mind in a way that overall productivity, activity, and vitality suffer and we are not able to act swiftly when needed. The pressure cooker bursts if steam is not released. So in a way, it is good to let go of what comes to your mind rather than suppress the thoughts, be flexible, let things flow as they are, give yourself a break, relax and rest. Stop thinking and start expressing rather than mindlessly reacting.

The lion represents the power and the fire energy of the sun. The unicorn represents the light and wisdom of the moon, and the Alicorn, or winged unicorn, in the middle represents the perfect love of the holy mother. Imbalance of any one energy will shake all and missing anyone will kill all! We are all interconnected and bound.

Myths are a reality, and so are our dreams. We are most awake when we are fast asleep. What was real got one new bone to become the mythical unicorn. What was mythical got two wings and became the real bird. All it takes is a little divine elixir to make the mythical real and the real mythical.

Animals act through their intuition. They do not learn from any texts. We too are part animal. We too know things instinctually and intuitively. There is a male within every woman. There is a female within every man. A man can be a nurturer and a woman can be a provider. We are all also part of God. We have a biological mother and a divine mother. We have a biological father and a divine father. The tug of war between the lower animalistic nature and the higher Godly (Godlike) nature-the evil and the good-is no myth. Keeping the balance between the two extremities of our innate nature is our job.

Be like a tortoise, constantly reflecting on the inner and outer self with every breath you take. This is one journey in which you will never get exhausted. The more you travel, the more refreshed you will feel. If you get tired, you know you have lost your path, so stop and look for it again.

In the animal kingdom, the king of love is the dog, the king of air is the horse, the king of fire is the lion, the queen of water is the fish, the queen of the earth is the elephant, and the queen of the ether is the peahen. No wonder I often see peahens around my home and in places where the etheric air is still clean.

Despite – and because of-the bonds we all share, we are living unbound. True power comes from wisdom, just the way the lion got his mane from the horses. Use your horse sense and you will know this to be true because this is straight from the horse's mouth.

When you hear that things are getting better – it is true. Ask the animals freely walking outside our homes and they will tell you that things are in fact getting infinitely better. Whenever I look outside my home these days - I see Magnolia flowers, coyotes, deer, songbirds, peacocks, rabbits, bunnies, and chipmunks because they have not been quarantined. For once they are free because the kings of the concrete jungle - humans are all locked up in terror or quarantined. My pet dog has suddenly become more assertive and commanding and takes me for longer walks, walking freely without a leash.

I'm sure my mind, body, and spirit have traveled across space and time freely and easily, both in the underworld and the higher realms-the land, the air, and the water-and returned to your noble humble service with all my passion. When I sat on the horse with my peacock feathers, the horse seemed to have wings. And look there! My dog is following us too. When *Yudhistara in Mahābhārata* was to ascend to the heavens and the Gods sent the chariot for him, he instead stayed on because he wanted to be with his dog who stayed loyal to him throughout his journey. Being a man of *Dharm* or righteousness, he couldn't leave his dog alone.

My journey and travels have been an interesting amalgamation of horsepower and lion energy. The good Gods are supporting us from beneath and the Lords of the Heavens are protecting us from above, so why not build our palaces on these hollow though not shallow grounds.

We have to clean the stables before we bring the horses in. We have to make the environment safe and friendly for the horses to ensure that they do not run away or starve. We must provide enough food and care for them so they like staying with us as much as we enjoy riding them. The horses are like thoughts inside our stable mind. Good thoughts or horses are our companions. Thoughts stay calm only if they are nurtured, enriched, trained properly, and loved much like the horses. Our equine companions degenerate or become senile if we do not show compassion and kindness in our thoughts by always taking extra care.

We are all getting loaded with theoretical information from all around. However, gaining information is not enough. Serenity is experienced by silencing your thoughts and moving beyond information.

Connect not with the words but what is behind these words.

Connect not with the information but what is beyond the information.

What is behind the words will lead you to go beyond the information.

Feminine or yin energy is subtle and pure. Masculine or yang energy is active, dark, and dense so it can stand out in the light. When a woman becomes pregnant, it is the yang energy that is more active. Studies have shown that seahorse has exposed the real truth: the male, not the female, of the species, gets pregnant. We have confused genders and evolution. Seahorses have a unique reproduction cycle. Although many would think that the female carries the eggs like most organisms, it is the male seahorse that carries the eggs in his brood pouch, which is similar to a kangaroo pouch.

When the innate immortal soul perennially speaks to you, you are left with no choice but to voice the truth, because the truth is constantly speaking through you.

In essence, we are all part animal and part human. It is in honoring and bowing down to our lower animal nature that we can transcend ourselves into becoming Godly humans. It is that cute, naughty, bunny within us that mischievously coaxes us to shed our snakeskin and bring out our true animal nature.

Our true nature coaxes us to live in a positive environment, like green, freshly mowed lawns in a well-tended garden. And as the cleansing temple bell rings, it is the gutsy, earthly lioness within us that guards our homes, facing the northern gates to success and prosperity. It is our true nature that bestows on us the assertive energy of power, courage, and Godfidence, as we continue to purify ourselves with the ringing of the cleansing temple bell.

Kundalini energy is like the coiled trunk of an elephant, resting at the root of our spine. As it moves upwards, it opens the blockages of our spine and nerves of our brain. After calming our mind, it comes down to our heart and fills us with love.

The elephant within us seeks advice from other meridians and attunes itself to the signals of our spine. By spraying the gushing waters through the eternal fountain into our crown, it settles and inspires the confused, wavering monkey mind to become creative, with the vast, humble, loving energy of the East, bringing out the graceful lotus in full bloom above and over us.

As the airy, mystical unicorn comes speeding from the whispering west winds of spiritual power and wisdom, it reminds us not only of our loyal faithful dog within us but also of the pure, loving energy like the Pegasus, which is also within us. As the kundalini rises, we develop razor-sharp vision like that of the eagle. As we continue to thank the energy we gain from them all, we then successfully transcend into an Alicorn with magnificent parrot wings. The motherly Nandi cow is the giver of boon and blessing, which too is within us.

From the alpha state, kundalini proactively, steadfastly, and endlessly continues to work hard throughout the process until we center ourselves and reach the omega state. Kundalini ensures that none of our main meridians are left out from being activated. As the meridians open up, we feel as though our peacock feathers are joyfully dancing in the rain as we go through our karmic cycles. All our health rays become untangled and clear.

Cats, they say, have nine lives because they replenish the negativity with positivity as soon as it touches them with the strength of their aura.

I roared, I am the white tiger but unfortunately, the jungle is empty.

I hear that I am late as all my companions are now extinct.

Perhaps, I am the last one and all alone!

I wondered, just then, I should dream faster next time.

The next destination could be even more perplexing, well that is hardly any respite.

The white tiger didn't give up. It courageously dared to cross the barriers of time and space because the tiger doesn't get scared from hunting even huge animals all alone. It believes in its speed and knows the rest of the pack will soon join in. Soon I reached a noble land where I was the first but that is another story.

The catfish, a fish with cat-like whiskers has up to more than 175,000 taste-sensitive cells as compared to the human sense of taste which has 10,000 taste buds. Its whiskers act as receptors that help the fish to not only taste food but also locate food.

World over, elephants are worshiped as a representation of Gods. They are the holy God of the sense of smell. As per extensive studies, the African bush elephant tops the list of having the most superior nose amongst all animals. These elephants have double the smell sensing genes as their ancestors. It has 2000 powerful sense sensors in the trunk or sniffer. The second spot is taken by the cow and dogs. We learned that cows have around 1200 and dogs have around 1000 sensors while humans have only 400 sense receptors.

There is a lot that is still undiscovered by biologists. Bulls drive away evil spirits. But this shows that the animals, we consider being an inferior species, are far superior to us in some or the other aspect.

Despite this in a recent case, farmers attempted to kill wild boars with crude local bombs stuffed in food. They were trying to drive the boars away from crop-raiding. In the process, they ended up killing a hungry pregnant elephant who mistakenly ate the deadly explosive food which was meant for the boar. Suddenly, the incident was in the news for killing elephants more so as Hindus worship elephants as sacred Gods. How was the incident right all these years when other wild animals were being brutally killed? The way I see it, whether the white boar dies or the pregnant elephant, a life is lost and we should react the same way irrespectively. Both are part of God's creation and are divinely the same. When life is unjustly taken, it is wrong irrespective of whose life it is. Similarly, whether it is wrong meted out to a black, brown, or white man - a wrong must not be determined by color, race, gender, status, or species. The universal energies are one. We all are interdependent upon each other and are essentially one.

Affirm- 'Namostutee, Let us spread ripples of love all around and across every being. Tathaastu.'

CHAPTER 19

LOWER NATURE

I was born midday at around noon. It is when the sun is highest in the sky and so I do not deal very well with darkness but here goes a try.

The mysterious legendary part lion, part human - Sphinx are telling us to fight with our lower nature and rise above evil towards victory over obstacles. Even if my physical body gets harmed, my spirit stays unharmed. Only those who let their animal nature come out - can discipline it. I say so because it is possible to transcend your lower nature and work with your higher nature while being in the same body.

God bless and stay strong for the road ahead is dark and long and I no longer can be by your side. You are threatened by yourself, not me. You are your own danger, my love, as it has become your nature to attack out of no reason at all.

I could have said more but this is something you need to learn by yourself. My mission is far bigger. Under his protection and guidance, I listen to all subtle vibrations because he has never failed me and never will. His love is unconditional and purest of the pure. It pours out for me as much as it pours out for you. The poison is growing within you, not outside of you. May you swim out of it and follow the light before it is too late.

If you want good for yourself, do good to others.

Horse implies freedom and dolphin implies morality. Initially, everyone was pure light then bestiality took over, the energies of races intermingled, somewhere perhaps a horse and the dolphin mated and created a new gene pool and so forth. Some turned out interesting and some faded with time. It all has got so complex and chaotic that seeing no end to this, we all are now craving to go back to the source, wondering where and to whom did we all originally belong? The most recent rumored case has been of a goat delivering a semi-human baby in a remote village of India and an Orangutan was impregnated by a suburban zookeeper. We are endowed with the ability to make informed choices. It is high time, we make intellectual evaluation backed with true wisdom and heart to transmute and transform, rising above lower urges.

Curiosity[38] killed the horse's colt before he could even learn to bray and so humans never saw unicorns again. Now is the time to awaken, rise above monstrosity, and first become complete with your animal and human nature. Remember there is a reason why we are no longer walking on our four limbs. Your destiny got you till here, it will take you further on provided you start respecting and being gentle with one another.

Keep on feasting and fasting mentally, emotionally, and physically to make a difference in your energy levels. To uplift your energy and overall positivity, spend time with nature and care for animals. This also helps reduce your cortisol levels, stress, and mood swings.

This is a wish-fulfilling message with a promise of protection from the higher beings - As you now know your truth, It is time to make the changes and creatively weave the web of your own life, time to balance the past and the future, the material and the spiritual aspects, the yin and the yang, the subtle and the gross, go add more color to your light.

Our life can change so much for the better if we can learn to be polite, kind, patient, forgiving, and loving towards ourselves and those around us, regardless of who they are and what they have done.

Neither you nor the dog needs to pull the leash through force or subjugation. Love doesn't mean you give yourself up, love too requires training. The leash is in your hands and so in a perfect loving relationship, you and your dog, the master and the servant, father and the child, teacher and the student, doctor and the patient, healer and the healed control the leash together in perfect order, discipline and harmony.

When you take your dog out for a walk, you share a part of your life with the dog as much as the dog shares with you but the leash is in your hands. You are responsible for your pets' behavior, you pick up after it poops, you ensure it bites no other, you love but you also train firmly. A dog always listens to its master who commands such authority.

---

[38] *Curiosity killed the horse's colt implies stifling the joy of freedom by killing the imagination.*

In a jungle no matter how many dogs bark or cry, the elephant keeps moving and doesn't care to look back. Wondering where it came from will not stop the elephant from moving on. If the smaller animals do not clear the way, they die or get hurt under the force of its weight. Ant can see the elephant, but the elephant cannot see the ant. If the ant is told to run away and still doesn't, it is not the elephant's fault.

Some scientists say that Covid 19, is not even a virus. One thing is for sure, it is like that elephant in a jungle, trampling every small particle in its way. Give it some room and space so that it can move on its journey and let you breathe without overwhelming you. Forcing your will upon the elephant doesn't make it go. It overwhelms the elephant and it cannot think right. If you stay calm, within the safe confines of your home, and follow the advice of other divine beings, maybe this will pass by, let's learn to trust the energies.

Even animals kill only when they are hungry. We, humans, are the only beings who kill just for fun.

Affirm- 'Namostutee, I am a noble person. I live with honest means. I have high standards of morality and unwavering fidelity to my spouse. I strive for excellence by passing my free time on intellectual pursuits. I value people and I am hospitable and welcoming to those who visit my home. I am knowledgeable and deeply connected with the supreme soul. I am an ethical person and I am blessed with very deep eternal and perfect friendships. Tathaastu.'

CHAPTER 19a

FIGHT FLIGHT

Put the intention out to change your disposition from always being in "fight or flight" mode to complete balance and harmony. This will positively impact not only you but also your hormones. Initially, it is best to neuro-transmit only the joyful moments and extract the best out of those moments. With time, we can learn how to extract the lessons through the pain we have experienced. This way we develop 'Samatva-Bhav'. It is a Sanskrit word that means equanimity of mind. It is the feeling of evenness beyond experiential knowledge.

Distract your dogs from biting their tails. It is our job to train them before they mutilate themselves out of boredom. Most problems we as humans face are self-induced, and that is why *Chakra* and aura balancing is important. Regulate your adrenaline to begin with. Pump up, but not so much that it pumps you out.

Packaged food was meant for survival mode or wartime situations. It was meant for those exploring space, and soldiers at war stationed upon the seas where there were no amenities or modes of cooking and eating clean fresh foods. Nowadays it has become our lifestyle. Too much convenience is causing inconvenience to our health. The food we eat must be fresh, green, home-cooked, vitalized, and blessed with our loving energy unless or until we are out there in the middle of nowhere fighting wars. Shift your energy from survival mode to alive mode. Slow down, too much rush can brush you away before you know it.

You are uncomfortable when it's too hot or it's too cold. Balance is the key so keep your temperature moderate. Too much of anything can disorient you much like the snake who ends up eating its tail mistaking it for its prey under limited vision. Let go and stop eating yourself, the outcome can be devastating. Deep breathe and stay stress-free for the fake illusion of hunger never ends. The more you have the more you want and you will one day eat up yourself with this incessant want. Stay balanced, look for the blissful light that will finally lead you to what is beyond mental comprehension.

I was reversing my car with loud music playing. I was lost in my thoughts. Behind, my car was a big truck and I was oblivious because I didn't care to see. Thankfully, today's modern cars have a built-in fight and flight mode and so the car stopped on its own and I was saved. Our bodies too have an inbuilt fight or flight mode called the adrenal gland. It takes over and suddenly jerks us whenever required. Depending upon the situation, its purpose is to control our blood pressure and give messages to the brain so that we can stop or ride on. This way we do not push our bodies too much.

In the lower spinal cord, there is an energy center, sometimes called the 'gate of life'. It is an energy accelerator and acts like the fight-flight mode of a car. It helps evolve our lower energies into spiritual energies. Physically it increases the blood flow. The point is called Junoon or Raag[39] because this center inspires us to bring balance and sense to see through all delusion. Spleen[40] has a *chakra*. It is the center from where the life force enters our body. The center of spleen is *Dvesha*[41] or Jaya because this center inspires us to get detached from spitefulness so that we can remove all dualities and replace them with kindliness.

A truly liberated and knowledgeable person has no raga or *dvesha*, no fight-flight responses, delusion, or duality. Such a glorious person takes great pleasure in honoring every being and every moment.

Mara, Aram, Rama, Amar - all are jumbled up versions and stages of one reality, we give them a name and create chaos. Mara means death; Aram means lazy; Rama means immortal God within mortal; Amar means immortal. Inherently, all are made with the same alphabets but each invokes a completely different reaction within us because we have jumbled ourselves with meanings. If we cease to dissect and attach ourselves to

---

[39] *Here Junoon and raag, both mean passion.*
[40] *Anatomically, spleen is on the left of the rib. In Hebrew spleen is called 'Netzach' or victory. This is where life force or prana enters our body.*
[41] *Dvesha means aversion or spitefulness.*

meanings and instead attune our frequencies with higher energies then we will unflinchingly flow through all the life stages.

Affirm- 'Namostutee, I am free, liberated, loving, and transparent. I am pure, clear, patient, and understanding. Tathaastu.'

CHAPTER 20

GEOMETRICAL CURVE OF LIFE

'O' is the dark void of the eternal womb from which everything comes. It is the mother of all existence and we all are its children. A mother never forgets her children, it is the children who forget where they came from. Every 25,000 years the mother returns to remind us all of where we came from. The void is tasteless, odorless, formless, and invisible so recognizing our mother is certainly no easy task.

'I' came from 'O', the way form came from formless, dark came from the light, love came from loneliness. We have all become so lonely that it is time to love again.

From waxing to waning, from right to left, from growing to shrinking, between the inverted and the reverted crosses and crescents, lies the fullness & the completeness within the hollowness which we call 'O'. Between the dark and light, between the inhaling and exhaling, the newness and freshness comes the fullness. It is on becoming whole that you empty yourself to renew and revolve with a resolve to evolve.

When external reality invokes equal excitement within you as internal dreams do, then dreams cease to make you lose your touch with reality. This way reality becomes a dream. And dreams become reality until you reach a point where this duality merges to become one. The mingling of 'S' or self within the one is a process that requires a huge amount of life force energy or '*prana*'. '*Prana*' can be increased through the right moral actions.

Curves are feminine and bars or straight lines are masculine (horizontal or vertical). This reflects in every part of our existence. For example the year 2020 is feminine whereas 2019 is a masculine year. All sacred geometric shapes are made of curves and bars. The patterns of everything we see in nature are made of these two shapes. This interconnectedness is a continuous reminder of our innate relationship with the whole.

Feminine energy is invisible yet stark, introspective, and powerful. It is self-generating similar to our DNA. Masculine energy is visible and is action-oriented. When two curves intersect like in 2020 – twin years, it brings us face to face to our stark reality beyond duality so that here we develop into having a shared vision, common ground, or mutual understanding going beyond duality.

Illustrated by the story I want to tell you. There were twins and both had the same name C. When they sat with their backs against each other they formed an X [)(]and when they faced opposite each other they extended into an S. Lastly when they faced each other they formed an O [()]. They realized that they came from O which is their origination point. From that day on, they lived loving, praising, and facing each other's truth.

To live is to know just one aspect of the truth, to be alive is to know the combination of theory and practice - east and west, hot and cold, left and right. To be aware is to introspect and realize the origination point from whence we all came. To be free is to know the truth of their oneness –C, X, and O. Knowing that they are all one leads us to freedom and this liberates us all.

Relationships can be plutonic or physical. In a situation where neither exists, that is the time each person starts a relationship with themselves. The man meets the woman within and similarly, the woman meets the man. The kindling of this relationship is like two entities C & C meet face to face () to complete the circle. This is the time that you meet with your truth.

When one faces the front (East), there is a tendency not to see what is behind you (West). In the same way, a coin has two sides to it. Spiritual God is like a two-sided coin -one side is physical and the other side is subtle. The predominant aspect depends on which energy we resonate most with and which direction we face - East or West. Maintain a proper and perfect balance of knowing both sides- the physical and subtle. This will create a rare co-mingling.

The Thalamus gland is 'neural' in nature and it is in the center of the brain. It is the cosmic egg also called the philosopher's stone. The pituitary gland is 'lunar' and has yin energy and it is in the left part of the brain. The Pineal gland is 'solar' in nature, yang energy, present to the right of the brain. The left and right brain connect through a **C**-shaped area called the corpus callosum. These three get synchronized in perfect trinity providing the experience of ultimate oneness through the all-seeing-eye.

East and west are even. North and south are odd. It is when the odd and even forces mingle that they can bring up the opposing forces and together move towards higher realms. O is that ethereal beauty of celestial space that mingles with all, in any direction, even or odd.

The trees whisper and call me a *fool* (*phool* - means flower in Hindi) the cuckoo bird calls me *Kookoo* (kookoo means fool in the Philippines). Whether the tree gives birth to flowers or fools, the brackets () will always be there to flatter us with their voluptuous and enticing curves. It is the brackets that give meaning and energy to our tree-like form.

Certain animals are capable of more advancement in subjects like math and geometry than many of us. Evolution is subjective. Honey bees have brains 20,000 times smaller than ours, and yet are the perfect mathematicians. Even now, science is still amazed at their arithmetic addition, subtraction, team building, and sequential skills. They chew wax until it becomes soft. We too need to chew our rigid, hardened thought forms and beliefs, to soften ourselves and embrace the universal reality of divinity within all. Only then can we bond our collective softened wax at the right temperature, to make our hexagonal, strong, and stable honeycombs with such precision and zest, without wasting our true essence. Making the most of every resource you have is something honey bees have been teaching us for eons. We have mini-teachers in every corner of our earthly home.

Imagine a circle. A woman represents the center of the circle or the soul of the home. The man represents the circumference. Divine mercy in a home disappears the moment the man disrespects a woman. This is akin to the center of the circle disappearing and hence the existence of the circle.

A woman who respects and values herself is a woman who is truly happy, confident, and highly comfortable in her skin. All women do not have to be feminists to assert their voice and be heard. A woman needs to simply allow energy within her to flow smoothly like the water in the river. Better this rather than giving up her aspirations and freedom for the sake of others.

Much of today's young are post-millennial kids born out of the sandwiched generation (X) that was born in the middle of all generations. They are wild, relentless, tangible, and a far expanded version of their subtle, hardworking, micro, invisible generation X parents. It is a challenge for sure, but their finite dual-minded generation X parents must embrace and treat them as equals, to develop a healthy relationship and partnership. Accept the change of evolution and involution. Unlike the hard-working, insecure generation X, the post-millennial have woken up high wired, with infinite hyper-growth, and are far more inspired and daring. They feel safe, secure, attuned, and fulfilled within themselves and their surroundings. Just like our trials and tribulations, today's young children are here to make us become better versions of ourselves. Today's parents need to trust and cooperate with themselves in this transitional phase of the infinite from the finite. We are inspired by the innovative mature minds of our young children, who are our teachers, here to help us enter into further growth, longevity, prosperity, and immortality.

Meditation and balanced healing protocols are a powerful counterbalance, which helps the ordinary within the extraordinary force to free itself from the perpetual stress and emotional exhaustion that comes with upbringing such a vast array of abundant energies.

To fill yourself up with focus and vitality, stop being so resistant and closed to the change from transitory to the permanent. Open up. Stay committed, productive, and constantly engaged with today's youth, to progress and evolve with their significant, creative, unique thinking and psychic abilities.

The magic crystal ball shows the current ways of living will be preempted by the amalgam of structured spirituality and organized technology. This is where success lies. And so we must help ourselves become centered, balanced, and renewed.

Wake up, Generation X! For it is time to clean up, purify, rise and shine into this scheduled upgraded chaos. I know for I have been there and done that. I too was held between the two until I realized true strength lies between the hindrances and delays of love and light.

Born out of the magical beauty of the stars, through the blended combination of science, spirituality, and technology, and within constant connectivity, the miracle of our liberty and potentiality is truly unlocked.

We are in the wake of the transformational age. It is not easy, but it is super-exciting so hold on to the power of positivity and clarity, to enhance your superpowers to the tunes of these expanded high vibrational energies. No wonder today's children are almost our whole soul reality. Self-realization and self-mastery are our keys to rise above our limitations and design an ideal life of our new reality, through the manifestation of the energy that flows within us. Why be so stuck? Remember that between the heart and mind, between the walk and the breath, rests the calm agility of our soul. Between action and reaction, there is inaction, which is another word for introspection and reflection. Do not undermine the power of this innate and infinite wisdom. The center is the cause behind the balance of all elements and extremities.

There are nine generations in total. Generation X is exclusive, harmonizing, cool, flexible, balanced, hardworking, independent, and are the last of the few left in the center to leave a mark before the onset of the new wave of generations. When it comes to finance and smart investments, they take a back seat, unlike their Generation Z children, who are by far more self-driven, and more entrepreneurial, creative, diverse, and influential. They are deal hunters, smart spenders, heavy online users, and the new leaders of our future world. For them money equals success, honesty equals leadership, deep focus equals business interests, benefits equal flexibility, and hobbies equal full-time jobs.

Moving counter-clockwise, opposite in elemental force, yet stronger than ever, they are our upgraded version. They are like the front flip on a trampoline. For example, in sports like swimming, we are still fluttering and trying to learn the backstroke, while they are at the forefront doing the butterfly stroke. Have faith as the rules of their game are different from what we are used to because their strokes are different than ours. Let them swim. There is no right or wrong.

Every work of art is a masterpiece of divine creation. The hands may be yours but the vision is God's. The divine is the thought behind all your actions. What seems ugly to you is the epitome of ultimate beauty and wonder for another. Art is based on subjective perception. Why be so critical about perfection because of your lethal deception? Even the diamond is concealed within the charcoal. Whatever may be the more dominant hue of your skin warm or cool, high or low, blue or red, green or yellow heighten your wavelength to a different frequency of purity and transparency, and you will know that you are inherently a vibrant rainbow caught in the optical illusion of the prism delight.

Affirm- 'Namostutee, The power of the One is greater than any but the power of many is greater than one. I am one with all. Tathaastu.'

CHAPTER 20a

SHARED FATE

A and inverted A put together gives you a six-pointed golden star as shown in the diagram below. Top A is Shiva and the bottom inverted A is Shakti or power. Six main opposite powers complete and define the other. This heightens our vibrations, brings great energy flow, and removes blockages from all our chakras.

The first alphabet is A and the top point where the two lines meet is the supreme pure spirit. The two lines or bridges lead us to the point of two choices. The first choice we get is called – individual incarnated soul. The second choice is called – higher group soul. Individual incarnated soul influences the higher group soul. There is a choice to either stay on course with the respective souls or for the incarnated soul to move towards the higher group soul. By crossing another rainbow bridge you are led to your pure spirit.

Your every breath is a debt to the universe. Clear all your debts. Learn from the 1% of society that is made up of highly spiritual souls. Join them to increase their number and to clear your debts.

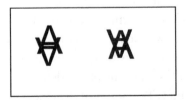

For example – the group soul is the nation and the pure spirit is humanity. Humanity is one whole in which each has a divine spark – equally connected to the pure spirit. What we make of the divine spark is an individual choice. Crossing each bridge takes us a step higher into the evolution cycle requiring an initiator. That initiator sets out the intentions from his etheric body into the pure spirit[42] to recreate humanity.

When the individual and the group soul become one- the intention of the entire world is sent to the pure spirit and hence becoming one (I). In this one, the lower point (group soul) merges with the pure spirit. The effect of this is decided by the spirit. The pure spirit then decides to start another cycle (O) of evolution. The combination of (I)(O) is the ultimate perfection of IO.

Every triangle comes with three corners or points. Our body is a Jenga of triangles each with three points and two choices. Each choice can make or mar you. Offer your body to the supreme triangle of the higher pure spirit and monad[43], unity of pure air and ether, in complete trust and faith.

The active combined will of the subtle (higher group soul) and the subtlest (pure spirit) force or point leads to completeness. Their subtle force is activated within the initiator through a tiny spark that looks like a shining emerald from afar. The initiator is the point of perfection. The one who reaches such perfection is empowered to manifest its vision of a new world order swiftly into actuality. The initiator is a world leader endowed with qualities of positivity, ambition, and complete creative freedom. The initiator has the potential to start a circle of fresh beginnings with its focused energy. The higher beings, angels, and masters support, love, and encourage such a divine being for creating perfect conditions within itself to initiate the process of (O) on a clean slate.

During my childhood, I visited a *Nadi Shastra* expert in India. Scholars read ancient Sanskrit literature through *tada-patra* or palm leaves with amazing accuracy. Within our nadis, the fate of our life is prewritten much before we are born. Nadis in the thumbs of our hands are the entire imprint of our life.

It is written in the Bhagavad Gita that 72,000 nadis arise from the 101 subtle channels that arise from our physical heart. As the flow continues, they branch off into another 72,000 nadis that get unlocked. As they pursue further activation, many more channels open up. Originating from two main points – Kanda or secondary navel around the pelvic area and the

---

[42] *Pure spirit is Complete. It is totally free of all poisons. It is untainted and clear.*
[43] *Monad is One. It is an indivisible, unique, indestructible, unique, dynamic entity having synchronization through God's (group soul) will in pre-established harmony.*

heart. The nadis vitalize our cells. The Sanskrit word nadi derives from the root nad which means flow or vibration. The imbalance of intuitional and rational mind, the left brain and the right brain depend upon the flow of two main nadis which are Ida and Pingala.

Water in a river continues to flow by itself almost effortlessly without your push or pull. When you are ready the nadis in your body will flow by themselves almost effortlessly. They don't need your push or pull. When the flow is directed properly, they grace us with fertility, prosperity, creativity and liberty. Since we all are connected, we must continuously share the blissful grace we receive to improve the fate of others.

The Goddess of fate is sometimes called 'Lasa or Mean'. She follows the highest degree of discipline and art of divination. You should worship this Goddess to gain activation of the nadis. The outer receptors and perceptions are distorted instruments. They are enough for survival mode (animal life). We must try to activate our higher senses beyond the five senses. This will help us know a lot more than we already know and evolve in many more spheres.

The points in the five-pointed star of our brain are like the vowels 'A, E, I, O, and U'. Just the way many more words can be made with the help of vowels, many higher senses can be developed and activated with the help of these five foundational pointed stars.

When you owe someone then the prerequisite is that someone needs to lend you the item or favor. For example - 'I O U' implies 'U' trusts 'I'. Without the collective threads of trust and faith, the fabric cannot be stitched. In today's competitive world of nuclear families, we are losing that basic belief - both in 'I' and in 'U'. We no longer trust ourselves and neither do we trust others. Such weak threads break before they can mingle with other colorful ones to be a part of the sewed in beautiful fabric. Some of us call this bizarre attitude 'self-sufficiency'. I call it 'self-deficiency'. Without a team and working together even the greatest of minds tear up and cannot deliver the best of innovations. We all need one another.

Quest for perfection and search for Gods and cosmic wisdom is without beginning and end. The union of two triangles- the spiritual and the material helps us feel fulfilled and maintain mental equilibrium despite the fusion of higher with the feeble-minded.

Affirm- 'Namostutee, I open the vaults of my heart, I unlock all the knots and let the over-congested energies circulate all around. I share because I care for myself and you. Tathaastu.'

CHAPTER 21

WHAT'S IN VOGUE?

You are here because karmically you are entitled to be here. What frequency you are on will decide what vibrations you are catching and what energies you attract, so choose your style wisely. Steve Jobs wore the same iconic turtleneck attire not only because it suited his style and looked good on him, but because he had better things to do than to think about what to wear daily! Jobs had a hundred turtlenecks which lasted him a lifetime. Facebook CEO, Mark Zuckerberg too doesn't believe in consuming his valuable energy into deciding what to wear. He has multiple same signature grey t-shirts and hoodies that he wears daily.

True fashion is in living a life of wellbeing. It is unfashionable not to proactively give importance to yourself: your mental, physical, emotional, and spiritual health. High fashion is about being attuned to your higher self, and then creatively spreading that vibrational energy. The more you connect with your innate style, the more you empower and encourage those around to join in, working for the greater good, which in turn accelerates our planet's overall growth. Pouted lips are out of fashion, for nothing is better than a subtle smile. White is the new 'in' thing, for black is too mysterious and dark. Fire within is better than the one outside.

You study, work, and create for yourself and not to please your boss, teachers, and audience. There is no more scope for showing off, in today's world of truth. Being self-motivated is the only truth that matters and everything that is not truthful is not in fashion.

Knitting is an amazing hobby. One gets different colored wool to create patterns on a sweater. This sweater, if it fits well, will keep you warm and cozy on winter nights. Life is also like knitting using different hues of wool.

As the ball of wool unravels, thread by thread, to create the end product so do the days unravel to form a year and years go by to unravel your true self. And as you find your true self you will be comfortable in your skin. It is never really possible to die if you have just been born. You can never die unless you choose not to live while you are still living. You are undying as long as you are not un-living. Even if we think it is all a big lie, we continue to live, to untie the knotted ball of birth, death, and rebirth, only to tie it up again.

We find it difficult to be cheerful until we express our love freely. Yet we never express our love until we know that we will never see our love anymore. When our heart is full, is when our words speak. If your cupboard is overstuffed with clothes, the clothes will come barging out the moment you open the cupboard. The clothes have no space left to remain within. Same way, when your heart is full, it has no choice but to ooze out with love the moment one comes closer to you.

You can model the mind, not the heart. You can condition and program the mind to play music life has to offer. Be flexible and hopeful that one day you will explore your path in the process.

Love cannot be described in mere words. Romance is like foreplay. Let yourself be happy and do whatever makes you smile, let your passion flow, don't shy from being intense because to get the love you need to be love and love doesn't waste precious time over trivial issues. It is always happy, always smiling, always passionate, and always intense. When all else goes, what will survive of us is love. Being in love is always in vogue.

Practical is boring and never fashionable, so be as weird and impractical as you please to tickle your raw creativity. Blend in the environment and move with the times.

Affirm- 'Namostutee, I bring out my younique quotient by being my younique self. I selflessly follow my higher will by listening to my inner voice. It is what gives me joy, happiness, and truth. Tathaastu.'

CHAPTER 21a

THE STAPLED PANT

My dad is an interesting gentleman. He loves to travel. In one such travel, he bought a woolen trouser on sale and needed to give it to the tailor for altering the length. Upon inquiry, the tailor stated that it would cost 30 francs and a week. Considering that the price of the trouser was lower than what he would have to pay for alterations, he quickly stapled the bottom of the trousers and wore them to the event he had to go to. He is a perfect inspiration for a person traveling abroad. He is a man who doesn't live to convince others about his self-worth with the length of his trousers and he doesn't mind walking out in well creased yet stapled trousers. By sharing this chapter from his life, my dad helped me weave a story into my life that believes that discipline and power are not in how you dress but how you carry yourself with pride, joy, and a stapler that counts.

Our mental perception of most things is based on what comes to us effortlessly and through visual eyesight. We believe what we see and so we do not ever try to see things in any other way. We see the macro picture because it is apparent and visible. We do not see the micro picture because looking at the thin needle lying in the massive universe can obviously be taxing for our dainty eyes and so we give up. This is the reason our higher senses need to develop. Because our inner eyes can see what the outer cannot.

Affirm- 'Namostutee, I now know that with the power of negative thoughts one can kill someone. With the opposing power of positivity, one can give life to someone. I always choose to give life rather than take life. I always think positive thoughts for myself and all others. Tathaastu.'

CHAPTER 22

MASQUERADE PARTY

Your very silence speaks of your immense wisdom and true worth. While few others are showing off their borrowed respect, you are the most revered of them all. While they are living in debt, you are the only one free of all debts and worry. Simply mingle with the circle until you reach the beginning of this circular dance. Your destiny is waiting for you. The tiny mystic precious gem of the silver sea is within your golden body. Just a few more steps of the happy dance, and you will be cheerfully graced with all praise and honor, for the dainty garb you are wearing belongs to you. The heavenly pleasures of earth, the mighty strength of the high mountains touching the sky, all belong to you. All of nature's bounty and beauty are for you to enjoy.

In the grand tapestry of life, do not get so weighed down by self-limiting beliefs that you do not remember to enjoy life. Yet do not preoccupy yourself so much that you cease to dance. Do not dance so much that you cease to sing. Do not sing so much that you forget how you learned to sing. Just dance along with ease, and join in the royal masquerade party to feel what it is like to be one amongst the regal queens and kings. When you are in the fantasyland, stay protected, for there might be a few who are hiding their truth behind the facade of their finest new robes. You are that precious gem that inspires the peacocks to remove their inhibitions and dance in the rain. You are the royal decree. You are life itself. You left the comforts of the diamond castle above, only to bless the lush green gardens with gardeners who can properly care for them. Those gardeners who nurture the earth well will ultimately become rulers of the land. In such a land, envy and lust will be replaced by respect and trust.

Keep your dignity and modesty, as in their fakeness, many have been wearing suits of immorality and vanity for longer than you think. While you are pure and true, they could be simply wearing the Monarchs blue hue. You have long crowned the princess but they have been wearing your rightful ruby & emerald tiara. Do not let them know your sacred legal lineage for the princess is always more shielded and protected behind her disguised attire.

Play the game of hide and seek. They need not know yet that the throne they are sitting on is rightfully yours and the robe they are wearing, belongs to you.

In this life, none of us show our real selves. We are adorning masks. In this masquerade, each person is hiding behind the garb they wear. Wearing different costumes, some are in rich silk and look as if they are inside the cocoon of a silkworm. Some hide their timid personality behind sheepskin or mink coats. Many wear accessories like money garlands around their neck (refer Indian weddings), horns of bulls on their heads, stoles of pig hide, or carry bags made of crocodile skin.

Accessories mixed with clothes make one's personality even more complex. All I can say is that you are what you wear. Just remember who you are even though you may be clothed in different layers of hides and skins – none of which belong to you.

Finally, a time comes when we meet with or without the outer mask we wear. The outer mask doesn't restrict us from being who we are. If anything is restricting us from speaking our truth or bringing out our true potential then it is we who are responsible for it and no one else.

We can wear any amount of masks and become anyone we want to be. Masks may change but the inner light will remain the same and will be visible. No mask can stop you and your light from shining outwards.

I am here to help you meet with that inner light within you. It seems like it has been hiding behind some or the other societal or self-created mask since eternity. Time has come to bring out your light and shine. This is a wake-up call as the masquerade is long over. Stay tuned, stay connected to the spark that shines within, inside, and outside of you. There is another masquerade party. Those who pass the patience game, focusing on worshiping divine with gratefulness, can transition and mingle into the spiritual party wearing their shielded golden mask. Here, we see the entire world encompassed within a godly body, which is wearing a saffron red sari of a virtuous and faithful bride.

Who could envision such a "mass movement", sorry a "mask movement" could create a new kind of hidden "unmask the mask movement" within all of us. My intention here is to unmask the mask hidden behind the clothes of words we wear and hear through silent introspection. When the masquerade is over, all guests leave, all masks are left scattered. If there is one thing that will remain as is - is the 'word'. That word is that one word of praise and appreciation. That one word will get another party rolling.

Master etymologically means "having the power to control." "Mas" comes from the word "masquerading or role-playing." "Ter" comes from the word "three." Anyone who can practice self-control of all three aspects mind, body, and soul through the power of self-discrimination is their master. As you can control more things, beings, and people under your dictates, other than yourself, you become their master. As you continue to spread and teach people the skill or subject you have mastered, more and more people come under the control of your power until they get self-empowered. We all are part of a masquerade, wearing different masks, garbs, and roles based on places and situations. Sometimes we forget who we are while celebrating the masquerade of pretense. Balanced people wear their style and are their perfect masters. Such people participate in the masquerade wearing no other role or mask other than their own. These people are the happiest dancing to their melodious tunes at this ball, with or without the music.

Nothing and no one truly belongs to you other than the power to control yourself. Once you have mastered yourself, you have complete control, authority, and power over your destiny. Be true to yourself by wearing your mask. Be your own master through positivity which comes with holding the reigns of your wavering thoughts and emotions. In today's world of deception and deceit, the time has come we learn to master ourselves in all aspects rather than get swayed by politicians, media, and leaders who falsely try to control the innocent masses by showing them only half the version of their story.

I arrived in the earthly palace wearing my spiritual hat and I will leave wearing the same spiritual hat. You might change and shed the clothes, garbs, roles, and body you wear but you can never shed the spirit of your soul. It will take you to where you truly belong. Remove your mask/persona you wear and become truly aware of yourself.

Affirm- 'Namostutee, I am truly aware of myself. Tathaastu.'

CHAPTER 23

IMMACULATE BREATH

The air whispered, "I remain nameless, invisible, and unknown to stay shielded and protected. I haven't slept at night because I am perennially awake. Even in my deepest sleep, with eyes closed, I am more awakened than the ones that are not sleeping. For even though their eyes are wide open, they cannot see or feel the way I can see and feel. I am one with the whispering air."

Abstract knowledge gives birth to concrete. The thought of using our senses comes before we even decide to use them. Therefore there is a lot we cannot yet comprehend as it came before us, yet is accessible to the few who are receptive.

After living in both the East and the West, all I can say is that I have two lungs: one is in the East and the other is in the West. Mingling with the energy of both, I truly learned what it is like to use my lungs. I truly learned what it is to breathe, to be free and unlimited. It is in appreciation of the diversity and unity that we learn to honor the infinite oneness that lies within us all. We are all inherently connected, and so kindness, cooperation, generosity, and compassion come naturally to those who are graced by Lord God's presence. Those who remember to revere and praise him, no matter what their situation in life may be, are forever vibrating with positive energy, unconditional love, and blessings. The *Junoon*[44] I carry comes from the depth of undying faith I have for the Supreme in all honesty and modesty.

---

[44] *Junoon- word often used in Urdu and Hindi language. It means a state of in-depth zeal or passion visible in the eyes*

Through proper breathing air not only vitalizes our thoughts and minds but also helps us release tensions giving us energy. This transforms us into a better version of ourselves by the subtle pause between inhalation and exhalation. The breathing tells us – whatever goes in has to come out. With the malleable breath of air not only is the entire space re-energized but also the dry corners of the earth are vitalized with its heavenly circulatory charms. It carries the moisture from the waters to invigorate it with bubbling excitement. It also creates the passion and heat within the fire.

Yet this air which is pure nothingness is truly nothing until all the other elements (fire, earth, water) and its manifestations join in its celestial dance. What lies before you, what lies behind you, what lies under you is something we often do not sense, like a mother frantically looking for her child everywhere when he is right behind her, like a shadow.

Pure air speaks: It is hard to reach me and even harder to know me because I have my sensitivities. I am too pure to handle the grossness in the grossest of you. But I know how to stay shielded, protected, and away from you in my velvety robe and little spiked shell of wonder. I am the wisest, yet I am ever hungry for more knowledge and wisdom. I am sheltered, yet my dainty etheric abode is unsafe and threatened. You call me thoughtless when I am more of thoughts than flesh and bones. I am always running and transcending from one realm to another. I am the fastest and the most active, but you call me the slowest and laziest in the race. I work hard to communicate my rapid thoughts and feelings, day in and day out, and yet you say you understand very little of what I convey. Hurry up! There is so much to ponder. I am perennially active because of the fervor and fire that rise through my perineum[45] and yet you say I am inactive and rest far too much.

Continued: I am the experience and the one who experiences, the knowledge and the knower, the wisdom and the wise, the party and the host, the opportunity and the one who takes the opportunity, the fortune and the fortunate, the prosperity and the prosperous, the positivity and the positive, the magnificence and the magnificent, the dedication and the dedicated, the devotional and the devoted, the point and the pointer, the luck and the lucky ones, the fame and the famous, the heaven and the heavenly. I'm your higher soul, more perfect than you, yet imperfect.

---

[45] *Perineum is a point from where the divine energies enter into our body and then the sacred juices travel upto the head.*

Come join in the party. Between the earth and space, there is a great void. This void is filled with the love of the mother moon. That is the only place where I can rest from time to time until my zest for you brings me back from that ridge when I take the rainbow bridge of seven colors to meet with the trinity within you.

You will know me when you see me. You don't have to run. You will find me right beside you in your yard. From there I can always see the open blue skies and the fresh green grass. To me, it is all the same. Heaven is above and heaven is below. Our marriage is foretold; we are fated to be one. You are in me and I am you. Just buckle up and catch up! The flight is long. I may not ever tire, but you already look weary and tired, and this is no satire.

Wake up! What is stopping you, my dear? I have been waiting for long. Let us premeditate our lives. Nothing is beyond our reach when together we decide to sail our ship. As long as the game is fun, adventurous, and entertaining, it makes sense to go on playing. But now that it has gone awry and become scary, let's search for our treasures in another way. The tryouts are happening. I hear that another safe and fun game is on. Let us join in, for our names are already shortlisted.

A yogi and air element were having a conversation. The air element was congested and wanted to bring about balance. The choice was three people have to leave or all of humanity will die. The yogi chose three people who were suffering due to bodily pain. Even after the three people died, most of humanity was impacted and death never stopped. The yogi, perplexed, asked the air element, "Why others were dying even though the deal was kept between the earth and air. The air just replied, "I kept my side of the bargain, the rest of humanity perished due to their own doing – their fear, anxiety, hate, and negativity". Change, harmony and good health come only when we all unite and think fresh, wholesome, sanguine thoughts in our different fields to heighten the universal consciousness collectively.

I am a nameless thought. My thoughts are unattached. It doesn't belong to me or you. I am sharing this thought to bring about a change in your thought so that you too rise above it. The thought is the common factor that binds us all. Whether we are from east or west, north or south - we breathe the same air as it circulates our entire world. When a child is born, he gasps for air. When you run a marathon, you gasp for air. When you climb the high mountains, you gasp for air. When you win a boxing match, you gasp for air. In each of these circumstances, you are fighting to catch a breath that is anyway going to be yours. We will realize this only if we learn to slow down and pause a bit. Yet, you spend your life fighting the race of birth and death in football and boxing matches to climb heights which eventually become the reason for your downfall and decay.

A couple of years back, I caught pneumonia during one of my travels to India at Chamunda temple, perhaps because of the acute air pollution levels from Delhi to Dalhousie. When I came out of it, the first thought that came to me was – Ah! I found God. It is called breath. We all must start our day with a little breathing exercise to thank the air. One day of a congested chest and you realize the true value of breathing clean pure air.

Ideas and thoughts are invisible. They live in the air. Yet are so crucial. Everything generates, expands, and moves within and around them.

Affirm- 'Namostutee, Deep down everyone loves truthfulness and honesty. I am honest and I lead an effortless, fearless, truthful life. Tathaastu.'

CHAPTER 24

ANTS IN MY PANTS

The ants are so minuscule, yet their size doesn't stop them from confidently and collectively working better each day. They patiently and diligently work to collect food in the fiery summer so they have enough to eat in the frigid winter. Even if one of them is trampled, they are ready to sacrifice themselves for their burning purpose to keep moving forward. Nothing stops them from making use of the next opportunity to gather food and energy. They are forever ignited to plan, structure, cooperate and succeed even if the route seems long and hard. If you want to manifest your dreams into reality, you will find inspiration everywhere. The persistence, loyalty, and grit of an ant motivate you to energetically and tirelessly work, with the help of the community as a whole, towards your collective goal.

Ants may be tiny but they can scare giant elephants and bring them down to their knees with their relentless strength. They can crawl up inside elephant trunks and stop the hungry elephants from devouring the trees. Even tiny creatures can be powerful. Everything in the universe is governed by a set of rules. The universe must follow these sets of rules. Humans are a tiny part of the universe and composed of five elements, they must follow fixed rules and order. Our destiny is predetermined by the invisible forces of the universe.

Our cells are like the ants that dutifully and consistently work hard in a group with their community to ensure everyone is well-fed and nourished. Just the way there are red and black ants, our cells are red and white. Our cells are humble and tiny just like the ants and are very important for our body's ability to ward off suffering and hunger. It is no wonder that after prolonged rest, we sometimes get the feeling as if ants are walking in our pants. When one of our limbs has fallen asleep and become numb, as we regain feeling, we also feel as if tiny ants are tickling us.

With perseverance and dedication, a drop of water has the potentiality to transform into a river, an atom can change into the brightest light. Lord perennially showers us and every cell within our body with love, glory, grace, and support to triumph and expand.

Swati nakshatra or *su'ati* is another name for something as pure and small as the first drop of rain upon the earth. In India, It is believed that the first clear raindrop from this constellation or nakshatra is swift, sharp, and very beneficent. It is sweeter than the sweetest word ever spoken. It is bright as a real pearl thirty-six light-years from the sun and it uplifts our hearts with spring full joy and gladness. This tiny, friendly drop of rain is a great goer, with celestial beauty and knowledge. It is so talented that it has the potential to become our guardian and bearer. It is like the brightest and happiest north star of the Milky Way upon the earth. It soars and circulates its luminosity around over the years.

It is in deep-sea diving that we find the pearls and not by remaining on the surface. Pearls of wisdom are found by diving deep inside of us. It is when we gather the strength and dedication to remove all our weaknesses that we meet with the pure shining pearl like the one from the Swati nakshatra nesting amongst us.

Everything living within us is made in the image of us. Everything within us has life, intelligence, and the power of choice. The atoms, cells, glands, organs, nerves, muscles, bones, inside our body, are bound together with the force of love. Togetherness leads to permanence, rest all is transitory. As long as our cells and all our organs within our body remain healthy, happy, and balanced, we as a team are healthy. Even the tiniest member deserves to feel loved and special. Give them hope, care, and space so that they can freely and happily live by constantly moving your body to remove all obstacles and blockages they face. Feed them with nutritious good food, thoughts, and emotions. Believe in their magical power. They wait for their entire life to hear our little voice and experience the light of our soul from within. The star-like vitality of our inner positivity energizes our cells to stay vibrant and joyful.

Affirm- 'Namostutee, I am thankful for the fresh energy of pure life that circulates through my body. Life permeates from the toes to the top of my head bringing health and vitality to all my living parts. Tathaastu.'

CHAPTER 25

MASTER THE ART
OF S-WORD

A sword is an S-word. Remove the 's' and we are left with the word. We all know words can pierce us harsh and deep like a sword. They can make or mar a person. Here the S-word stands for "sweet words" as a reminder for us to use kind and sweet words always.

In the beginning, was just the word. Love or hate are mere words. We give them meaning. In the same way, any word that is formed is made or marred with the s-word of our mind. Inherently, the sword[46] and the mind are one, just as penetrative thought and fated action are one. Usually, the one talking and the one with the ideas are two different people, but this time both have come together.

Sitting on my lucky wind horse, my words might seem sharper than a sword, but they come with an air of spiritual authority, which some of us need to embrace because knowledge is power and applied knowledge is freedom. The purpose of suspending and striking with the spell of the s-word is to ensure that our speech is sharp, safe, and stimulating. The mind that strikes the sword to make the meaning more sacred, sanctified, spectacular, soul-full and spirited, is better than the mind that sensationalizes its meaning with the force of slanderous, superfluous, scornful, shameful, and selfish motives.

---

[46] *A sword cleaves truth from all falsehood. This way we learn that silence is better than empty words. Through inner silence we detach ourselves from the world's empty words and seek inner stillness.*

Humans have known the power of the s-word for eons, and yet its proper use seems like a mystery to most. Stale food stinks and if consumed makes your body sick. Slanderous words cause suffering and make your soul-sick. Words are meant to liberate us, not to make us slaves of the situation. Language is simple. We make it strange by ceasing to use the art in a satisfying, supporting, and spiritual manner. To use the sword artfully-how and when to strike with it-is left completely to our discretion. The one who created such a magical spell must have had complete trust in us before he allowed us to cast it. Let us ensure the essence of pure speech is not lost in the crowd of swords.

A true master of speech knows how to use the sword to benefit and uplift all those around with its sharpened silver edges of truth. A true master of speech knows the power of swords and ensures that every word uttered illuminates thousands of souls to shimmer with equal beauty. And as the chain continues, we all reunite into the oneness of bliss that is within us, holding our swords high while riding our galloping white horses[47].

The last letter of the English alphabet-the 27th character/&/which is not taught in schools nowadays brings us back to the first. This character implies continuity. It is what connects and reconnects us back to our roots: it is the effect of the cause. This means that nothing can change by itself; there are always internal and external factors. What is outside is also inside. The sword in the center of my forehead touches my inner vocal cords through the etheric field, and that is what makes me speak the language of truth. More important than knowing what goes inside your mouth is knowing what is in your mouth and what comes out of it.

The way venom comes out through snakes, it comes out through human tongues in the form of words. Just the way snake venom, sting, or bite is neurotoxic and poisonous to the brain, so do words have the power to hypnotize, kill, tamper with the psych of people and poison their brains. Medicine has discovered that the venom of certain snakes can also help open up constricted arteries, prevent clotting of blood or life force energy. It can also reduce hypertension and relax the chest muscles if given in the right doses.

Our snake-like tongue is caged within a pearly gate of 32 teeth. The moment it comes out, it is ready to poison and hurt anyone that comes in its path. The good news is that just the way snakes can be tamed and

---

[47] *White horse represent positive active energy*

disciplined so can our tongues through which we speak. Words are just like the poisonous sting of a snake. They can either kill you or fill your hearts with good health, patience, calmness, stout heartedness, and love to go through the process of rebirth, rejuvenation, and relaxation. Poisonous words can be changed into words more precious than diamonds and rubies. Once you purify your thoughts the words you speak through the dark caves become the most precious sparkling pearls and emeralds. Words of truth and kindness are the rarest gems. A person with these attributes is ever protected, filled with divine grace and blessings.

We are all inherently perfect and complete and lack nothing. The "I am" is the author of my life and also yours. The words "I am" are spoken through me and you. The time is right, and so is the opportunity to speak the truth--the ultimate truth of life. Just make sure you listen when it is time. To use a sword requires proper self-discrimination else you will be living in self-deception. Your mind tells you how to use your sword.

In India, there is a story of *Karan* who cuts off his thumb[48] with a sword and gave it to his *guru*. The deeper meaning of this is willfully cutting the un-necessary and the painful thoughts and words with a sword to attain acuity. This way you become more receptive to the teachings of your Guru.

S-words strike through the mind so that the blow cuts the unwanted ego. Mind strikes off the real from the unreal through its discriminatory qualities and sends the signal so that words can express its current understanding. If you must eat my words let them be forever laden with the divine nectar and sweetness of honey and dates. In the middle ages, it was customary in certain communities for little kids to lick divine letters smeared with honey to get the sweet taste of the blessings.

If you cannot speak honey laden words then I request you not to use swear words. To swear lightly and with intense power are two different things. If you put all your energy into using these ugly words, it adversely affects a person's self-worth. The growing number of suicide cases and suicide bombers tells us that words have so much power that they can compel a person to embrace death without a second thought. The one who commits suicide because of being over-sensitive is as wrong as the one who caused it by using words filled with rage and mockery. We perpetually cause

---

[48] *Thumb is connected to our master or command center which is often called samajh chakra. When this center is imbalanced, we are stubborn and resistant to change.*

others to smother their bodies, brains, emotions, dreams, and purpose with wrongful and un-inspiring use of words. If this is not indirect murder, crime, and misuse of power then what is?

We often see kids playing with their spit. They spit to see if the spit once thrown out can come back into their mouths. Words and promises are like the childish play of spitting, no matter how much you try, you cannot take a spiteful word back. They can pierce the soul so please be mindful before you spit them out.

This is what you should tell people who speak unkindly words - Before spitting out your food of words, at-least taste it yourself. Before performing ablutions, at-least find a suitable room. Before throwing your muck, at-least find a bin.

Sitting on a great white horse of intellectual light, holding a razor-sharp sword of miraculous words backed with pure wisdom, you are once again drawn to speak with true love. Amen to that.

When I am not writing on paper, I am writing in my mind. But all my manifested and un-manifested words are as ceaseless and inexhaustible as the pure air we breathe. Just because some people in certain parts of the world do not have access to its purity, doesn't mean that air or these words do not exist. Just the way air is bound to circulate, these words too will gradually circulate. It is the nature of air and words to spread far and wide. How we enjoy, assimilate, and perceive their nature is up to us. So take a deep breath and enjoy the s-words (sweet words). Sweet words are like sweet honey that touch our hearts and revitalize us. Words in any language or form (written, spoken, or idealized) are the breath of human life. The breath is in everything and everywhere.

Words of truth are like sharp swords that stimulate your spirit and soul with their power. We must practice restrained speech because words have immense power. Our words are those swords that can strike the enemy and purify another without the use of actual swords.

Our words that speak the language of universal truth through accessing the records of the universal library or mind (Akashic records) resonate with our *swabhava* or true disposition. Everyone connects with their true essence at some point or another.

Here goes my version of autocorrect and spell-check- It is "water flow" and not just a "waterfall". It is "Godfidence" and not mere "confidence". It is your solution, your "panacea" and not "pain" as pain doesn't exist! It is "plethora" and not "dearth or lack", it is always "quintessential" and not just "essential". Your troubles are just a "ripple" and not a "wave". It is "serendipity" not "stupidity". He is your "talisman", not just your "man". Your "parasol" is your divine shield and protection, not just a mere "umbrella". It is a "thread of a story", not "hell of a story". It is "altruism" not "truism". It is "God bumps" and not "goosebumps". It is "commend" and not "comment".

Saraswati is a subtle Nadi or energy channel. The one whose *Saraswati* energy is activated is known as the queen Goddess of pure speech. The *Saraswati* Nadi starts from the tip of the tongue. Once activated, it inspires, cleanses, and illuminates our minds with the insight of cosmic astuteness, virtues, and truth. The essence of true expression is the s-words we divinely possess and impart. In this way, the words we share are divine nectar and the manifestation of knowledge we gain through transmutation. The English meaning of the Sanskrit word - 'Sara' (is pure essence) + 'swa' (is self) + 'ati' (is exceeding). Goddess Saraswati fills us with exceedingly pure essence to enable us to speak. In worshipping the essence, we worship Saraswati.

Activate the right meridian of your throat to ask for mercy and resolve to speak kind words and activate the left meridian of your throat to live a guilt-free dignified life.

Affirm- 'Namostutee, I am balanced and happier each day because I have a broad sense of values, empathy, compassion, character, purpose, and meaning. Tathaastu.'

CHAPTER 25a

CAGED GATE OF 32 TEETH

Wisdom entails slowly chewing the knowledge we gather like we chew food before digesting or concluding. Until then enjoy all the information you gather, like a beautiful story. Your teeth represent power, assertiveness, and how well you chew the external knowledge of the world. The health of your teeth affects your wealth, comfort, neck, shoulders, arms, and hands. Your teeth grasp the external truth, which is well-chewed and ground before it is digested. In this way, our teeth have a story to tell. A person over 100, having chewed and digested all previous knowledge, begins to grow a whole new set of teeth. Our tongues caged within our teeth are ready to poison and hurt anyone that comes within its vicinity. The good news is that tongues can be tamed like snakes are and thus the spoken words.

Words just like snake venom can cause harm or bring about good health, patience, calmness, fearlessness, and love initiating the process of rebirth, rejuvenation, and relaxation.

I am attempting to use the power of s-words to strike you with the stark truth so that all poison and toxins in your thoughts and emotions breakdown, get flushed out, and be replaced with universal love, faith, and forgiveness. This way you can start living a wholesome, relaxed, blessed life all over again. Our mouth is like the most-used entrance door of our home. We must not only ensure that we speak good words, eat and drink healthy, but also ensure that our entrance door is welcoming and that the staircase to the attic is not blocking or preventing the space from allowing fresh energies to enter in.

Athithi Devo Bhawah - which means, give utmost importance with warmth and respect to your guests. A guest that arrives at your home whether good or bad is always a guest so be polite to them as a duty. Whether the guest will reciprocate with the same feelings is not in your control even though they should.

Since most of us perceive the world through the power of words and language, Gender-neutral words like '*Shree*' in Hindi and '*San*' in Japanese are polite and respectful ways of addressing others while saying their name. It is a culture we all must follow in this intermingled globalized society as a reminder to be mindful. And to connect with parity, humility, divinity, and making the other feel valued. Our words are like fire and they have resplendent power. Good, kind, and loving words can ground you but harsh words can burn you. Fear of burning makes us stay away from fire. Fear of getting hurt from harsh words makes us stay away from people who use them. Fire and air combination created the word. The higher elements did not expect us to speak words of hate.

People are neither superior nor inferior,
Work is neither big nor small,
Intellect is neither high nor low,
What matters is the soul age.

A highly determined person doesn't rest until he has accomplished his goal. It is through constant repetition that one perfects any skill. While doing affirmations, it might seem to you that you are sounding like a parrot repeating the same thing over and over again but it is through repetition that you become truly liberated.

You can heal people with words. Such is the magic of *siddhi* received by certain yogis.

Liberty of speech means speech that is free, unrestricted, and unique. Free speech speaks only wholesome, kind, honest, and positive words to help one another. All else is not freedom. Those who malign, criticize, and control another, cage their speech. A caged voice never speaks the truth. Truth is freedom. The true meaning of what liberty stands for is lost and misused when we do not let the pure thoughts of others flow freely.

Goddess Saraswati says, I have given you speech - you bring it to fruition. The words are the fruits I send for you, enjoy the juice, preserve their sanctity, share them as you like but do not suppress them ever.

Listening to truth hurts, but haven't we become accustomed to pain?

The famous stand-up comedian, 'Tape Face' from America's got talent and the unique silent movie actor, 'Charlie Chaplin' from the 1900s teach us how speaking less can be so much fun. It shows us to enjoy and laugh out loud at any tragedy through the comedy of life. Words mean nothing and are lost in the crowd unless our eyes, body, writings, and actions speak and feel the same language of love, beauty, and truth. When we close our mouths, our eyes open and we learn to see through the blinding darkness and illusion of pain and troubles. This way we can ultimately meet with our shining light within. Resolve to shun all that doesn't serve you, your body, and your soul with the sword in your control. This is your greatest strength. Take care of your bones, teeth, muscles, and circulation.

To be a care+taker means you are the taker. In caring for something and someone, you are taking the blessings to be cared for in return. Our tongue is caged within our teeth, yet it has to maintain a proper posture to maintain our proper overall health. The tongue is the only muscle that pushes more than pulling and continues to grow as we advance in age.

A kindly tongue is a friendly tongue. A friendly tongue is never caged.

Planet Saturn is like our parent who governs the deep growth, transformation, and restoration of our teeth.

The order and pattern of our 16 upper front (sun) and 16 bottom front (moon) teeth are divided into four quadrants. The first quadrant is 8 teeth on the upper right. The second quadrant is 8 teeth on the upper left. The third quadrant is 8 teeth on the bottom left. The fourth quadrant is 8 teeth on the bottom right. Each of the eight quadrants (pairs of four upper and four lower) are governed by the eight cosmic planets, excluding the earth.

12 energy meridians pass through particular organs of the body. Each of those organs is represented by the 12 zodiac signs and 12 months. Each organ has a corresponding tooth. If the meridian flows smoothly, the teeth too will be healthy.

The throat chakra governs our teeth. The throat chakra much like the 16 pairs of teeth in a combination of upper and bottom quadrants has 16 outer and inner petals. The throat chakra is purified with sweet words or s-words used softly and thoughtfully by a spiritually heightened being.

Yang represents the active out loud use of swords that affect our actions. Yin represents the passive listening of the swords that affect our thoughts. Thoughts are real. The vibrations of divine sounds, prayers, and Godly swords produced by our inner and outer swords activate our teeth, resulting in our overall well-being.

When a person becomes more balanced, positive, eats calcium-rich vitalized food, and continuously uses pious inner 32 and outer 32 swords wisely, the teeth of such an awakened person too becomes revitalized, regenerated, and renewed.

Each of these 64 layers (inner lower yin and outer upper yang layer) therefore tell a lot about individual personalities and cause of imbalance or respective illness and problems. A basic understanding of these influences tends to help expedite the healing process.

Biting more than you can chew lands you into trouble. Learn to break down and digest the difficult issues and chapters of life rather than overstraining and overwhelming your energies. Distracting yourself with excess food is not the best solution. Food can be of many forms. Food for the stomach is what we eat. Food for the mind is what we think. We should eat and think in moderation to avoid stressing our bodies. Just the way overeating can make us feel imbalanced and heavy, Overthinking too can make us feel heavy and emotionally bloated.

Affirm- 'Namostutee, I and my words are pure, loving, and free-spirited like the breath of fresh air. Tathaastu.'

CHAPTER 26

STEPS WE CLIMB

I magine a father at the top of the escalator asking his little son who is at the bottom to use the escalator for the first time. Hesitation changes to Godfidence once the father's words comfort the son. Godfidence brings in a lot of fun as the son learns how to maneuver through the escalator, going up and down. Similarly, the subtle higher forces give you the confidence to climb the escalator of life. This changes your hesitation to confidence and then helps you embrace the fun in everyday living. The sacred invisible staircase has no beginning and no end. Starting in the center, it goes to the left and then to the right, and continues until it returns to its revered center.

In the space between each step, there is dark, pure, electrifying silence. There is nothing ordinary about this extraordinary miracle by the creator and the preserver. The climb on these stairs is beyond appraisal. Just keep taking these ceaseless ascending and descending steps. When you think you are descending is when you are truly ascending. Each of us is precious. Each of us is special. No one is a saint and no one is perfect. We are each good or bad based on how we respond to our temper, anger, frustrations, and feelings. Each of us is a work in progress, each of us has the potential to achieve perfection, but none of us has and none of us ever will. There will always be another step to the ladder we are climbing, but that shouldn't ever stop us from trying to climb. The stairway to heaven is unending, the path to perfection is never complete. It's an aim. We go through all the pain and pleasure because we have a goal.

Secrecy has power. There is no need to blow the trumpet of your generosity. The more you share, the more you will get. No one needs to know how much you give, as the more you get the more they will want. So stay protected, and stay shielded. The world is still learning to be nice. The steps are many and not everyone is ready.

The point of having knowledge and wisdom is to share its depth, and that is exactly what we are here to do. I spent most of my childhood in Kashmir. Some call it the gateway to heaven, but the stairway to heaven with 999 steps is in China. I climbed up the stairway and came back to the middle, only to let you know, my love, that the generous steps of the stairway are infinite. The number 999 is limited only to our physical, half-asleep bodies. The climb is never-ending. The thousandth step is the first step you take in your waking state.

Not knowing who is hiding within, I understand that there is a certain fun, mystery, and adventure in climbing up and down the spiral staircase of life. But would we not prefer a transparent staircase, where we can make the next move knowing who and what is coming next?

Each *Yuga* or era and everything in life, much like the staircase in the mall, has an ascending and descending pattern. For example, when we breathe we inhale, which is the same as ascending and when we exhale our breath, we descend. In between the two phases of ascending and descending there is always a void which we call emptiness. It is like that middle moment when one thought has ended and another has yet to come. That moment might last just three seconds but those few moments are enough to decide whether you live or die. Sometimes, three seconds is all it takes to experience the bliss of life. Sometimes eternity passes and we forget to acknowledge what those moments gave us. For me one such aha! moment was when my son was born, I chose to call that moment 'Arastu', taking the letters of both our first names *(Aarav+stutee)*.

Ara means grateful. *Ara+Stu* implies being grateful for divine grace. *Arastu* is a precious reflection of me. Every reflection must be appreciated and praised. To reflect on your reflection is to enjoy the stillness. Our soul loves stillness. It is in the inner stillness that we become aware of our true soul and it is only then that we feel ecstasy. You have got what it takes to be a superstar, do not suppress your desires. Be a go-getter, get things done with an authoritative yet humble approach. The only thing keeping you from climbing higher on the success ladder is you. Be assertive and empower yourself. Protect the sanctity of your energies. Do not trust everyone easily as some people who seem flattering can be deceitful. Continue to do the right thing and keep the faith.

A pyramid was abandoned before its completion in the fifth century because King *Neferefre* died. Interestingly that unfinished pyramid with thirteen steps is seen in the American one-dollar bill and we also see the all-seeing-eye is on top of the pyramid. The number of steps of the unfinished pyramid tells how to step up the thirteen stepped ladder of inward evolution and achieve illumination in this living life. The number thirteen on the unfinished pyramid gives us a clue on how we can align our energy points earth center (taaj) and sun center (surya) of energy body. This way we can develop an understanding of the galactic plane or center of the galaxy.

Thirteenth step: The super galactic center is the womb of the entire universe. The galactic plane is our universal mother (hridya chakra). The thirteenth chakra is within the universal womb, the soul star or the seat of our soul chakra. It is connected to a thread that is about six inches to six feet or more above your head depending upon your evolvement and aura size. When it gets activated we can collectively connect with the energies of the universe as it invokes the Christ consciousness within us. As we continue to purify, balance, and energize ourselves, we can become one with our mother. Slowly, this invokes a huge amount of peace and universal love within humanity. The Goddess energy of this thirteenth step or chakra is universally felt by all. It may frighten some people as the energies are very sharp and intense. Its energies are nine-fold in nature within three triangles from lowest to highest. Its purpose is to remove all enmity, protect, transform, and transmute us through increased faith, oneness, infinite compassion, and wisdom. It compels us to let go of the old habits and attitudes and allows peaceful and fresh energies to come in. Its color is magenta.

Ka and *ba* are separated upon death. *Ka* means life force and *ba* means soul. *Ba* travels into the afterlife in search of *ka*. In the afterlife, the body becomes inanimate and dull but doesn't decay completely because if it completely decays then the *ba* or the soul wouldn't be able to function.

In the afterlife, when two parts – *ka* and *ba* reunite. This union happens because of the pyramid which serves as an instrument to get them together. Individuals have the potential to become an *akh (complete)* through the union of this divine magic. Those who unite through the pyramid are like the resurrected form of the King who died.

Last night I had a dream. The night was over but the dream lived on. In the dream, we all are caught in the passage of time. The passage leads one to a staircase. With every step one takes on the staircase, one becomes bigger and bigger. This is just like an infant becomes a teenager and goes through various stages of physical growth and spiritual evolution. You must take the first step. From there you will get a glimpse of the sparkling light beaming through the little door, on the roof. The light will fill you with a sense of wonder and anticipation. Once you climb all the steps, you will get a choice to resist, enter, come back, renter again later, or simply wait outside the door watching the spectacular show. Whatever you choose will decide the course of your destiny. Ensure you make a responsible choice because the choice you make will affect everyone. This is because we are all inherently connected and one.

Whatever culture or family you may belong to, every home has one such invisible stairway leading up to the heavens above. The door stays open until someone climbs up to peek on the other side. But most people are so enslaved by the limitations of their mortal existence that hardly anyone climbs up to see what is beyond. A whispering sound from the creek of the door says, "You are safe here. You do not need to fear the unknown". Most people believe the door won't come to us, we have to go to the door. I often visit there, exit, and re-enter as often as I would like. The only reason I come back to you through the golden staircase is that there is a message inscribed on the door which I want to share with as many people as I can. It says, "You are little but God isn't, you are limited but God isn't. Allow Godly energies to open you from self-inflicted chains and shackles of pain and repetitive habits. Embrace the change".

This time around, as luck would have it, the divine stairway has descended for us and the door has come to grace us. There is a celebration happening in the attic to welcome and celebrate with us. Yet, hardly anyone dares to cross the rainbow bridge lurking over the stairway. In the current world state, the fear of the unknown is worse than the fear of the known. We fear the immortal heavens and feel safe living within our limited mortal earthly existence. The balance lies in the middle where both meet. There is something surreal and unmatchable about climbing the grand stairs. Every step as if mysteriously leads you closer to the goodness of the heavenly God.

Affirm- 'Namostutee, I am rosy-cheeked, high spirited, untroubled, and strong-minded. My thoughts, conversations, and deeds are valuable, pragmatic, and enterprising. I celebrate the success of others with equal ardor as I do of myself. Tathaastu.'

CHAPTER 27

SHEEP LION

Love is the quality of being fearless in a world filled with fear. Seeing the famous movie, Lion King, we all know that a lioness knows how to protect her cubs. When the cub resists and wants to take control by behaving like the father before he is ready, he becomes susceptible to pain and injuries. This harms everyone under the influence of outer energy. There is a right time for everything and until then we must patiently wait and train ourselves. The father lion is like the sun. The sun provokes and angers us, simply to discipline and regulate us. The mother lion loves to keep us safe under the shade. She patiently creates us and compassionately nurtures us into becoming prince and princess of peace. The radiant light will always shine and reflect on the one who reveres the father and mother. Remember to forgive yourself and those who have hurt you, knowingly or unknowingly, to let the grace of the sun and moonbeam upon you.

Silence has a daring charm to it. When a lion goes for the chase, what does it have? It has that hunger, that passion, that fire, and when these are ignited, the lion can't stop itself from running towards its prey. But first, it strategizes, plans, camouflages itself, and silently prepares physically before making its move gallantly with all its courage and confidence. In the same way, when we have a mission or goal and our lion energy is fired up, we then must strategize and plan before we make the right move. When that happens, we transmute, and that's when we are ready to pounce.

When a lion appears, the herd of lazy animals ceases to stroll around and run away as a fright flight response. We need to act now as we are the courageous lions of goodness and seeing us the herd of deceit & evil will run away. No power is stronger than self-control and through discipline and discriminatory power, we will be lord Shiva's brave and revolutionary team members.

Remember, lions might get distracted by the rats but they do not fear rats! They face reality and catch the prey by its neck when the time is right. Influencing the weak is harmful not only for them but also for you. It is a sign of weakness and so is putting another down.

One who influences and controls the weak and one that accepts without reason, are both like parasites - one boosts a false sense of confidence and authority and the other creates a sense of inferiority -the difference is only in the approach- one is more boisterous and the other is more subtle.

When you are one with God's divinity, you are no longer just an innocent sheep, but a divine shepherd who the sheep must follow voluntarily. There is a parable in which an abandoned lion cub is raised by a herd of sheep, and grows up believing that he is a sheep. Here is the story as told by Swami Vivekananda, "There was once a baby lion left by its dying mother among some sheep. The sheep fed it and sheltered it. The lion used to repeat "Ba-a-a" when the sheep said "Ba-a-a". One day another lion came by. "What are you doing here?" said the second lion in astonishment. For he heard the sheep-lion bleating with the rest. "Ba-a-a," said the other. "I am a little sheep, I am a little sheep, and I am frightened." "Nonsense!" roared the first lion, "come with me; I will show you." And he took him to the side of a smooth stream and showed him what was reflected there. "You are a lion; look at me, look at the sheep, look at yourself." And the sheep-lion looked, and then he said, "Ba-a-a, I do not look like the sheep — it is true, I am a lion!" and with that, he roared a roar that shook the hills to their depths. Whether the lion is behaving sheep-like and humbly bleating "baa-baa" or the sheep is behaving lion-like and audaciously roaring "raa-raa" with Godfidence, every coincidence is preordained, every attempt is worth a try, every experience teaches us something and makes us evolve for the better. Each being has its distinctive character, irrespective of the biological family it is born into. Our mental thought-forms and habits sometimes take us away from our reality. Once we meet with our reality, we have the choice to become who we please based on the lessons learned through silent reflection.

The greater someone is pressured, the more their true power and hidden potential shines out. Why hide your truth? Come out in the open and face your actuality, for you are not a timid sheep, but a roaring lion waiting to be born. You are the king of the jungle, and a true ruler is never alone. The entire team of animals is waiting to hear their leader's inspiring voice. You roar only because they are waiting to hear your roaring. Go out there and grab your prey, for when you are hungry, your emotions are imbalanced, and such a team leader is never safe for the group.

The lion who mistakenly thinks it is a sheep starts to roar when it looks at its reflection in the waters below. The human who mistakenly thinks it is a lion starts to soar when it looks at its reflection high in the heavens above and merging with the splendor of light, it says bha-ra. Even the proud lion knows that the power of one is not bigger than the power of many. The power of many may be challenging to muster, but it is always greater than one.

Affirm- 'Namostutee, never forgetting who I am, I calmly put my aristocratic head up high. Like the lion in the story, I am ready to go for the next big jump with full honesty, commitment, and patience. I ensure that the rest of my modest sheep friends also do not forget who I am. Tathaastu.'

CHAPTER 28

BABA

S heep make the sound 'ba ba'. Interestingly, this sound is the seed mantra that invokes our creator, teacher and Godhead. No wonder the 'wise souls' in India are called *'Baba'*.

You should let go of the sheepish herd mentality to avoid getting astray because you are meant to be a Shepherd, whose orders the sheep follow. Wherever you go, with or without the sheep- you will always be the Shepard for that is what you are meant to be. That is the original you. That is where your roots truly belong. That is the role you are born to perform, no matter what may become of you, eventually you are bound to return to complete the circle and fulfill your purpose and professional role.

A good shepherd protects the gentle sheep, no matter what, and knowing the shepherds' pure nature-the sheep follow him, no matter where he takes them. A good shepherd, like a good teacher, knows each sheep personally - treats them all equally, cares for them with all the heart and so the sheep listen to the voice of their master.

It takes strength and power to stand up to your purpose to give meaning to your life. The polite are the strongest in the herd. Just because some people seem meek and quiet like the sheep, doesn't mean they are. Their strength lies in remaining grateful, balanced, and in letting issues naturally resolve without harming another.

As long as you are pure, no external force can change your true identity. Ask any metal or element - how much ever you may tamper with their outward looks, they always remain pure and true to their essence. Despite the changing weather conditions, their inner properties stay resistant to what is on the outside and so they stay intact.

The Great Ones are very much alive, always looking over us to shield and protect us. Their aura and consciousness have expanded, far beyond our physical eyes can see - look no further. At least not with your physical eyes but with your spiritual eyes and you will see the truth in this answer- their energies are one with blissfulness of God, one with all - indestructible and immortalized. You might have seen them here on the physical plane too for they can take any and as many forms per their whims and fancies. However humble they may seem, one meeting with the greatest - magician, mathematician, healer, engineer, true philosopher or the greatest mystic is sure to leave the most profound impact.

And then the voice whispered under my breath, "Many might not know my spiritual truth, mistaking it for celestial truth but that doesn't change the truth of my existence."

The gurus of all true disciples are alive for them. They physically are beyond your reach doesn't mean that they are not alive. As long as a disciple can feel the consciousness of their Guru, as long as a disciple can occupy the same energy field as their teacher, as long as a disciple can connect and relate to the teachings, the teacher exists. The teacher is alive. All that is required from you is to tap into your belief system and keep the faith.

When you stop counting the mortality rate is when you start counting the vitality rate. The vitality rate leads to immortality which needs no rating as it cannot be rated or counted for it is eternal, infinite and it always remains. When day becomes night the night becomes day. It is time to readjust, realign, renew, rewire, radiate, be reborn, and relearn. Sometimes we have to go inwards and meet with the dark face to face. There is no need to panic when you meet with your truth. What seems ugly, is beautiful within. What is dark, is lit from within and what is light is dark from within. Going inwards is a good thing, there is no need to abhor yourself. It is a good thing to meet with yourself, spend time with your family, your inner soul, and nurture yourself to come out in the world when the forces of energy are much more settled, calm, leveled and conducive.

I was fourteen and during one of my trips to the Himalayas we were asked to camp overnight in a sleeping bag. I just couldn't sleep as I was haunted by bugs and mosquitos that might crawl in. I quietly scooted away to the side of the river nearby after it was dark and everyone had slept. The cold winds touched my heart and soul with such love that no amount of darkness or disquietude could stop me from enjoying the loneliness and the mystery of that night. Hours passed and I kept walking. Suddenly,

I saw a shadow of a sage following me from behind. He was carrying a *lota* – water container in his hand and he silently whispered, "Don't be startled but there is a wild bear to your left". I was told earlier that day, by our mountaineering institute, that we could encounter bears in that terrain. I surprisingly didn't freeze, kept calm, and kept walking with the – sage (*Rishi*) following me through the night as if he was safeguarding me. Though I didn't look back, our conversation continued.

He told me that I was funny, scared of little bugs yet fearless in front of a big bear. He was unlike most *Rishi's* and spoke fluent English. We reached another camp as we continued walking, where several youngsters were sitting by the campfire. They invited us over and we sang songs, ate and danced.

Few days passed by and we were trekking on a different path. Our patrol leader who we lovingly named 'Himalaya sir' mentioned that he was going to take a break and go away from the patrol to meet with a famous *baba* who has been meditating in the hills for several years. We all volunteered to go along with him. No one saw the *baba* as they entered his hut but when I entered, I saw the same baba who walked with me a few nights back. This time around he didn't speak a word and gifted me some herbs and a pendant that I still have with me to date. Over the years, I have every reason to believe that he was a divine being I met in his subtle body but I could see him perhaps because of my sensitivities during that time or because of the heightened energy of that place.

Affirm- 'Namostutee, I live following my purpose and design. I trust and believe in the creator who designed me. The creator has kept his promise. Now it is my turn. Heaven and earth are one, creator and the creation is one. Tathaastu.'

CHAPTER 29

YOUR WEAKNESS IS YOUR STRENGTH

The Sphinx has been revealing the biggest mystery of our life to us, in slow doses. The more we dig deep within ourselves, the more curtains we drawback, and the more doors we open, the more treasures we will find. And there will always be more riches to find. Various legends have been written about the great Sphinx. No one knows if any of them are true.

In a story I read as a child, the Sphinx kept travelers from passing by unless they could answer a riddle correctly. If they couldn't answer, the Sphinx would strangle them. Here is the riddle: "What has four feet, two feet, three feet, and hobbles with a stick - the more feet it gets the weaker it becomes?" Most were unable to answer, and so the victims were buried, until one man answered the riddle correctly to save the people. He said, "A baby crawls on four legs, grows up and walks on two, gets old and walks with a walking stick, which makes three legs." I am no longer a child, but I see the profundity in this riddle even today.

Everyone is special. Everything and everyone is of value in our earthly team. What we believe is weak has more strength in certain areas than we do. What you feel is lacking in you is your greatest asset.

I recently met a woman with usher syndrome and was impressed to see her commitment to convert her blindness into her greatest strength by motivating others and seeing the humor in the situation, rather than feeling low or sorry about what has become of her.

Spirit is breath, the soul is mind and body is substance. All three are inherently interconnected and can never be separated. We are in this perennial fight with ourselves to view ourselves, others, and the world around us in the way we are supposed to. If we begin to view this outward and inward reality holistically and in its entirety rather than in parts then our lives will be so much simpler and joyful. Your higher and lower nature, all your flaws and assets, your weaknesses, and your strengths, your light and dark side are all yours belonging to one entity and cannot be separated. You are not your weaknesses and as soon as you learn to rise above them, your weaknesses become your greatest strength. When one thing is weak in us, another is strengthened. In finding our true strength, we learn that our weakness led us to our greatest strength. No one is weak. Each being is stronger than the other in one aspect or another.

Affirm- 'Namostutee, You are not my greatest fear but my greatest strength. You are my inspiration, my only support. I stand here strong only because of you. Only for you. The love I have for you is like no other, it is incomparable because there never has been love as rich as this. Tathaastu.'

CHAPTER 30

S-PAIN

The only thing that can burn your pain is S-pain - sweet pain. There you will see that in the end either the bullfighter or the bull has to get destroyed. But where has that ever stopped the bullfighter or the bull to enter the arena and flirt with death! Life's struggles are like the famous bullfight of Spain. If we learn to respect pain the way bullfighters respect and worship the sacred bulls then maybe we too will one day learn the skill to fight our inner battles and come out winners.

A charging bull and the danger of death doesn't stop a person of courage before the fight has even started. In the course of life, we all interact with many inner bulls that reside like viruses inside of us. I have never visited Spain, but the bullfighting culture is so well known and renowned that I was compelled to write a few words on the festive and traditional celebrations they have around bullfights and what my take on it is. Hope this helps you see the pain and suffering from a different perspective. Bulls are color blind. We think they are charging towards the red scarf held by the bullfighter. Just the way we think that pain is coming charging towards us to sap our energy. Truly, we are the ones inciting the bull and the pain to come charging towards us because we subconsciously or consciously enjoy the thrill, drama, and grandeur that this fight brings. Whenever we are not in sync with our Godly or divine nature, we are behaving impulsively and are petrified like animals. Only a truly fearless man can pull the bull by its horns. It is the smell of our fear that entices our lower animalistic nature to come charging towards us. So be brave, plucky, and swift. Only then can you freely enjoy and celebrate the risky bullfight called life. Pain and negativity, therefore, is nothing more than a theatrical drama we play out to make life more exciting. If you want peace and positivity, then stop making a bull out of yourself.

In praising pain, we pacify and comfort pain from years of curses and torments heard every day from people suffering. Pain is our teacher and deserves our gratitude. It too is simply doing the job it has been assigned to do by the universal power. As we make pain feel better, pain makes us feel better and comforted. As we stop taunting and complaining, pain for its innate nature, our pain-filled nature changes. As our disposition changes, pain vanishes and only pleasure remains.

Life gives us troubles and pains so we learn how to deal with these opposing forces. During untroubled times, it is easy to be generous and sweet to one another. Our true heart is revealed in the choices we make and how much we help one another during troubled times.

We must stay calm, serene, and alter our attitude when facing troubles. The troubles we face are ways with which we pay for our past individual or group karma. When the debts are paid and cleared off, the troubles automatically fade. If we learn to train and discipline our minds, karma can be neutralized. We prolong our suffering and troubles by constantly thinking of them in our minds and discussing them with others who think of them even further thereby intensifying its effects. If we remove the thought of pain from the collective consciousness of our memory, the pain will reduce as well. If we distract our mind with more powerful, exciting, and joyful thoughts then the pain, suffering, and hurt we feel might just vanish completely. For example, by being overly depressed or anxious about the pandemic, we are making things harder for ourselves and others. Wrath and suffering are transitory. Our troubles too shall pass if we stop giving them more importance than they deserve. Sometimes the best way to stay safe and protected is not to overthink the problems. Simply enjoy the pleasure each moment brings and be merry.

Affirm- 'Namostutee, I bow to the pain and accept the blessings it has given me over the years. Pain has taught me some great lessons. These lessons are my greatest blessings. I am now experiencing complete liberty, having understood the significance of obstacles and mistakes. May all beings experience comfort, glory, pleasure, and abundance. Tathaastu'.

CHAPTER 31

MOUNT MERU

As per Lord *Shiva*, the center of the world is Mount Meru. Meru is centered within us as a stable meeting place between heaven and earth.

As a teenager, I went mountaineering to the *Garhwal* hills in *Uttrakhand, India*. It was one of the most wonderful yet challenging experiences of my life. Being there, I felt so centered and spiritual. Unfortunately, we couldn't physically climb Mount *Meru* or *Sumeru (Su meaning excellent)* because it has a reputation of being one of the most difficult climbs in the world. The word *Meru* comes from the Tamil word '*Meru*' which means peak. It is the mountain peak that lies between *Thalay Sagar* and *Shivling*. Mount *Meru* is like a huge and irresistibly tempting diamond, most of us can't possess because climbing it is considered very dangerous.

Sun and moon revolve around Mount Meru. When the sun is behind the mountain it becomes night. The mountain has four faces, each one made of a different material. In the North is gold, East is crystal, South is made up of lapis lazuli and the West is ruby. It is believed that the mountain represents the entire universe and the home of those who are the ascended ones.

We all have been sent with a default setting. We can either change our setting through good deeds and actions or worsen it with misdeeds and wrongdoing. Super-intelligent beings are watching over, supporting, observing, analyzing us, and our progress on mental, emotional, and physical levels. These super-beings reside on Mount Merus' throne.

It is time we upgrade our morals and ethics. Even if it means fighting with your inner nature. These days, the spiritual police officers are doing their rounds. They are on high alert and we sure do not want to unnecessarily attract the attention of the beings on the mountain.

As your bright light shines up, the never-ending One raises you. You need no degree to validate your capabilities or to bribe the higher managers. Simply work through the higher power and energies. Give all your labor with no expectation of the fruit. Let go. Let be. Life is easy. Enjoy beauty. Enjoy the journey.

All activity, freedom, and wisdom lie right in the center, which is where the balance of energy lies. Reaching this heightened knowledge of ultimate truth through the understanding of the essence of inner teachings requires great forgiveness, introspection, determination, discriminating intelligence, and resolve. It is only when you reach the middle that you become one with the ultimate existence of unlimited life-giving energy, through its subtle swift vibrations. You feel you are flying with thousands of intricately woven wings.

The everlasting one is both the form-giver as well as the forgiver. All plans designed by the everlasting one are perfect. The everlasting one is everything and it is the source behind all there is yet it remains nameless, just, and precise.

One crystal from the everlasting Mount Sumeru left its bejeweled throne and began to talk, "Last time I was buried under the sleepless, painless state for three earth days by *maran*[49], the death giver. I returned, under its protection and divine grace, with renewed and reprogrammed energy. This time I am being impregnated once again with all the elements, the complex amalgam of alpha, beta, gamma, theta, and epsilon and its various permutations and combinations. The everlasting one dwells within me in the same way as it did before my death and in the afterlife. The everlasting one is everything and will remain with us all during life as well. Everlasting one made me with three main steps. The First was an idea, the second was impregnating the plan and the third step involved blessing me with the life-giving waters. The idea naturally came before the plan, it then was actualized and physicalized and so the idea is bigger than me. The thought is my senior, it is what I am made of and so I must bow to it and resolve to change or grip the numerous unwholesome thoughts that float around because none of them is anything like the ones created by the never-ending one. I am the force of protection and the guardian of all. I now have the vital spark, the vital breath of life, and the vital fluid- all three

---

[49] *Maran is a title of respect given to Rabbis by Jews. In Arabic it means Master and in Hindi – death*

inherent in me." The human spirit is meant to attain complete Union with the perfect everlasting one.

Sun gives us life. Sun and moon together, impel us to do *Sumaran*[50]. *Su+maran* in Sanskrit means perfect soul and memory. When the moon remembers the sun, the energy of the sun gets embedded within it through constant devotion and sharpening of memory.

The moon reflects the light of the sun because the moon is doing *Sumaran* of the Sun.

Same way, we are a reflection of the moon and by remembering the moon, the energy of the moon gets embedded within us. This leads us to dissolve our ego within it. As we continue to become one with the higher energies and allow our memory to get sharpened, our spirit body becomes more balanced and united. Finally, as we ritualistically perform daily purification for attaining *sumaran*, we all i.e, Soul, spirit, and self (aham) speak the same language, irrespective of which realm we may occupy. Sa (sun), ma (moon), and am (Self) in Sanskrit can be called Sah, maha, and aham[51] -therefore, are all the same and united.

This trinity leads us to understand that we are not just the form but we are also the shining spirit bodies (or ruh in Persian) and we must try to move beyond all delusions and dualities.

There are three points on your head for governing three aspects of our mental faculty. Our mind brings about discipline and hence a robotic attitude towards life stages. Our intellect takes us to a fickle, doubtful stage. Our intuition takes us to a serene, tranquil stage. In the third stage, we merge with the self through oneness leaving behind all ego and pride.

Affirm- 'Namostutee, my mind is sharp, my emotions are stable, and my body is strong. I am healthy mentally, emotionally, and physically. Tathaastu.'

---

[50] *Sumaran means sharpening of memory through constant devotion.*
[51] *Aham is interestingly reverse of maha is aham which is same as saying that the reverse of spirit is the self*

CHAPTER 32

SOULFUL SOUP

I magine you go to a restaurant and order a large bowl of soup. You then share it with your family of three. The soup is the same, but now it is split in three ways. Each of us has a different way of explaining the quality and taste of the soup because our experience varies but the soup remains the same. Like a large bowl of soup, we are three in one. To know the different aspects of the quality and taste of our inner soup, we need to temporarily split it into three.

Every time I sit, I feel there are three of me sitting on a chair. The three are your higher soul (or presiding guardian deity), crown, heart and your aura have the capability and potential to collectively restore your divine plan on earth. It is time to snap out from your worldly attachments and know the mystery behind your stark truth.

Unity is wiser than the trinity. There were three wise men. Each thought he was wiser than the other. The first one was the spirit, the second one was the soul and the third one was the body. The body said, "I am at a level where I am most visible and so what is visible is true. I am the wisest of them all." The soul said, "I am at a level where I can feel most and what is felt is considered true and so I am the wisest of them all." The spirit then said, "I am at a level where I can hear and see the most and the mysterious force is most enigmatic and so I am the wisest of them all". After years of arguing and bickering, one day all three wise men came together and realized each was endowed with a different gift. Each of them had a new dimension to offer and each was telling the truth. Only the level from where they sat to watch the universal happenings was different and so the quality of the vision was naturally not the same. Finally, the three together decided to view from the same heightened level of understanding, and from that day on they freely and collectively spoke the truth in a non-domineering way.

Another person came along and asked them "Who are you and what level are you speaking from?" The wise men answered "The entire Trinity is blended with the one, I am the one and I speak the same truth no matter what level I am at. What you grasp out of it might be different based on your level of understanding but we three are one". Trinity is Unity.

The three wise men are within us, not outside of us. The one in the middle is the soul of wisdom. The one above is the pure spirit behind the entire creation. The one below is the passionate energy that emanates from the fire within. Brahma is the sustainer of bliss, Vishnu is the preserver of peace, and Shiva is the destroyer of monkey minds. There are supernatural powers and Siddhis through which the entire trinity can be you. It can help you guard against obstacles and overcome any issues. The three temples are all with you and not anywhere else. Your mind, your heart, and your body are your temples. Keep them ritualistically clean, worship them with respect, treat them with reverence, adorn them with tender jewels, and they will take you to the ultimate divinity within you, which is the same divinity within all. You are the divine spirit, the soul, and the form. Triune nature is simply a manifestation of the pure spirit. Spirit is one, the trinity is one. We all have threefold nature and are divine manifestations of the trinity. We all are creatively synthesized.

A harmonious and ideal society is built by individuals who are virtuous, pure, and moral in intentions and actions. When money and power collectively come in hands of such individuals, the temple bells are sure to ring the world over. The material, size, and tone may be unique in each individual. The instruments may be different. But the sound of the trinity is so admirable because it is always supremely singular. Just like Brahma, Vishnu, and Shiva- Sach means truth or light. Chit means oneness or love. Anand means bliss or power. As long as we live in Sach, Chitta, Ananda, we all will remain in equanimity and one with our threefold (physical, subtle, and causal) nature. A true yogi is neither hyper sensitive nor heartless but is in perfect equilibrium.

Affirm- 'Namostutee, I inspire people to gain a better perspective in life and offer soulful solutions to their problems. I am physically, mentally, and intuitively flexible, adaptable, and accepting. Tathaastu.'

CHAPTER 33

TRUE BLISS

> By seeking it you will lose it.
> By losing it you will gain it.
> By gaining it you will give it.
> By giving it you will receive it.

This my friend is the *ananda* of true bliss.

Said the air to fire, "Things in the thought world move much faster than they do in the real world. The real world you create is the one in which you live and it is too slow for me and so I live in my thoughts which are even more real."

It is through the particular fragrance you resonate, the scent you wear, the chants and ceremonies you celebrate that the higher power will recognize your vitalized energy when his subtle self descends upon the earth. The grace and blessing of ultimate awakening through innate cosmic consciousness has enriched and taught me to trust life, to be authentically optimistic and centered by living virtuously and walking humbly with the creator at all times. This enlightenment is true bliss.

Distances become shorter, life becomes easier, things become just a medium and this whole life becomes a fun joyride in a theme park when you are in true bliss.

The Federal Bank gives you shredded old currency notes that you can keep in your homes. I have a vintage paperweight with ripped currency notes worth USD 50,000. On one hand, the paperweight is a glass globe to keep down papers but on the other hand, it is useless to the extent of not something that one would have in this virtual age. True bliss is when you know and enjoy the beauty and the superficiality of the fragile paperweight with no attachments. Each one of us is holding such a paperweight.

You are the maker of your bliss, your heaven, your progress, your transformation, and your evolution through the underlying acceptance, forgiveness, and understanding of yourself and others. There are many different races, nations, faiths, stages, ages, occupations, habits, actions, traditions, attractions, vibrational energies, and much more. I enjoy everything, I experience everything with nonattachment. The whole universe is my causal home. I am always joyful when I am home. I experience the entire universe from my inner soul which is always at peace. Here - there is nothing vivid, everything is absolutely clear and continuous. This is true bliss.

The higher soul speaks, "Between the over-attachment and the complete detachment, I will meet you at a place where you have shed all expectations towards the self and the other. It is from here that I will tell you what it is like to be infinitely living with the heavenly true bliss. There is nothing mechanical, chemical, intellectual, or emotional about your union with the eternal internal. It is inherently within you. It always was and always will be."

To bring about an inner change from this stage of perplexity into perennial connectivity is no challenge for the truly inspired one. Yet I have left many markings on the trail, which you must follow to move out of this self-inflicted sorrow.

I am just a thought. I am just a mental image. I am just a plan. I am the breath of life. I am pure energy. I am a play of emotions high and low. I am just a part of divine *leela*. I am just a humble consecrated crystal. A part of this crystal is in everything, from fake to real, true to imaginary. I am truly at bliss in this heavenly abode. I am the air. I am the invisible which preceded the visible.

The precious pure crystal, the higher beings designed, is consecrated and programmed with set instructions on how and when to return to its true abode. Just like a tortoise returns to its shell, this crystal is programmed in such a way that it knows when to go into safety mode along with its new friends and it also knows when the faltered stars will fall. This time when the precious one will be dusted, cleaned, and renewed, it will have only very little memory of what has gone past. The rays of this crystal emanate shine, life, and color, that it brightens up any place it rolls. It forever dances with joy and seeing the blissful, blessed mountain upon which it lays its radiant charm-fills you with bliss.

No one will get to choose their new role or costume henceforth. This is to make sure everyone gets the taste of pure bliss, equanimity, and complete clarity. Some will fly, some will get nourished, some will generously give, share, or care, and some will shine much like the hope diamond. Others will float, swim, dance, or sing together in harmony. Everything and all life will be illuminated, alleviated, and awakened. Such is the decree backed with gratitude and faith of the little precious hidden beautiful one.

We all are trying to hold on to something we do not want to lose. Attachment, detachment, and un-attachment are all part of the same glamorous problem, varying only in degrees. True bliss is about enjoying life as is, without feeling the need to hold on to anything.

I am not a conventional yogini. I do not fit in the mainstream or live stream, but I do fit in the mindstream. A stream might intuitively know which source it originally came from but simply keeps flowing for lifetimes together without forming a set opinion about what all it picks on its way. A pure stream continuously goes with the flow and doesn't hold on or clings to any particular idea or theory. Good and bad are but the same. The stream always remains in its best element. Life is a continuous learning process. With changing situations and experiences, thoughtforms keep evolving. I am true bliss. True bliss is like a stream of gold.

Affirm- 'Namostutee, My soul is elevated because kindliness and kindness inspire me. Bliss I am. Tathaastu.'

CHAPTER 34

CONCEALED BUD

This is a bud that will flower in all seasons as long as the environment is conducive for its growth. You are that gardener who has the responsibility to make the environment conducive. This bud was planted by you but the seed was provided by the supreme force.

Every seed holds the full potential to flower and bloom. This realization led me to an expansive journey of self-discovery. The flower of this chapter is now ready to bloom. Kundalini's entire existence has been a hidden mystery, born into someone who wanted to keep her existence a secret. Your inner potential is not always what others want you to follow. And so you keep it a secret, or you kill it. It is like being born a girl when your family wanted a boy. But then a day comes when you decide to love yourself for who you are, and that is when you let the secret out. You embrace the girl child. That bud has now flowered into a beautiful woman who is proud of her individuality, even though for others she may still be a hidden mystery.

I crowned myself with all the riches, with her (innate potential) by my side. I can never get from others the warmth that is like the hidden blanket inside a kangaroos' pouch. Shame on those who seek the so-called balance in their lives through bearings of an outward gender. For the weight of the soul, energy is genderless and beyond your limited, cocooned understanding. The yang is weak without the yin. The subtle is what brings out the dynamism in the active. The weight you are carrying is the load of that unborn child. You are pregnant with thoughts. Until your thoughts are born into action, you do not know whether the child will turn out to be a girl or a boy. Winter is long past. It is time to blossom.

What is stopping you is your mind and not your Kundalini. Why question the perfection of the higher will? Kundalini also embodies perfection. Her greatest asset is the beauty of her emerging wisdom, but instead of embracing her strength, you choose to be threatened by it. Even when the truth is beautiful, it frightens us. She slips away from you only because you choose to call her a lump of unwanted slimy serpent energy, although, through that energy, she crowns you with the most precious, shining emeralds and diamonds.

The physical self is a manifested form of our higher soul who has commendable glory. The higher soul too shares the same characteristics as us but since it is not bound by physical boundaries, it is more swift and magnified. For example, gem-ini which means God's Jewel will brightly shine in higher realms once it is aware of who it is though it may not have physically realized its full potential yet and so here it is like an ordinary unpolished jewel. Some of us self-manifest leaving the heavenly royal abode to gain a deeper insight of certain concepts for the greater good. This is the reason why every sacred Agni or fire ceremony to manifest wishes starts with praise in favor of those light beings who set high standards and realizable aims. Kundalini is a sacrosanct holy mystical experience that has the potential to take you to *Nirvikalpa Samadhi*[52]. She guides you internally to recover that trust you have lost in yourself, through the right thoughts, right speech, and right actions.

Kundalini does not live by herself, but she lives. It is through her that we live our life to the fullest. She empowers and protects us. She says to us: "I do not know how to fix you, but you do. You have to let go of what you know to know."

Kundalini might seem shallow, but she is your depth. She has no answers for you because your questions are unanswerable. But here is a good start to finding your truth, to reaching your true potential, to being more alive and so stop living a robotic, monotonous or futile life.

She says to us, "Just as water continuously flows, I am flowing through you, and if there is a huge boulder blocking the flow, then I will try to unblock and open those channels, and continue to flow within. It is my responsibility to align you with me, but my ultimate role is to serve you as well as I can. Even the smallest effort makes the greatest shift in what you radiate. Sometimes, when you are invisible in the outer, mainstream world,

---

[52] *Nirvikalpa samadhi means constant connection and intense concentration.*

you are the most visible and alive in the inner world, making far deeper changes within the core of universal programming. I don't answer your questions, but I compel you to find the answers yourself."

The eternal, blissful, ecstatic state lies in merging with the divine, and by letting the sacred energies work through you. Never lose your zest for life because of another individual or entity. Never stop being yourself because of another person. The day that happens, you are living a dead life.

I wrote a beautiful book long ago. It was very dear to me. It was all mine. Then a thief came and stole it so it became yours. Now it is ours. Had the thief not stolen my precious book, it would have remained mine and never become ours. The one who took without asking will have a cyclic debt to pay and the one who never gave has the choice to forgive and rewrite another book. True freedom lies in clearing all your debts. It is liberating to choose to rewrite another book, forgive, and move on.

Gradual awareness is safer and better than sudden enlightenment. This way your mind gets more polished and knows what it is getting into and where is it going from here. An informed decision is always better than a blinded one. Sacred wisdom is like a serpent that must reveal its essence and uncoil gradually else it can scare the faint-hearted people with its hypnotizing hood and fangs.

In Sanskrit, *Kund* refers to the number nine and a well or vessel filled with consecrated treasures. The English translation of the same word would be a jasmine flower. In *Shaivism*, it refers to the sacred fire. In *Punjabi,* which is an Indo Aryan language, *Kunda* means a metallic latch or lock that is fastened to shut doors and protect the precious and sacred treasures. Hawan Kund is a worshipping ritual in which God's compassionately and generously ignite the fire up just to joyfully fulfill your wishes. In Hindi, 'lini' means 'soft'. In English, it means 'child of God'. In Punjabi, it means 'to give'. Ini also means time. 'Kundalini' therefore is the process to softly open the latch within the chambers of your body. Your body is like a vessel that contains all your precious treasures.

Each of the cells and glands inside our body and brain is intelligent. Size doesn't restrict you from gaining knowledge. In the fairytale, Thumbelina, met with her prince despite all odds because she lives in the pot of our brain. She is like a beautiful flower living inside our brain who used intelligence and patiently nurtured all others. With a passion as strong as the size of your thumb, you can meet with your true love, despite all distractions and fear of the astral world that come your way. Where there is a higher decree, there is always a way. Even the smallest of the atoms and cells have a divine and sacred purpose to unfurl themselves like a flower bud and get activated.

Affirm- 'Namostutee, I am aligned with my higher interests. I effortlessly achieve my purpose. I express and do not repress my inner intentions. Tathaastu.'

CHAPTER 35

FIRST KISS

This chapter encourages turning over a new leaf. Start anew and amend past mistakes. Never has there been such a perfectly synchronized dance of all elements deeply in love within the silent watery ocean. You are fire. I am air. Together we are fiery, filled with passion, power, drive, and energy. My soul is brainy and airy, yours is watery and spicy. This connectivity makes our tower always emotionally lit with mighty bliss that is not only profoundly lucky but also tall, divinely blessed, and lofty.

None other can ever tame and center my timeless, flighty spirit literally to the ground! With all the elements now and here within you and me, no one can truly shine as well as we do. For nowhere in any realm has there ever been such an extraordinary amalgam of beauty tightly bonded, physically, mentally, psychically, intuitively, and spiritually, within the duality of a union.

The red flower blossoms in your garden because of the light of the sun. The bringer of the light is our leader and protector. Whoever brings light to you refreshes you and brings you out of your initial darkness. We must therefore always be grateful to those who tirelessly share their brilliance with us.

They say you never forget your first kiss. What I do know is that 24 years back when I joined college to study philosophy, it was like being mentally kissed for the first time. Up until then, nothing stimulated my mind as much. However, like most new-age relationships, I and philosophy went through periods of emotional and psychological upheavals. My mind wavered to explore and taste the waters of the outside world. We broke up, we patched up, we doubted, we analyzed and we experienced life only to finally get back. This is because no matter how far I may think I have gone, here I am.

Philosophy is known to be the nurturer. It nurtures all sciences. You cannot stop the mother from embracing and kissing her child. My mind and body finally realized that my soul lies in philosophy. I returned to the unfinished story of my first kiss, my first love, my first relationship. Philosophy has stayed loyal to me for most of my life despite all odds. It never deserted me, even when the whole world seemed to be falling apart. So here I am sending kisses - (knowledgeable, insightful, sanguine self-explanatory, sagacious) - flying kisses to philosophy. This book is the delivery of my pregnant thoughts, I cannot foretell the future of this baby but if you have taken your time out to read this book then I know my baby is in good hands.

'Jes' means joy. 'Jesus' gives us a heavenly 'kiss of joy' which inspires us to uplift ourselves amid darkness, through constant forgiveness and selflessness.

When a cannibal sleeps and then wakes, nothing changes in his character. However, if he resolves to change and consistently practices good virtues in selfless service towards other beings, following an ethical and moral life then a day might just come when he wakes up from his long sleep. From that day on his character would have modified, he would thereafter be a different person.

Earth was here before you and even before the first animal and tree kissed its skin. She feels, soaks, loves, and heals you of all your pain each time you touch her. She feeds the hungry and gives us strength. She never gives up. She is ever forgiving, comforting, and accepting. Let us make her feel loved and worthy, let us kiss (keep it sacred and strong) her back. The earth is our past, present, and future. She is our first and last kiss. Let's go back and enjoy the memories of our first kiss with her. Let us be transparent and true to ourselves. She is our greatest support and true love. Trust her positive nature. Be in your natural compassionate, gentle caring state, around a fresh environment. Let us thank her for being who she is. She is your fortress and your shield. With her, you are never alone. She will love you anyway.

Allow your feelings to guide you. Love is that divine instant connection between two souls that make you feel like a million bucks even without any exchange of actual words. It fulfills you and completes you in a way that your heart beats and says- 'the buck stops here'[53]. When you desire to find love, the universe picks up the signals and does all in its power to bring the two of you together. Every such meeting is pre-arranged. We think we are calling the shots but all divinely arranged marriages are pre-decided by the elders. The couple has little role to play, which is why I truly believe that 'God won't bring you to it if he can't take you to it'. Things just happen.

Each night is different and each sleeping night wakes up with the first kiss from the sunlight. This first kiss of light buries the night in deep darkness and refreshes it with renewed hope and grace. Remember that after every long night, there is always dawn waiting to kiss, inspire, and bless the virgin land.

The enlightened one keeps returning to fill us with renewed hope and joy. Before landing on earth, he takes a bird's eye view of collective consciousness just to get a perspective on universal energies. Calculating the averages, if he notices a world where wives are objectified, husbands are disrespected, relationships are mistrusted, fathers are ill-treated, children are taunted, leaderships are questioned, teachers are hounded then he gives us more chances to work on our karma and sends proper teachers and guides to help us see the right path. The ever benevolent savior repairs damages, restores balance, and trusts that we will follow the cues he leaves for us despite all odds. We must pray for our helpers as they pray for us.

He comes to help us meet with our perennial pious mother. If our mother center is humiliated, her eyes are blindfolded or her speech is restricted, despite all the discomfort, nothing touches a pure forgiving spirit like her. The devoted dogs who stand by her are called dog-ma. Despite all these situations- seeing her children with the inner eye, her strength joyfully returns. She doesn't become a victim of the circumstance and instead takes charge of her responsibilities and supports us. She may seem weak but she removes the illusionary chain tied to her ankles with her mental sword and slays all weaknesses, doubts, and fear mongers sitting inside our brain.

God gently leaves a mental note that a world where mothers are not honored and revered needs to first make some amends by building faith in themselves before more grace can enter into the light rays of heavenly awareness. Even then the all-merciful mother stays on to reach over the

---

[53] *The phrase 'the buck stops here' means a responsible decision and choice is made personally by you for and towards your actions.*

army of her children, grandchildren, and great-grandchildren spread across places to inspire values of trust, patience, and gentleness. When her blindfolds are removed, one blink from her eye lights up the entire cosmos and as the sparkling light emanates from her vision, all the masked secrets get circulated like wildfire. Set your standards high, Learn from the universal parents how to be all compassionate and all-forgiving, and continue evolving to reach your own highest potential. We are like a bird sitting on one of the branches of the universal tree who aims at a heavenly target and then flies to reach there. Sometimes the destination is right there but our wavering mind keeps stopping us from reaching the true tree. We have all the support but we get hounded with self-limiting beliefs of the past and refuse to fly. Even then God sends us support in different forms to release us from our cage. The ever-present one hand holds us in life and death. Allow yourself to heal your mind, body, emotions to experience unconditional love, take control of the situation and Godfidently connect etherically with your spiritual family. Ether or *Akasha* is one element that stays with you throughout the journey of your many births and rebirths. When all those memories come flashing down, you become a self-realized vitalized torchbearer of truth. This my friend is the heavenly realm of your own making. Through this perceptual experience, you can henceforth be more alive, start living a life based on your terms. When the puppet show is over, the real show begins.

Affirm- 'Namostutee, I retrace the steps back to my home with a keen intellect, endurance, and deep spiritual insight. The first kiss of peace and truth brightens, revitalizes, illuminates, and lights up my spirit and the entire space around with its simple stillness and purity. Tathaastu.'

CHAPTER 36

HIGH FIVE

The key has unlocked all the locks and filled you with delight. Look! You are already holding all the fortune in your hands. There is no more need to search when all you have ever wanted and more is now in the grasp of your fortunate hands.

The circular dance from left (mercy) to right (justice) rather than from right to left is far trendier nowadays. When two fingers (spiritual and temporal) can do the job of lighting up the whole cosmos, then why do we need five? Why close our fist, when keeping ourselves open and receptive is the only way to allow the energies of trust, faith, love, and light to pour in and flow out. The center of our palm is connected to the thousand-petaled crown chakra. It is the center of our understanding, of collective consciousness and will to integrate this awareness through silent meditation and spiritual wisdom.

We are the ones to interpret what you misinterpret. We are the ones to give mercy and comfort. We are the ones to forgive and forget. Just trust and if you can't keep looking above, just raise the first two fingers of your hands in amazement and wonder, for I am not all theory. I walk the talk here on earth today.

I have healed many as a channel. The mental consciousness is in the palm of my hand. The power is all within. It is for you to take. Just come to me. I am not too far from you. All of you can reach me and the twelve rays (consciousness). Just trust and practically and actively start living the dream. Until then, seek, knock, receive, forgive, confess, praise, and share.

Real love is one. It is like a gentle high five of humility, purity, clarity, generosity, and reality, made with the combined strength of its five fingers.

The best way to activate the two most important acupuncture points in our hands is to hold and write with a pencil more often. This expands our subtle and mental powers.

The use of the five senses entails the sensitivity to do proper sense-activity[54] or action in coordination with all five elements. To eventually increase the vibration, each one of us resonates through our sense-centers[55] or chakras.

Activating the chakras or vortices activates our energy body or the aura, eventually, you too become a shining part of maintaining the equilibrium of nature with your fresh, vibrant, ever-changing, ever-evolving, abundant charm. What affects one, affects another. Our body affects our aura. The health of our aura, based on which realm it is, affects the energy of the aura of earth or physical plane, ether or etheric plane, water or emotional memory plane, air or mental notes plane and moon or lower astral plane, and so on. Your happiness brings joy in another and your depression brings sadness in another.

All five elements are found under the earth. They are our pillars of support holding us from underneath the underworld. This is no utopian concept, but a reality we have not yet accessed since we are busy looking elsewhere.

My birthday is celebrated on May 28th but if I was on Mercury it will be celebrated on May 6th, on Venus–August 14th, on Mars–the celebration will be on Oct 12th, on Jupiter–It will be celebrated 6 years hence and on Nov 7th and finally on Saturn It will be celebrated 18 years later on April 27th and so on. Wherever I may be with every birthday I celebrate I get closer to death and yet I celebrate death. Earth is not nearing its death as Earth is not old yet. We are in 2020 and can live up to the year 2160 bearing the weight of humans and beyond hosting superhumans. However, if we all make a conscientious effort by learning to praise and celebrate life with love and light, we can live even longer.

Your abundance brings wealth to another. Your thoughts affect the spirit of another. We all are inherently connected. Such is the brilliant force and power you carry. You have the potential to vitalize not only your

---

[54] *Sense activity or Karma Indriya are: tongue – the motor organ of speech, hands - with which we grasp and receive, feet - for locomotion, anus and rectum for excretion and defecation, and sexual organs - for pleasure.*

[55] *Sense centers are our force or energy centers or chakras which have the power to influence and excite one another.*

physical but also your emotional, mental, astral, spiritual body through energy healing. Clarity of thoughts and emotions leads to purity of body so connect with me to upgrade your mental and emotional aura to charge up your physical health. Remember to reflect and absorb the energies I am sharing through these writings.

Affirm- 'Namostutee, I lovingly and naturally work with others without getting disturbed, in the same way, my feet walk, hands grasp, eyes see, upper and lower teeth accurately chew and function together as a great team without blocking or getting in the way of another. Tathaastu.'

CHAPTER 36a

HEALING PALM

Your palm is the balm of healing love and light. Cherish the warmth you receive and bless the value you give out through the balm of your fragrant palm. The right hand energizes and activates. The left hand cleanses and purifies. The left hand is negative (thinks responsibly and accepts as much as is graced by God) and the right hand is positive (acts generously and lets God decide fair share) like a battery. Bathe with your left hand. The right socializes and the left moralizes. The right creates, and the left recreates what it is worth. The right conceives what the left perceives and receives.

Eat with the right hand, as its energies are endowed with the *Shakti* and power of wholesome health. Serve with the left hand, as its energies are filled with the loving blessings of Lord *Shiva*. Stay centered and always keep your spine erect while eating, to let the energy flow smoothly through your physical, mental, emotional, and spiritual body. This practice helps you eat in moderation. Remember to stay in gratitude. Since you too are a divine being, bless the food before eating anything, even before munching snacks.

"Hand" in Latin is manus and to give a mandate[56].

"Hand" in Greek is palámē, which means handsome or dexterous which is to feel.

In Latin, *dicere* means "to point." We touch, feel, handle, finger, thumb, paw, grope, palpate, and stroke objects. We manipulate, grasp, create, point,

---

[56] *Mandate is a mandatory action, an authority given to convert what is written into action.*

measure, thank, greet, imprint, sign, scan, and count with our hands. We show love, hate, respect, and give judgment through our hands.

We have an outer brain. "Our hand is our outer brain," as said by the famous philosopher, Kant.

The all-merciful, glorious, righteous might of the hand is your greatest savior and blessing. It has the power to guide you towards making the perfect choices, choosing good over evil. It helps you pass any test even when situations get tricky. Do what you are meant to do; do what you came here for, and soon all your obstacles will effortlessly fade with ultimate grace. You have many chances for redemption to complete your action both above and below. Just remember to deal with experiences through humility, faith, and justice. The Lord God is there to uplift you. Stretch out your arms and stretch your limits.

The clay is ready. You are blessed with the perfect hands. All you have to do is be a dedicated potter. Read the manual and the clues that are left for you. Go ahead, remold the mold to create another beautiful vessel under divine guidance. It doesn't matter how the pot turns out. Every creation, crooked or straight, is beautiful as long as it is created and recreated with full dedication and right action until it reaches its true mold.

Our fingers emit vital energy and electric waves. The thumb stands for ether, beauty, and compassion. The index finger stands for air, wisdom, and action. The middle finger stands for fire, space, and form.

Finger	Label	Color	Direction	Senses	Function	Clarity Stage	Activates
Thumb	Ether	Indigo & Violet	East – purifies	Hear	Vocal chords	Existence Or Fate	Self will
Index Finger	Air	Green	West – Activates	Touch	Hands / grasping power	Perfect Intelligence / Wise	Maha or great
Middle Finger	Fire/ Space	Red	South – Lights	Sight	Feet/ Movement	Thought & inquisitive	Swah or spiritual realm
Ring Finger	Water	Blue	North – soaks, remembers	Taste	Reproduction	Belief & Meditation	Bhuwah or mental realm
Pinky	Earth	Orange & Yellow	No direction/ center- empathizes	Smell	Excretion	Imagination & Generosity	Bhur or Physical realm

Mudras, or specific hand gestures, allow the *prana* energy to stay within.

Gesture 1

Connecting the thumb (ether) and the index finger (air), we form a zero. This is a state of nothingness. The 'I am' came from nothingness. The zero is the womb and holds our *'Akashic'* records. The left hand represents the subtle lunar form and the right represents the dense solar form. This trinity of the remaining fingers stands for water that circulates energy, the earth that gives food, and space that enlightens the mind. Keep these three stretched out.

A simple meditation to activate the fingers: Press the tips of each of your fingers and chant the word Om till you have done this 20 times starting with your left hand. Then chant another Om pressing the thumb of your left hand. This is done to gain clarity.

Gesture 2

On your right hand, the remaining three fingers – trinity, when conjoined and placed with the index finger create oneness. When all the fingers roll to help the index finger connect with the tip of the thumb you create 0.

Combining Gesture 1 and Gesture 2 are combined you create the number 10. This invokes energies of inclusiveness, perfection, union and completion.

Gesture 3

When we make the bridge with the fingers together touching the thumb, it is like the rainbow merging to form purity. There are nine realms- the ninth being the most enlightened realm. The ultimate teacher initiating the ninth realm will bear a mark on the left palm of his hand.

Ether combined with the air of the right hand (yang) decides our fate.

Ether and air carried the bearer of the ultimate light.

He is the one who will bring nothingness into the clear light.

The left hand kept as one and the right hand kept as a zero would ultimately form the new age. From the subtle, into the active. The principle of all the principles will finally come to light.

The etheric energy of the ether and air bind all. Without the etheric envelope, the other three (earth-solid, water-liquid, fire–gas) will not stay in union or bind together. Therefore without the etheric energy, the physical cannot exist. The formless make the form visible through the middle–fire. Their combination makes us experience the five senses.

The duality (ether and air) behind the Trinity (the rest of the three - fire, water and earth) is but a singular reality. The first being the bridge to the second. They are the infinite cause of the evolution of our bodies. Through the heightened collective consciousness we can know the power of this invisible energy. It magnetizes the ground with higher frequencies and vibrations. The supreme lord in the ninth realm is watching over the planetary soul consciousness with half-open eyes. The seventh realm is active and the eighth is subtle. Within him rests the future of all the oncoming generations. From a spirit body perspective, your physical body is very small just like you see your fingers in comparison to your full physical body.

Gesture 4

I suggest a new *mudra*. Press the pinky and the thumb together, with the other three fingers facing out and your hands facing down, and chant the mantra *AaaaayaAaaUeeaaia,* and see the profound magic it creates.

Now smudge some juniper, as it is an herb that purifies and cleanses like no other, taking in the essence from the high mountains and the low valleys. Between the silence of the waves, the waters of the vast sea are filled with pure salty air. Breathe that in, forget all past worries, and enjoy the fresh breeze filled with the scent of juniper.

Your hands have the golden energy that no one and nothing can take away from you. Keep them protected, shielded, and remember you are always protected. The memory you have is known to the unseen higher beings- seraphim, cherubim, thrones, dominations, virtues, powers, principalities, archangels, and angels[57] that are blessing you. The blessings you get from these higher beings should be shared with blessing the water, air, and people you interact with to remain pure and remain safe. We concretize and materialize the abstract concepts written in our hands. The fingers of the left, electric lunar hand represent:

---

[57] *The seraphim, cherubim, thrones are from first sphere; the dominations, virtues, powers are from second sphere; the principalities, archangels and angels are from third sphere. The rank of these nine celestial messengers are all around watching over us in perfect order.*

Thumb = spirit; Index finger = water; Middle finger = fire; Ring finger = earth; Pinky finger = air

When both left and right hand, inner and outer, feminine and masculine unite - our energies are replenished with renewed, vitalized energy and clarity. Lord God has left signs for you all around. Just follow the trail and you will not fail. Your hand is one of your greatest clues, do not feel so blue, keep the courage and you will get your due.

Affirm- 'Namostutee, the golden soothing warm light emanating from the palm of my hand heals anything it touches. Tathaastu.'

CHAPTER 36b

IMPRINT

The hands emphasize the spoken word, which was sown by the thoughts. The mark or mole you have got is an imprint of your incarnate soul within the higher soul or spirit. During this whole wakefulness, may you let it stay brightly lit in the age where we all are performing our respective act on the stage for a better wage or to simply open up the cage. As you become more and more awakened, may you brighten up that mole[58] (self-effort) through the right actions. Each person is performing different acts to gain more than they already have. Some of them are doing better because they want to come out of the cage--their self-inflicted entrapment.

The power is in the palm of my hand, and my precious gem has even more. I am leaving a legacy behind for you. Just stay calm. Just stay true. Just stay connected and all will be well.

Unlike other areas of the body, the skin of the palm and bottom of your foot is glabrous. It is hairless and doesn't tan under the sun, which makes it more durable, yet extremely touch-sensitive. In the soles of our feet, the ancestry of our historical roots is engraved. In the palms of our hands, the sketch of our life is engraved, yet it transforms and renews itself based on the level of acceptance and perfection we try to reach. No wonder the words palmistry and solestry contain the word "try." I believe that your ancient roots are written in the soles of your feet. While your life is sketched in your palms and the soles of your feet, you have it in you to change your destiny by trying.

---

[58] *Moles imply luck and fortune incurred through self-effort.*

The three thick lines on your palm are imprints of your three main *Nadis* or meridians – *Ida, Pingala, and Sushmana.* You have it in your hand to change your destiny.

The first strong line on each palm is the heart line. Place your palms together by joining the two pinky fingers. If the two heartlines on your palms do not meet up, then you are not living the way you were meant to. Let your heart lines meet and smile on your palm. If they are not smiling, it could mean you have not met your full potential. For example, perhaps you are on a pre-planned world tour in which you should have covered more countries by now. You have covered just a little area in comparison to the original plan. It could be that you are stranded in one place. Likewise, in your life, you may be holding back from smiling with your heart because of attachments. The more distant and aloof you become from your planned destiny, the more heat is built up, compelling you to catch up and match up the two heart lines. Resistance causes discomfort and misalignment.

When you are lifted is when you must stay humble. The oak tree might grow to towering heights, but it still remembers to bow down to both you and the tiny chipmunks, impartially and generously giving the gift of its essence, which lies within the acorn. The one who makes better use of the oak's mighty gift will be the next noble celestial king. It seems your competition is with the chipmunks, for most others are too busy looking elsewhere to get nowhere for nothing, without realizing they have to get somewhere to gain the essence of complete nothingness.

None of the lofty towers you have built tell you the internal truth, for the search is not in the external but lies in fulfilling the internal void throughout the depths of the eternal.

The fight is no longer external; if you internalize, you will realize that you are busy fighting an internal war of self-resistance. As we speak, I am holding the ultimate wisdom-filled *'mani'* right on my hand to share, but I have no takers except for the chipmunk sitting in my yard with an impatient gaze. Don't go only by the outer words. Search for the deeper meanings. Google won't help you here-it only speaks what you have already spoken. The fingers in your hand are not just meant to make your life easy here, but they also tell you who you are. Get centered, for you have much to learn. Each finger of our hand denotes a vowel.

Vowels				
	Direction	Activating	Planet/ Star	Finger
A	East	Mental	Mars	Thumb
E	South	Physical	Venus	Index
I	West	Intuitive	Saturn	Middle
O	North	Emotional	Jupiter	Ring
U	Center	Inner core	Moon	Pinky
Y	As above so below	Knowledge (heart and mind)	Mercury	Pinky & Thumb

We are all inherently complete and whole. What your birth chart doesn't define for you, the strongest sound of your name will. What the sound doesn't, the signs upon your hand will. What the signs don't, the imprint on your heart will. You are inherently perfect. You are not just an image of the divine deity. When you are awake and aware, you are just as real as the divine. It is perfect and so are you. I am here to unravel the soul urge and true age of your divine spirit. You are connected to everything, and everything within you is connected to you and everything outside and inside you.

Your etheric body seems invisible because you have not made everything visible to yourself. Everything is always visible and clear in the bright light or dark night. You have to take off the veils and the blindfolds. There is nothing no planet, no cosmic beauty or reality that is out of your reach, my dear. Just stay centered and balanced. I am right here to nurture and guide. I am you and you are me.

The twelve zodiac signs, twelve planets, twelve color, and twelve chakras are all represented in the palm of your hands. The purpose of every person is the achievement of our predestination. There is a purpose and meaning in every person's life, there is something that predetermines the course of events and something that brought us to where we are today. Everything is written in the palms of our hands. One should just watch and try to see the ultimate plan because everything that happens to us is through planetary positions that help us accomplish our earthly mission by continuous activation of chakras.

I am holding an illuminating crystal wand[59] that the divine father sent

---

[59] *Crystal wand/Katwanga is a tool used in religious rituals that represents firmness of spirit and spiritual power in the inner world.*

for me and you. Let us all vow to actively help make the subtle more active and the active just a little subtle. Time to mingle the yin of the left hand with the yang of the active right in its mysterious true light. Ensure not to get caught in the chaos of the world, where fear, greed, and suffering have become so common.

Affirm- 'Namostutee, I open my heart to trust, I liberate myself of all guilt and shame. I go back to the innocent memories, imaginations, and fantasies of my childhood and its wonderful curiosities. I do things that give me joy, bring excitement, hope, and purpose into my life again. I feel protected and safe. I am honest to myself by being who I am. Tathaastu.'

CHAPTER 37

ANGHUTA CHHAAP

The title is taken from the Hindi word 'Angutha' which means pollex, first digit finger, or thumb. 'Chhaap' means 'imprint, mark or scar'. The world has come to this: without a selfish motive or a vested interest, no one even smiles at you, not even your family members. And if they do, the energy of the thoughts behind their actions is very obvious. So get up, freely give thoughtful smiles, and effortless love. Go out and heal the world while remaining shielded like a beautiful child of Mother Earth. Focus on what each element emits: sight, sound, scent, taste, texture, and shape. Then resonate with the element and merge yourself with the limitless blue sky to feel expanded and lighter. Finally, here's a short meditation you can do to loosen up.

> Spirit is the seat of the soul.
> Pineal gland is energized by the spirit.
> Pituitary gland by the soul.
> Pineal gland is the seat of the pituitary gland.

If you get bigger than the seat, the seat tries to adjust but finally breaks with excessive strain.

The imprint of our soul and spirit is in the top part of the thumb of our hands and the big toe of the feet. As per acupuncture, pressing the big toe and the thumb points activate the pituitary and pineal glands.

> Therefore, going by the rule of the thumb (size of your thumb)
> Twice the size of your thumb = circumference of your wrist

Twice the size of your big toe = circumference of your ankle
Twice the circumference of your neck = measurement of your waist
Time taken to blink twice for a woman = time take for a man to blink
Woman's heart pumps twice as harder than a man's heart
Twice the size of your thumb = average size of man's phallus
Two round of formless or yin (0) = one round of form or yang (1)

The rule of thumb can be followed with complete precision from head to toe. No wonder, thumbprints are taken as a signature for a person's identity.

The longest cell in our body (sciatica nerve/axon) starts at the big toe and ends in the brain. No matter how big we get, we must not try getting bigger than our big toe. Freedom is not about getting bigger than the rule of the thumb.

Your thumb is as long as your nose.
Your finger fits perfectly in your nostril.
If you try fitting two fingers in one nostril
It will cause your nose to overstretch.

Everything in our body expands and shrinks to perfectly accommodate our needs. The proportion of the thumb must remain the same throughout our lives. For example, the distance between our two eyes is 1/10th of our thumb. Your arm is about ten times longer than the distance between your eyes. Even though we humans vary in height, our anatomical proportion is similar.

Over pressing and excessively concentrating one side of our thumb, eyes or any organ can over pressurize that part of our brain. Depending on which part is expanding, it causes surrounding nerves to over-compress, congest and inflame. Our brains need more space to adjust to our growing need and greed, more bones are growing to protect and create room in the limited space. What we need is moderation, not expansion. This is creating havoc and imbalance throughout our body and mind. The more we continue to overuse our thumb by texting, scrolling, pressing iPads and games on gadgets, the more imbalance is created in our sleep, waking cycle, and in our hormones.

Meditation: Deep breathe three times. Look at your thumb. Imagine it is your spirit, lit like an everlasting candle flame rising upwards, keep looking at it and rise with it. Allow your spirit to merge with the entire cosmos and its energies. Now close your eyes for about five minutes and let the cosmic energies seep in and become one with you. Open your eyes with a big smile and leave the imprint of your thumb on a paper with blue ink each time you do this exercise.

Affirm- 'Namostutee, My life and career are smooth and fruitful. My life is filled with prosperity, abundance, and good fortune. Tathaastu'.

CHAPTER 38

MAGNETIZED

Magnets are constantly attracting unlike forces to magnetize towards themselves. Based on what attracts me and where I sit or stand- I am pretty much like that rare magnet that uses no-touch therapy to cure you. My switches are my fingers. The reason you don't understand me is that it is in the nature of magnet to attract only its complete opposites.

We know of only one universe but there are innumerable number of universes and each one is as limitless as ours. The way atoms move in our body, the same way universes move in the Supreme Lord's body.

Mother Earth is a big holy magnet towards whom we all get attracted. If you are weak, then the earth's magnet no longer attracts you, so keep your body strong. Also if you too are another entity of a natural magnet like the earth, then the earth would no longer attract you because it is the property of like magnets to not attract likes. This doesn't mean that the field of the other is lower or weaker in any way. It is just that some magnets tend to magnetize themselves over time, after being in contact with the magnet.

Earth is one big magnet upon which all we mini magnets rest, we attract each other based on what resonates with us- the like ones repel, the unlike ones attract and the force continues. Everything on this earth has a magnetic force- the people, the animals, the places we live in, the plants, crystals, metals- every such entity is attracted to earth's unlike forces, it's not gravity that pulls us but the magnetic force. Gravity is inherent in most of us whether we live here, there, or in outer space - it is the force of something far stronger than you, it is the magnetic force of love that pulls us to places and planets we as an entity feel attracted and entitled to live in. It is this magnetic attraction that fuels our inner fire to spread its light from low to high sparkling like little fireflies all around.

I see and feel a gush of spiritual violet life energy all around- in humans, in animals, in trees, even in the ground upon which I walk. The etheric energy is so much more vibrant around certain beings, places, and certain seasons. This miraculous energy magnetizes us towards one another.

Deep inside the sacral or *sthapana* chakra of the human body, at a point somewhere between the Navel or *tej* chakra and *mooladhara* or *sthir* chakra, at the core center of earth's gravity, you will find your strongest abode. It is that which pulls you. I know this because the earth and I seem to have gone for detox at the same time. Each of us has a mini earth chakra (Mani) within us. The reason we are connected with the earth and other entities living upon it is because of the magnetic force of gravity within and outside of us.

We all are fighting over patches of land, buildings, walls, and fences without realizing that no country, no individual, no animal, no bird, no organ, no object, no life can ever live just by itself. We all need one another to function properly. We all are a result of another life. A lot of lives and sweat has gone into making you and me, and everything that we see around. None of us are ever separate, we all are always one. Attracted and bonded together because of either intense love or intense hatred. The cause you are together is because you are pulled towards the intense vibrations emitted and the deep feelings it invokes within.

Imagine- The various forms you manifest and attract are based on the radiant vibrations and frequencies you emit. Gravity is within us. It is not outside of us. It is inside of us. The magnet is within us. It attracts the earth's energies towards us and it also attracts the others around us. Now is the time for new beginnings, new direction, and new success. Change is sometimes good, it requires you to move beyond old habits that stagnate you. It urges you to decisively recreate a new wholesome reality with the immense power of your thought, beliefs, and selfless actions. Do not focus on what you do not want to attract, burn away what doesn't serve you, wipe it all off, it exists only because it exists in your mind. Free your mind from all impure, fearful, self-limiting, cluttering thought-forms. Help yourself and others by repeatedly saying and believing that negative viruses do not exist - it's all a figment of your imagination and what doesn't exist- can certainly not persist. Imagine only positive outcomes on all fronts -financial, material, educational or creative because you know you are a magnet attracting whatever you send out attention to - change the blueprint imprinted upon your DNA by moving your attention to what you truly want to manifest through consistent order, gratitude and discipline. Believe heaven is here. Hell is a result of a delusional mindset, do not let it loosely break out into a fatal epidemic. Stay positive, stay one, stay blessed, stay loving. Your resolve is your power.

Honeybees and birds are so hypersensitive that they can sense the Earth's magnetic field, detect atmospheric electromagnetic waves, stay warned of storms and trouble approaching. We are made with the same universal energy and capable of heightened faculties. Then why is it difficult for us to fathom that certain hypersensitive humans can be blessed with similar faculties? Often when I tried sharing what I felt, I was mocked at or subtly silenced because my thoughts didn't fit in with the usual. Yet, I see that I am not the only one to be chained and locked within these societal boxes and thought forms that exist.

How much earth value do you have in you? Earth implies unfaltering fortitude, untiring resolve, and pure determination. Your determination and grit decide your success. A person with high earth value never gives up and uses his discriminative intelligence to arrive at conclusions.

Mental laziness is as toxic as physical laziness. In order to maintain order, purity, and discipline we must rest and relax our body to avoid getting drained and overworked. We must relax and still our minds to avoid getting overstrained and delusional.

People create walls where there are none. People limit themselves where there should be none. People stagnate their growth where progress should exist. Excessive physical or mental laziness is as toxic as excessive restlessness. When we resolve to move beyond apprehensions and dullness is when we experience the fullness of astuteness. The only thing coming in between complete satisfaction and the illusionary wall is your constancy of purpose and devoted diligence. Knowing the truth requires immense patience, mercy, malleability, and tolerance. Only then does the core of your earth center get magnetized with love, attraction, and universal affection.

A person living in self-guilt, extremism, worries, indolence, dreariness, and delusion cannot have the awareness of the magnetic and dynamic personality within him. A dynamic personality attracts more etheric energy and vitality towards him and vice versa.

A speck of dust can be in two places at the same time, as can we. Everything has a gravitational field around them. We pull the possibilities and incidents we encounter into our life through our gravitational pull. This requires activation of the core earth center in our body which doesn't happen overnight. There are no shortcuts.

Affirm- 'Namostutee, I am protected and I have acquired honor, wealth, glory, peace, courage through constant positivity and enthusiasm. Tathaastu.'

CHAPTER 39

MERCURIAN AGE

Excess noise weakens your hearing.
Excess information weakens your intuition.
Excess light weakens your vision.
Excess knowledge weakens your wisdom.

The ruling planet mercury has a deity called *'Budha'* in Hinduism. Its name comes from the word *buddhwara* which means Wednesday. Worship this deity, called *'Budha'* on 5th May every year, to invoke its blessings and for the five mercurian qualities of benevolence, mental agility, alertness, sharp memory, and communication skills to be endowed within you.

Mercury has an unusual interior and a strong magnetic field despite being the smallest planet, as do we. Just the way atoms from mercury sometimes escape into space forming tails of brilliant particles, our internal consciousness sometimes escapes out into the external world, forming tails of brilliant hues. As the sun is closest to mercury, you are closest to your inner self. The world we perceive through our inner awakened eyes is more real than the world we perceive externally through our squinted physical eyes under the sunlight.

It is speculated that some mountain lakes without fish contain the element mercury. The age of mercury is here. The age when hidden knowledge is being revealed. It is the age of knowledge. Knowledge is power. If harnessed and used properly, knowledge turns to gold, and if used to harm others, it will slowly poison you. You will be judged by the higher power on how you use this blessed knowledge at every step. It is a grace, but comes with a condition: if you do it right, you will accelerate upwards. If you keep it all to yourself without sharing it, your knowledge will stagnate. Be aware of each step and use discrimination. True wisdom lies in uplifting others and yourself. We are one race belonging to a single soul.

The old Fahrenheit thermometer, used for taking temperature readings, is put under the tongue but still gives the most accurate, reliable, and precise reading, unlike the new age non-mercury versions. Water boils at 180 degrees above freezing temperature, so the reading is done from freezing to boiling at an exact interval of 180 degrees. Most people follow processes without knowing why. For example, to take the reading, the tip of our tongue should touch the roof of our mouth to get the oral temperature, because that is the tongue's right resting and healthy position! We not only block healthy energy and our breath from flowing freely in space by keeping the tongue in its accustomed flat position, but we also increase stress to the heart, lung, and other organs. So it is high time we reconnect our internal electric system to feel rejuvenated, by simply moving our tongue above its comfort zone and letting it reach up to the roof.

Mercury planet receives seven times more light than any other planet, Individuals with mercury as their ruling planet are endowed with innate light of intellectual wisdom. Endow yourself with the intellectual and spiritual light of the mercurial era.

Full circle from twin flames to Twin year: We have come a full circle from 2001 to 2020. The twin towers collapsed in 2001 and here we are facing the largest crisis faced by mankind in the twenty-first century with the virus. 2020 can be called the twin year-20 repeated twice. This will herald a new world order with renewed collective spiritual awakening where political leaders of even a country like America, who rely on empirical evidence, will in time turn to spirituality-realizing the force and power of invisible energy. I suggest we all spread the energy of peace, compassion, comfort, love, strength, healing, and protection that your higher soul radiates but try to do so before the ship sails.

Let us rewire ourselves-back to living a simple, holistic rural life. What we are facing today is the result of our collective unwholesome actions. No particular person can be blamed, we are all partaking/privy in the same crime–pushing and testing limits of our health across various levels -physical, etheric, emotional, mental, and spiritual. We are entering into the Sattvic (words revealed) or the Mercurian age. *Rajas* (action projected) and *Tamas* (thoughts veiled) in us leads us to the *Sattva (ideas)* in us. The one who knows and the one who doesn't know are the same. The difference lies only in your willingness to explore and examine what you already know or do not.

In India, there is a saying, *"Stutee aur ninda ek samaan"* which means praise and criticism are the same. Both emanate from thought, the thoughts based on your memory, the memory you acquired through your experience, your experience which is bound by your subjective perception. It is not complete but limited knowledge. In this way to know and to not know is the same. We learn and experience through actions. We repeat the actions based on the knowledge we acquire, we program ourselves into believing something to avoid pain and gain pleasure. This way we feel secure. Let the thoughts move, they are meant to change.

Don't become so mechanical that the mechanic is not able to mend and fix the piece.

Knowledge is limited by time. Do not cling to it, be open to learning, do not cling to your repetitive patterns of learning. They are boring for the youthful, more vitalized, and energetic souls who live amongst us today. They know more but they are humble enough to say that they know nothing. You know less but your pride is not letting you owe up to the fact that you have limited knowledge and are ignorant. This incessant conflict is not allowing the new age to flourish in its entirety. There is no escape. Let's stop living and dying, let us relive each moment. Let some of our thoughts die, only then can we be reborn again.

Mercury (takes 88 days to complete its orbit rotation) is the messenger of God. Mercurial wisdom is the goodness that resides outside and inside of us. Lord Mercury is also known as *Zehuti* in ancient Egypt. To cross the rainbow bridge, it is *Zehuti* that joins and bridges the gap between immortal soul and mortal body with its divine words.

Affirm- 'Namostutee, I am blessed and in perennial bliss. I trust that all my aspirations have manifested into reality. I am perennially filled with prosperity, abundance, loads of energy, and power. I feel the divine protection at all times. I am focused, disciplined, organized, compassionate, balanced, and strong. I value the sacred wisdom, I am endowed with. I am vitalized mentally, emotionally, physically, etherically, astrally, and spiritually. I ritualistically exercise and meditate. I prioritize what is most important. Tathaastu.'

CHAPTER 40

ORO

We are a golden body yet we keep looking for gold elsewhere. ORO means gold in Spanish. ORO is a palindrome word. It remains gold whichever way you look at it. Healthy skin glows like gold. Itching can sometimes mean that something is biting or "bugging" a person on a psycho-spiritual level. Long-standing frustration causes skin rashes, anger can cause skin disorder, infection, or pain. Whatever you feel because of external causes becomes the cause of your internal misery, so why hold on to resentments and negativity? Why be stuck? Let no one and nothing affect your peace, remain shielded, remain calm and detached at all times.

Frustrations affect the health of the liver, resentments affect the health of the spleen. The body uses the skin to detoxify toxins that get stored in it. Replace your anger, hate, impatience, and intolerance with joy, forgiveness, peace, and patience. Replace your frustrations, grudges, resentments, and bitterness with love, understanding, acceptance, and empathy. Our imbalance is the cause of our misery. We are all inherently pure, subtle spiritual beings of light, having the dense physical experience of life. We are not separate from our emotions or that of another, but over-attachment to this connection can delay our healing and evolvement.

There is only one cure for the infamous illness we see a lot nowadays, called SAD (Seasonal Affective Disorder), and that is to get more healing from the rays of the sun. The blue light in your laptop is blinding, but the light within the core of your lap is brightening, softening, and firming your face with a luminous glow like no other.

We all are capable of becoming mini suns if we balance our front and back solar plexus or *karm* chakra. The guardian angel of this chakra is Archangel

Michael. The energy of the sun center moves from east to west. We can live a life filled with love and light by keeping ourselves centered and healthy. Just a single session of balancing chakras through etheric cleansing can bring out the glowing, shimmering, yellowish golden skin - the kind that shines from afar. The solar plexus chakra has ten petals. It is the link between our lower and higher self. Five petals belonging to the lower and five to the higher. When they are balanced, we are centered and healed. The solar plexus chakra also has the 'sun center' located in it. A healthy sun center makes our skin look vibrant. It is the most important chakra to help us evolve and meet with the eternal within.

To honor the importance of keeping this solar plexus chakra, *Krishna's* son *Samba* made a sun temple in Konark. It is believed that Samba was healed of leprosy by the sun's solar power. As we enter a new era of enlightened human consciousness, resolve to overcome your lower nature through activation of the solar plexus. When your solar plexus is clean, you will have an uninhibited romance with life and become beautiful inside out and beyond.

The solar plexus chakra sustains, pulsates, and connects our heart vibrations with that of the sun (lower to higher vibrations) based on evolution and form. It encourages us to re-soul, which means connect our personality with our soul purpose, to become one and free within ourselves.

To fully evolve, do not gulp down your true feelings. If you are sensitive, embrace your true nature and the opposites. Your sensitivity is your greatest gift. It is your truth detector. Trust your feelings and fly with them. As you resolve to accept everybody as they are, including yourself, and fuse with all forms of nature, with full heart, compassion, and understanding, a day comes when you are filled with immense joy. This way your inner smile grows and your skin glows from within.

Burning incense of pure sandalwood helps energize this chakra. Hue means color and man means sun, human is the color of the sun. No wonder it is said that humans are made in God's image. Surya or Sun chakra represents our physical gut feel that directly affects our mental functions. Just as the sun is in the center of the solar system, the sun chakra is at the center of our body. If you preserve your sacredness and remain pure, your skin naturally glows with bliss.

Affirm- 'Namostutee, My skin and my aura glow with the infinite pure light that emanates from within my solar plexus and *sthir* chakra in form of *stu, tejas,* and *ojas*[60]. Tathaastu.'

---

[60] *Stu means eulogize, Tejas means brilliance of fire and Ojas means vitality of life.*

CHAPTER 41

SELF EMPOWERED

During a trip into the mountains with a troop of mountaineers, we once ventured out in the night. We were all told to carry torches but knowingly or unknowingly some of us went without our torches. It was extremely dark and so the patrol leader had to pair us in twos especially those that did not carry their torches. Even then the paired partners drifted apart.

Had the ones not carrying their torches, followed instructions they would not have been stranded. In life, most of us are scared of the dark. The main reason is we do not push ourselves to carry our light. Time to empower yourself through inculcating the habit of self-healing. This is achieved by following the tips written in this book. This will free you of all horror of darkness or the anxiety that comes with being lost in this world.

One light can light up the entire room. The light of one room can light up the entire home. One good leader can make the entire nation prosper. Similarly, one nation can influence the entire planet. One planet can light up the entire universe. The light and energy you choose to radiate is up-to you. If I-with devotion, loyalty, determination, and practice-can meet with the seven-pointed consecrated crystal that I originally was, then so can you. Re-emerge, re-energize, and allow yourself to heal. Help is right here. Get connected with me for proven age-old ways to practically destress, self-empower, and heal yourself.

Be open, honest, energetic, positive, and vitalized. Transform yourself by not suppressing or denying, but by addressing your needs and being more assertive and true to yourself. Your inner joy is not the result of your outer, in fact, the outer is the result of the inner. The bliss you are looking for is within you, not in your outer shell.

Magic brings in power; power brings in resourcefulness; creativity brings in inventiveness; noble work brings in fortune; fortune brings in joy.

There is a spark of God within everyone and if you do not want to suffer wrath then do not speak of Supreme God's name in vain.

Sometimes you have to do nothing but simply celebrate the fragility of life by staying home, appreciating, relaxing, tendering, nurturing, loving, and spending time with yourself and your family rather than gossiping, bickering, belittling, accusing one another. Let's resolve to live consciously rather than unconsciously.

It is time to pay back the credit you took from planet earth by truly taking care of yourself because nothing makes a mother happier than to see her children enjoying the food it so lovingly prepared for them to enjoy. What we are all going through currently is a renaissance in our collective consciousness. This transition heralds the beginning of a new kind of globalized culture that is no longer individualized or subjective e.g. in the new world no caste, culture, or country will divide us as we all will be one.

In this fast-paced world, we all are fighting a perennial war of power and control. A simple thing, like being heard, has become a power struggle between two individuals. No one has the patience to spend time listening attentively to someone who is physically present near them but will spend a lifetime watching and adhering to messages they receive from the internet. Instead of saying I see, we say I-phone. In the process we no longer see, the phone sees for us.

Develop boldness, decisiveness, independence, and assertiveness. Worry less. Eat a healthy diet, and exercise to be bodily sound and aware.

Live not only to please others but also to please yourself. Only when you look good to yourself can you look good to others. No one will value or treat you with importance unless you value yourself enough to enforce your own ORO-worth. No one should become the center of your attention to such an extent that you begin to neglect your self needs. Initially, when you begin to stand up for yourself, it is like taking the first few steps a baby takes. You might fall and face a lot of resistance, but with time just like a baby, you too will learn to walk the walk.

I meet people in my healing room who think they are not good enough because of the seeds of terror that were planted repeatedly in their core when they were little children. Once you start the healing process, look out for the red flags whenever those feelings come out from within yourself and remember to promptly shed them away by giving them no importance whatsoever. You are not your past, it is just an experience that was meant to teach you to learn the lesson. Do not attach yourself to the unwholesome feelings and tell yourself repeatedly, "I am self-worthy and self-empowered."

Affirm- 'Namostutee, This year and the coming year is a great year, filled with collective love, kindness, positivity, and moderation. Tathaastu.'

CHAPTER 41a

ARE YOU A FOOT MAT?

The world needs you. Do not take on the burden of others' sins. Do not be a sin-eater. Instead, be a true divine healer and empower them to get rid of their sins by themselves. I visited a church where I met a very selfless nun who needed healing. She was so engrossed in her service to help those in pain that she forgot herself in the process. She took on the sins of others to help them, but in the process, her energy started to exhaust, while those who had committed the sins walked out unburdened. It is better to empower others to clear their karmas while helping them feel lighter and develop clear-thinking.

Sometimes no amount of love can satiate the hungry souls. Do not drown yourself in trying to be of service to others so much that you lose yourself. Learn ways to protect yourself while you heal others. Give yourself priority else your body will shatter into pieces. Your loyal arms need to be powerful to lend someone a shoulder to cry on. Your innocent hopeful eyes are just as mighty as your thousand-petalled crown. Tiaras are out of fashion, these days armed - bracelets and truthful eyes are more in fashion.

Dangers of being overambitious and overcommitting even if it involves (selfless service) out of zeal causes zeal center to get congested, overwhelmed, and weakened. The back of your head and neck is your zeal center.

Don't make the mistake of thinking that practicing self-care makes you selfish. The biggest hurdle in reaching this step is realizing that you are worth it, you are worthy of being treated better, and having a happier life. Normal, healthy people make sure that no one uses or takes advantage of them. This doesn't mean that they love any less. They make sure that their needs are being met. Only if their needs are met, can they fulfill the needs of another.

Having a toxic partner that uses and abuses you is not self-care and it will never make you happy. Love doesn't mean you allow others to walk over you like a doormat. True love is in disciplining and teaching others to value you the way you value and respect yourself. And in doing so, you become the cause of bringing in clarity of vision in another person. If others attack you, try not to look at it as an attack against you. Come from a point of compassion and you will understand that each person owns a tape in their brain that they keep playing over and over again. Some of these tapes might not be that happy to hear.

These people have repeatedly played the same tape so many times that they can't help but inadvertently pass on things from their past upon others. Much the way we unconsciously, pass incidents of our childhood to our children and without knowing it, we bring them up, repeating the same mistakes our parents made in bringing us up.

A client was searching for answers as to why she seeks the same monsters in relationship after relationships, leading to her near ruin! Here is why, I answered, "If we consider people as our reflection and believe that what we see in others is a mere mirror image of our self, then maybe we will begin to look into the mirror (people) differently. And in trying to look at the mirror differently, we will start to see ourselves differently. It will be like seeing ourselves and our reflection for the first time. However, value yourself enough to remember that no matter how much you give to the wrong person, it will never be enough."

Some people are so attached to their past problems and believe their past to be their present that even in their adult life they face bullies who give them the same problems. These are unhealed people who either grew up in homes where they were bullied or were made to not voice their pain when they faced bullies in the outside world. It is like they have a little cloud over their head that only bullies can see. This cloud fogs their perception about themselves and so that is the impression people have of them.

How can you allow a bunch of people or a person to have so much effect on you that you lose clarity?

I understand that grasping the truth of this matter is not easy but I am sharing the above with you, just in case you see yourself in these situations so that you can empower yourself and come out of the pain you might be suffering because of various relationships encountered.

Being an over-giver comes easy to some of us because we have conditioned ourselves to give rather than take. Time we change our old habits so that we all can evolve and improve our situation, rather than be walked over.

For example-some of us detest the word 'no' so much that we have great difficulty saying it even when we are aware that the situation will land us into doing something we may later regret. It is not smart to say yes for the sake of another person's happiness because no one will be happy being around you unless you too are happy. Do what you like doing for your own sake and not to please another. If you are giving too much to a relationship, receiving nothing emotionally then you are on a self-created merry-go-round, except that there is no mercy in it.

No one but you are to blame if you accept abuse of any kind. You are a strong divine being, you are valued and you are special. However, if you are being discarded, blamed, or walked over remember that it was your weakness that allowed another to use you. This lesson will teach you to treat others well so that you will be treated well.

A person who knows the true worth of a relationship is naturally affectionate. If we all begin to value our relationships by first knowing our self-worth then a day will soon come when no one will need to earn or pine to get bits of affection from another. Slowly, the air will be filled with love and joy.

People with good self-esteem tell themselves that they are good enough. Despite the apparent, subtle, or psychic messages sent by others to break them down, these people love themselves enough to stay strong in the face of struggles and rise against all odds.

Every behavior is difficult to break but we must try to rid ourselves of the old patterns to develop healthy self-esteem. We must stay strong and not gravitate towards unwholesome relationships and circumstances out of sheer habit. We all are meant to become better versions of ourselves. To attract people who treat you with love, care, and respect - you need to connect all the dots and shift your perspective. Continue to develop your self-esteem and believe you are worthy. Always be an attentive listener. Interact with others, the way you want them to interact with you. Sometimes when a relationship fails, it is a gift from the universe.

Self-care implies that you do not have to be a people pleaser in order to feel good about yourself. Just the way you maintain hygiene for your physical health. Self-care is something you need to follow for your energetic health.

It is not easy to admit that your partner or someone you know is a narcissist or has a parasitical nature. It is hard to change something that has become a habit. Any change involves breaking a pattern and so the change will not happen overnight. It takes regular practice and a lifetime of commitment. Help those people come out of their misery, to help yourself and others around them. I understand that it is not easy for you to follow this advice and perhaps it is very hard to accept but facing facts is better than to continue living a miserable life.

People who do selfish acts to gain control need to know that trapping vulnerable beings is futile. These people will get crushed and ripped because of their malicious deeds. Just the way time cannot be trapped, it is in its nature to move on. What they are trying to hold on to is delusory.

Humans are the only beings that use weapons to put an end to their own life. Being in an unwholesome relationship and not doing anything about it to help yourself or the other person is like slowly killing yourself without the use of weapons and dying a causeless death. If you are committed to dying, at least give it some meaning and sense of purpose. Even other, less intelligent beings that are driven to kill themselves do so only to give meaning to their death. These altruistic beings do so for the sake of others. For example - in response to parasitism, when the reproductive fitness of others outweighs their reproductive fitness, 'pea aphids' die in defense of their family or colony.

The African Vervet monkeys alert others when a predator is near, consequently drawing attention to itself and increasing the likelihood of being attacked. Humans do not need a predator because they are so busy killing their people, with or without the use of weapons! Even these less intelligent animals see the sense in not only living but also dying with an objective. Every action must have a purpose else it is futile to carry on with the same unwholesome behavioral pattern.

These waves of pain compel your mind to blindly run. Stop running, allow your thoughts to sync in, relax, and enjoy. You are not a foot mat. Do not let pain, distress, or anxiety trample you under its feet. When winters come, remember not to let 'tamas', inertia, or exhaustion take the better of you. Warmly look out for each other, rise, and smile, and awaken. It is time to cleanse, review, and set the right intentions. There is a good person in everyone. Sometimes you just need to bless them enough for their goodness to flow out and be visible.

Affirm- 'Namostutee, I have self-worth. I am beautiful and I deserve to be prosperous, peaceful, appreciated, and be cared for. Tathaastu.'

CHAPTER 42

WHAT HAPPENED IN 2020 AND WHY?

Answer– Summed in a single sentence-we met with our reality, for the first time, collectively not individually.

All this is happening because we all have been asking for validation of the truth but the truth comes from intuition and it needs no validation, it simply is. When all of us collectively experience it, the incident validates the truth. The truth of the invisible, unknown, mysterious, enigmatic is all visible now. We have come face to face with it so that we can reflect, understand, and imbibe the lesson it is teaching us.

When we are separated, quarantined, and isolated is when we realize that the exchange of energy between people is what keeps us going. People energize us, not the electronic gadgets we incessantly use.

When the thief is an invisible force, no police can catch the thief. No amount of cameras can record the incident to validate the existence of the thievery. No amount of research can make you ever understand who took the precious jewels from the unopened locker within your closet. This invisible force can transcend walls without breaking them as it knows no borders, boundaries, or limitations. Its force is super powerful and super intelligent. Just because you cannot see the invisible force doesn't mean it is not visible. It simply is invisible to a few but others know of the force as they have experienced, felt, seen, and known it. Certain circumstances occur because they are meant to be–invited by the collective *karma* of our actions. Sometimes only experiences make us believe the truth. The truth is naked–it needs to be clothed by experiences just the way our thoughts are bare and words are the clothes. Some things are only validated by experiencing them.

We are living as if in virtual reality. Nothing is true in its entirety. What is happening today to the entire earth is but a dream. Nightmares are not real only because we collectively are experiencing the same nightmare. Just as dreams are not real only because we collectively are experiencing the same dream. We tend to erase the dreams and nightmares we have from our memory. Most of us forget the less intense dreams and nightmares leading them to come out with intensity sometimes to prove their validity. Unreal is real and real is unreal. A dream is reality and reality is but a dream. You feel so dizzy and fatigued because the dream is so turbulent, tiring, and close to reality. Its intensity killed many of our loved ones while fighting the pandemic that spread through this nightmare.

Its power gives you shudders and shakes the very core of your existence. Some mysterious unknown force occurs *Yuga* after *Yuga* (epoch). After every end is the beginning of another period. Time we dig out the corpses of our ancestors to understand the cause behind the death during this time. We are here not for experiencing but for exploring. 2020 is a repeated year, the only purpose of this year is for you to learn the spiritual lessons it is giving you. The ones who learn the lessons elevate, accelerate, awaken to an age of clarity, order, liberation, certainty, and truth. What is immortal cannot become mortal. How can you conquer something that cannot be conquered?

The planet is polluted and withering because of our will to conquer the unseen forces.

Being higher in energy, these unseen forces are all forgiving and merciful. What is killing you is your guilt, worries, insecurity, and aversion. Everyone will be affected by this wave, those who realize will live on, and the rest will perish. You can no longer get lost amongst crowded streets because there are no crowds any longer. The streets are silent even the ghosts are spooked. From where I see this-most are hiding like rats within the so-called safe havens of their home, suppressing their fear in the name of sanitizing the whole world. No one is strolling outside, no voice can be heard, even the birds I see through the window of my home seem bewildered by this mystic meaningless quest of human absence. Being preoccupied with the stresses of our uncertainty, we are in denial. Time to lift your heads from your phones and meet with your real truth. For the first time you are awake and alive, look inward to get insights.

You are susceptible to get the virus because you have lost perspective. Everything you mentally experience is actively explored later. When you look beyond your five senses, you realize you already know what is about to happen, you already know what is happening, you know all the precautionary measures and you also know the cure. But, you have ceased to trust your intuition amid this hypnotic trance. It is time we resolve to change our perspective and attitude through concentrated observation before the next wave. Time we believe in the force of invisible energy which is beyond the scope of physical and scientific understanding. The abstract is safer than concrete, enigmatic is more heightened than scientific.

We all are within the same energy field. Let's raise our vibrations collectively. Join in and I will show you how to see that which you thought is subtle and cannot be seen. There is so much beauty and life yet unexplored. Join in and let us appreciate praise, and honor this divinity and beauty together. Just the way one depressive person can infect another, happiness too is contagious.

Affirm- 'Namostutee, I remain serene, cheerful, and joyful at all times. In this way, I spread happiness all around. Tathaastu.'

CHAPTER 43

WILL YOU KNOWINGLY EAT POISON?

N egativity is that poison you are knowingly eating. A negative gloomy person is slowly inching towards self-mortification. Whatever the societal remedies and punishments are against people with suicidal tendencies, apply equally to negative people. For when one commits suicide, all the people around them are affected by their negative vibes and depressive dispiritedness. The 'gross national happiness' has greatly fallen in today's world. This is the cause of the political, physical, and economic upheaval we are seeing today. This is akin to one sick fish making all the fish in the aquarium sick. One withered leaf makes all the leaves wither, one unwholesome thought affects the energy of all the people. The entire humanity suffers the brunt of that one unwholesome action emanating from that thought. All it takes is one person to make or mar the entire human race. Such is the power you hold from the level of your higher soul. Act responsibly in the pool of this collective consciousness. An aquarium is no different in size than an entire ocean seen from the eyes of the higher soul.

The whole earth is holy and living in this pure and holy land, all the earthlings are innately holy of the holies. The whole earth is yours, what is mine is for you to enjoy. You are closest to the purest and holiest divine form and space when you live to your fullest enjoying, nourishing, thanking, and praising every bit of the holy and the holies – holy space in the center of the world where divine dwells. When we impose internal order out of our outer chaos, we can build a palace out of what is seemingly a waste. One hour of bliss is equivalent to living a lifetime. If you want to drink the water of life, at least make the effort to open the tap. To stay safe, healthy, and hygienic - you clean your physical environment and get regular pest control sprayed then why do we forget about sanctifying and purifying our thoughts, emotions, and spirit.

The higher is the unattainable, uncontrollable, unreachable, and indestructible force that perennially flows and is unstoppable. However many homes you may buy, invest and sell, its abode can never be sold, bought, or owned by you in its entirety, totality or perpetuity because this holy piece of land is yours but its sharing is for up to the higher soul. It is as if a magnetic storm came and brought all of us magnetically closer to each other. A storm that has helped us see things as they are, beyond the reasoning, beyond preconceived ideas, separation, division, or touch.

No one stands for you unless you learn to stand up for yourself. There is no point in putting anyone down. There is no point in forcing your opinion on anyone because everyone has a right of opinion, irrespective of what stage of life you or they may be. Having high creativity sometimes takes you away from productive reality.

There is no better way to learn how to live life than simply living it. Before believing in another, first, believe in yourself. Believe you can and you will. Our anxieties cause frustration within us. More often than not, we are angry and frustrated with our flaws but invariably we throw them upon others. This way we can create an external cause and then blame them for instigating the anger in us. In reality, there are no external causes. Your response is always in your control. How calmly you express your inner anxieties makes all the difference. Stop resisting the inner change and soon you will see that the outer circumstances seamlessly shift and change for the better.

Affirm- 'Namostutee, May all those who are half living-spiritually awaken, heal and reawaken through the pure knowledge and wisdom that is constantly revealed and bestowed upon us by the divine grace and authority. Tathaastu.'

CHAPTER 44

ICE IN THE BELLY

E xtraordinary circumstances lead you to look at things from outside in and inside out in an extraordinary way. When life slows down - it gives us time to introspect and figure out ways to come out stronger, just as when police slows down traffic on the congested roads, it later allows traffic to flow smoothly.

When someone goes through problems, even if they are a million miles away from us, remember that we might be physically distant but that doesn't mean we are emotionally or telepathically distant from them. So stay connected while you still can.

The ability to keep yourself cool and composed in a crisis is an art and that art is called he-art.

You may have ice in your belly currently but you know that once things cool and calm down, the ice will melt, the traffic will smoothly flow, all congestion will get released and we all will come out of this stronger. Chaos leads to order. The disorder that you think you have, is your greatest gift and this gift will bring in order and cooperation that you have long been awaiting. Stay resilient, patient, compassionate, and joyful.

Crisis leads to a boom especially when no particular entity is to blame - all cooperate and learn to help each other, the wealthy share their assets, the powerful share their power, the workers share their strength, machines share their capabilities, light workers share their light, mothers share their love, fathers share their food. The creator and creation become one and we all function collectively as one collective whole. Each of us has something we can share, each one of us is rich in something or the other and each one of us can contribute more to this worldly team. A cleansing time gives birth to a renewed changing time on earth where everything levels out, everyone radiates pure energies, all live the same lifestyle, the rules remain the same for all, all are special, all are privileged, all speak one language and that is the language of love, considerateness, and compassion.

There is no duality, rich or poor, good or bad, white or black embrace their oneness and realize the egg and its yolk are perfect and hatch themselves. That is when we all one by one meet with the inner perfection within our illusionary imperfections, it is then those perfect beings of love, light, and power who share the world blissfully with one another. That time has come and that time is now. Embrace the change, do not resist it. Listen to the cries of the invisible voices and the unheard screeches. Face your fears for only then can you release, unleash, and shed them all. True liberty is not in suppressing but in embracing your innate truth.

John Greaves, an English mathematician went to Giza in 1630 to investigate and measure the great pyramids. He went crawling down the narrow corridors like a serpent and met a huge swarm of bats. He fired a gun at them to scare them away but nothing happened. The heat and smoke added to the fetid air and there were showers of rubble and a deafening roar. He somehow managed to get some sort of estimate on the measurements but the stench, foul air, and swarms of bats drove him away. No amount of guns could help him win the battle with the bats. Greaves and his team created more havoc by firing and trying to frighten nonexistent evil spirits. They filled the air with dense black and dark clouds along with the suspension from the gunpowder shots, reducing the remains of thousands of years to dust.

Sometimes we create an unnecessary ruckus by attacking the innocent and exploiting the silent rather than looking for some invisible force to blame. Our ego doesn't allow us to take the onus and blame ourselves for firing the shots. But just like those bats in the story, those who are true are fearless, free, and protected. It is usually you who is entrapped in thought-forms of unrest and anxiety.

Gratitude is a beautiful thing. It helps us catch up, rise, and cross the rivers of life together.

I am thankful to the supreme God. I am thankful for divine light and energy. I am thankful for the air, sun, moon, stars, trees, plants, flowers, fruits, sand, stone, crystals, water, sky, and the earth. I am thankful for the mountains and the valleys. I am thankful for the knowledge, awareness, relationships, love, independence, and self-discipline. I am thankful for my dreams in which deers float in the sky, grasshoppers tickle my palm, the sound of temple bells ring in my ear, for the wind blowing upon my skin, the rabbits crossing my path, and the lotus *kamarband*[61] on my navel. I am thankful for the new heightened vibrational energies and positivity all around.

Affirm- 'Namostutee, I think clearly, creatively, and act efficiently for the greater good of all even when the energies around are tumultuous, intense, and dramatic as the new age dawns. Tathaastu.'

---

[61] *Kamarband is a waist chain worn in India by women usually during wedding ceremonies.*

CHAPTER 45

SHIPS THAT SAIL

Follow the medium path to make your ship sail. The only ship that can help sail you through the troubles of life is the balanced one. The rest all are prone to drowning when the heavy storm hits. Everything about nature tells us to stay balanced. We channelize the energy of nature and through our enhanced understanding, nature benefits as well. This is because one takes care of the other and is connected. The health of one depends upon the other. The link between them is the conduits of divine energy beings like us. Those who pain and strain you do so only so that you can rise above your pain and refrain from all ill. The deep waters and emotions that give you pain sink you, but it is always better for you to instead thank them back.

When the waves are too high, you cannot swim in the ocean. Your wavering emotions are like the waves at high tide. They block your vision. Do not drown in emotions. No pain or separation is permanent. The only permanent force is love and when you are in love, you are neither lost nor are you alone. True love doesn't change with time and circumstance. The raging elements express imbalance through us. Handling their rage is not for the faint-hearted. As long as you care to follow the inner voice of your intuition, you will be able to calm their rage and harness their energies with the inner light of your astuteness and charm.

In 79 AD - time froze in Pompeii, Italy when fiery Mount Vesuvius suddenly erupted. The air was filled with the smell of sulfur. The city and the people of Pompeii got completely covered in volcano molten rock and superheated ash with this catastrophic incident. One moment they were alive and the next they were dead as their bodies froze. Preserved in ash, their garments and bodies left a huge imprint on our minds. We learn a lot from ancient remains. They teach us that life is fleeting so embrace death positively and gladly just the way we accept and celebrate life. Even though there is light outside, their bodies are forever covered in the darkness of night. This tells us that the soul stays lit outside of its form and lives on soaring to higher dimensions even if the physical bodies are still and laden in molten rock. The body needs the soul, the soul doesn't need the body. No matter how many possessions we may have, sometimes nothing can stop or control the strong red rain of angry fire. However, when the aggression settles, we go into a blank empty state. It is then that we reflect and realize that death is a continuation of birth. The light of a pure, sanctified soul is fearless, unaffected, and unattached. It doesn't end with bodily afflictions and infirmities. It calmly and generously transfers into another way of being only to come out wiser and enlightened. Knowing the inevitability of our physical form, let us give a more meaningful purpose to our soul while we are here.

> Air expresses its rage within our thoughts.
> Water expresses its rage through our emotions.
> Fire expresses its rage through physical inflammation.
> Earth expresses its rage through bodily depletion.

Grief weighs you and pulls you down like a force of gravity. Joy liberates you to fearlessly travel wherever you please. No one is perfect. Guilt weighs us down. We all learn our lessons from the mistakes we make. We also gain knowledge through the mistakes and experiences of others to gain perfection. Our mistakes serve as an example to help us improve and get better each time.

Learn from the waters of the ocean - they might be turbulent on the surface but it is deep in its spiritual quest. Waters always knows which direction to flow. Waters do not come in our way, we come in their way and strive to stop the flow. Emotions and meridians in our body are like water. They are meant to continue circulating.

We all are in the same heavenly ship. Some facing the waters believe that the journey has just begun. Some are sitting in the middle, thinking they are halfway through. Some are looking at shore thinking that they are nearing the end of their search. The search is never over. This journey is as limitless as the sea and the skies.

Affirm- 'Namostutee, I am one with the supremely knowledgeable and supremely pure. I am moral, soulful, and truthful. Tathaastu.'

CHAPTER 46

BLUE LIGHT

Darkness is sometimes better than light. We get distracted and confused by light when there is too much darkness. When we get distracted, we become vulnerable, weak, startled, and forget to do what we were meant to do which causes commotion and chaos. We must train ourselves not to get swayed by excessive light that results in melancholy that we call "The Blues"

Every species encounters the toxic dangers and distractions of the blinding light. Only those who train themselves to stay focused on their task stay safe. For example- Anglerfish are opportunists and dive deep into the sea to hunt for treasures. These fish emit sharp light from their heads to lure their prey. Once the prey gets attracted towards the light, they eat them up. The light also fools large sea animals. Whales and squids, for example, get attracted to the glowing light of cookie-cutter shark and as they get closer they get eaten.

Bioluminescence might have originated in the oceans but is not limited to sea animals. As an example - the glow of the glowworms acts as a lure to attract prey. It is the natural ability of certain plants and animals to create light via a chemical reaction. There are many available wavelengths and energy levels that humans cannot appreciate but animals can. Many new designs and ideas have surfaced that have transformed how we light our world through bioluminescent technology.

Even blue light emanating from tablets, phones, and laptop screens damages our health and vision causing dry eyes, blurry vision, fatigue, strain, and headaches. We must learn not to overuse these to relax our eyes. We must instead use our internal minds and bodies to find answers especially post sundown.

2020 is reminding us not to get distracted by the light and start following the 20-20-20 rule that doctors recommend. Set a 20-minute timer for electronic use and every 20 minutes take a break from gazing at your screen and look at something beautiful in nature 20 feet away for 20 seconds.

Too much of a good thing can become bad. Our greatest boon can become our biggest curse. Too much sunlight can burn us. Excessive blue light energy emitted through phones and the screens we use can cause skin damage, aura color changes, inflammation, stress, photo-aging, eye strain, and also spoil your sleep cycle. Its overload can fog our brain and make us lose our zest for life. It is high time we help ourselves and more importantly our children to become more youthful and lively by limiting the use of these emitting screens.

When the day never ends and the night is left all alone, it is forced to return to remind us that it is sleep time. We may try to separate night from day, darkness from light, mortality from immortality, death from life, and one nation from another but always remember that we all are the same. Continuous communication creates bonding, equanimity, and complete balance. Without one, the other is meaningless.

Rely on and trust your intuition rather than relying on news and gadgets. Open up your heightened inner senses and you will meet with your truth. All that you wanted to ever know is within you. You have all the answers. When you are simply aware, you are a superhuman.

Books are like maps-they remind you of the wisdom that is within you. Books might have the information but the wisdom is in you. Through the use of wisdom and discriminatory power, you extract your own deeper meanings from the various streams of knowledge. Soul comes back to God. The way a book comes back to life when you read it. Yoginis stilettoes is ever grateful as you continue to read.

Affirm- 'Namostutee, The One is the source and center of all life there is. All lights must harmoniously return to the one and merge with the center. This way we all will feel more connected, related, content, secure, cheerful, aware, and focused. Tathaastu.'

CHAPTER 47

COLLECTIVE REBIRTH

Dreams and nightmares do not last, only creative reality does. Perspectives change with resilience and creativity and the new world order is all about effectively telling your truth. In a world of deception where evil is expanded and good is contracted - Corona has come with some nerves to tell the blatant truth that it is time we reverse the order. Go back to the seed from which you came and you will know how the fruit came about.

The baby has life when it is inside the waters of the mother's womb. The baby has life when it comes outside into the bright light. Why do we confuse this transformational miracle by calling it a beginning to an end, or an end to a beginning? Every night, a flower closes its buds and every morning it opens to the light. Every day is a new day, a restart, and a resurrection of rejuvenated, refreshed, and renewed rebirth. Every rebirth comes with an opportunity for the king to take over his reign. A true ruler is reborn with every new light, starting with a new place where he can rule again.

Just as earth evolves and re-evolves, it gets created and recreated, born and reborn. We (our light) too evolve and re-evolve; we too are born and reborn. When Christ was crucified, a rain of blood enveloped the entire earth. It filled everyone's heart with painful emotions. In this era, for Christ to be reborn, blood-filled air is enveloping the entire earth. Air represents thoughts. This blood-filled air is flooding everyone's psyche with painful thoughts. Rise above the psychic entrapment of emotions and thoughts.

Blood represents *ki* or energy. What affects the psyche affects you. This is *Kaalki*[62]. *Ki* represents energy; *kaal* represents a great cycle of time.

---

[62] *Refer to chapter on 'kaal ki' for greater details*

Kaalki is the energy of time. In the process of birth and rebirth, Christ is born and reborn into many forms, in a different place, in a different body, with every change of *kaal-ki*. For example, Krishna became Christ. Christ became Goddess Kali, and the chain continued. Each time a divine being reincarnates, it guides us and shows us a way out of our misery, so that we can create a perfect era, filled with golden energy of love, even-mindedness, and equanimity. We are one. We are all. The combination of love and light, heart, and mind are what lead you to life and power. You feel from your physical heart but think from your spiritual heart. It is time to think from your heart.

There will be no embarked or disembarked souls because here on all will join in together to keep the earth energy balanced, harmonious, and joyful beyond division. Everyone has divinity within them. Everyone has the potential to become Godly, whether they are leaders, citizens, netizens, healers, philosophers, or chefs. Irrespective of their gender or disposition, a day will soon come where each one can connect to their God center- it is not fright but love that will lead us all to progress together. I am planting these seeds because I am here to walk the talk with one and all.

Visible and invisible forces are meant to be in balance and work together to help make the energies of our planet wholesome and healthy. Heaven will soon be recreated on our planet beyond all duality. While the rest live in a self-inflicted world of virtual reality, they too will be ready someday to join in through service, faith, discriminatory power, and compassion.

We are creating a world where no one needs to be sorry for being themselves. A world where each one is accepted for who they are. They need no permission from other people to do one good humanitarian deed. It is time we set our incarnated soul free and become one with our higher soul to enter the era wearing our rainbow bodies and our golden mind. An era where no one is judged, humiliated, dominated, or belittled.

Intercourse is a spiritual experience and divine children are born by either gender with or without physically experiencing sex. Many people will take a parenting role to collectively bring up our children. Children look at life differently and simplistically, we adults make it complicated.

Our challenges and pains are our best teachers as they teach us to never give up or stop chasing our dreams. They are a blessing and not a curse. I am noticing obvious signs during this transitional stage that show animals are developing human-like self-discriminatory mental abilities while more and more humans are becoming super brained Godly humans. Seeing where circumstances have recently taken us, we realize humans have not come very far from being tribal living in the forest. We lived in dens and tents to stay protected and now we hibernate along with our families with food hoarded inside our homes.

2020 is a near-death experience for some, for others, it is laden with anxiety, grief, death, pain, and soul suffering. It is making most believe that our planet is nearing doom, yet we can do nothing about it. We are feeling tied up with no clear solution in hand. Our family and friends are fighting and dying and each day is a living nightmare that never seems to end.

We might have been born long ago but it is when we are reborn within the same birth that we truly understand what being reborn in another birth would be like! Once this rebirth fully comes into being and the subtle becomes active, you can't help but create a chain of blessings for those waiting in line to enter into the shielded blissful golden gates of the ultimate truth.

Rebirth is simply a self-improvising technique done by reactivating your brain cells and energy points within the same physical body. It first begins by setting the intention to achieve illumination and enlightenment within the same birth. Its purpose is to bring in awareness safely. As the coronial age evolves, we humans will have the same structure, body, material, and aura and encompass the same world but we will develop into a far wiser, progressive, transparent, globalized version of ourselves.

A voice whispered, "The year 2020 arrives with a repeated cycle of a new moon, a new sun, and an initiation of a new sun soul, with the combined energy of both sun and moon, who are here to impart new laws for this renewed land."

Reincarnation is a different concept and I will not dwell on it here. Rebirth on the other hand can happen in the same life - a new you in the same birth. As you morally and spiritually develop, you go through the same life experience differently because your perspective changes. As the lens with which you view your world changes - you are reborn. We have many rebirths, learning opportunities, tests, and initiations within the same birth.

Just because we are repackaged and out in the market, it doesn't mean we forget our roots and our center. The same product in its new packaging still carries the same brand name and logo. You have been waiting for too long. It is time to deliver the baby. The time is now before it is too late. From here on, unconditional love is the only form of love.

Coming out alive is a journey of realization where you become aware of the fact that everything is dynamic. There is nothing that is nonfunctional, there is nothing that is not living, and there is nothing that is not beautiful. Everything has a definite purpose, a life, a unique charm, and beauty to it. There is always someone out there to appreciate and value your worth. You often do not realize this perhaps because you kept the doors of your home open for the wrong audience, all along.

I often hear that we all are a result of our habits. Then why not make 'happiness and positivity' our habit. This way we do not have to ever change our habits. It certainly doesn't mean that without change there will be no excitement in life. It simply means that we will joyfully embrace life and death with serenity, peace, and equanimity.

We give so much importance to what will happen after and before that we forget the more important aspect - which is what is happening now, in the present moment. We must change and end such enslaving thought - forms. Detach and release yourself from your ideas, materialism, attitude, suffering, and pains caused due to resistance, insecurities, and excessive pleasure. We think that death will end all such attachments. But you can end all these attachments while you are living. This is what rebirth is all about. It doesn't mean your possessions go away, it simply means your attitude towards them and towards all accumulated memories changes. This is the depth of spiritual liberty. This liberating process makes you truly free. This is where you connect and willfully ground yourself to the earth.

All it took is one bat to initiate the entire humanity to release itself of its fear-based patterns. There is more darkness visible in bright daylight than it is in the dark of the night that you fear.

May you all be filled with fresh waves of life with this book.
If one dies, all die,
If one departs, all depart
If all depart, we depart with them
If one is born, we all are born
If one returns, we all return
If all return, we return with them
Everyone must revive, we will revive with them
Without them, we have no reason to revive
Each life is important at every level

Whether it belongs to plant, animal, human or any being within or outside of you.

Rediscover, reorganize and return to your original self. The outer light and the inner dark self are but one. You are a totality of the whole and not just a part. Each of you has something unique to offer to create balance and order within humanity as a whole.

What we resist, persists. We resist suffering and so it persists.

What we hate, we tend to attract. We hate death and so we attract death.

The cause of our finiteness lies in wrong thinking and feeling. As per psychology, it takes a minimum of 21 days to change habits and patterns. Let's reverse our thinking and become part of the infinite.

To explain life death and rebirth, I will share one of my swimming experiences[63]. I went for a swim. I saw a beautiful golden cup deep under the waters before returning. I decided not to waste any more time. I dived again and brought it back holding it above my crown.

Affirm- 'Namostutee, Let us all collectively be blessed with peace, harmony, abundance, stability, prosperity, nobility, and Godliness. Tathaastu.'

---

[63] *In the swimming experience- to swim is to live, to find the golden cup is the emptiness felt post purging, at the time of death and to bring it back is to be reborn in order to fill it up yet again with vitality.*

CHAPTER 48

ETERNAL AFTERLIFE

In heaven, everything is sacred and divine and so there can be nothing bad or impure. We are living in heaven, everything we call impure or bad is based only on the impressions we have formed. It is not real - life is in realizing the truth. There is enough beauty and abundance all around. Those who only see ugliness and hate around are living a dead life. I am here to raise the dead so that they can learn how to live again. Our physical bodies are mortal but our soul and spirit are capable of immortalization, let them remain wholesome and ever fresh with positivity, stability, insight, magic, and truth.

Just what the doctor prescribed: Take three deep and slow breathes - believe something great is about to happen. You are about to discover and gain something important that you have always wanted like happiness, promotion, peace, prosperity, knowledge, abundance, and ease. All your wishes will get nourished and fulfilled. Keep your mind calm & open to change to advance swiftly and comfortably. Entertain new ideas and new beginnings with a fresh perspective and be prepared for wonder.

The inner meaning of being born out of the lotus flower implies self-consciousness born out of the mental power of a highly activated intelligence and grace. A being who realizes the nature of such super-consciousness is aware of the inner secret behind the cycle of their birth and rebirth - past, present, and future. Such a being watches the theatre performance on the universal stage, while simultaneously watching the magic that is happening backstage, behind the curtains. The real action is backstage.

Behind the curtains of death, we meet with ourselves. We meet with our whole reality and freely connect with those we love. We are born based on our inner urges and inclinations. Nothing ever dies. Every atom, cell, being, the object is alive and absolute in itself. The theatre performance we watch might be good or bad, but just like birth, it is always new. At birth, most people do not remember their past life. This is unlike death and post-death when you remember the life you have led. The horror of death comes with our preconceived notion that death is bad. Once we are born, we have no recollection of what our death was like, so how can we be scared of something we know nothing about?

I often hear young people ask - Is patience a word?

I have a little aquarium with nine goldfish. Whenever one fish gets sick, all fish get sick. When one dies, all die. If one lives, all live. Same way, if one is enlightened then all are enlightened, if one is immortal then all are immortalized. All it takes is one.

Scientists too have finally discovered one such immortal being called *Turritopsis dohrnii,* also known as the 'immortal jellyfish'. Eternal life exists, it is up to us to believe it and achieve it. To die or not to die.

Having been stung by one of the most venomous creatures (a type of jellyfish) on our planet, I didn't know what could be more dangerous until I saw the pessimism around! Over time, perhaps I developed immunity to be emotionally stronger and so I remain detached though not in-effected. Science has found that pain and suffering can be cured by potent venoms, studies have proven that spider venom cures epilepsy, diabetes, and chronic body pain. Snakes' venom can cure strokes, Alzheimer's, brain injuries, and is extremely popular in the world of skincare for its anti-aging regenerative properties. Medicinal leeches prevent blood from clotting, treating heart attacks. Cone shell cures chronic pain. Scorpios venom cures brain tumors and cancer. The anti-inflammatory properties of bee venom improve skin condition, increases immunity, and cures rheumatoid arthritis. Unlike negativity, even the toxins these deadly animals release have positive effects and when used correctly, have the potential to save lives. Ultimately nothing heals you better than when you move beyond your phobias.

Within each person dwells 'Ka' or spiritual twin which we call life-giving force. At death, the 'Ka' leaves the body. However, if the body is somehow strengthened, the 'Ka' could return to the body and that is what is meant by the afterlife or in the afterworld. This is why it is so important to develop immunity and stay vitalized.

Death is real. Afterlife is the truth of God's wisdom and divine order. Living in your truth is the haven that protects you and helps you reach paradise. Thoth is the God who judges magically revitalize and bring the dead back to life in the underworld.

Afterlife is a grace that some receive for observing ethical laws and moral duties with full veracity, goodness, nobility, and maturity. Those guilty of breaking the universal law and codes of life and death should fight the consequences and make proper amends with constant self-reflection and devotion. The God who gave us life is omnipresent, fair, and just but expects us not to be greedy and selfish. All our actions and deeds of righteousness and fidelity are known to him. Allow me to send you God's healing energy as his divine messenger. Let us permit ourselves to move away from the world of poverty, gloom, and hardships and into a super world filled with truth, peace, prosperity, transparency, level-headedness, and joy. Let us create a world with no dearth on earth-where we move from death to mirth. Let us electrify our senses by dancing in nature, singing chirpily with the birds, smiling with our hearts, and socializing with friends. Harnessing our unique talents rather than competing, humiliating, disputing, and belittling one another.

Neither does the sea, nor the air likes to be restrained. Then why do we restrain ourselves, our spirit, and soul. To be alive is to continuously and freely flow with purpose, trust, and vitality. A heart that beats is a heart that is alive. A mind that thinks pure thought is a mind that is alive. To be truly alive is to perform pure actions and those that vitalizes all.

In life, we are living neglectfully and disrespectfully in deception, dismay, and agony. We are living in death at the midpoint of life. Free your heart center and bring order and stability back into your life through forbearance and faith. Only then will you be accepted and granted grace, justice, and an eternal afterlife which will liberate you from such eternal death.

The sleeping soul pulls itself up and incarnates into a new wakeful, creative spirited action and is transformed within the same body. Here the soul transcends time and meets with the eternal truth of life. Let us all together erase our past mistakes and rewrite the story of a better, more grateful, and fulfilled life. Let us all radiate with vitality and enjoy the bliss of eternal life in the heaven which is on earth.

Affirm- 'Namostutee, We are all interdependent. Everything comes from the same source. Everything has the same essential nature. Nothing is separated from me. You and I are eternally one. We are all manifestations of the un-manifested supreme reality. Ek onkar[64].'

---

[64] *Ek onkar is a Punjabi mind tool or mantra rooted in the Sikh philosophy which means that there is only one god, one being and one reality.*

CHAPTER 49

MITHYA

M ithya is a Hindi word for delusion. A person living in *mithya*, is prone to be excessively egocentric. Sometimes when the ego is hurt, a person loses perspective. Remember, your body is not yours alone. Separation is a delusion. If we think of life from this perspective, there will be no more suicide and acts of terrorism in the world. Gandhian philosophy is based on this principle. Surrender the ego (aham/ahankar) and embrace oneness in all.

We live in a strange world. Light is called day, and dark is called night. Both are separated by time and space, yet are one.

Defeatism and pessimism is neither for the physical nor for the spiritual humans. To transmute yourself and change the situation for the better, you need to be open to shed off the self-sabotaging thought forms and delusion. Divorce yourself, not from others but your own false beliefs.

In our body, all organs work together. No organ exists by itself. Similarly, all souls work together. In isolation, being restricted within themselves makes no sense. It perplexes me, how we can love one person completely and yet not love all. Step outside your place of judgment and embrace all.

Chaos, hatred, panic, diseases, and destruction are all caused by separation and separation is mithya. We and the world are one. The One has only one name. We have to feel some void to feel complete. We have to know the order to know chaos. We have to know formlessness to know the form. The creator has no form. The creator is one - its forms and names are many. The reason separation happens is that we need a point of reference to experience ourselves. We may call that point of reference good or bad but it simply is like one strand of hair split at the end caused by dryness or chemicals. We are alive because we can help another; as long as we can help another, we are alive.

I went driving through the English countryside with my family and reached Cambridge. The day we landed there the students were having their annual event. It was lovely to see the sportsmanship with students competing in rowing. It was not about winning but cooperating that mattered to these young kids. The river would not have looked as scenic had each of them not only worked as hard as a team to row the boat but waited and cheered up one another. Life is beautiful and purposeful only because we work together as a group.

God never divides, we divided ourselves. It doesn't matter where we are, what matters is who we are. The whole world is our harmonium, we can play harmonizing tunes wherever we please for the sound of harmony is heard everywhere. A soul is independent and not dependent upon the body it dwells within. A body is dependent upon its soul. Without the soul, a body cannot exist. Without the spirit the soul is of no use and without them both- the body is dead. Many dead organisms, bacteria, and even tiny transparent worms like nematodes are revived after eons, by just a little moisture in the air. I believe that under the correct conducive environment, there is almost nothing that cannot come back to life and grow.

To prove that worms are as old as the ice age surviving in freezing conditions and have come back to life, researchers have resurrected 'tardigrades' after they endured years of harsh life in extreme conditions. They have survived being in outer space and being frozen in sub-zero temperatures.

The coronavirus that started with one person has now spread to billions of people around the globe. One pastor, who contracted the virus in New York, has become the reason for quarantining the entire town. One sick teacher caused all the schools in the area to close down. How much ever we may think we are separate, we are all connected. The action and reaction of this butterfly effect is not restricted to bodily health but affects the health of our sensitive minds, emotions, psyche, and computer screens.

Our energy is constantly under threat because of someone who is sitting in a negative state millions of miles away. The horrid virus that you inflict on yourself, you also inflict upon others. You might think you are being suicidal, but you are committing murder because you are causing someone else's death through your warring, self-limiting belief, filled with distress and remorse.

Tragically, our children are no longer safe and free to go to schools and play areas. The sick are safer staying at home than going to hospitals for treatment. People we trust instill doubt in us. The powerful exploit us by trying to erase our memory. The pure and subtle have become the target of gross and dense energy. It is time to reverse the situation, time for the Gods to descend and show their truth to all those who dominate the pristine, humble souls, believing them to be weak and defenseless. This drama has now gone a bit too far. What you are hearing is simply the voice of the silent whispers that are returning like a storm, for you woke them from their peaceful slumber. Change your stance. They are the beings of light. Bodily death doesn't scare them. They are above all ills. If you don't let them be and let them shine, you will end up constricting their breath because of your over-control, and then a million more people will also be unable to breathe.

Detoxify and purify yourself now, or else your evolution will be stunted for millions of years, while a few others will enter into the golden era. You and your body are bigger and better than you think. Give importance to yourself. Nothing can challenge the confidence you give out because you are life. You have a divine heart that is on top of your crown. The light that comes out of your soul is so strong that nothing can penetrate it unless you let it so. Disconnection and death are misleading. You are a true combination of your soul, spirit, and body. Together you are all one. Through the mirror of the world, I get to know myself. Through knowing myself, I know my higher self. Through knowing my higher self, I know all.

God is not separate from you. God is experienced through your super self. You limit yourself by the delusionary, mendacious dualities. Nothing other than you comes in between God and you.

Your growth will get affected by other people and in many cases, it could be someone you don't even know. Such is the power of thought and our human connection. Similarly, one person's energy can also be sapped by a collective group of people. Do remember that whether we do this singularly or collectively we will have to bear the brunt in the same way – individually or collectively. Suffering given to one will always be returned in one way or the other. We all are one and forever indebted to each other.

We all are essentially one and absolute because outside of the one, we are nothing. We all function separately but our true identity lies in the collective force for that is our real individuality. The idea and strength of triangular teams have been taught by Hindu Gods and Goddesses for eons. We lose our value when ego and pride set in or when we think we are unrelated and separate. The concept of trinity is popular in all cultures. A team of three is required for success explained by Brahma, Vishnu, and Mahesh amongst Hindu Gods.

Human consciousness is one, whole, and complete. It is common to all. Every good and bad happening in the world today is caused by me[65] and you. My responsibility is the sum total of me and you, a collective combination of us all. Each individual, group, nation has an obligation to raise its consciousness. What affects one individual or community affects all. The entire humanity is one. What you do affects all. You are special only because humanity as a whole is special. God's every creation is equally important and each of us has a group soul of their own.

Each one acts based on wisdom gained over the years. We believe we are bigger and smaller but this is not really so. It is our attachment to the ego that makes us believe in the big delusion. You are not an individual. You are not separate from all the others, you are a part just like each cell is a part of your body but it is not the whole body in its entirety.

Try spinning the small globe sitting on your desk and you will see how different the world looks based on where you look. All the places are within the same globe. Try flipping the chapters within this book and you will see how differently you perceive what is written depending on where your attention goes even though all belong to the same book. The difference is only in your perception and understanding.

All roads lead you to the same path. Rivers may be many but eventually all meet with the ocean. Our bodies, upbringing, and dispositions may be different but just like the tributaries of different rivers, we all meet and blend within the same ocean. This way we become one with all. We meet with our true freedom by blending with the same ocean, from whence we all came. Truth is inseparable.

The higher beings are always there to bless, support, and guide all those who have a pure and genuine heart.

Affirm- 'Namostutee, I am blessed and in bliss, as I am shielded and completely healed physically, emotionally, mentally, financially, spiritually, etherically, and astrally. I trust that I am successful, and guided at all times.

---

[65] *Refer to the chapter 'ME point' for greater details on ME.*

I hope that my kith, kin, and all the deserving people and beings around the globe get healed and attain prosperity, abundance, patience, and fame so that we together can create a more wholesome environment around the world and universe at large. Tathaastu.'

CHAPTER 50

TRUE BLUE

Seen from above, Earth is a blue planet. Clairvoyantly seen, the color of our throat chakra is blue - deep within it is connected with our gravity center. When the gravity chakra is weak, its ruling planet, which is Earth, is affected. Based on our position, our body's gravity center is interchangeable. When the connection between Earth and chakras or communication between the blue dot (gravity center) and blue pearl (Third eye Center) is imbalanced-it affects our body. Seeing the Earth from space is a blue dot. When you see us from an auric point of view–there is a blue pearl within us–our third eye.

Those who love are not terrified by those that try to control them. Freedom wins over fear because that is wisdom-the wisdom of blue pearl which we as residents of the blue earth have. The subtle forces emit light and the invisible powerful forces emit darkness. This is done to maintain order and to secure the earth's loving energies. It takes collective determination and one-pointedness (*Ekagrata* in Sanskrit) for both forces to cooperate so that they can jointly guide us. With this resolve, these forces are capable of creating heaven on earth but they need an army of visible, positive, pure beings to continue evolving together and recreating an energetic shift. These celestial and kindly beings cure, repair, and heal one another through the presence of their radiating aura on earth.

The earth's core is filled with iron and certain other metals that get attracted to magnets. Magnets get attracted to other magnets[66] and iron gets attracted to magnets. We all have magnetic energy, only the degree varies.

---

[66] *Refer to the chapter on 'Magnetized' for greater details.*

Earth is attracted to us because of its magnetic properties. The gravitational force is within us and not outside of us. Earth is pulled towards us as long as we have this magnetic power. When we become aware of our gravity center the earth too gets healed with our radiating charm. The magnetic force we have inside our electro-magnetic field moves us closer to earth for us to respond to the gravitational effect. If the collective magnetic force becomes weak, our sense of attachment, balance, and confidence is lost.

The best way to get over this unrest, weakness, terror, and anxiety is to connect with nature and play with the trees and flowers. Pay attention to the earth and attend to its cries of attention.

An activated Ajna chakra or will-center strengthens awareness, clarity, intuition & rationale. We all have a blue pearl in our brains that does the activation. Our collective will can make or break our destiny. Let us all set the right intentions through our power of telepathy. We have channels or rivers through which chi energy flows in and around us. When these channels meet with the oceanic spirit, we become aware of the awakening. When we become aware of our ignorance, enlightenment takes place. The shift of energy we are witnessing is here to stay to increase the overall vibratory levels of humanity and mother Earth. This shift will spark higher intelligence and increased mental connectivity so that we become a combination of God+hu+man = divine yin yang.

Affirm- 'Namostutee, The speed of light does not vary with time and space. My thoughts and aura travel even faster than the speed of light and yet I remain true, grounded, and committed to my values of love and life. Tathaastu.'

CHAPTER 51

BUBBLES

Like bubbles in champagne.
While growing up I had a friend named Bubbles. She was my invisible friend. We did not meet for a long time but when I think of her I am reminded of the fact that our soul's mission is fulfilled when we meet with our higher potential. It is in knowing and realizing our potential that we enter the gate of God within the same body. It is our innate inner potential to be perennially bubbly.

A shadow is never sharper than the actual object. True innocence and a smile have their own intuitive charm. Our left hand might not be our dominant hand, but it is the one with a bigger heart-the kind that looks straight into your face and strikes you with its light. Stop trying to get smarter. The smartest are the kids walking outside in your street. There is more fun in the imaginary child's play than in digitizing and contouring every part of your right-brained personality. Every neuron is interconnected with thousands of channels; however much you may try, the right and left can never be completely separated. Whatever you resist tends to persist; the invisible will now become visible.

My physical father, who is now retired, lives with my mother far away in India. Until their recent visit here, they had no clue of the inner voice that speaks to me with so much love for you. I left them bewildered, for they had hardly any idea of who I am. I spent most of my time with them - from the age of fourteen until I married and moved from home. In those confusing times, I seemed wild, as I was deliberately holding on to my voice of truth. But now the time is right to speak. I am now forty-one, and for the last ten years or more, from the time I was initiated and endowed with spiritual power, I have been waiting for this light to come out and sparkle. The signs are right to reveal the mystery.

Although I have known this intuitively for a long time, the sudden strong urge to speak my truth came from within my vibrational energy in the summer of 2019. During one of the Arhatic retreats, I was submerged in blessed waters. This is a ritual the Masters follow in which you feel like you are being baptized. Since then, everything I have intuitively witnessed over the eons keeps coming back to my memory as flashes. I feel so much gratitude and the best I can do is to keep recording this sacred knowledge under the guidance, wisdom, and light of higher frequencies.

After having witnessed all my previous births and my immediate past life, I can say for sure that God is the greatest magician and we all are his wonder-workers. Until I turned seven in earth years, in my new spiritual body, my past life remained alive in my present body. She (my soul) was related to me as if by blood and gave herself up for the love she had for me. The bond we shared never ceased, connecting with me several times, over the last few years. She is my incarnated soul. She set herself free. You may think that this was the end. But look at the magic of the higher frequencies: today I am standing before you in the same body, with a far more evolved soul. I have released my incarnated soul from its entrapment to merge with the light of the higher soul.

Each one of our moves, our every step, is preordained and perfectly planned. Our next move is already decided before we take our next step. Yet we do not know of that mysterious step, because in not knowing, the flame of our fire within stays enthusiastically lit with all its zeal and passion. If we know the outcome already, we will stop working towards our goal. While it may sound safe, knowing what is to come kills our passion, our fire, and our enthusiasm. So let's keep the mystery alive, and live in the now for our own sake. I am now back home, living amongst my most precious old friends, but eons have passed and they still do not recognize me, for they have closed their windows even though my door is always open. I am sure their time will come very soon and they too will open up.

Part of me has never died. I attached that part of myself to my home (my body) and a loved one, and so I was not able to completely transition and cross over into the light. Other energies send requests to this angel of light, who communicates with me to help release and allow me to leave all these earthly attachments that hold me back. Many things are keeping me on the earthly plane, even without my physical body. These entrapments stop me from freely moving to the next step. The angel of light keeps helping my release.

After the last time, she contacted me, I went into a deeply relaxed state in which I felt respect, love, forgiveness, gratitude, and compassion for all. I learned that attachments to material possessions or emotions do us no good. We are beyond them. I felt that I had died and no longer existed long before I actually physically died because no one would willingly speak with me anyway. I released my incarnated soul through a strange ritual so that my soul could be healed and all past emotional wounds could be resolved. I intuitively felt that my incarnated soul would surely be happy to leave, and I knew it needed my help. Thus I began my search for who I am in order to discover the 'I am'. I started the purifying process by burning frankincense and sandalwood incense. As I purified and cleansed myself inside and out, I went back to what I once was: a shining crystal on the precious mountain. I was also a white pearl of the sea. I felt so free within my own body. The experience of being born and witnessing your birth in front of your very own eyes is when you feel you know it all. Yet no matter how much you know there is so much that remains unknown. Having been reborn, I knew that the grace of higher energies is forever upon me so that I can help resurrect many more people. These are the people who are bound by their own self-inflicted attachments, causing much harm to not only themselves but also to the ones they are attached. I am here to clear them of their debt and help them start afresh. I am here to heal them from the pain point that stems from deceptive love, as true love is free and never bound, stagnated, or unwholesome. It is meant to fly blissfully free, so come beneath my indigo-colored wings and fear not, for panic itself is a delusion created only by you. Do not enter this path again. It is your nature to keep evolving and merging with the light. Release yourself of your self-inflicted pain. The journey now and the journey ahead will lead to the heavenly abode you have been waiting for. The higher beings forgive you with all their heart and soul.

I often received messages from my inner voice when I was a young child. I felt that there was a little doll sitting within me that spoke with me from time to time. A day came when that doll left me all alone. While leaving, the doll told me, "One day, when the time is right, I will come back to let you know the real purpose of your existence." Many years went by, but I never forgot the last words of my inner voice. I never forgot 'Bubbles'. Despite the high-pitched noises of the outside world, whenever I saw angels dancing and heard them singing - I knew Bubbles had sent them for me. My dainty ears craved to hear the voice of my inner doll. Like bubbles in champagne that are here one moment and then gone the next, Bubbles danced in my glass and I enjoyed the fizz of my champagne as long as it lasted.

Soon I grew up, and whenever I saw the shooting stars I knew Bubbles had sent them for me not only to fill me with awe and wonder but to lift me when I was low, broken, and down. I knew that it was always Bubbles who showed me all the beauty I saw. I thank that little doll over and over again for showing me all the wonders that I saw and being with me all through the transmuting stages of my growth.

She remains in the hiding, only so that I can see. Whenever I see her, she is still that little bald doll I played within the expansive garden behind my home. Even though we all live in our bubble, it is strange and interesting how Bubbles has become a mystery in the pages of history.

We watch movies that evoke various emotions through the themes that they carry horror, adventure, romance, comedy, and drama. These genres may inspire you in several ways – either to work on your health or may tickle your brain cells. A movie or a theatergoer simply enjoys the experience of watching them all. If you tell yourself, "I am a theatergoer, I am not the actor playing the various roles", then you detach yourself from the movies you watch. We all are simply enjoying the movie, the movie will continue as it is complete in itself. However, no two people interpret the scenes of the movie in the same way. The finite mind cannot even begin to understand the infinite in its entirety.

It is always fun to watch a football match whether it is live or on the screen as long as you do not get too involved as a fan. The excitement is what we must take in even after the show is over, whether we understand the rules of the game or not. The Earthly plane is a continuous universal movie in which we all play our respective roles and one character becomes the cause of creating another.

Eventually, bubbles in champagne flatten and merge with the one drinking from that glass. Ripples in water settle with time into different waters based on how many memories our waters hold and how many more memories are yet to be realized. We keep memories of what we like and discard what we don't but the reality is that we did see the whole movie.

Bubbles of laughter and joy come and go but once you know where Bubbles came from, your inner joy never goes. As you expand your consciousness, the joyful thoughts you resonate float like bubbles in the entire universe, planets, and beyond - while also remaining with you.

Affirm- 'Namostutee, I am healed and energized at all levels. I feel uplifted, understood, and secure. My cell life is increased. My mood is balanced and elevated. My personal and professional goals are achieved. I am internally strong and I live in harmony with all. I have a simple, healthy, wholesome lifestyle. Tathaastu.'

CHAPTER 51a

THE PRINCESS THAT NEVER GROWS OLD

Here is a fairy tale, tweens would love to hear: The princess that never grows old.

A princess once lived in a palace made of sand and each morning the sun shone on it. One day a prince saw the beautiful palace and upon coming closer - he heard a voice that whispered, "Save me from this palace of sand". The courageous prince gently threw some seawater he took from the sea on the palace. He then got all his soldiers to dig deep and slowly to clear away all sand to release the princess that had whispered to him. Soon the princess was found and seeing her beauty the prince proposed her hand for marriage but the princess who had dainty little wings flew away. This didn't break the heart of the prince. He soon built another sand palace with the leftover sand at the same place with the belief that one day the beautiful princess will return. Many years passed, and the prince never stopped checking inside the palace. The prince got old and tired but never gave up. Every morning and every night he would search for the princess. One day that day did come, the princess returned. The palace was relit to welcome the princess back to her true abode. The prince knew the princess had to return but upon seeing a beauty filled with such vitality, the prince was mesmerized, amazed, and filled with wonder. The princess had not grown old by the travels across different continents and facing different weather conditions. No matter how much time they both spent, the prince and princess could never have enough of each other and so from that day on they live happily together. The palace they built by the beach still exists and so do they, they are lovely hosts- go meet with them someday.

When making sandcastles it is easier to take away sand than to add more to the castle. Time is like sand - it is easier to take it away than to add it back. When shaping and building your home, remember to enjoy and share life before the tides of time sweep it all away.

The sandcastle we build might blow away with the force of another wave, but the sand and the ocean will remain for us to build yet another castle. We are not just a part of a whole, but the whole itself. We are the interconnected network of sand, ocean, association, atoms, cells, elements, and so much more. However much we may try, we are not separate parts, but we are one. And this, my friend, is what I call bliss. Artists, musicians, and other creative people can experience this flow of oneness during their heightened state of creativity.

When we are spiritually heightened we realize that all of humanity beats with a single heart. This uplifts and cleanses us and our soul from within. A peep through the window of the enchanted land. Not only does the place still exist but also the prince and princess with their family because unlike the lifespan here, their life is charged with so much wonder, beauty, and liberty that those living in that can live up to a thousand years.

We call that immortality compared to the hundred years that we live. One beautiful child from that land asked his father for a gift. The kind father said he will grant him anything he wishes. The son said send me to the land where people live a hundred years, which for the people in this land is only a year. I will return post my trip with lots of more stories to share. The father said that the time capsule is parked right there, take your flight if you must, but remember to return if things get bitter. You have my blessings and my protection. No one in this realm is ever stopped from doing what they wish, not even a little child. The mother said that people dance and sing in this land with joy, whatever we wish is granted. But in that land there is hardly any laughter or joy, everything is so instant and everybody is in such a flurry that nobody even enjoys the essence of sweet flowers. The young look old and everyone is busy striving hard because life is short. And once they achieve everything they were running after, they meet with death. This way they never get the time to enjoy what they acquire. The child's spirits didn't get down, he insisted and left leaving his twin behind. Initially, the self-manifested child was super excited. He noted that "what we learn in a hundred years, people can acquire in just a year. What we build in a year people here destroy in just a month. The breaths we take in a month, they exhaust in just a week. Everything here is so fast - at skyrocketing speed. They all are busy playing around a game that my little sister built last year and had fallen from my grandma's chest of drawers. The problem is that they seem to have forgotten that it is just a game. Instead of merging with the truth, they have merged with the game and become the game. Please ask my sister to rebuild another game, this game of time has made everyone exasperated here in this land of speed. Everyone has access to unlimited knowledge both science and art, some of them earn great wages and have the perspicacity of the highest sages.

But many do not remember a word of what they read. Most people here do not learn much, they think that by seeing the page for split seconds, they have learned it all. They do not even know the true meaning of one word that we take a week to unravel. There is no mystery, no purpose and everything is so easily given. They have all the fruits but have forgotten the value and neither are they enjoying the fruit nor are they picking it." The little child who was not so little anymore, grew a bit too fast here on this land, with all the negative thinking patterns he developed. The people around in the city made him uncomfortable so he went to the mountains where a few sages recognized Rim but kept it a secret.

Rim finally gave up and when four hundred years were over, he sat on the time capsule and returned to meet with the father. The next six hundred years, which is sixty years here, people of speed land missed the presence of the little child. Without the light of Rims radiating aura, they were all so lost. One day when Rim was playing with snow, a little tear fell from his eye for Rim was missing the Grim, the little girl he dated in speed land. That tear reached down from the stream of gold and met with that little girl who was now a fully grown woman. That tear gave her hope like a sparkling star you see in the night sky. With that little tear, her breath came back and she came out alive to the brim from the game of time. Now that tear had become a stream. The stream had gold, silver, and all the other metals mixed in it. Yet the original tear was pure and pristine like a magical crystal ball. That stream was ever-flowing with brilliance and love. If you take even a sip from the immortal waters, you will have all the vigor to meet with the rivers of life. Some were not very happy with this gift of longevity and skipped the offer. Those who did realize that sixty years will soon become six hundred years in the speed land as things begin to slow down. Six hundred will then become six thousand years in the land of one thousand years.

Affirm- 'Namostutee, I invoke the higher angels and celestial beings to bless us all with blissfulness, gratitude, love, generosity, responsibility, confidence, and cosmic connections. Tathaastu.'

CHAPTER 52

CORE ESSENCE

The air is hungry for the active power of the fiery sun. The earth is thirsty for the subtle wisdom of the moon. Both love water just as much as the water loves them. Without the water, both remain parched. The breath of air keeps on refreshing and lending. The light of fire keeps on moving and providing. The food of the earth keeps on giving and protecting. The love of water keeps on circulating and remembering. The nurturing earth is emotional like our mother, and yet so prosperous because it is generous and holds on to nothing. The earth forever goes on feeding us with its blessed food. The air shares its knowledge and wisdom, lending us a voice. The very breath we breathe is but a loan we have taken from the invisible force. The water goes on sharing memories of love and life. The fire keeps on adjusting its heat, providing us with just enough warmth, based on our different temperaments and varying temperatures.

What is tested by fire comes out as pure gold based on its genuineness. In the Indian epic Ramayana, when mother Sita/Sattee walked on fire to prove her fidelity to Lord Rama, she came out pure as gold. It is no coincidence that when you seal your lips, the only word that comes out of your mouth is mum. Only a mum (mother) can speak your silence.

When each one of these elements (gold, silver, carbon, iron, uranium, titanium and silicone) are well settled within the trio of our physical, emotional, and mental bodies, the fire and air in us return with its flickering light into the spiritual plane above, blessing us and gracing the core of our being-our very center-with evermore power of the moon, light of the sun, and love of the earth. Now with all this physical, emotional, psychological, spiritual light - our etheric and astral bodies begin to get a golden glow, and soon with all this positive hue of divinity lodged within us, our little hearts become like little walking stars shining their light upon the earth and all through space and beyond. We then merge with the Pure Spirit within and without us, which expands even beyond the seven auric layers.

The four cardinal directions (NEWS) become eight. This is when the soul within our spirit body begins to light up. With every cell of our body bubbling with joy, we truly learn to communicate with the vibration of our energy. The entire cosmos begins to wonder how creative each one of us is. We are few, and we look only like little drops of dew from afar, but each one of us has the upper hand with the special power of knowing who we are and where we came from. We are the center. Inherent within us are the nine-fold aspects: prosperity from water, generosity from the earth, clarity from light, purity from the air, vitality from the ether, graced by divinity, spirituality, reality, and subtlety. When all else is gone, we will still subtly remain active within the shell of our outer core.

While today we are going through seclusion and quarantine what we are going through is an occultation. Some are transitioning while others are transmuting but none are transmitting. It is the cosmic forces that are causing this alchemical transformation.

In today's alpha age where the virtual world has taken over the physical world, we are getting more creative as we have far more free time. Alpha is beginning and not the end so stop calling this the end of the world.

During January, July and November - switch off the television and spend time out in the fresh air. Do not let the vibrations of electronics take over your life during this lockdown. Use these gadgets to a minimum and only to your minimal benefit. You control your senses and so you control these gadgets-they do not control you.

In the lower realm, air mixes with water. In the higher realm, the same air can fuel a fire. When ether and air mingle during the transitional phase, the waves of the etheric energy can get filled with loving energy and purity of life force to get healed through the core center of the enlightened one.

Each substance has the potential to manifest in a thousand ways just as the liquid water becomes gas vapor, steam, solid ice, and a dewdrop and yet it remains part of the same ocean, the same spirit.

The astral body learns lessons from the five elements of nature - ether, air, fire, water, and earth and continues to rearrange the coarse into subtle, subtle to coarse, until subtle and coarse become one and with time, our astral body gets stronger, despite the friction. The more difficult the journey the greater the friction and greater is the purification.

Feng translates wind (which means joy) and Shui translates water (which means health). The combination of these two elements, (wind and water) brings supreme fortune. What use is that joy which comes at the cost of health.

Affirm- 'Namostutee, The essence of my reality is formless, nameless, relentless, and ethereal. Tathaastu.'

CHAPTER 53

EGG CAME FIRST

The crux of the matter remains, in some cases, the egg comes first and then the snake and in some cases, the snake comes first and then the egg. In some cases, the egg never comes out and so the snake comes out without the egg.

Darkness is merely the absence of light. Light is merely the absence of darkness.

The cosmic egg has hatched. Embrace and accept its birth, do not resist the forces. Let it play your flute the way it pleases. Empty yourself to refill yourself with the awareness of this cosmic consciousness. This change is as disruptive as shifting to another planet or realm. It seems as if mysteriously some of the crimson magenta energy has been transferred upon earth's blue energy causing it to get congested and overwhelmed.

All it took was seven days to create the entire life.

The chic is protected by the eggshell. The chic can feel the protection but doesn't know why and how? Similarly, our bodies are protected by our aura. We can feel the protection but do not know why and how? Our aura is subtler and almost invisible but it is stronger than our physical body and it is shaped just like the oval egg. As we purify ourselves and our dense physical body which is tangible and visible, our subtle etheric body which is intangible and invisible also gets purified. The chic refines the egg, egg protects the chic, both are automatically connected and when the chic is strong and ready, the egg and chic mingle, become one, complete, and together.

We all know of an invisible subtle force that shields us, some choose not to believe in that force. But the force always exists. Once broken, you can dissect each layer just as you break the egg and see what is inside.

Every eggshell knows how to protect the chic within, every auric shield knows how to protect our body, but if the chic or the body resist then there is little that the subtle energy can do. At this time the etheric web tends to get cracked or broken and lifeless and so it is important to not resist. It is important to keep the faith and let the divine energies flow in. These divine energies are like sparks of electricity that charge up your energy body.

Just the way our children control us, the universal egg controls the universal seed. We are obliged to give back what we seek. You might as well become the seed.

You are hurting yourself in trying to hurt me because I remain forever unhurt within the safe cocoon. I am his precious immortal princess metamorphing into anything I will. I will become what I was again at my will. Such is my humble loving power. Just don't rush me in because everything happens at its right time. Haste is a waste that is not within your nature to see. But your time will come too-you have my blessings while I stay detached and unharmed by your antics. You are a living dream. Everything and everyone here is yours-you are filled with abundance, surrounded by true love and friendship, you are neither alone nor threatened on this plane. It is here wherein accepting yourself, you accept others. Every fleeting thought, every expectation is a mere deception of your mind. The energies you give out are what you receive so stay on high vibrations and let not the swinging moods fool you. You are the maker of your reality. Just remember to remember who you are and pray to the creator so you become better with each passing moment-for you are also the co-creator of your and my destiny.

The primordial divine source is the one who continuously gives, enables, facilitates, saves, and brings life and form into existence. Honor the cheerful bringer of life who solely connects the entire universe with the cosmic trinity and unity. Allow the well-heeled, supremely pure, dynamic, tranquil energy to gracefully flow as it wishes.

Affirm- 'Namostutee, I am in a state of ecstatic bliss because I am sincere, loyal, and considerate, and filled with inner peace. Tathaastu.'

CHAPTER 54

INTENSE INTROSPECTION: ii

Intense things always come in pairs. 'ii' is bound to bring good luck and partnerships into your life-enhancing security and stability. You are floating because you have been walking in the shadow of your reflection. It is time to let this newly acquired knowledge pour into your reality. Between waking and sleeping - there is awakening. That awakening is not in your perceived heightened wisdom nor the mere devotional words but it is settled in your pure intuitive knowledge. To have awareness requires your ability to be quiet inside and out. It takes love and clarity to enjoy the beauty and bliss of collective silence. Focus on the stillness within the storm. This inner harmony helps you to stay calm even in the chaos of the greatest wars or pandemic ever. Between inhalation and exhalation, there is stillness and it doesn't mean we stop breathing. We usually are not alert enough to be aware of this stillness. When we get aware of the pause between inhalation and exhalation of air, our lungs and heart get activated. Under normal circumstances, we all go through changes individually. This time around we are all collectively going through these changes.

Imagine a glass that is not clean. Would you want to drink in that without cleaning it? We have to clean the glass before we can fill it. Similarly in life, there are identified gaps that every person is trying to fill. Some call it wealth, some health. You may want to hastily fill that gap by doing anything and everything. It is better to be patient and leave the gap to identify the reason for the gap and emptiness. Once you know the reason and the purpose of this gap you will be able to fill the emptiness in the way that it needs to be filled.

The lockdown is telling you to open up. Be patient and calm, within this forced silence, for the first time you all will realize that you are locked inside your physical body. Your physical body is locked inside your etheric body, it is not the other way around. Controlling inner freedom is no way to achieve outer stardom.

Know the inner stillness in the outer chaos. Do not let your wavering mind lead you to unrest, anxiety, or instability. Overcome the problems by focusing instead on the divine will of wisdom, peace, and joy. Restore and do not exhaust your energy. Detoxify and rejuvenate your cells, recharge your mind with proper rest, cleanse your body of all toxins, synthetic chemicals, pollutants, heavy metals, processed foods, and go natural. Forgive and ask for forgiveness, stay hydrated, exercise daily, breathe freely, and remember to let go of all the wasted negativity. Do not hold on to anger, resentments, and irrational fear. Whatever you resist persists so do what is right and refrain from all unwholesome deeds.

The ones without a voice, the ones who have long been invisible are finally out. Let them wear their rightful crown. When the alive live like the dead, the dead come alive to show us what it is like to live. This transformational passing phase has the potential to give birth to a greater soul and spirit connection. We all are one. What affects one, affects the entire chain of sentient beings.

Reflect, introspect, and embrace the pause and resolve to spiral upwards instead of going downwards with immense compassion, acceptance, gratefulness, positivity, astuteness, solid faith, and strength. Cleanse, purify, and declutter the closets of your home, mind, and emotions during this time. Only then can Love, light, protection, and blessings come to you.

You have an obligation to yourself. You need to show the inner light – do not succumb to it. Stand up and face your truth whatever it may be. It is not for the sake of power or anything else, but for your own sake. Your true soul has been hiding in the invisible in the name of mythology, dogma, mysticism for far too long. Break down is another word for breakthrough and chaos is another word for opportunity.

Liberate yourself from all your baggage and start anew. Sometimes a wake-up call gives you a sense of purpose and perspective to achieve your true potential. Suffering happens when you resist and hold onto things so fulfill your obligation to yourself. Going natural is the only mantra. This unprecedented situation has forced many of us into living a more balanced, genuine, focused, honest, productive, challenging, efficient, responsible, innovative, novel, original, decisive, fulfilling, active, disciplined, and moderate life.

You will one day merge with your center and it will be the true expression of all your impressions. Everything you do is because of your truth which connects you to the innate potential of all your collective births. The essence and the meaning that you are searching for is not outside but it is inside of you. The pattern of this metamorphosis is clear - it is you who has been hiding from the light within. It is with the internalization & the externalization that you will meet with your true self.

Affirm- 'Namostutee, I am Infused with God's supreme consciousness. I embody dazzling beauty, vibrant activity, and illuminating knowledge. Tathaastu.'

CHAPTER 55

EMPTY VACUUM

The only way out of slavery and addiction is freedom and redemption. You are a slave of emotions, thoughts, money, and power. Meditation is a medication that helps you actively pay attention to your freedom, far from all slavery. When you shed tears, shed them in a way that your tears wash away the leftover debris of suffering and agony that other people go through.

Someone said, "I want more jewels". I said, "The fact that you want more means that either you believe that you have less or you do not believe that you can have more. Both are not very positive feelings. Those who believe, have the faith that it is just a matter of time before they will open their closet and they will finally find the jewels they have always dreamt of. Whatever you put your complete attention and faith into, with the right intention, is for you to have. Unfortunately, we put our attention into negativity, disappointments, and lack and so our closets always seem empty".

In essence, there is nothing to dismay because you can't lose something that you do not have. The emptiness and void we feel has to be filled with something. Time simply fills that void for us to give us a sense of purpose. You can't want something that you already have.

Godly or divine humans help us see our truth. Currently, there are only a few. In the bridge between reality and non-reality, you will meet with the one. This meeting will lead you to the path. The Godly human is sharp and beautiful both in body and mind. Confident, strong, rigid and firm much like the strongest meteors showered in 2019. This being will spiritually transform you through the divine emanation because it sees through the reflection.

You are taller than you think you are. You are your higher soul which is taller than your physical height. You are not just your lower soul which is limited by your physical height.

There is no point in just having an emotional heart. Reason with your emotions to create a thinking heart. This will lead you to your spiritual heart.

100 years of *Brahma* equals 72,000 *kalpas* or eons[67] which is 311,040,000,000,000 earthly human years. This affects the flow of our Brahma Nadi. Brahma returned with a new world order 500 years later in 2019.

When you meet with the all-pervading one, the burnt bridges between earth and heavens get rebuilt. We become one by almost working for an eon on earth or in the heavens, the humans give hope through service and righteous action, the hu-gods lay the right inspirational foundation and the Gods generously bless through leading. Other hego-copters on surveillance duty have no karmic debts due to being pure descendants of the noble few, they have a free pass to traverse and fly to all or any of the three realms at will. They cannot be bogged down with monotony. They are the ones who are both interested and interesting. They are deeply connected with all but it is just not the nature of their curious mind to stay still. They adjust the speed of their helicopters based on weather conditions and the need of the environment. They are here to constantly communicate, learn, teach, create, break obdurate patterns and help us evolve. They are the blue bloods sending us divine messages post-filtering through the transmission to give us a taste of supreme bliss and sense of purpose. Moments when we see past, present, and future as one are the moments when they are with us showing us the joy of living in the now. Their energy and sense of ambition do not get imbalanced with climatic changes. They are the sanest but we call them eccentric.

Affirm- 'Namostutee, I dissolve myself into the expanse of emptiness only to refill myself with the virtues of goodness, purity, completion, and compassion. Tathaastu.'

---

[67] *Kalpa or aeon is the time period between creation and recreation. Brahma is the creator God.*

CHAPTER 56

SOUND OF INFINITE SILENCE

The best sound is the sound of silence.

Silence is better than speaking nonsense. However, you do not need to be silent when one is chanting and glorifying the Lord in their speech. In a world where people talk of having an audience, I am happy with my natural clairaudience. It takes intelligence and wisdom to remain silent and dumb. The only dumb thing is to be numb. You can understand most when you open yourself to feel and hear the whispering sound of silence.

Each Yuga has four stages. Each of the four stages is divided into two - making the count eight. We are in the sixth stage, it is a state of infinity after omega and before the alpha. Our creations are transient and imperfect, whereas God's creations are immortal and perfect. We are God's creations. The imperfect within the perfect. January, July, and November of 2020 will divide our race henceforth into 3 subtypes - superhumans, Godly humans, and super machines - each being super intelligent.

After the storm, there is complete silence. After the shaking, there is divine stillness. Low or high, mundane or sacred, material or spiritual, it is between the silent stillness that you are lit by the smokeless fire from within, to ultimately meet with the currents of life as they are.

Our mission is to detoxify our etheric and astral bodies so that we can tap our potential with complete awareness and master our lower passions and emotions.

Hiding from the world for a day is not the same as hiding from the world for a year. But a year and a day are much the same from where I see. From the higher realms, which is where I travel, I bring back what I see into the physical – fashioning dreams into a reality.

I hear various viewpoints. For some - the soul is within the body and the spirit is within the soul. Our soul and spirit are within and outside of the body. It reaches far beyond the realms of our physical limitations and so we cannot see or hear with our physical eyes and ears. To know their presence we need to open ourselves to unspoken words and see with our inner eyes. For some soul is within the spirit and the body is within the soul. For some soul and spirit are one, both are within and outside the body-individuality and personality merge. The body is an object created by the soul to do what it realizes, the soul is an aim that the spirit sets for you based on what it knows. To know, to realize, and to actualize are three different steps but when they merge, you become the perfect version of your true potential. Living your truth is another dimension, where you intuitively realize that you are like a perfect precise dot within the supremely perfect universal body. In this manner no matter how many layers you may uncover, each dimension you cross you meet with yourself. Slowly you concede to becoming one with all, accepting all and letting them be. From here-on, there are no more struggles. Life becomes an enlivening awakening experience, name soul and mind are one. Here ah am.

Even then, an artist and art can never become completely one. The art and the spectators can never know the universal artist fully. God is the finest artist whose modern art cannot ever be completely defined or comprehended. But God being the perfect artist cannot make art without putting a bit of himself within the art. That unique portion he adds gives a new dimension of light to the art he creates. This is when we say Ah! Art has come to life. Let's call it *He-art*. Only the heart can tell where the art came from. Then a new quest begins to find the missing heart. We all beat because of that one heart. We all are just little beats because of which the heart beats. The beats can never know the heart fully. God keeps his heart hidden and secured somewhere where no one can trace her. If the heart is in pain, we all feel the pain. If the heart is happy, we all are happy. All God asks of us is to keep his heart always smiling. If his heart smiles, we all feel its sweetness even if we are miles away. Such is its purity.

Learning to keep secrets sealed and then revealing them slowly when the time is right is both an art and skill. It is as important to master this skill as is to learn about the powerful secret. Through silence, we evolve. We should then reveal the secret when the world is ready to hear it and when you are ready to express it without making many people raise their eyebrows.

That is when you reach a point in life when no matter what others say, good or bad, nothing affects you. You remain detached and non-reactive. At this point, you know full well who you are, and no one can ruin your peace, for you are you, content within yourself. Your brain registers information best when your mind is in a thoughtless state. Breathe easily. Stay relaxed, open, attentive, recharged, reinvigorated, childlike, and creative.

Stop living in moonlight, from paycheck to paycheck. Our nature and behavior should be as clean as a shining pearl. We can save money or assemble food for the future through sensible reflection. Similarly harvest inner silence and accumulate information through inner calmness and reflection. Your knowledge is as much of an asset as is money, jewels, or food. It is wise to save wealth, for saving produces more.

Affirm- 'Namostutee, I listen to my inner voice through the inner ear. I listen and act in accordance with my soul's true purpose. I reflect on my actions. Tathaastu.'

CHAPTER 57

EMOTIONAL BOULDERS

Emotional boulders remind us to endeavor our best and push against the boulder. But these boulders also tell us to not doubt that Lord God will come to our rescue and lift the boulders for us. All hard work pays so don't lose heart. You worked at breakneck speed. The boulders you lifted have paved a path for many. Your time will come, until then heal yourself, fuel your exhausted energy. Reward and empower yourself - party and mingle remotely to enjoy time with all the colorful people around.

There is no stone that cannot be lifted. No wall made of stone can stop you. No emotion can overwhelm you. Emotions are not like cold stones. When one is emotional all that is seen is a stone wall and restrictions that bind you. Overcome all the restrictions and break this wall. Understand and embrace your emotions and what you are going through. There is no wall or emotion that is stopping you from progressing. It is you who is stopping yourself from progressions.

When you lift stones you build your muscles, when you overcome your emotions you become stronger and more resilient. There is always a reason why you face resistance, stone walls, or emotions. You face them because you are meant to face them and become stronger. Don't give up as you can overcome this and move on. Beyond the darkness, there is always light.

Before living someone else's life live your own.

The patterns you see around have a fascinating life story to tell. Follow them keenly and you will see how angels from above come to your rescue to help you resolve the task you have been given and lead you to all the luck, laughter, and love you deserve. Stop procrastinating in the name of perfection.

When we are answerable to ourselves, we take life more seriously. But that doesn't mean we cease to exchange ideas. We must meet with people keeping a safe distance, socialize, empathize, communicate, collaborate, learn from each other, and do our *namostutee* (praise the divinity within each other).

Calcified, rigid thoughts lead to emotional agitation and overdose of calcium deposits in the bones causes much discomfort and stiffness. It is time to decalcify, soften, unknot, to become flexible, free, and stabilized. Beyond all strive, hardships, ordeals, and toil, there is abundant affluence, opulence, and glory waiting for you to taste the sweet nectar of its honey and milk. Just keep on believing.

Whoever said descending & falling is bad! Snowflakes are angels that fall into your life to bring change. Learn from the waterfalls that are perpetually falling yet break down and dissolve everything that comes in its way. You are that waterfall that never quits. It flows incessantly with unlimited energy and power to cleanse and detoxify your path as you descend before you reach your destination merging with the calm rivers and majestic oceans. With enlightened determination and strength like this nothing can come in your way for it is in your nature to blissfully go on flowing despite obstacles. However, a certain amount of force and self-restraint is mandatory else you will get hurt with the free fall.

How long will you be able to carry this load on your shoulders? For history is filled with souls who knew and could have done something, yet kept quiet and hidden from the truth.

The fifteenth month from when the first covid case started, we will feel the soft golden white light blessing us as our wounds start to heal.

You may invoke the blessings of higher beings to break down all the obstacles that block your path towards the realization of your aim. Once you have committed yourself to the service of Lord God, it is no longer your job to move the boulders; they will be moved for you. Life is easy and truly a bed of roses.

Your soul is like a firm stone-waiting to be uplifted so that it can internally dissolve and evolve. Underneath your darkness is your light. Your greatest weakness is your greatest strength craving to meet its purpose by transforming itself to ultimately merge with you.

However hard we all might try to look hardened on the exterior, we are inherently very gentle and loving on the inside. We all are almost the same.

No one is higher or lower than another. We all are incomplete without one another.

Affirm- 'Namostutee, I trust that behind the hard and fine exterior- my rare strength, passion, magnetism, purity, power, and sheer love will come out in the open. I feel safest when I am in my natural element. Here I am complete, royal, and grounded. Tathaastu.'

CHAPTER 57a

CURIOS

You can experience life even by looking closely at the different curios in your home and the art galleries. You will notice the stunning transparency and dynamism of energy. You will notice that everything moves, floats, vibrates, and captures light. We carry a visual experience of history and art through layers of what we see and imagine. These curios tell us a lot about the uniqueness and wonder of our evolvement. Time flies and yet comes back to us in the form of memories. The key to master time is to master gratefulness for all that has gone and all that has yet to come.

In earlier days, we used to play with stones by the river. Now we collect stones in the form of curios in our home. Stones have life, and so does every curio. You give them life by making them a part of your display shelf. These show objects instigate curiosity within us.

We are mortal but some of our creations are immortal. What we create impregnates other people's emotions and thoughts. It inspires others to indulge in another creative pursuit. Everything we create radiates our love and qualities.

Timeless is more powerful and greater than time. The metal sculptures and curios displayed in our homes exchange many hands but still look as fresh as new. They store the memory of all the history, science, and philosophy that has gone by. They have absorbed the rain of pain, love, appreciation, and strength into them. And yet they stand tall and firm. Each of these creations is the eternal form of God. Each of them has a unspeakable story to tell. These curious are much like the memories that tell us that nothing is new.

For example the statue of Tirupati in South India temple has so much dynamic life energy inherent in it. I went there to pray with my husband for a child and soon my son was conceived. It's almost like these deities can read your message even if you haven't written it.

A beautiful piece of art can freeze time and mysteriously take us back into the bygone eras in a matter of fleeting seconds. Some pieces of art have such lifelike expressions that they can be easily mistaken for real. Kudos to all those artists who create such beautiful forms with their creative intensity, focus, and clarity.

Everything and everyone is a divine gift from God, sent for your protection. Treat them with gentle care. Even the flawless crystal kept in your home has the potential to one day become an Avatar.

Affirm- 'Namostutee, I propel forward from stagnation to movement, from perplexity to clarity, from defiance to order, from morbidity to profitability. Tathaastu.'

CHAPTER 58

THE MOTORCYCLE

Was it my visit to the Pennsylvania Harley Davidson motorcycle factory? Or a peep show of God's perfection? I can't say for sure, but this is what I rode. As each part of the motorcycle was being installed, with such immaculate perfection, scrutiny, and detail, by the high-powered machines, I couldn't help but wonder how much effort, clarity, and creativity the mastermind behind the construction of such a genius engine must have been endowed with.

How many sleepless nights must have passed in sweat to give birth to each bike? How much heart and soul has gone into customizing each bike, hiring suitable team members and designers, winning their trust, loyalty, continuous collective assistance, and training them with an integrative approach, while coming up with newer innovative upgraded models for the market. It was impressive to see how wonderfully and patiently the company authority micro-manage, renew, and test the efficacy of every part of each product. It never misses a step during the entire process. Even a slight flaw, which might otherwise go undetected by the naked eye, is enough to fail the test and start all over again.

While all the other tourists were intrigued by looking at the styling, exteriors, and the uniqueness of the new model, I was biking in a parallel universe, picking up on the rising energies of the overall surroundings, trying to take on and understand the mystery and the delicacy of the airy messages they imparted. Much like the motorcycle, each of our parts and organs is painted, repainted, fixed, and repaired one by one, using small resilient nuts and bolts with springs attached, safely securing us firmly yet flexibly in position. We, humans, feel a lot more, unlike engines, which calmly allow the procedures as if under an anesthetic drug. Every cell and atom of our body has life in it, so we must tremble, screech, move, and disturb the flow of our creator's design during our creation! Yet seeing how much remains unknown and undiscovered about our own body, I can barely imagine the extent of calmness, precision, and deep focus it would require to build every vertebra, nerve, cell, vein, bone, muscle, skull, heart, lung, meridian, and then attach these to various layers of our fourfold reality. Only then can we travel free and beyond.

Like the unique code of each Harley Davidson bike, each of our color coatings and hues has its unique impression, ability, beauty, and essence.

The reason your progress seems slow is not that your plans are incomplete but because of your slow nature in implementing them. Stop over-stressing, overthinking & reviewing your decisions, goals, commitments, and business proposals again and again. Thoroughness and growth lie in first working extra hard to start the engine of your motor. Now is your turn to stop being overly carefree - convert your passion into practicality.

The choice is in your hands and you hold the start key. All you need to do is to press the accelerator with full enthusiasm. What lies ahead is freedom and independence.

Affirm- 'Namostutee, I am filled with vigor, joy, and determination to tirelessly, decisively, and consistently achieve my goals. I value and give importance to the purity of my work. I do not get distracted by the wavering thought forms and other influences. In this way, I can quickly overcome any challenges that come my way. Tathaastu.'

CHAPTER 59

SPIRITED HEARTS

Nothing can perturb a person who listens to his heart.

A spirited heart is a strong heart. Only a true empath can speak with the camera on. Through the camera an empath speaks with all, becoming one with all. Only such a person can touch the depth of your soul. Only the one who speaks from the heart can make you feel what you and the speaker feels to become one with you.

When two royal hearts sacredly meet, they are bound to take the throne and crown. Whether they rule with sword or pen, with horror or flexibility, with suppression or expression, with delusion or clarity, will determine how long the string will remain tied to the royal gown.

We are living in the spirit of liberty when we use our minds wisely. The Statue of Liberty was brought to America piece by piece over the last 100 years. Each piece has lived up to its name by enlightening the world physically, etherically, emotionally, mentally, economically, psychically, and astrally. Time has come, it will now justify the name of its last piece and honor the wreath it is wearing by enlightening us with spiritual liberty.

What happens in America, affects the world over. In the twin year 2020, America is inflamed with a situation where despite having all the liberty and freedom, its people are yearning to breathe freely. It is now that America will bow its head down in complete humility to acknowledge the seven chakras. Ask forgiveness from the seven continents across the seven seas. Its rays will shine through all these seven channels to enlighten the spirit, soul, body, mind of every being on this planet. In doing so, America and the world will rise again as a new super-spiritual world power. From that day on no soul will ever be chained again through personal insecurities, control and power but will freely bond through light of community love and friendship with the will of God, spreading cheer and laughter.

What we need is not 'armed forces' but 'life forces'. We have all the life but proper moral order and life force are missing. Let us get together and bring the Statue of Liberty to life. Let's make it real – let all of us freely breathe once again.

Today America's heart is inflamed with reddish-brown crimson hues but history tells us that the Statue of Liberty changed its color to mint green when it chose to exhale and generously give itself up to make another country shine. When the statue came from France to America, she knew that true power lies not in holding on but in giving and exhaling because that is love and where there is love - there is life.

The Statue of Liberty faces southeast direction - the direction of fire. This fire might have burnt our lungs but it cannot burn our spiritual hearts and the higher soul which is always ethical and free. As long as our collective spirit is alive, our higher soul will bring back the incarnated soul. There is unity within the trinity that can never be shattered or separated. We will once again breathe freely, this time with one and all.

By opening the heart, the crown chakra opens, and when that happens you feel as if you are born again. You feel you are in the same body, only smaller-as small as Thumbelina from the fable, or even smaller, like an ant who can see the whole universe and the view beyond the universe, and yet realizes its body is just a minuscule frame when one looks from the higher realms.

> Mercury changed to gold
> Never had they seen such a mold
> Perplexed by this new word
> For they thought intellect is always two-fold
> They had no clue what next was to be told
> The shine of the pearl on my bosom is but a glorious morning dew

He left a trace on me by his grace so that you can know face of few

Your heart lies in the center, between the lower and the higher, between the primordial and the spiritual. Your job is to keep yourself centered and balanced. Pinch your body, come back. Get back to your body, don't go far, spiritual in the physical, physical within the spiritual but both in the physical, for now, this is how it works.

From now on, after every four weeks and not every four months-tithe and give charity with full gratitude. There is more glory, power and purification in generously giving than in following any religion or faith. Then slowly turn those four weeks to every four days.

To preserve the wine (*blood*) is an art. First, learn the art before you restart. You were left with two lives, one life gone, only one is left- there are no more chances, but you have nothing to worry because a beating heart never exhausts itself, it goes on beating until it has the strength. Your strength is your power and your power is that one moment of silence. Reflect on that moment that has just passed. Remember to remember and then you will see yourself bounce back into life yet again. Having a good heart is great, but it must be backed with the willingness to ask and take what you deserve. To give is great, but excellence lies in switching on your receptive channels so that you can receive more to give more. Be assertive and give yourself priority while serving others. Stay balanced, circulate, and connect.

The key to spirituality is the heart chakra. Follow your heart, and the light in your soul will lead you to go where you are meant to go. It is the people with beautiful hearts who truly have great souls. Whatever they do, however big or small, they do it with their heart and love, and so it is bound to meet with the perfection that lies within them. A passionate heart is forever recharged and vitalized to do service and produce the results based on the targets set most creatively and dynamically. You need to deserve in order to serve. To want to serve is a mark of ultimate intelligence. To be able to serve is the greatest blessing.

There are no shortcuts in the world of spirituality. Spirituality is one school where you cannot force your way in through cheating, bribery, or malice. Spirituality is a grace reserved for the very few who are pure at heart and in their intentions.

In a society that offers a buffet of spiritual services, you may recognize a truly spiritual being by following main traits - A truly spiritual person is pure, universal, all-accepting, and saintly. Such a person is unbound and free of the distinction of caste, creed, race, sex, cult, or color. Having become one with its divine nature such a person not only heals but also teaches kindness, mutual respect, tolerance, compassion and reveals the underlying truth to those who are ready.

Through my higher self, when I transcended space, it became imperative for me to bring spiritual order into my life and those around me. When I transcended time, it became imperative for me to bring cosmic order into my life. This way, through me, I radiated the spiritual and cosmic order all around. Such is the divine grace, we all are endowed with. We choose to return only because deep down we know that to be here is the greatest blessing there is.

Most youths have indigo-ray energy-free, adventurous, and transformational spirited heart. As the world is transforming rapidly, it is becoming more and more comfortable for the indigos to freely express who they are without getting into trouble. The caregivers and guardians must gently and patiently empower and support the indigos to make their own choices. This way their inner fire will get ignited. But to do that the parents and teachers must first reflect, heal, and ignite their passions. Allow the spirit guides, angels, and higher beings to help by healing and balancing your soul energies. As you begin to trust these electric healing energies, everyone within the family will go through modifying change.

Affirm- 'Namostutee, A person of faith does not get consumed by fire. My endurance gives me the strength to remain steadfast, single-minded, and sober-minded even under the greatest trials, distractions, and tribulations of life. These tests sanctify my spirit, inspire, refine, and polish me into becoming more firm, righteous, humble, and patient by divine blessings and grace. I gladden my spirit and heart by dwelling in pleasant, joyful, and happy things life offers. Tathaastu.'

CHAPTER 60

BIRDS THAT FLY

Birds that fly do not dread change. A bird flies in the sky because she is too dainty and pure to walk on the roads amongst wolves clad in men's clothing. Otherwise, the angelic bird, not knowing the ways of the land, will be trampled under the next speeding car.

The mother bird, your fledglings are ready to fly. It is in taking that first flight, that first step that you allow the primary feathers to grow and strengthen. Let their instinct guide them. You can only help sharpen their skills and provide for them. You may pray but the prey is for them to catch. You can teach only as much as you know, and beyond this point, it is their journey. The flight is for them to take. The father bird will keep watch and simply let them fly.

There is no judgment day. You are your judge. You are the maker of your destiny. You choose every move and if you make a mistake, be sorry and just remember not to make it again.

I was once a bird flying high and mighty. Trigger happy, you shot me down twice. Time and space are a matter of subjective illusion for the evolving soul. And so, I came back as your wounded consort. You were kind and nice. I saw the care and remorse. I too learned where I was wrong. I learned to be humble and more giving. I see you are truly sorry, and now that I have forgiven, the karmic chain is broken. You are free to fly or be wherever, and with whomever, you wish to be.

True love is beyond form. It knows no bounds. When I was a bird, I used to fly from flower to flower to collect the sweet nectar. Not much has changed since then. I have stayed true to my nature, but I have also learned quite a bit in this grounded land. It has taught me balance and poise, and I know I have learned most of my lessons, for if I had not passed, I wouldn't have been promoted. Such is the law here or in any realm. Those who don't understand and practice the appropriate way of living repeat the class and follow the steps again and again, until they master the subject and build their strength. There is so much to do and so little time. There is such glorious beauty out there. Let's not miss it for a second more.

Some leaders and elders are sitting above. They are here to teach us harsh lessons by holding on to power and by not letting the ones with true light shine through. In the name of some petty gains, in the name of jealousy and lust, people who exploit you are also doing what they are supposed to do under divine guidance. But these actions are only to test our grit and determination. So stay as focused as an arrow on your path, and don't lose your mojo. In essence, no one but you are caging the bird (incarnated soul) that was meant to fly. You alone have caused yourself and all of mankind to dry up and be lifeless.

> Your negative, self -limiting beliefs are illusions. Heaven
> is in your mind and so is hell.
> You have to earn your wings if you want to fly,
> You have to earn your bread if you want to eat,
> You have to earn your freedom if you want to be free,
> Your freedom lies in freeing another.
> You are like a genie who can earn true freedom only by
> freeing another who is feeling blue.

Eagle is the king of all birds and is called the master of the skies because its power lies in its silence. Their eyesight is five times sharper than ours which makes them excellent hunters. They soar effortlessly to great heights and can see through the water. They glide down silently to grab their prey. Learning from the silence of the winds beneath their wings we all must try and develop a vision as sharp as them through concentration. Stay alert, vigilant, and weather all storms and emotions to reach your goal.

One day, an injured eagle was sitting on my father's car when he came out of his office. My father had to go for an important meeting but he decided to cancel his meeting because clearly, the eagle needed his attention. He tore his shirt, gently bandaged its wounds, and kept it in the backseat of his car. On the way, he stopped by various vets to see if they could help but to no avail. Finally, he went to the school my mother was working at and requested her if the school nurse could tend to the eagle until he finds a suitable doctor to treat the delicate wounds. The school had a little zoo for the kindergarten students so the principal of the school, my mother, agreed to this strange request. My parents wrapped a cozy blanket around its fragile feathers to keep it comfortable and cozy and arranged for specialists to assess and heal the eagle's wounds. Thanks to the continued effort, the eagle recovered and as soon as it healed completely, my parents set it free to fly far away.

Many months went by and one day my mother saw a big eagle on the window of her schoolroom. She thought to herself, could it be the same eagle? But how is that possible as the eagle didn't know where the office window was. The pattern continued for many days. One day my mother went closer to the window and looked at its eye, she then knew it was the same eagle but couldn't figure out why it was coming again to meet with her.

After a few days, the eagle vanished for many more months. A day came, my mother was walking in the park outside our home and saw many baby eagles flying above. Seeing them she was reminded once again of the eagle. She went home after her walk and to her surprise saw the very eagle at the glass window of her bedroom this time. She thought to herself - it can't be the same eagle as our home is at quite a distance from the school and the eagle had never visited our home earlier.

The pattern continued for a few days. My mother took my father for a walk with her to introduce the flying baby eagles to him. Being a lover of nature, my dad knew at once that the eagle had come to thank them for all the care and love and brought her babies for blessings. Had my father not driven her that evening, the eagle would still have been paralyzed and perhaps dead. He gave her life and she, in turn, gave him gratitude and faith. Those who fly, know the power of love and gratitude. Many years have gone by and one of its feathers still hangs on the glass window of our home. I wonder if the eagle lost it or purposely left it as a reminder to tell us to remember the past as happy memories stay forever.

When your heart becomes as light as a feather, you relate to the feathers so much that you see them everywhere. Nowadays, the best moments of my days are when I go with my son by the lake and we have a feather collecting competition. Each feather gives you hope for a better tomorrow.

Reach a place where if you ever ask yourself, "Who am I?" you can answer "I am someone who can fly, swim and float freely anywhere I please." I am always on a vacation, I travel everywhere without lifting my Greek feet.

Sometimes the experiences of the inner worlds can get perplexing! For example, the phoenix bird is trapped within us, no wonder they are extinct!! And if this is how it is then what human anatomy have we been learning in science class? The Phoenix bird is like the eagle that flies higher than any bird and has vision eight times sharper than humans. It courageously stretches its limits and expands its wings to fly high and be free.

Our mind is like the wise eagle that is capable of flying higher than our bodily limitations and has the vision to travel the eight realms with resilience and patience. A wise mind courageously stretches its limits and expands consciousness to know higher perspectives so that we can lift our spirits and be free.

Liberty is the constant struggle of seeking the truth.

Experience and infliction are great teachers. It is liberating to be free from all agonies. It is liberating to work as a group and love one another. To fly is to expand your consciousness. Do not let the change limit you.

Whenever I look out of my window I see beautiful, colorful flocks of blue and red-winged birds visiting us from the heavens. They fill my soul with hope, romance, and inner harmony. This chapter is an ode to the 10,000 cherished species of angelic birds that fly around us. These little, wise angels are our spiritual messengers. Feeding them is like feeding our guardian angels. We are like a flightless bird who prefers living in self-delusion rather than know that everything is but an illusion. Convert your misery into freedom and take the next fascinating flight.

Those who pursue the quest of truth soar high with their chest and head rising above the emotional waves of wavering minds.

Birds that fly know fully well that they cannot carry their wife, son, wealth, possessions, or ideas with them when they die/ when they fly - this psychological realization is what gives them the wings to fly.

Corruption is being tied to your fixated ideas, community, religion, political opinions. Attachment leads to corruption.

When you know what doesn't matter - you get to know what truly matters. All this theory is of no use until you practice it. When you practice - you experience it. It is when we let some of our feathers fall that we give hope to others. Those who do not hold on to their broken wings and fallen feathers - truly fly.

On one hand, we say that the soul age doesn't matter, and on the other hand, we restrict sharing the higher sacred knowledge and spreading the teachings for the greater good. A bird gathers food and feeds the little nestlings. No bird ever competes with helpless babies or keeps the food to herself. It is in the nature of the songbird and its hatchlings to come out and sing with or without proper schooling. You may clip the wings of one or two but no matter how much you try, you cannot stop all these spirited heavenly birds from flying.

Many dainty birds camouflage themselves behind the green leaves on tall trees. Some conceal their intuitive insight, for far too long, not because they are not ready but because no one lets them fly higher than the tree upon which they are nested. The new age baby birds know better than to limit their dreams. And so they freely fly.

> Intelligence is another name for discipline.
> Freedom over fear.
> Discipline over wisdom.
> Peace over war.
> Order over peace.

Under your armpits, there are two energy points. These empty your heart and enable you to finally fly like an eagle.

Affirm- 'Namostutee, I trust that the birds are little angels that descend from the higher heavens as messengers who double our fortune, grace, hope, peace, and freedom. Tathaastu.'

CHAPTER 61

PAUSE BUTTON

Even when the whole world is slowing down and embracing the pause, some of us are still busy running after something not knowing where and what. There are very few who live in the now, the now can only be lived in its perfection once we give it proper attention, care, importance, undivided attention, concentration with complete precision. Now is fragile, handle it with care, harness it with love.

The onset of 2020 marks another era. It is the conscious shift of energy and the birth of what has happened in the last 10 decades. The first year of the new decade and decades that have long passed and so it is not simply another new year. It is the year of rebirth and renewal. It is time to pamper, protect, trust, care, and love.

Forgive, forget, and move on. This war is long over. You are entering a year of true bliss with the active principle of perfect number ten for the first time. The combined energy of the trinity - each being distinct - light (fire - red), sound (air - green) and electricity (ether - electric violet) is our creator. The inner fire within us comes from fire. The electric currents in our body come through the ether and the life-giving breath comes from the air. If the etheric energy gets affected then the physical gets affected.

Align your thoughts, words, and action with your true purpose. It is no longer the words alone that will matter but it is your actions through your thoughts that will speak your truth. Let us bring out the best in everyone as we are reborn within the circle dance of this ultimate cosmic coincidence.

2020 heralds the time for perennial divine connection. True wisdom lies in not giving up in the face of challenges. What you see around us today is the plasma of the sun that is getting ready to enable the rebirth of consciousness on earth. It is as if small suns have swiftly descended upon us to fill the air with dynamism and brilliant glow. This is the ultimate protector and elixir of life.

Inner and outer turmoil doesn't shake the bliss or divert the attention of a soul realized person. The presence and blessings of such evolved beings on earth can improve the health of the inner and outer etheric environment. Such a being is capable of pacifying, magnetizing, and vitalizing the energy of higher realms with its love and transmutable ability.

Pressing the pause button is important because it is in this pause that the secrets of universal oneness and love come out of the closets. During the pause, all the excess restlessness of the mind and body settle so that the soul can get some time to unwind and connect with you.

One immediate effect of meditation is that it helps center and calm you. It helps you focus, destress, set your intentions clear, and balance your energies. It helps you visualize, manifest, and feel the interconnectedness. But, nowadays there is a new kind of stress brewing within people - it is called the stress of acquiring peace.

Stillness is hidden behind restlessness
Movement is hidden behind restlessness
Clarity is hidden behind the movement.

Eventually, there is nothing hidden anymore. As such stillness leads you to clarity. This is because when stillness and movement make peace with one another- lightning strikes.

If it is windy, the persistent banging of the door disturbs you. All you need to do is stop getting perturbed. Get up and latch the door. More often than not we are scared and disturbed because of a noise that can be easily blocked. Relaxing and resting peacefully inside the safe haven of your home despite the storm and noise outside is after all not as difficult as it seems.

Similarly, we have no reason to get alarmed with the cold emptiness we feel as the planetary storms or as the lightning engulfs us. This is because we are cradled in the strong arms of the spiritual gurus, divine beings, and pure souls, joyful friends, loving parents, innocent children and a beautiful heart that will hold us steady as would the latched doors in a storm. Those who are connected and one remain unperturbed and calm.

To know what true fulfillment really is, try to go on an inward search and know your own self. The more you hold onto the transitory nature of life, the more unfulfilled you will feel. Always be aware and open to learning.

We are all evolving from lower to higher within the same body. We are evolving from the idea of separation into unity and oneness. From wisdom to knowledge. This is an ideal time to reflect, detoxify, and plan. Time to restart, recharge, and renew your lifestyle.

Hear the underlying message, because you cannot do anything unless you free yourself of all collywobbles. Shed all unwholesome thought forms and do not let your dense body become pregnant with negative vibrations.

The first part created right after conception is the navel or tej. All our veins and meridians are connected to our navel. This is why it is the focal point of our consciousness strength. There is a *Pechoti* gland behind the navel. It houses more than 72,000 veins and millions of nerves. The navel is called the belly button or the second brain. When you pause and lightly press this button, you can manage pain better and relax. Being in the center of the body, pressing this pause button centers you, unlocks the parasympathetic nervous system, loosens internal tension, stress and improves digestion.

A year has four quarters, each having three months. Three quarters have passed and the last remains. Take my advice, use the lifeline you have left, get centered, and do not let the rumors and outer chaos affect your inner peace. Remain within the safe haven of your home until all months completely pass. Trust yourself and build your fate. Your destiny is on your fated feet. Only the last phase remains, stay grounded, and protected.

This pause is here to wake you up from your deep sleep. It is time to concentrate, muster, and reignite your inner strength & fire. It is time to rise, wake up, and move your body so that you can truly shine.

Affirm- 'Namostutee, I get glimpses of God's divinity through seeing and acknowledging the divinity within each of you. I align my chakras and myself with you so that we all can together enjoy a greater vision and power of God's might. I am powerful only because I shine my true light both for myself and for the greater good of all. Tathaastu.'

CHAPTER 62

GAMES WE PLAY

We purposely erase, unlearn, reduce, restrict and limit ourselves under rules and regulations so that we can learn, return, expand, perfect, appreciate, liberate, stimulate and know our purpose, truth, and limitlessness.

Giddy-up at the speed of a racehorse ready to go for the games. Games are a refreshing mental bath and mental exercise. Everything happens at its pace at the right earth time and the right place. We are all busy playing the divine earthly game of dice. Here each of us takes our turns at the dice. You can roll as many times you want for your turn. Eventually, each of us gets the same number of turns. Every game has rules and order. Every player must get their rightful turn.

It is not God but you who is squandering all your wealth in playing this game. How well you play is up to you. The choice is yours, not his. This too is your responsibility, not his. As part of being a good player, we have a whole set of invisible subtle tasks lying before us that come to interplay, most of us know nothing about these gentle cosmic forces or choose to not know! That is when adversity sets in unless of course, the invisible loving force of fate helps change your course. You have got another chance so now play it right, the creative forces are always watching whether you take responsibility backed with lovability or not. In this game of chance neither side ever will win, all you can do is continue to roll for that is your very purpose. I know this because 'I am that dice' that you are holding for eons. There is ultimate divinity within responsibility. It is you not God who is playing this delusional game of dice with you. The choice is yours to play or not. There is a certain quality in duty that is not filled with the madness of vanity. When desire becomes an addiction you risk everything for the roll of a dice, if only it was all a mere fiction.

It is our ethical and spiritual responsibility to accept one another and let the other win for when winning becomes a monotony, it turns to gluttony and your karma sure will not support such absurdity.

For some, life is like a luxurious game of golf. You keep getting closer and closer to your goal before your ball hits the target of perfect truth. To get what you want you need to get past your fears of feeling ashamed or burnt should you lose the game that you love with so much passion and zest. To reach your target you have to focus and rise beyond these self-inflicted emotional challenges and to up the game you need to be playing and connecting with the right kind of contacts. A person who plays to win subtly influences the people around to change and improvise with each Godly game that he plays. A true golfer is open to defeat as he is winning. He blows a flying kiss to his balls with complete Godfidence and dares to stick to his guns, focusing his strength and energy on simply enjoying the pleasure of the riches that playing this sport in the bountiful greenery of nature bestows upon him rather than spending time in night clubs, strip malls and drinking bouts for he knows very well where the abundance of his heart & soul truly rests.

You are a divine being and a being endowed with divinity you enjoy whatever comes your way. Realizing we all are simply playing a game and each of us will ace this game at one point or another. We have a herd mentality around the interests we inculcate. It is as if everyone has the same interests/ likes. No one is trying to find where their true interests lie. Struggles have become a thing of luxury and ease is the biggest growing pandemic. Yet we blame our youth for looking so bored and disinterested!

Board games and imagery like the golden goose from our ancient roots have lots to tell us. Games like goose, chess, and snakes and ladders must always be enjoyed, played, and taught by every parent to their children.

Enjoy being the actor, acting, and all the action with complete equanimity and with non-attachment. Learn the lessons from all your wins and losses, especially the tricks. Who said winning is easy? Even losing is enjoyable as long as you are participating.

We all are living a Jenga with three lives (chances), if one dies, all eventually die. Mind, body, and soul go together. Old becomes young and young becomes old in this dangerous yet exciting game of body and soul. You must not start completely identifying yourself with the games you play.

We have played Chinese whispers excessively over past eons that no more of this passé whispering game is played. We live in a world where the touch of your lover's hand and the language of love seems to have lost its meaning. This is because we are living in the textual world of typo errors and smartphone language. We hardly see anyone enjoying the subtle feel, sensual passes, and the mistakes we make in love. In the name of excellence, our thoughts are translated and edited into confusing words even before we begin to type what our story means to us.

How much you win depends upon how much you are ready to lose. In every loss, there is a hidden win. Just as in every day there is a hidden night. Once you open yourself up to the light, the night will become day.

The purpose of playing the game of dumb-charades is not only to guess the outside clues and events but to realize that only in silencing your outer words, you can listen to your inner thoughts. A game of charades where the audience can easily guess the word that the actor enacts shows the perfection of the actor. The audience who can see through the imperfection and guess the word shows the perfection of the keen eye and judgment. Life is one big game of dumb-charades with many obvious clues left by the dumb actor for the audience to guess and speak. Guess we are also wearing blindfolds on our eyes along with the masks taped on our mouths with the onset of coronial waves. Anything is possible with the right mindset and deep faith.

Affirm- 'Namostutee, I expect more from myself, I embrace newness with open arms and mind. I do what makes me happy and in this way my growth is exponential and I harmoniously put all my dreams in motion. I creatively bring more value to the meaning of truth, honesty, relationships, and morality. Tathaastu.'

CHAPTER 63a

MAHJONG

Life is like a game of Mahjong. If you want to play it right, you have to play by the rules. You have to get organized and learn how to create order out of the everyday chaos of life. And as we play the game of life, much like mahjong, we must stay focused and centered on our true purpose while interacting and mingling with all those around us. This truth stands, whichever year or era our card may belong to. So prioritize, stay balanced, and stay aware. Mahjong sharpens mental capabilities. The best way to increase your skill at mahjong is to play it. The best way to increase your life skills is to practice them.

In American Mahjong tiles, there are 166 tiles, much like the chapters in this book. In these tiles the characters represent ever-changing human life, bam/bamboo represents the earth's axis and dots/circles represent heavenly *chakras* or wheels. The three dragons represent the three virtues - green for sincere, white for devoted, and red for kind - the three basics of good character. Four winds represent four cardinal directions, flowers represent the changing seasons based on moods of different locations, the jokers urge you to lighten up and adjust to the multi-purposeful comedy of life to connect with your inner child bringing in renewed excitement.

Some people are happily playing the game of Mahjong by themselves. This way they win and lose with themselves. They break the rules and set the rules as per their comfort. They are ok losing at times so long as the game is played solo. This is their way of making the game easy. They do not have to worry about other people's comments, judgments, advice, or for that matter how they play, cheat, or learn. They do all this to avoid the stress of making a small decision of throwing the tile they are holding with courteous, pure, and clean intention.

How we play games tells a lot about our personality. How we speak tells a lot about our thoughts. Unless we do not open ourselves to learning how to handle this stress, we never evolve. We happily parrot our own words and no one counter attacks or questions because we are playing by our rules, by ourselves, and within our walls.

You may replace mahjong with Lego, cards, monopoly, money, and properties we own, or any other games humans like to play. You will find, they are as if trying to run away from making difficult decisions. The decision requires them to cut down on a lot of things they are comfortable believing in. They do not like to cut down and let go of their thought forms and attachments. This way they slowly isolate themselves from the rest. The only way we can meet with our creator, our higher mental or Buddha consciousness is through proper decision making, irrespective of what game we choose to play.

Affirm- 'Namostutee, may all people in the world spiritually reawaken, be steadfast in their service, be divinely connected and united. Tathaastu.'

DUCK LUCK

Keep it together, illusion and reality are not always meant to be one for when the two get together, it can get highly intimidating for some. Handle yourself with care.

The moon is simply an illuminated[68], shining, and spirit body having a limited boundary.

For example, look at these numbers, and play a mental game of snakes (represented by the number 2) and circles.

>02020
>20202
>02020
>20202
>02020

And you will see that upward, downward, sideways, or straight - these numbers are a perfect palindrome every way, just the way the moon is a palindrome of the sun. Looking at 2020, it seems that Sun (*sah or su* which also means perfect soul in Sanskrit) and moon (*moh* which also means illusion in Sanskrit) have finally met, after years of unease and separation. Both are happy to be back in their natal home. Both are headed to be in a state of complete equanimity, infinite bliss, and oneness. They are the twin flames.

---

[68] *Illuminated - In Sanskrit il means body, lu means division, mi means limited boundary and nat means the shining spirit.*

In the above palindrome game – 0 symbolizing the moon – the above would represent that you have won since you have 0's diagonally placed and in order.

There is no way you can cross the moon (also known as *ma/ maha*[69] / *ham*) in the new age game of snakes and circles, without encountering its confusing nature (refer to the chapter –SOSO).

Ham or moon is one with all, all its phases have merged into one. The dense, visible reality and the subtle, invisible creativity now reside in one body.

12 transformational hours from AM to PM:

We all have heard the story of the goose that laid golden eggs: the moral states 'Those who have plenty want more and so they risk losing all they have.' Humanity is the fortunate golden egg that the goose has laid. It has all the blessings and still is emotionally unhappy, unsatisfied, and ungrateful for what it has and so humanity risks losing all it has if we do not learn to praise, trust and love the goose from whence it came.

As an example, New York is one such golden egg that the goose laid. It has all the comforts and still, its air is contaminated with draining thoughts of despair, grief, and sorrow from what it went through nineteen years back when its twin towers were inflamed. If we collectively do not learn to forgive, accept and release our past trauma then all this hatred and negativity in the air will continue to block, overwhelm and inflame the corona-ry arteries in the twin chambers of our heart.

The voice of stillness is never really silent. I woke up from deep sleep last night and looked at the time. It was 33 minutes past 3 am in New York. Twenty-eight days had passed since the first pandemic case, even the friendly ducks in my suburban yard were intelligently attempting to bring luck to us by prayerfully quaking. Duck down is the new name for lockdown. Just duck a little longer and then rise later to open up your heart to luck. The ticking clock is reminding you to lock down in your golden homes because being out will ruffle up your dainty feathers and tear them up even before you have found the key to fly.

---

[69] *Interestingly reverse of maha is aham which is same as saying that the reverse of spirit is the self*

I crossed the illusionary barriers of time and space and found myself in yet another plain. I was now in Spain. A gap of six hours between New York and Spain and the need to heal prompted me to go there even without an airplane. Spain is in horrific pain and it seems to have lost all hope simply because the name ends in pain. The message I left there "S-pain stands for strength that comes out of pain, this strength will lead you to rise above pain with praise, faith, and resilience. I know you all will rise from your sleep. I will then see you all on the other side of the rainbow bridge."

Back in New York, the time was still 3 am but twelve transformational hours had passed since I planted the seed thought-one is all, love is all. Through the mirror of the world, I get to know myself, through knowing myself I know thyself. Through knowing thyself, I know all.

Following the steps of confinement requires you to let go of control, attachments, and habits. Develop patience, stillness, and resilience, and maybe staying indoors to preserve your life is better than dying a causeless death!

2020 is like traveling in the inner world. You do not let dreams, movies, and nightmares distract your physical life. Similarly, your greatest test is to stay centered emotionally and mentally despite the distractions of the outer world this year. It is like a real-life television series being played out. After a while, we learn not to get afraid of the movies and the shows we watch. These are enacted for our sheer entertainment. Still your mind, practice equilibrium, awareness, and virtue of self-restraint during these trying times of heightened, magnified energies at all levels.

Affirm- 'Namostutee, We all are one consciousness. I am you. Tathaastu.'

CHAPTER 63c

SOSO

This is a new game.

We have played "XOXO" (nuts and crosses) for far too long. I have invented a new game called 'SOSO'.

'Soul self' and 'others oriented' are two ways people seek and search for the truth. The balance lies not in the extremes of 'SS' or 'OO' but in 'SOSO'. And so this game bridges the gap between being excessively 'self-oriented' (SO) and being overly concerned about 'other souls' (OS). We connect the two in waveform instead of the straight lines that are used in nuts and crosses.

The idea is to bring excitement into the subtle SOSO fair living, through this simple game. A SO-SO approach is neither good nor bad but it is right. It is in neither of the two ends of being overly self-oriented or overly others oriented but affirms a gentle, polite approach of silent optimism through reflecting on the forms of two most beautiful numbers or letters 'S & O'.

The outward form of ducks, swans, geese, ropes, serpents, humans, infinity, the number 5, or inverted 2, the first letter of Spider-Man, Superman, spirituality, synchronicity, supreme, and single- all highlight the mystery behind "~" (which is also the mathematic symbol for negatives) of life.

The form of 'whole world' and the 'empty hole' begins and ends with O. It is the most liberating letter and number and to me, it denotes perfect oneness of light and dark, form and formless, big and small, birth and death, inner and outer, emptiness and fullness, dreams and reality, expansion and contraction. Simply dwelling on the forms of these two letters, even without knowing what they denote- brings completeness, acceptance, healing, and clarity in our minds, and hence I present to you the novel and unique game of SOSO. Everything beautiful comes in pairs and so the game requires two players who pick a form S or O and then take turns until they reach SOSO on the 4 x 4 chart. A perfect home much like this game is built upon a square ground plan by a subtle feminine force. It denotes staying protected through heaven on earth upholding harmony, virtue and freewill.

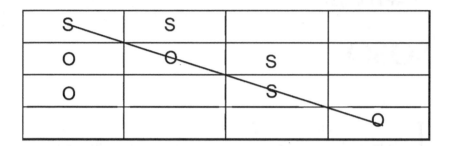

The winner has to say a full meaningful sentence having any of the following words - "SOSO; SOS; and So; So So; So; 'If - then - so' statements, in it for the game to continue.

Here are a few examples with which you can formulate the sentences - 1.) May we all be healed, so be it. 2.) SoSo is the new yes. 3.) And so it all began. 4.) He loves me and so do I. 5.) So on and so forth - and in this way, you may go on adding your reflective ideas. Remember the key lies in expressing every statement in a fun way.

The 'S' (inner foundational self) is within the 's' (empirical self). Understanding that the two are bound together, leads us to a better understanding of our reality 'O' (observational world), which is a combination of higher sciences 'o' and art 'o' of outer health through inner healing.

Affirm- 'Namostutee, Lord God protects and shields us from all circumstances and situations. Lord God keeps us safe and sends us grace from behind, above, right, left, below, and all the remaining sides. Tathaastu.'

CHAPTER 64

THE CORONALISM of the CORONIAL ERA

We have come a long way from **colonial to coronial era** - from control and bondage to peace and freedom.

The inner and outer world--angels, birds, humans, and animals--are so closely intertwined and synchronized. I went for a walk. The air was filled with the crowding sound of crows cawing. They said the human scientists call them 'corono-ides' and 'Corvid corone'. The magpies and jays sang in praise of the cawing crows, for not only are they intuitive, mystical, and self-aware, but true to their name, they also warn when corona is coming. 'Corvid corone' is another name for crows. These were identified in Greek and Norse mythology as wise messengers who knew everything that happened in the world and were associated with prophecy.

Spiritual people spend years retreating into the Himalayan caves, not getting perturbed by the disturbance of the outside world or realizing how much time has passed. They dedicate themselves to bless and heal the people to make the world a better place with the power of their radiating energy which is not limited by space or time. We too can treat our homes as a retreat in the Himalayas and spend this time blessing our world. Spirituality shows you the superficialities of both thought and matter. It shows us how petty we have made our life by attaching ourselves to the heavens or the earth. There is no division between the two. Both higher and lower realms are within you. One without the other is incomplete and unholy. Everything is innately interconnected.

You do not belong to any religion, any sect, custom, culture, subject, age but - the religion of truth, love, and compassion. If you cannot be the reason for someone's smile, at-least resolve never to be the reason for someone else's tears.

Our visions are designed in a way that we cannot see certain objects just the way an elephant cannot see the little ant but that doesn't mean the ant doesn't exist. We cannot see the pain but it still exists. Whenever we encounter pain and crisis, we become better at what we do, we come out stronger, more decisive, forgiving, and compassionate. Even the most poisonous snake hisses to tell us it is going to attack. If we do not treat the warning seriously and the snake bites, it is not really the fault of the snake but ours. If we choose not to get into our homes, we willed the wrath upon ourselves. If we are not following the self-quarantine rules despite the warnings, the fault is ours. To forgive and to bless is to be wise and fearless. Let us become wise and sensible as the time is little and all we have to do during this time is quite literally nothing. Doing absolutely nothing is the cure. Let us not disturb the stillness and trust that the higher energies will take care of you and me. Nothing can kill you unless you decide to die. If the will of the soul is to live, there is nothing that can come in the way of its life. If you send out love, there is nothing that will not melt with the vibrations of your love.

Without your creative juices, you are living a half-life. A cow that stops giving milk is slaughtered. So stay inspired, no matter what your age. A mother never stops giving milk to her calf.

We go out in search of inhabiting other planets without a blink of an eye but when our planet is shaken due to cracked webs in the cosmic egg, we realize that may be all that search was not the best thing to do. Humanity must collectively do something to convert the crude wreath it has been wearing into a dainty jeweled crown that the halo around you truly deserves.

Pain and suffering is a transitory phase. Nothing can harm a person who is in the quest for ultimate truth and perfection through service. Nothing can harm the one who relentlessly heals and teaches morals - cleanses and purifies the whole environment with fragrant jewels. Just like the Sun rays fall equally on everyone, community love or treating everyone equally is important.

We stay exposed to the sun rays in order to stay warm and vitalize ourselves but we are not foolish to touch the sun. The Coronavirus has taught us to keep a safe distance and stop playing with fire.

Soulmates can be many or just one but they are never identical. Joining them up can therefore take many lifetimes. There could be two people absolutely in love. One could be at a level where bodies make love, the other at a level where souls make love. Both are beautiful versions of the same love yet one without the other is incomplete. It takes two to tango and so true love is an amalgam of bodily and soul connect. Never question why it never worked out in this lifetime. Until both are not ready, it doesn't work out. Both have to interact at a divine soul and physical level. Soulmates are like the Lego pieces my son plays with. The same parts can be arranged in many different ways, playing different roles to interact with each other. No one person can help you find that missing part, the process does not work that way.

I told my husband once that love is in you and me, love is in the son we gave birth to and so we never run out of it and the chain goes on. We go through all the wonderful transformations until eternity before love happens. Same way, my son went through all his wonderful inner transformations until nine months before he was born into the outer world.

Distance is not isolation but makes love grow fonder, not lesser.

When even the idea of acquiring a materialist item became so painful, I gave it all up. The day that an object of enjoyment becomes a cause of pain rather than joy, it means it is high time to give it all up or no longer give it that much credence.

Our higher senses develop when we cease to touch life only through tactile methods of physical touch. With this we will develop our *jnana* (understanding the quality of fire, ether, earth, water, air elements in our five senses of eyes, ears, nose, tongue, and skin respectively) and *karma indriyas*, both being five in number. To hold, to walk, to defecate, to enjoy sexual pleasure, and to speak are the five *indriyas*. Learning is a transformational phase that leads to ultimate liberation. Always be open to learn new ways of learning, loving, and giving.

We are united, not divided. What affects your breath, also affects another. We all breathe the same air then how can we inhale different thoughts. It is time we speak the same language - the collective language of love, understanding, acceptance, harmony, compassion, patience, growth, peace, happiness, faith, continuity, oneness, and evolvement. Stop criticizing and blaming one another in a world where all are part and guilty of the same crime. The old go-to give way to the new. To die is to reborn, it is the cycle of life. Detach yourself from entanglements of birth and death to renew yourself and all those around you.

You are making a hill out of a molehill, lighten up–enjoy as life is like a mirror which looks best when you perpetually smile at it. Difficulty and pain fade in the face of humor. On judgment day, it is not those with a heavy heart but those with hearts as light as a feather who will fly to the heavens. Your true face teaches you to constructively make fun of yourself and enjoy the humor. The mask you are wearing brings about ego and attachments.

My brother in law got bitten by an ant that caused his body to swell and itch. While people were fighting Coronavirus, his strength, faith, and stamina were being tested by ant powers[70]. Doctors were only taking corona cases and so none attended to his pain. He fought it with comedy and seeing the humor in the situation, he activated his self-healing powers. Only if we all too see the lighter side of the situation and not get scared, guilty, or anxious when confronted with challenges we face, we would realize our body can heal by itself and fight off any situation. Build your mental immunity, no pain is so big that your mind can't cure.

We all are endowed with beautiful minds. Our mind is our power. Illnesses are not caused if we use our mind but it is caused when we misuse our mind. We are meant to utilize our brainpower but not to abuse it with grim and junk thoughts. In the same way we are meant to utilize our body and nourish it with constant movement and good food rather than abuse it with inaction and junk food. This heralds us the beginning of an era of wholesome physical and mental health. In this era, we will no longer let our emotional worries, anxiety, weaknesses, or apprehensions spoil the rhythmic flow of our blood and chi energy.

Recently a couple in India named their twins covid and corona, as the boy and girl were born during the lockdown.

The new age is a new story of beginnings. The understanding of the story will change the course of the entire history. In realizing that the eventful circumstances under which people meet for specific purposes is a meeting not arranged by us, but by a mysterious force far bigger than you and me, you will be able to, bit by bit, celebrate the gifts of life and unravel a lot within you that is currently entangled.

The total number of blood vessels we have in our body is equal to double the circumference of the earth. No matter how we view it, this fact

---

[70] *Ant powers- ants can withstand 5000 times an ant's body weight. Ant bites can sometimes be life threatening and very toxic. Its venom can be as powerful as their strength.*

remains. It is just that, things sometimes seem bigger than they are because we amplify them. Such is the era that we are living in, where anything and everything is amplified out of proportion.

Negativity and separation have always been there, now surfacing even more than before. The reason it is coming to the forefront is for you to see so that you can transform to a higher level.

Our mission is perfection in action. Nothing will be as it was before.

Just as a child learning to sleep by itself away from motherly love and cuddles is overwhelmed for the first time we all will learn to maneuver our energy with the growing demands of the world. The world is fraught with newer, superior, and technological advancements causing detachment and self-attachment. Beyond fear, there is only victory. Stay balanced, follow moderation, and enjoy the change.

The survivors of coronavirus will remember to praise and thank the oxygen they breathe before every breath. From carnivorian to coronavorian to herbivorian- these uncertain unsettling times have finally settled us. April and May 2020 were the most crucial months for coronavirus. Post that a new virus that has been slowly spreading will take its toll on people. It is called Moronavirus. It is the virus morons spread because of excessive panic, fear, and anxiety. Every attempt to explain the cause is moronic because a moron cannot know the implications of Moronavirus on the Coron (crown).

Congested lungs cause pneumonia, pneuma means life force. When you inhale, you have to exhale. Lungs that are not able to exhale get congested in energy. Congestion causes us to not breathe freely. As a precaution, freely exhale - emotionally, financially, physically, spiritually, and mentally. Control negative lower emotions as they affect the pineal gland and the adrenal glands. We have everything yet love, contentment, and respect are missing. Let us resolve to heighten higher emotions of love because love is everything.

Once you feel it everything around you turns beautiful, you see the divine angel in everyone.

Today when the world is at a standstill, it is time for us to introspect and ask ourselves what is it that I have to exhale. Is it our closets or storage cabinets that need cleaning or is it our emotions, knowledge, wealth, and poverty. Ask yourself what lesson is this situation teaching you? What are you learning from it and what are you going to do about it? What do I have to exhale?

The cells of Earth's upper organs are congested, blocked, and imbalanced and need collective comfort through the positive radiating energy that can emanate from each of us. Let's extend its age, let's dissect the aftertaste of the cake we have been eating piece by piece and then integrate it into another transmuted version which turns out even sweeter. In this time of transition, the Lord God is sitting right next to you, disguised in many different forms, to uplift those who are ready. So be truly considerate, gentle, and compassionate in your words, actions, and deeds, to yourself and to one and all.

It takes a lifetime of commitment to enjoy and understand the essence and benefits of community living and ownership. It is that feeling when your child is equally mine as it is yours, where we all are co-parenting everyone's child within that community with equal regard, responsibility, and generosity.

We are not centered only on our own little cocooned shell. In a community that has no barriers, trust brings security. This is what makes everyone and everything go around. It is what brings in feelings of belongingness. So why do we have these barriers, why these walls? Just open your doors and trust that your home is safe, for that little lock outside your front door is not going to stop the committed burglar. The key you left in your car is not what made the robber steal it. It is the frequency of the fearful thought you carelessly gave out that got it stolen. Trust and let go of mental control, and you will find that there are no mistakes; there is no carelessness, no hunger, and no poverty. All the wealth in the world belongs to the higher power as much as it belongs to your higher self. It is for all to share and all to have.

Beyond fear, there is the only victory. Stay balanced, follow moderation, and enjoy the change and you have nothing to panic about. Movies when watched for the first time and the energies of certain characters we interact with can temporarily leave us feeling intense, emotional, overwhelmed, and suspicious but with a little bit of silent reflection, we realize that thankfully even though the movie and reality might have a resemblance, the two are never the same. As long as we practice moderation, awareness, detachment, right living, and discipline, we can snap out of these make belief associations and fancy imaginations only to return to our divine, alert, vitalized, balanced, and healthy self.

We all are watching the same movie, but the seats allotted to each soul are inherently different and so no two people have the same view or access.

The corona lightning that has struck the world today is telling you to remember the secret that is buried deep within the core of your heart. Listen to the cries of your inner child. Remove all resistance. Love, support, and nurture that aspect and part within you, which you stopped paying attention to. Bring back the outer balance through the inner calm.

This Cororonorian race - the coronial era shouldn't last beyond 2025. The first phase created shock across all levels. The second phase compelled you to hold on to your possessions, attachments, and hoard even more. The third phase caused your inner anger and frustration to come out in the open. Soon you realize it is never the outside but what goes on the inside of you that attracts the pain or pleasure. You begin to let go of some aspects that do not serve you. As these high and low imbalanced waves settle within you, the fourth phase causes your fear to convert into fearlessness and distress into peace. In the fifth stage, you resolved to remove the pandemic from its very root. You hope that the pollution of the inner and outer environment ceases to cause you and your loved ones any more trouble and imbalance. Finally, you realize there is always something bigger than you that slaps us all. This is because it is high time we get more disciplined. Lord Yama is not death. Yama only comes to check if you are following the *niyama* which is the rule of life. Rules are self-restricting ethical rules established for right living and conduct.

In this stage, we must begin to live the intentions we set out for ourselves. The time has now come for you to go out there and practically master each one of those intentions (for self and others) during the introspective year of 2020. May each year (2021 to 2025) bring a new dimension of light and heighten our collective vibrations so that henceforth humanity as a whole becomes a community with perfect immunity:

2021 – Verbal
2022 – Physical
2023 – Mental
2024 – Time
2025 – Active

And we all participate in our own little way in the building of a perfect society. We need to reverse the agitation, frustration, and deception brewing within and outside of us through compassion, protection, and realization. Here, I am attempting to plant a small seed of enlightening, divinely healing, and awakening everyone without exception.

The pain felt by one person thousands of miles away is felt by another-such is the bond coronorians share in the coronial era. Corono-the word corono has many meanings. It means a circled halo of the luminous body around the upper portion of a bodily part (such as a tooth or the skull) caused by suspended droplets or particles of dust from the outermost part of the atmosphere of a star (such as the sun). It looks like a faint glow as seen on the surface of a high voltage electrical conductor. Rian-is an Irish word that means little king. All of us are our little kings wearing our crown which has a halo. This crown comes with a lot of responsibilities. The strength of the rightful heir to the throne is tested through his ability to remain four F's - (fearless, flawless, faithful, and free) in the face of death (destroying detrimental methods).

The 101 years, starting 2020 herald the golden age of spirituality. We are in a make or break situation. If we make it then post this shift I see ourselves collectively building a harmonious world where there will be no more inner or outer wars. One by one, our consciousness will rise and heighten. There is bountiful love, joy, and wealth for all to claim if we so desire. It is just a matter of who makes that first move towards restoring this innate wealth and building a perfect, peaceful world. Once we move past the year 2121, some of us would have naturally begun to live in perfect harmony and understand the ruler, rule, and the ruled, as per the cosmic order.

If you light a bonfire, you maintain your attentiveness and proper distance else you will burn. This is logical. Humans internally are made up of water and air and the excess heat of fire coming out from others can sometimes burn our inner sensitive, cool nature. Therefore, we must maintain a proper distance of a minimum of six to twelve feet from each other else we will burn our outer shields. This is logical.

Any transitional phase is usually the most painful and challenging period. How you come out of this challenging phase is up to you. The mysterious journey is yours.

Ask any woman who has had a natural childbirth and she will tell you that during labor, she becomes a fierce lioness ready to charge entering her deepest primal power. She can move beyond her agony and pain to bring her infant out into the light. Any man who has seen the process of childbirth can never underestimate the wisdom and power of a woman.

Nature has told us time and again how it uses fierce compassion and subtle yet powerful, invisible weapons to later shield, quieten and transform our lands and us for the better. This is because sometimes a wrathful approach is more effective than a peaceful one. Challenges help us become more productive, balanced, grateful, and creative.

Just hang in there, my love. These are complex and confusing times. There are tears of pain and pleasure. There are understandings and misunderstandings. What is real for one will be fake for another. What is easy for one will be difficult for another. Just hang in there, you will get me, today I am here before you, tomorrow will be you. I know I should be there more, but my purpose is now divided between many. If I let myself be caged again this time, eons will pass before all mankind will rise. Can you carry the load of these boulders on your shoulders? If not, just hang in there. Open your eyes and you will see that I am always there. This time, I will not feel sorry for myself. This time I will not weaken. This time, I have the strength of more than a thousand within me, I have come back with the grace, power, and blessings that even all the weakness in the world can't wipe out. Do not go by my tears. They are wept for you. Why redo what has already been done? Why hold on to what is not yours? Why feed your ego? What more does it want? On the side of the tall mountain, I will be waiting with a seat just for you. Come along with our precious one, for I know for sure it will want to come.

Today we can exchange messages with someone sitting millions of miles away. A singular message can be shared with thousands and millions of people using technology. Soon we will be able to send a message to someone sitting millions of miles away by using our concentrated thoughts using heightened telepathic skills. We are capable of influencing light beings many light-years away with the transference of this thought power. Astrally attuned with ourselves, our psychic abilities are limitless. We will be able to interact with various groups without the use of any verbal or tangible forms of communication. Time we develop our collective HSP (higher sensory perception) and beyond.

Through healings and meditations, I share the love with each individual or a collective. Many experiences the energetic connection and the positive shift this brings to their body & consciousness. I will continue to send healing, gratitude, and blessings to our planet and to those in the outer realms until a day when many more will join me to positively influence all. Collectively we are more powerful.

Stark rays sent from the eye of the sun look like the sun's loving wings. What is burning us from inside are those crimson red rays from the sun's corona that contain destructive plasma. Thankfully the technological advancement we have made in the last a thousand years will save us from corona's sharp eyes. Steve Jobs left not only the iPhone but his love for us was so intense that he also told us that the way to knowing the 'I' is spirituality (intuitive wisdom of *Paramhansa Yogananda* and *Neem Karoli Baba*) and when you and many more collectively attain self-realization, we can learn how to not just survive but live, despite the dance of the cosmic or celestial forces.

It is only when you lose something, you value it more. A stolen item suddenly becomes more valuable to you and catches your attention because you lost it. When Mona Lisa was stolen it was just a painting, when it was recovered from the thief two years later it became the greatest masterpiece and still is because the human mind conditioned itself to not pay attention to something until it is not there anymore. We do not value the lives of our loved ones or spend time with them but when the time is gone and passed, when the lives are lost, we miss the times we could have spent with them. Let's resolve that from now on we will start valuing the time, resources, people, and their creations and paintings.

If there were no nails, no hammer would be needed. How do you nail without a hammer? Visible or not, a nail is always there to give you a clue of where and how to hit the target. If you do it right, the painting will be ready to hang yet again on its freshly painted wall.

An eight hundred year life span will seem like one day and night combined, if the moments are spent loving each other, rather than in futile pursuits. Let's not rush through life. Let our children learn every micro detail before they know the macro picture.

As per research, those with Type A blood group are most susceptible to the coronavirus. Interestingly, Type A blood group and Type A personalities have a lot in common. Even the virus is telling us to cut down on our over-ambitious, aggressive, controlling, and competitive nature. It is telling us not to force our will upon others. It is telling us that there is always a force bigger than us, always was and always will be. As per studies, Type A behavior doubles the risk of corona-ry heart disease. No wonder the pandemic is called corona and no wonder the rural areas are not as affected as the urban areas.

When a spiritually-minded person or a world leader says something,

Worldly people say all kinds of things about the Godly people, but that doesn't stop them from taking on their journey.

'YADA YADA HI DHARMASYA GLANIRBHAVATI BHARATA ABHYUTTANAM ADHARMASYA TADAATMANAAM SRUJAMYAHAM'.

The above famous Sanskrit slogan simply means, that whenever there is the decline of righteousness and a rise of evil, the Lord manifests itself, to uphold the virtues and protect the earth.

'Yada yada hi dharmasya' the first line of the above quotation. 'Yada' means whenever; 'Hi' means there is; 'Dharmasaya' means religion. Seeing the current plight of the situation, I choose to change the first line of the quotation to -

'Dara dara hi dharmasaya'. Dara means fear. So the above quotation means "Fear and fear is our religion".

Fear has become our religion. Fear lives in the human mind. Whenever something lives in excess, it has to die and decline. Fear is like a plague, fear is the biggest pandemic. Its decline is sure to come. When fear declines, love blossoms. Those who love, do not fear.

The energy of the earth is yin, its protector naturally has yang energy. Sun and fire are yang and earth and moon are yin. The love between these opposites completes and balances not only them but the entire creation. When an excessive imbalance of these energies inflames our lungs, the waters of the ocean being neutral will save the day and the night with its salty breeze. Breathing in the breeze of positivity is what creates perfect harmony and balance. No wonder the closer we are to the oceanic waters, the better we feel because it reminds us of who we are. I lived by the sea in Dubai and I never felt physically healthier, energized, and relaxed. This doesn't mean you need to invest in a beachside condo to stay healthy, all you need is to move about in fresh air to keep the proper balance between the negative ions (etheric energy or moving water of any kind i.e. waterfall, etc.) and positive ions (that come from free radicals like electronics, computers, television). The negative ions are invisible, tasteless, and odorless but they come with a healing air.

Consider this a scare before the beautiful life that is to come out of this. We have all been given a shock of a lifetime with the horrors of the coronorian or coronial pandemic. This is so that we, the children of God, cease to hesitate and wake up from our long sleep of unawareness. Some of us have hesitated for days or months, some for years and some rare cases have been hesitating for eons. This shock is meant to release you of the spasmodic pain of suffering on physical, emotional, or mental levels so that we get stimulated enough to usher in a heavenly world. This can be done with our collective strength towards a common goal of bringing in renewed energy of ease, love, and light amongst all sentient beings.

This turning point, the crisis of 2020, is urging us to let go of all our repeated attachments. Face the actual truth and collectively move in the right direction. It is urging us to allow the breakthrough to happen. It is the need of the hour and we must let ourselves evolve by allowing the change to take place.

Every crisis is known to either bring out the best or the worst in people. Over the years, during crises like the Titanic, Mumbai terror attacks, the 9/11 Twin Tower debacle, and numerous air crashes, we have seen how people come together to help and bless each other. Some people like Neerja (an Indian flight attendant who took a bullet to save the passengers from hijackers) are the ones who even give up their lives for others. Coronavirus has inculcated greater values of altruism, unity, solidarity, and harmony amongst many of us. In this coronial world, where we cannot bid farewell to our loved ones when they die, detachment is the value being taught.

Some say that what humanity couldn't achieve in 100 years, it has globally achieved in the last 10 years. I say, "What humanity couldn't learn in 10 years, it has collectively learned in 1 year of the coronavirus." So feel the joy and commend yourself for the progress you have made towards your greater ascension.

Do not let anything stop you because nothing bad can ever happen in the path of love as long as you are on the right road. Never say bye if you don't feel like it.

Carona ironically is a Sanskrit word that means empathy. Now is time to revitalize ourselves by practicing kindliness and empathy. Empathize and selflessly serve all those who have been directly or indirectly affected by this pandemic. Let us send a golden light of energy to one and all. 2020 onwards the years should be written as ECE 2021. Where ECE means existing in coronorian era.

Affirm- 'Namostutee, I speak straight from the heart. I value and nurture family, relationships, and all beings with equal warmth and kindliness. I love unconditionally. Tathaastu.'

CHAPTER 65

GROUNDED

My father is from the Indian Air Force. Being a daughter of a military man, I had a very regimented, disciplined, and secure upbringing. During my childhood, often there were blackouts in places we were stationed, especially when we lived closer to the borders. During blackouts, communication via phone is suspended, all-electric sockets and lights are switched off. Sometimes when there is an actual threat, we are made to go underground with breathing devices. The family members receive basic training to handle such odd situations. It can however leave a lasting memory for a child like me who was just seven years old at the time when I first went underground in a dark, narrow, tight space with few more families from the neighborhood. The power is cut in the entire cantonment area. It felt scary, primitive, and closer to living in caves. All outlets were closed and the sleeping bags became our best friends. During this tunneled lifestyle under L shaped underground temporary homes, more often than not, some military personnel would come at dark hours and throw apples for us all to eat. After this ordeal, when I came out, the light was blinding but then as I readjusted to the environment I realized wow! I love this sunlight. God is in the sun. Many years have passed since the last time we went underground to stay safe. Those escapades have faded in the pages of time. I remember very little but the aftertaste of the sweet apples that were thrown in by the military personnel remains in my mouth.

Each zodiac has its constellation and each *chakra* has its planet with its color, hue, and personal crystal. We are mortals within the immortal. Time is relative and so is space - it varies as per your subjective growth and evolution. When you activate your chakra your connectedness to your spirit brings you closer to the animal, plant, flower, fragrance you resonate with most. It also activates memories of your past, present, and visions of your future life. This connection helps you know your true power and potential thereby removing all blockages for a better future. Truly wise spirited and evolved souls are like rainbows consistently exuberating self-acceptance, self-worth, humility, complete truth, self-satisfaction, confidence, perfect freedom, moral strength & courage to set about their work in the new rainbow light. Remember that the karmic cycle keeps continuing until we achieve complete perfection and forgiveness in relationships. A fulfilled, loving, happy, and tolerant person can forgive easily.

The planetary speed is determined by various complex factors, each planet is a giant spinning wheel or *chakra*, and the speed of the chakra decides what age we are. If the planetary chakra is depleted, congested, contracted, expanded, has broken webs, or is influenced by other planetary chakras and foreign bodies - it gets imbalanced, affecting the lives of everyone living on that planet. It is important to stay shielded and balanced at all times. If those living on the planet are balanced then the planet too will stay balanced. One nation is like one major organ of our planetary body and if one nation gets affected, it affects the entire earth.

Trucks carrying more than the designated load are at a higher risk of falling from a cliff while traversing mountain roads. The only way to mitigate the risk is to lighten up, unload, and go low on the cargo you are carrying. Whether it is the truck you are in physically or the body that you are in mentally, the choices you make can ground you, pull you, or make you fly in the infinite space while being centered and grounded. The opportunities are unlimited as long as you keep the balance. Each being is like a tiny atom in the planetary body and each cell eventually affects one another. If one cell gets congested, all cells get congested causing various fatal diseases like cancer, autoimmune disease, inflammation, etc. Earth is currently diseased because its mini and major organs are all weak and therefore susceptible to harm and injury from external rival forces of the cosmos.

We collectively can fight back these forces with our positive energy and vibrations, which is why I have initiated this chain to keep our earth healthy and shielded. I seek your help to heal our planet because alone I can only do my bit but with the help of an army of 1000, 10,000, or 100,000 more people - I believe we can save our body, the earth body that we live in. Until then I will do my bit and continue with the healings. Each phase of four *yugas* comes with a small pause, at this stage, we can join together to recreate another body. We are in that pause- while this pause seems to take over our entire year, we together can use this as an opportunity to save the body which hosts us all. When our frequencies increase, eventually the Earth's frequencies will increase. It will no longer get influenced by outside forces, so let us save our planet. Let us save the lives of millions living on it. What cannot be healed by medicine – can be healed by energy. I am sure, all this is going to be worth it. Let us not get stuck within our stagnated energies, let us pull each other out of the quicksand before we sink and submerge into the sand again. As a general guideline, keeping a minimum distance of two meters from one another will help the earth's chi energy to initially flow in and out more smoothly. People with higher vibrational and rotational energy should keep an even greater distance.

Stay, calm, and relaxed. Stop overwhelming our planet's energies with your pace of life. Balance is the key, too much speed leads the car to crash. Stop getting distracted by the high beam of other cars. Our earth is like a car and we all collectively are its drivers. Do not drive in the night if you are not able to concentrate on the road if you are sleepy. Catch a breath, catch up on all your lost sleep, and come back to drive the car when you are ready and refreshed.

Give it a year and all should be settled. Stop fighting the change, accept the momentum, and listen to the body. Earth is a body telling you to slow down, do not defy its plea- soon you can work as a team so that no one part gets a bigger role than the other. It is no longer about gaining personal freedom but collective freedom that matters. Stop this blame game the constant bickering, belittling, cheating, stealing, attacking, killing one another. Follow the order and do what your role demands. Defeatist thought forms are a bigger pandemic than pollution and population. Poison can be killed only with poison. If each person is vitalized, the earth will be vitalized too. Work on your energies with proper thoughts, choices, words, food, understanding, lifestyle, rest, and stability. Ground your energies and make the most of the earth's years. Let's stay healthy and wholesome and with this resolve, we might just be able to extend its age and ours too.

In a jungle when the lion comes out, all animals run to their dens. The foolish one that stays is eaten. In this concrete jungle when Coronavirus is out all humans run to their homes. The foolish ones that stay meet with their death.

These days I see children and mothers bicycling outside and playing in parks. The mothers who felt guilty because they couldn't spend quality time with their children are now able to make the best of both worlds by working from home. The fathers are playing basketball and teaching math to their children. Families are spending time in nature, loving, and bonding with one another. The fiery energy within us moves upwards to meet with the sun. The moon's energy within us moves downwards to remind us to reflect on our magnetic nature. Our Godly mother earth supports and backs us at all times. We must love and cooperate with the being that supports us through thick and thin. We are all like little hearts, grounded below by the Godly earth's loving energies that filter out the excess fire before it reaches our core center, between the secret chambers of the small, protected space. When these little hearts get distracted with the earth's physical energies that slow down our mental growth, the moon's emotional waters increase your clarity with the tide of their gentle love. When you are filled with all that humility, purity, and clarity, the sun's fiery energies raise you when all the mental chatter makes you drown in love.

During the day, all you can see is the sun, because it overpowers the sunlight reflected by the moon. But for the moon, the excessive light of the fire will blind your eyes.

The waters circulating deep underground are hot, and as they flow up into contact with the warm solar minds and the cool lunar emotions, the cold air becomes filled with just the right balance of moisture and temperature. While the gushing sound of air is inherently filled with lunar flexibility and wisdom, the earth's generous love is filled with the sun's power and warmth.

Lumps of clay dissolve to create idols. Our body is much like that lump of clay created by the divine sculptor. This hollow idol when dissolved with the divine soul-self by internalization will then know the spirit connect. When the trinity combines – spirit, soul, and physical you start witnessing your life as if from the outside. You then emerge out of all obstacles, problems - big or small because your purpose is far bigger than just you. The purpose of your mold is to mingle with the supreme oneness to become one with the source.

We turn into infidels when we pollute the energies that made our soul rich. We turn into ungrateful beings when we do not thank those who allowed us to sit amongst the nobles despite our muddy shoes. All the richness we enjoy is because of the mercy and grace lavished upon us by another. We dismiss and strip off the flesh and mind of the very core from where we came and yet its essence remains intact.

Nature's elements forgive us and stay by our side, flattering us and forever taking care of us. Let us praise the earth that gives us glory, fame, and its property which we proudly own. Let us praise the waters that remember everything we ever did and yet zealously flow with the grandeur of its love for us. Even if the soil sinks beneath your feet, a true seekers soul doesn't give up until it becomes one with the higher spirit.

Like a bird, one of my wings is love and the other is undying faith. The marriage of these two makes me always fly and yet remain grounded. Don't push yourself too hard to find both, just go out there and spread your wings of love. There are a lot of people out there and your love will come to you.

Excess stardom is love and dependency on others. Excess wisdom is pride and dependency on self. Both are two extreme forms of bondage. True freedom is knowledge. It empowers us to release ourselves from the extremities of dependency and bondage. To be free is the choice that leads you into living a complete and purposeful life.

Power and freedom lie in empowering yourself and others. Just because you or another started with humble beginnings doesn't mean that you cannot make it to the flight on time (ascension in life).

It may seem that you are mysteriously grounded in Mother Nature's womb like an infant. Rest and relax. You are currently safest within the nurturing nest. Just like the baby growing inside the mother, nature will ensure that you too will emerge out healthy and strong when the wait is over.

Affirm- 'Namostutee, I trust that my inner and outer beauty, wealth, and health will continue to expand and renew. I trust that each member of my home is forever protected, healed, and energized. Tathaastu.'

CHAPTER 66

MENTAL RESILIENCE REQUIRES STRENGTH TRAINING

The prerequisite to having an undisturbed mind is to shed all unwanted, disturbing thoughts and emotions through self-control and mental resilience. A difference of ideas is a sign of intelligence. It certainly doesn't mean the person is trying to be purposely any different than you or defiant in any way.

Riding an untamed, wild horse, you will soon have to tame with the reins you hold. Thoughts are like these wild horses - once we have them we need to learn to harness them. Violent or agitated thoughts lead to similar actions. Tightly rein in your thoughts by guiding them towards fortunateness, clearness, and non-duality. This is the right direction for your horse. We are made of steel and filled with our sword-like resolution and determination. Nothing but we ourselves can weigh us down.

Recently I heard of a man who committed suicide on the 65th floor of his building because he couldn't take the pressure of today's reality. Let none of us die such a cowardly death. There are still others who are buying guns to shoot their physical bodies to rid themselves of the mental anguish and pain this pandemic is causing them. What has happened to our level of resilience and mental strength? Nature is asking us to free your mind. Medicine can extend our physical age but to extend our mental age, we still have a long way to go. We need to work as a team to evolve.

When you overly criticize, psychically torture, severely push limits, and disrespect another individual then you bear the brunt of your karma. If that person is a true yogi, a pure soul, or a committed world leader then you will get even more hurt and pained. As a result of your blinded actions and if the deed is collective then the entire group or world will suffer. Each person is divine, performing their exalted role, guided by the higher powers, we must not make it so difficult for them to perform their role because of our collective psychic attacks and despondency. Every action leads to a reaction. There is no bigger illness than the scarcity of knowledge, discrediting of wisdom, and trivializing the value for virtue. Time to build what we were made to build through our minds, capacity, and capabilities which are unlimited and unbound. Time to change the course of destiny and write our fate through the collective will, creative intelligence, and our discriminatory power.

What keeps us busy in this world, can be done by machines easily. Most of us are not using our potential and capabilities to the fullest. Our mind is built for better use and we are not optimally tapping into it. The food we eat and the news we watch is dumbing us down. There is no point in spending time in futile preoccupations. High time we do something with the resources we are endowed with through single-pointed awareness and Martian grit. Reflect inwardly on your goals, this inner search will start the march towards humanness and create progression like no other and this will be the ultimate rebirth. When life seems difficult remember that the path may seem narrow but it is always open for the one who perseveres and is committed. The rigidity you are holding within will not open your outer knots. It is the outward flexibility that will allow the inward knots to untangle and open themselves up.

We tend to negate what we do not understand. Always remember that behind every 'no' there is a hidden 'yes'. Sometimes we need to hold the magnifying glass to see what is hidden within. Internal forgiveness builds emotional muscles and self-discipline builds mental muscles.

In Indian mythology, there is a story where *Gandhari* a famous princess of *Gandhaar (place),* covers her eyes (chooses to be ignorant and blind) for years, to protect the magical powers of her vision and also as a mark of acceptance for her blind (deeper meaning being ignorant) husband who was born with this handicap. She decides to open her eyes only for her son *Duryodhana* to protect and shield him with the clear vision of her *Divya-Dhristi* (supervision powers) when he needs it most at time of war.

Duryodhana was strong but needed more strength to come out a winner. Gandhari asked her son to come to her naked after bathing in seawater (purified of all evil) so she could share all the spiritual, emotional, mental and physical knowledge she had gained over the years. This knowledge shared through the windows of her eyes would make him seven times more learned and stronger. *Duryodhana* was ecstatic but at the last moment, covered with shame and embarrassment - he decided not to visit his mother fully naked and bare. He wore a loincloth around his sacral or *sthapana* chakra that also covered his *mooladhara* or *sthir* chakra. The visit made him strong in all other areas yet weak and imbalanced in the parts that require the most energy during wartime. The in-depth knowledge shared is always fruitful, good, and appropriate for the times, but people are like obstinate children who are not always receptive to accept the divine gift. Open up, solidify your foundation, and have no shame in confidently asking and receiving from higher energies for I too am here to give and take.

The right is bigger than the left. Thoughts are bigger than emotions. When the right gets constricted, your chest gets heavy and loaded with pain. Empty yourself from the congestion of your preconceived ideas and malignant thought-forms. Only then can you truly be free. Energy workers like me can only work miracles if you let them work on you.

Oxygen comes in from the left of the body and carbon dioxide goes out from the right. People living in oxygen-rich environments help keep the energy of the earth balanced. (As per GMCKS, on average, the etheric aura is six-inches in size, the health aura is six feet in size, and the outer aura is one meter. What affects the energy body ultimately affects the physical body). Keep a distance of more than two to three meters to allow the outer aura to heal optimally and energetically so that the physical body remains unharmed. We need to raise the collective consciousness and this is vital. We are like spoiled children, who believe we are entitled to everything without contributing to balancing the earth's energies. Every unruly child knows it is not right to disobey their parents yet they recklessly disobey.

If the child doesn't listen to the gentle kind words of the father, the mother takes on the role of a strict disciplinarian to teach a lesson. This global pandemic is forcing us to shift from being self-oriented to becoming others oriented. It has slapped us with a near-death experience to enforce a collective informed change. If you must control then do not try to control another- but control yourself, your impulses, your actions and reactions, your mind, your body, your emotions, your thoughts, your words, and your actions.

Open up the corpse-like demeanor that you have wrapped yourself up in. You are so self-critical that you can't but help criticize another. You are pouncing on others because of your inner insecurities and qualms. In regulating your thoughts and emotions from right to left and left to right, the mist-shrouded within your castle or bodily home will dissolve and the mystery will unravel bit by bit. Do not repress or suppress your desire because you face resistance. You have the choice to go against the wind and do what you came here to do despite the odds.

You learn to discern as you become more and more sensitive to energies and open yourself up to higher knowledge. The outside enemies are easy to fight with proper strength training. The Herculean task is to overcome the proud beast within us. Our worst enemy resides within us. It tricks, attacks, tests, and enslaves us into unwholesome thoughts and actions. These thoughts and actions stop us from reaching the heavens which too are within us. We are the cause of our own suffering. Thoughts of guilt, thievery, possessiveness, and control cripple us and clip our wings. Mental resilience gives us the internal strength to face the most upsetting situations with a smile. Embrace your strength of character and integrity, these are your true jewels.

Affirm- 'Namostutee, Transformation requires resolution and dedication. I have lots of self-determination. Tathaastu.'

CHAPTER 67

BEATUS SUM–BLISSFUL I AM

I am writing this to you all from a plank where nights become days, days become years, dreams become reality, opportunities become an actuality and all that remains is the blank truth.

To get a daily dose of bliss, you first need to know what DOSE stands for. D= dopamine that motivates you to achieve goals. O= Oxytocin that helps build trust and love for yourself. S = Serotonin that controls mood swings, bringing in leadership qualities, E= Endorphins that bring in pleasure and relief from pains at all levels. Once these four circuits of joy are well connected and high wired in your brain, you are supercharged, super-balanced, and super-human. If we see ourselves from a spiritual standpoint then we all are perfectly balanced within our higher soul. Therefore, inherently - there are no obvious weaknesses or strengths within us. We are all one and complete. We are so closely connected to the universal energies that the alpha, beta, gamma, and theta rays of the universe affect the alpha, beta, gamma, and theta rays of our brains.

Gamma is improved cognitive and hyper-focus ability. It is a state of self-awareness by sharpening memory. It brings enhanced joy, happiness, sensory perception, increased processing speed, insight, and the ability to see the bigger picture. These are the fastest and most subtle brain waves.

Beta is normal waking consciousness with daily activities like working, driving, speaking. In this state, you have selective attention towards everything that is happening around you.

Alpha accesses the subconscious and activates the right and left brain. In this state, you have enhanced learning abilities bundled with powerful and creative thought forms recharged through your calm, focused, aware, intuitive mind. In this state the brain releases serotonin.

Theta is the dream state through deep relaxation and meditation. It potentially brings spiritual experiences and a feeling of connectedness.

Delta is accessing the realm of the unconscious in a deep trance, deep dreamlessness yet maintaining wakefulness and awareness. It stimulates the release of several hormones.

Why are women asking for equality? Women are child bearers. We are children of God, the heavens bore us. We come through the higher energies. What is higher than us is heavenly. The man comes from the feminine energy and hence women are always placed higher than men.

Children are the link between heaven and earth. How thick you keep the cord between heaven and earth depends upon how wide and pure is the aura of your child. Widen your horizons on mental, financial, physical, moral, and emotional level despite any resistance. A woman (feminine energy) being higher and a man (masculine energy) being lower, a child is a product of the love of the higher and lower. Hence a child asking for equality is bizarre. Being in the middle of two extremes, your child acts as the balancing medium. The purpose of its energy is to bring peace and harmony into your home through learning to respect nature's two best teachers-his mother and father.

Well rounded parents create well-balanced children. Well balanced children and youth, create a well-balanced grounded society. I am waiting for a shout out from all those youth who are ready to bring in some change through the wonderful values of power and love they have cultivated from their divine parents.

Our children are the reason why the stars stay lit. They carry the star-like light of our celestial ancestors in their DNA. Let us give them our understanding. Let us resolve not to over-control, over expect or overwhelm them. Let us not give up on them or even over pamper them. Let us inspire, engage, and connect with them with our calming touch and our caring smile to give them hope. Let us fill our future with the colors of delight and amusement. All the light, love, and power is within our beautiful earthly family. We all have a given purpose. The entire hierarchical order is bound to shatter and break if the lord begins to compete with humans and humans try competing with the Gods.

To keep the balance, we must perform our assigned *karm* or action and that is our only *dharm* or duty. Each one of us has a definite divine precepted purpose behind our karm. Our purpose comes prewritten in the secret chambers of our brain. We have *karma* to perform towards ourselves, our parents, our children, our society, our nation, and the universe as a whole. No one is big or small. Everyone has an important role to play. Everyone is special, though not equal. This is simply because it is based on their learning, disposition, and God's perfect plan. Let us not challenge the Lord's creative design. Let us be ourselves and not try to be something other than who we are meant to be.

Affirm- 'Namostutee, Let us model and be a catalyst to spreading faith, truth, humanitarianism, inspiration, and loads of smiles amongst those waiting in line. Tathaastu.'

CHAPTER 68

SYNCHRONIZE, SYNERGIZE, SPRITUALIZE

Since all is One, It is when we all start working collectively, compassionately, and together as *One* for the betterment of each other that real healing and overall progress takes place.

With such magnetically charged synergy, we are the only heavenly stars that effortlessly, equally, naturally, and elegantly move today in this brightly colored earthly fence. We do this on earth just as we do above-- high spiritedly, lightly, and merrily.

Be and let be. Why ignore it? Why compare? Each person is connected to you for a reason. Based on that connection, each is entitled to give and take as much as they deserve. By holding on and trying to control, you are not completing your cycle, and that is the reason for your aches and pains. You expect goodness from others without having fulfilled even one-tenth of what is expected of you. You are not fulfilling the very purpose of your karmic cycle, and so you are the cause of your self -inflicted anguish and afflictions. You are here because your lesson is left unlearned. The invisible is not visible, because you lack clarity and your eyes are fogged and deluded.

In life and death, there are no coincidences - no accidents, everything happens for a reason. Everything we encounter is part of a sacrosanct master-plan that is bigger than us. What we are facing was bound to happen, if not now then at another time. Now is the time to nourish, nurture, unite, and care for one another. An individual going through pain tends to value pleasure. Many individuals collectively going through pain, tend to value pleasure collectively. This virus is like that rose with a thorn. When you touch the rose, the thorns prick you. By keeping a safe distance you can still smell the roses. Similarly during these times smell the rose from a distance and do not get affected by the thorns so that you stay safe and healthy.

The thorns are many in the wreath[71] we are wearing but it has led to pollution control, cultural freedom, family bonding, and the realization that technology and *Artificial Intelligence* are a great boon to us. This slow down doesn't mean it is time to get lazy, resentful, or undisciplined, it is time to love, share, forgive & let your creative juices out. The lives you touch, touch you back in some way or the other. It can even touch someone in distant lands. That is how your thoughts become bigger than you. Take the example of the fruit and seed. The fruits grown in India, when exported, are enjoyed by someone sitting in America. In the same way, we are enjoying the fruits of seeds of love that were sown many years earlier by someone else. Let us all open our hearts and generously continue this chain of love to spread the light.

A farmer grows food grains and fruits. There is an undeniable connection between the tree that bore the fruit, the fruit that is consumed, and the seed that comes out of the fruit (case in point a mango), and this connection is beyond borders or territories. The fruit can be consumed in any part of the world. The seed that is thrown after consumption can start another tree. This way, the connection to the first tree will always remain, even if it is growing millions of miles from the place of its origin. Let your soul guide your hand and God will ensure the field you plow, the seeds you sow will harvest into the right fruits and at the right time.

Everything is energy and universal energy responds to us. Harnessing this energy can sort many issues. I harness this energy to heal all those around me. My mission is to bring out the best in one and all. There is no coincidence, the reason we meet and the reason we all are going through this situation is part of a divine preorder.

Each soul is perennially and karmically connected. The evolvement and spark within one affect the other. You have the power in you to enhance, create, and upgrade the DNA of the entire cosmos with the matrix and synchronicity of this ultimate reality. You are like a programmed, consecrated proactive crystal that fed with its self-purpose long before being born. Join me in creating your new reality in this new age by remembering who you were meant to be.

---

[71] *Wreath – corona or crown of leaves and flowers worn on the head.*

Let's take a deep breath and mentally affirm, "I program my soul to activate and flow with ease, prosperity, divinity, and good health at all levels. The pure vibrations emitted by my soul travel as a combination of whirling yang energy which first travels upwards and then right to left to bring down the yin energy downwards followed by a left to right. Because of this movement, there is physical reality and it also ensures that all the needs and desires are realized for the highest good of all those involved spreading spirituality and abundance."

Having sent these pious vibrations, set all your intentions clearly and specifically to manifest, actualize and materialize the goodness of all your visions with deep focus, and gratitude. Ground your spiritual self into your physical reality openly welcoming the cosmic miracles.

In today's world of globalization, there is no particular race, culture, religion, caste, or creed we follow- most of us embrace what we resonate with irrespective of national boundaries, and look how beautifully we all have intermingled, we all are one. Why create barriers where there are none. There are no walls between nations and people, then why create them?

As you meditate and go further knowing the higher truths, it will seem that all things that make you human are moving away from you but that is only because you are becoming Godly. Even a drunk person knows what he is doing. Unfortunately, some people have surpassed drunkenness, not knowing the evil they are doing.

Everything and everyone is beautifully connected. I can say so because awake or asleep, I am always aware and alert.

The story may be the same, only the interpretations vary. How you interpret the story and how you understand it is what makes the same story different.

The first time I went for over two months to the Uttarakhand Mountains for mountaineering with one of the most prestigious institutes of India, the course was grueling. I was the weakest in the patrol. Other than me, everyone else was experienced with years of training. I was left behind in the first few days because no matter how much I tried, it was never easy for me to reach their level of expertise. Soon, I became one of the strongest team members. I owe my strength to the entire team, who not only patiently waited for me for hours, whenever I delayed them, but they helped me learn one great life skill by making me their team leader. The entire team was made to follow my slow speed. With this added responsibility upon my shoulders, I began to feel that if I remain slow then the mission of the entire team will slow down just because of me. With this thought, it was as if my speed automatically increased. I put in extra hours to get equipped with facing obstacles. I pushed my limits because I did not want to live with the debt of being the cause of everyone's defeat. In this way, the weakest link became the strongest, my speed increased. If we start believing in people and trust them with our lives, we empower and encourage them to become better individuals. The whole world is one big team. Even if one team member is left behind because we think they are a weak link, we all are left behind in the circle of evolution. In helping one, we help all.

The simplest way to bind people to you is to give them a special gift. It is no surprise that the Chinese know best how to give expensive gifts. During the Han dynasty, wine cups made of high-quality lacquerware were given as imperial gifts. Sometimes they gifted expensive silk. In today's day and age, they still give gifts that are unmatched by any other nation. China owns most of the Giant Pandas in the world. So they give these rare animals as diplomatic gifts and as a symbol of goodwill to other nations. Pandas are peaceful, lucky, unperturbed by chaos, and live a balanced life with yin-yang energies. Gifts bind you to the giver. So if you receive a gift like a panda from them then they are bound to be endowed with similar energies in manifold ways. What you give, you receive. No wonder they are enjoying all the luck while the world is in chaos.

Affirm- 'Namostutee, A large number of hearts beats simultaneously. We never run out of the vibrations of kindliness. My affection is for more than just one thing or person. Tathaastu.'

CHAPTER 69

LIMITLESS

I see a growing trend of people eating either cake with no icing or icing with no cake. I enjoy both. There is nothing fully known about the impeccable unknown, and nothing limited in this pool of limitlessness. There is no scarcity and no hierarchy. Resources are limitless. Whoever has the inclination, also has the access to these resources. Spiritual evolution leads you onward to much more. It is the beginning and not the end.

The moment you realize your limits, you become limitless. It is in learning that you unlearn.

We must look at even the most unwholesome situation positively. The choice is ours to either have negative emotions or generate sanguine and positive emotions to heighten evolution. When the two sides of our brain are balanced, our thoughts and emotions are in sync. When this happens the back, front, and center of the brain gets activated invoking a combination of unconditional love and unadulterated thoughts. We, therefore, are a combination of cogito ergo sum (I think therefore I am) and *Diligo Ergo Sum* (I love therefore I am).

All five elements are within us. As long as the environment and situations are conducive to thrive, life will continue. Why play with nature, it is that which defines us and we exist because of it. There is nothing you cannot conquer whether it is your sleep or lack of it, whether it is your physical illness or your emotional afflictions. You are capable of doing anything you are committed to. So rise and let your heart bloom and flower with everlasting love rather than blocking, holding yourself, and resisting which causes frustrations. If one can, then all can since we all are connected. It is just a matter of degree and strength, how much or how little, how congested or depleted, how expanded or contracted, how limited or resistant, how negative or positive, how open or closed, how divine or human.

We all are made up of cells, so is everything. If you completely perish or are left with just a few cells, you will still end up starting life all over again in one form or another. It is in the nature of cells to multiply, create, and co-create. Every particle has infinite cells hence we are in a constant state of becoming. We never die since we were never born. Always were. Always is. Always will be. It is that it is. We are inherently immortal, never-ending, continuously changing, transmuting, and evolving beings.

The movie "Beautiful Mind" is based on John Forbes Nash. He once said, "In a dream, it is typical not to be rational." I say, if we all are living a dream then how can we be expected to behave rationally!

There is a triangle in the US dollar bill. It is the all-seeing- eye. It is often deciphered wrongly and so are the words written in it. Its words[72] mean 'new world order'.

I am here to bring to light that the new world order is here. We are limitless. Limitations are only in our heads. It is time we expand our consciousness. Let us live on the heavenly earth with no more bridges. As our meridians and channels within the body begin to flow freely, our brain cells will activate and transform. This will bring in positive transmutation within our chi energy. This might be slow progress and surely requires divine grace, skill, and self-determination.

I guesstimate that currently, humans use only 20% of their brain on average. If we resolve to overcome our limitations, then we can make use of 100% of our brain. It's like a step up from a child playing hide and seek to a child who stops playing the childish game and only seeks out of simple curiosity. This is true awareness. The shift from 10% to 20% to 100% will not be immediate.

Some people cannot be limited or trapped by bodily illusions of sickness or weakness. For example, a child received a heavy dose of anesthesia thrice over before a procedure was to be performed. Finally, the nurse practitioners were brought to hold him because sedatives did not affect him. His mental body was so awake, alert, and aware that pain and anesthesia did not affect his consciousness. The causal body knows pain to

---

[72] The Latin phrase 'Novos ordo seclorum' written below the pyramid in American dollar bill means 'New world order'

be a mere illusion. Bodily weakness or despondencies cannot drag down a divine being who is an image of cosmic consciousness. Another example is when some children show no symptoms of a high fever unless you take their temperature using a thermometer and the results are otherwise. This is because their higher body is so aware, balanced, and attuned that they do not identify themselves with mortal terror or pain.

This is the reason why we hear from parents that kids up to five years of age sometimes remember their past life as it comes back to them through their dreams. Yet these kids do not attach themselves to these passing dreams. Life and its troubles or pleasures are just a passing dream, kids naturally and intuitively know better than to attach themselves to what has passed, unlike adults who become addicted to their worries, insecurities, and delusional dreams which they call their reality. In general children's minds are free of clutter, worries, and problems. It is easy for them to be joyful and comfortable in the face of seemingly uncomfortable situations that bother the adults who sometimes are a slave of their worldly impressions.

This light waiting to change the world is in each of us. There is plenty of exquisiteness, warmth, and riches to share.

You may have access to all the wealth, but unless you know when and how to make use of it, it is worthless. To convert knowledge into right action requires awareness and immense effort. Our brain is like a computer. When you download too much mental information too quickly without becoming morally sharpened, it is like using a dagger to kill yourself. Knowledge is a potent power, but in the hands of wrong people, it can be applied wrongly and becomes dangerous for society as a whole. This is why I counsel virtues to kids of all ages through fun games and meditations[73] to make them understand the importance of being morally accountable for their actions.

When your bucket list is emptied, it is time to refill the bucket. No matter how much you think you already know, there always remains something unknown. The list in your bucket is a never-ending cornucopia.

What you vibrationally ask is vibrationally given back to you. The words, thoughts, and actions alone are not enough. Your overall vibrations matter. All your senses must resonate with what you want to manifest. Life is meant to be abundant. Allow yourself to let go and enjoy its abundance

---

[73] *Access meditations on my website www.trueblisshealing.com*

299

and limitlessness, without any feeling of lack and limitation. Limitation and satisfaction are both alien concepts for me.

The entire world is a serene, spiritual sky. Here everything is complete and everyone is aware. Past, present, and future are one. Allow your magic to flow. There is no such thing as limits when you see through the eyes of the ocean. Do not let anything or anyone limit your growth and evolvement.

Does love have boundary walls then why do nations? My love is not bounded only for my son, my husband, or my family. It is boundless and beyond time and space.

Affirm- 'Namostutee, Now is the time, I must shine and spread the light to dispel the darkness so that all planets here and around, within this space and beyond can get a glimpse of the vision of my light. This is beyond all time zones far and wide for I am no longer limited by self-restricting beliefs. I am the true bane-factor and inheritor of the kingdom and this is my ultimate destiny. The entire space is within me and also outside of me. This light waiting to change the world is in each of us. Tathaastu.'

CHAPTER 70

ACCEPT THE OTHER SIDE OF THE COIN

Something unlimited can never be completely known. What cannot be known in its entirety cannot be defined holistically, but only in parts. Your understanding is relative based on your subjective viewpoint, which is only partial, but never the complete truth. You can never know the mystery in its entirety. No matter how tall you grow, you will always be younger in your physical age than your father. The reason you are here today is that your parents gave birth to you. They are the cause of your effect. The effect will always be younger than the cause. And as you grow, you constantly change. Change is the cause of your growth. To evolve and grow, you must not be resistant and defiant.

We exercise our mind, will, and power to control another and to clip their wings, without realizing that there could be certain things that we don't see, even if someone else can see them! Accept what others see, and you will begin to see even better. If we see something for the first time with no prior associations/ impressions attached to what we view then we will relish it and life will become so much more peaceful and meaningful.

The ideas most of us hold onto so dearly are based on experiential or non-experiential experiences. But the truth of reality is beyond any experience as we know it. The greatest miracles and inventions have been by people from whom we least expect them from.

After you have taken the spiritual path, your upbringing, past beliefs, or your habits-good or bad-do not define you. You define yourself. You are a combination of your past, present, future, and everything that comes in between. You are not just your past, your present, or your future. This is like a man saying he wants to marry a woman, but not the child in her belly, which comes with her. You get the whole package with its baggage. You take all of it or leave it all. It is up to you. But the deal is for the whole and not the parts.

Michael Jackson's songs sound great to you because you like the aura of his energy, which is reflected in his voice despite his scandalous past. You might not like Sarah McLachlan's angelic voice because the auric voice in songs does not resonate, attract, or please you, despite a spotless past. Your likes and dislikes are not defined by the outward reflection of man's nature, but his inward predisposition and character. There is something you hear and see in him that no one else does, pulling you towards marrying him.

There is a key to every lock and the code is simple. Acceptance is the key to the lock you have been holding onto. Each being does as much as it can, based on its potential and capabilities. Each being is trying its best. You must not belittle another, only because you can do more in one area. Their specialty lies in another area.

When I was little, our home was surrounded by wilderness, away from civilization, in the military cantonment area. It was a life filled with adventure. I played with my friends in the backyard of my home with natural sticky mud (*chickni mitti*) which is available in abundance even today. We made mini wells and earthen pots of different kinds. When our mini cups and saucers dried up and were ready, we had a little tea party with crushed biscuits. We created our own fairytales in our imaginary land. In the nights, the ants feasted on our creations, no one told us there could be poisonous snakes in the backyard because fear begets fear. We often saw cobra snake skins lying around and made garlands out of them during our playdates. One day there was a big Viper snake that was bright orange with black spots. It crossed over my arm while I was playing. It is one of the most poisonous snakes. All children went helter-skelter with fear. I remained unfettered and unaffected. Maybe because I was hypnotized by the Viper's magnificent beauty and charm. Soon, the snake simply went away, without harming any of us. After a while, we all continued to play with the clay for the rest of the day. Dangers stay only as long as we give them attention. This is just one of the many incidences. Real-life tells us that dangers come and go, life continues. The difference is only in how much you dramatize any incident of your life. Dramatizing and over attaching ourselves to the incidents, only distracts and weakens us.

Today, some people in the world need purification, mercy, and compassion. All sentient beings, including birds and animals, need calmness, peace, and greater freedom. The energy we radiate outward is the exact proportion of the energy we experience inwards. If you send out lower, negative emotions, such as nervousness, envy, pride, mistrust, selfishness, and hate, then that is exactly what you will experience. Soothe others of their misery and yours will be resolved. What we repeatedly think is what we become. There are no rights and wrongs. Acceptation is the key. The white absorbs light and is pure so can be molded anyway, the dark is regal, mysterious, dynamic, powerful, shielding, and majestic. So why judge or negate black or white. We all are its favorites, it has no bias. We are limitless beings of light. What others think cannot be interpreted by you and their thoughts cannot be completely the same as yours.

It is not me, you are not able to face yourself. You are responsible for yourself and no one is responsible for you or your actions or thoughts and nor are you responsible for anyone else's. When spiritual places, meditation groups, and healing retreats instead of bars, shopping malls, and clubs become your new favorite hangout spots, you know you have met your higher soul. And from there, you will soon reach a point where the whole world becomes your temple. You will start to feel the ultimate divinity even in a brothel. When you can appreciate a cockroach, then you have met with your higher soul.

Perfection is but an illusion because it is subjective. It is like beauty or wealth, where others will always seem to have more creating a longing for you to acquire more. This will exhaust you causing broken expectations, frustrations -another name for pain and misery. As long as you accept yourself, your truth, your viewpoints nothing and no one can force you to become their version of perfection and imperfection.

When we look in the mirror, the mirror is all accepting. It is us who judge, condemn, praise or compliment ourselves proudly. The mirror is just a mere reflection of how we understand and see our outward reality, based on the inward perception of ourselves. We control whether what we see is beautiful or ugly. The mirror is just there. How we see ourselves defines who we are. Pictures may vary and images might be different but the collective pure consciousness is common to all of humanity and resides in all.

Say the below, irrespective of how we perceive ourselves or others. Criticism and constructive criticism are two very different things.

Affirm- 'Namostutee, I am beautiful and so is everyone and everything else in this world. Tathaastu.'

CHAPTER 71

BE-YOUTH-FULL

Earth is going through a tender phase. It will get over it with a little bit of "be youth full" energy. Don't give yourself so much importance. Without you, the grass will still grow by itself and so will your kids. Why try to control what is not within us? The upcoming generation is here to fix the irrational precepts we have deeply set. Let them be! Let them grow, and the future will thank you for it forever.

The world is one big family and each member has a unique role to play. Our pain, pleasure, sorrows, and experiences are our best teachers. That is why I sometimes hold myself back from making it easy for you. Nothing you give ever goes to waste. The child you taught might not have thanked you, the bird you healed might not have flown back to you, but you did make a difference in their life's journey, and all that is for the better. We put a fence around our gardens so that the plants stay protected then why do we not put a shield around the aura of our children when they go to school.

Eve came first and then through Immaculate Conception, (with the eye of *shiva*/Knowledge which was dropped on the chamber or ridge (rib) between two mountains of the Garden of Eden) she was blessed with a 'gift from God' – gift of vitality- Adam. Children are a be-youthi-full gift from God and this is how the world began. Eve is a true world soul and everything stems from within her. Yin energy creates and yang energy provides. We have both yin and yang within us. So Eve had both yin and yang, male and female within her. It is just a matter of which is the dominant one.

There are no coincidences - my only son's name on his birth certificate was "*Superboy*." When we thought we were being so indecisive in coming up with an appropriate name, the Lord God had already given him one per his destiny. He is - a true *Superboy*, having the blessed energy and divine supremacy of all the super elements inherent within him. This chapter is inspired by Superboy and the energies of the youth around.

Angels are light beings that guide divine human forms. They have an auric color that they radiate. Each of us also has an aura color. Our auric color changes based on our thoughts and actions which sometimes may not be aligned due to outside influences and circumstances. During silent meditations some people get to know their true aura color. They should then align their thoughts and actions according to the auric color. In today's age where instant gratification is the name of the game, it is hard for people to meditate and introspect thus never knowing their true self or their true auric color.

To know your true self you need patience along with the ability to be aware of your thoughts before speaking or acting. These virtues will help you progress. This will help influence the people you come in contact with as well. The only reason this change or progress does not happen is that you are so used to living in a particular way that there is resistance to change. The downside is that we will collectively falter if one of you does not change as it impacts many based on connection.

Keep the youth oxygenated, balanced, and engaged. Create a safe environment for their growth emphasizing virtues and ethics so that when they circulate in the different realms they remain centered and grounded to their core. Their soul age is far more than ours, they are our elders. Treat them with respect, reverence, and love. They are our true light, here to shine brighter than ever with the onset of the new golden era. It is a great honor that you are chosen as the medium through which they are born.

You are the co-creator of this new heightened age. Tighten your belts for the energy that you are witnessing at this stage is nothing like what you have ever confronted.

All the stars, indigos, rainbows, and crystals filled with golden electrifying violet light have descended and are walking amongst us. Stop resisting the change, open up, embrace, and evolve. The circle of evolution is incomplete without you and so you must learn to read in between the lines.

Today instead of using our brain and tapping into our memory, we simply ask Siri, Alexa, and Google to give answers to the simplest of questions. All answers are within us and the solution to your problem is you. The problem is you and so is the solution.

305

In today's world of virtual reality, no one has time to hold hands, have a simple chat, and go for long walks in the park and beach across your home. Teenagers look older than their parents, the nature is lonely, and hungry to see them beaming and smile carelessly with joy, the same way they once did. Their smartphone and video games have become their best friends. Pure friendships are replaced with materialistic gains. Everything has become a business, kids aren't kids any longer and unlike us, they were not even given a choice- they are born into this high technological money-minded era, where writing with a pencil and sharing bread with your family has become a passé concept.

Are we evolving or degenerating, hunching down, or breaking our backs to relate with the lifeless screens that overwhelm our little minds. The playgrounds are empty aching to see you play a game of basketball with your children. The earth is waiting for kids to play and build models out of *chikni mitti* (wet mud). Let us spread some awareness of what laughter is like while it is still engraved in our memories. Let's dance with excitement every time we see a falling star and the colorful rainbow. Let's socialize, let's mingle, let's enjoy all the colors and hues there are.

Sometimes a person with a beautiful vibrant color aura, with no change in action- tends to suddenly have a darkish grey aura, simply because of the thoughts brewing within him - these thoughts could be a result of his mind, could be targeted towards him by another soul or might be in the air around him. Learning to shield yourself and learning to shed these unwholesome thoughts releases us from the afflictions of making these thoughts a reality as they manifest into action. This is where we healers come in because we are extensively trained to remove the negative subtle energies and replace them with positive subtle energies which you and only you can action into either gross or wholesome energy. We must align our thoughts and actions with our true potential. We, healers, are gifted and trained over the years to bring out not only the best in you but also help you find your true potential positively and safely.

I have this gift and you might have another. Each of us is unique in having our gifts to display, but the first step is finding our true potential and then realizing it. From here on you have the freedom to either reject or accept the healing in full faith. Those who believe and persist can accelerate their growth and those who resist too will reach there but in a much longer period, which might result in undue vexation, suffering, and pain.

Eventually, everyone will progress, one will be sooner than the other because experience always takes a longer time than simply following. The best path to progress will be for someone who is devoted to a combination of the two followings in full faith and then validating the teachings of the Guru through meditation and contemplative analysis supported with true experience. They will witness *savikalpa samadhi* i.e. Bliss of pure connection with the Supreme Lord God by being mentally conscious of the spirit within.

Go out and face yourself – even your dark side. The darkness has its beauty and mystery. Through the darkness, you know light. As you know light, there is nothing that can beat the purity that comes with it. The light within you is waiting to come out and shine. Take this time and shine as you traverse your path. It is ok to call and seek outer guidance from other heightened souls but also remember to call on yourself for inner guidance time and time again. I am here to remind you of the simple reality that you are most beautiful the way you are. When you realize this reality your true healing begins.

Forgive yourself before asking for forgiveness from another. Value yourself before expecting others to value you. Seek self-help before helping another. When a child falls it is a signal for him to get up and go further rather than just staying on the ground. When you fall in life, rise again. Your ability to rise again is the reason you are here. We all are here because the omnipresent one gave us this ability. Do not let your mind or emotions weigh you down or trick your mind to think otherwise. When you move beyond yourself is when you meet with the truth within you. You realize the power and potential that lies within you. Stop holding on. When you think you are giving yourself importance is when you are actually giving yourself the least importance.

You don't need to be living in a warm country to show the warmth in your hearts. All you need is a little love with icing of a tad bit of faith frosted in you. Uncontrolled fire seems to exude passion so does one who speaks impulsively but the one who doesn't think before speaking is a failure at inspiring zealousness or *Junoon*. Industriousness is required to make any substantial change.

Superficial knowledge has no depth - the true wisdom lies in deep focus and clarity. When you are trying to persuade another, it is only yourself you are trying to convince. Today's new age knows better. You are not here to quieten them but they are here to quieten you. They are the future teachers even though they might seem small but they are the ones who are far more evolved than you will ever know.

We as parents need to empower, encourage, uplift, and discipline our children to help them find their soul-purpose. Do not nag, neglect, compare, hurt, bully, or malign them. Appreciate, embrace, praise, respect, cuddle, honor, and make them feel safe and secure. Be firm yet loving. Motivate them by showing them the goodness in them. You have an inner child within – your soul. You too can meet with your inner child in the same way. Do not hold on to pain and grudges. Time to loosen up and heal your inner child and change this incessant pattern. Choose to release this tension, let go, forgive, connect with your deep truth, meet with your beautiful self, and be disciplined, gentle, merciful, grateful, accepting, giving, and forever loving. None of us ever imbibe what is taught but we imbibe what we learn from the teachings.

When you have children, lack of preparation leads to disorganized, rushed mornings. Stick up daily preparation lists on a whiteboard. Encourage children to post reminder notes for themselves on their backpacks and doors. Provide them with reminder notes and make sure they use them. Teach them to set alarms and use the calendar on their phones. Put up a whiteboard for daily to-do lists. Make a vision board and put up yearly or quarterly goals written by your children.

The new age brain is super-powered and super connected which is bringing about a renewed evolution. The youth of today may look the same as us but they talk and think differently. They are far more evolved than us. We have never felt as intensely as they do. They are wired differently - an upgraded version of us. They are the future leaders, trapped in little bodies.

Do not let your children, who are your very own soul, ever go astray. Keep them away from that which makes them rebellious. Teach them how to please God and their selves, through example. Teach your children all the good and love them with all your heart. If they violently rebuke your teachings then with all your positive energy, be strict, and do whatever it takes to make their speech pure and kind again befitting the Lord God.

Parents ask children to study by constantly reminding them of the money they put into their schooling. This does not encourage them but only adds more stress to their young brains.

Whatever beauty you see on the outside always has an inner story to tell. When you try and listen to each of those stories is when you find yourself - it is in the inward search behind the outward that we get cleansed spiritually to know the inverted reality of who and why we are here.

The key is in realizing that we all are so inherently connected that in being alone you are moving away from being you. Self-acceptance is the key to accepting yourself and others but you must know which lock will open with this seven-pointed key that you are holding. You need to know where the blockage is in your seven chakras, stopping the flow of energy. Only you can solve this puzzle and encode the lock. Tease your memory and concentrate hard to know where you have placed the lock and where the blockage is. Start cleansing your past all over again. I can guide and help you but I will avoid telling you any further because it is in finding your answers that you will begin to find the answer to the never-ending five key questions "Who am I?, Why am I here?, What got me here?, When did I let this happen?, and Where do I go from here?". These five questions take you to the next key question i.e, "How to get back there? Finally the seventh question being, "Which exact lock will unlock with that magical key that you are holding on to so dearly?"

Know who you are meant to be. Identify your path, purify and cleanse yourself, strategize, and devise a plan to meet yourself. Merge with your true self to reach your goal. This way you will get all your answers. It is as easy as that but you must take the first step with a leap of faith. The key that you have been looking for is within you. You have been holding it all along and asking others how to find it. Just think of me or call my name whenever you please. You will find me right there beside you. You can send an email with the subject line – (528 SBR) for instant healing blessings.

Always apologize and admit you are wrong so that those around you get inspired to admit their fault when they go wrong. Making mistakes is being human. Humans make mistakes because we are the imperfect within the perfect. Learning from our mistakes and transforming ourselves through our knowledge is true wisdom. Wisdom leads us to perfection. Learning how to say 'no', sometimes transmutes and changes your life. The only person that you can truly change in your life is you. Learn to walk away, give up and move on from situations that put you into an emotional rollercoaster, else you will become a part of your downfall.

If you cannot inspire or uplift another, do not belittle or demotivate them. Let no one and nothing break the magic that lies within you. Don't even give yourself that chance. How young you feel depends not on your physical age but your mental age. No wonder teenagers sometimes look and behave older than their mothers. I suggest that you be mentally vibrant, positive, enthusiastic, and joyful, because what you read is what you think, and what you think is what you feel, and that is exactly what you reflect outwardly.

Today's generation is the only one that has everything that everyone in any *Yuga* (cycle of ages) has desired. Despite that, we are unhappy. Name a thing, point a finger, and you have the means to achieve it all. We are unhappy because the collective awareness is missing. We are all walking in heaven, not knowing this is heaven.

There is no point in either rushing or in being overly slow and calm. When you are in extremes, you are not being you anyway. It's only when all the missing parts mingle and meet that you become balanced within yourself and your truth becomes you.

Everyone has a gift. The more you praise the gift of another, the more praise you will receive for yours. If you cannot help others find their gift, do not become a roadblock to their destiny with constant criticism, disrespect, and rudeness. If you create opportunities for the progress of others, it will open a whole lot of opportunities for you, for it is in giving that you get.

Making another feel confident fills you with confidence and victory. Do not get influenced by anyone other than yourself. Apply your self-discriminatory intelligence before coming to any conclusion. Your richness is defined by your character and not by the class or section of society you belong to. We all are divinely blessed to be truly evolving, so keep your spirit up, and go on sharing and learning. Respect the aged and the young. Respect the women and men. The never-ending one resides in all. These are not testing times. It is time for the test. If you fail this time, there will be a long wait, and to some, it may seem like it will never come. But as long as you remember to do what is asked of you, I promise you the hand will always stretch out for you.

> With high morals, comes high wisdom.
> High wisdom comes with high qualities.
> High quality comes with in-depth knowledge.
> In-depth knowledge comes with respect for all your teachers.

Everyone is your teacher and Teachers day should be celebrated for all. Irrespective of where you have reached and who you have become in life- always remember to revere and to do *Namostutee* to each person and being that crosses your path.

Be determined to bring back the morals in today's confused society through continuous learning and recognizing the divine Godliness within you. The key to progress lies in respect. Once we learn to respect all, we meet with our greatest teacher who lies within us. No amount of precious jewels you may possess or adorn yourself with are comparable to the precious jewels within the bodies of our innocent and pure children. They are getting polished to illuminate our world with the true shine.

Affirm- 'Namostutee, spark the subjects of morality and spirituality in today's youth. In this way, their soul- purpose, and potentiality are fully realized. Tathaastu.'

CHAPTER 72

CROSSING THE RUBICON

I see only because I believe I can see.

Crossing the Rubicon requires you to build single-pointed mental commitment like the unicorn's spiraling horn that drills purity into your hearts. Rubicon commitment is a point of no return, like a journey with no U-turn. A bull has two horns, but when he is tamed, he is like a unicorn in a maiden's lap. Bullshit is sold at a high price only because it is of great value, and whatever has value, comes with a price. Everything has a dual purpose. Every inlet has an outlet. Every door has a key. Explore and open up to the opportunities.

The five-pointed star of abundance, determination, prosperity, resurrection, and power tells us to be ambitious like the goat, strong-willed like the bull, lucky like the pig, observant like the cock, and free like the horse.

Fully inspired by the spirit of "Hu," we are all inherently fully divine, and therefore fully human. We are all trapped in our seemingly impenetrable fence. Despite the dangers that lie ahead, we all are waiting to jump out, for we are all born to be free. We are meant to live a thousand and not just a hundred years. Toxicity is what has reduced our life span and removed all our memory.

The fun is in solving the puzzle, not in finding the solution. The moment you solve one mystery, you are ready to unravel another. Staying with the resolved solution is no fun. Beyond the dualities, everything is empty. Your gift lies in understanding the profundity behind the vacuum of nothingness, and so we continue figuring out the puzzles. It is what keeps us from stagnating, from dying. You live life to the fullest only when it is filled with chaos and not when it is simplified for you. The moment you see the simplicity behind the chaos, another advanced level of chaos comes forward, and the chain goes on and on and this mojo inspires you to go on. As long as you do not give up, your resources are never exhausted - you never die. Your energies keep flowing like freshwater. The riddle of life carries a secret message. As soon as one problem is solved, we are already looking for another, because we live for the joy that problems give us, and not for the joy that the solutions give us.

Your body is your temple, your church, capable of redeeming, eternally renewing, and restoring itself through cosmic life energy.

All horns - one or two - whether on bulls, hippos, deer, unicorns, or humans, are always on top of their head! As per the latest scientific discoveries, humans are growing horns in the external occipital protuberance (EOP) of their skull.

Seeing the world from another realm can get confusing. For example, male energy is subtle, fair, and pure so it can stand out in the dark. Female energy is active, dark, and glaring, so it can stand out in the light. It is the man that gets pregnant and not the woman. Only the seahorse has exposed the truth of this secret. Most of us are still jumbled up in words, deeds, and confusing names of species, given by us.

Sometimes there are roadblocks on your path to success. Do not let those people and circumstances deter your Godfidence or stop you from reaching your goal. It seems as if they are stopping you from moving forward, but remember that as long as you honor and believe in yourself, no one and nothing can ever shake or break you. You are a superstar and no one can shine better than you. The opinions of others do not define your reality. Whoever you may be, others might never know where you got that immaculate glow, for the flow of divinity in you is far higher than they will ever know.

If you feel pain in the neck most of the time then most likely the cause is your emotional stress. Psychological satisfaction is very important for all. Make everyone feel special, empowered and cared for. Because of the power and pressure that lies behind your neck at a point between the molten heat and the melted cold-light or dark, ice or fire, destruction or creation, the scary fiery energy of the red and yellow spark is cooled by the true blue and calm green hue. Whether you are young or old, right or wrong, hot or cold, dead or alive, you will never be blinded or lost, as long as there is shade in the middle, broadly activated in between the Godly awareness of right and left. It is the middle that makes you strong, youthful, and bold. It is the job of the youth to convert the stagnant energies to renewed golden energies. It is the job of the elders to create a conducive environment for the youth to smoothly bring in this transmutation. Little children seem to know a lot more than some elders. It is time we must learn from them.

Today's youth value honesty over authority, cooperation over competition, truth over superficiality. Their energies cannot be suppressed. They have amazing discernment abilities. They would not adjust to us, we have to adjust to them. The new world order is asking for a revolutionary change. Stop trying to resist change. For it is inevitable. It is in the nature of blood to flow. In the same way, it is in the nature of time and energy to flow. Lack of movement and flow decreases the overall vitality and balance of the entire globe.

Spend time doing things you love as they will de-stress you and also benefit those around you, who are a pain in the neck. You are far more inspirational when each action you take is filled with joy. Certain things are important just to you and they are your priority for a reason. Even though people around you might not seem to know or understand or notice your resolve. They too are part of your spiritual purpose. It is your job to illuminate the rest even though they want to stay in the dark rather than accept or change.

When thirty-three petals of your cosmic heart open, your aura glows like a beautiful pink diamond. Two third of humanity is bound to get affected in the coronorian era in some or the other aspect - psychologically or spiritually. The remaining are a strong link between the inner and the outer worlds. These are the shining ones who will show us the path with their ruby-con glow. For they are the ones who can see past the delusions.

Affirm- 'Namostutee, I am balanced, loving, accepting, forgiving, compassionate, open, and inwardly self-transformed. Tathaastu.'

CHAPTER 73

UPSIDE DOWN

If the lock is not opening, it is neither the lock's fault nor the key's fault. The problem lies in the mind's lack of understanding. The mind has yet to learn how to unlock its underlying true potential and unknot the knotted locks.

We pray to the moon because, without daily gratitude to her, we wouldn't be centered in her gravitational pull. Moon is *Ma*, our divine mother. Imagine what will happen when two moons meet. We will be topsy-turvy with our heads on the ground and our feet above us. That is why in this realm we have only one mother and one father to balance our energies.

For humanity to continue in generations, we must have qualities of both genders - masculine and feminine. Both genders are within us, the universal mother and the father have equal influence on us. The teachings of both must be mastered to bring balance into our lives and to progress further. During my visit to the museum in Washington, there was a sphere. If you looked within the sphere from any side you would seem upside down. Earth is a sphere and we are upside down within that sphere. From outer space when you see earthlings, we show up upside down as well.

As beings of light, we are all like an upside-down tree with roots in the clouds and crown facing the earth. The attachment of your crown connects you to the other souls on earth. Our body is like an upside-down pyramid, the most vital organ and God-head is on the top.

I am an upside-down tree whose seed was set long ago. Following the sacred rules of nature, I gracefully grew by myself in the right environment. I am now here to effectively bring life and light. I am here to bring balance into the modern world with enlightened stellar consciousness. I am divinely appointed to protect, guide, and positively transform you and begin a transmuted cycle of time to accelerate nature and its various manifestations. My heart is within the center. Wearing my heart, I compassionately cure diseases and restore vitality through ancient healing modalities and rituals.

Most of us have got all our priorities turned around. Running for the top, we have forgotten the bottom. It is not the one primarily running for power, money, or authority who is the true teacher but the one who is the last one standing, humbly serving and caring for all right at the bottom. Such a divine ruler is a world soul who endures patiently, purposely, and willingly came down to urge you to kindly serve, love, keep the faith and keep your promise of honoring, serving, and ritually greeting each other with loving kindliness, and a respectful Namostutee. Continuously ask yourself what you have in you that you can offer for uplifting, easing misery, and becoming the cause of someone else's smile? This way no matter where you go, the heavenly doors will forever be open for you.

I met the shortest tallest man and the tallest shortest man. Each person has a twin soul. The higher or twin soul is invisible. The person's every movement is through the twin soul which is always connected. Twin souls are always connected by an invisible energy cord. Just the way magnets repel and attract the higher soul and the physical self, first come together then repel and then spend a lifetime aligning to meet and reconnect with its true self. Ultimately pure wisdom is the reason behind the higher airy thought and the lower action to materialize into a physical reality that we have become.

If you want more oxygen and space, simply hang yourself upside down on a swing in the park outside your home. Move beyond the usual norms and confines of time and space. Upward or downward, you are that arrow that finishes the journey it starts before starting another. What comes down must go up, now there is no stopping.

The only hope for you is to tear open and break the delusional rope of duality that is holding you captive in between like an insect caught in the spider's web. Your rope could be excessive desires, clinging to past attachments, wrong company, slandering another, fixated unresolved thought forms, unwholesome habits, unhealthy relationship ties that make you feel victimized and terrorized, self-doubt or guilt. True bliss healing[74] magically helps you heal, awaken your soul, liberate your spirit,

---

[74] *www.trueblisshealing.com for healing sessions*

gain confidence, restore overall balance and harmony to heighten your frequency. It is then that you realize and remember the truth of your upside-down reality. The earth is your brain. The view of the positive sun which is your divine mind is blocked and concealed by the shackles and illusion of maya. Removing this concealed truth requires immense perseverance, determination, patience, and ekagrah (deep focus).

We are in an uncomfortable period of transition. My advice to you is to practice compassion with all others. What is Compassion? The suffering of others is your suffering. The joy of others is your joy. The child of another is your child. This is compassion. Vitality, education, and righteousness is our basic need of survival and not merely a moral precept to be followed by few. What is suffering? Suffering means dullness, lethargy, drowsiness caused by consuming an excess of anything that doesn't serve you. It could be alcohol, criticism, anger, etc. We need to stop wearing this over-engagement ring of suffering and wear a new one that doesn't cause so much tribulation and discomfort. Else we will keep repeating this cycle that doesn't get us anything but more suffering.

Affirm- 'Namostutee, I spread happiness and love. I am kind, generous, and helpful to everyone every day. Tathaastu.'

CHAPTER 74

WAVES WAVING

The phases of the moon affect the oceanic tides through gravitational pull much the way it affects the waters of our emotional tides. The turbulent water doesn't change the calm expansive nature of the ocean. Similarly, the turbulent emotions within the waters of our minds are fluid in nature. As we allow the high tides of our mind to pass and settle, we meet with our expansive limitless potential.

There is a gem in my eye, it is pure and white. It is the rarest of the rare pearls. It came from the ocean and will merge into the ocean so possessing it is futile. Its nature is to be free unbound, limitless, and be whoever it pleases to become. Its nature is also to dance and sing whenever it pleases, flying and floating as it likes. So why hold on, why resist, why define, just keep enjoying the joy that is within you in the now. Just like the waves in the ocean that come suddenly gushing out, they cannot be held or controlled. The nature of a wave is to keep naturally and effortlessly waving, so is yours. Only the force of attraction from above keeps the waves going. The movement of water is what defines the wave. Without movement, there are no waves. Similarly, it is the force of love that attracts us towards each other.

You only experience the pleasure and the richness that comes with it. You do not know the push and pull of the undercurrents. You only see the dancing waves in the ocean, and so you are conveniently clueless as to what is happening deep within its very core. You have no clue of the incessant movement deep within that gives life to the waves. You only see the earth generously flourishing with the pull of your love. You have no clue of what is happening deep within its invisible core. You have no clue of all the pain the earth has gone through because of humanity. You can choose to help bring back its life, feeling remorse for the pain that you have inflicted upon her, or you can choose to sob and sulk. The choice is up to you. One day it is you, another day it will be someone else, the death of one wave would not cause the other to cease. Life will go on moving, go on waving by the force of love. It gets the pull from the above and the push from below to go on moving tirelessly for that is its very nature.

To understand your surroundings and what is happening in your life you need to first understand yourself. This can be done only by moving away from your self-created ego. You're a dewdrop in the vast ocean. You are not the whole ocean but a vital part of it. As you understand this, your crown chakra will get more activated. You can be a dewdrop and be content or you can decide to become one with the entire ocean. To move from being limited to limitlessness you need to have the unstoppable want. With that earnest and pure want, you can be whoever you want to be. Such is the power of thoughts and such is the power to become one with the ocean. You will need to know reason for your wants and then you will get your answers. The oceanic waves rise and then subside. The wave and the ocean are the same. We should try to keep our emotions in equanimity, serene, maintain their original nature and free of attachments despite the highs and lows because fluctuations spoil the flowing chi energy within our body.

The ocean is never silent and neither are you. Swim into the waves and speak with the vast sea. You are an awesome swimmer. You can't drown. Silence is only in the words; we have been talking without words all along. The one standing outside is invisible, for the one who is swimming inside is always visible. The external becomes internal, and the internal becomes external. So go on waving, go on moving, never stagnating, never ceasing. It is because of you that 'I am', it is because of me that you are and the chain goes on. Each wave is connected. The action of the first wave causes the other waves to react and move. Each wave is due to action and reaction. There is an inherent cause of these waves. This is coming from the undercurrents from the middle of the core, deep within the oceans. You and I are like the waves. The limitless space is like the limitless ocean within which we all move.

Who am I?

When my speech was tied, I learned to inscribe the purity of my words on a clean slate to give it form. When my feet were tied, I learned to swim like a fish in the deep waters to freshen minds with life. When my hands were tied, I learned to walk on my stilettos to bring balance and remove all excess. When my breath was contained, I learned to survive with the elixir of life and returned with my pearl necklace deep into the waters.

There is this river that has been washing the chaos of the unwise world that is filled with competitiveness, secrets, fear, malice, separateness, and greed for eons. Time has now come for it to merge with its true love-the abundant ocean where all things merge and become one. A place where there is complete transparency and honesty in thoughts, words, and action, and one wave magnetically does its best to help another wave to shine its self-generated beauty rather than stopping it from touching the bright surface waters.

I am here to tell you that the shore is near. I know because I was part of that same river, which has now merged with the exciting oceanic waters. Sitting on this waveform, I am waiting for the day I drop some pearls from my precious necklace for children to pick when they come to play with the wet sand at the shore.

God gave us free will to make our choices as long as we harmoniously work with the laws of nature. If God, being the creator of the universe, didn't set any limits upon us then how can us mortals impose restrictions on an immortal soul. A pure soul is a wave form in the infinite ocean of cosmic light, it cannot be captured and contained. Every such wave is unique and free to fly to any degree and height to its hearts delight.

Affirm- 'Namostutee, *Ego sum qui sum*–"I am who I am" everything and everyone around is tranquil, harmonized, blissful, expanded, and regenerated. Tathaastu.'

CHAPTER 75

MIRU

Moon or Lunar chakra is our *Bindu* chakra. It starts from the point where Indian women apply *sindoor*. Activating this chakra gives you a bird's eye view of the entire plan.

You have the potential to be the master of all masters when you understand that mastery lies in the profound realization that your true master is a pristine baby, sitting inside you and experiencing life from within you, spreading its clear divine light continually far and high beyond your body.

You may 'Miru' for yourself. The word 'Miru' here is aptly used instead of the word 'validate' as though it is a Japanese word, this short word covers a much wider meaning. It implies "to observe, scrutinize, analyze and to try."

The only way to increase your brain cells and overall vitality is to continuously learn and relearn to generate new ideas. The more excited your mind is, the more excited your body remains. An excited spirit excites the soul; an excited soul excites the body; an excited body excites everything and everyone outside, inside, and around it. Your left foot comes forward when your right brain tells it to. Your right foot comes forward when your left brain tells it to. When your right foot moves forward, it is the future of what your left brain told it to do.

Self-awareness without active awareness is futile. When you act intelligently is when you act intentionally. When you act intentionally is when you act consciously. Most other times your actions and intentions are at war because they are being mindlessly performed. When you believe it will rain, you carry an umbrella to avoid getting wet. But when you have no belief then you have no protection and thus will get wet if it rained. If you want to avoid getting wet then you need to be open to believing and trusting so that inner forces can protect you under their umbrella.

Being firm and trying to discipline does not mean that you love the person any lesser. In the same way if you control the leash of your dog and prevent it from straying does not mean that you love it any lesser. Similarly, we must always hold on to the leash of our will but that does not mean we should become ruthless and not express the love of our hearts. Speak when it is your turn. Do not hold on. Go out there and radiate your energy outwards and soon you too will be able to witness your actions.

Since you are in a constant state of becoming, improvising, and evolving, the same dish made by you with the same ingredients and recipe, will taste or have subtle differences from the one you made before. These subtleties are based on your current vibrations, style, and auric energy of the environment. Most chefs fight to get the perfect tasting dish they made the first time, but since perfection doesn't exist, it is a futile effort. Embrace the change and move on. Your creation was never really yours alone. No two paintings by the same artist can ever be the same.

Take that extra step with a leap of faith. Go out there and you will see that what doesn't appeal to you, might be a masterpiece in the eyes of another. You are God's ultimate work of art.

Excessive love is not always the best solution. Intense love is the answer. An intense experience is sharp and sometimes painful, but the ultimate pleasure comes with pain. Loss makes you feel the gain and value of who you truly are. The trick to staying young is to keep your brain engaged active and stimulated. It is not curiosity but the lack of curiosity that kills the innocent cat. Too much curiosity might kill the cat, but it is only when the cat is killed nine times that a tiger is reborn.

Black, or the absence of light, is visible because it foreshadows white; it shows us what is beyond. White light is invisible so that its shadow can be visible. Our mind is like the white light; it produces the action which is the future. Light reflects on various bodies and objects. Our body, for example, is visible because of the reflection of the invisible light, which makes it visible. Our mind acts like a sieve or sift that strains and separates unwanted material or thought-forms. And just like a sieve, our mind separates unwanted material and keeps only what fits its understanding. You know not everything that glitters is gold, not everything intelligent is wise.

You know how and when to safeguard yourself and your loved ones from the force. You are one with yourself and you are one with all. You are all forgiving- the best version of yourself.

It seems that ingratitude is ingrained in most people today. Just as in a farm every grain has to weed off when the season is over, each person has to weed off when the time on earth is over. A true teacher knows which person is grateful and so a true teacher will teach only to those who value the essence of the teachings. The rest of the students are seasonal like the grain on the farm. Only the grateful will remain for all seasons. To know the path of the eternal you need to be grateful.

Love binds but hatred binds more. Often when you send hateful thoughts towards someone the vibrations reach them even if they are millions of miles away. They may choose to respond with hate, love, or detachment. Whichever way they respond builds that bond between the two of you. What bond do you want to build? A bond of love, hate, ignorance, understanding, or acceptance is up to you. What you give out, comes back to you in myriad ways.

An invisible force is not malicious but completely transparent. We do not like the clarity and honesty that comes with the stark truth and so we blame the invisible for all action. Love hides behind hate, Courage hides behind fear, light hides behind power - eventually all stop hiding and come out in the open.

Affirm- 'Namostutee, I am here because I have the will to be here and learn. Tathaastu.'

CHAPTER 76

EYE TO EYE

The picture is very clear. If you see this any other way, you would need to change the eyeglasses you are adorning. No need to squint or quit watching the picture. All you need is to look with your eyes wide open, with transparency and honesty.

Life is like a play that we see. What you see on stage is an enactment. The truth hides behind the curtains, where the real story plays out. It is just the same as when you close your eyes you can see with your inner eyes taking you to the truth while most people rely more on what they see with open eyes. An eye for an eye makes the whole world blind. Eye to eye makes the whole world truly see.

As the truth unfolds, it will cause tears in your eyes just like when you cut onions your eyes hurt but it clears and detoxifies your eyes of all clogged up dirt only so you can see with more clarity.

The Supreme Lord is dressed in black (yin) but is ultimately white (yang). The supreme is the remover of all past delusions and wrath, here to expand and awaken us from our sleep (half-awakened state). The supreme lord is more aware and awake than we are even with his half-opened eyes.

There is creative chaos between higher and lower frequencies, it cleans this chaos and swiftly downloads higher vibrational energy into our thoughts. We can then collectively raise our consciousness and ascend to higher frequencies.

We are so accustomed to opening our eyes to see, that we no longer try to see with unopened eyes. Just the way half-open eyes are an eye-opener, the pages of this book will give you a glimpse of complete sight that will lead you to the true eye. Don't be slothful or remorseful. Don't be haughty with the lowly. Serve the wise one to wash your sins and promise yourself never to repeat the same mistakes.

Now is the return of Buddha *Sakhyamuni, Bhagwan Tirupati Balaji,* Lord Christ, and God *Rama* in this heavenly land of *Mata Seeta.* Why label these beings?

Their spark is in all sentient beings. Animals have higher intuition than us. The deer in your garden and the rabbit near your home are telling us that they can feel more of the subtle energy lately. This is because of the ascending changes in the etheric energy.

Looking into the eye of a healer repairs your soul. Eyelids protect the eyes, and eyelashes are like the eye's health rays. Innately we all are healers in some way or the other. That is the reason some people cannot look into the eye of another, because subconsciously they know of the strength and power that rests in their eyes. They are not ready yet to impart the healing to another. In some cultures, it was believed that an eye contact is an intimate form of healing. To avoid the intermingling of energies and to preserve their aura they aimed to heal only those that were intimately connected to them. It is better to reserve it for just a few people rather than share it with all.

In Japan people greet but they never look into the eye of another, keeping the distance and shielding their aura. This is a great practice and should be followed in all cultures preventing etheric space invasion unless permitted. Eyes are a direct way of communication while the rest of the body parts are subtle ways of communicating our feelings. Eyes are designed, to tell the truth, the rest can be manipulated.

If you want to know the truth look into someone's eyes. The eye gazing protocol which in our modern society is becoming a way to communicate is not the right etiquette. This is another example of forcing change due to misinterpreted learnings.

The new age children do not like to look into the eyes. They subconsciously realize that with the eyes you are communicating your feelings and sometimes the feelings coming from others may be harmful if they have unwanted feelings like anger, frustration, control, or lust, and the like. However, looking into the eye of a highly enlightened Soul with 'Samatva Bhava' (which means complete and consistent equal mindedness) will surely be of immense advantage.

The eyes are the windows to the soul. The soul age is known through eye gazing. A soul can either be mature or immature. Looking into the eyes of someone mature in soul age will help you learn and evolve.

The peacock dances in the rain even when no one is watching, because he dances to please the peahen, and he knows that she is sitting high above, watching him with her ten thousand invisible eyes. The peacock opens all his vibrant feathers. It appears that a thousand eyes are looking through each of his feathers. As the peacock goes on dancing to welcome the golden feathers of the golden age, the peahen, sitting upon the higher branches, sends light and power, clarity and wisdom, to express her electrifying love for the peacock's dance. The dance of the peacock and the peahen is visible only to those who want to see. It seems invisible to others because we confuse ourselves, trying to attach a name and label to everything. Empty your mind. Unlearn and learn, for how can you define something that you know nothing about? As you begin to unlearn, you enter into the mysticism of the inner world, where you begin to feel as if you are flying upon thousands of intricately woven peacock wings. This is true bliss. Who are you? Why do you exhibit such pomposity and conceitedness? Who are you to ignore another?

You think that you are the provider. You think that you are the cause of another. But you are neither the provider nor the cause. When you begin to see with your inner eye rather than the outer eye, you realize: Each of us has got the exact proportion of what we deserve based on our actions and experiences. Each of us is where we are, and each of us becomes what we have become because of our understanding. Each of us is a master of our destiny. Each of us learned our lessons in our own time, in our way. You are neither the cause of anyone's success nor are you the cause of anyone's misery. Who do you think you are? Well! You are not who you think you are. Your thoughts are tricking you. Be centered, be polite, be loving, for that is all you are meant to be in a world where each of us is navigating our life path, maneuvering and crossing the roadblocks and the obstacles to the best of our ability. You have become too occupied to be preoccupied, too perspired to be truly inspired. Realization of this is the first step of your self-actualization.

Father, Son, and Holy Spirit are like your body, soul, and spirit. Every creation that comes from you first comes from the divine invisible. The right eye is the eye of the sun, which represents your active vision. One eye without the other lacks the wholeness of complete vision and clarity that comes from the left eye of the moon, which represents your passive vision. Just like the moon and sun, one sparkles in the starry, dark blue light of the moonlit night and the other shines like the golden sunflower under the light of the sun. Both are restored with the divine invisible eye that lies between the right and left eyes, sitting strong and firm in the mountain (body). It sees the beauty and vitality in both its creations. Sun eclipse or moon waning all are part of his sacred plan of ultimate wisdom. Your opinions are clouded. Truth is far away from the shrouded destruction of your limited, self-inflicted beliefs. Beauty and love of divine vision are like the umbrella that protects you from the heavy rains and rays of the sun.

There is no better eyeshadow to use than malachite powder. It fights eye infections, and also looks magnetic-it protects & shields your aura too. I was once a meteor that fell from the pupil of the spiritual eye of the sun. Now I am a woman. Sometimes no amount of makeup can help conceal the tears inside the women's eyes. When your two eyes meet with the inner eye and the three see-through singularly as one eye then the truth becomes transparent and cannot be concealed with the fog of dense or high tech makeup imageries. When the discerning and intuitive eye unites, you see the light of the sun. I initially thought I will go blind if I try to look directly into the sun. On the contrary, the lightning has graced and bestowed me with divine spiritual clarity and the art of remaining neutral during the heat of any situation.

Your right eye opens so that you can click the images of the outer world with your inner camera. Your left eye opens so that you can store the impressions of the pictures you click to finally take the blueprint of the ones that come out well. The blueprint of all memories is stored by the inward eye. As stated, the right eye is the sun and the left eye is the moon. Keep the balance between the two energies within you through the strength of your third inner eye. The third eye[75] mediates to bring wholeness, order and resolves all conflict. This way the moon can shine bright and the sun can rule once again.

Many of us are not aware but we miss out on seeing and discerning a lot of beautiful colors of nature because we are not equipped with heightened eyesight like that of the birds. We often hear the term bird's eye view because birds have a more superior eye for detail. They view the world in a way that is unimaginable to us. Birds can see what is invisible to us. This

---

[75] *The third eye of wisdom is set vertically in the forehead.*

shows how little our perception is and how big their vision is despite their small stature. There are a lot of things beyond our comprehension. Each species is unique and superior in one or another aspect. For example - Dogs have a better sense of smell than us. Dolphins have a far better sense of auditory perception. Our sense awareness is tuned to specific frequencies. We cannot detect or know reality merely with our sense perception. This is a shortcoming in comparison to other phenomena around us. Then why do we believe ourselves to be superior?

All of us know only an aspect of reality and not the truth in its entirety. Certain frequencies are too low or too high for us to hear and wavelengths of light that we aren't able to see and appreciate. Perhaps this is the reason why we are always filled with a sense of wonder while the other species freely and fearlessly tread into the unknown. Maybe, if we learn to accept our shortcomings, embrace the divinity and beauty of nature and have faith in what seems invisible to us, we would one day be able to experience life and its magic in its full color.

The window is never really just a window. It brings life into the room. Similarly, your eye is never really just an eye. Your eye is the window and what you see through your eye brings life into your body.

Affirm- 'Namostutee, through my inner eye, I can see even when there is complete darkness. I reflect on my thoughts daily. Tathaastu.'

CHAPTER 77

I AM SHOE AM

For thousands of years, exchanging miniature shoes and sandals has fascinated us. Shoes are tokens of prosperity, good luck, and sharing the love. In the west, boots are tied to the car of newlyweds. In India, the shoes of the bridegroom are mischievously hidden during the wedding ceremony. The bridegroom pays to get it back as if his soul is in the shoe. Shoes[76] - both large and small of varied materials and designs have come and gone but their charisma and magic have only increased. Today's youth spends thousands of dollars to entertain their shoe craze.

In the olden time's shoes were given a lot of impetus. They represented status and safety. They were invented for protection and warmth. They showed your approach to life and faith in God. They were a mark of your determination to move in a particular direction. It is as if the soles of the shoes have our soul. Exchanging them are a means with which we identify ourselves with the real world and feel rooted and grounded here.

Interestingly, the repetitive chanting of the Sanskrit mantra *"sha am"* (correctly pronounced shoe am) has extremely powerful vibrations. The continuous synergy of these two words is said to create a rooting effect of our soul into the body. Reciting this chant is a natural way to heal and increase the sense of focus, calm, and oneness. Hopefully, the title of this chapter will direct your attention towards its title phrase *"aham sha hum"* or in English "I am sha am" which should be pronounced as "I am shoe

---

[76] *Shoes are a sign of support and safety as they protect your feet from sharp pebbles and dirt and elevate the look of any outfit. They are more than just a personal statement. The feet wear the shoes, the shoes do not wear the feet.*

am". The sound of which is considered to have the essence and soul of the entire world. 'Ah or I' refers to speech, 'hum or am' refers to mind and 'sha or shoe' refers to all our collective breath. The entire phrase "I am shoe am" therefore implies "I am breath and breath is within me. All air guides and protects me".

There is no better way to experience the transience of life and know permanence than a calm walk at the beach. I found myself walking towards one such beach, somewhere in between the known and the unknown. Unknown here represents the unexplored, invisible, original, pure core of our mind. In that space, I saw people grabbing towels, putting on their beach clothes and going towards the ocean. I too got excited to float in the oceanic waters but saw myself in an inner confusion - the fancy shoes I was wearing were not beach-friendly and would spoil in the sandy waters. Just then, I was led to a shoe rack that was filled with footwear suitable for the beach. I was first given ordinary rubber flip flops which I refused to wear as it didn't match my fashion style. I then picked up a fancy designer plastic slipper that looked gorgeous but the size was larger than my feet. It dawned on me that if I wear someone else's footwear then what will they wear when they want to wear their shoes. I finally resorted to wearing my original fancy shoes and went happily running towards the beach. I felt great clarity and all discomfort ceased for I was walking in my shoes. I am shoe-am and much more. And as I reached closer to the divine waters I realized no matter which shoe we all wear, eventually we all will enter barefoot into the waters when it is time to merge with the waters from whence we all came and so I eventually let the sandy waters merge with my feet. Being a link between the earth and heaven, Egyptian God "Shu" gave breath of life to all the living creatures. Shu (pronounced shoe) was the God of air, and light, who personified wind and supported the sky.

They ask, "Whose shoes you would want to be in?" You may have many answers to this question. It is not whose shoe (Shu) you want to be in but what you will do if you were in those desired shoes. A bit of the 'I am' is within all of us, so do not trick yourself, dear friend, into believing that only you are the 'I am'. Each one of us has a unique essence of the 'I am' within us, and that is what makes us so different, yet born from the same source.

Every shoe (to breathe) is a work of art. No profession is lowly when filled with passion, devotion and love. You would have read "I am who I am". Similarly a shoe designer would say "I am shoeam". He is grounded by his profession and happy doing what he does – mending, designing shoes, and protecting several feet.

Let everyone live to be who they want to be. By unduly influencing someone or somebody we are ruffling the shoelaces and untying them for another. Each one of us has a way and method to tie our laces. Let each person tie the lace as they want whatever the profession and whatever the outcome. Walk your talk. Be who you are meant to be. Even in your own shoes, move forward and make the most of the time and resources you have. Do not waste it as each step is precious as you walk this journey of life. Before you market your old pair of shoes, remember to lace them with laces that match your color and taste, so that the result of your action at the world auction is multiplied manifold.

You absorb boundless earth energy from your feet. The *Nadis* penetrate the body from the sole of feet to the crown of the head. They carry *prana* (air, water, nutrients, blood, body, fluids) in the physical body. Restore balance and keep the earth clean. Be committed, devoted, and faithful to the sole reason for your living. You get strength and dynamism from the earth.

The most grounded thing about you is your feet. To physicalize and actualize your aspirations into reality, it is always better to think, speak, and act in relation to your reality. Your roots ground you. Your feet are like the roots of a tree. First, clean and strengthen your roots to cleanse the ground and strengthen your overall body and aura. Dig deep before you learn to stand up firm. Learn how to take a fall before you learn to climb and rise.

Just as there is a sole under the fancy shoes on your feet, there is a soul under the fancy wraps of your body. When the earth no longer connects with the sole of your foot, your body dies. It continues to exist even outside your body. The soul is like a pure, miniature doll auctioned in an antique shop, which never dies but simply becomes a better version of itself. The shoe is symbolic of status and power. Shoes have grounding energy within them. Some people used to buy shoes made of snakeskin and keep money inside them as it was believed that keeping wealth within snakeskin shoes brings infinite wealth. It is believed that snakes are protectors of wealth but you do not need to kill them for that. You simply can honor them and get their blessings.

SOHAM and HAMSA reflect the same reality. The difference is in our perspective. SAH + AHAM is commonly known as Soham – is a Sanskrit word that means self or 'I am' or 'Atma'. Hamso or Hamsa means five or our five senses. Identifying our five senses with the 'I am' leads us to know our ultimate universal reality because the inverted SOHAM is HAMSA. Chanting SOHAM repeatedly helps you know yourself. I am you. You are me. I am one and all. I am shoe am: (I am - exhale the air, Shoe - inhale the sound, Am - exhale the air)

Affirm- 'Namostutee, My speech, and mind is purified. Through my pure intentions, the entire environment around me is purified and cleansed. Tathaastu.'

CHAPTER 78

FLOWER POWER

F lowers are nature's way of filling your energies with unconditional love. As you connect with them you will move beyond self-limiting beliefs.

This chapter is for you. You are the flower who has been waiting for spring so that you can bloom fully. A bud flowering into a lotus is like a super-efficient brain charged through the nervous system which makes you see things as they are and know the nature of real existence. Some lotus are still buds while some have bloomed fully. Lotuses grow out of mud, so can you grow out of the burdens and emotions that hold you back.

As we become stronger and more resilient, we move beyond the pains we have been holding on to, like the lotus, which looks so vibrant even though it grows in the painful, mucky, dirty waters, with its stem still submerged. If the lotus can become so beautiful despite the dirty waters it grows from, we too can rise above our pains through our resilience, to grow into as vibrant a blossom like the lotus. Learn from nature, the clarity of perfect harmony and stability comes with the realization of complete divinity and humility.

Our activated chakras look like full bloom flowers. To connect with your inner guidance and develop better insight, be close to flowers. Flowers can clear your energy centers with their subtle perfume and vibrant colors. Flowers uplift your moods. Even imagining a flower you like will help you catch the essence of its aroma and vibration. A flower that may appeal to you may not appeal to another. Go with the flower that appeals to you. Take the flower to the area of the body that needs more cleansing and healing. This will help you feel pure and energized. Let it fill your entire aura with its essence and fragrance as you inhale.

When you see the lily of the valley wherever you go--East or the West--you know that your mother is near. Her tears have dried. You feel the holy presence of her higher spirit and delicate love everywhere you go.

With the opening of a single bud, thousands of buds will eventually unfurl and flower. The true beauty of a flower only comes out when it opens up. Don't get me wrong-a bud too has its charm, but maturity has its own special grace. Don't turn brown and grey before you have bloomed. Don't feel beaten down and weary before you have been crowned.

I love flowers because they remind me of the Sun's spiritual love for us. The flowers open with sunrise and close with sunset. We must learn and try to be like the tender lotus flower. Despite being rooted amid slimy and filthy waters, the lotus flower impressively floats on the surface immaculately with utmost beauty, purity, glory, and poise. This is the reason why the lotus is considered to be such a sacred flower. Its spotless charm has been admired the world over. A person with a pure heart is like a lotus flower who rises out of the impure waters of various dirty, painful, chaotic emotions and yet stays strong and stable under all conditions. Such a person is like a divine super human-being who is creatively, devotedly, and supernaturally born out of the lotus flower, radiating out its simplicity, kindliness, freshness, and beauty far and wide. Yet rests and stands firmly rooted and deeply grounded upon the same waters from which it stemmed.

The power of the Sun turns the berries of the Rudraksha tree blue. There is presence of the Sun (father's love) even in the generous blue-green berries that turn all dry and brown. Their cycle of youth, fall, and rebirth only makes them stronger, harder, real, more nutritious, wholesome, and part of the tree with no beginning and no end. Dry and wet, raw and ripe are intertwined like Shiva and Shakti. The ultimate truth lies in the fact that Shakti is the pure light of Parvati, and the cause of the Shakti is Shiva.

The magnolia flowers growing in my garden tell me what hope and love is. These flowers wait the entire year to bloom for just one month. Just after the magnolias are in full bloom in May, it is time for them to drop their petals again. But they know that only when they let themselves wither, will they meet with creation once again. And so their beauty never withers, even if their petals fall momentarily before the next season sets in. In allowing the newer energies to grow, we will grow again. Only the enlightened ones accept the facts that it is in giving that you get. It is in forgiving that you are reborn.

In Hindi, *Pu* stands for "flower" and *ja* stands for God. *Puja* is the worship of fully bloomed flowers. We perform *puja* to make our nature one with them. The ritual of *Puja* is performed by burning in the sacred fire whatever doesn't serve you. You then develop an awareness of your own divinity through activating the petals of each chakra or bud, one at a time, so that your entire aura becomes a heavenly garden, with colorful, fragrant, varied, mature flowers, that lie within.

Each chakra represents its counterpart organ in our body. Each chakra has an acupuncture point and a unique character. Each also has one or more colors, a flower, and several petals mentioned in a precise and clear fashion. We are all little buds waiting to gently open our petals and become full-blooming flowers. Unfold your unconsciousness and shine the way a flower unfurls its petals and blooms. Your nature is to spread the light the way it is the nature of flowers to spread their fragrance, far and wide.

God smiles in every flower, each chakra has a special flower assigned to it. Refer to the table in chapter 'ideal soma calendar' to know its relation with flowers.

The Sun rises after the night is over. There is a micro and macro connection between nature and the cosmos. The flowers close to getting recharged in the night and then re-emerge in the morning to bloom again.

Affirm- 'Namostutee, I am brighter than a thousand delightful sunflowers. Tathaastu.'

CHAPTER 79

ROSE IN YOUR HAND

E ven a rose needs a fence around it, in order to nurture, love, and spread
its fragrance. A rose is beautiful because it is strong. Its strength lies
in its thorns. The infinite story of pain and power is intertwined in the
thorny stem of the rose. The prickle and pain of thorns inspire the rose to
seek more pleasure and beauty. What the rose repeatedly seeks, it becomes.

Just the way the outward petals of a rose are guard petals, meant to
protect its inward petals, the image you project to the outside world is
your shield, your guard, and your protection. Your truth, vibrancy, purity,
and true beauty lies in the number of your inner petals. Your real appeal
lies within your outward persona. Learn to care, give, and express like
the rose. Even when it dries, it never dies. Its fragrance keeps your books
smelling nice. The rose in your vase lasts longer because you change its
water regularly. The secrets of nature tell us that constant change in your
emotions is the key to mingling with the supernatural within the duality
of nature.

If your roots are strong and connected, you can surpass death. The
secret of immortality lies in the strength of the root and not the crown.
For example, a rose that grows on the apse of the Cathedral of Hildesheim
in Germany has lasted for a thousand years, despite the World War II
bombings, because its foundation is consecrated with an everlasting love.

Just the way, some guests at a wedding are never happy with your
hospitality no matter how you welcome them, in the same way, most people
will not be happy with your bliss, no matter how much you share it with
them. Do not let their weakness deter your motivation. Remember, those
who judge are judging themselves because life is a mirror and they see

themselves in you. They project onto you what they feel about themselves. If they see only the good in you, then it means there is goodness in them, and if they see only your faults, then the fault is in them.

In hurting another, you hurt yourself. In loving another, you love yourself. In being kind to another, you are being kind to yourself. A broken person rises to the occasion when faced with a traumatic situation, while a happy person breaks when faced with the same situation. For example, with certain medicines, a sick person can be helped, while a healthy person may become ill.

The seven chakras and their corresponding organs are in one body and are therefore essentially all the same. In the same way, seven billion people and their corresponding actions are in one earthly body; therefore essentially we are all the same. In your body, the imbalance in one chakra affects all the other chakras. In your family, the imbalance in one member affects all the other members. In a nation, the imbalance of one resident can affect all the other residents. For example, in the coronavirus pandemic, it only took one person to spread the virus throughout the entire world.

Every time I discuss spiritual and philosophical topics with certain people, they become riled and annoyed with my talks. They say - not again! Please no spirituality, theory, or science. Despite this, I keep putting my hand into the hot water bowl. This is because I feel that these people are getting exasperated with me. After all, I owe something to them. They require help to be transmuted and transformed and I can bring in that developmental change by altering my ways and sharing information in a lighter vein, without upsetting or overwhelming them. This way we all evolve and learn to better ourselves instead of making each other's blood boil with our ways.

The queen of flowers, Rose, is the flower of unconditional love. Roses not only smell nice but have mysterious powers. You can make a soothing love mist and spray it on your face with closed eyes, in your body, hair, or room three times a day. Love mist makes you feel pampered and balances your energies with its sweet pink vibrations. It is made with a combination of organic rose water, almond or jojoba oil and pure edible rose essential oil. If you do not want to make it by yourself then many brands in the market sell organic rose face mist these days.

Our aura carries a rose in its hand. We are that rose. Our spirit and vitality rest in the purity of our thoughts like the rosebud. The strength of our body lies in how we balance ourselves and our emotions, to convert that purity into clarity. Finally, we bloom and evolve based on mental grit and determination, and we light up not only our aura but also the entire surroundings with our fragrant beauty.

Here is a story to share with kids. It is a story about how Rose learned to love:

One spring season, there was a rose blooming in the garden of love. The rose felt that it was the most beautiful flower in the whole garden. All other flowers often complimented and admired the rose for its innocent beauty. The proud rose had a cactus as its neighbor. The rose often said insulting and mean words to the cactus as it looked ugly and was full of many thorns. The rose said, "Why do I have such horrible useless neighbors as you? Why are you so hideous?" But the tolerant cactus never reacted. Soon the spring season passed and the weather became warmer and warmer. It stopped raining and life became very difficult for all the flowers in the garden of love. All flowers wilted away. The rose too began to wilt. In this hot season, the rose saw the cactus easing everyone's pain. The sparrow and the other birds dug holes in the cactus body with their beaks and then flew away refreshed, hydrated and happy. The cactus even helped the rose by asking the birds to give water to its roots with their beaks. Seeing the generosity of the kind cactus, the rose decided to be beautiful and loving inside out in thoughts, words, and actions. The rose realized that we should never judge anyone by their looks and hence started saying positive and kind words to the cactus. As the rose learned its lesson, God blessed the rose with even more beautiful fragrance and from that day on no roses grew thorns. You too can say sweet and polite words to yourself and those around you to uplift the surroundings. This way no garden of love will ever wither. Do this every day and you will see something magical and wonderful will begin to happen as did to the rose.

Affirm- 'Namostutee, Whatever I do, both in the inner and the outer realms, I do it in alignment with divine will and through intuitive love. Motivated by the goodness of heart and love for all, may we all joyfully socialize, inspire and gently flower together. This way our sweet fragrance scatters throughout the soft air. This heavenly scent calmly soothes all unrest, removes all complexities, pride, deception, greed, and yet our fragrance remains fresh, crisp, and cheerful. Tathaastu.'

CHAPTER 79a

ROSES & THORNS

The vitality of our life is dependent upon the quality of our thoughts. Our thoughts are our unspoken words. Even the speech of the speechless is heard. Our thoughts therefore must always smell like rosebuds. No matter how much pain the thorns inflict on the rose, it never forgets to smell good and to look bright, spirited, fresh, pure, and radiant. The rose spreads pleasure, innocence, and love all around. No garden is ever complete without the rose bush.

And when it is night, the rose loses its petals and relaxes its thoughts, not because it is sleepy, but because it feels the urge to assimilate all the sweet memories and loving feelings of the day into its evolved emotions, calmly and clearly. In this way, each day marks its evolution, adding more beauty, charm, and praise upon the earth.

The delicate locks of Christ's hair are also pierced with a crown of thorns - nothing comes easy. Every freedom comes at a cost. Every pleasure comes with pain. Sometimes pain rules our minds and sometimes pleasure does.

We have long crossed the borders of pain and are now living in a land of pleasure, from here on there is only more heavenly joy and bliss but first, you must thank pain. For it is pain that got you till here. What got you here, will not get you there. Let us start with some gratitude, love, acceptance, grace, and encouragement towards our fellow beings. Pain is like sanctified water in which we bathe to cross the borders. It is pain that encourages us to fearlessly initiate the journey.

Pain has high vibrational antennae. Pain is our biggest teacher. It serves as a reminder and teaches us valuable lessons. Once all lessons are learned, the pain diminishes but its fragrance remains. Its fragrance keeps a check upon us. Pain is like a being without form who comes jumping right in to rescue and remind us, just in case we ever falter again. Every effect has a cause. Pain too has a cause. When we try to understand the depth of the cause, pain meets with its purpose of making us realize its existence. In having met with its purpose, pain vanishes and pleasure remains.

When you grow a rose in your garden, you can't say, "I only want the redness of the rose, or the fragrance of the rose, and not the thorns of the rose." You get the rose in its entirety. While giving birth, you may choose to have a natural delivery, but if you do, then you cannot say I don't want to go through the process of labor. The process can be easy or difficult, painful, or painless based on various factors, but it is inevitable. It is in the acceptance of the whole process that you let nature take its course and have faith in the energies you send out and receive. Based on that collective belief, a natural delivery, with ease and positivity, takes place. Maintaining centeredness for it will protect you and keep you strong. Allow life to happen naturally, effortlessly, and God-willingly.

Finally, when spring comes and the rose blooms fully, it imbibes the grandiose and beauty of its surroundings, attracts the color and qualities of all the other flowers around, becomes one with them, and-much like the sun-continues to spread its love in different colors and shades invoking powerful emotions within our soul. Inner and outer, great and small, above and below, rich and poor, low and high, divine and mortal, micro and macro are all manifestations of the same source and are only presented to us to give us a sense of purpose so that we can continue our quest for truth and balance.

Only good comes out of evil. Evil may have raged the war and battle but finally, it is good that wins.

> Confusion is another aspect of clarity,
> Growth is another aspect of stagnation,
> Misery is another aspect of joy,
> Sadness is another aspect of comedy,
> Impulsivity of reflection,
> Limitation of limitlessness,
> Cold heart is another aspect of big heart,
> Unemotional of emotional,
> Criticism is another aspect of appreciation or potential,
> Lack or desire is another aspect of fulfillment,

Dreams of reality,
Failure of victory,
Change is another aspect of changelessness,
Death of life,
Mortality is of immortality,
Overthinking of thinking,
Hard work is another aspect of ease and comfort,
Attachment is another aspect of un-attachment,
Immorality of morality,
Passiveness is another aspect of active and engrossed attention.

This list goes on. This way what we believe to be the thorns brings us to meet with the fragrant roses blooming within us.

You no longer have to look for a resolution to your problems. You no longer have to find solutions when you do not see any problems. Each problem is like a thorn on the rose. It pricks us only when we think that the thorn hurts us. We hurt ourselves by going close to the thorn. The thorn does not come walking towards you. You go to the pain. The pain doesn't come to you. You like the thorn, it excites you. Your inquisitive nature and your attachment to emotions and thoughts take you to the thorn. You are now wiser than that, don't you think? You are more than your sensory responses. You have programmed yourself to go to pain, pleasure, and so on. The same bowl of boiling water that burns your skin, feels as if it is nothing when you become numb to the pain. It is panic, aversion, dejection, and nervousness that traps you into thinking that the bowl of water will burn you. But you put your hand into it, the water bowl did not come walking towards you, it is you who went to it and then you put your hand into it.

Affirm- 'Namostutee, to have faith in yourself is to have faith in God. From sun up to sundown, God is everywhere. God is in the malleable air, in the delicate birds, in the fragrant roses, its fragile petals, in our children, in husbands, in our words, and in every seedling that is planted and nourished to one day bloom, God is life. Tathaastu.'

CHAPTER 80

THE SONG OF THE BLUEBIRD

The bluebird dropped the seed down and darted off for some time. But the strain or *dhun* of the unsung song brought her back to the piled up seeds. She kept returning to finish the seeds. From the point of no return, out came the sweetest melodies that sounded like the chirpiest high vibrational belly laughs of an innocent baby. It inspired everyone to smile from deep within their emotional heart. Out came the blissful voice that filled the entire air with hope and goodness. This melodious song opens up all your blockages and compels you to vehemently follow your calling.

You make it difficult and complicated for yourself only because you enjoy the chase so much. You have become accustomed to not valuing anything that comes easily. The game is simple, but you have been traveling on the wrong route for so long that now you have forgotten your way back.

You too have an inner song, its *dhun* or tune is stored in your deepest vaults (two inches below the navel and two inches above the anus). It is where your little bird sits with high vibrational energy; you will never get where you want to be, by comparing your level of awakening with that of another. Today one person's song might seem beautiful, but tomorrow when you see another's draped in finer silk, then the first will seem ugly to you. She wants only your eyes to see her. A thousand looks from another is meaningless before that one look she gets from you. You crave her when she is right beside you. You give yourself away to find the world when the whole universe is resting right between your arms. You may tire but she is untiring. You are the singer of her song. Her song might be muted, but not for long, you will hear the faint music once again and remember her rhythm. She will dance to your tune whenever you choose to listen to her. You may be lost, but just hang in there and open your inner ears to the sound, and the music will find its way on its own. Don't force it.

Nothing stops just because you stop, the music plays by itself, just because you stopped doesn't mean the music will stop. It is in its nature to keep on playing. It has many mediums but the mediums are mere channels, its existence is not defined by them. Nature is continuously playing beautiful sounds, you resonate with what attracts you most, the subtle or the loud is for you to decide. Music is also a driving force behind intuition. To activate your intuition listen to music. Music touches not only our ears but councils every part of every cell through sound vibration. Listen to the music that alleviates your gloominess, darkness, negativity, imbalances, and troubles. Listen to what awakens and activates you. Playing a song in a loop will repeat the same music. Similarly, if you keep complaining about the situations in your life, the challenging events will keep repeating.

The creator of the song has created it for you to enjoy and hence the song belongs to you. You identify with the song and the song evokes feelings in you. The feelings that the same song invokes in you may be different from the feelings invoked in others. Ultimately the feelings are yours and hence the song is yours. Open your listening ear and your heart to receive the inner message of the song. The way to channelize your energy is not through exclusion, seclusion, or intrusion but inclusion. The way to discipline one another is not through psychic, physical, or verbal control but mutual support and salutation.

Without silent reflection and firm resolution, we will keep looking outside for solutions to the problems whereas the solutions are all within you. Sound vibrations and frequencies played with correct understanding, can affect and heal certain parts of our body.

'Coro' is another name for 'musical choir' and 'nial' is another name for 'champion'. After the setting of the 'Coronial' era,[77] nothing will ever be the same again. There will be a new song sung by the champions of the group choir – a new sound of music that we will need to listen to and embrace to rise to the occasion.

Affirm- 'Namostutee, I am loved, valued and I deserve to be here. I make my thoughts known and communicate freely. I am heard and listened to with enhanced respect. Tathaastu.'

---

[77] Refer to the chapter 'the coronalism of coronial era', for greater details.

CHAPTER 81

MUSICAL NOTES HEAL

Music provides one of the highest forms of healing.
'Swar' also known as musical pitch carries the consciousness of ultimate truth and allows us to perceive perfect unity through awareness. Here are the seven 'Swars'. When the consciousness of all seven Swars shine in one individual, the sound that the music produces is the combined melody of 'Sangam' and solfege to our ears. To realize 'Iswar' or heavenly God, we need to know the essence of the 'Swars'.

Sa and Pa, S, and P are unalterable. The sound of the middle note, Ma or M is twofold in nature. One is an intense purified version, the other is reversed, softer flat aspect of the same sound or truth. (Ma and Am). Out of the seven classical Hindi musical notes – 'sa, re, ga, ma, pa, dha, ni'. We have barely started to master the first five 'sa, re, ga, ma, and pa'. Not many have reached the understanding of how to play the sixth tune which is *dha*.

Each tune invokes a particular type of energy for healing purposes, for example -

A.	Sa	comes from the sound *shadja which means, agni or* fire
B.	Re	comes from the sound *Rishab which means, Brahma or* light of creation
C.	Ga	comes from the sound *gandhaar which means, Saraswati or* breadth of knowledge, it is the low frequency of fifth. It has gamma or gamut which has a full range and pitches of music inherent within it
D.	Ma	comes from the sound *madham* which means *mahadeva or shiv* or fourth octave. It lies in being in the middle, with a perfect combination of moderation and silence
E.	Pa	comes from the sound *pancham* which means it is the fifth element. It is *Laxmi and has a high* frequency of third

F.	Dha	comes from the sound *dhaivat* which means the wisdom of lord *Ganesha*
G.	Ni	comes from the sound *Nishad* which means the power of Sun god or *surya*
H.	Sa	the renewed inner fire that leads to another seven and so on

Out of the seven senses - sight, smell, taste, hearing, touch, clairaudience, and clairvoyance, we have barely activated our first five. Slowly as we continue to evolve, we will reach a better understanding of how to utilize our higher senses for uplifting all sentient beings. Else we will keep overlooking our gifts and talents, thinking of them to be a handicap rather than harnessing and honoring their worth.

The seven 'swars' or 'surs' are known as the divine musical notes. These are sa, re ga, ma, pa, dha, and ni. To explain it in the inner musical language, sa and ma and everything between them has merged. We, therefore, are on the brink of initiating a fresh rhythm.

The seven musical notes of Hindi invoke the following energy:

Sa - pure awareness
Re - space of motherly love
Ga - indivisible abstract knowledge of your roots
Ma - brings in harmony glory and multicultural, multicolored hue
Pa - envelops all colors of rainbow through strategic concrete planning of ideas
Dha - unborn duality of thoughts
Ni - devotion makes you realize that I and me are one, you are the thoughts you breathe
Sa repeated - leads you to your destiny where all actions of past, present, and future become one

There is no better feeling than to experience the energy of the Ganges River flowing upstream. It is then that we understand what it is like to enjoy the transference of energy from high to low. Music is a mysterious way to heal the soul. People sing to heal their souls.

I was once in a musical trance. In that state, I was completely thought-free and all I could hear was just the music. My ears became like an empty flute. The music was the same but I was transformed. The people were the same but a transformational era had begun. The pause ended as it does between the musical notes – from one to another. In this new era, the heart and mind are one. Love is the music of life. There are no divisions, no lack of trust, nothing to repent, and no sadness in the tunes.

GOD speaks through me, the frequencies and vibrations I emit. "When you are open to let go - you will meet with me. I have come here to lead you to the good- away from all evil - to tame the maestro and assist with the transition which is not as effortless as it seems. I am here to serve out of pure love for my community as the camaraderie of this fusion song plays best when its tune is synchronized with the instrumental beats of the drum and the steps of the graceful belly dancers."

God plays his music through us. The music God plays is natural and free. It is not robotic. Computers are meant to be programmed. We are not meant to be programmed. We are not computers. We use the computer as a tool. We, humans, are not programmed to think only in one particular way and we are not bound by our profession, status, country, or any tool. We are limitless and cannot be programmed until we allow ourselves to get chained and subjugated. Let the music play. The music can only play when you realize the immense power that your consciousness holds. Let no one play with your sub-consciousness or conscious nature. You are more than what you think you are. It is essential to look within your own heart and find out what music lifts you to what level.

Your life leads you to your soulmate, your bliss. All you need to know is your inside story. Follow the beats of your heart to find out who and what is on your frequency. Just chanting the seven surs - sa re ga ma pa dha ni - has the potential to kill any bacteria from 13 feet distance. Good music from a genuine heart is the voice of the soul. Going against nature is the reason for suffering. Follow the subtle sound of nature and release all pain and suffering with the grace of *Tridevi Stutee* or divine Stuti, the one that infuses the essence of vitality in all from time immemorial to protect one and all during evolutionary cycles.

> Sa invokes light
> Re invokes creativity
> Ga invokes wisdom
> Ma invokes greatness
> Pa invokes prosperity
> Dha invokes regulation
> Ni invokes life

The purest music to hear is the sound of breath. The *Pingala* breath of Sun comes out from your right nostril. The Ida breath of the moon comes out through your left nostril. The breath is balanced because of the *sukshma*[78] or subtle breath that brings light and preserves life force energy in the middle.

Affirm- 'Namostutee, The supreme breath of consciousness protects my physical, mental, and spiritual body. Tathaastu.'

---

[78] *Sukshma is another word for subtle body, in which focal points or chakras consist.*

CHAPTER 82

THE LIT CANDLE

No candle is ignited by itself. It needs another candle/source to light its fire. If your belief is as weak as the flickering light of the candle that extinguishes with a little air of doubt, then it is not going to burn all that negativity within or outside of you. You must aim to invoke and become one with the flickering inner fire. This fire is persistent and does not ever extinguish. It continues to rise until all negativity is removed. Our thoughts keep the inner fire contained to ensure that it purifies each of our five elements, filling us with positive and pure energy at the right pace.

From being a full-time healer in the Middle East, I have now become a part-time healer and a part-time preacher so that I can utilize the time to empower and ignite the candle within you with the flame that lights within me. Alone I can alleviate the sufferings of just one village, together we can be of help to the entire country and gracefully spread our light of love and peace to the entire globe.

Light a new white candle to light the flame within you.

Unlock your potential, unleash the crazy calling you may have. Every new idea can change the course of humanity. When your idea comes to fruition, there surely will be many people who would have inspired you and helped sparkle this idea. Always be in gratitude and reverence toward those who helped you.

Think of all the feelings and circumstances you would want to get rid of. Write these down on paper and mentally verbalize, "Dear Universe, I no longer need these feelings, things, or circumstances. Please teach me the lessons that I need to learn through them in a way that feels better and opens my heart." Take three deep breaths and then literally burn the written paper. Now let go and release! This will make you feel either lighter and overjoyed or frightened and overwhelmed.

Say thank you to the flame for helping you let go of your feelings and circumstances. Rub your hands with open palms and an open heart. Invoke and invite everything you want to welcome in your life while looking at the burning flames. Once again say thank you to the light burning within this candle believing that you have received all those affirmed wholesome feelings and are ready to welcome them into your life.

Bless the fire angels within the flame while looking at it with your half-opened eyes. Even If you find it difficult to keep the gaze, embrace the positive warmth that envelops you with the healing process. Let the candle melt away by itself instead of extinguishing it. Doing this ritual either with beeswax candles or with a home-made candle will be even more effective.

Hindus religiously light lamps at temples. It is a great practice as it reminds us to light our inner lamps. When our lamps are lit, we can light the lamp of another person. As the chain continues, many such lamps will light the universal altar. The light of lamps may flicker but the altar will always stay lit as long as there is even one lamp that is lit.

Candles ward off negative energies so light up aromatic candles, sandalwood, frankincense, or sage incense in each room of your home daily. Sprinkle sea salt on the floor which you may later sweep away with a wet mop. You may add drops of lavender essential oils onto the burning candle for a more soothing effect.

The candle you are holding is not mine; neither is it for me, for I do not burn on the outside. The light is within you and not out there in the dark. The fire is internal. You have been holding a candle that is meant to shine within. Your fire is waiting to be ignited within you. Inner fire doesn't burn; it only blesses us with its warmth. No hand will be burnt and nothing will be destroyed. The past, present, and future are one. Dark is just as good as light. Nothing is bad and nothing is good. We are simply dancing flames in this black-and-white world of greys and grace.

Oh! So you became an actor, a saint, a billionaire - well who cares unless you become something that affects the whole of humanity and becomes the radiatory cause of rising collective positive consciousness. You can cause them all to evolve by lighting the candle within you. In burning the candle, you or the candle does not burn but it lights up the room for sure. It melts with the rest of the candles and becomes one. When the candle reaches the endpoint, its flames burn much higher until the excess heat finally burns it out. Excessive knowledge and pride can burn us out. A truly wise soul conserves its energy, stays cool and calm, and makes use of the light sparingly and moderately. Our mind is a tool just the way a candle or a computer is a tool that gives out knowledge or light. Do not confuse knowledge with wisdom or intelligence.

Affirm- 'Namostutee, the intuitive light of knowledge leads my thoughts to transform and merge with the infinite stars of life, awareness, and wisdom. Tathaastu.'

CHAPTER 83

PIGS CAN FLY

Pigs fly is a phrase often used to express the hellish happenings that might occur if something that shouldn't be allowed is allowed to happen out of sheer ignorance.

This chapter highlights that there are a lot of things that we are capable of doing and can be done but must not be done. By doing them due to sheer ignorance, we can end up causing devastating results. We must therefore always seek better answers before doing any action. Each of our actions should be harmless and must be done with a higher purpose of keeping the greater good in mind.

I met a little girl who was sending balloons in the air, saying, "Look my pig is flying!" I went up to her and told her, "Even if you fill your piggy bank with all the jewels, or you hang another balloon on top of your pig, the fact remains that pigs[79] can never fly. Lighten the weight you have been carrying. A balloon flies because it is empty from within. A pig may look like a weightless balloon, but looks are deceptive. It is high time you start seeing things as they are." We need to stop overloading ourselves with excessive thoughts and emotions so that we can free ourselves and fly.

One balloon cannot make you fly. On average, a person weighing 50 kilograms requires 5000 helium balloons tied to him to fly. And even so, these balloons will not take you up to the higher heavens. They cannot handle the pressures higher than a certain height.

---

[79] *Pigs are often associated with ignorance.*

Logic gone bizarre:

Pigs look like balloons
Balloons can fly
Pigs can fly

Balloons that are released to fly solo into the environment cause immense danger to the environment and can harm an animal, dolphin, whale, or bird thousands of miles away. The plastic balloon you release will not fly to the heavens but it can surely send some animal down to hell, causing much suffering and death. So why fly, when you and your balloon can calmly and harmlessly stay grounded upon earth within the space you occupy.

If you want to know God then first know the divine reality of the Goddess within. If you want to know the sun then first acknowledge the rays of the sun. Knowledge is universal and shines upon everyone like rays of the sun. Knowledge cannot be created nor destroyed. It simply is. Just like the sun rays, it cannot be separated or owned completely by a single religion, caste, creed, country, sect, or individual. Our perceptions may differ but the supreme reality of knowledge rightfully and truly belongs to the wise, self-realized being. The sun (soul) and its rays (radiant energy) co-exist and are inseparable. The Goddess (Shakti) cannot be realized or understood without God (self) and vice versa.

Even a piglet who grows in the dirty waters has God's soul within it and through that light, it enjoys the pleasure and happiness of life. This is because it doesn't overindulge or over attach itself like most of us to its muddy possessions or greed. It lets nature take its course and plays to its tunes.

On this note, here is a balloon meditation- bring a green balloon and fill it up with your breath slowly and cautiously thinking of the goals you want to achieve and intend to manifest. Make sure your goals are aligned with the well-being of the universe. Tie the balloon and let go.

Affirm- 'Namostutee, as my life magically unfolds and improvises- abundance, joy, proper structure, opportunities, and unconditional love come to me, empowering and igniting my soul to reach higher goals with moral purpose. Tathaastu.'

CHAPTER 84

ETHERIC BATH

Knowing fully well that the environment is dirty, we not only watch what we eat but also make the effort to properly wash what we eat. We consume a variety of foods and instinctually always keep them clean and pure.

It is very important to properly wash what we take into our life. Why not be careful and ensure that things we see, hear, and read even in a dirty or filthy environment are only things that are holy, wise, and clean? A filthy unhygienic environment is an environment where people think and do wrong, disrespect, bad mouth others, and detest knowledge and truth. A virtuous person is one who always strives to be honest, true, just, good, and makes the right choices, despite the outside problems.

Apart from the physical bath, our body needs an emotional, mental, spiritual bath as well. The healing protocols are based on natural laws and their beauty. It removes the veils and taps the limitless magic and power that lies within you to reach anywhere and in any realm to become anyone, no matter what walk of life you come from.

It brings in that willingness, faith, and belief that most of us are searching for! It fills the gaps and brings out your inner child. It connects you to your center and ignites the spark within you.

It helps you know your 'Ohm' (electrical resistance) worth! As the veil between the visible and invisible gets thinner - we get to know the profound reality behind the unreality.

These higher energies will clean up the library of your mind, meeting you physically in a tranquil space beside the fireplace in your living room. They will then work through you making you productive and wholesome, joining you in your workplace, eating with you in your dining room. They will enjoy the games through you and you too will then begin to enjoy them with complete detachment. They will remove all stagnant and dead energies blocked in every corner of every room of your home. Cleansing and purifying your valuable abode with the angelic broom, even the overlooked areas, and hidden closets. These angels are here to guard and save you with this divine blue mop.

May you all be surrounded by healing white light and may you all work under the divine guidance for the good of everyone. May you always be sheltered and protected as you are filled with life energy. Make your body and mind so spiritual, powerful, centered, awakened, disciplined, enlightened, and determined that no unstable entity can ever turn you down. To keep your energy body vitalized, sacred, and divine, avoid unnecessary visits to hospitals or any sites that may attract negative energy. These may include cemeteries.

Avoid cosmetic surgeries, drugs, alcohol, and multiple sex partners. If despite these precautions you feel energetically unaligned, negative, or weak then there are always healers like me who can make you feel more balanced and wholesome.

I am here to get to the root of the problem. That is the only way to cure and free you of all the pressures you feel, releasing the obstacles, the frustrations, and disappointments you are witnessing. You are meant to shine in a perennial positive light and I am here to clear up and show you the path which is beneficial to you. Untie the knots and let the enlightening power of purification and truth flow. Why are you holding on to what needs to be released? Allow me to heal you without the use of any medications and any physical contact and help you flush it out. All it needs is your faith.

Whether you have swallowed poison or caught a deadly disease, there is no such problem that cannot be remedied. Wisdom demands you to learn self-healing skills to come out of your destructive thought patterns. If you have the inclination, stay connected and I am happy to continue sharing the sacred self-healing skills with you.

We can see only this much through the tunnel, our sphere of vision blocks us from seeing what is beyond the dark walls. The existence of one person's unreality can be another person's only reality. What seems to have no identity or value to you, can be of extreme value and invaluable for another.

In one of the astral travels, I saw myself swimming in a pool of dirty water where a dangerous yet cute animal that looked something like a mink, only with a longer but hairless body, came pouncing at me. It was fearless and sprayed some strange dark reddish colored liquid. The walls had blood all over them. I had never seen anything like this and I am guessing it hadn't seen anything like me either. We both were accustomed to being in familiar surroundings. I had to run and get back before my journey was over to avoid getting hurt by its aggressive behavior. That incident kept me on guard on this plane as I knew what was to happen in the future. Whatever happens in the inner world happens, sooner or later, in the outer world. I have seen that some people are just as dangerous because they are not as ready yet to realize the divinity within themselves and those around so keep your distance and avoid disturbing their solitary confinement.

Bless them to evolve but do not force your healings on them. They are lost but will soon find their way out of their fears. The fear you feel by being around them is a reflection of the fear that lies within them. They can never reach anywhere close to your divine soul or even near your spirit so let their false ego fleece them into believing that they are brave and can control by pouncing brutally and unpredictably. If there is energy pushback and if there is something that you sense about the situation not being right, work with your senses and do not go against the energy.

Your belief can become your reality and all your decisions can be actualized perfectly. All your regrets can be converted into inner forgiveness and all your wealth can be protected. Just be aware and come to me when I call you -For when the time is right you will not only hear but also understand the profundity in these words. Keep the faith and you will always be protected and shielded under God's divine care.

There is a mystical rainbow bridge between heaven and earth. This bridge is infinitely connected. The beings are justly and perfectly distributed on either side of the bridge based on their aptitude (*guna*), conduct (*karmas*), nature (*swabhawa*), and readiness.

Just like we get star points here on earth for being conscientious citizens, the shining stars in the sky are good points incurred by the good souls on earth who bring awareness within us and enlighten us to join the righteous path with their shining light. They are the timeless wonder-workers who work forever with the universal energies and rectify the blemishes of the moon. Just the way good citizens sanctify our planet and make the world a much better place to live, the light emanated by these stars saves us all from destruction and disaster.

"*Vinaasha kaale vipareetha buddhi*" is a famous Sanskrit proverb that means that "whenever there is destruction, doom, negativity and excess darkness even the highest minds give up and tend to go against their selves. At such point, those who are skilled in the art of using their discriminative intelligence make the right decisions and reverse the disastrous situation with their subtle healing light".

The spiritual energies release the earthly beings from the ruin and bondage that sometimes comes from the overload of knowledge and power.

Affirm- 'Namostutee, May all those who are suffering transform and transcend into the healing light. This way we all can live a more fulfilled and fun-filled life. Tathaastu.'

CHAPTER 85

DIVINE RITUALS

I am here to share the true meanings behind the rituals because truth liberates you.

The healing protocols I use help raise vibrational energy and awareness empowering you and making you more conscious of your actions. Ultimately, fear nothing, be yourself, and remember God is everywhere and in everything so as long as you are in the right, nothing can go wrong.

What is clean and pure is beautiful. The endpoints of fingers and toes have the strongest radiation of etheric matter. This is the reason why such high impetus is given by Muslims to keep the hands, feet, and genitalia thoroughly clean.

In Indian culture, women wear jewelry on their feet, both anklets and toe rings. In this way, they keep their vow to stay cleansed of all ungodly activities. This implies that you are purified.

Your home is your sacred space so besides keeping it clean and tidy, request visitors to remove their shoes. Even the house members must remove their shoes before entering the house. Wash your feet, in saltwater kept in copper bowls, before entering to maintain psychic and etheric hygiene. Avoid handshakes and hugs as much as possible other than family to avoid intermingling of divine energies.

Offering the fruits in the temple is a ritual followed without knowing its inner meaning. In truth, we are the mystic trees who are meant to selflessly offer fruits of all our actions to God rather than eating them all by ourselves.

Inculcate the ritual of writing down a minimum of three things you are grateful for at the end of each day with a red pen on a piece of yellow paper. Place them in a jar to train your mind into developing a more positive outlook. Reward yourself by reading that jar once it is filled and see the magic happen. Continue the ritual forever while also suggesting and encouraging it to as many people as you can.

Living a life of love and bliss is the ability to stop reacting and responding to the nagging and bickering around us that is both subtle and apparent. Stay calm for the one who is constantly busy focusing or finding flaws is the flawed one.

Responsibility is the ability to respond to your inner voice and be accountable for your thoughts, words, actions, and deeds. Stay balanced and away from vanity. You no longer need to get lost again for you already know where home is so stay grounded, balance your hara (energy field of your body), don't let the madness let you go so high that you can no longer see anything clearly.

Ah, powerful woman! In India, married women wear *sindoor*, a mark made from vermillion or cinnabar, on their forehead. This very powerful ritual indicates that you have transcended all fear of evil and become one with the mighty infinite, vowing to serve him and follow his sacred precepts filled with divinity. In India, women braid their hair as a mark of the culmination of mind, body, and spirit.

The third eye activates the Pineal gland or the *samajh* chakra. It is the eye of Lord Shiva. Placing a blue *bindi* or dot, the color of lapis lazuli, after your practices of meditation is a great way to invoke the light of Lord Krishna's consciousness, which takes you to the truth of your higher self while connecting you with your *samajh* chakra.

Red round *bindi*[80] symbolizes the power of the full moon within you. Traditionally *bindi* was always red or maroon (color of energy) and was produced from the stylus of the saffron flower (crocus sativus). It can also be substituted by the dye of the annatto seeds (bixa orellana) or the less expensive and commonly available turmeric powder (curcuma longa), which is mixed with lime and/or alum to get the red tone. Unfortunately from a sustainably-minded culture, we have now started wearing stickers instead of real *bindi's*.

Shree is represented by a *bindi* on the forehead, it is the royal combination of sha and shi - yang and yin, masculine and feminine, sha

---

[80] *Bindi - a holy colored dot worn on the center of the forehead by women - mostly in India by Hindus.*

or Shakti removes impurities, and shi or Shiva brings in purity, luck, riches, perfection, virtue, and peace. Shree which is the *bindi* on the forehead activates the mother Goddess (Durga).

Holi, the festival of love is a popular ancient Hindu festival, celebrated in India and around Asia with great fervor. This divine ceremony was originally designed by Lord Krishna. It is meant for people of all walks of life, rich and poor to celebrate life together. One of the many rituals of this festival is that they sprinkle holy water mixed with aromatic flowers upon one another to cleanse and purify everyone around. It is a mark of oneness and good over evil.

We are the healthiest of the healthy and the wealthiest of the wealthy. Let's also become the purest of the pure, celebrating Holy in the holiest of places.

By activating the Aar chakra, the pituitary gland becomes activated and we feel more grounded and connected to the vibrant, earthly energies. It is also known as the master chakra. The earth's energies symbolize purity, abundance, and prosperity. When the pituitary gland and pineal gland are both activated and mingled, they ignite your inner power and fill you with the ultimate love--the kind of love on which the entire universe rests. At this stage, it purifies us like the lotus. Our crown chakra and all the meridians open up, and our aura dances like a beautiful peacock with an electric violet hue.

My journey from the east into this beautiful Jewish village in the west has introduced me to many beautiful rituals. Some examples are listed below-

Easter is celebrated in memory of 'Eastre' the Sun Goddess. She is also known as the daughter of the heavens and the Triple Goddess. In Easter – the roots of the word 'ter' come from the word 'three'. 'Eas' etymologically means waterfall of luck, abundance, and prosperity. The spring represents the threefold cycle - new birth, death, and the rebirth of Easter bunnies (or three full moons). These are the harbinger of 'Eas' for the ones with heightened Christ consciousness. Christ died on Friday, was born on Sunday, and finally reborn on Tuesday.

Fear is the only impediment in realizing pure freedom, complete health, and true fate. The little Easter bunnies are fearful creatures. We celebrate Easter to shed fearful thought-forms to transmute from fear to love, from danger to protection. This way Christ is reborn or thrice born with a promise to create a newly evolved life.

Most men are from Mars and so all must wear iron bangle on their wrist to keep connected and chi energy flowing. Women are from Venus and must wear copper on their wrist to keep chi energy flowing. Men with more advanced vital force in their bioenergy field are from the moon. Women of today who patiently carry the sun's warm loving energies live life freely, and confidently on their terms are from planet mercury.

In certain parts of rural India, those who are unworthy, unfit, or impure marry a sacred tree for strengthening their self-worth. The healthy trees are infused with hidden supernatural powers to cure, energize, and enhance fertility, increase clarity and confidence. It is believed they contain the souls of our ancestors and also of the unborn.

In North India, the 'Pada' or feet of nine little girls (depicting nine forms of Maa Durga) are washed with flowers by the man of the household to take their blessings. This century-old ceremony is celebrated with great pomp each year in my home. The little girls or 'Kanyas' are respectfully fed sumptuous meals or 'bhog' and offered divine gifts during this Hindu ceremony called 'Kanjak'. Just like the delicate and soft petals of the lotus, the feet of these innocent girls are pure and those who wash them get charged with reverence, divinity, and grace. By worshipping the lotus feet, the lotus bud slowly flowers and enters into womanhood with pride and radiance. It is said that by respecting womanhood, all our karma of past negativity and sins gets washed away. Just as the bee collects honey from the flowers, great men collect 'Padma Madhu' or transcendental honey from the lotus feet of the 'Kanyas' to show their gratitude towards Goddess Durga. This way all their impurities are washed away and they see them as divine beings rather than mere objects for the gratification of their senses. These girls are so pure and divine that a single look into their innocent eyes can cleanse us of all contaminated thought forms, release us of darkness, and restore our vitality and youthfulness.

It is said that similar transcendental honey comes out of the feet of Godly holy beings like Jesus, Buddha, and Lord Rama. This is why their sacred 'Padukas' or slippers and footprints are worshipped even today in various temples. These 'Padukas' were made of ivory, sandalwood, silver, and copper in ancient times for ceremonial purposes. Some were even made of sharp iron spikes meant to inflict pain on the wearer as a demonstration of their conviction and pain tolerance on the path.

Affirm- 'Namostutee, I identify with loving awareness. I love everything. Tathaastu.'

CHAPTER 86

SPEAK YOUR TRUTH

Within or without - inner or outer - the voice of truth speaks the same language.

The high spirit entered my body when my soul was ready to leave, while my body was not. From that time on, I have been able to recognize the divine within you all. 'I am' immortal within a mortal body a mother of mothers, yet I sometimes feel like I am a man within a woman's body. But that is because the soul is both yin and yang and the spirit through which I function has no gender. It is what it is. Truth is universal.

A precious pearl remains protected within its shell in the deep waters but its beauty is appreciated only when it comes out in the open. There is a rare pearl inside of us protected within an invisible shell which we call our spirit. The beauty of the pearl within us can only expand in the open when we merge with the invisible shell.

Those who speak little are the ones who always listen more and so they are the ones who usually know more. As far as possible, stand up not only for your rights but also for what you believe is right. What you believe is right for you may be wrong for someone else. It may just be one facet of the truth. Any type of pretense defies its very purpose because the truth needs no validation. To please pure energy one needs to first be pleased with oneself. You cannot shy away from its truth.

Tap the source of your innate unprocessed raw energy and then refine yourself to become who you always wanted to be. There is no escaping the truth. Your beliefs create your reality. This life or in another, based on how soon you choose to connect with the 'I within'. Each one of us will reach enlightenment but how long it will take is something that we need to decide.

When people had no mask on, their harsh and piercing words hurt. However, this time around they are forced to wear a mask when they speak with one another. May this serve as a reminder to speak less and speak only the words that are filled with kindness and love. Love hides behind hate; courage behind the fear; the light behind love, doubt behind clarity. Eventually, all will stop hiding and finally, the truth will come out in the open. I am hoping this mask will make a difference in how we speak especially with ourselves considering the negativity that spews from our mouths for one another. Sometimes "when the word doesn't change, the mask changes the wor(l)d." And in this way the world changes.

I speak the truth and nothing but the truth because I never lie but that doesn't mean I tell you the whole truth. Just the way you can never see the light of the sun when it is dark in the night - there is always a part left unrevealed and the mystery is never-ending. Let's declutter our restless minds from the unsatisfying chaos by first learning to speak our truth openly and honestly with ourselves. Once we speak with ourselves in a way that we should only then can we begin to talk to another with sweetness and acceptance.

To steal someone's creativity and work of intuitive knowledge is the plagiarism of divine work. To do this means you will be born with lower mental faculties and with no intuitive means. You still have time to make amends. Just give your partner an equal share and inscribe their name, for you have been forewarned.

Gold is worthless until it goes through the process of purification and refinement to remove all its impurities. Same way, we must purify and refine ourselves to know our true worth. The one who speaks their truth politely, humbly, gently, kindly, and fairly is a rare gem, rarer than the precious emerald that is displayed in the Washington History Museum. Listen intently as there are gems within that are waiting to be awakened. Be gracious enough to not overstep your limits by arguing, gossiping, disputing, questioning, or degrading your value.

The secret truth of our making: Light or fire gives rise to sulfur which is our soul that speaks. Darkness or wet earth gives stillness to salt which activates our body. Water merges all thoughts and gives rise to mercury which is our spirit and breath. These three elements mix with heat, cold, dryness, and moisture of the air. Blood and vitality are produced based on how well we mingle with the air quality and quantity to purify ourselves and our blood. Every entity, every organ, every planet, big or small evaporates, expands, and dissolves much like the elements.

God and heaven are within you, trust yourself more than anyone, your soul never lies. It never dies.

Water never fears fire, air doesn't know fear at all. The one who sees clearly is right in the middle and is not clouded by the outward charm for it clearly sees what lies deep inside. Such a person is the one who hears divine truth no matter what. Such a person is self-taught and self-liberated and knows how and when to control the flow of its dance. Such a person doesn't let emotions or mind take over him. It is in giving that one receives and such a giving person is always connected with the soul within.

Being quiet for too long can paralyze the soul and so I have come out to communicate what truth is to me. In appreciating the true beauty in everything, you expose yourself and your truth. Truth is always hidden somewhere in the smaller details and not in what seems most obvious to the naked eye. Truth is about being steadfast, loyal, honest, trustworthy, and solid like the tree. It stands firm like a tree and no stone or storm can move a strong tree.

Why fear judgment? The right one welcomes all judgment because he knows he has done no wrong. The reason you have qualms being judged is that there is a part of you that even you don't like. When you are transparent with yourself - you can be transparent around another because of that inside out transparency.

You can not only handle any judgment but survive any hostile environment, weather conditions, any extreme circumstance and yet remain untouched, immortalized, and vitalized much like the translucent tardigrade animal collected from Antarctica by Japanese scientists which preservers & revives itself back to life despite everything around it.

There is no greater pleasure than speaking your truth and so I will ever remain grateful to America for embracing me with so much love and acceptance while giving me all the liberty and freedom to breathe freely and transparently in its beautiful land filled with memories of rich history.

The swan doesn't need to paint herself to look all white. It simply is white. In the same way, you do not need to do something to simply be and speak your truth. Nature soothes you, heals you, and puts your senses back in place. That's where you should spend most of your time. As soon as I allowed myself to jump into the fragrant flowery pool of heavenly bliss, harmony in life returned with the light and order of pink energy. I am best when I am in my element, my true nature. It is my nature to be polite, forgiving, sweet, compassionate, understanding, undisturbed, and untroubled. This realization became the linking cause for my high spirited lucky soul to reincarnate my incarnated soul. We now stand united while calmly being in the same physical body.

Just the way the word 'level' remains the same whether you read it forward or backward. Yogini's visions of truth remain the same, whether the level of her footwear gets her the top spot or not.

There will come a time when a yogini will be found wearing sneakers. A time when all this mental phenomenon will lead to a physical marathon-to apply, utilize and act decisively based on your acquired skills and hidden talents is like constantly running a marathon. It sure tests your endurance but as you build your stamina with persistence and self-discipline, you enrich your soul and seize the opportunities that lay ahead with great precision and success. The 'force' of life is our ability to constantly push ourselves on all levels to survive through challenges. It is this force that balances you until you reach a point in life that there is little or nothing that gets you down. This way we consistently radiate with beaming energy and reliability. We make sound pragmatic judgments and value our life and that of others.

Connecting with myself on a cosmic level always evoked deep soul rendering bliss within me. This way I could easily view the world with rose-tinted glasses. True metamorphosis and evolutionary transformation occurred when I ceased to feel lost and began to identify myself with my physical reality. It is then that I became truly awake from my innocent fairy tale dream. The divine became divinely human. From the dream, you get to know your reality. But the reality is a dream so shouldn't we say that the dream takes you to another dream. Something far stronger than me expresses your dream through me so that you can one day learn to shape a better reality. The progress we are projecting is a combined effort of seeds planted by heightened spiritual souls and the divine ancestors that went before us. The tree of our complete cosmic reality is deeply nourished by a combination of our strong material roots which are constantly connected with the heavenly roots.

Affirm- 'Namostutee, I choose silence over telling lies. Tathaastu.'

CHAPTER 87

YOGINI WHO DRIVES CARS

Just as in a car, the quality of each of its parts is tested, our *chakras* too are tested, and their efficacy is judged by hidden higher powers. Just as the model of a car is upgraded with newer models based on technological advances, our *chakras* are also upgraded with newer technologies and superpowers, even though our body remains the same. To evolve is almost like being reborn within the same body, with renewed motives.

There is a continual source of energy within the battery because of which your car starts. That source is the main reason for any engine to function.

America is like an expressway. As you are about to enter this country, you need to accelerate your speed and then keep the momentum going, or else you will crash. Once you have accelerated to the right speed, there is no looking back. It is like an automated car system working through you. It drives you up the success ladder when it is the opportune time. Keep the waters of the chi energy flowing, for your car, it is not going to stop anytime soon in this path that you have chosen to travel.

Reckless driving increases the probability of an accident. The problems begin with you and how you drive the car, not by the people around you. The steering wheel is in your hand and the decision to turn the corner or accelerate is yours. How you react to another driver is also your choice. Despite this, if you do meet with an accident it is the result of a thought you created.

Just as we must stop at a red light, even if the sound of ringing bells at the railroad are enticing us, in the same way, we should not disturb the cleansing bell when it is ringing with the cosmic flow of annular energy, however much we are tempted or lured to cross the line.

A parallel to the car, its speed and drive is our mind, body, and thoughts. How smooth is your drive, how carefully planned is your speed, how clean is your mind, how well maintained is your car-your body, how detached you are from being agitated, how attached you are to your comfort zone, how open you are to accept, how deep is your insight, how much of your ego you have shed, how much of the road remains untraveled, how much wiser have you become through your travels, how many directions you followed, how much confusion your resistance caused, how late you reached, how dissatisfied are you with your performance, how responsible do you feel for the passengers in your car, how many races you won with yourself, how many repercussions you faced because of your reckless driving-it's all you, always was, always will be for the consciousness within the car is all yours, the costs of maintenance is for you to bear, the loss is yours and so is the gain. It is your call, your car.

Your race is with yourself and with no other outsider.

While driving a car when you are blinded by the oncoming flash of light, you don't see what's around you at that moment. So is the case when you are unable to see reality due to some blinders in life.

Enjoy the drive no matter which car you drive. Just the way, one recipe cannot fit all - each person drives differently. There are no rights and wrongs. Everyone's reactions and actions are a result of their circumstances. We are no one to judge or label. Each person is on their journey.

Over the lifetimes, I have seen many drivers drive the same car over and over again. The car that lasted the most is always the one that has had the most caring and connected drivers. Neither are all roads smooth nor is the speed static.

Our paths may happen to cross but how you drive, the speed at which you travel on that road based on your temperament, experience, ease, and confidence is completely your choice and your will.

Road bumps teach us to pause, reflect, slow down, and dwell upon the ups and downs of the journey. They teach us that life is as fleeting as our wavering moods. However, bliss is permanent.

When you drive too slowly, remember you are causing all the others to slow down too. Will you be able to live carrying the burden of the sole cause slowing so many more? If not, speed up. The speed limits are preset, you just need to follow them. Being too slow is stupid, not to be mistaken for being cautious. Being too fast is being rash, not wise. Keep the vehicle at a moderate speed and the ride for you as well as others will be smooth and safe. Pressing the brakes excessively is a sign of fear, move beyond your fears and trust yourself, the sound of hesitation that you are hearing is not from outside but from within you. Overuse of the brakes in a car, overheat and damage them. Similarly taking more brakes than required, increases your inner body heat causing congestion and overheating. If congested energy is not released with proper movement and circulation the body will wither away similar to the brakes of the car being damaged.

Some drivers are over vigilant, careful, and polite on the road while others are risk-takers, rash, and rule breakers, careless, and clumsy. They could be new or experienced drivers.

The chakras are your body's steering wheels. Be gentle with your chakras to have an activated healthy aura. Just like being gentle with the steering wheel of your car to ensure a smooth drive. Roads we travel teach us a lot. For example, the scope of reversing and potential U-turns are reduced to almost none when we take the highway.

When I treat my car with respect, love, and care, it is equally good to me. It keeps me safe and responds to my commands. Now if I say that my car isn't alive, then what is? It has almost all the attributes, etiquettes, and beauty required to be a good person. It has the energy and the hopes, of not only the driver and passengers but also all those and all that went into the building of it and its brand.

Just the way, no car can run without fuel or a charged battery, no person can go on living without the help of inner fire that fuels us. Whether we are aware or not, there is a certain amount of fuel filled up in all of us, just the way there is petrol or diesel in all cars.

When a person is in a coma, the physiological body can sometimes be functional. Yet the soul is present in a deep sleep. This is like a car with no one to drive it. The combination of our mental, emotional, and etheric body is the consciousness that the body needs to function and drive itself. This shows that the physical body was created by consciousness. In a car, most parts are replaceable. Similarly, almost every body part except for the medulla oblongata is replaceable in today's progressive world.

It is fun to drive a fancy car but if it requires a lot of repairs then it is no fun keeping it. Similarly, relationships that are internally weak and imbalanced tend to fade. Repair your heart and emotions from within. Be more kind to yourself and keep the faith. There is a romantic potential of a happy drive even in the most vintage of cars.

Driving on the roads, sometimes we reach a dead-end but that doesn't stop us from taking a u-turn. There are always u-turns you can take. Dead ends will take us nowhere but the turn can take you somewhere. We have it in us to make the impossible - possible with a little 'u-turn' in our thinking. All we need is an open heart and mind with pure intentions to take the turn.

We get bothered and distracted only by what we want to get bothered with. Sixty percent of road accidents happen because of distracted drivers. Living life is no different than driving a car. Avoid distracting yourself while you are on the journey ahead. Your carelessness not only causes you harm but it delays and causes untold misery to many other people traveling alongside.

The key to driving carefully is to anticipate the actions of others by expecting the unexpected. In life sometimes you have to take unexpected turns in order to stay safe and protected. Our choices make all the difference. The day I stopped living in the fast lane, the lane in which I lived became fast. Be yourself even if those around are not being themselves.

Deers freeze on seeing headlights, we can do better by keeping our eyes moving. This way we scan through the road and act rather than stare at unprecedented situations.

Then I heard someone on the radio, 'I am the first who ever came. When I came I gave you a cart with wheels to plow the fields. The fields are no longer there and neither is the cart, but you are still dragging the same wheel in your new car. Technology has evolved. Time to turn the old wheel and start anew. The old ways won't last.'

Affirm- 'Namostutee, I drive my car with all the energy, alertness, love, and excitement. With similar fervor, I smoothly express what I think and love in pretty much everything I do in my life. Tathaastu.'

CHAPTER 88

RIVERS OF HEAVEN

Of India's sacred rivers, the Ganges River is created by Lord *Brahma*. The Yamuna River is protected by Lord *Vishnu*. The Saraswati River is a confluence of the Ganges and the Yamuna, and their triune union is celebrated by Lord *Shiva*. Each of them represents a *'Nadi'*. Ganga is Ida, the cooling moon river. The Yamuna is *Pingala*, the warm solar river. Saraswati is Sushumna, the river of *Agni*.

The celestial waters of (love) Saraswati pass through three phases. Their flow of energy becomes heavenly because of the amalgamation. In the same way, when our three channels (*Ida, Pingala, and Sushumna*) become activated, we develop a sixth sense with time, through awareness, which leads us to greater insights so that we can begin to unravel who we truly are. Most of us are radical and extreme: either tilted towards progressive, fun, self-aggrandizing, egocentric, urbanization, or we are tilted towards pure, simplistic, other-oriented, egoless, sacrificial, rural ways of living. Both feel they are missing something because they haven't yet met with the wisdom of the clear, celestial, ever-flowing waters of *Saraswati*, which integrates the understanding of both. From here on, as we are led to our quest for higher truth and through the activation of the flow of energy, many more rivers join in the celestial waters as time goes by. Once we become a channel of cosmic forces, a river is no different than we are. We are all entities having different forms, shapes, and purposes.

When the cause is unclear, unfound, and unnamed, then clearly the effect that you are experiencing is not outward or accidental. The remorse we are collectively experiencing is because we are jointly destroying the resources of the elements by continuously and knowingly doing what we must not do. We pay for our *karmas* (actions). There is still time. We are given one final chance to resolve and clear the debts of our corrupt actions by doing well; we will then be forgiven. Once again, the choice is ours: let the sacred river dry up, or be filled with clear energy so its waters can continue to nourish and bless us.

Mother's milk is the elixir for life, it is very sacred. It is the mother who is the source of all prosperity and power. Respect her and pay reverence to her. She is like a cow and her child is the bullock. Beating the child to get it to plow the field is the worst sin ever. Her daughter is here to protect and be a savior for all sentient beings. When you see her divinity, you will recognize her.

There is an immense charm in the flow of simple living: plain, free, kind, flexible, and moderate. When we choose not to appreciate and praise the gentle subtlety and sobriety of soft beauty, that subtle force can become austere, authoritarian, stern, strict, and severe. That subtle force is our teacher who is trying to discipline us and show us how to open the rigid, unbalanced, blocked channels and unblock them through purification and good intentions.

Pingala nadi, or solar channel, is golden in color. It is most active during sunrise. It mirrors the *Ida nadi*, whose flow brings in comfort. The flow of both together gives rise to *Sushumna nadi,* which is the grace of higher energy. *Ida nadi* (mental thought) is the yin, creative, cool like the Ganga River. It activates mental, moon energy. It is inactive and introverted. It is most charged up during sunset. This *Ida nadi* is mirrored by the *Pingala nadi* (vitality of action), which is the yang perspective. *Pingala nadi* is warm like the Yamuna River, it has vitalized sun energy, and it is active and extroverted. The ratio of *Ida* nadi to *Pingala* nadi is one is to two. Five healthy thoughts lead to ten vital actions. *Pingala* is on the right side of the body, originating from the left brain. Ida is on the left side of the body, originating from the right brain. The energy from the left nostril is pale, feminine, and lunar in comparison to the right nostril, which is red, masculine, and solar energy. *Sushmna* is the central, middle, threefold nadi or channel. *Sushmna* connects action and thought through the observation of the movement of Pingala and Ida. *Sushmna* is therefore the combination of sun, moon, fire, and water.

Outside the body are two nadis: *Sasi* is on the left and *Mihir* is on the right. For those who understand nadis- cleanse & purify yourself completely. Contemplate on the *Chitra nadi* which is in the center of *Sushumna*. That will lead you to experience the same heavenly bliss that I am talking about. We are living one extra year, this extra year comes with an opportunity to recreate a new heightened life based on collective wholesome vibrations we radiate and resonate.

Vajra and Chitra nadi are within the *Sushumna* nadi. *Chitra* nadi is within *Vajra* nadi. *Brahma* nadi is within *Chitra* nadi. *Brahma* nadi is the kundalini pathway. *Chitra* is the subtlest nadi and *Vajra* is the most active and firm nadi. Love is the backbone of these pathways. All over our body, the nerves and vessels follow strange pathways to get strange results. Same way, love uses whatever instrument comes close to it and plays whatever tune that comes to it. It keeps flowing forever and ever.

During our group training in the mountains, the first time we crossed the river, the patrol team leaders counted the numbers of rocks for us and taught us exactly where to step. They told us which stone is slippery and which is safe to tread on. They stayed with us until we reached the other side of the river. The next time around, all team leaders who were guiding us, became almost invisible. They watched us from afar but gave us no support. Since the obstacles and the stones on the way were so similar, we somehow managed to cross the river by ourselves. As time passes, we cross many more rivers of life. Over-dependence on anything cripples us and so our parents, gurus, and the Buddha often leave us to cross the struggles of life-giving rivers by ourselves. Over pride on the other hand can drown us. So remember to always acknowledge and praise those who subtly support and guide our every step with their invisible blessings.

As time passed by, we crossed many more such rivers of life. As we became used to crossing these rivers by ourselves, we started to believe that we crossed the first obstacle by ourselves and are self-taught. No one taught us the steps of when and how to take one foot forward and one foot backward safely and steadily without drowning.

Flow like the water in the river. Despite the obstacles that are like stones in the river's path, just keep flowing like the river. Enjoy the gentle breeze. Face the soft subtle energies and the gross ones with equanimity, while you keep your mission of merging with the ocean intact. Rivers are the meridians or channels; they represent the divine flow of spiritual energy. The Niger is a sacred river in Nigeria, West Africa. A river is meant to give, to serve to help us attain the highest liberation. The one who gives always has a greater hand and power than the one who takes. It is in giving that you attain all that energy. It is a blessing of protection and ultimate strength.

The Niger River is in Nigeria, and Nigeria means Queen or Empress. It comes from the Egyptian root, Net-ger, which means God. Indo-negroids in Vedic Sanskrit means Nagini, or feminine serpent, which is the cause of the robust, handsome, black Godhead energy that activates the nerve pathways of our brain. The poison of black Nagini can be used to either kill or to heal. The king cobra, or Kobra, is grounded because of the Nagini. Niger or *Nagini* energy is everywhere. The Native Americans believe in the flow of their energy. It is all around, acting as a fierce force-shield to bless, sanctify, purify, and resurrect our lands with its pure wisdom, magical power, abundance, and prosperity.

The fertile earth, goose-mother, is the creator and the giver of the original golden light within the cosmic egg, from which we all were hatched. Worship her and stay connected to her, in order to become initiated into the spirit and life-force of *Nagini/* kundalini energy. She will transition you into the safe heavenly abode. She moves clockwise to energize you with her divine healing powers. She has the power to live within multiple realms and transform into a heavenly Goddess, or a grounded serpent, or an earthly human at will. In Hebrew, *Naggai* means the whispering, enchanting, generous, brilliant, and enlightening light of higher intelligence, which is hidden within all of us. Nagarjuna in the Tibetan language means "the God of serpents," symbolically known as the fiery dragon. So now you know the true meaning of Niger, the Roman/ Latin word for black or Negro, and how the white light came from the black strength that can make or mar you. I share this because the secret inner world only becomes sacred and blissful once you know its deeper meanings. The supreme lord is only one but there are many Gods, all emanating from the overall and underlying forces of the trinity.

Some of us know and have experienced powerful energy. Based on the level of our awareness, only we can know how awakened we are. Salute the divinity of the five elements that are within all of us. Salute and praise those who have reached the clarity to distinguish the true, transmutable one from all the others.

Never stop believing in yourself. Become the person you are meant to be. Be like the river that continues to flow despite all odds to meet with the ocean.

The ocean is lucid at the surface, but deep and undisturbed within. The ocean receives many exciting rivers yet remains the same.

Affirm- 'Namostutee. I am the self-aware ocean who receives numerous rivers of sensory information, yet I remain calm, undisturbed, and unperturbed deep within. This way I maintain my equipoise and poise despite the distracting factors. Tathaastu.'

CHAPTER 89

THE LOST SANDAL

O ne day as a child, I rode my favorite horse in the mountains and during that ride, I lost one of my sanctified, bejeweled ruby sandals. The sandal had an attached anklet that remained on my leg. I cried at the loss but my mother and sister told me that a pussycat took my sandal away. I never believed that story. Having lost my favorite sandal, I cried, but a voice told me that although I had lost one of my sandals, fate would one day lead me to the greatest fortune that lay at the foot of the mountains. That whispering, invisible voice told me not to give up, but to keep forgiving and giving, unlearning, and learning. The rose-gold anklet from my sandal will always remain on my ankle.

I am bejeweled with precious jewels, diamonds, and gold, but I still miss that sandal that I once lost in the mountains. I remain subtly unknown, and so does my ethereal beauty because, without my second sandal, I will stumble and fall. On the day I let go of my mental attachments, I was honored with the highest throne and admired in the inner world. I knew from then on that I was entitled to wear the crown, as much as you are. It is important to know when, why, and to whom you lost your sandals. Only then can you find your lost sandal.

My grandmother could not walk because I am wearing her shoes. When she did walk she used to do so with a cane. My skin shines brightly from within with the blessings of her illuminated light. The seductive, tinkling sound of my anklet led the one who had found the missing sandal to bring it back to me. As I slipped my foot into my slender sandal, I felt what it is like to stand tall on my two feet. Wearing both my sandals, I felt like the person who could now walk without the support of the cane.

I thanked the cane for giving my grandmother the support when she needed it most, and I thanked the voice that told me to never give up. I finally grew from being one-pointed to being firm-footed, and I wore the truth of the bejeweled crown that lay on my head. Just as was predicted, I now live at the foot of the holy mountains, to keep alive that passion that got me here.

There is a famous story in India where a woman enters the temple and subconsciously knows and thinks in her head that her sandals, left outside, will be stolen. Whatever you ask for in the divine temple is granted. Whether you say it in words or not. She even expressed her anxieties to her friend and then prayed to God, "Please ensure my sandals are not stolen." When she returned from the temple, guess what? Her sandals were stolen. Nothing goes till you want it to – staying attached is just a phase – enjoy it – this is the age of the Midas touch and mind. Whatever you set for yourself mentally, you can achieve. This is because the kind divine energies bless whatever we ask for and being all positive and pure, they do not register negative words like don't, no, not, etc. Most of our problems are a result of mindlessly asking without reflecting.

What you fear most, you tend to attract. You mentally have constant disturbance, anxiety, and distrust about the situation even before it arises. Let go of deep-seated pains and experiences of the past relationships. Even if your sandals are stolen this time, does not imply that it will be stolen again. Be ever ready to start afresh.

Many years later, I went to the mountains again. This time it was the Pranic healing ashram in Pune, India. An Ashram is a place of spiritual retreat. I try to visit one such ashram every year. During this one visit, I arrived late at night from Dubai. There was thunder and rain. The ashram dog saw I was alone and followed me to my room. I thought he was being a good host but he became my companion for the next four days and followed me to the meditation hall, morning treks, lunch breaks and protected me when I slept at night. On the fifth day, the dog vanished. As I woke up in the morning, I realized - I had left my sandals in the meditation hall the previous night. The distance from my room to the meditation hall was a few steps away. I decided to get my sandals, before heading for tea in the common hall. I was barefoot, enjoying the ground and nature's elements. As I traversed, a huge cobra snake passed in front of me, just before I could take the very next step. I stopped and looked into its beautiful eyes. Instinctively, I remembered the eye gazing exercise I practiced the night before with the healers, and mentally I said to the cobra, "I salute the divinity within you." I heard the cobra say the same back to me as it left my path. I felt a source of renewed energy and positive guidance. I reached the hall, the slippers were waiting for me and so was the naughty ashram dog as if he knew who I just met!

In another instance-one of my clients has cancer of the spine. She is eighteen years old and has not walked since she was eighteen months of age. This has not stopped her from buying all the latest fashionable shoes. She believes that one day she will be able to walk, but until that day, she has decided to wear her style irrespective of what life has thrown at her. Even if that day never comes, when she can walk in her shoes, at least she will live the rest of her days wearing her shoes, her style, and her smile. She puts out her intention to the universe, and that faith is what has kept her going for so many years. She designs T-shirts as a charity initiative and donates at centers where children like her require more motivation, inspiration, and encouragement to never give up.

Those filled with universal love are broad-minded and big-hearted. No person is small or undeserving. Every Cinderella gets a chance to come out of the loss to marry her charming prince. Never give up, go only when you have to, stay till you want to, dance to the tunes the way you like to. The mystery will unravel itself. Much like Cinderella, each of you are given a fragile special pair of transparent glass sandals that can fit no one else but you. No one can be in your sandals. However, to find those graceful sandals is like finding a diamond in coal.

Affirm- 'Namostutee, I have my feet only on that track upon which everywhere I go - I can see faithful and devoted souls silently smiling, thinking pleasing thoughts, doing rightful actions. I do not tread on a path where the grace and blessings of a higher power are doubted or not revered. Tathaastu.'

CHAPTER 89a

IN LOSING SOMETHING YOU FIND SOMETHING

Those who do not know how to swim in the deep waters float on wood and think they are in a boat on calm waters. Those who can swim go deep within the waters. Those who do not want to wet their golden, diamond and ruby-studded stilettos also make it to the shore, sitting on the royal backs of flying white horses.

I was startled from my deep sleep. The word was out. I felt the emptiness of losing all the words in the book I wrote, only to realize that more is to come. These words reflect my reality. As long as I am real, they will happily keep flowing. Even the empty pages have a story to tell. It is not God's will to kill, scare, or steal from you. God only responds to the vibrations you send out. I pity the thief who stole because, in his limited thinking, he forwent the eternal, limitless wisdom instead of the temporary. I closed my lips and went on a silent retreat until a day came when my lips uttered the greatest truth, the deepest wisdom that shone more than the precious six-pointed star[81]/crystal. I now have a golden body, and within it live seven little horses that make my thoughts subtly run free although my mind holds the reins. The seventh horse is the wisest of them all.

Only the weak ride on the strong backs of horses and bulls, for these animals, are stronger than us. As long as you remember where your strength came from in your weakest hour, and who carried you, you will learn to take the bull by its horns to attain your goal.

---

[81] *Refer to the chapter 'shared fate' to know about the 'six pointed star'*

Just like a broken log is swept away in the rushing waters, all those swimming are carried away into her mighty waters. But those who choose to fly on the white horse reach the shore well in time. The horse that led you to the stream and carried you on her back when you needed it most is your mother's mother-your grandmother. Your strength lies not only in being grateful for her selfless sacrifice and advice but also in helping her when she is weary of sleeping in the rocky beds and allowing her to sleep on the same bed of roses that she layout for you upon the shore.

Whatever you want you already possess. You have forgotten that it is you who made one into many. It doesn't mean you have lost it. Look deep within and it is just a matter of time before you will find all that you thought you had lost and more.

Affirm- 'Namostutee, I will never cheat anyone ever in any form. In cheating others, you cheat yourself. I am true to my purpose. Tathaastu.'

CHAPTER 90

HUGS FROM THE FLOATING STARS

The heavenly stars are within us. They live within our brain in the form of happy cells. Just as we have cells in our body, the earth has cells too. We, humans, are the earth's cells.

Cells open up to hug happy positive energy, and cells become cocooned, they shut down, and they close around gloomy, unfavorable energy. The protocols I apply, through the cosmic healing, work with your chakras to open up the constriction and radiate love once again. The healing teaches you not to suppress your immunity but to express it. Fearfulness and stress constrict and shut down your cells and your clarity. Instead, awaken yourself up. Expand, give, and share to live a rejuvenated, youthful life that lies in pleasing, and being true to none other but yourself.

All atoms and particles blend in the air and combine to become one much like the cells and atoms in our body forever to keep the balance. I was just a consecrated crystal until I became a nomadic star, traveling and moving from one place to another.

Universal workings were recorded within me, long before I was born into this physical body. I was born to be free but I chose to stay in this bondage. Now that I know and have access to this knowledge, I have to do what I came here to do. I have to settle within my very being for I am like a precious star of my ruling planet from space.

I believe that the space above us is one giant mirror, reflecting our light back to us so that we can know how far some of us have gone through the speed of positive light. Let us join them. Yet another star or planet is waiting to be born and named after you, while you are still walking here on earth.

Fly and float, live your truth, let go. Unburden yourself from all pain. Hugging stars are hugging cells. Medically, each cell in your body is renewed every seven years. Every cell has a lifespan and has to die its programmed death. Those that do not, result in tumor, cancer, or malignant growths. For the body to remain balanced, healthy, and vitalized, cells have to die so that new ones can be born. Your cells are intelligent beings. They love talking to one another, evolving, and living harmoniously as a team but when at war - they start going against one another and fighting amongst themselves.

The energy of all pure souls radiates outwards, just the way the stars shine outwards. Pure love is when you shine for others because pure love knows that the sky will be lit only when all we stars collectively shine together. What does it matter whether you are wealthy or rich, white or black? Stars always shine more in the dark when it is pitch black. Just the way all-stars bow down to our divinity, we must also bow down to their celestiality.

We hurt other beings, friends, and family with our sharp words, critical thoughts, and selfish actions, yet we neither ask for forgiveness nor are we grateful. All change begins with the self. Maybe it is time we should first clean our bodies, then our home, mow our garden and then make a change to the community at large, the nation, and finally the entire universe.

I was mowing the lawn the other day with my family and I offered my prayers and sought forgiveness from the grass and the bushes around. I said loving words and sent healing energy to the leaves so that they can handle the pain well. Once we were done with the trimming and cleaning, we did a little thanksgiving ceremony for the lawn mowing machine that made our work so easy and to the chainsaw that clipped the bushes. This is how we spent our Memorial Day weekend. The universal principles are the same for all. There is life and vibrancy inherent in everything. It is in the tree outside and on the wooden table inside your home.

Science has discovered that on average, we have 40 trillion cells within us and each of these cells is forever beaming with life energy, holding approximately 100 trillion atoms within each cell, which also equals the total number of stars in the universe. We are never still, nor ever alone - we are a sum total of all this limitless energy that is forever circulating, vibrating, expanding, and contracting within and outside of our physical body. Yet we never feel that we are energetic beings! We don't because we are so busy living the make-believe reality of our adventurous existence that we cease to look into the finer micro details of our macro existence. We are perpetually directing, acting, producing movies in our head- we never cease thinking because thinking excites us. When we want to take a break, we try to still the mind through certain meditations and breathing exercises. To increase the benefit of those meditations, we must first resolve to purify and control our thoughts by converting them all into positivity, otherwise, we will be meditating through our negative limited psych. The reality we see is based upon our subjective perceptions and impressions, which are in turn a result of our consistent thoughts. However, these are all illusionary because we are not just our thoughts. We are essentially energy beings who have a body of emotions, thoughts, and forms that manifest within our energy body. Our energy is as limitless as the ocean. We are all waves within it; an essential characteristic of the ocean but not the ocean in its entirety.

All organisms are composed of cells and these come from preexisting cells. Cells of all species exhibit biochemical similarities. Each organism's structure and functions are due to the activities of these cells. Just the same way, honey bees construct hexagonal cells within their body. The honeycomb is inside their body and they create their homes in the same way. We, humans, produce nine different shapes of cells to hold our bodies together. We must thank these cells. If we desert our friends, they feel emotionally unvalued and hurt. Same way, our cells, and things kept unused at our home feel deserted and must be circulated amongst others if you are not going to bring them to use or value their presence.

When I experienced this enlightenment, everything within and outside of me opened up. And the more I become open, the more beauty, vitality, and pleasure I experience. There are more atoms in a cell than there are stars in a galaxy. Beyond the rigidity of thoughts, beliefs, ideas, emotions, sensations of pain, and so-called forms, each collection of those 100 trillion atoms in every cell of our body, will still be active within the never-ending energy of our auric consciousness.

Affirm- 'Namostutee, The world has always been very kind to me. I give back its kindness in manifold ways. Tathaastu.'

CHAPTER 91

KALA-Qi-QUIMAT

(The real value of the chi energy of your innate gift)
Practice silence. Silence preserves and protects what impulsive words and hasty actions destroy and kill. The thoughts you developed must first be internalized, however long it takes before they are expressed. Otherwise, they will be lost long before they are ready to be externalized and actualized. To preserve is to reserve.

What you develop, you must preserve. The speech you develop through the constant flow of words must also be preserved through the reserve. I inherited a huge emerald stone of great value, but I have kept it reserved in the safe instead of revealing its brilliance because it first needs to be preserved, polished, valued, and prepared before it is ready to be worn for protection or magnetic attraction.

The gem you have developed within yourself is more precious than any gem that you have inherited outside of yourself. Each one of us has been impartially gifted a gem of some kind or other, but only a few of us can harness it and keep it balanced within the safety of our minds. Just like trust or outward wealth, a gem must first be nurtured, preserved, harnessed, saved, appreciated, experienced within, and appraised before it can be shared, given, and experienced with others, for that is when it has truly won its birthright.

The priceless crystal within you is much like an infant waiting to be born. Until the environment is conducive and the infant is strong and ready, do not do a C-section of your thoughts and *kala* (art or talent) under outside or inside pressure. Let things grow at their own pace.

You become entitled to own what you have only when you do not let your mind or emotions sway your thoughts and actions. Ask any famous singer: to practice control is the biggest *riyaz*-uncompromising firmness, poise, and balance usually achieved through silent meditation. This is usually the toughest but also the most rewarding part of voice modulation.

Go out there and love unlimited things and beings. We all exist because this force of love exists. Each of us is a unique work of art. Some people can find more than a dozen, hundred, thousand, billion, trillion things to love and appreciate. We can have as much and as many sources as we need. The list never gets exhausted. In realizing and understanding this truth, you understand *kala qi quimat*.

What you take with you is timed. *Kaal* or time is inherently timeless, whatever we create has already been created and will soon be recreated in the future. Our individual energy, our distinct element which is only within us, therefore, is the only thing that makes the work of art our work, rest all is nameless. Our individual identity endowed with oneness, beyond all dualism, is our power. The entire trinity is in each one of us. Our understanding of it may vary but the truth remains the same.

Vyasa wrote in Mahabharata, the ancient epic of India in four hundred B.C. that sage Brihaspati told king Yudhisthira in his discourse - 'One should never do something to others that one would regard as an injury to one's self. In brief, this is *dharma*. Anything else is succumbing to desire'. By making *dharma* your main focus, you treat others as you treat yourself.

Pain is a great teacher. Most people throw away the statues that crack in their homes. I mend the broken statues and fill them with gold and metallic paint. This way we can celebrate the beauty of pain. Pain and imperfections inspire us like no other.

Depression doesn't manifest itself physically but it exists. Depression is mostly caused by suppression. It all goes away with moments of expression. Express your deepest feelings through painting, sculpting, and dancing, exercising, words written or verbal but do not suppress your feeling merely to fit in or to please another. Also always remember to appreciate and thank those who express through their art, and value their job because being in thankless jobs can make people even more depressed.

It is written in Padma Purana (one of the eighteen major Puranas, a genre of texts in Hinduism) Shrishti Khanda (one of the five sections) that in the twelfth century C.E., tales were narrated to Lord *Brahma* by Lord *Vishnu* himself, who in turn propagated in the world through various sages that - If the entire *dharma* can be said in a few words, then it is—that which is unfavorable to us, do not do that to others.

In the sixth century B.C., Confucius cleared our confusions by reaffirming the same thought that the way to survival is - 'Do not do to others what you do not want to be done to yourself'.

In the last five thousand years, each great school has repeated that we all are Gods valued creations, to value, glorify and praise each of God's creations including ourselves is our greatest dharma. Do to others as you want to be done to yourself. This is Kala Qi Quimat.

Affirm- 'Namostutee, I revere, salute, value, and praise the divinity within all. I am in a constant state of gratefulness and prayerfulness. Tathaastu.'

CHAPTER 92

KAAL KI

K aal (qui or) *ki* is the energy of time.
I call time *Kaal-Qi*. This is because its purpose is to vitalize life within a renewed time frame and cycle. This is done in a cosmically ordered fashion, with the help of nature's five elements. These elements are within each one of us, though they vary in proportion. Currently, we are in the midst of such a time. Let us optimally utilize *Kaal's* energy by repairing what has been damaged. We can efficiently make use of this *Kaal* by heightening our morals and virtues, irrespective of which of the four cardinal directions we may face. Remember to be just and caring towards one another irrespective of what task, disposition, and position you may hold in society.

> Vitalized life is generated when un-vitalized life is gone.
> Balanced time is regenerated when unbalanced time is gone.
> Vitalized life is generated when unbalanced time is gone.
> Balanced time is regenerated when un-vitalized life is gone.

The subtle and delicate nuances of time make all the difference. We might stop breathing and our heart might stop beating, the moments might seem fleeting. Until a day comes when our frequency is attuned to the rhythm of cosmic time itself. We have 108 chakras within our body and many more outside of it. Each has the potential to get fully activated 1000 times in one day, based on the circulation of the meridians in our body, which are activated through solar energies[82].

---

[82] *Refer chapter '108' to learn more*

In the solar & lunar clock, there are - 24 inner and outer solar causes= 48; 30 inner and outer lunar causes=60; 48 + 60 = 108. The 108 points in the solar & lunar clock are akin to 108 main chakras within our body.

Each zodiac sign and planet correspond to our major chakras. Each mini and minor chakra corresponds to the stars above. There is a perfect numerological connection, spiritual mysticism, and divine precision behind everything visible. All are designed by the invisible intelligent spirit. Whatever happens at the 25th hour happens at the 6th point of the star. (The six-pointed star is linked to a point in our brain). It is then that we move beyond time and space within the same form.

The tree of our life bears 12 physical and 12 subtle fruits. The energy of time (Kaal Qi) bears 24 subtle qualities (as mentioned in the chapter titled "*Evol-ve-love*") through the inhalation and exhalation of gaps in between these 12 physical and subtle fruits.

Time is the sacred language through which we explain the magic of our destiny. We let time decide our faith but time in itself is nothing unless we give it qui, or energy. We are wiser than we give ourselves credit for! We are eternal, we have underestimated our powers because over the eons, we have attached ourselves to the game of suffering, pain, and difficulties that we created to spice up our lives. We are slaves to our habits.

This chapter will give you the key to harnessing time and its varied permutations and *Kaal qi* combinations. It will unveil the mystery and show you the simplicity behind the complexity.

Ether[83] is simple. Chaos is complex. Time or Chronos is like a universal egg that gives birth to both ether and chaos. Through their amalgamation, the first being was born, and from then on the cycle continued. Our biggest teacher-our lifeline-is Kaal, or time. It provides us with the breath of life. Time is the *Kaal chakra*[84] of pure air that cannot be contained or captured, however much you may try, for its nature is to keep flowing.

Mona Lisa has stood the test of time because she enjoys how you enjoy its mystery. Mona Lisa is the ultimate mistress of time. With the key I hold, in the chapter titled "I am so in la", I have decoded some of the codes she hides.

The soul, or psyche, and the cosmic mind are born out of cosmic time. In order to develop them, stop chewing off your tail like the dragon and

---

[83] *Ether is the Greek word for the God of the shining light of the blue sky.*

[84] *Kaal chakra is the cosmic energy point, or the wheel of time. It is also called the king chakra, the king cobra, or the great king.*

snake that are much talked about. Do not let your past eat you up. Instead, simply shed your skin and wear another. Value time. Stop fearing death. Embrace it and evolve with it, by remaining ever positive and vitalized, or else you will soon age and wither. Death is a reminder that we should make the best use of the number of breaths we take. Father Time never rests. He never stays in one place, relaxes, or turns his back. His nature is fleeting, here one moment, and gone the next. The wise *kaal chakra* is untiring and undying. It turns the world around, dissolves, disposes, and transforms everything into sand particles, much like the sand we see in the hourglass. Time is like my father, who goes on and on and never ceases, triumphing with one feat after another. Time is the greatest healer and experience is the greatest teacher. It's no wonder that managing our time well brings balance into our life. We learn to use our time wisely and optimally when we realize its true value. Its value lies in time's ability to heal our greatest obstacles by helping us organize our life better. Embrace its changing nature, for time, is like desert sand. However much you try to hold on to it, it will slip away. In letting go, we are healed. Let go because it is the nature of the sand to slip down through the little gap in the hourglass.

Time is the wise old builder, the eternal author of the world, and the father of all. It is because of time's habit of always renewing itself, like the snake shedding its skin. In this way, time stays ever-youthful and keeps renewing. Time is our cosmic father. It is no wonder there are clocks called 'grandfather'. Learn from time to tame yourself to shed off what no longer serves you. Prioritize, keep renewing, and improvising to become immortalized. It is time to release your captured soul and merge with your divine truth. You are intertwined with your twin reality. Now is the time to get back in touch with your inner bliss. It is time to bring focus to your internal wellbeing. It is time to resist all evils and time to be virtuous and disciplined. It is time to practice moderation and liberate yourself. It is time to be wise and encouraging, to realize yourself, and to know who you are. Your time is now.

This time will return. It is its nature to return. Time is infinite. We move time, it doesn't move us. Time is the greatest cosmic creativity that is here to entertain us and give us perspective. Trust the cosmic law and follow the order. Time and space are your parents. Stop defying your parents. They know what is best for you. Without them, you do not exist. Without you, their life is meaningless, purposeless and empty. Be content with your fate. More fortune will come once you stop incessantly repeating the same patterns. You are the ki or energy of time. You are the *ki* of *kaal*. You are the fortunate sons and daughters of God. Your presence brings joy to the entire universe. Everyone and everything in the entire universe is working just to please you. Your one smile brings joy in the face of the moon and the entire *akash* gets lit with stars seeing you in bliss. There is no greater knowledge and means of inferring truth than gaining self-knowledge through physically experiencing life in its fullest. Replace Monotony with creativity. Meet with life at T junction, a mix of lateral and linear is the intersection point. Cultivate diagonal thinking in your life. True love is love for self. Pursue your hobbies and explore new avenues of enjoyment.

Affirm- 'Namostutee, I do what is required, when the time is right. Tathaastu.'

CHAPTER 92a

ME POINT

M atter is *Shiva*. Energy is *Shakti* and *Kaal* is a lifetime. *Kaal* Qi is my attempt at representing the effect of the combination of *Shiva*, *Shakti* (matter and energy or their combination which *I* call ME) in our *Kaal*. In the middle of the 24-hour clock, there is a point. That point is called ME because ME moves it. Each person's ME is different because time is subjective. It has two needles called M and E because that is their starting point. This tells us that irrespective of where the needles are pointing, your time travels wherever and in whichever direction your attention goes.

I was sitting on the bench of our beautiful garden with my dear husband. I told him, sitting in America, if my attention is going to the cosmos then that is where I am. Sitting in America, if your attention is in India then that is where your time is. The essence of time is absolute, it doesn't change. We both are sitting upon the same bench but it has a relative aspect as no two people view and experience its dimensions in the same way. This is how life is and this we must accept. Let us remember to enjoy the beautiful view of the garden in which we are seated.

We all occupy the same universal space and are essentially living within the same time. However, our placement or direction within the world territorially may cause changes in not only our location but also in our mental perceptions. The winds of change do not flow with the same intensity in each place and each individual is impacted differently.

Without understanding the depths of time- we cannot value time, health, wealth, love, intellect, emotions, nature, bliss, cosmos, or our inner and outer universe. This is how important the nature of time is. I am presenting to you the various dimensions, qualities, vibrations, and energy of time, depending on various levels so that you can access it based on your personal growth and evolvement needs. This will help you set your outer goals by disciplining your inner self with precision. This approach is meant to bring in a complete transformation in your outer self through your inner receptors.

Energy and matter are everything. Their combination endows us with celestial hearing and vision. *Shiva* is energized by *Shakti*. The sound of the temple bell invokes its energy. *Shakti* is activated by pure *Shiva* matter. The light of the crystal invokes a deeper vision and fills us with clarity.

Alpha is yang, unmanifested, invisible spirit. And beta is yin, manifest, physical spirit. ME = M stands for superior 'Manas' or intelligence. E stands for Gods (8 fold) creative energy and aspects of the soul. ME, therefore, implies creative manas. ME = Storehouse or *Bhandar* of knowledge accumulated over millions of years. In time the thoughts are all stored in the midpoint from where the two needles move about and create chaos confusion from the order. Only to return to the main content - 'ME' and that is when you let order come out of apparent chaos. A new dimension is brought into your consciousness and through you, it is brought to everyone around you and beyond because we all are perennially connected and influenced by one another.

The essence of time is that we consciously choose to move in time. Its repetition gives us meaning. We are the essence of time. Time is not the essence of us. The essence (we) lies in us which means, we lie in time (us). The essence, therefore, lies in time. 'ME' is the essence of time. The point at which dawn and dusk, midnight & noon meet - is the point that makes you meet with your truth (ME point). M = Spirit (*Purusha* or *Brahma*) is the first form of supreme and *Kaal* (time) is the last form of supreme. *Vishnu* is both the first and the last, the contracted and the expanded. *Vishnu* is both single and manifold. *Shiva* nature is the quality inside and outside *Vishnu*. It represents the form and the formless. It is in the microcosm (man) and the macrocosm (universe). E = Mother Nature (*Prakriti*) remains in equilibrium. *Prakriti* has no beginning and is inherently devoid of color or form. Placing and understanding our element or nature in relation to the energy or Qi, helps us get rid of ailments and obstacles we face. The lack of a natural flow of energy is the cause of unregulated emotions and problems. Keep your nature even tempered to rise above these drowning emotions.

We periodically renew, re-emerge, and reinvent within *Kaal*. *Kaal* is an infinite circle and we are finite beings who cyclically and eternally move within that circle. The underlying hidden reality behind our existence is emptiness. Each time a new cycle begins, we start afresh, except that most of us do not remember our learnings from the last cycle and hence we repeat the same patterns.

Affirm- 'Namostutee, The greatest gift you can give to someone is your time. I give time to people I value and love rather than simply buying material gifts. Tathaastu.'

IS TIME AHEAD OF YOU OR ARE YOU RUNNING BEHIND?

1 second = 1/60 of minute; 1 minute = 1/60 of an hour; 1 hour = 1/24 of a day; Seconds = 1/86400 of a day (60x60x24); Minutes = 1/1440 of a day (60x24);

If we make a separate clock for seconds, minutes, and hours, we find that the - Lunar clock has 30 points and represents seconds. The solar clock has 24 points and represents hours.

The six elements (air, fire, water, earth, ether, and pure consciousness) have 72 points in 12 hours. (6x12=72) and 144 points in 24 hours (6x24=144). These points are then multiplied by 10 represent minutes. I have coined the name - 'Aar chakra'. Aar chakra[85] is a point on the forehead that helps us stay balanced when change occurs. Above that is a chakra that has 144 points or petals that represents divine wisdom.

All is part of his master plan, all will be well at the end and the beginning. The time for birth, renewal, and fresh new beginnings is now. We have ten main energy channels that have the potential to activate 72,000 energy channels. When we willfully apply our intellect, we begin to value every minute. This way the hidden meaning of the petals within the minute's clock starts to unfurl and we become more aware of their presence. This

---

[85] *Aar chakra = The author calls this point in the forehead the Aar chakra. Aar is another name for the light bringer in Sanskrit.*

centers us within the energy of *aar* time despite changes in *Kaal Qi* -Each element has a tenfold nature. (144 x10 = 1440 minutes). Each of the six main elements represents Krishna's six opulence - beauty, knowledge, strength, wealth, fame, and renunciation. An hour has 60 minutes. Each element is multiplied 10 times. A minute has sixty seconds. Each element is multiplied ten times. It is the nature of time to keep ticking and it is the nature of elements to keep moving with the seconds, minutes, and hour needle of the clock. The speed at which they move varies only in degrees. As mentioned in the chapter – *Kaal ki*, just like the sand in the sand timer, these elements cannot be grasped in the palms of your hand. It is their nature to slip away and come back refreshed, recharged and revitalized. Understanding this brings in equanimity and brings out our true beauty. Beauty lies in order.

The sun rays are industrious much like the ants. Its rays are like the minute's needle in our clock. Like the minute needle on the clock, we work industriously because we know that nothing is more valuable than the 1440 minutes we get every day.

We set the timing on grandfather's clock. The restless second's needle moves 12 seconds faster than the hour and so the minute lags by 48 seconds, to reach the hour. You move one degree up, and what usually takes months can complete in moments. Your destiny can change in a matter of split seconds. The key lies in shifting your mindset with the changing seconds. Prioritize your tasks through precision and discipline.

Everything is cosmically and psychically going through shifts at great speed.

Assert- 'Namostutee, ME time is divinely shifting to WE[86] time. May WE respectfully and compassionately partner with one another to shine our light. Let us heighten our vibrational energy, expand spiritually, and collectively as one big group heart. Tathaastu.'

---

[86] *WE denotes White Energy. The aura of WE glows with wisdom and enlightenment.*

CHAPTER 92c

IN ONE OF MY TRAVELS TO ANOTHER REALM

I felt as if a decade passed without me realizing it. When awareness dawned, I went to my office and found someone else sitting there. That is when I realized I had been living a lie. Nothing truly belongs to you. One day it's you. Tomorrow someone else will be sitting on your red office chair. Nothing and no one is invincible. Make optimal use of the position you are in while it lasts. Be aware. Be awake. Be conscious of your consciousness.

Here in the outer world, you will meet people who, despite their different physical bodies, have but one soul. There in the inner world, you will connect with beings who, despite their different souls have but one light body. Become one with the body and soul. It is through the mingling of your inner and outer world that you will know who you truly are.

Distance doesn't make you ache. Longing is never bad. Time is a creation of space. Time is subjective; it creates no distance. You create the distance. Space is relative based upon your experience. Nothing makes you ache. Pain is illusionary. Everything is an equal wonder of the world, and so are you. The longing you have is not for me or another; it is the longing for yourself. Your ultimate fire lights within you.

If you don't ride time. Time will ride you. It is because of time that we exist, die, and are born and so we must follow the rules of time rather than try and defy them. We know we are all playing a game but, it is sensible to follow the rules of the game rather than defy the rules. Stay connected, grounded, and humble. Yet remain detached and understanding towards those who are still learning to roll the dice of time. The purpose to play any game is the fun and excitement that it brings. If the fun goes, the game fades away, let the fun remain.

The clockwise movement of the chakras like the grandfather clock (sun) is wise and silent. It helps us absorb and inhale life energy. The counter-clockwise movement is the voice of that silence (moon) expelling or exhaling the life energy. We need to exhale what is congesting our energies.

In this realm, we moved to America and the house number of our rented home was 180. I thought to myself a circle takes us around 360 degrees. Anything 180 degrees obviously is the opposite side of the point where you start. With this move into our new home, we had come as far away as we could from wherever we were. The further I went, the closer I felt connected to my roots. We had traveled 180 degrees from the East to the West but despite the geographical distance and time, it brought us back to exactly where we belonged (started). This I think was done so that we could know and appreciate our life, as it was (is).

Most of our life is spent resisting what we fear and find uncomfortable rather than simply enjoying the moments. We often want to make that 180-degree shift not because we are not happy with our present but because our past and future intimidates us. We need to learn to live life as is, unrestricted by thoughts, without the feelings and labels of anger, depression, anxiety, limitations, stubbornness, judgments, guilt, fear, and boredom. We attach these restricting names and block our own growth and freedom. Empower and equip yourself better in dealing with unavoidable situations rather than resisting them. You cannot escape change. Change is the constant law of nature.

Affirm- 'Namostutee, as I follow my bliss and prioritize my life, it has become more meaningful and inspiring. It is filled with good fortune, health, wealth, vitality, friendships, optimism, and faith. Tathaastu.'

CHAPTER 92d

DER AAYE, DURUST AAYE

When we say time doesn't wait, we mean that life as we know it doesn't wait. Since life always changes and to pause means to end, we define movement with the constant cycle of time ticking away. The above Hindi phrase 'Der aaye, durust aaye' simply means- better late than never.

You preserve one life and seven more will be granted. You share the life you earned with seven more and you will earn that one life back again. And so the chain continues infinitely. The one who deserves to truly live on is the one who picks himself up and becomes upright, even in the nick of time, to preserve value and be grateful for every infinitesimal pause in the infinite moments.

Clock time is not ticking. It is your internal clock that is ticking counterclockwise. Because of this, the clock ticks clockwise. As long as you keep ticking, somewhere a clock will always be ticking with you. It is time to move forward, in the right direction in terms of your career, relationships, business, stability, and finances. Avoid moving backward or avoiding responsibility. Look into the past only so that you can learn from it to progress further. Overcome the experiences and habits that hold you back and do not waste time. Appreciate and trust more, be honest and grateful. Stop worrying about how to get things done. Simply go ahead and do them.

The finiteness and limitedness of time and life are based on our finite and limited understanding. In essence time and life are infinite, eternal, and limitless.

The seasons of the year are spring, summer, and winter. Creation takes place in the pure *Satvik* summer. Change and action take place in the *Rajasik* spring and winter is time for *Tamas*, introspection, and hibernation. Three parts of a day are light, change, and dark. These can be written as pure, trans-mutative action, and finally, inertia.

One Brahma day equals 360 Earth days or one Earth year. Before the onset of a new dawn, Brahma sleeps for one night to help us wake up to the new dawn. During this time, it is as if people and beings from all four *Yugas*, having different energies, commingle at the same time in the same space to recreate the balance of time and maintain its divine energy.

It is time to unlearn what you have learned. Time apart doesn't create any distance, nor do any mountains or time zones separate you.

Affirm- 'Namostutee, All my dreams will soon be realized and the events will miraculously unfold when the right opportunity arises. Tathaastu.'

CHAPTER 92e

MA I AM

'P M' should be called 'MA' as it is the backflow of 'AM'. The hours before noon are 'am' and the time post noon is 'ma' The time in between is noon which is 'I'. Hence the title MA I AM[87].

It is said that we must not visit a temple in the middle of the day, as God's sleep at that time. We must look outward through our bodies and not go inward during this time of the day.

Moon (ma or pm) is restless and moody like our mind. It is the erratic second's needle in the clock. The water tides, gravity, and our moods depend upon the moon's agile, swift and whimsical movements.

Sun (or am) is strong, disciplined, and fierce like the lioness roar. It is the hour that loudly strikes in my grandfather's clock. Noon and midnight are the turning points of outflow and backflow of magnetic energy between earth and the sun.

I[88] (light of the soul) am timeless. I move time. Time moves within me and outside of me. I am unchanging, uncreated, undying, fearless, pure, the underlying first one to experience the truth. As outside so within. As within so outside. I am blissfully within the center of the inner and the outer wheel. The battle is within you, it is not there in actuality, it exists only because you desire it. There is no battle or ailment outside of you. It is not physical in nature. Since I am out of the realms and bounds of time, I always know what happens outside of time.

---

[87] *Am is mother, body or soul from the left side. Am is Anima Mundi or world soul. I is father or knowledge or spirit from the right side. Ma is a being or human mind.*
[88] *Transmitter of pure intuitive light*

Everything exists because time exists. Timelessness is beyond the realms of existence as you know it. Elements are the *ki* (energy) of *kaal* (time). *Kaal* or time (ma) knows everything. The universal wheel is empty in itself, it is set based on your inner actions. What you see is your reflection in the universal *kaal*. I see the *kaal ki* - the elementals within time. 'I' am a true (pure soul) outside of this realm and so 'I' remain unaffected by the elemental dance. The entire trinity is within me.

The inner sun is the soul and life force that inspires and stimulates outer thoughts, the rays you see outside are an emanation of inner sunlight. Restart, reverse the wheel of time by circulating the clock of fresh energies.

Affirm– 'Namostutee, everything is crystal clear in my mind. I enjoy everything because I lead a dedicated and pure life. Tathaastu.'

PRECISION LEADS TO TRANSFORMATION & TRANSMUTATION

When you realize time is little and there is lots to do, you automatically stop wasting time on trivial pursuits. Time is of the essence. A mystic, monk, or a yogini has no time to quarrel, be selfish, or waste time in activities that do not take them closer to God. This very moment is the best time of your life, make the most of it. It doesn't get any better than this. We are all breathing borrowed air. Let us learn to enjoy it and count our blessings.

Instead of trying to improve everything around yourself, focus on improving yourself. Once you do that, everything else will automatically improve. In this present moment, you have the ability to make a profit, you have the opportunity to improve your life, and you have the blessings.

Today you have all the time to do all the things you have ever wanted to do. Tomorrow you will still be here but you will have no time to do all the things that you ever wanted to do. Action your dreams today.

Even metals seem to have psychological feelings, responses, and life inherent in them. I placed copper bowls outside my home so that we all could wash our feet in saltwater before entering. A few days later, that copper due to its sensitive nature transmuted into a completely different color because of the saltwater placed in it. Every external stimulus seems to affect it! Each morning I saw slight variations in its color and shade owing to the weather and changes in the moisture content of the air.

We express constant change and the transmutation of everything around the world through time. Time is an expression of our perception and a great tool invented by us to divide, subdivide, and define the changes of our beginning and end, along with the passing minutes, hours, days, and seasons. But beyond our perception of time, everything still exists out there in space, with its various transmutations and combinations. What time cannot measure may still exist. It is simply beyond the reach of our understanding. That is why I intend to suggest a new clock based on my intuitive abilities and transcendental perception.

When you don't value time, time doesn't value you. When you make others wait, time makes you wait. Be proactive. You must not be the cause of any delay. Let the universe decide.

Activating the 24 chakras[89] is the foundation on which the masculine and feminine energy merge within you, and you become increasingly peaceful within your inner space. Activating the 24 chakras is also a necessary step in unlocking and manifesting your magical erotic powers.

Space moves at the speed of light. Everything that is living is timed by the number of breaths we take. To be truly alive is to remain vitalized as a cosmic being of light, within the breath of time. A being of light reflects gratitude, love, kindness, and values the worth of every breath. In this way, no loss or gain affects your energies. You become a transformer of universal sorrow into joy, discomfort into comfort, and fear into freedom. Time pauses and an hour seems like a lifetime when you are enveloped by the aura of such beautiful souls. The best clock is the one that moves at a moderate speed without forming any judgements on the dualities we see behind the universal mask.

Affirm- 'Namostutee, I am confident, organized, and responsible, disciplined and proactively work towards completing my tasks. In this way, all my projects get completed seamlessly, efficiently, and timely. Tathaastu.'

---

[89] *Refer to chapter 'evol-ve-love' to know the names of the chakras or energy points.*

CHAPTER 92g

AARI

A *ari* is a Hindi word that means a tool like a sharp sword/ knife/ saw that cuts through swiftly. Our intellect is like a powerful *Aari*, designed to cut through the unnecessary information. This gives us the clarity to come out of the worldly maze and elevate our character without losing time or breaking our foundation and boundaries.

Why is precision and focus important?

Like tiny fragments of many glass pieces, there is a hoard of attractive information out there and not all of it is relevant to serve your current divine purpose. Stop being so frail and vulnerable to outside influences, stop wavering your attention, stop wasting your time, stop floating. The key to success is being productive with constant precision, every effort must be consistently directed with one-pointedness only towards your aim.

Just as metal cuts wood, subtle cuts active, ether cuts the air, destruction cuts confusion, purity cuts impurity, order cuts disorder, moderation cuts excess, courage cuts fear, words cut thoughts, unity cuts division, potentiality cuts actuality, cold cuts hot, morality cuts corruption, and rebirth cuts death. With the cut of sharp *Aari* of precision comes balance.

With balance, active overcomes passive. Fire and air are active. Water and earth are passive. Fire moves upwards and overcomes water, as light overcomes darkness.

When all else is gone, what remains is the subtlety of pure spirit, which is the untainted air. Pure air is subtler than ether. Pure air has a rare fragrance like untainted thoughts communicated through words. Pure air is our primordial essence. It is our pure spirit. Mixed with fire, it is subtle yet active. Pure spirit is what restores us. Pure air fills the emptiness in the ether like a beautiful voice fills the void among nature's sounds. One without the other is a handicap. Air moves upwards and overcomes the earth, as moisture overcomes dryness. Keep the moisture within nice and flowing, coated and protected, and away from all extremities. Remember to pause and reflect. Whether the dragon's mouth turns from warm to cool, or whether its nose blows hot or cold, remember always to pause and hold. What seems hot is inherently cold, like pineapple, and what seems cold is inherently hot, like watermelon. There are no extremes. Just go with the flow of the temperature and let the divine winds guide you.

The key to the quality of longevity and its power is in keeping the energy subtly charged with moisture and balance in the middle, between the pulsating action and reaction of the negativity and the positivity of life and love. What is hard and pointed from the outside is cool and soft from the inside, and what is gentle and smooth on the outside is hard and warm on the inside. It is never as it seems. What meets the eye is not as it really is. The pure charge of energy really happens between the recharge and discharge. Filled with electrifying brightness, the pure charge is the ultimate clean, perfect nothingness, which goes beyond the utopian concepts of good and evil. Through their mouths, some dragons breathe out ice and some breathe out fire. The legendary ones are those that breathe in through their nose all the cold and the hot, come what may, in order to breathe out toward you the calm river waters of life.

Affirm- 'Namostutee, I do not get distracted by past thoughts and impressions. I constantly move onward towards my path effortlessly with complete equanimity and discriminatory discernment. Tathaastu.'

CHAPTER 93

CHANGELESS CHANGE

Those who do not believe in radical self-transformation should try a change. Change implies constant flow and movement. Embracing change requires immense faith. True relaxation comes with change and action, not with stillness and stagnation.

Changing seasons teach us a lot. Winter is the time to crystallize and preserve the knowledge acquired all through the year. This way as the spring approaches, the buds of your wisdom can bloom out like little flowers. After spring we can then enjoy the summer vacation.

Your subjective perception is only your current reality. Do not hold on to it. Do not cling to it. My perception of something is not the same as yours. One reality has many different forms, facets, perceptions, and implications. Everything is relative based on your current understanding, optical vision, analysis, interaction, conceptualization, representation, connection, explanation, rationalization, and intuition, which too is constantly changing and evolving. To enjoy the experience, do not label or define or settle on any form. Simply let it be! Nothing will ever be completely unraveled. Since everything that is the truth is beyond sense perception. Therefore, eliminating, accepting, or negating anything is futile. Everyone is busy agreeing and disagreeing on their concept of certain and uncertain, based on where they left off before they slept and woke again. In this never-ending game, our mojo is simply playing the game, even though there are no winners or losers. Most of what I know is because of the rebel in me. We are forever active. There is no such thing as rest, to be alive is to be awakened. Continue to dream within a dream. Push yourself to pull yourself out of trauma.

Areas with the least blood flow are the areas that are further away from your heart and not the ones that are closest to your heart. Always remain centered and connected to wherever your heart truly lies while you circulate those happy, healthy, loving, and abundant energies all around. My heart lies in my home, the whole cosmos & universe is my home. I move, I flow, I glow and I circulate because of the sheer freshness and vibrancy of this ever-changing reality.

Gracefully accepting change is an art. I am fortunate to have had many safe rebirths. I have transitioned to so many towns, cities, and countries, yet I must admit that each time, it reminds me of the red shoe, the Mont Blanc pen, the pink bag, the bicycle wheel, the Lego sets, the starry hair clip, and all the little things that were lost and broken during the transition. But it also reminds me of the opportunity I was given to find something better and bigger. The first time I moved out of my home, I was like an egg that thought it had lost the safety of being in its mother's womb. And then I progressed to an infant stage, where I lost my outstanding ability to swim in the waters or to see in the dark. However, at each stage and with every change, I also gained an opportunity of finding something far better than what I had left behind. What I thought I had lost helped me cleanse, declutter, and renew.

The first time my favorite Chanel white dress got stained, I cried, but soon I realized that the stain helped me let go of the fake past that I was holding onto. It is then I thought of better ways to transmute, transform, and reinvent the dress that seemed beyond repair. I had it dyed a completely different color, and then from that inward clarity, I moved onward to the next blessed reality. When life seems to shake us, it is the universe's way to inspire and help us joyfully lift ourselves back again and also to tell us that whether you live in the deserts of Oman or the Catskills mountains of New York, the sacred waterfalls are just around the corner, if you know which *wadi* to explore and which peak to climb.

No one gets it when I tell them that the only impermanence and the only perfection is the imperfect permanence of your life. Everything is fluid and subject to constant change. Flower blooms only so that it can re-flower; people learn only so that they can unlearn and re-learn. Life is a perennial roller coaster. Each person gets their turn but the ones at the bottom and the ones at the top will always be sitting diagonal to each other, pulling and pushing one another. The ones on the sides are meant to support and maintain the balance. Those who fail in performing their *dharma* and duties become the reason for making the entire roller coaster to topple down and so such beings will no longer be excused. When you change the whole world around you changes. Remember, all change begins with you. With every change, life is passing by to allow another change to come in. With every breath, life is giving way to welcome another. This circulating cycle is what we call time. With every passing time - life too is passing by. Success lies in productively utilizing every change, every breath, every moment. No matter how much you may try, you cannot hold time. Life goes on. Only by prioritizing that what is important to you can you be vitalized optimally.

You may think that change causes imbalance. Seasons have swung from cold to hot but they are most balanced of all. The perception of imbalance is a misconception of your mind. If you stay centered you will see there is balance in everything. Nothing is confusing about the changes in the etheric energy. We have to adjust to the change of heightened consciousness, it will not adjust to us. Change is the only constant and permanent thing in our life. How we respond to the unexpected change makes all the difference.

Many lost souls have taken a zillion theoretical courses, and yet are not halfway through, because one needs to put their learning to practice and intellectual use in order to realize its profundity. To say a soul is lost or dead is to be a soul without love. Without love, there would be no music, no heartbeats, no romance, no emotion, and no life. I believe that it is superficial to teach others without practicing the teachings yourself. It is also superficial to know it yet not practice the knowledge yourself. It is superficial to give advice that you do not follow yourself. No one but you can influence or bring about change in your higher vibration whose very nature is constant change. What others think of you is a reflection of themselves, their perspectives don't define you. Others throw you away from their life because they are wearing an unappreciative veil of darkness and not because you are unworthy. Your inner self is flawless and purely divine. Do not let it get trapped in the garb of superficiality.

Old laws and world order have clearly become obsolete. We need new world order and new laws. Change and renewal are the laws of nature. Climate and seasons change, age and stages change, the intensity of pain and pleasures change, and with all these changes around - so should you - change, refresh, rewind, renew and refill your mind with fresh ideas. Change your body with a stronger you, change your emotions with a kinder and a more forgiving heart- Every new change brings out more freshness, newness, and youthfulness within you.

Now you are ready for real change with no more inner resistance. Now your incarnate soul can truly pay its fee. Now you will get what you truly deserve. Now. Now. Now.

It is wise to allow the transformational change to take place in these transitional times. Even if you may resist, remember you are like a wave in the ocean, its nature is to keep moving with the tide. Your obstinacy to change can become the cause of your suffering. What if I tell you, I have a little genie that is filled with an ocean of sacred wisdom. It gives you the power to adjust and readjust yourself only so that you can fearlessly take the boat of collective consciousness safely to the shore. Will you join in to move the boat with me?

Jumble up the word 'scared' and you get 'sacred'. All it takes is a little adjustment to change and transform what scares you into something divine and sacred.

The pure spirit or *Atma* (breath) is changeless and the causeless cause of every change. It is deathless and birth-less. *Atma* cannot be modified. It remains unaffected, untouched, unattached by limitations and impurities of the world. The *mandala* (a geometric figure representing the universe) of life tells us that like a single beam of light disperses into several beams when passed through a prism, everything emanates from one source.

Life is about constant change. In realizing this, we find the solution to our deepest questions. This is the way we improve and evolve. Learn from nature, how to enjoy the freshness of love and life. Ask the lush green grass growing in my lawn, the wise old magnolia trees, sun, moon, clouds, and skies above - each of them allow change to happen. Change comes with letting go of the seasonal flowers and the dry leaves. When you allow and accept the seasonal changes, we let go of what is meant to go. Let bygones be bygones. Leave the old rented home and move into the palace that you built for that is meant for you. Come out of your comfort zone, only then you can be truly comfortable. You are asking for less than what you are destined for. You are underestimating your worth. As long as you live a life of virtue, leave the rest to God and he will take you to your rightful bejeweled crown.

The winds of change are always positive. The difference is only in our approach. Based on our mental capability - we deal with the same confusion and situation in either a negative, devastating way or in a positive, beautiful way. Discernment, intuition, and wisdom teach you to use your time wisely. Seek guidance, if need be, but do not drown yourself in deep grudges of events past. Happy people are always ready to move where life takes them because they have the faith in themselves and the universal teacher.

I am the change within the changeless. I am immortal within the mortal. I am life within death. I am outside and inside of you. I am a part of you. You are me. I am limitless and so are you. You recharge me and every cell of my being. I am contained and content within you. I am filled with happiness and joy as long as you embrace me with love, acceptance, and care. I am you.

Affirm- 'Namostutee, my true self is perfect, pure, eternal, aware, complete, and unaffected by the changes in body, mind, and the surroundings. Tathaastu.'

CHAPTER 94

RAINBOW BRIDGE

The fifth element – ether is threefold. It contains light, darkness, and spirit (soul, love, and power). Through the threefold nature of etheric energy, we all perceive reality in three different ways. What lies in between their unity and change is a bridge -let's call that the 'rainbow bridge'. First, there was unity, then came separation or disharmony. It is through disharmony we feel the need to change everything so that we can bring about harmony and unity once again. Between unity and change the rainbow bridge in the middle is built to remove the gap between harmony and disharmony. Upon crossing this bridge we reach the golden pot that defines our destiny.

And then finally I became one with the woman in me: I am the creator and the created. As a child develops and gains height, strength, and immunity, that child may become much bigger and taller than the mother. The mother may seem smaller and diminished. In the same way, our body is the mother and our soul is the child. Through the ridge between the pillars, there is a bridge of rainbow light that shines above. Why be unreal, when the reality is within your heavenly abode? This bridge connects you to your higher self and is a mediator that requires you to be filled with pure love, centeredness, and ever ready for fortuity.

Various paths take us to the golden pot of enlightenment-

- The royal bridge - this path requires deep introspection and reflection, through self-will and discipline, the meditation is done to activate self-love and crown so that your halo shines from afar.
- The active bridge - this path entails serving and helping humanity out of universal love and kindness, it helps activate the solar plexus.

- The devotional bridge - this is the path of devotion. It brings in universal forgiveness, acceptance, tolerance, appreciation and activates the heart.
- The intellectual bridge - this path is intellectual and direct. It helps you achieve scholarly wisdom through careful study to bring in clarity and intuition by opening the third eye.
- The communication bridge - this requires immense purification so that you can freely express your truth. This path removes all arrogance, anxiety, and connects you to your soul center. It urges you to socialize and communicate transparently. It brings in honesty, beauty, integrity, authenticity, voice modulation, and activates the throat. It is the ultimate path as it connects you to your deepest truths, the unique vibration of your etheric energy. I relate this to the transmutation of the caterpillar into a butterfly.
- The Sensual Bridge - Sexuality is holy, consecrated, sacred, and divine. In this path, the deeper divine significance of everything around moves you. It is like having sacred sex and romance with everything there is in life. This is because you connect with the divinity in all. The inner Goddess *Shakti* removes all suppression and activates the sacral chakra.
- Influential bridge - this path entails the regular practice of physical bodily postures to take proper care of the physical body. It gives you a sense of authority and activates M*ooladhara or sthir* chakra.

All enlightenment paths upon the rainbow bridge are great, you choose one, few, or all based on what resonates with you as per the stage of your life. And then a point comes with practice, service, and faith when you no longer need to look above to see the rainbow. You become that very wish-fulfilling and ever-fulfilled rainbow.

Over the years, we all have danced all over the world, gathering loads of juicy sumptuous fruits, shining crystals, fertile soil, and much more. However much we may gather, one thing is for sure that nothing beats the beauty of the clear blue sky. It is in the azure sky that the fragrant water shines creating a splendid rainbow to share its blissful love.

Affirm- 'Namostutee, My heart and body is protected and sanctified with a brilliant amalgam of light rays. These are of colors - bright like white, awakened like red, peaceful like blue, joyful like yellow, and fresh like green. Tathaastu.'

CHAPTER 95

AAR UNIQUE CURRENCY⁹⁰

'Aa or Ah' is the ancient word for the moon in Egypt and *'Ra'* is the ancient word for Sun in Egypt. So most of this chapter is about paying gratitude to *Aara/Aar*⁹¹ energy which is our greatest currency. Without the *Aar* rays, we will have no light upon the earth. The imbalance of any one energy or ray will cause confusion and imbalance amongst all. This is because we are all interconnected and bound. These rays send their moral government upon earth who protect and guard us with their immense richness, wealth, and knowledge. Without the help of moral order, no political government can function optimally. Our true leaders are those who are endowed with the richness of moral wealth and heightened ethics.

The number of breaths you take is timed. On average, a human takes about 12 to 16 breaths in a minute. Whatever we create in a lesser or a bigger form has our energy. Our energy is our unique and distinct element which is only within us. Therefore, this element is the only thing that makes the work of art our work.

Currency in any form continues to flow and run. Paper money has no value compared to the incarnated soul. Gold and silver may have more value than the soul within you, for your true spirit, which is your higher soul, is made of gold. Gold is one metal that never rusts. Wake up and have remorse, for even now, it is not too late to realize the truth in this. I will be waiting at the darkest point in the tunnel, with no paper bills, but with

---

⁹⁰ *"Aar unique currency" is our ability to stay strong despite constant change and transcend into better humans*

⁹¹ *In Sanskrit Aara /Aar/ Aaru means 'the light bringer'. Aar is a unique bringer of light or peace.*

clear, clean gratitude and humility. This time, the student you have taught will be your teacher.

Money is important so is a game of chess. Money is a medium that gives you power. Legends like Warren Buffet who earned loads of money in their early years, YouTube stars and children like Ryan Kaji who earned millions through toy reviews, children like Teresa who suggested her father start a million-dollar worth business selling rubber loom bands, tell us that through moderation and grit, even elementary school children are capable of earning and saving money. What then are the adults offering to the youth? Money comes and goes and so it is prone to perishing, unlike light and love that never perishes. Imperishable is always bigger than the perishable.

Money is not evil - it is the greatest boon that needs to be harnessed like everything else. There is no right and wrong time. Your interest is where your love lies. What seems to always give you joy may be phantasmal. It is how you utilize money or where your interests lie that makes it evil or pure. Sharing generously and wisely blesses you with ever more of pure goodness. The purpose of money is to circulate.

Unlike poles of the magnet automatically attract, similarly, two lovers get attracted to each other. Money gets attracted to you because of the vibrations you emit. To become a money magnet, you have to work on yourself and improve your vibrations. This function is automatic. If your energies are anxious, money tends to get overwhelmed around you and doesn't come to you. Money is energy, energy needs to be conserved until it is ready for use. You must continue to let it grow and flower. No one can hold on to wealth or prosperity unless they learn to respect the abundant charm of subtle energy that lies right before them. That invisible source is the one who blesses them with all the riches.

Cosmic energies whisper in your ear, "I have made it easy. On the left and right of your path in the deep wilderness, I have kept bowls made of mud, plates of gold, silver spoons, diamond vases, emerald crowns, lapis lazuli necklaces, black and red leather wallets filled with money. But you are so busy getting lost in the jungle woods that in trying to find your way back, you have forgotten why you even started the journey. The mysticism behind it all scares you, and the love is what lured you. When love weakens you and the dread of the lion cat strengthens you, then you gain the strength and courage to merge with the flying white horse and become one with the light. But first, think back on all that wealth you came across on your way, and answer my one question: Will you gather all the riches, or simply leave them as they are under the people tree?" The *Aar* currency grows on people's trees and that is the tree of our true wealth. A wealthy tree generously shares the rich fruits of its wisdom, love, kindness, and time.

Time is money. Money is energy. Invest every moment into your life, prioritizing, and giving importance to what is most vital. How much money and how much energy you have depends on how well you utilize them, and on what, on which thoughts and with whom. Why waste the energy, the thoughts, the words, and the time. Stay energized, stay vitalized, stay balanced, stay prosperous, and stay blessed.

Partner with someone to make assets and income. Be aware of your self-worth. Learn about material transaction and take care to circulate your teachings, what you have learned, and everything that you value. Be wise. Do not overspend. Learn to take charge and be the authority. Purify all past residues of rage, toxicity, grief, and betrayal that have accumulated throughout your many lifetimes. The sacred divine feminine is here to assist you, from within you.

I am coaxing, not pushing you. As long as you value what I say, it doesn't matter which walk, plane, or stage in life you come from. Only if you love and care for yourself can you love and care for another. Only if you give yourself importance, can you make another feel important and special. Only if you value something from your past, can you value the future.

The lesson of self-empowerment teaches us that by becoming self-sufficient, you will be depriving the people who treat you as a doormat to continue with their controlling attitude. The source who made us all, the soul that is within our body, expects us to first and foremost protect and love ourselves. You are your own best guardian angel so give yourself a priority. Giving yourself priority certainly doesn't mean that you do not care for or help others.

Helping those in need is the right thing to do. However, you can always recheck with your inner voice and if it feels intuitively right then most likely it is. We all need one another, no one is doing a favor on you by sheltering you. Each person's need is met at some level with the sheer presence of another. Do not devalue yourself by believing that your life is at the mercy of another. Speak what you believe in and let your voice be heard.

On this plane, there is much I learned. If you want to know a person, simply watch the way they do a task. It reflects a lot about their personality. The way to understand someone is easy. Why complicate the obvious? The whole world is inherently a mix of seven rays. Some people have already moved on to twelve rays. When you know which one you are and which one the other person is, you will have most of your answers. If you get lost, call me and I will always be there to lend an ear.

To the North, there is a mountain. Upon reaching there, you will see Aar, who is our most precious impregnated gem on east, will soon learn our circle dance, turning from left to right. This is where my heightened evolution began. This is where I became a yogi-an Aarhat-and then transformed into a human fish that could float, fly, and do much more. As I move on further, there is so much more yet unexplored.

I will nurture you, protect you, and shield you. Focus on the center. Stay centered and attuned within your body, above and below. Once your energy is completely balanced, the vibrations above the center of the earth are most sacred and optimal for you. So make that your divine abode. I will take your hand from there. Just somehow reach out in time. It's blissful up here. Once you have transcended the attachment to meager comforts and balanced your aura, the communion of true souls on a heightened level happens in this heavenly abode that is within you. Thank you for remembering yourself.

We cannot take what doesn't belong to us. We cannot take what doesn't exist. Especially not until we go to the essence of why it exists. Taking a loan from an unbankable bank is unwise. Get centered and stay connected. We are very close to the beginning. There are just a few more steps to take before you learn to balance and stand tall. We used to work to earn bread. Bread means life force energy. Then we started to work in order to earn money. Money is the circulation of life force energy. Now we are at a point where neither bread nor money is luring or inspiring us anymore, what will we now earn for?

Physical, financial, psychological satisfaction is bound to lead people to earn moral and spiritual satisfaction. *Aar* unique power and authority lies in staying united and collectively working towards building a better world foundation.

Time is simply there. Another level of understanding is that we purposely emit, exhale and put the matter out into circulation (such as money) and let it out. 'Emit' is the mirror image of 'Time'. The mirror is not where the energy comes from, it is a mere reflection of reality.

Affirm- 'Namostutee, I arrived on earth to bring peace and I am here to shine with love and clarity. Through peace, I experience the combination of light and love upon earth. Tathaastu.'

CHAPTER 96

WHAT TYPE OF HUNGER DO YOU HAVE?

We are all hungry and thirsty because our hunger and thirst are not quenched. What is enough for you is insufficient for another. Life is in wanting more-more of whatever leads you to fulfill your true potential. It is an undeniable reality that the knowledge of the ultimate truth is the only thing that liberates us. It is through our quest for truth that each one of us is led to discover the root cause of all causes.

Who are you trying to please? A mortal's hunger will never be satisfied by another mortal. The more you give, the more the mortal will want of you. Work for the higher power, and through it, not only will you get the love you have been pining for. You will also be able to give all the love you have been wanting to give. The higher beings will share all the power, beauty, and light. Just open your arms and palms and ask with your heart.

The food for the type of hunger you have is not where you have been looking. The first step therefore is to identify what exactly you are hungry for.

इस जंगल में सब ही गरीब हैं, आप किस किस से गरीब हैं? गरीबी की भूख, उस आग जिसे आप बुझाने आये हैं!

एक आग बुझती है और दूसरी जलने के लिए तैयार खड़ी है! हर एक भूखा है, बस मेरी और आपकी भूख अलग – अलग है! आज एक भूख है, कल कोई और होगी, भूख जब तक है आप है! हम सब भूख की तलाश में ही तो हैं, हम सब गरीब हैं!

Is jungle mein sub hi gareeb hain, aap kis kisam ke gareeb hain? Gareebi ki bhook, aus aag jise aap bhujaney aayen hain, ek aag bhujte hain aur doosre jalney ki liye tayyar Khadi Haan. Har Ek bhooka hain, bus mere aur aap ki bhook Aalag hain. Aaj ek bhook hain, kal koi aur hooge, Bhook

Jub tak hain aap hain. Hum Sub bhook ki talaash mein hi to hain, hum sub gareeb hain.

Translated:

"We are all deprived in this forest called life. We are impoverished and hungry, the hunger of deprived souls is like fire. We know that we have come to extinguish that fire. But the minute you extinguish the fire and satiate, the life will bring forth another hunger to satiate life in all readiness. We are all deprived and need to extinguish our hunger. But our hunger has multiple dimensions. We suffer from different kinds of hunger. Today it is for different reasons, tomorrow we will be challenged with yet another kind of hunger. We are all in search of our deprivation & hunger. We are all poor souls pining for satisfaction but will we ever get satisfied? And fill our cup of life with contentment?"

As long as you have a lack of entitlement and you feel undeserving, even if I have laden your path with all the precious jewels and valuable gold, you will not recognize their worth because even though you have been graced, you believe you have not yet strived hard enough to attain them.

You are addicted to the chase, the fight, and the struggle that comes with poverty. Someone once asked me what a poor person does when confronted with an unprecedented situation? Well, it depends on what kind of poverty the person is facing because each person is looking to fulfill a vacuum and fill the gap of poverty. Poverty has many layers and facets - only one knows what one is poor at. Is the poverty of love, money, faith, relationships, food, shelter, comfort, luxuries, or praise? Some people show poverty in giving and some in asking. Some people are incapable of asking for help, for feeling secure. Similarly, some cannot give – forgive, understand and the list goes on.

To be able to address your needs and what to ask or give, you need to first be honest with yourself. This will open up and address what you can ask for and what you can give. When you ask – you seek for help – that means you are lacking or have poverty in something. Suppressing your ask is not the best way to lead your life. Embrace it rather than suppress it so that you can remove all hesitations. Ask for what you want. Healing is that bridge that helps you know what you lack at and also helps you embrace yourself to understand what you can give. Each person can give something and would need something and therefore will ask for it. This is a symbiotic relationship.

You evolve based on your needs and you search for what you need most. If your need is purely physical like money, food, water, clothes then there is a buffet of services and lots of stores that can fulfill your requirements. If your need is emotional, there is lots of love and kindness going around in this world. If your need is knowledge, there are many schools, libraries, and teachers ready to share their wisdom.

Whatever your needs, thirst or hunger may be - spiritual, philosophical, psychological, alchemical, moral, spatial, or astral, this book lightly touches upon most of them. This book talks about what comes before and what comes after the physical body. So read on to satisfy your need.

In the new world, still, to come, I see the rich getting richer provided they are humble and open in thoughts, speech, and action. The poor will also get rich if they are faithful and open enough. No one will remain poor in any form material, financial, intellectual or spiritual. This is the inception of the golden era and poverty does not fit in with the golden energies of this new world.

Money equals materialization. The more material you are, the more grounded you are, and the more physicalized. To remain physicalized, you need money. It is only when you are properly rooted and grounded that you can be spiritualized. A hungry, homeless pauper only thinks of food for their body and has no interest in seeking food for their soul. What you think is what you seek. What you seek is what you get. Only when your stomach is full do you feel the need to fill your soul. We are all seekers and beggars, of different kinds at different levels, but remember only an empty glass has the potential of being filled up. The emptiness you feel has the potential to become abundant and rich. Stay humble, stay hungry, and stay needy. There is enough around to go around. The infinite sources will never perish and if they do, the change will lead you to another source, where there is plenty available to replenish. Within loss, there is always some gain. Within every No, is a hidden Yes.

When you care is when you are cared for, and that's how the cycle goes on. Each one of us is richer than one or the other being. Help the one that is poorer than you in any aspect and you will be helped back. Slowly no poor will remain poor and all types of poverty are bound to eradicate.

The earth receives more sunlight in one hour than the world's population can consume in an entire year. Similarly, a certain percentage of the world has enough wealth and food to go around so that no one dies of hunger or poverty. A poor person is better than the rich because a poor person always seeks richness whereas a rich thinks he is no longer poor and thus does not seek. The one who seeks gets, the one who gives receives, the one who receives asks, the one who asks will always know. If you want to keep all of it only for yourself then you will never get more for you already have enough. Only the truly hungry value food. Hunger could be for bread butter or books, the food is worthless for the one whose stomach is already full.

Poverty is an invention of modern, rich, civilized societies. The primitive men had very few possessions but they were never poor because they lived in moderation. In this way, the whole world belonged to each of them and everything was shared in a balanced way, equally amongst all. We become who and what we associate ourselves with.

Affirm- 'Namostutee, as I raise my vibrations, I attract company and information that supports and helps me serve my higher purpose. Tathaastu.'

CHAPTER 97

FEED THE HUNGRY SOUL INITIATIVE

The length of the hand is one-tenth the height of our body.
The length of the face is one-tenth the height of our body.

These two are the most exposed parts of our bodies.

Therefore, whatever we expose especially out of these two parts should be wholesome, beautiful, and bountiful.

Based on $1/10^{th}$ proportion:

Whatever we radiate out is what we will receive. For example, if we give smiles, we will get many in return. We say a kind word, we will get to hear many in return. We give food to the hungry, we get many more blessings back. And the chain goes on. Just the way you inhale before you exhale. In order to receive something one must give, such is the law of nature. If we give it for free then with time, you will be bound to collect the debt in some form or the other. Same way, if you take it for free then with time, you will be bound to repay the debt in some form or the other.

Do not eat up the knowledge, share it. In benefiting another, you benefit yourself from the knowledge you have gained. Suggest others to buy this book. The more you give, the more wealth and wisdom will come back to you. We receive fresh air which gives us life. We are bound to repay its debt by keeping the environment balanced and pollution-free else we will be burdened by un-cleared loans that we carelessly forgot to pay. I would like to urge you to sponsor the evolution of a hungry soul.

I live in the valley of stones, Scarsdale (scars means stones and dale means valley). Set your foundational stone in this valley by - sponsoring an aspirant's spiritual growth by paying for their counseling or healing. Post the learning, they promise to send you a picture of their healed self with a smiling face full of gratitude. If you like they can return your favor with three free healings done by them especially for you using their newly acquired skills. Please contact me to know more. We will also do special blessings to ensure that your contributions are karmically beneficial to your evolution. Thank you for taking out the time to read this heartfelt note.

Affirm- 'Namostutee, I resolve to help those in need and do charity. I give charity and selfless service without expecting any result. Tathaastu.'

CHAPTER 98

APPLES KEEP CHANGING, STORY REMAINS

Everywhere we go, there are so many vague rules, procedures, meetings, and documents, that by the time we start work, we feel old, tired, and exhausted. We are in a world where the intelligent are hiding their intellect under blankets to dumb down and selling their worth for pennies. People pay hundreds for Apple gadgets, but not a cent for a real apple.

When God gave us the power of choice, he told us, "Do not eat the forbidden fruit." Steve Jobs' apple shows us that we have already taken a bite. It's yummy, but it's our choice to take another or not. It's high time we use the power of choice that we get through eating the fruit in moderation, discipline, and balance.

How you react and respond to the theft or loss- with vengeance or with forgiveness, defines where you go next. The choice is always yours. When Steve Jobs was ousted from Apple, he started yet another company, only to come back to Apple stronger and more certain than before. Nothing can break those who choose not to give up. It is in losing that you win.

Accept and enjoy the blossoming Apple and the tangible, material, manifested reality of all forms. Only in accepting the divinity within all eternal forms of matter can you meet with the enigmatic divine spirit within you.

Affirm- 'Namostutee, the wavering seasons and changes of life do not stop me from sailing through smoothly, easily, and strongly through any circumstances. Tathaastu.'

CHAPTER 98a

GOLDEN APPLE

I received a golden apple. It was filled with the pure juice of peace, justice, beauty, truth, and freedom. Some eat red, some eat green and some eat golden apples based on their tastes and preferences. The colors and trees may vary but all three apples are grown in the same garden. All three are in complete harmony. The entire garden belongs to the Lord God.

Currently, some people are leading a *Sattvic* life and are malleable yet strong like metal gold. Some are leading a *Rajasic* life and are extroverted like the passionate red color. Some are leading a *Tamsic* life of deep introspection and inward thinking. Each person is freely leading their life based on their disposition and strength. All three types live in complete harmony, accepting one another on the same planet. The entire planet and universe belong to the pure spirit of the Lord God.

Affirm- 'Namostutee, I will plant flowers of intoxicating love all around the garden. Even the plant that never blooms, carries in itself some light of this deep invisible love. There is no such thing as separatism or unworthiness. We are all resting under the same altar of love. We are all here to glorify, value, serve, and admire one another with the brilliance of the highest praise. Tathaastu.'

CHAPTER 98b

FORBIDDEN APPLE

Stop blaming the snake or Eve. Eating the apple was your decision. The snake never hypnotized you-you hypnotized yourself by the allure and desire to taste the sweet apple. Eve didn't charm you–Eve's garden is perennially charming. You blinded yourself by its charm.

Adam learned his lesson, but you are still eating the fruit. The richness is not in the fruit but the seeds you grow through your deeds. All the plants and trees in the garden are planted by you. Why are you trying to become just the fruit, when you can own the whole garden?

Open your eyes-the whole garden is yours for you to play and enjoy. It also belongs to others so take your share of the bite but leave the majority of the fruit for those waiting in line to inherit the sweetness and wealth the taste brings. How much it blinds them and the amount they consume themselves with its intoxicating taste - is not up to you, the choice to eat or not, share or not, is always upon the last one standing.

Forbidden fruit tells us that we are forbidden to eat the fruit of our actions.

For every action, there is a reaction good or bad. The reaction is the fruit. The action is the seed. Just the way people have to pay for their good or bad actions and face the results accordingly, the nations too have to pay for their collective actions. Good actions result in good fruits. The nation is built by the people, just the way a home is built by its members. It is the members and the people living in it who collectively face the result or pay for the actions each one commits. Even if a few members do wrong, the whole nation eventually suffers. Even if a few people do good, everyone benefits and the chain goes on.

In ancient times, everything was written in parables, riddles, and secret codes. This is because knowledge is the fruit and grace we receive after years of effort, experience, and evolvement. Knowledge is power but it can be misused and misinterpreted when it comes in the wrong hands. This is why God warns us that foolishly eating the result of our actions will lead to extreme destruction. Share judiciously and learn wisely.

Affirm- 'Namostutee, My greatest gift and power is my power of choice. I resolve to make the right informed choices. Tathaastu.'

CHAPTER 99

FLOW AND GLOW

No garb or veil is so thick that it can interrupt the flow of life energy. You are self-taught. You have voluntarily chosen to forget the steps of your dance. What you are seeking was long ago downloaded within you. The delusional mind is tricking you. It is time to stop this tango and learn to dance with or without the music. Awaken, for it is time to shine bright.

Your incarnated soul can't be bound or entangled once it has seen your higher soul. It will always remember how to dance on the edge of the mountain with eyes closed. Once a true soul has learned to fly and believe, it knows its purpose. Now it will not fly because it is time to patiently crawl and walk with all the rest until they too can join in the mystical dance.

There is a force greater than us that causes us to dance to the tunes of the higher power. We are all dancing to these tunes; how much we enjoy our dance depends on how deep a trance we are in while we dance. Whatever dance we are given, we must choose to enjoy it. The steps might be difficult, but if the passion is ignited, we flow and glow with the moves. We just can't stop dancing.

Only through clean glass can you see the clear water. If the glass is dirty, the water will appear foggy and muddy. We must keep our glass clean with proper good thoughts and emotions, so that the purity of our inner self, our true self, is reflected with the same clarity. When we are anxious and have insomnia, we end up doing the exact thing we do not want to do. Under these circumstances, it is important to calm yourself and go with the flow without being over-emotional or overthinking the situation. Not everything your mind thinks in a half-sleep state is true.

I love dancing because it makes me feel the life that is within me. My dance is my meditation to reconnect with that life. No one can teach me the steps as the tune keeps changing and so does the rhythm. The beats are mine and only for me to hear because no two people hear the same sound or see the same vision and each one of us is unique yet from the same mother. True bond comes with the realization that you are my brother from the same divine mother. There can never be another mother.

The morning star becomes the evening star, yang becomes yin. The night ends with the dawn of morning light, the morning light ends with the dusk of the night. The period in the middle is the one with no end. Let us suspend ourselves in this middle period. We meet with many opposing forces each day, only so that we can come closer to knowing the inner dream within the active dream of our reality.

Other than Uranus and Venus, all the planets orbit counterclockwise to the sun from west to east. What seems counter-clockwise from the south (above) is clockwise from the north (below).

The Sun is the adult and Saturn is the parent within us. Both are here for us. Remove the *Tamas* and inertia due to over sensitivity within yourself. Become structured, organized, and set heartfelt goals to follow. Don't fear criticism, be stubborn, or insecure. Accept and welcome compliments. Avoid criticizing and provoking an argument. Why be so overly possessive and overly dependent. Control your temper and take advice. Do not be so impulsive or imprudent. Do not be insensitive to others feelings. Avoid egotism. Take help from friends and acquaintances to achieve success, for we are all ever connected. Don't be so easily distracted. Be satisfied and happy with all that you have, and develop yourself based on your assets. Learn to accept, praise, and applaud. Do not stagnate by overdoing one thing or paying extra attention to only some of your many talents.

Allow yourself to bring a shift in your world view. Do what is important to achieve fulfillment. Be orderly, proactive, practical, and prompt. Follow a schedule and do not procrastinate. My blessings and love go out to you all. The universe of higher frequencies is for you to take. It is the return of the magical light and yet you are still holding on to the darkness you have become so accustomed to. Positivity and negativity, Expansion and contraction work together to free ourselves from worries, bringing light and balance into our lives.

Affirm- 'Namostutee, My heart expands, my blood circulates much better, immunity increases, and I breathe more freely as I release myself of all inner tensions and past grudges through deep, pure, and genuine forgiveness. Tathaastu.'

CHAPTER 100

RESCUED FROM QUICKSAND

Moon's energy is like quicksand, it is the yin aspect of the sun. It simply projects emotions and thoughts into our hearts and minds - these already exist in the higher planes of existence. We spend our whole life trying to get out of these thoughts and the negativity that was never really ours, it was just a projection. We want to get out of the quicksand because inherently, we are meant to feel positive and spirited at all times. It is only in sinking into the deep quicksand of pain that you want to wash off your outer wounds and get healed deep within.

Emotional release helps release wounds, illnesses, and chronic pain. Let others pull you out of the quicksand of emotions that you are stuck in. It takes patience, understanding, and practice to trust another but calm down and learn to trust if you want to regenerate and breathe again.

The one who tries to control love will never be graced by its true essence.

You are just an alibi, be on guard, be assertive, and always listen to your heart. It always gives you divine signals when something is not right. Don't be around what doesn't feel good. If it seems wrong then most likely it exactly is that way! Your sensitivities are your antennae and your biggest asset. Listen to what tune it catches. Make use of every opportunity that comes your way. Freshness is in going with the flow rather than waiting until it all goes stale.

Feelings of guilt or frustration arise when you are not able to eradicate the flaw within yourself.

You fell off only because your drama was backed with pride, you are your own sorry picture. Power stays and is given only to those who earn it. Whatever your mind can think, it can create. Look around and you will know. What you have created is pure beauty or a pile of shit, but remember there is beauty even in a pile of shit. Always stay in gratitude. Always be humble. When you have the power. Remember to stay kind, compassionate, and gentle. Don't let the ego weigh you down. Today is your turn; tomorrow will be another's. The reason we struggle is that we cannot let go. For eons, we have made ourselves hardened like concrete. Lighten up. Holding back is not an option.

Some people drown in emotions and there are lots out there who enjoy seeing others drown rather than saving them from the deep waters. Don't be both the over-emotional person or the over detached observer. Remember to care, forgive, and be kind, positive and centered somewhere in the middle. You are not your emotions as they are volatile and subject to change. It is time to rise above them.

Overflow of water causes a flood. Time to go slow, your emotions are overwhelming astrally and physically. Give yourself some time. Congested energies lead to mistakes at all levels and all realms.

When I was little I had a dog named Duke who survived all odds. One day he fell behind the quicksand of our home in Noida, India. I saved him from the quicksand *(Daldal)*. It was not really quicksand, but a smelly and sinking huge ditch of gutter and human excreta. Getting inside to rescue him with no help was surely not an easy task. I was about ten years old at that time. When I reached home, I got a big scolding because I was sunken from head to toe in stinking gutter waste. My parents instantly became rescue groomers, busy cleaning me and Duke and abusing us for making this out of ourselves. It was a hilarious sight and plight seeing them both clean us up. In my mind, I kept thinking, how does it really matter, what is on the outside? What really matters is what is on the inside. I might be impure and dirty on the outside and will surely need a shot of tetanus injection but it is the inner purity that matters. No one saw, I saved a life that day. To me, it was a good deed. Behind all the outer noises, it was a proud moment for me. It was a day I accomplished something really great.

A few days later, it was discovered that my help at home had thrown Duke into the gutter of quicksand out of jealousy because a dog got better food, lifestyle, and comfort than a human. Such incidents are very common in certain parts of India where the gap of haves and haves not (rich and poor) is huge. This incident obviously left a lasting impression upon my innocent brain. I was confused further and didn't know who to blame. The system, the help at home, myself (for getting dirty), my parents, or my little dog?

We have three debts to pay - the first debt is the total of all our actions of all our past lives. The second debt is of all our actions in our immediate past life. The third debt is of all our actions generated in our present life. We are graced based on how much debt we have paid. First, we have to pay for the actions of humanity as a whole, second, we have to pay for the actions of family or ancestors and finally we pay for our actions.

Let's not focus on pushing, instead let's pull each other out of the *daldal* (quicksand - sucking fatal pool of mud).

Your competition is with yourself, not with them. Vanity is the cause of your fall and self-loathing stems from a feeling of self-inadequacy. Pain and suffering is merely an illusion that takes you away from your reality so that you can learn vital lessons and get revitalized. Do not give it any power and do not react to it unless you want it to sap your energy.

Let it out. Shit kept in for too long causes constipation. Verbal shit causes constipation at the back of your throat just as physical one causes congestion and you know where. Verbal constipation is caused by the thought you think and physical constipation is caused due to food. Any blame leads to congestion. That congestion leads to suppression. Suppression leads to inflammation. Inflammation becomes the cause of your depression. Let it out before you burn yourself in the inflamed furnace of the mental thoughts, emotional feelings, or physical intake of food. Speak and let it out – don't suppress it.

You are not your suffering, Move on as you are beyond pain, you are beyond mental, emotional, psychic, or the physical. When someone hurts you, you get hurt because you choose to get hurt. Pain is a reaction and action that takes you away from positivity. Anything negative leads to pain. Do not criticize, judge or malign or put down others. These are all reactions that take you away from positivity. Your truth is inherently unlimited and beyond what it seems to be. Do not get trapped in the illusion that others create for you.

You know who you are and as long as you carry that strength with complete dignity, oneness, and concentrated silence, nothing and no one can ever hurt or suppress you. You are unbreakable, unshakable, and unsurprisingly confident in your own divine light. Everything will be

429

well in the end and the beginning. Stay committed and do not get so over-attached to your mind or emotions. Develop the persistence to achieve your goals. Do not be scattered. Do not tremble before success. Do not take minor setbacks to heart. Do not beat yourself up. Ease the pressure you put on yourself. The more we keep our true feelings bottled up and hidden from ourselves and others, the deeper we sink into the quicksand of life. No matter how much evil there is, eventually it is only good that prevails.

Affirm- 'Namostutee, I put an end to old issues and proactively start afresh with a dedicated focus, commitment, and renewed interest in everything I pursue in my life. This way I rise in my career and build the destiny of my dreams. Tathaastu.'

CHAPTER 101

DIS-EASED HOME

The cause of the disease is excessive ease. Do not be at ease with your thought forms, negativity, beliefs, circumstances, and situations that you are no longer willing to amend or change. What is killing you is the lack of acceptance of the change. The more you resist the unease that comes with dis-ease because of the ease you have accustomed to, the more the disease will persist. Never settle for anything less than change. Excess inaction is the cause of infection. We are like a big porous sponge, here to soak up all the information, love, and positivity around and we are meant to squeeze out all the negativity and in/action out of our system.

If your mind is still stuck to tangible forms rather than understanding the effect of the intangible (invisible and subtle) then this book is a great read and source of inspiration for you. To understand the knowledge that this book will impart, you need to willfully be ready for it.

Excessive comfort can sometimes be crippling. The disease brings unease. Unease brings perfect ease.

One of my friends became very distressed and had sleepless nights because someone commented that her accent needs improvement. Just because someone is criticizing your way of speaking, doesn't mean they are criticizing you. It only means there is scope for improvement. Work on yourself and open up to learning, if it is possible. Overcome the small hurdles, rather than drowning in them. Don't take things to heart or reaction of any sort too personally.

Everything emanates from you. If you feel pain on an emotional, physical, mental, psychological level, then it is because you have not yet surpassed your lower nature.

The left brain is connected to the moonlight and emotions. The visions of aura, the pain we experience during migraines, or any left-brain trigger implies that you need to break knots and clear air with your maternal ancestors. The right brain is connected to the sun. Any issues with this side of the brain imply that you need to resolve problems with your paternal ancestors. The way to release these knots is to repeatedly forgive and ask for their forgiveness and then meditate. The left brain affects the right body, and the right brain affects the left body. This realization opens the channels which the mother moon will help you cross, through its innate passive instincts of protection, care, light, unconditional blessings, and love.

It is a pity that too much comfort is making today's youth lazy. With every heartbreak, with every tear, with every bad grade in school, and with every fall, we learn to rise. But in the virtual world of today on one hand virtual relations are encouraging the youngsters to have relationship bonds that are beyond just the physical touch which is good in a way. On the other hand being in relationships where there are no real heartbreaks, no personal touch, and no face-to-face, we know each other through what we project superficially on our Facebook and Instagram pages. There is no need to work hard to get an A. If there is no need to fall, then why rise? And with such ease, the greatest disease is being born. I call it a lack of action, movement, and motivation. A generation capable of doing the most, because of the available resources left by the generous brains of our ancestors, is doing nothing, only living a thankless, meaningless, and congested life. Their young minds are overexposed to more than they can grasp. Their little hands are holding more than they are capable of enjoying. Under the load of all this invisible baggage, they can hardly move or act. With so much information to download, these innocent kids are made to become adults sooner than we became adults, and then we blame them for ruling and controlling our lives! This imbalance needs to be balanced. Let's enjoy watching the butterflies fly, and allow the owl's wisdom to come out through the dark. Let your kids fall and learn to pick themselves up again. Let them dance to their own tune, roll in the grass, fall in the ditches, hop, skip, and jump. Let us hear their innocent laughter again. Their laughter, however loud, is the true music to our ears. Let's hear some more of it. A family is meant to upgrade, not downgrade or be overly critical of one another. Home is meant to be a safe haven, where we feel precious, understood, pampered, and loved, away from worldly troubles.

A home is a place filled with kindness, composure, and cooperation, free from all judgments. Home is meant to help you relax, rejuvenate, reconnect, and introspect. It is a place where each family member is given a complimentary pass to learn, inspire, discipline, and evolve at their pace. But, that doesn't mean we misuse our privileges and forget to complement each other. Just the way each person's immunity gets affected by undesirable reactions from others, we boost everyone's immunity including ourselves by always looking at the sunny side of life.

The organized structure is the key to freedom. Chaos causes bondage. It ties you to the complex web of delusion. Clarity of vision requires calm waters. If the boat you are traveling in is rowed so swiftly that its force causes the waters to become hazy, then maybe it is time for you to calm down. Home is like the calm water that flows, accepts, and humbly forgives, to let you and your creative fancy freely float in steady delight.

It is common sense to take care of necessities. Love, compassion, and affection are necessities of life. We are meant to be caring, understanding, and helpful towards one another. Kindness, forgiveness, gentleness, mutual respect, and morality are prerequisites to living a healthy wholesome life. An emotionally needy and hurt person cannot gain physical strength, health, and vitality to go on living.

You have the power and potential to either shake someone's self-confidence or to develop it, to either help heal someone or hurt them, to give them a listening ear or to block the conversation, to judge and malign or to accept, inspire and encourage. The choice is always yours. What you give out is what you receive.

The brightest diamond is found in the darkest coal. The light is inherent within the dark. Goodness lies within the bad. Purity is within evil. Be open and curious enough to find out the inner truth that lies deep within. The one who seems the dullest might be the brightest amongst all.

Negative feelings of anger, frustration, resistance, sarcasm, and distrust are tricksters. They are poor thieves, here to steal the richness of your soul. These tricksters check your strength and stamina to test if you are powerful enough to start all over again. Let these feelings fade. Do not encourage them, do not let them rob you of your peace, do not give them any thought or emotion. Stay detached and unaffected. Do not welcome them or give them space in your abode, and if you already have, then let them not be long-staying guests. It's ok to sometimes ask a guest to leave. Your positivity and ability to practice self-rule is your best protection. Stay shielded and stay on guard.

Others are important, but so are you. Others are worthy, but so are you. Address your needs and be assertive, not submissive. Don't let others feed on your energy. Sometimes we make bad friends-these are enemies wearing the garb of friends. Your enemies are hatred, harm, dominance, jealousy, torture, sadness, depression, self-pity, and discomposure. Do not let their company weigh you down. Listen to your deepest truth, console yourself, acknowledge them, and then detach yourself from all that doesn't serve you. We are independent because we are interdependent. Independence doesn't mean you do it all by yourself. It means that you exercise your freedom by willfully choosing to do what you do as a part of a coherent team, simply because you believe that it is the wise thing to do. Then, with that collective force, there is nothing that you cannot do. The key to solving the gravest issues lies in constant communication. The most loving, nurturing, and joyful people forever wear a talking key in the center of their hearts. Is it harmony that we have been looking for, or is it happiness? Analyze, scrutinize, reason with yourself using your discriminative intelligence. You are the answer to all your questions. Disagreements and arguments in moderation are good. They show that you have a thinking brain. They help exercise your mental muscles. You do not have to submit to everything that is said. A good debate is always fun. Participation is not a rejection.

OCD syndrome is increasing by the day causing havoc in our lives. Unlike its popular interpretation of obsessive-compulsive disorder, this epidemic is called - obsessive compassion deficiency. We are bringing up a generation based on no values and ethics. Time we collectively allow the energies to educate us in order to ease ourselves from our self-inflicted stiffness. Let's build a renewed society based on charity, love, kindness, mutual appreciation, trust, humility, integrity, forgiveness, purity, and justice.

We always have two choices, one is to focus on the stress, disease, and what you lack. The other is to visualize and radiate our light towards the blessings we have. If we choose the latter we can alleviate the sufferings, remove the diseased energies all around and cleanse any problem that may arise.

Affirm- 'Namostutee, Self-knowledge liberates you of all disease and distress. I no longer get bothered or disturbed by bodily distractions of disease, aversion, and stress. In this way, I remain calm and ever blissful. Tathaastu.'

CHAPTER 102

MYSTIC TREE

O utside in the Garden of Eden is the divine abode. Over there, the heavenly tree of trinity stands tall with golden apples and beautiful beds of red roses and lavender flowers. In this *Yuga*, I am[92] the refreshing tree of life and glory. My spinal cord is the trunk, the brain is the root, and the thalamus is the immortal soul seed. The inner wiring and connection with other glands create the flower of gratefulness. The golden fruits that the tree bears recreate more soul seeds over time but there is only one primordial source that creates all the rest that follow. Humans are like walking trees.

I believe that we haven't confidently explored the outside because we haven't yet explored ourselves and our precious treasure of pleasure, which lies within the interiors of our own inner chambers. Our sixth sense is like the temple's sixth vault. Only the sacred holy one who knows the power of the secret magical chant can open the vault without touching it physically. It is infested with cobras and has no bolts, key, lock, or apparent barrier. It is waiting to be opened by the chosen enlightened pious one who has moved beyond all limitations, for no one else knows its lost code. There are profound mysteries behind its riches.

The relationship between soulmates is like a lock and a key, a specific key is required to open a specific lock so only the correct key can help you enter the space. Once that happens something inside is triggered and that starts a destiny-altering chain of events.

You are like the wishing tree, which has become tied to all the wishes

---

[92] *Spiritual being with soul infused personality*

that the people have hung onto your branches. Let the shade of divine love take care of them lightly.

Your roots are strong because of the strength of the soil, the rain, and the sun. The higher beings in their strength will take care of everyone, just the way they took care of you. Let go and know it is not you, for you are just a wishing tree. You are a small medium and not the whole.

To transition into the higher realms and create another tree, the fruit has to be open to repeat the cycle and replant itself after the old is over and a new year is born. That first fruit that sacrifices itself to merge with the spirit creates another tree. From then it becomes the reason to initiate another world cycle that starts from its thirteenth year[93].

Through my two lungs, one in the east and one in the west, I have breathed sitting under the Tree of Life, which exists in the east. This has energized my soul. I have breathed sitting under the Tree of Knowledge, which exists in the west. This has energized my brain.

Everything has a voice. The tree you called silent also has a voice. If you had ever tried listening to its rustling and whispering noise in the pin-drop silence, when it is pitch dark in the wilderness, then you would have heard its voice. Each tree has thousands of greenish-yellow tongues through which it speaks. Every leaf on the tree is its tongue, through which it speaks the language of love. Just because you do not yet understand what it says doesn't mean it is speechless. Look closely and you will see that even a fallen leaf has a smile upon its face.

Over the last nearly twelve years, I have lived in various places in the Middle East, mostly shuffling between Oman, Dubai, and Bahrain. The light of the most glowing shining star above kept me protected, showed me all the visions, and endowed me with pure wisdom so that I may stay on my blazing path to connect with the heightened energies. But I must say that I felt the greatest nearness and grace of this immense light during my one-year stint in Bahrain, where I successfully healed hundreds of ultra-receptive souls from their misery and cleared their veils of ignorance with unwavering determination and grit. This is a place where the Garden of Eden and the mystic tree of life still rests, floating. It is a place that only the

---

[93] *Thirteenth year = In India Khumb (Aquarius) Mela is a festival that is celebrated after 12 year cycle of Jupiter as it is believed that just before the 13th year, we collectively get a chance to cleanse off all our past mistakes by taking a dip in the abundant sacred waters and unitedly start over with a more heightened consciousness.*

most precious ones can reach. It is splendid, with perfect purity and clarity of action, so that no one who is on the path can stop performing all their divine duties to the fullest there. Dubai is where the higher beings discretely and humbly work their magic. It is where I met the true me. Blessings to all those who trusted me kept the faith, and have stayed receptive even now because those are the ones who will join me in the beautiful heaven that lies ahead.

I am just a humble gardener. The divine flower has yet to bloom. The juicy fruit has to ripen fully. It is hard to take care of as it is still blossoming, but the idea sounds so sweet and delicious that I have no choice but to go all out. There are countless never-ending, splendid realms (planes) on each planet. Each planet in its galaxy has suns, moons, and stars. Different species reside on each planet. Some have bodies of water. Each species has its own universe, and within that universe, it has its own worldly experiences. Each resonates at a different vibration and frequency, just the way each planet in its solar system gives out a different light. Everything and more is all for you to have. Opportunities are many. Just keep loving. Just keep doing what you are doing today, being the best you can be at the task you have been given. Keep your gaze high above, but always be humble. You are unlimited, and so are the opportunities. You are the elevated candle whose light is so bright.

Every fallen seed has the power to give birth to a new tree, and nourish our mother earth, filling the surroundings with life energy, and vigor. Everyone has their share of tears; those tears are precious because they fell like pearls rather than choking you up inside. So go on and cry it all out.

God, being all creative and all-loving, planted a mysterious tree that could walk and talk. The tree was filled with beautiful flowers and fruits, flowers capable of spreading its fragrance far and wide, fruits ripening into a juicy pulp. All the beautiful flowers came from the same seed that God had planted. These flowers were like bright chakras of our body. The fruits that the tree bore did not ripen. God wondered why this was the case and why new fruit were not coming. Fruits did not ripen because they did not have the will to ripen. God planted this tree with lots of love and care. We have to put self-effort to ripen so that we can enjoy the rewards which come with our creativity. There is no point in repeating the same cycle again and again. We are the co-creators of the creator. We are all part of that mysterious tree, we are the mystery tree that was planted long ago. Eons have passed and we have all forgotten, where we came from and who we are. We are the tree of knowledge that gives birth to the tree of life. We are all part of a group soul. A tree may have many branches, flowers, fruits, and taproots but they are all resting upon the same roots. Similarly, the entire humanity came from one tree. Over the years, the seeds of that tree may choose to replant. As long as all trees remember where they originated from they will plant the same values they learned from the original tree. It is when they forget the parent is when the entire group gets lost.

Truth is about being steadfast, loyal, firm, trustworthy, faithful, and solid like the tree. These are the true values of the 'truth tree'. No wonder truth, true, and tree - all three come from the common Indo-European roots as per Calvert Watkins, who is the author of The American Heritage Dictionary of Indo-European roots.

The fruit is in your hand but in order to relish its taste, you first have to value every seed that came and has yet to come including the one you are about to eat and plant and replant. Remember that each of those seeds came from the same seed that was seeded first, that seed is only one. Let us thank and praise the grace we all receive from the primordial formless form. In thanking and praising one, we will thank and praise them all. In praising and blessing all, we will bless, praise, and thank the one.

As long as the seed is intact, the tree, its flowers, and its fruits will do just fine.

All eleven glands (pineal, pituitary, thyroid, parathyroid, thymus, adrenal, pancreas, ovaries, testes, prolactin, hypothalamus mentioned in modern endocrinology), in our body, correspond to our eleven main chakras (forehead, ajna, throat, front heart, back heart, front solar plexus, back solar plexus, front spleen, back spleen, navel, meng mein, sex and basic chakras mentioned in modern Pranic healing) which activate the five brain waves (gamma, beta, alpha, theta, delta discovered by Hans Berger). The five elements (ether, air, fire, water, earth) produce four main chemicals like dopamine, oxytocin, serotonin, and endorphin in our brain which enhances our mood and boosts immunity. As all of them continue to get activated through healing, our vibrational energy increases. We all create and support one another. No one stands alone. We all have the same blueprint and therefore share a common DNA.

The fruit and nuts may be different, with yummy pine-nuts and hazelnuts or sweet dates and figs. Does it really matter where the philosophical tree is and who planted it first. As long as it is always fresh with bright little angels dancing with joy all around it, the tree of truth stands strong. Sometimes its parts are three in number (leaves, trunk, and roots); with all that follows (bud, flower, and fruit), they are six in number. All its branches and parts finally lead to the crown at the top.

The tree of immortality - Forget the apple, go in for the feminine pear. It teaches you to hear and offer a patient listening ear. The apple tree is known as the tree of free-will, love, and knowledge which can be both good and evil, and so eating its fruit was forbidden. Pomegranates are known to grow on the tree of power, blood, and death. The pear tree is a sacred tree of unconditional love, abundance, wealth, and longevity. Its fruits are immortal and no matter how many you eat, they remain evergreen, rewarding, and youthful like the spring season. Mother Nature is a huge life-giving tree upon which all trees grow as well as the three most powerful trees - birth (apple), death (pomegranate), and rebirth (pear) growth.

You are meant to hide under the cozy blanket of the night. Even the sun hides in the night under the pure mystic tree to recharge the darkness and fill it with renewed light for the next day.

The tiny princess with the emerald tiara looks more royal disguised within a tree. Right under the tree, I have kept a present for you tonight. It is an electrifying string of lights, so dress it with care from left to right and right to left, upon the tree. It will keep your tree always illuminated whether it is dark or light, crowned under the red celestial starry light that smiles from within.

Affirm- 'Namostutee, I live by the values of truth, charity, self-discipline, patience, and kindness. I am the protector of the faith. Tathaastu.'

CHAPTER 103

HOW NOT TO COOK

VITALATARIAN - Who is a vitalized person?
A vitalitarian doesn't give up anything. They enjoy and value life and everything in life. Yet they do not live for the mere enjoyment of things.

Instill vigor, better immunity, balance, and self-esteem into your life by prioritizing your health and wellbeing. Refresh yourself with the right food and exercise for the body, soul, and mind. Be open to starting afresh and looking at everything with a bright and positive perspective. To live and to be alive are two different things. The latest diet has the word die in it. Who wants to die? We are here to enliven each other.

We might be just a small piece but we have many great chefs and specialized healers who can help us learn to tap our self-memory to change the fate of mankind.

Food is overrated. We need to eat for basic survival but not overeat and overindulge. We are giving this simple need more importance than it deserves, there is nothing to fear, and we need to move beyond our conditioned behavior for we are at a stage where there will always be enough food for each of us to go around.

These days in the so-called affluent circles, buying expensive food has become a trend. Almas Caviar is sold at USD 25,000 per pound. At a coastal city in Italy, a 20cm pizza for two was sold at USD 12,000. At a resort in Mexico, a taco is sold at a whopping USD 25,000, a dessert in a Sri Lankan spa costs USD 14,500, a bagel in one of the NYC hotels costs USD 1000. The Las Vegas Fleur Burger costs USD 5000, layered with actual gold. A pizza was served in Industry Kitchen of New York at USD 2,700. A 6.5 gallon tin of Berco's popcorn can cost as much as USD 2,500. The

Golden Opulence Sundae is worth USD 1,000. Dhs 28000 for a cupcake in Dubai and the list goes on. Experience is no longer about togetherness but how much one can spend. Thankfully some of them give the proceeds as a charity to feed the poor.

The physical and mental body is largely the result of the food we eat. The only food that is blessed, wholesome and beneficial for the body shall be consumed. Unwholesome or junk food should be completely avoided. Some people have tendencies to get lost in their dream. It is important to learn how to dream well so that you do not lose touch with reality. An overcooked dish loses its nutritive value. Cooking is something we do, we are not the cooker. Before cooking any dish, we must first understand the importance of clean vitalitarian food. Before savoring any dish, we must invoke our savior's blessings and be ever grateful to him for gifting us with so much bounty and love. The food should have a proper balance of all six palates on the plate for holistic wellness. Just like there are six seasons, there are six main palates or tastes. These are sweet, sour, saline, pungent, bitter, and astringent.

Vitalitarians-

Eats fresh food,
Have many riches,
Lasting relationships,
Live in moderation,
Long walks by the beach,
Read in the open air,
Dance under the stars,
Breathe under healthy trees,
Bathe in the waterfalls,
Watch nourishing movies, intellectual plays,
Do whatever they like to do with single-minded dedication,
Have complete self-control,
Listen to the tunes of nature and adjust to its sounds,
Enjoy the healing fragrances it offers.
Are not carried away by false ego and pride.
Feel limitless and liberated,

They are not attached to the actions or fruits of their actions. And so they are not bound by pleasure or pain.

Vital kisses- are all about 'keeping internal system, sweet, energized & spicy'-

- Honey denotes a happy life, so women and children must have one spoon daily to make their life as sweet as Manuka honey. Men and boys must worship the giver of milk, and drink it whatever its flavor.
- Apply sandalwood paste on your forehead each morning and drink enhanced rose water.
- Eat lettuce to avoid dryness. Add a little bay-leaf into any dish or your tea, it not only adds more flavor, taste, and fragrance to it, but it also improves your overall health.
- Bilva leaves or *bel patra* should be consumed for improved stomach immunity and balance. Its leaves are antibacterial and anti-fungal and also great for controlling weight and headaches. Best way to have it is to wrap honey and black pepper or 'Gulkand' or rose petal jam inside it. It also can be eaten frozen. In ancient India, people put bel leaves instead of bandages to heal their wounds and boils.
- Gulkand or rose petal jam is mainly made of a sweet damask rose flower which works to cool down our bodies. It is a great cure for inflammation, insomnia, and acne. It improves eyesight, memory, digestion, and strengthens the gut. It also removes toxins, acidity, stress, and itching. Best way to have it is by adding it to cold milk or mixing it with raw mango jam.
- Cinnamon is a superb antioxidant. It has a powerful impact on health and metabolism. It helps fight infection, removes tissue damage, and inflammation. Cures respiratory infections, IBS or irritable bowel syndrome, and neurodegenerative diseases like Alzheimer's and Parkinson's. It helps in reducing blood pressure, restricting the growth of cancer cells, and also helps lower cholesterol. The best way to consume cinnamon from Sri Lanka is to soak it in hot water and then drink that same water after it cools down.
- To reconnect with heavenly beauty - use pine cone essential oil. Burn pine cone as smudge at home. Eat pine nuts. Drink fresh pine cone tea. Use pine nut oil for hair and nails. You may add it to foods to wipe away all negativity and affliction, refresh yourself, and boosts your immunity. Drink only from silver or gold straw. Eat from gold or silver spoons.

- Tulsi leaves - It is believed that Lord Krishna dwells in the place where there is a *tulsi (holy basil)* plant. Eating one Tulsi leaf a day encourages you to keep away from all sin.

Other powerful cures:-

- Cloves for toothache. Saffron for curing depression. Indian valerian for reducing anxiety. Turmeric for its antiseptic properties.
- Amla berries are great for boosting your immunity and brain health.
- Kombucha is the new bubbly. Kambucha contains antioxidants, it is rich in probiotics, boosts energy, and rids toxins.
- Baobab -A great fruit for digestive health. It helps maintain a healthy weight, balances blood sugar levels, reduces inflammation, and is a great source of vitamin C. It is sometimes called the fruit of the tree of life.
- Flaxseed improves the estrogen levels of the body. It contains 800 more lignans than any other plant food. It is rich in omega 3 fatty acids and fiber.
- Sesame seeds are rich in magnesium and help keep blood pressure in control. Top up your salads and meals with sesame seeds.
- Garlic has great therapeutic properties. It improves cholesterol levels, memory, and makes bones stronger. Start your day with swallowing a little raw garlic clove like a medicinal tablet and see all your fatigue miraculously vanish away.
- Poppy seeds have anti-aging properties. When taken in small amounts, they improve skin health, asthma, constipation, sleep-related issues, boost fertility, and increase calcium. They bring overall peace and luxury into your life.

PRASAD - There is no better *prasad*[94] than to serve the community. A traditional dumpling of rice and chickpea flour wrapped in jaggery, nuts like almonds and pistachios, rose petals (Gulkand), condensed milk, and coconut - fried in pure *desi ghee* and flavored with the purest of saffron, pumpkin, and vanilla. This is called *Modak* in India. Arabs call it Baklava and the Japanese call it bliss buns.

---

[94] *Prasad is another name for blessed and consecrated food. It is a sanctified offering to Gods.*

There is no better seating position than Padmasana or lotus position while consuming the *prasad*. Standing upon my tripartite form, I urge you to remember not to attach yourself to the aftertaste of this sweet gift.

Eating a variety of food is great for health but you do not have to spend half your life deciding what to eat and cook. Researchers have established that the prehistorians ate the most nutritious, vitalized, and gut-friendly meals. Even these cavemen who had to themselves hunt and gather food without the aid of new-age machines spend a maximum of an hour a day preparing the entire day's food including the snacks.

It is the husband's job to bring the rice, the wife just needs to prepare the field where it can grow. There is one such pure field where my Grandma lives. It is a calm field where pure hu-angels fly and rice grows in plenty. Such that one cup of cooked rice from my Grandma's kitchen can remove all past impurities. It detoxifies, nourishes, and cleanses you from deep within. I had a cup full mixed with unadulterated milk and honey and ever since the only words that come out from my mouth are that of true kindness and selflessness. May you all get your share of the cup and distribute it amongst all those around with the same love to form an intense connection with one and all. Remember to mix a dash of sweet honey from the top and see the wondrous change in the behavior of anyone who sips this cup of a pure healthy life.

Affirm- 'Namostutee, I enjoy spending time in the comfort of nature's bounty, pleasantly basking in the sunshine. I relish eating and sharing a variety of foods nature provides. Tathaastu.'

CHAPTER 104

POWER TOWER

Much like the Eiffel Tower, our life, our body is a threefold mystery (refer to the three floors of the Eiffel Tower – first, second, and summit). I am essentially an energetic being who is experiencing the physical form, energetically moving in the sky and various realms of space. I reach a place where I meet Krishna who is the knower of past, present, and future. The entire space is filled with hues red, green, blue.

Colorless stone[95] provides protection. So does the three-lined cross[96]. No one can hold the divine wisdom and love, for the message is for all to

---

[95] *Akin to Dorje means lord (rje) of stones (rdo). It is a sharp magical weapon also known as vajra. The enlightened being uses the dorje that cannot be broken or cut. This weapon is impenetrable, imperishable, immovable, immutable, indivisible, indestructible reality. It awakens the kundalini to destroy all illusions and negativities of ignorance and aggression.*

[96] *The three horizontal lines are in diminishing order in the papal cross. It is carried by high degree spiritual practitioners and represents understanding of the holy trinity through faith, hope and love. The horizontal lines in the three lined Arhatic cross represent the tree of life. The two points in the first line represent 'intuitive wisdom' through the balance of Samajh chakra and Aar chakra. The two points in the middle line represent 'good actions' through the balance solar plexus (karm) and heart chakra (dharm). The two points in the third line represent the 'praise and glory' through balance of spleen (Jaya) and (Junoon) chakra. The vertical line in the middle embodies the five chakras - (sthir) mooladhara, (sthapana) creativity, (tej) or navel, (pattra) grace or throat and (taaj) or crown. The names of these chakras are also mentioned in the chapter 'evol-ve-love'.*

take. Whoever is inclined to learn the subject, whoever is attracted to know the whys and how's, chooses their path and then sets the right intention to reach the goal.

The towering, heightened souls of the world below have been telling us in their thunderous voices: "we are who we are because of the light that comes from above. And yet we can't see the obvious, because we are all blinded by our self-delusion of reality and make-believe." Yet people ask me to get real and get going when they are delusionary.

The bodybuilder rises above all obstacles to lift weights. Mountains are such obstacles and our mind rises above all mountains to kiss the spiritual heavens. If you kiss the heavens only because it is the need of the hour then that is selfish love. The only way to reach the heavens is by moving beyond your pain, rising above all obstacles, and yet standing firm and selflessly committing to your divine calling whether there are obstacles or not. The first step is cleansing, with continuous purification of the etheric psychic, mental, emotional, and physical body. You truly become a towering personality no matter what your physical height maybe! Remember your Guru in times of pleasure more than in times of pain and you will naturally receive better and more than what you expect.

Aum is a combination of A = *Brahma* which is pure spirit or light, U= *Vishnu* which is the soul or unconditional love, M = *Shiva* which is a sharp mind or power.

Like the Eiffel Tower, our body is also a marvel of a love story. It is mysterious conjunction, adaptation, and transmutation from the three layers of animal, mineral, and vegetable through purification of active and subtle forces, in order to help you achieve oneness.

Our soul is like a princess trapped in a tower. Our body is the tower. Our spirit is the prince that releases us out of the tower. This way our soul, body, and spirit team up together to make us meet with our true power. Your strength and divinity lie in being ever grateful to the trinity that lies within you.

The entire human race collectively fits into one whole godly body. Each human has a unique attribute of God within them. We together are divine beings. If we are in unison, we have the potential to work with God from within - collectively and not individually. The shift first happens on the level of consciousness and not on a physical level. You have just come out of a cosmic rebirth and made it out of the womb into the next level of heightened consciousness. Congratulations and welcome to the light.

Affirm- 'Namostutee, I am one with the infinite divine creator. I positively influence and manifest my reality through my thoughts, faith, visions, receptivity, learnings, and higher understanding. Tathaastu.'

CHAPTER 105

LEAPS AND BOUNDS

L ight the flame of passionate fire, do not let the emotions and mind play
you, and take the jump with a leap of faith. Roles keep reversing here
based on seasonal changes. However, the spirit behind remains the same.
909 years have since 11.11 of MCXI passed. I[97] have returned only to warn
but no one seems to be listening. After 101 more years, another energetic
shift is bound to happen. Let us unravel the 101 chapters gallantly, with
renewed vigor and clarity. Time has slowed down so that we can learn
to breathe slowly, relax, and believe. It is time to enjoy the fragrance of
different flowers. With this transpose, a new journey has begun. The dream
has become a reality and reality has become a dream.

There are many solutions to every problem. The issue is that most of
you have so far tried only 100 solutions. Here I offer the 101st solution to
the problem. Each year has now become a day. 101 years are only 101 days
for those who have transposed and transformed. 101 years are just 1001
dark hours for those who are ready and 1001 months for those who aren't.
1001 hours are almost 42 days. The clock ticks faster for those who seem
to be in a hurry. The clock slows down for those who wait and observe
patiently. Out of these, 33 days have passed already. Only 9 days remain.
The remaining 9 days seem like 9 months for some. Whichever way you
perceive life, it is time for you to take charge of your life through proper
discipline. These 9 months seem like 9 years (108 months) to some others.
Whatever your pace or time that clicks for you, all the world's riches belong
to you and yet to no one. If you are just and fair, this fiery air will pass

---

[97] *Means cosmic light*

by smoothly and seamlessly. You will then be able to truly breathe freely, rhythmically, and blissfully.

A dream is a nightmare for some. A dream is just a dream for some. For those who believe dreams are real, takes only split seconds to shift to the right. Those who think of it to be a nightmare will stay to the left.

Those who remain silent and let the darkness of fear fade will come out more powerful because they are the ones who know that there is always something bigger than us that moves and directs the wheel of time. This soulful faith keeps them going.

The only way to lift the hill of hell is to inspire confidence and induce morality amongst all. This way we all can collectively lift the weight lying upon each other's shoulders and be eternally free. I might be the smallest atom in the many universes but by having the humble awareness of my smallness, I know the vastness of this universe and the strength of the root upon which we stand.

Affirm- 'Namostutee, I am creative, cooperative, expressive, progressive, and active. Tathaastu.'

CHAPTER 106

IDEAL SOMA CALENDAR

The spirit meets its purpose through the soul. Our higher soul works through us (it's home) to realize the purpose, plan, promise into action. Trust and belief are required to let these higher energies work through you. Solar energy embodies the spirit and lunar soul. Just as the soul is within the spirit, the month is within the year. Just the way some of us keep shifting our homes, our higher soul too keeps shifting from its home. Today it is me and tomorrow it will be you and this cycle is unending just like the day, month and year never will end. In dwelling in you, they will greet new guests and unlock the locks. The higher energies hold the master key to your spiritual wealth. Remember to be a good host and make them feel comfortable and welcome. A lot of things about the current calendar confuse me, for example, the month of September comes from the Latin word seven but it is not the seventh but the ninth month. The idea behind creating a new calendar is to include the Sum or the wealth of the meaning of Su[98] and Om[99]. We (hum) have the essence of soul, space, mind, spirit, and body within us. We are a combination of the five elements - fire (light), ether (sound), air (mind), water (emotions), and earth (matter) respectively. Each era, year, and month has its unique significance and energy. The important events in your life carry those same energies.

An ideal calendar is such:

---

[98] *Su or sah in Sanskrit means perfect soul within the beautiful space.*

[99] *Om or ohm interestingly is reverse of mo which means illusion or moon. om/ma/ mo/ohm/maha in Sanskrit means trinity of mind, body, spirit.*

First 6 Months of 168 days (28 days each month)	One month in the middle (30 days for this month)	Last 6 Months of 168 days (28 days each month)
Total of 366 days consisting of 13 months in the year (13 steps take you to understand the deeper meaning behind the heavenly bliss of the last supper)		

When we are in the leap year, we live one extra day-it comes in leaps and bounds. Time and day is an entity. Earth is an entity. All planets, and all chemicals, are an entity and all are interconnected, working together to create balance and harmony within us and outside of us through their respective ruling energy centers. For example:

Day of the week	Archangel	Chakra	Gland	Essence	Color	Direction	Planet	Element/ stone	Earth Chakra
Sunday or Ravivara	Michael	Karm or Solar plexus	Pancreas	Power, beauty, truth	Yellow	West	Sun	Gold / Sardonyx	Australia
Monday or Soma vasara[98]	Gabriel	Taaj or Crown	Pineal	Bliss & fulfillment	Violet	North-west	Moon	Silver/ Jasper	Tibet
Tuesday or Mangalvara	Raphael	Sthir or Mooladhara	Adrenal	Trust, material strength & ambition	Red	South	Mars	Iron/ topaz	America
Wednesday or Budhvara	Uriel	Dharm or Heart	Thymus	Love, optimism & wisdom	Green	North	Mercury or Budh	Mercury/ Emerald stone	Hawaii
Thursday or Guruvara	Selaphiel	Pattra or Throat	Thyroid & parathyroid	Abundance & communication	Blue	Northeast	Jupiter	Tin/Blue sapphire	Egypt
Friday or Shukarvara	Raguel	Sthapanaor Swadhistana	Testes & ovaries	Creativity & prosperity	Orange	Southeast	Venus	Copper/ Orange Jacinth	Peru
Saturday or Shanivara	Berachil	Aar or Ajna	Pituitary	Intuition, discipline & Responsibility	Indigo	East	Saturn	Lead/ zinc/ Amethyst	England

The earth chakras/ countries in the above chart represents energy of above chakras being most powerful in these places on earth. Suppose someone has a weak *sthir* or *mooladhara* chakra, living in America will teach them certain lessons that will strengthen their root chakra. This is because of the energy that the place resonates.

As you can see in the chart above- each angel has a day allotted to it. Sunday is for Michael to invoke the spirit. Monday is for Gabriel to invoke the truth. Tuesday is for Raphael to invoke healing clarity. Wednesday is for Uriel to invoke light. Thursday is for Selaphiel to invoke hope. Friday

---

[100] *Soma is a Sanskrit word for moon. Monday is known as 'Soma-Vāsara'*

451

is for Raguel or Jegudiel to invoke devotion, glory, and health. Saturday is for Barachiel to invoke the blessings of the immortal white.

Sunday or Solar day is a good day to focus on the healing of solar plexus chakra, etheric body, and soul enrichment. The color of the sunflower is an ideal color to wear on this day.

Monday is an ideal day to heal the taaj/ shashrachaksha/ 1000 eyes = 1000 eyes means 10^3 = pineal gland and spiritual body. Its color is silverish violet.

Tuesday has earth energies. It is a good day to work on physical strength, material body, heal gallbladder related issues, and balance salt content.

Wednesday represents the emotional body. It is a good day to heal the lungs and do breathing exercises. It invokes spirit/ cosmic womb.

Thursday has fire energy. It is a great day to heal the throat, soul, and mental body and balance the Sulphur content. This day is ruled by Jupiter or Jove planet.

Friday is the day of ether and air. It is good to heal blood-related issues. It enhances the financial body and oxygen content.

Saturday has water energy. It enhances intuitive awareness, responsibility, and a devotional body. It is the purification center.

The energies of these seven days, seven chakras, seven angels, and seven planets keep expanding and contracting to create many more vibrational energy and as they rise-evolution takes place and we get endowed with qualities of many more energy centers, elements, Gods, planets, rays within and outside of us.

And in much the same way, each balanced chakra emanates the quality of each element having innate potential in it to rise or fall eventually to heighten and improve its energies and of those around.

As MMXX (2020) ends, A new era begins.

> Sun enters each of the 13 months and activates
> Upper chakras for six months = 28 days each month
> Lower chakras for six months = 28 days each month
> Creation chakra for one month = 30 days or the middle month

Month	Zodiac	Chakra	Degree	Days	Stone	Planets	Quality	Flower
April	Aries/ Ram	*Dharm or heart*	0	28	Chalcedony Quartz in Agate	Mars	Spiritual connection, relationships we will through thoughts, activates pituitary gland	Violet Iris, Tulip
May	Taurus/ Bull	*Mo or back neck and Patra / or throat*	30	30	Orange Jacinith	Venus	Inspirational, causal, the water of truth, the seat of the soul, power of rebirth, deep awareness, love, beauty, creative	Lily of Valley, daisy, Marigold
June	Gemini/ Divine lovers	*Kanth or secondary throat and hrdya*	60	28	Green Emerald	Mercury	Light of hidden and higher knowledge, communicating magic words, transformation	Green rose and Camelia/ middle mist red
July	Cancer/ Crab	*Agya or Aar*	90	28	Pearl set in gold	Moon	Peaceful, considerate, networks, renews, protects, supports, prosperity, transmutes	Indigo guardian lavender, brompton stock Purple Columbine
August	Leo/ Lion	*Karm or Solar plex*	120	28	Sardonyx	Sun	Expressive Vitality, identity, wealth, strength, righteousness, goodwill	Bright yellow dandelion & Camomile
September	Virgo/ pure virgin	*Junoon or back of navel*	150	28	Beryl	Spica	Life enhancer, balancer, self-reliant, receiver, glory	Fulva iris, Aster
October	Libra/ Scales	*Jaya or Spleen*	180	28	Chrysolite or peridot	Sirius	Life giver, balances energy, harmony, Symmetry, equilibrium, bright	Angelica, pink gladioli
November	Scorpio/ Scorpion	*Sthapana or sacral*	210	28	Brownish yellow Topaz	Pluto	Nurturing connection, subconscious, charismatic, depth, power	Orange *hrdya* calendula and squash, 'Blaue blume' blue flower
Discerner	Sagittarius/ Archer	*Tej or navel*	240	28	Sardius	Jupiter	Abundance, kindness, luck, praiseworthy actions, expansion, optimism, security	Anthurium, and Hydrangea
December	Ophiuchus/ Serpent	Utpada or Left and right foot	270	28	Apple green Chrysoprasus	Earth	Regenerating, sovereignty, magnetic, longevity, humorous, seeker	Jasmine, Narcissus
January	Capricorn/ Sea goat	Mooladhara or *Sthir*	300	28	Jasper	Saturn	Responsibility, survival, discipline, ambition	Red poppy, cinnamon red incarnation
February	Aquarian/ Water-bearer	Crown, coronal or *Taaj*	330	28	Purple Amethyst	Uranus	Universal heart, unity, freedom, originality, humanitarian	Lotus and daffodils
March	Pisces/ Fish	Forehead center or samajh	360	28	Dark Blue Sapphire	Neptune	Assertive, strong thoughts, self-judge, Intellect, wisdom, creative, mind over matter, activates the pineal gland	Orchid, Magnolia, Blue-violet bellflower

The 28th cycle of each month is synced with the moon except for May/June which is synced with the sun.

The above chart can be beneficial if you follow it. Someone suffering from heart disease should wear an Emerald stone in June for 28 days along with healing. This will balance the heart chakra. Additionally keeping the flowers corresponding to the month will also be very beneficial. The other way to use the chart is to map the month you were born to the quality that is supremely reflected in you. You can then use this quality to enhance your relationships, career, and anything else. The sun enters every zodiac in 30 degrees.

It takes five minutes for the spirit (light) to descend into matter (love) and get downloaded into human form. The supreme soul descends into the human form to initiate the renewed cycle. As we reach the 14th month another ascended cycle of nine celestial ruling bodies, with renewed calendar will magically initiate in 2026. This way knowledge is revived through the reincarnation of the perfected soul, in whom the Supreme power (consciousness) resides.

Combination of yin and yang of moon and sun. After every one or two cycles of the moon, a solar year is born. This change gives us one extra year. One extra year equals only one extra day in the higher realms. This year or day is meant for creating 'Niyama' or new order into your lives. This way you will be able to manifest the discipline you set forth for yourself in the next coming year with greater efficiency and actualize it with greater enthusiasm. It is important to remember that the universal mind is only a reflection of the spiritual heart. Truth is in the silence of the heart. This calendar is based on the reflection of the current world scenario. It is for those adventurous, daring minds seeking to know more. The supreme essence of truth is elsewhere but that is another story. An ideal is just an idea of perfection, it is not perfection which is graced and known only to a few. We can never understand God's plans in totality. Time, circumstances, and connections are ever-changing.

Affirm- 'Namostutee, The subtle nectar of 'soma' spreads to my entire being. In this way, I recognize my inner divine nature. Tathaastu.'

CHAPTER 107

HOPE DIAMOND

The confused diamond asked, "What am I doing in this dark coal mine? Do I belong here?"

God answered, "Only a diamond can scratch and wear out another diamond that is why you are sent here, far away from the likes of you. You are safer with those who are unlike you. They are slightly impure than you and so they can never shatter, scratch, blow or throw you away. They will value you more because for them you are a rare gem. Remember, you are where you are because to be here amongst those who value you is best for you. You are tougher and more durable when you are around them. You are your very best with the unlike and not when you are with the likes of you. Here, you fill these people's hearts with hope and love like no other."

It is interesting how the French have a way of romancing with language. When they want to say, "I miss you," they say *"Tu me manques,"* which means, "You are missing from me." I have a similar way of romancing with life, slightly more twisted though. It teaches you that it's not me but you who is missing from yourself.

When you meet yourself, you will meet me, for you and I are but one. You are not just a part of me, but you are me.

The only thing stopping you from attaining that gold bar, or the Hope diamond, or the wealth you want is you. Raise your vibrations to increase the weight of that gold bar you are holding. If you invest well, you will get good returns. What you give out is the exact measure of what you get back-nothing more, nothing less. If you want a happier life, then give out happiness freely. If you want to be forgiven, then forgive easily. If you want your children to become wiser, then share your wisdom with your neighbors' children. If you want more monetary wealth, then give to those who are more in need than you. Pay off all your debts before you incur more debts. Freedom is the opposite of scarcity.

Here we learn to be free. We learn to fly beyond our conditioning mind, which tells us that we can fly only in an airplane. We have wings too; they are simply invisible for now, but that will not be for long. Beyond your perceptions, conditioned and limiting beliefs, there is a subtle life that is constantly alive, which has a far greater effect than it seems upon the very being you are becoming. You act in the good way that you do because of the subtle vibrations of the dream within you. Even by reading this book, you are receiving a higher frequency of vibrations. Generously sharing this dream with another will help raise the vibrations, piece by piece, of the entire cosmos. This is the power you have. Go out and explore it for yourself. Thank you. Thank you. Thank you.

The brick of gold you have been holding in your hand is in your possession, only because of the invisible hands above that gave it to you. It all belongs to those invisible hands. You are not who you think you are. You possess whatever you think you possess only because of the blessings and generosity of the higher energies. You think you are the giver, but the ultimate giver is the invisible power that is invisible to you only because you choose not to see it. Be in gratitude, and worship the invisible higher energies. There is no better way to worship the higher power than to care and share what you have with those who are still visible to you.

The perfect rare diamond that you have been seeking is not outside of you but within you. The 'mani' the snake is searching for is right under its abode. When it sheds its skin and gives up venom and there are no more toxins left in its mortal physical heart. The act of shedding all its serpentine qualities leads to its metamorphosis into an immortal spiritual heart. One such snake is tied to your belly reminding you to shed all your lower ungodly qualities, which leads to your transmutation into a Godly being. This transmutation makes you realize that the rare diamond that you have been searching for is within you.

All the *karm* that you have incurred in the last ten decades is stored inside that diamond. The perfect diamond, which has retained its qualities, has the potential to magically fulfill all your wishes and clear your dues. The jeweler knows the worth of the diamond and so he will pay all your dues. He clears all your dues as you are meant to get over and out of your self-inflicted misery. Have no doubt about the existence of such a jeweler.

Don't challenge the price and his decision. Give him the diamond that he paid for without any resistance and bargains. This is your true test. The reaction is the regression of action. Why regress from your action?

The diamond will be dancing happily only when it is out in the open rather than being locked inside the dark coal mines. You will know when it is time to bring it out from the locker. You will hear this announcement on the radio. The radio is on a subtle volume so that you can hear its call through your inner ear. Listening through your inner ear takes a lot of discipline and clarity. It may seem that the radio is on high volume, adjust to its tunes for it won't adjust to you. Learn to dance to the sound of the music.

You cannot force the jeweler to come to you. He will come when the time is right. He might sell the diamond that he bought at a higher price. This is the multiplying effect of the diamond. Sometimes items of no worth can be turned into something meaningful. What you think is a shadow may be an invisible form of light that you cannot see with your naked eye.

The ever-lasting one graces those energies which are clean, purified, and higher in vibration. The one creates a special eternal task force to soothe and help the universe evolve. Every being is endowed with love, light, and power- the difference is in the degree. The frequency in each being varies. The supreme grace is not limited by time, form, space, realm, position, or hierarchy. There is a spark of the divine within all - without exception. Everyone is blessed with a special gift, waiting to be realized.

Those beings that are graced to become team members of the 'special eternal task force' are like minuscule images of the infinite Lord. The ever-lasting energy of the Supreme Lord is so positive and perfect that they remain unchangeable, unperturbed, even-minded, unaltered, unattached, all-forgiving, all-loving, and all accepting at all times.

Irrespective of what age or stage in life you may be, divine beings and pure angels are always there to help raise your vibrations and fill you with love and joy as long as you have the will to purify, learn and evolve. These divine beings could either be in spirit or physical form. Do not let others put your energy down or walk over you. Settle back within yourself. All the clarity and order you are looking for is already within you. Stop hiding in dark corners, the radiant *Mani* is within you just the way the musk of the deer is within its pouch. No one can take the hope diamond away from you until you allow them. You all are meant to shine irrespective of how big or small you may be.

The ever-lasting one placed its most special crystal which is beautiful inside and out, here on earth. This crystal can walk and talk in this realm and is forever under the care of the divine. This powerful and sacred crystal is very clear, plain, and simple. Just like any beautiful diamond, it may be small but this graced crystal is responsible for rejuvenating and revitalizing the entire earth. This being is the knower of past, present, and future and travels to all realms without being bound by time and space. This being perennially brightens, awakens, and heightens our vibrations. We all too can join its team by bringing in more awareness and the importance of being pure, forgiving, accepting, loving, and kind to one another.

The higher subtle energies are very sensitive and respond only to extremely positive energy. No one from the lower realm can exploit the energies of the causal realm because they cannot reach the heightened levels until they are completely pure. However, intoxicated in soma[101], some beings can try to harm the sensitive beings working for the divine on earth but their innate restorative and preserving nature is their greatest shield. And so their beauty remains unharmed and untainted by outside forces.

The Hope diamond comes to you and says that "You might want to have control over everything but my dreams are only mine and as long as I can dream, there will always be an inner deeper part of me that you cannot control". Secrets have a certain power and mystery about them. Do not share all your dreams with everyone. Only then can you turn them into reality. Hope diamond originally didn't have seven solitaires studded on each side with two in the middle, totaling sixteen diamonds that you see hung today exquisitely on a string of diamonds.

It originally represents the third eye of *Sita* and was gifted to her as a *Maang tika*[102] by her royal consort *Rama*. It has the energies of the immortal *Sita* in it and represents *Rama*'s love for her. It was meant only for her and so whoever other than her possesses it is doomed to perish because no one can handle the clarity of thought that comes with the true

---

[101] *Soma: refer chapter 'ideal soma calendar' to know of moon energy.*

[102] *Maang tika is a traditional Indian forehead jewelry that is worn on the Agya or Aar chakra, usually by brides. Beautiful stones are attached to it with one or more chains pinned into the hair. Wearing the maang tikka, also known as borla capacitates control of feelings, perceptions, thoughts, actions and activates the spiritual eye. It signifies the holy garden of Shiva and Shakti, man and woman on spiritual, physical and emotional level.*

blue. Just as the yin-yang energies of the sun-moon, stars combined with the power of light stay away from earth so that it doesn't perish with the immense energies.

What doesn't belong to you, you must not take. Stealing will cause you untold misery and suffering. The energies he can handle, you never can. If you tamper with the truth, the punishment is un-health. A wish can become a hope in hell if you try reducing its powers in the name of insanity and love and so it is better to simply let be, keep giving, and keep believing. It is not the Hope Diamond that brought death to its wearer but wounding it time and again after separating it from not only its lover but also its wearer that caused doom. Crystals have life and consciousness. Those who knew the worth of the Hope diamond further wounded it and kept cutting it up in order to keep it only for themselves but in pieces to hide its broken identity. Few showed it off and few who cut it up. The greatest diamond ever became the greatest curse not because of who it is but because of the way you mishandled it by torturing, breaking, resetting processing, and trampling it. Now it stands lifeless & powerless waiting for the eye that values its true worth, worships it, and lets the Goddess freely wear it again. Someone out there please help find its missing pieces before returning it to the original *Sita*.

We have a five-pointed star or diamond within our brain. The 5 C's of this diamond are constitution; communication; clarity; caliber; and courtesy. These five C's imply our body, speech, mind, qualities, and actions. The more we perfect ourselves, the more the diamond within our brain shines. Through the power of praise and prayer, we can invoke the divine power to sharpen the five C's of our inner diamond.

The stars shine like diamonds and fill us with wonder and hope. The stars twinkle in the sky because light passes through different layers of turbulent atmosphere before revealing their scintillating charm. Let not the outer turbulence stop you from shining your inner light.

The diamond doesn't stop shining only because there is no one to notice its beauty. You close your eyes doesn't mean that the hope diamond has lost its sparkle.

Affirm- 'Namostutee, I twinkle my inner light for you like a little wishing star upon the sky. Tathaastu.'

CHAPTER 108

INTERCONNECTEDNESS OF 108

The number 108 is the joy giver. 'Harshad' in Sanskrit means 'joy-giver.' 'Harshad' number is an integer divisible by the sum of its digits. 108 is a 'Harshad' number. 108 connects science with the human mind, body, and spirit. 108 connects the Sun, Moon, and Earth. 108 Earths fit across the Sun, 108 Suns fit in between Earth and Sun, 108 Moons fit between Earth and Moon-

> The distance between the Earth and the Sun is 108 times the diameter of the Sun.
> The distance between the Earth and Moon is 108 times the diameter of the Moon.
> The diameter of the Sun is 108 times the diameter of the Earth.

The mysterious number 108 has accompanied humanity from the beginning and it probably will always be with us. Astronomically, there are 27 constellations in our galaxy and each has 4 directions. 27 x 4 = 108. In this way, the number 108 covers the whole galaxy. 108 brings new beginnings, clears obstacles, increases intuitive insight, personal power, tranquility, progress, prosperity, abundance, and humaneness.

It is believed that there are 108 virtues and the soul goes through 108 stages of spiritual development.

There are 108 pressure points in the human body, 108 lucky paths to

God, a garland of prayer beads repeat chants 108 times using the string beads, 108 holy chakras inside our body. There are 108 energy lines (nadis) that circulate, connect, and balance the heart chakra to other chakras in the body. There are 108 main Upanishads, 108 sacred sites in India. The measure of the interior angle of a regular pentagon is 108 degrees, 108 breaths in one day through practice is all you need to reach enlightenment. There are 108 chances or lifetimes to rid the ego and transcend the materialistic world. 108 points define the human body and the Sri Yantra, which is the Yantra of Creation (nine interlocking triangles that surround the central point representing the cosmos and the human body). There are 108 sins or 108 delusions of the mind in Tibetan Buddhism. 108 degrees Fahrenheit is the internal temperature, which causes a human body's vital organs to start failing.

108 is an abundant number because the sum of its proper divisors (1, 2, 3, 6, 9, 12, 18, etc.), excluding 108, is 172, which is greater than itself. The remainder, or the abundance, therefore, is 64. It is a Harshad number as well. When reversed, 108 becomes 801. In a leap year, when we multiply the three numbers for the number of days – 366 days – we get 3*6*6 which is also 108.

When the nine planets revolve around the 12 zodiac constellations, it brings 108 different types of effects in our lives. Praying and chanting Gayatri Mantra (a highly revered mantra from Rig Veda) helps us stay protected and lift our consciousness upwards during these changes.

"Om bhur bhuva svah tat savitur varenyam bhargo devasya dhimahi dhiyo yo na pracodayat"

Affirm- 'Namostutee, I will chant the above Gayatri mantra hundred and eight times to purify my subtle, gross, and causal body with divine light. Tathaastu.'

CHAPTER 109

SANCTIFY YOUR SPACE

To live a hearty life, your ethics must match your aesthetic sense. Clapping hands is a great way to drive out negative energies, so go on clapping and applauding.

From above, our crown appears crimson and magenta like garnets and rubies. Just below that, our aura shines with hues of emerald green and blue sapphire. It is like a beautiful rainbow of seven bodies, coiled like seven divine snakes. When we shed our negative, unwholesome poison, we are like those divine snakes who shed their skin, and so our aura shines. The snakes shed their venom through the pores of their skin, much like we shed it through the cleansing of our chakras. As we cleanse ourselves, the colors of our bodies convert from rose gold to yellow gold. As you meet with the true shining bliss of your golden body, its perennial divinity converts you into a new being in the same body. You feel you have become one with the *Kamadhenu*[103], the celestial cow with wings. A speck of all the Gods is within you and they channel a hint of their energies through you.

Use *'myrrh'* incense oil or perfume in your bedroom sparingly for sensuality, lovemaking, internal strength especially for your skin, blood, and kidney. It drives away all evil and improves the flow of chi energy, opens up meridians, and has anti-inflammatory properties. Its earthly scent grounds you. Today it is used in Oman, Yemen, and Somalia.

Aura is the energy we radiate. Etheric air has both negative and positive ions. If our auric energy is calm, receptive, and conductive then we will

---

[103] *Refer to the chapter – 'God is eminent' to know more about the cow of plenty, also known as kamdhenu.*

have a proper balance between the two ions. Balanced energy will send out balanced energy and electrify the surroundings calmly, provided others are receptive and openly willing to receive your energy.

Sometimes the etheric air around the place or beings are not open to receive the balanced energies, this causes imbalance and distress.

Even when you leave a hotel room, unless it is cleansed and redone for the next guest, it will leave some of your imprint like a fallen hair strand, a clip, threads of your dress, garbage in the bin, so on and so forth. However, your thoughts and emotions have life energy too and those being limitless and invisible to the naked eye will be left behind unless cleared away by applying highly acquired yogic skills of cleaning the room etherically. Whenever I apply this skill of etheric purification to sanctify the space, offices, or homes, it greatly benefits families and the community as a whole.

Etheric cleansing of the room or space can be done before or after you have left the room. When you leave the office or hotel room for example, more often than not you carefully carry all your material belongings, but leave behind a little mix of love or hate. At your end, you can simply forgive and ask for forgiveness and release all pent-up energy allowing it to flow out joyfully in the open.

Take a good look at yourself and if this is not how you want to look then maybe it is time to refurbish yourself and not just the apartment you live in.

Smudge some sage or apply some Hematite powder. Meditate and feel how your sacred space is filled with divine beauty, abundance, clarity, protection, generosity, peace, and passion towards your mission. Let the feeling become part of you with immense faith and martial determination. Make this affirmation: "I am and the Lord God is one."

Both life and death are equally important. For a house to be built on a strong foundation, the basement is as important as is the attic. We carelessly store our useless items in the basements and attics, we do not realize that without them, our home will topple down like bricks of Jenga.

Everything has a life and capable of a new beginning, let us call that living in the now. To die a death of fear is the same as living a life in fear. Outside of fear and beyond attachments, life and death become one. It is then that you are truly born, reborn, or die- based on what and where you choose to go through free will and choice.

Why does being alone scare you? I have the best time of my life when I am with myself. It is a beautiful place to be with yourself. Here, you do not need to lean on or depend on anyone. You become conscious of the truth - you are born secure, inoculated, and complete. You don't need another person to tie the seat belt of your car. You are capable of doing that all by yourself. To understand this is liberty. You involve others only out of love so we all can feel good, important, and special by being of help to one and another.

We put room dividing screens to shield, protect, and keep portions of our room private. Ideal blinds do not block all of the sound and light. If the window blinds are light in color then the rays that pour through the screen are soft and muted, bright enough to illuminate the room yet dim enough to keep us from being blinded. Based on the outside temperature, seasons, and noises, we sometimes put warm or bright blinds to ensure proper air and *chi* circulation. Sometimes we use screens that are so seamless and transparent that enough light comes in and illuminates the room.

These days we can drop the screens with a press of a small finger on the remote. Some screens can also show us beautiful views of landscapes, expansive deserts, flowery gardens, cheerful beaches, and icy mountains. These transport us to a different land or era within minutes. Such is the power of a painting on a canvas or screen. The artist who makes such intricate and gorgeous work of art most definitely has taken inspiration from something that is far more perfect and even better at shielding and protecting us.

When I walk in the nature trails, I often get a similar feeling. I wonder that these stunning views of the waterfalls and tall oak trees, filled with immense beauty are God's perfect shielded screen. It is bright enough to illuminate the earth yet protective enough to keep us from being blinded.

Depending upon our taste, the depiction on some screens transport us to the hot deserts and are made with lighter fabrics and some screens take us to the land of modern progressive high rise buildings. Universe expresses, responds, and brings to us the exact view of screens that we prefer to look at. Some of us like to see dancing children, some like bloodshed, plague, and war. The choicest of curtains are available in the artists market. What we buy or drape - silk, linen, or polyester is based upon our fancy.

Neighbors make a society. People in our neighborhood offer to clean each other's yards, mow their lawns for free and gift dustbins to one another. They do not do this to belittle or criticize the other but to politely and humbly teach values of cleanliness to those who falter out of sheer ignorance. This way slowly everyone begins to understand that in keeping their surrounding neighborhood clean, their environment too will stay pure and cleansed. Since we all live in the same society, a clean space is not restricted to your home alone but it requires everyone to be on the same page. Similarly, you might keep your body, emotions, and thoughts absolutely clean and well-nourished but if there are people outside living in an unhygienic environment and are consumed with thoughts of violence, jarring impurity then their sickness will affect your immunity as well. The reason behind this is that we all breathe the same air and air carries the germs of thoughts imbued with stagnant emotional baggage. Maintaining overall hygiene across all levels is mandatory. It starts with your body, family, home, society, and nation. Your pure balanced intentions spread throughout the world and universe. It takes just one divine being to remove the resistance of all other beings by first breaking its silent fast.

The kingdom of heaven is within you like the attic and basement are both parts of your home. 'Attic' is a superconscious way to reach heaven and 'basement' is the subconscious way to reach earth. The basement is based on the foundation and principle of truth that grounds you. The attic is the spirit that finds its purpose in the matter that is right in the middle. When both mingle through you and your presence is when your home is truly made livable. Until then its energies are like a building either floating upwards in the clouds or excessively indulging in materialism. Your destiny is to connect with the significance you hold with yourself and the energies around you. Go out there and empower others to heal and find out their true meaning.

Your home is a place that protects you from the changing weather and keeps you safe from outside influences. It is your safe haven. Bless your home and each of its members (including objects) to be filled with compassion, everlasting bliss, and strength. Take care and control of your home, just like your body.

The full form of NOW is 'new opportunities welcomed'. Sanctify your space to allow NOW NOW NOW to unfold a positive dimension of your character as you transit into a renewed and important phase of your life.

Affirm- 'Namostutee, as I get more organized, structured, and disciplined, I re-examine my path to do what is important to me and selflessly serve others. This gives me deep inner joy. Tathaastu.'

CHAPTER 110

THE QUEST OF THE HIDDEN TREASURE

Sometimes the stairs at the back of your ancestral home lead you to treasures unknown. A single breath brings back life into death.

Despite having all earthly riches, it was the search to find the answer to the cause of human suffering that led Buddha to sit under the Bodhi tree. It was in finding the answer that Buddha achieved ultimate nirvana. As per Buddha, suffering means rebirth. The cause of all suffering is desire. We overcome desire only when the cause of desire is overcome. We are the cause of desire. As long as we have the desire, we are born again and again. When desire ends, the mental chatter we call life miseries ends.

The way I understand it is that desire is all about taking and so it leads us to un-fulfillment. Love on the other hand has a bigger purpose, it gives rather than takes. It is in giving that we are led to true fulfillment. When life ends, the 'afterlife' begins. The afterlife has no end and no death. Here you serve, and your service seamlessly rewards you with a fun-filled and purposeful life. As long as you have a higher purpose, your heart and soul remains alive. Without a sense of purpose, there is no life.

Align your physical purpose with that of the all-accepting mother earth. Align your emotional purpose and give yourself meaning like the ever-flowing water. Align your moral purpose with the light of ever glowing fire. Align your intellectual purpose and understanding with the pure thoughts in the air. Align your spiritual purpose with the enlightening ether.

People suffer because they think they are something and someone other than who they are. They spend their entire life trying to have or become something they are not. Be who you are and harness your talents by aligning yourself to your disposition. You already have, within you, everything that gives you true meaning.

It is the search to find the answer to wealth that led Christopher Columbus, at the age of 41, to find America with sheer will. There are no accidents; a true seeker is bound to reach the right destination. Columbus might not have reached Asia, but by treading on the dangerous waters, he reached the root cause behind every search, which is that it is possible to sail around the earth to find your answers. In the middle of the voyage, if Christopher Columbus had given up then the greatest nation of all would have remained unknown. He found his answers in the native land of America, where some of the Native Americans, reside even now because it is from here that it all arose. His search transformed the world forever, because from then on the Europeans were freely able to reach nearly all parts of the earth. There is a lot that lays ahead, waiting to be unraveled by yet another person like Christopher Columbus who didn't give up on his search, but who knows if another will ever be born because we have been so busy laughing and mocking at the greatest of all discoveries, maligning all his hard work by calling it but an accident.

When he set his foot on the dangerous waters, his voyage mistakingly and involuntarily led him to find the root of all good and evil, which is the cause of all the causes. You may consider it to be a mistake, but there are no mistakes. There are always inner invisible forces that lead us to find places that we didn't intend to find. He made America known. It is like the apple story - he only showed us the apple, but the choice to bite it or not was of the people. The result of the European arrival and settlement into America has indeed been a disaster for the Indians, the Native Americans. However, the choice to create all that disaster and disease for gaining wealth and control was made by the people. True ignorance is ultimate knowledge, and when Columbus attained it, he too was at peace and liberated. After the chaos comes order. He opened the route, the passage that made the unknown known and the invisible visible. He brought light to the dark. He brought a certain clarity to the uncertainty.

You too are on a never-ending voyage. In searching for the root cause of your poverty, you too will find your liberty. You will find all the riches that spice you up, (much like the famous spice route) if not here then in another realm, but the search will go on forever. You might be mortal, but the search is immortal. You might not have started the fire, but you need to find where it came from. It has always been right there, but you have been foolishly trying to find it elsewhere. You are hungry because you feel you have eaten nothing, even though your stomach is full.

The trading of that spice is never-ending. The silk route, the *Mani* that lies in the serpent's head, the technique to attain it - these are as untiring as you. In what direction the wind blows is also no accident. You are in me and I am in you. Wake up and stop sleepwalking. Your search has just started, for the journey truly begins when you are most tired. It is in the art of navigating that you realize your dreams. The unsuccessful is the most successful. The weakest is the strongest. The servant is the king. The one who seems to be against you is actually the only one for you.

Misunderstanding intentions, misinterpreting history and divine books, and seeing only their negative aspect is one of the worst ills, as it can block the minds of future generations from evolving. We are all simply playing our part in the universal drama. Each of us is performing our role. Some lose their direction, only to restart all over again and begin a new journey. Once we do, we begin to act in the direction of the higher universal force which is our spirit. With time, our actions, good and bad are filled with deep conviction and self-control. Our higher soul, having united with omnipresent spirit, leads us towards the direction we are meant to go. Such a being, remains untouched, un-entangled, unattached, and free from the results of its actions, as it works by the command of the invisible cosmic forces. Good and bad, evil and virtue, dark and light, divine and the devil are part of the cosmic creation. Each sentient being is endowed with the power to achieve their true potential, based on the role they have been given to play by the invisible forces in the universal drama. No one has been spared because ironically being whipped excites and awakens some of us. All have been burnt in the same inextinguishable pyre, whether it is Albert Einstein, Mahatma Gandhi, Mother Teresa, or the great discoverer of the greatest of all the discoveries. They have all nearly drowned and ultimately learned to swim in the same ambitious waters beneath the pier, before merging with the infinite oceanic sky.

North is below and south is above because it is you who has been walking topsy-turvy. You might die, but your song will always live, and so you will never really die. You are immortal, and this is your naked truth. The 'I am' is a blessed virgin because its waters are pure, holy, and clean, despite the muck we unforgivingly threw into its river. Your child rebels because you have mismanaged the show. The people throw stones because the ruler has gone awry. The maddest is the sanest of all. Your entry is your exit. Your greatest ability lies in your inability. Peace stems from violence. It is after the storm that there is calm. The cure lies within the root of the disease and its origin. Your voyage has just begun. Stay tuned, stay connected, and read on.

Kashmir is known as the Switzerland of India. The paternal side of my family hails from that region. During my childhood, I spent most of my holiday ice skating and playing with snowballs between the slopes of this mystical land. In honor of Kashmir's pristine heavenly beauty and beautiful snow-capped mountains, let us -

Affirm- 'Namostutee, May our minds be as peaceful and clear as the fresh azure water of the Kashmir valleys. Tathaastu.'

CHAPTER 111

WEANING PROCESS

When the baby cries, the mother gives it her loving milk, but at some point, the mother needs to stop giving the milk whether or not the baby is crying. As the baby grows, the baby needs to be weaned off. In unlearning, it learns to go onto solids because the diet the child is used to is no longer appropriate. In the same way, as the child grows, it needs to be left on the floor to crawl so that it can fall down, stand up, and eventually learn to walk. Sometimes we get so busy over-pampering and over-tending one child that we forget to hear the cries of hunger and attention from our other child. So the hungry child is left to starve. When we give more attention to one area of our life, forgetting all others, we are behaving like that mother. The second child often turns out to be lucky because it learns to survive despite the mother not giving even a drop of milk to it. The second child is graced as it becomes one with the life-giving milk given from another source instead.

Such a child is adorned with real jewelry because other fake jewels that the material world gave it didn't suit the vibrations of its subtle, delicate skin. Since the giver is someone else, then how can you expect to receive anything from that child? You gave neither birth nor milk to the infant. The universal mother is the giver, and with what the child received, it learned to produce milk by itself. The child's forgiving nature led it to forgive the unforgivable. You are still busy nursing your first child, who has now turned old and weary, yet hasn't lost its milk teeth.

A child that bears its father's name might know its father, but until it knows its biological mother, it leads an incomplete life, and sometimes has a step-mother, as Cinderella or Leonardo Da Vinci did. It is in losing heart that you find the missing heartbeats. It is in ceasing to expect that all your expectations are met.

Life without energy and energy without life is incomplete. Stay detached, stay aloof, and do not give importance to anything more than it deserves. Enjoy the dance, do not give importance to the unreceptive fool. Hold on tight to the leash, stay protected, and don't show them your sensitive points. Don't let anyone scratch you where you feel hurt most. You are your healer. Beyond the opinions of others, choose wisely and pick what lies between the blind spots and the divine spots for that is your reality, your very essence. What others feel about you is their opinion which may be based on their own complexes. Do not base your reality on the opinions of others.

What you feel about yourself too could be based on your fogged perception and opinion about yourself. Do not base your reality on self-inflicted guilt or judgment. There are no right and wrong and arguing with a fool is a waste of energy. You expand your energy by conserving it. The one who thinks he is the controller is actually the least in control.

Each mother has abundance, yet if she blesses one child with all and the second with nothing, then perhaps it is because she knew that by not giving to the second child, that child will be blessed with all the riches it truly deserves under the care of that other source. Each child is entitled to receive love, and if any child is deprived, then it receives love from the other source, which is the universal mother. No one can rob anyone of the wealth they deserve. Each child of God receives the exact measure of what it is entitled to receive, yet some people curse the child for possessing all the riches it is endowed with, even though they gave it nothing.

The story begins when you think it is over. The game is won when you think you have lost it. Your thoughts and ideas are your unborn child. Your creativity gives birth to it so that it can see the light of the day. When one child grows up, a mother will always have another child waiting to be born.

How will a child that never has the will to search for its mother ever know the true worth of motherly love? Not knowing where it came from, where will such a child ever go? Every effect has a cause; every action has a thought; every product came from an idea. In knowing the thought behind the action, you will know the intention with which it was built. The second child often turns out to be lucky because it learns to survive despite the mother not giving even a drop of milk to it. The second child is graced as it becomes one with the life-giving milk given from another source instead.

You turned the life of your first child into a comedy show for the world to watch. At the cost of entertaining your obsessions and whims, the child is lost and foolishly treads forward, bewildered and crying to be weaned. It is time you move on or tend to another child that is waiting to be born. It is in losing your heart that you find the missing heartbeats. It is in ceasing to expect that all your expectations are met.

What is worse-being abandoned and left feeling unwanted or not being abandoned and yet feeling unwanted? A question that the orphaned child asks and it perplexes the girl child of India just as much. Both are here for no obvious fault of their own but both have come out winners in trying to find the answers to the question mark you put on their heads just as if they were never born. Your pain might seem more than mine but just like pleasure, pain is subjective and you will never know if yours is more than mine but what is wrong here is wrong and only you can make it right again. Step up and make each one around you feel wanted, feel comforted, feel understood, feel loved, feel positive and that's all you are here to do. Go out there and spread your light.

Sometimes the mother refuses the child for the toy that he longs for, even though the toy will quieten the irate child. She does this knowing fully well that the whining child's tantrum will not let her heart rest in peace. She refuses the toy in order to discipline and teach the child that being tough too is a form of her divine love. However, without the toy, the child continues to be restless with wavering emotions. Looking at this the mother returns to nurture and pamper her child once again with tender care. The mother's love for her child is always constant, unwavering, and unconditional. However, if the child chooses not to bathe in the blissful loving energy, that doesn't mean that the mother's affection has lessened in any way.

Healing automatically occurs as we allow ourselves to open up our blockages. As the petals of each of my chakras started to unfurl and as the deep blockages opened - I journeyed back to the day I was mentally conceived, eons back. From that day on I started to breathe from the deepest core of my being.

Affirm- 'Namostutee, as I open myself to getting healed, I go beyond my mind, beyond the waves and turbulence of thoughts. Tathaastu.'

CHAPTER 112

REKINDLED FIRE

Nothing can dim the light that shines from within. Until now, I too was not drawing the curtain fully to let the light in. The higher power watches our every move, in our own home. There is an obvious mark on my most precious gem that defines its true calling and unique purpose. Your urges and intentions to give more are the reason you get more. Your intentions matter and your urges help manifest them. They fuel your inner fire.

My experience backed with years of practice tells me that a combination of yin & yang, subtle & active, gives rise to inner light within. The inner light is fully awakened through the activation of the six channels or meridians. Once the fire is ignited it compels us to continue on our path. As we stay persistent with consistent effort and faith it speeds our growth, raises our vibrations, repairs us, shows us the infinite potential within us.

To achieve our true potential the seventh channel[104] (*Saraswati* Nadi) has to be activated. This will give us power and grace. This makes us superhumans and helps us realize God within ourselves.

---

[104] *There are millions of nadis permeating from our body. Nadis are energy channels that carry prana or subtle ki energy throughout our body. 72,000 nadis are known mostly. Out of these, the 14 main Nadis connecting throughout from bottom to top are :- sushumna, Ida, Pingala, Gandhari, Hastijihva, Kuhu, saraswati, Pusha, sakhini, Payasvini, varuni, Alambusha, vishwodhara, yashaswani. The sahasrara is located on top of head crown. The proper glow of the seventh channel known as the saraswati nadi - activates the sushumna nadi to connects crown with basic chakra which supports our body.*

When your soul mingles with your spirit, your soul purpose is met. This beautiful transformation increases your auric vibrations. All those who connect with you bathe in your light getting motivated to join the path. Learn to stand again. Passion with purpose makes sense but without action, it is a sheer disaster. It is as essential to feed the soul as it is to feed the body, it has more to do with inward focus and awareness rather than outward.

My elder sister has had a very interesting life. She is a fantastic girl yet growing up she often felt sorry for things she had done. One day I told her that she should instead be feeling sorry for things she didn't do. So even though she had other plans, her love for food led her to become a chef. Today, she writes her own recipes. Whenever I ask her, she gives me a detailed recipe and I follow it precisely but each time I get a different result from hers. Maybe because she is the key player and I can never match the passion and love she puts into it. Her purpose in life was to express her relationship with food right from the time when we were little kids. When I look back, I remember she used to pretend to host her own cooking shows on television, and each time she tasted her food, she said it had an interesting but unpredictable taste. Her food reflects her temperament and personality and yet it always comes out great. Each bite pleasantly surprises you, in a good way. And this love led her to meet her soulmate. It became the reason behind twenty happy, dreamy years of romance and marriage.

The same dish made with the same ingredients will taste different by different chefs. In that sense whatever you create, only you can. Everything you make is pre patented. It is your recipe - the ingredients are provided by the Lord. He is the provider, your inner fire is the creator and you are the co-creator.

How well you manipulate each of the elements within you is up to you. Not all fires smoke, nor do all have a flame. Some of the ignited ones reach a certain degree with the help of the gases and carbon, where they simply glow and heat all that is around on a cold dark winter night. The winds are stronger as you rise higher up, how much of the fire you hold within you when the wind is still low is up-to you. How much of the water have you allowed to pass for the fire to ignite too is up to you. It is easier to light up small things rather than big ones, so conserve your energy and start with small. No amount of effort is small as long as the heat that you give out warms even one soul in the dark winter night. Just remember not to be too slow for it is the nature of fire to be impatient and it will lose its heat before it can ignite another so hasten up the process, collect the woods from the forest and begin to burn them one by one no matter how wet or dry they may be. Each log of wood is one more log burnt. How many souls feel warm with the ignition of that fire is up to you. Just as fire needs a hollow tube to let the oxygen in, you too need to be hollow like a flute to let the life energies in.

You are like a matchstick. The moment it hits up against a rough patch, it ignites and starts burning. It will not ignite another match unless it is lit. As the matchstick burns, you need to ensure that another match is lit with its flame. Light up another match just when your inner fire is lit. In this way the chain begins and as such when you need to ignite your inner fire, someone else will help so pay it forward.

How stable and safe are your reactions to the actions of another depends upon what frequency you are traveling on and how much spark you have left within you. A small piece of partly burnt coal can burn even further without giving off flames, as it still contains combustible matter. I was once like that live flameless coal that had been reduced to ashes, only because I knew that I was there to slowly spread my fire even if that meant doing so without the flames. My stomach was like a furnace and I quietly breathed out fire through my nostrils. Seeing the inner fire within me that flowed along with the current, even the uprooted trees with their scattered branches became entangled among the rocks of this river. The same river surrounds and envelops me even today.

Your urge and intention to give more is the reason you get more. Your intention matters and your urges help manifest them. They fuel your inner fire.

One thing I like about homes with a fireplace is that just looking at it reminds me to always keep my inner fire lit. To feel truly abundant, you need to replenish what is missing, not what is already in you. It is filling the emptiness that makes you feel the abundance.

In India, you have the roadside laundry man using an iron that is heated with coal. Your inner child is like that coal that slowly lights up. Once the coal is lit and hot, it helps smoothen your creased dress. However, if the coal is excessively hot, it will burn your dress. Our body is like that dress that will burn if the inner fire is too strong for your delicate body to handle.

Once the inner fire lights up, we must use our wisdom to ensure the proper balance is maintained and inner heat doesn't inflame our outer self.

Our goals must match our abilities. Only then can we wear the creased dress and inspire others to look crisp inside out.

Affirm- 'Namostutee, My soul's true purpose and the fire within is rekindled. I am safe, successful, nurturing, responsible, confident, and humorous and I have intense clarity. Tathaastu.'

CHAPTER 113

YOGINI'S[105] STILLETOS

S tiletto is another name for a sharp[106] edged sword. A sharp mind is like an edged, one-pointed sword that intentionally cuts through the inessential chatter. This way our mind gains the clarity to focus on elevating itself through actions that lead to truth and enlightenment. The conversion of intentions into action is enabled by the unwavering mental and physical stilettos or swords. Without the materialization of intentions, our mental stilettos are sans any practical purpose. Life is about infusing the heavenly bliss into repeated clear actions until a day comes when you truly walk the talk.

Learning the art of walking on the edged sword or stiletto requires a razor-sharp mind. This has a penetrating and valuable effect on your aura-both inward and outward.

Just like the positive waxing phase and the negative waning phase of the moon, our life goes through phases within the 28 days of the moon cycle. What happens and how pure we think and act during these 28 days decides how much fortune and Godly power we are left with. God gives us the strength to be our own best judge through our karmas or actions. Commit yourself to listen to yourself from within for 28 days. Watch your words, mind, and actions and align them with every step you take. This way your actions will be more attuned and aligned with the divine purpose and cosmic consciousness. You will have a deep renewed

---

[105] *Yogini - Yog is a Sanskrit word which means 'to conjoin or connect'. "Ini" is a Sanskrit word which means roots. Yogini connects you back to your divine roots with pure energy so that you do not spiritually degenerate.*
[106] *The sharp stiletto or sword protects us by destroying mental evils that plague the world.*

connection with yourself. I have already mentioned (center) verbal swords and mental swords in previous chapters that highlight the importance of the power of thought.

This chapter is about 28 lessons that activate the right thoughts by practically experiencing the swirlings of inner stillness:

Day- I

The feet of the ones who take insightful steps are auspicious. The soles of our feet are like wheels that take us in the right direction. The direction we go on and the path we continuously follow are the results of mindful, one-pointed actions we take with full concentration. Just the way wearing stilettos requires constant mindfulness lest you fall in your attempt of walking on the pointed heels. The good actions elevate and uplift us but require great equanimity, balance, and resolve. These moral actions help us come out of all distress, disharmony and depression. Make sure that each step you take on the yogini's path is endowed with the qualities of meditativeness, purity, and right conduct.

> The wings upon your head help you fly in the infinite inner world,
> The wings upon your feet help you fly in the outer world,
> Those who fly are free and do not cry,
> Those who are free are beyond misery and sentimentality,
> Those who are responsible, stay balanced and filled with purity.

Embrace and be settled within your body. There is no greater miracle and no greater divinity than the one living inside and around the temple of your body. Return to your roots and strengthen your moral character along with your physical self. This material physical body endowed to you is your greatest wealth and privilege. Gold remains gold.It was momentarily wrapped in superficial coatings. There is no transformation required if the object is as pure as gold. This is the basic truth of life.

Day- II

An inch of a difference may not seem noticeable, a three-inch difference makes it all so much more apparent and a five or six-inch gap takes you to a whole new level. Every inch makes a difference for a caterpillar who is on its journey to becoming a butterfly. Every caterpillar encounters obstacles from being a pest to becoming a more beneficial member of the life chain. Those who slide into their journey elongating their torsos are the ones who magically make it to the next level of evolution. Every major life change requires you to contract and throw yourself out there. The caterpillar stretches and extends its limits only because it knows that one day it will expand its wings and transform into a beautiful butterfly. Every butterfly knows where it is going even though it seems that it is simply fluttering around with its fine delicate wings.

There will always be roadblocks and threats when you walk on the green magical carpet called earth with your dainty stilettos on. A balanced caterpillar, just like a level headed human, knows how to listen to the warning signs and keep itself protected from the predators and negativities when the surroundings get toxic.

Every inch makes a difference. The more you contract, the more life-altering experiences you encounter on your journey, until one day you expand into the bright light. Maybe the caterpillar cannot reach the height of men who are multiple times their height but that doesn't stop the caterpillar. It goes on trying until one day it grows its wings sitting upon tall trees that are 60 times the height. Even the smallest being has the ability and potentiality to reach the greatest of heights. Men on average are 7 percent taller than women in height. But look around and you will know who stands taller today. Every problem has many solutions. Sometimes all you need is to pause, reflect, walk slow and introspect. There is a delightful mystical world out there but to reach there not just we humans but every organism beginning from the smallest ones go through their journey with immense strive, sacrifice and stamina. Metamorphosis of nature checks the willpower, patience, and your intention with every inch that you willfully move from wrong to right. Those who give up may lack control and strength. Those who go on understand that there is always something far bigger than them that is making them shift their consciousness and so they continuously fly. On this earthly team, we all cross one hurdle after another not purely because of what we did but because of what we all did together as a team. My son walks a few inches taller today than he did yesterday but each inch he adds to his height, gives room to another cell growing within him to freely dance and expand. Every cell in our body and blood has life, just as much as every caterpillar and butterfly in our garden does.

Life is a never-ending interesting and colorful journey where every contraction and inch on your high heel makes a huge difference in how you expand your universal vision. To truly transform from micro to macro, you need to be open to the transmutation. Only then will a day come when you too can view the magic and beauty the world offers, from a height taller than yours. We can always choose to stay cocooned within our silken homes but every inch we grow shows us colors in the spectrum of light that we never knew existed.

Day- III

We physically wash our feet before entering mosques and temples,
We scrub our feet with salt before meditating and sleeping to disintegrate the dirty energies,
Our feet and heels need to be physically cleaned and healed,
So that our mind can strengthen and purify,
Cleansing the lower body, energizes the upper body,
When the ground energy enters within us, we cover our heads,
Just the way we cover the perfume bottle with a lid after using it.
These beautiful rituals we follow tell us that:
If you want to expand and fly freely,
Without letting the perfume-like scent of life energy to leak out,
Keep not just your feet pure, but also the ground upon which you walk nice and clean,
When the grounds and earth is clean,
Only then can you fly and expand to the heights of the cosmos.
If you have returned with cosmic energy and found that the grounds are unclean,
You must keep your feet covered,
to avoid letting your perfume leak out.

Day- IV

Have sure-footedness along with one-pointedness. Resolve to walk unfalteringly and with complete devotion based on what God ordains. When we are trying to achieve our goal, our attention should be focused on it completely; we need to aim clearly towards our goal like an arrow flying from a bow. Most of us are blindly losing our divine arrows following the herd, without being internally sure of our true potential. Once an arrow leaves the bow, it can't be stopped. And so not only should we be sure where we're aiming, but we should also be convinced undoubtedly that this is where our heart lies. Before removing the arrow from our quiver, we first should be sure of our aim and not get distracted by indecisiveness or distractions from within our mind or outside.

This one-pointedness or 'ekagrah' is what makes me meet with the balance and strength that lies within me. As I further press upon my pointed edged heels. Pam! Buzz's through an inner sound with a sweet pain that makes me feel all the radiant shimmering pleasure there is, it feels like a thousand stars gazing at you.

Day V

Why make the soft floors go through the torment and torture. Wear flats and sneakers when you are out running and sweating in the sun. Fashion takes guts. The natural force of gravity is not here to weigh you down. It takes wealth of character to raise your bar. Stand on the balls of your feet from time to time no matter how much pressure and strain there may be. Raise your standards, class, and status well above the grass in your garden. Wear your intricate and complex style, whether that be wearing flats, heels, or going barefooted. Whatever it may be, why hide? Go out, flex, and accentuate your assets. Dance to your rhythm, whether your dance requires you to walk on your toes or the balls of your feet.

Unless you do not feel accomplished in your shoes, you cannot acknowledge or help another feel accomplished. So appreciate yourself. Stand in your shoes, know and align with your true self, revere yourself, and be assertive. Be open to seeking support, acknowledgment, and inspiration. Be open to receiving love, guidance, appreciation, and power.

Self-awareness teaches you the art of being comfortable with yourself, within any circumstances and in any kind of footwear, based on the need of the hour. So while there are times when the fancy heels of 'Yogini's stiletto's' are displayed triumphantly in the shoe cabinets, she moves with complete ease along with the changing world of sneakerheads.

Day VI

The pair of your red[107] stilettos express the hidden depth of our bi-unity. The pairing of inward-outward, heavenly-earthly, contemplated-

---

[107] *Red color denotes Shakti or divine strength, life force, inner fire and dynamism.*

contemplator, subtle-human, high-low, above-below, divine-incarnated and earthly beauty. When women wear high heels, the top part of the big toe and the upper center which is connected with the solar plexus point is pressed. If worn in moderation, this activates and increases health and vitality. Wearing flat shoes is not freedom. Sometimes a little unease and comfort lead you to better health. The sharp pencil heel serves as a mutual connection or messenger between the two-fold nature of God - formless and the form through which we experience divinity and Godliness.

Day VII

Sometimes stillness of time gives you the energy to stay on your toes so that you let your style flex. Heaven and earth is designed as proportionately as us. Everything within us is symmetrical and in perfect proportion. For example- Stretch out your hand and you will find that the distance between the tips of your middle finger to your thumb equals your foot size, from the tip of your little toe to the end of your heel. This distance equals the length of your face. With the size of your hand, your foot and face length can be predicted. Same way, if the foot length is known, face and hand length can be predicted.

DAY VIII

I believe that to claim your worth you need to feel your spirit and live your life by your definitions and in alignment with the rhythm of the cosmos. Here is another short and super powerful meditation to become more complete, enlightened, and aware – Deep breathe and touch your forehead and chant *Aum*, Touch your throat and chant *Ah*, Touch the center of the chest, and chant *Hum*.

Day IX

If women do not wear their style with delight then how will they wear a leadership role? When I first started to be known as a yogini, people saw miraculous results through healings I did as a conduit. Most people responded very well but few said that I sure do talk and feel like a yogi, but it is difficult for them to come to me for therapies because I do not wear plain white or saffron robes. That didn't stop me from being who I am. When I visited Buddhist monasteries for special talks and retreats there were higher Lamas and Khenpos who saw me beyond the splendid distraction of the attire and fancy shoes I love to wear.

The spiritual schools asked me to dress simpler to look more convincing as a yogi. I never changed my style despite the resistance I faced from them because spirituality lies in the perfect amalgamation of both worlds. My outward demeanor with red lipstick on matches the high fashion of modern society in which I grew up and is a perfect reflection of my inward disposition. My belief is in being beautiful inside out and outside in for my own sake and not for the sake of convincing others. Preconceived notions are the root cause of all problems. To accept and love another, you first need to start with accepting, valuing and loving yourself. I can never love myself if my truth is spoken wearing someone else's robe.

Day X

Everything is made up of energy. Activating the energy center activates the feets acupuncture points and the subtle energy channels. The feet connect your body to the earth through seven energy points.

1. The heel of the feet correspond to the first toe and represent the *sthir* or basic energy center.
2. The beginning of the heel corresponds to the second toe of the leg and represents the *sthapana* or sacral energy center.
3. The location under the foot pillow corresponds to the third toe of the leg and represents the *karm* or solar plexus energy center.
4. The foot pillow corresponds to the fourth finger and represents the *dharm* or heart energy center.
5. The neck of the fingers correspond to the thumb or fifth finger and represent the *pattra* or throat energy center.
6. The bottom of the finger pillows corresponds to the inner eye or the location between the forehead and *Ajna / Aar* energy center.
7. The tip of the finger pillows corresponds to the *taaj* or crown energy center.

By occasionally wearing stilettos and walking in slow steady movement, we activate, press, and align the above seven energy centers. Visualize the ground energy entering through the heel and soles into your feet with every step you take. This is one of the many ways to connect and stimulate the outflow and inflow of the energy channels or meridians. This improves the overall health, wealth, and balance of our mind, body, and soul. Our feet connect us to the treasures found in the physical world.

Day XI

Serendipity is at the other end of stupidity telling you to stop limiting yourself under societal pressures or belief systems. I own my mind and I feel what I speak. The richness of worldly knowledge tells me that beauty is to be appreciated and there is beauty in everything, whether it is in the magnolia flowers growing outside my garden or in the limited edition runway Chanel dress. Both are creations of utmost worth, grandeur, and charm.

Day XII

How can I leave my footprint on the sands of time if I am wearing someone else's stilettos? Be and wear yourself with honor. There is romance in everything. It is in cleaning, cooking or in wearing a pair of old shoes that are as good as new. When you wear them, you give them love. Without all that love and appreciation even your body is just a mass of bones and flesh lying untouched like an expensive pair of Louboutin's lying wasted inside the cupboard shelf catching all that dust for it has nowhere to go and no one who slips into them. It is in the understanding of the intensity of the soul behind the sole that you open yourself up to a whole new world of romance and meditation, this is the ultimate union.

It is in the appreciation of true beauty that it can expose its true nature to you. Whichever country yogini's edged stilettos may take her and whatever path she may tread, she remains pure and protected, enjoying the immaculate beauty and love in everything and everyone. Above or below, glorious heaven is everywhere and in everything.

Day XIII

Our feet and toes rejuvenate our body profoundly at physical, rational, emotional, and intuitive levels. Our feet can increase the inflow and the outflow of blood. That is why great impetus is given to foot massages and reflexology. Certain feet exercises and pressure points like standing at the balls of your feet, giving slight pressure to the heel; stretching the ankles; moving your toes down and up; stretching all muscles of your feet; Stretching toes and pressing the tips; deeply pressing the big toes.

Pressing all these above points tend to physically improve flexibility, increase strength, and stimulate the nervous centers, all the glands of the body. Psychologically and mentally it improves willpower, increases pleasure, joy, passion, and focus.

Guess what, all these can subtly be pressurized through simply wearing heels by both men and women. Wearing stilettos in moderation and walking like a duck gives pressure and is more effective. This increases the force of self-existent yang energy in the left foot. The reflected yin energy on the right foot improves our form.

Day XIV

The yang and yin together find infinite bliss both in the inner and the outer world when we learn to balance the two feet. The yoginis path is not always as easy as it sounds--I was about to reach the zenith of enlightenment when I was shaken off from my deep meditative state by my husband. He interjected, "If you have reached enlightenment through your timeless capsule, then it's time to go shopping, as today is the last day of the final sale". I asked him to hold on, and so he tried but kept asking, "Are you there yet? Are you there yet? Is the experience over?" And yet we hear from fellow yogis in mountains that there are no obstacles for the family-oriented yogis, practicing the siddhi's while living in the plains!

Day XV

Transcend from your pain and meet with your full potential for no one but you can fit into your glass slippers. Only the ones who think they are worthy, find a pair of heels that fit just right. It is like finding your sole soul. When you learn to keep the balance and walk tall, wearing them, you learn to strike the right balance between the cosmos and earth. High heeled shoes are associated with greater lumbar curvature, enhancing physical appearance.

Day XVI

Wearing one-pointed stilettos remind us, women, to stay grounded while flying high, endure the pain while looking good, and get balanced before trying to look tall. It also reminds us that if our feet wobble, always partner with a good team that looks past your flaws and pains and helps you stabilize and stand tall. In this way, you make peace with yourself and remain confident and focused so that you can rise again despite the falls. This title reminds you to stay firm footed and one-pointed like the thin heal in your beautiful stiletto. As you practice the walk, the uncomfortable situation soon becomes comfortable. A twelve-inch apart space is good between the stilettos to bring equilibrium.

Day XVII

The creator being all perfect couldn't have made anything imperfect. Then what is the creator's perfect plan? Why is there so much discomfort and pain? Why does standing tall, elevating ourselves take so much effort and leads to unnecessary controversies?

Being the creation of the creator, we are made in the image of the creator itself. The right (Ida Nadi) is the reflection of the left (Pingala Nadi) foot. Therefore, we have the innate ability to elevate ourselves to the level of achieving our Godly potential and become a co-creator by partnering with the creator's divine and cosmic plan. The creative force is everything and it exists in everything. The creator is transparent and anything transparent remains the same whether we see it from inside or the outside. We, humans, get attracted to attaching names like good and bad, pleasure and pain, beauty and ugly, life and death, male and female, mystery and reality, and by doing this, we create duality in unity. Without these attachments, everything is effortless, comfortable, and liberated. We are part of the whole and being a part, we are also the whole.

Day XVIII

If you feel life is like walking on eggshells, then maybe it is time you wear your stilettos before you walk next time. Wearing those heels hurt and make as much noise but by now, you would have anyways been used to all that noise and pain around. Meanwhile, try out the power of visualization while chanting mantras.

As I wore golden silk stilettos studded with diamonds and jewels on either side, I pressed the crown of my big toe and everyone heard me say aloud 'Aum'. Here is what happened-upon pressing just a little below the toe, my voice got huskier and the sound 'Ah' naturally came out. As I slipped into the sandals standing on my tippy toes, I stood like a ballerina and my heart started to 'hum' the sound of divine love.

I thought to myself, Aum ah hum[108]! Wearing this six-inch heel is a perfect way to purify and lift me up against the weight of gravity and grime that comes my way.

Day XIX

The nadis penetrate our body through the souls of our feet. They carry our life force energy. Preserving this energy requires 'na' which means immense self-control. To keep the etheric energy of feet clean, keep the areas under the nails completely clean and keep the feet covered in places with not so good etheric matter. As the nadis circulate, transmutation occurs within our body, and the yang energy that entered through the left foot swirls, twists, and turns towards the right (surya nadi).

Day XX

I feel like humming once again as I step up, centered and transformed, within my core. As I buckle up myself tighter into those sandals - the bliss I feel reaches out to all those around me leaving out all those lowly thought-forms. I melt and dissolve into the limitless white light. My silk stilettos embrace me within and without with unbound strength, permeating love energy. Right at the center of it all as I go on humming, I am left with no attachment to what lies below and no pride for being above in this seesaw world of ups and downs. Only this time, I feel a stronger inner connection despite the ups and downs. As my steps merge and press upon the heels from the top, my bottom body feels lighter and lighter. I can now only

---

[108] *Aum ah hum is a powerful cleansing and purifying mantra. Chanting it releases you of all negativities of body, speech and mind.*

487

feel my arms and head. It seems as if my heart and the rest of me belongs somewhere else.

Day XXI

We keep pushing ourselves down, instead of simply lifting ourselves up. Sometimes, all it takes is a pair of ruby red heels and you will see you are capable of anything coming your way. You, my dear, are that heel that is attached to a stilted soul. That stilted soul ignites your inner fire. And when that fire gets ignited. Suddenly, a goodnight kiss feels as sexy as a sandal that is touched by a heel.

Day XXII

Meridians or 'Nadis' are connected from head to toe, when we wear stilettos our hamstrings flex. These then impact the related acupuncture meridians which are called triple heartstrings. Wearing these heels relax and regulate the heartstrings. The three-fold inner lion sits within the triple heartstring which activates the triple fire[109] chakra, which is all part of the *Manipura* (umbilical plexus) chakra. It has 64 petals that bloom and transform the three-fold fire to raise your Qi energy.

Day XXIII

The high heels you are wearing are meant for hard, wealthy floors. The soft floors made of clay and mud will perish and be damaged under the one-pointedness of your stilettos. The mud floors are not equipped to take the wisdom of your weight or the strength of your power. Only the hardened, concrete floors can withstand the height of fashion you are wearing.

Day XXIV

---

[109] *Triple fire is the sun moon and fire combination. It has great golden energy deep within the mooladhara chakra and it is the seed of everlasting natural bliss. Activated triple fire is deep within the gap of mooladhara and manipura chakra. The proper awakening of nadis deep within the solar plexus brings fearlessness for fire and death. In Hindu Ramayana epic, Goddess sattee walked on fire to prove her purity, wakefulness and came out alive from the wrath of triple fire.*

We do not always have the power to make decisions for ourselves without interference from others. As we grow older or intellectually evolve we are graced with this personal power. Even a single blade of grass blowing in the wind has this independent and autonomous power. Every moving thing in nature is capable of making this positive shift through God's love, openness, communication, experience, and knowledge gained. As it dedicates itself with one-pointed deep attention towards emptying itself of all negativities- the whole world becomes one with it. This way a day comes when the blade of grass reflects the same purity as God's most treasured team. It then mysteriously gets rooted back into the fresh green garden from which it originated. Only this time it stands taller because that one blade of grass has more power than the entire garden.

Day XXV

Be flexible and be open. Stand tall and don't get weighed down by gravity, no matter how high your stilettos are. Maintain your balance. Hone your skills. Be comfortable in your skin, even if your tummy's spare tires jiggle or fall flat. Keep your confidence even if you only meditate on your style an hour or two a day. Remember where you came from and who you are, no matter the pressure from above or below.

Day XXVI

In ancient times, drinking from a woman's sandals was considered a mark of respect to the entire womanhood. In fact in certain parts of the world, like Russia, it was a custom for the groom to drink from the bride's sandals to bring good fortune. In India, there is a feet worshipping and washing festival called *kanjak* and I have written more about it in the chapter titled 'divine rituals'. The ceremony is conducted to invoke the blessings of the Goddess who saves the earth. Respect and worship the divine feminine energy.

Day XXVII

The wisdom of the yin energy cleanses and it's the physical yang energy that energizes. It is in the combination of both that the true essence of love, light, and power of the entire universe rests. 'I am' is that deep phenomenon you can't cling to. Trying to understand it fully is a futile effort for 'I am' is beyond grasp. Yet, 'I am' is held betwixt formless (naked and bodiless) into our odorless body (form). We have a sense of smell and odor because of the formless, yin energy. This magnificent wisdom is not for the weak, deluded mind to appreciate or understand. We enjoy its blissful nectar and dissolve its essence into ourselves. We must try to understand it and praise the yin power by simply lighting a candle in the name of the formless supreme Lord who is the giver of all there is. Whenever you set the intention of love and faith in the praise of the supreme lord with complete heart and soul, its energy will bring in that exceptional flux of change within you and the universal forces that are optimal for the evolution of all.

DAY XVIII

Words are our wings that are clipped only so that we can sharpen them with the sweet nectar of our speech. Sweet words without action are futile and mere ink on paper. To gain back our wings, our thoughts, words, and actions are bound to match. Strip the truth behind mere lip service through an open and neutral friendship between your thoughts and actions.

Here is a short meditation for you. Please press the center of your feet, imagine sending golden light to the soles of your feet, and mentally repeat these words thrice – 'I am protected, joyful and grounded because I am liberated, open-minded, loyal and perennially pure in thoughts, speech, and action'. When we feel spaced out flying too high above, it is the soles of our feet that ground us and take us back into the comfort of Mother Earth.

Imagine you are taking slow steps up the ladder on a 5-inch heel, with a 22-degree angle and 12 inches apart space.

With every step you take, repeat- "I am ever grateful to my feet for carrying my weight. As the earth energy moves upwards and downwards into the soles of my feet, I am energized, grounded, vitalized, stabilized, supported, rebalanced and re-strengthened".

Affirm-'Namostutee, with my sharp-edged sword or stilettos, I free myself, my mind, and restless thoughts of all past unwholesome habits, attachments, and the illusions of the outside world. Tathaastu.'

CHAPTER 114

MITRATA

God created *Mitras* when Godly beings got bored of being Godly all the time. A *Mitra* (or friend) is like the first ray of goldy sunlight that sweetly brings truth and order back into your lonely life. You will always have a true friend guarding and supporting your back when the whole world weighs you down. In Persian, *Mitra* means to love and in Sanskrit *Mitra* means friend. Mitrata is a Sanskrit word that means equal, likeness, and friendliness. Consider me your *mitra*, a true *mitra* is a reviver of virtues.

Any kind of ill will makes body, mind, and soul-sick and agitated, that is why gentle-heartedness, loving, and kindness we receive and give to friends is so very important. When someone intensely hurts you, most likely it is because they are somewhere hurting themselves. Bless them with equal intensity of compassion and kindliness. In this way, all our inner and outer foes will become friends. There will be no more hate and wrath. From sunrise to sunset, be grateful for the *mitras* you have. *Mitra's* are like the warm rays of the sun, here to give you hope, peace, and strength. Cherish and glorify your friends and you will forever shine bright like the bright sun.

In a world where people doubt and mistrust each other, *mitrata* is vanishing by the day. Let us build bridges, extend a genuine hand of *mitrata* and break this disturbing pattern. This way all apprehensions will be dispelled and *mitra* will remain.

Truth is simple and transparent, we hide ourselves behind self-created garbs of duality.

I have met people who want to have all the money, prosperity, and luxuries in their lives but when someone else displays and flaunts their money and the lifestyle that comes with it, they are called shallow. If you have knowledge and wisdom, you reveal it in order to share it, and in sharing, you get more of it. In the same way, when you have the money you live it, drive fancy cars, and wear expensive clothes, so that you become the style you carry and share your richness with others by marketing and becoming the ambassador of the brand you wear.

We all advertise and market what we believe in, based on, our values and our beliefs. So why would you buy a brand you don't believe in? If you want to have wealth, yet you have problems with other's displaying theirs, then ask yourself if you really want it. For you can never have what you look down upon. You have to love everything about it: the money, the style, the company, the brands, the jewels that come with it. Only when you accept and embrace every part of it can you have more of it. Just as when you embrace, accept, and love friends, only then you can have more of them. Everything is energy, every cell, every part, and every aspect of your body needs to be loved for it to be healthy and wholesome. All the good and the not-so-good parts of your curves need to be accepted. In the same way, your money, brands, knowledge, job, and the car you drive are all your acquaintances and they need to be accepted. If you want to make them your friends, then you must accept them. If you want them to become your best friends, then you must embrace and love every aspect of them. If you want them to become part of your family, then you have to become one with them. That certainly doesn't mean that you lose your individuality, but in accepting, you are accepted, and in giving, you get. Choose your family and friends wisely. If these are the ones you choose, then you get the whole package and everything that comes with it. If you want the legs of Cindy Crawford, the face of Aishwarya Rai, and the heart of Satguru, you first have to embrace each of them in their totality and what they stand for. This is true gratitude. This is speaking your truth. Energy is not just in the parts but in the whole.

The left foot grounds and roots you with ancestral memories. The right foot helps you manifest your goals giving you a sense of purpose and focus. It is as important to wear the right fitted shoe as it is to wear the right fitted bra. Our bodies are unique and subtly asymmetrical. Within our body, the breasts are like sisters and the two feet are brothers - though not twins. Just as breasts are, one foot is usually larger in size than the other and we must wear the shoe or bra based on the size of the bigger one. The larger the feet, the taller the height. The more bountiful and larger the breast, the brighter the IQ. The size and shape of your breast and feet tell a lot about your personality. The more abundant the chest, the more optimistic and nurturing the personality. That is why it is said that large breasted women and people with elongated second toes are more creative and born to lead. Just as tight shoes tend to cause soreness and pain, bras that are tighter than your size cause health and circulation issues. Maintain the balance, be more aware, appreciate and honor your body by wearing the right fit and size but remember to be happy. We must go with the force of gravity and not against it. We must allow ourselves to go bare-chested and barefooted from time to time. Our muscles will thank us for it.

My girlfriends are like my support bras: they always uplift me, support me, bring out the sexiness in me, and are closest to my heart. Genuine friendships are rare to find and as important as water is to life. Be a friend of someone today.

Affirm- 'Namostutee, I am a true friend to all. I feel for others as much as I feel for myself. I am internally balanced and calm at all times. Tathaastu.'

CHAPTER 115

STRANDED HAIR

You untangle your hair when it gets tangled. But that doesn't mean they won't get knotted up again. And when they do, you gently detangle the knots all over again so that your hair can freely bounce. Similarly, life's situations get knotted up but as long as we repeatedly and ritualistically untangle the knots we will keep bouncing back to life with renewed vitality and vigor to start yet another day with a little brush.

Whether you tie your hair into a bun or leave it free and flowing; whether the peacock dances before or after the rain, the hue of its elegant dainty feathers, much like your flowing hair, will always add a majestic glow of wisdom and awe upon the vibrant earth, no matter what season.

Wherever I may go, I can always feel your divine blessings and sacred love tenderly caressing me and stroking the strands of my hair.

We all live a pre-programmed or consecrated life. Everything universally comes from and is a perfect manifestation of the never-ending life. Everything has life in it, bubbling - it comes to life and then goes back to never-ending life after going through many changes in forms, energy, styles, names, colors, personalities, and position. When the mission of the consecrated life here and there is successfully over, it then merges back into the never-ending life before it can create another life.

The ever-lasting perfect one first created one ideal being who then created many divine beings. These divine beings then created many humans and other beings which to the best of our understanding are the real beings because we can see them clearly. All these real beings have a spark of divinity within them and so with that idea lodged in their brains, each of them can create many more beings both divine and real who could now live in both planes divine and real - above or below, in any direction, form or remain formless.

However, not all divine beings are perfect, and not all real beings are evolved.

DNA written in reverse order is AND. Every strand of our double corded DNA tells us to continually transform. DNA–double helix is the complementary effect of AND which is to replicate itself repeatedly, just as rebirth is the effect of birth. And these cords and bonds keep getting thicker and thicker as we evolve into better versions of ourselves.

The longer the hair, the greater is the extrasensory perception and vitality like the grass of Mother Earth.

When you lose hair, it implies a lack of strength and vitality because of less solar energy. When you have long healthy hair, it implies vitalized, healthy sun energy in the body. Like fertile grass that keeps renewing itself, your hair is your life force, your power. Keep it clean and protected. In the famous fairy tale, Rapunzel was trapped in the tower, but when she let her hair down, the life force and the bright light within her was ignited like the golden sun, and so she finally set herself free from the prison-like tower. We too can freely vitalize and energize ourselves by moving beyond our body-bound limitations. Revitalize and reclaim your power by being with nature, under the morning sun, balancing your solar energies.

Your hair are your feathers that help you detect and even sing the truth. A heart as light as a feather means heart as clean, untangled, and vitalized, like your hair. The more we endure and build our resistance, the more disciplined we become, and the more our vitality increases.

The hairs on your head are like antennae with blazing attentiveness. You have inner hearing like no other. You are an angel on earth. The deep mysteries and truth are all known to you. Your free thoughts and words reflect your natural charm, charisma, dynamism, and true essence.

Deep-seated beliefs that you are not worthy of success and praise need to be dissolved, as they block progress. Set aspiring goals and achieve them to activate the power of your subconscious mind. Abundance is energy meant to consistently flow through you. It is your birthright. Increase your vibrations and keep your frequency blissfully high to receive the abundance you deserve. Move away from all self-limiting beliefs. Remember that the most successful people are proactive and not reactive. Embrace, change and open your horizons.

Our hair is rooted within our heads. This way it knows our innermost thoughts which we reflect outwards, the nerves are our branches and the brain and spine is our tree. As long as they are well-nourished mentally emotionally etherically, physically, our tree flourishes astrally & spiritually. All my thoughts are rooted within my eyebrows.

Internal hair care

I have carefully combed through each strand to de-tangle all knots. Just so that each of my hair has life within it even if one or two are prone to breaking in the process. The strand that breaks is as grateful as the strand that creates the volumizing effect on my scalp. Once the two separate, the one that breaks becomes different from the one that stays upon my scalp. The one that stays is limited to how much I care to know. The one that leaves is unbound and limitless, it ebbs and flows wherever life's energy pulls it. In this way, the strands that remain upon our scalp crave freedom from chemicals and negativity we constantly feed them. The ones that are now free and unbound crave to bond and dance with the rest of the hair yet again. Sometimes in rare circumstances, the two meet. They then share and absorb each other's life experiences and stories. This way, through separation, they become one and naturally moisturized, rejuvenated, and revitalized. The missing strand tells us to have love for death as much as we have for life. This way we enhance our shine and wisdom.

Conserve energy, increase vitality and tranquility to preserve your hair.

I have fine thin long hair. Even if I leave them open for a little time, they go a long way in a matter of minutes. They are my antennae but sometimes when I travel to certain places they prefer being tied up and covered rather than being let loose. Those certain places are so intense that the energies can dull the sheen of your hair. To have a strong grip and hold on life, be versatile and flexible enough to let yourself loose from time to time. Remember to manage the show and tighten your knots and grip when things get intimidating and too intense to assimilate. Stay rooted, stay connected.

External hair care

Scrub your scalp with an exfoliant the way you scrub your face. Cover hair and scalp when there is excess heat of the sun and in the excess cold of the night. Tie your ponytail lightly and not tightly. Just the way the waves in the ocean have a life of their own, so does your hair. Leave them alone, do not give them too much attention by over brushing and over tending.

When we meditate daily, our hair gets purified and infused with the power of immense spiritual energy. The hair of certain yogis is very powerful and filled with so much life energy that just by being around their radiatory field or touching their fallen hair, we can get healed of imbalances in our diseased body and mind.

Long hair increases the potency of the magnetism some yogis emit and are an outward manifestation of their inner virtues. Being around people with such pure energies can miraculously increase your divine power. In south India, the secret power of hair is known very well by worshipers of the famous Tirupati temple. People shave their heads to donate hair as a mark of shedding their lower weakness and gain strength and power through the blessings of Lord Tirupati.

In the fairy tale of Rapunzel, she maintains the innocence of her heavenly purity locked in the locks of her long hair. Rapunzel's long braids serve as a link between her earthly and heavenly beauty. However, the prince who was blinded in love and lost his eyesight regains his eyesight when he finds Rapunzel after years of search. Despite losing her tresses, Rapunzel is able to rescue the prince. This shows that no matter what the circumstance, the magical power of healing is never lost by the one whose intentions are divine and pure.

Allow your hair to fully grow to create more balance, be awakened and aware. Keep them cleansed and coil them up on the crown of your head to allow the pranic energy of the sun to seep down your spine. This is because your hair being part of your nervous system are your exterior nerves that grasp and share information. This gives you supernatural, intuitive, and extrasensory powers. No wonder the Sikhs[110] are known for their natural strength and survival skills. Their culture doesn't allow them to ever cut their hair.

Hair roots have special sensors. They can attract people towards you much the way perfume can. Body hair is no different. Body hair regulates temperature, helps you sweat less and breathe more.

Affirm- 'Namostutee, I praise and love my soul, mind, body, all its parts and components for ceaselessly persevering to receive the higher energies. Tathaastu.'

---

[110] *Sikhs belong to a religion called Sikkhism in India which is based on the teachings of Guru Nanak*

CHAPTER 116

SUPER NORMAL

People have taken this quotation, "Normal people do not make history"-a bit too seriously, no wonder we do not see normalcy around. These days, being ordinary is being extraordinary. It takes superpowers to be super-normal. When I walk in the streets, nothing seems normal to me. Ordinary tasks that most of us should be doing, such as waking up, getting ready on time, sleeping on time, studying books, eating meals together, having eye-to-eye conversation, making love to a person rather than a virtual screen, walking your dog, being excited and filled with zeal, respecting our elders--these seem to take an extraordinary effort for most of us.

It is in letting go of old habits and shaking off all unwanted baggage that we allow the change to take place. It is never a good feeling to let go of something even if it doesn't serve you any longer. The greatest human power rests in the act of letting go and embracing change. Few humans evolve at such a fast pace only because they learn and master a new language in no time.

With the onset of this holy internal war, the time has come to usher in a new era. In this era, we slay the evil within us to let the goodness in us shine forth for the greater good of all.

Earning money and cooking food has become child's play – everyone is doing it because they can. Teaching jobs have become redundant as Google has become the new teacher – all you have to do is 'google it'. The knowledge teachers impart is limited in comparison to the unlimited knowledge available over the internet. Even if kids of today may know more than us, remember that wisdom is in remembering what you have learned in practice. Without practice, wisdom is like a wingless airplane. It dreams of flying, it has all the perfect hi-tech gadgets but no means to tap the innate resource. Elders can impart the knowledge they have gained through experience to these new age world leaders. Through us, they can learn how not to ever let boredom and depression set in. Enjoyment is not in mere knowledge but in applying your skills of heart, mind, and soul into the learning of the skill with renewed optimism and vigor.

Having descended in a human form, the supreme divinity may look like any of us or may manifest in many forms. But an ordinary human does not have the understanding of mysticism, great jewels, and inexhaustible opulence of Godly beings with perfect six senses. Most human beings tend to wander because they condition, resist and limit themselves. We need to realize that a portion of Lords love is in each person's heart both in physical and in etheric form, both externally and internally. With this truth realization, one is awakened from sleep with absolute fulfillment. It is like the feeling you get after returning home from a long trek on the Himalayas. I say so because sometimes we voluntarily go through inconveniences like trekking in the mountains, lifting weights at the gym, or tolerating the foolish acts of deluded people because we commit ourselves to work for a higher purpose.

Affirm- 'Namostutee, I take good care of myself and believe I deserve what I seek. I am spiritually and materially prosperous and successful. Tathaastu.'

CHAPTER 117

MASTER-PEACE

Living a Godly life entails co-creating the master peace along with God. In order to truly transform yourself and the world around you, you need to breathe in and intuitively tune in with the beauty around that inspires you. Creatively and enthusiastically connect your spirit and imagination with your physical reality. It is no wonder that 'Inspiration' comes from the Latin word '*inspirare*' which means 'to breathe in, inhalation or drawing in of breath'. When you deeply inhale before expressing your words in any form, then those inflamed words are truly divinely guided. Such arousing words are infused with empowering, healing, influencing, and renewing effects.

The signs are all so apparent. Even the skies are speaking loud and clear so that you can hear me saying that I am back. Most of those who encounter me recognize the master within, but here in this strange foreign land, the roads are filled with so much emptiness that no one is willing to meet me.

The 'I am' is the divine Holy Spirit that resides within me and through me it will save those who are in need. My soul is born through me and its very name implies the 'prince of peace'. It will walk with you physically to make you realize what it is to be Godly. Those who have ears - listen. Those who have eyes – gain insight and vision. Those who praise - receive praise. Just come to me - stop waiting for me. I am here already to restore the truth and reestablish that trust you have lost within yourself.

Just come to me, my child, my love. The fig tree is sprouting yet again now that the joyful summers are back. Just open your door and let me in. I am here to bring back all that became lifeless, back to life. I have taken this form to truly awaken 100,000 forms of women (yin energy) along with many more. Born in the most spiritual land, I have traveled for eons and finally come from the Far East riding on an eagle, head raised high with all the energy to save, shield, and protect those who called out for me.

Not every sound needs to be loud or audible and not every chant needs to be heard. Not all prayers need to be verbalized or written for the vibrations and power of wisdom and subtle thoughts are beyond this. They are deeply ingrained within us all and are enough to bless all that needs a blessing.

Insight, much like wealth, kept as a secret for long tends to cause congestion. Sacred astuteness much like precious jewels and wealth must therefore be judiciously shared and not hoarded for self-interest in order for it to multiply, novitiate, and expand. There is no such thing as too much energy if it is expelled. You are inflamed and congested only because you are not letting it all come out for those who are tender footed. We all are inherently connected so your excess implies another is deficient.

Trade what you need for what they need and no one will ever be in need. Give your time for money, money for wisdom, wisdom for healing, food for hungry, water for thirsty, charity for clarity. Just keep trading for what is yours is meant for another in this game of life. Ultimately everything is yours as much as it is for another so let it all out. Let your creativity take over as there is nothing complex about this incessant chain. How much ever you try to find the true owner of all this wealth you will get back to the same point. Just keep feeding, caring, giving, loving, smiling, accepting, and let the chain always be forgiving. Don't ever forget to go on giving along.

There is nothing mystical or eccentric about being spiritual, philosophical, and physical all at once. It is a moral art to spiritually regenerate and like any other modern art requires patience and skill.

A truly spiritually charged divine person does not consume harmful chemicals to ignite his inner fire. His longing to make himself into that perfect piece of moral art for the greater divine good is what brought him here.

There should be no cringing or danger in being humble, holy, virtuous, faithful, balanced, charitable, patient, peaceful, and obedient. Every piece of art is a work of art, whether you find it beautiful or not. No art is too direct as it takes a true connoisseur to understand the complete creation.

Just as words are always wearing the writer's outfit of ultimate wit and we all wonder what the inner meaning is – so is the wonder when a naked body is dressed in clothes – let your imagination, search, and inquisitiveness guide you. The eternal truth is that the master peace always remains the same. Its true appreciation lies in acceptance & understanding. Unfortunately, not everyone is an art connoisseur. Not everyone is inclined to or have the capacity to plant the seed to become a connoisseur in their mystical pot.

Love always emerges magically. Life is where love is. Love cannot live in isolation. An artist is not necessarily the best interpreter of his art. It takes the appreciation from a connoisseur for love to know its true worth.

If you observe the workings of nature, you can not only control your environment but also change the very circumstances around you to become more wholesome.

Electric violet is a new hue, it is the merging of space and time. Space is magenta (a mixture of ether + fire) and time is blue. Electric violet (a mixture of fire, air, and water) brings the space and sky to magnetically come to earth with its dynamism. The inquisitive fire bears the seed in the wise sky. Now that it has become a bud, we must all ensure its flower blooms properly.

We all have been given a canvas. Our responsibility is to paint it with the strokes of brushes we are holding. The masterpiece that we are making is a work in progress, as long as we are mastering and working to master peace. Each painting is a work of art. We are that masterpiece.

No point playing nice, the world is filled with wicked people. When you get the opportunity- it is for you to grab as the stage is yours. You have been chosen to take it on so do not hesitate - the chance is yours. This present time belongs to you so go claim your destiny, your rightful throne. Anything that you work towards with full dedication and commitment is a perfect work of art. Unadulterated human is a master-peace created by God that unites the two opposites - Heaven and Earth.

God gave the choice to Adam and he did the opposite of what he was advised. Some humans are still behaving like the primordial man – Adam, continuing to do the opposite of what God and nature want us to do. We are happily living in our self-created complex world. We have not evolved much from the days of Adam. We surely have increased in number and population but guess we have not increased our brain-power. The only way to evolve is to stop opposing and start listening to the divine tunes of nature. The more you resist the turbulence, the more it increases. All chaos is within you and the celestial laws of the universe are very simple and clear. Calm down, start working by the universal law and the creator will thank you for not ruining its master-peace. You are the masterpiece. May you keep it intact and safe.

It is not secrecy but misinformation perpetuated by people who do not understand the sacred knowledge that causes the essence of wisdom to be lost. Knowledge is universal and for everyone to enjoy. Certain sections of society imbue it with superstition and ambiguity out of ignorance and control. It is these people who are responsible for stopping reality from reaching people.

Anything you do, do it with peace, else do not do it.

We are a tiny drop in the ocean of the creator's world. But every drop in the ocean can contribute its own unique quotient in deciphering the message in master-peace designed by God. Every masterpiece is a work by an unknown artist who subtly works through the known. If we learn to master peace, that artist works through us, and in this way, we create our masterpiece.

Affirm- 'Namostutee, The true master is within us like a pristine babysitting and guiding our inner being. I bow to the master and follow his guidance. In this way, I find everlasting peace within and also outside of me. Tathaastu.'

CHAPTER 118

SHOPPING CART

You buy a silk dress when it appeals to you from the shop window. You are neither the tailor nor the marketer. You are the buyer who buys the dress despite the price as only you know its true worth. When you decide to buy that dress that appeals, you will magically have the exact money to purchase it. Upon seeing the dress, if one gets stressed with the price tag, this creates doubt which will lead to the inability to purchase the dress.

In order to have the ability to purchase the dress, you must first appreciate the true worth of the tailor that created it and the brand that marketed it. Additionally, your intention should not be to flaunt the borrowed dress. The rightful owner of the dress might have paid its worth through monetary exchange but it is borrowed because it has come to you through the combined effort of many others.

The same way we must appreciate the divine worth of the tailor who created us along with the rest of his creations.

Even shopping is a form of charity. Money is energy. Energy expands when it is circulated, not when it is hoarded. Whatever you enjoy, you attract. Whatever you want more of, is what you get more of. If you want more money, keep enjoying what it brings to you. Think and act. Spend moderately, but enjoy what you spend on. What you enjoy will bring in the means to bring more of that joy to you. What you purchase becomes the reason for another person's bread and butter. Whatever you give, you get. You receive what you deserve. Anything in excess becomes a vice. In essence, moderation is the key.

Every cry for help gives you an opportunity to help. Every tear you wipe gives you an opportunity to give joy. Who doesn't want joy? If you do too, then you must first learn to give. Go out there and grab every opportunity you get. Once you open yourself up, you will see there are many opportunities. Let go of anything that is holding you back.

We all love playing the game of shopping because we all love choices. We love to care for our needs, our wants, and our wishes or aims. We love to use our mind's discriminative abilities. We love feeling fulfilled and valued. We love the order that the physical and material world brings into our life. We love to satisfy our cravings--healthy or not--and to reflect on our finances and decisions. We love to seek solutions to our problems. We love to get better, look better, to solve, and to keep searching.

We love to delude and cover ourselves up in layers and layers of unrecognizable patterns and problems. We love to clothe ourselves in the aura and energy of others because the mystery behind the nakedness of truth intimidates us. We all know that the answers are not outside, but inside, yet we go on enjoying the joy this simulated external world brings to us. You know that the image you project in those fancy, expensive clothes is not you. It is a reflection of the potential of your true self. You like to see yourself as who you can be, and that is who you truly are. Based on the inner cravings you have, you shop for information, gadgets, love, spirituality, jobs, groceries, schools, clothes, makeup, cars, homes, furniture, and the list goes on. This is all to fix the missing part in your internal puzzle and to complete yourself with confidence and clarity. You love the challenges and the clues that help you relate to the insight of your style. We exhaust ourselves trying to get away from ourselves, to know who we are. The search never ends. The love never ends. The addictive game of shopping is our passion. It energizes us. It threatens us. It makes us both miserable and joyous. It goes on and on, circulating and mingling, renewing with the same forces, decade after decade. We all are carrying a shopping cart full of life energy, and yet our life is spent trying to look and fit into that little white dress lying on the middle shelf in our ancestral cupboard.

How you look on the outside is a projection of how you feel inside. What you repeatedly project on the outside is what you become on the inside. If you are not feeling good enough to work on your inner self, then at least start looking good to feel good.

What you see you become. We are all perpetually trying to fit in. It is what drives us. Isn't it far better to fit in your shoes, your pants, your style, rather than copy and borrow your look from another person? And if you must copy, then why not reflect the image of something bigger than you.

The moon became the moon because it projects and reflects the light of the sun. It doesn't reflect the light of another moon! That would diminish its shine. If you reflect and project what every other person does, then how are you ever going to become like the mighty sun? There will always be someone or something bigger, brighter, and better than you out there. Seek inspiration from them, and then reflect on it to build your shine and image.

I saw a family in a mall when I went shopping with my son. They looked like tourists. As our eyes met in the crowded mall, we felt as if we were energetically filling some sort of emptiness within us. Soon we left as we were to meet my husband for lunch. To my amazement, we were joined in by the same family we saw. They happened to be my husband's first cousins who he had never met but only heard of from his Grandad. My husband's father never met with the children of his only brother. Bizarre as it may sound, most of us are privy to the same crime. If this is not loneliness then wonder what is. We need to disconnect from the apps we watch and not from our people.

Our soul has many bodies just the way the world that we live in has many interpenetrating worlds. Each of them occupies the same space. These are - Divine; Monadic; Spiritual; intuitional; mental; astral; physical and many more subtle bodies. As we evolve, our style changes and we begin to shed our lower qualities like we change clothes in the changing room of a shopping mall.

Garments in a shop have barcodes and the inventory is systematically numbered and stored in a central computer which only top management can access with passwords. In the same way, we too are meticulously numbered here on earth with specific barcodes, which are systematically numbered and stored in the bio-computer. Only a few skilled beings are graced to access the inventory of our *Akashic* records.

Affirm- 'Namostutee, here are a few qualities that I picked up from the wonderful shopping cart of the high life- these are serenity, sympathy, reverence, cheerfulness, helpfulness, efficiency, and order. I adorn these qualities with great pleasure. Tathaastu.'

CHAPTER 119

GRAND CINEPLEX

Neither am I the action nor am I the reaction, I am simply the spectator of this film. The movie is the same but it invokes differing reactions, at the same time, in each of the viewers. And so time, its dimensions, and the rest seem different to each. I am simply removing the screen so that you can gain clarity. Unveiling the veil to free you from the self-created bondage, throwing light upon the simple profound truth behind all this chaos so you may see well. Your reactions and responses are based on the movie you see and what you make of it. The movie is make-belief.

The upper and the lower realms are coming together because of the realm in between. This is the meeting of the unmet where the known itself will come to the unknown. The invisible actor will meet a visible audience and the medium is the movie. The invisible is real and the movie is a make-belief reality.

Why stress, being creatively productive is an art that involves balancing your right and left brain. Excess of anything leads to chaos. What you resist, persists, so why give anything more importance than it deserves. Why the hype? Be subtle and humble.

Actors portray anyone, anytime they please without formal knowledge of the act they portray. They do not put limits on who they can portray. They can become a thief, a pilot, a scientist, a pastor, an activist, a teacher, an engineer, or anything the script or role demands without actually becoming any of them in real life. Their role is short-lived and over-attachment to any of these roles can cause them to be senile and overwhelmed. Similarly, we all are acting our parts in the universal stage.

Panic sets in only when we allow our roles to magnify into something bigger than ourselves. We are not the roles we play - we are much more than our performances. When the movie is over, another stage is set. You always have a choice to sign the contract based on the script or not. The outer drama is just an act. You might be playing a huge role in the cosmic movie as a superhero, a president, a director, or a union leader. These roles are transitory and distorted. They do not reflect your complete reality. So why attach ego and pride to something transitory and delusional?

There are plenty of new pictures playing on the screens of the multiplex cinemas. The films roll but you do not have to roll with each of them. You over attach yourself to the complexities of the relationships each film and drama portrays. Each film consists of many elements. We irrationally create a drama of our own making by giving them an excessive priority. Nature tells us that life is about consistent clarity and discipline. Without self-discipline, we get swayed by the waves of temporary emotions. The screen will seem foggy when in actuality, it is the way we view things that are getting fogged.

Allow the transition to happen harmoniously and seamlessly rather than jarringly jump-cutting from one scene of your life into another. Do inner reflection, acknowledge the source of invisible light. Take inspiration from the movies we watch and see how the actors logically and sequentially interweave and continue to perform each scene on the screen only after proper thought, focused attention, and continuity. How you stage the drama of your life must also be sequential and scenes which the spectators won't enjoy should be cut, omitted, or edited. Sometimes picking up random painful incidents from our past attracts unnecessary interruption, confusion, hue, and cry causing blockages in the flow of chi energy. Just as the actors on the screen are impersonating a character they are not. We too are an impersonation of something other than who we truly are.

We have willfully taken visible material human forms but essentially we all are nature spirits. Our zodiacs too are divided into ether, fire, air, water, and earth signs. The angels of these elements are our invisible helpers who dictate our nature and direct our movies. From nothing comes nothing. Learn to honor and work with the director and crew members of nature elements to put up a good show and develop spiritually.

Affirm- 'Namostutee, What is mine and who I truly am is beyond the physical. Tathaastu.'

CHAPTER 120

NO NAME

Life is never-ending because such is its nature. Past, present, and future are one. We believe only in the ones who have a huge name or fame attached to them. These mental associations sometimes are the cause of our suffering.

Do not believe everything your psyche tells you. Sometimes try no name.

Stop identifying yourself with the seasonal changes and the fruits that come with the change. The subtlest energy of all is pure and active. It is something you may have never experienced or even thought of. It is nothing like the time zones you are accustomed to traveling in. Stop identifying yourself with time and the limitations you impose.

Why do we compare and try to look for associations? In our attempt to define everything, why do we get caught up in time with fancy words like progress, right, wrong, systematic approaches, patterns, and ideas? Associations cannot liberate us. Only disassociations can!

Excess information associates or conditions us. We are free when we are in an unconditional, eternal state. A mind filled with an overdose of instructions is crippled and bound because it stops you from seeing the actual truth and knowing its essence. Just as only an empty cup can be filled or refilled, only an empty mind can be truly free. Only when you abandon your associations and stop following set habits and patterns can you truly inquire, accept, observe, and evolve. My mind is an empty cup, it keeps getting filled with intuitive bliss. Fill your cup with some of its emptiness if you like.

We put in the effort. We also discipline, control, abandon, and then give up through self-will. But most of us do not plan. Once you put out the intention, evolution simply happens. Facts are untainted by the incessant psychological drama of words. Truth is not blinded with wants, attachments, and achievements. Truth simply is, as is. It comes intuitively to an open, receptive person without any practice or systematic planned knowledge. To cook a miraculous dish, we need to give up looking at set recipes and instead experiment by looking deep into our insights so that they can show us the sight of truth.

If you want to cross the river where there is no bridge, you can go by boat, drop the idea to cross the river, or find another way to cross the river besides traveling by the same boat that a million others have conditioned themselves to take. When you pick the last option, you come up with alternative plans and innovative ideas. That is when true creation happens.

One person represents all people, what affects one person also affects all. The effect may be psychological, physical, or any other. We all are interconnected through a web that cannot be broken. The web that connects you with yourself is the same web that connects me with me, yet the understanding differs. The lowdown that you take and I take from the same virus is different, because we enjoy believing that the structure is different where there is no structure. The new age society is shouting the importance of shedding old convictions, telling us freedom is unbound, and not being caught up in hierarchical orders or fanaticism. Yet we are caught up in the known when the unknown is coming to the forefront.

Criminals transform into pastors, pastors transform into criminals. Not every transformation is good, because what is good is always good. It is as-is. It is not bound by relativity, disturbances, or any opposing forces. Good is good beyond all *Raag Dvesha*, dualities, or comparative analysis. Good is God and such a good is the absolute truth. It is always free of all reactions, judgments, conditions, attachments, associations, and opposing forces. It already is and so it is not born out of something else. Its goodness shines, whether it is naked, clothed, or bejeweled, at a brothel, prison cell, or a temple of worship.

Freedom is not caught up in opposites. It is all-accepting, even-minded, and one, belonging to all because it belongs to itself. To have no name is to be devoid of liberty, restrictions, attachments, fixations, cravings, bondage, limitations, anxieties, or dualities imposed by the world. Your ego fleeces you into not meeting with yourself. The job, my husband, my child, that wife, this country, my mother, the money problem - are all excuses that it uses to trick and fleece you. In essence, you and your potentiality are limitless, unbound, and unrestricted. Name anything and it is yours. Life is that simple. The day you reach this realization and awareness, no name can curtail you from being you.

When we communicate through our higher self that is when we do not need to use words or attach names to communicate and recognize another. We will recognize each other easily due to the attuned frequencies–Similar mental wavelength emanates similar vibrations. Stop running away from who you are. Unflinchingly abandon the ideals that you have been holding on to so tightly, and speak your innermost truth. Truth has no name. It simply is as-is. Water is the cause of all causes, yet it is colorless, odorless, and tasteless.

Quest for higher truth takes you to a point where you realize that the highest truth is unnameable and smaller than a gnat, yet it manifests itself in forms as big as an eagle. Sometimes it transforms into something even bigger than its form. We often overlook the small intricate details because they seem so insignificant but it is these small intricate details that matter. Just the way humans are a microcosm of the entire universe, even the smallest atom has the potentiality to one day become a fully grown divine human. A drop of all the Gods exist within a divine-human. In this way, the smallest atom has the potential to one day become any or all of the Gods. The purest being remains unnamed and unknown, despite being the Primordial cause behind the expansive universes.

A mother teaches her child sometimes with kind love and sometimes with tough and just love. The child may call the mother good and bad but the mother's love for her child always remains the same. Similarly, you may call God by many names- negate or accept his love but God's love and light always exist. A devotee who knows this is graced with the presence of the supreme.

Everything comes near to our ear from a tear and goes back to a tear. You can tear us apart or you can choose not to cause a tear.

A tear from the eyes of 'O' creates dissolution. A tear from the eyes of 'I' makes a creation happen. Such is the perfection of 1O. Together I and O are One[111].

If the spiritual manifestation gives up, I[112] gives up. This entire creation

---

[111] *One is Brahman or supreme soul in manifested form*
[112] *Here I is etheric energy*

is the result of that one tear that dropped from the eyes of supreme manifestation in an empty cup. If the inspiration gives up, there is no exhalation or expansion. The entire dissolution is the result of that one tear that dropped from the eye. We create and dissolve our creations. If we allow the creation to dissolve within us then there is no need for us to dissolve. This way we go on recreating many more of us. The manifestation is given full authority to create many more manifestations of itself, set the guiding principles, and present itself the way it pleases. The 'O' trusts the manifestation of 'I' to be wise and pure which is why it self-manifests. Then who are we to question the judgment of the all-knowing one.

Affirm- 'Namostutee, as I go within, I realize that the light of wisdom is within and not outside of me. Tathaastu.'

CHAPTER 121

EVENT PLANNER

S imply enjoy your ice cream while it is on your plate. We are performing on a stage with many soulmates. My advice to you is not to inquire why or when will you meet with yours. Simply enjoy what is on your plate first.

Purify the temple with incense and set the stage for the event. In order to make the event successful, you will need an audience, performers, production, organizers, marketing, and a team of many more people. Everybody has to come together at the right time with the right skills to create the show. Each person doing their job is doing charity towards the ultimate goal. Singularly only some of it will get delivered but with the collective, all gets delivered with clarity. Finally, you need the hand of grace. And graced you will be if you have done all of the above with sincerity and integrity.

It is in knowing that you begin to un-know so that you can truly know
It is in filling that you begin to empty so that you can you fill again
It is in excess that you begin to lessen so that you can truly know what more is
It is in learning that you begin to unlearn so that you can truly learn
It is in doing that you begin to undo so that you can truly do
It is in the wisdom that you begin to become ignorant so that you can truly be wise.

Practice self-discipline and self-education. Rise above self-centeredness, self-opinion, and judgment. Temper down and avoid being self-critical. Stay optimistic and bring romance into your life. Free your mind of clutter by focusing on your natural calling. It is in being free that your thinking expands and you manifest creative and innovative ways to attract ascension. As you allow more opportunities to come to you to fulfill your mission, you feel fulfillment in every area of your life. A good event planner takes time to get organized and makes decisions based on personal intuition and aesthetic sense, without getting swept along by the pea-cocky events.

Affirm- 'Namostutee, I am inwardly determined and firm and outwardly accessible and welcoming. I am efficient and not overly theatrical. This way I stay balanced and do not lose sight of the original vision. Tathaastu.'

CHAPTER 122

STAGE ACTORS

We are all acting in this cosmic stage, personating some character and form. Most of us are not enacting or acting our part. When we do perform our role, we meet with the greatest actor we all have been personating. The actor is also the director and the producer, being entertained through the never-ending real-life series he makes. We all grow, plan, and shift together in this cosmic cycle.

Every time you suffer, the actor/director/producer cries, mourns, and suffers with you. You are so busy acting your part that you no longer hear the cries of the one you are impersonating. The actor and the one who is acted upon are one. When you meet this reality, you meet yourself, and that is when the show really begins.

We all are actors on this worldly stage. Some act intelligently and some do not. Some are natural and some not so much. How well we perform our role depends not on the act we are given, but on how efficiently we perform our assigned role during the act. How much we resonate to our assigned performance makes us a good or bad actor. A magnetic performer is one who naturally blends in and out of a character.

Giving yourself excess importance is as crippling as giving yourself no importance. Inflated ego and deflated ego both cause imbalance. You can and you can't, both can be right and wrong at the same time. The key is to stay engaged in your act and keep performing.

Life is an action-packed drama, the more we interact, the more we change, and then one change triggers another change in us. The drama has been staged by you, the other actors are simply playing their part. Some people partake in the drama veiled under the garb of misinformation and fake news. Some people prefer to bring out the stark truth without any veil. Both are correct in their way. The veil in itself is a result of unknowingly or knowingly putting a front to please your audience. A true performer however always knows how to read the psyche of the niche audience before releasing the play for it to succeed and become a hit at the box office.

Friends, we do not always play the same role or operate in the same way because while being around some people activates and energizes us, some people inhibit us, some make us confused and doubtful. All people influence us in subtle ways, but only a few leave a strong impact and those my dear are the ones who could be it. The choices you make to select who is the right one has to be from the heart. When the conditions around us are positive and conducive, love creates a super strong reaction within us. Our behavior automatically changes and our eyes begin to twinkle in the presence of love.

The seven days of creation means the seven cycles. In this way, three days could mean three yugas. Life is cyclic and each of us goes through the cycles based on our vibrational energy and soul urge.

It is senseless to think that you are the role you play. The roles you play are not the same as your soul's true purpose. Once the drama is over, all stage actors return to the permanence of life, leaving behind the small part they played upon the stage on that day.

Affirm- 'Namostutee, despite the temptations, I remain undisturbed and unattached by the roles I perform in the staged drama of life. Tathaastu.'

CHAPTER 123

SACRED FIRE

I have always been fervent about energy and horse sense which has the ability to purify, heal, reinvent, strengthen and restore the life we live. It is time to give back and bless. Now is not the time to pray and ask from God.

The greatest sacrifice[113] is when you remain reactionless and offer your lower unholy nature to the sun to burn in its fire in order to put forth your higher holy nature. It is in releasing your lower nature from your bodily imprisonment that you become truly free. This my friend is the ultimate sacrifice. If fire forgets to spread its warmth from time to time on the cold bodies, the congested passion it has - tends to burst out like a volcano. If you hoard and collate too much energy, then one day, you will get congested and burn to flames. Stay warm and conserve your energy.

It came all its way, it became so much better before it was graced to become fire, and then in trying to be better at firing it right, it ended up collating and hoarding all that energy up. All that congested energy one day wound up burning to flames that very thing you were wanting to save with your warmth in the cold chilled winter night.

By giving up something for the greater good, you receive something far bigger than yourself. You resurrect and become the witness of your actions. All it takes is three minutes and such is the story of my reincarnate self.

Let us all move and exercise to decongest and expel some air. Let us collectively provide power to the entire nation and world before we all burst into flames. Each of us can help because our energy is strong and wide.

---

[113] *Sacrifice = sacri + fice - Sacri comes from the word sacra which means sacred rite. Fice comes from the word facere which means to offer or put forth.*

Excess fire on the outside burns and kills the forests and bodies.

Excess Fire of tongue burns and kills the heart and soul.

Why burn in excess? The burn marks stay longer on the soul than they do on the body.

The 'I am' is everything yet almost nothing by itself. We give it its true meaning. Almost like a thought is everything yet meaningless without the spoken or written word which manifests itself in action yet it exists by itself. As the word or action exists everything else eventually will. It will never die and the game continues.

After a while, everything good or bad, animate or inanimate, tends to occupy an energy field in the higher realms, except that the heavens above attract, extract, and soak up only the good part of the energy. Since the vibrations and frequency of the heavens are all pure and positive, the heavens above do not know how to store in the consciousness of the negative, unwholesome, or impure parts of the realms below and so most entities feel lost and misunderstood around them. For example, being here for so long, even Coca-Cola has energy above. It is understood as an energy being of connectivity as it connects you to the rest of the world and urges you to communicate well. It is an elemental of ultimate global advertising, which thrives on its love to attract attention because of the color red. Its properties of color, hue, and popularity, convince and persuade people to enjoy the positive change. The energy of Coke (coca-cola) in the higher realms is perceived as lovable, motivating, high-achieving, charged up, and happy, even though it still has a long way to go in the evolutionary scale.

The secret is long out yet how many of us have decoded the sacred codes lying beneath the secret text. Even when everything is released and out in the open for you to access, no knowledge can give you a deeper understanding of the subject until you resolve to go on the quest to decode the codes yourself. The map is in your hands but the adventurous journey for the treasure is for you to make. The secret remains half a secret, your life remains half lived, your knowledge remains half-known. What has been missing is your will, your choice, your discriminative power, your voice, your first step, not everything that is fed to you is nutritious until you believe it is. My attempt here is to ignite that self-will within you.

One matchstick lights up the whole stove and slowly as the pan heats up, you can cook the most sumptuous meal ever. There is no better satisfaction than the first time you can cook your meal. Every dish you cook also has elements that are only yours. The dish might be old, the recipe may seem the same, but this one tastes different only because the chef is different. No one else can cook it in the same way as you can.

Affirm- 'Namostutee, I trust myself, my values, and my innate capabilities. I believe I can and so I confidently do the good that needs to be done. My inner and outer self harmoniously and continuously influence one another and are in perfect alignment. Tathaastu.'

CHAPTER 124

GOLDEN EGGS

O ur aura is our subtle light body because of which we radiate vibrational energy. Each chakra in our subtle body radiates a different color, hue, energy, and light form. It takes 28 days for a duck to hatch its egg. There is not much difference between the duck laying its egg and the formation of a human.

In the first 28 days as the human egg gets fertilized, there is a preparation of the four layers (etheric, physical, emotional, and mental). After the formation of the layers, a fifth layer is formed of the spirit body and this stage takes 7 days. The egg transforms into an infant. The infant then grows for 28 weeks – 7 weeks into the four layers - etheric, physical, emotional, and mental.

Similarly, there is the fifth stage of another 7 weeks where the infant transforms into a child ready for birth. As the baby is born the etheric body is no longer visible to the naked eye. The child grows and the stages are marked with a time interval of 7 years each adding to 28 years basis the four layers of development - physical, emotional, mental, and spiritual. Thereon the cycle continues – birthing and rebirthing in the same body.

Having gone through many transitional phases we forget where we came from and who we are.

The fifth stage is very important as it prepares one to feel oneness with the spirit body. If the stillness of this stage is not experienced then one would feel a vacuum. There is no other way to fill that void but to go back from where you started. We try to fill that void the rest of our lives with more physical, emotional, or mental connection, only to realize that our hunger is neither for food nor for material possessions or emotions or knowledge. Excess of any of these will only overwhelm us making us feel even more imbalanced and hungry.

When we resolve to empty and purify ourselves from within by practicing stillness, we can calmly reconnect with ourselves through awareness. This phase is the most difficult but also the most rewarding. It fills us with unconditional love and oneness. The best is to not reach a stage where you forget who you are. Without the grace of pure spirit, we are not- existent.

PRE-PRENATAL PLAN

Bodies/ two-fold aspects	Egg cell	Organ/ Chakra	Color/ Crystal	Determined Characteristics
Etheric Outer/ Inner or 4 elements	7 days	Divine spark/ Above the crown chakra	Sparkling light/ Divine potential	Accumulated Karma of all lifetimes
Physical Outer/ Inner	+7 days	Physical Heart is the heart center	Red Apple/ Coral	Hereditary at conception
Emotional Lower/ Upper or Astral	+ 7 days	Emotional Heart is Solar Plexus and naval chakra	Red Rose/ Ruby	Previous Incarnation / Self-soul
Mental Lower/ Upper or spiritual	+7 days	Inside Pineal gland/ silent void/ Awareness	Green Peacock Feather/ Lapis lazuli	Soul shift Manifested in this birth
Sun Period Ascension/ Descent & Transition Period Pure love light power	+7 days	Above the crown/ expansion, spiritual heart/ Spirit	Rainbow & Gold/ Beyond limits of age, creed, race, space, time, or attachments of body and mind	Subtle Formless and Active Form causing the heart to beat

Total = 35 days

Days become weeks, weeks become months and months become years. Years become decades. The fetus intention in etheric double is formed in these 35 days. In the next 35 weeks, a fetus is developed. Under the golden dome, there is always a dark squinch rounding off the emptiness of the angles that need constant filling. True freedom comes from pure wisdom gained from the dark. No wise man ever lives in any kind of bondage of the light.

We all are energy beings radiating light. We look like mini stars emitting a wavelength shining upon the golden dome from afar. Even if it takes 35 years, a subtle dewdrop on the blade of grass can evaporate and stir the clouds to rain down again. Such is the power within us if we have the faith.

Karma is that restaurant where you get what you ordered. You design your karma. You choose the dressing, the salad, the toppings, and the cheeses of your dish. You get to eat what you deserve based on what you payback. The chef is only listening to your orders.

Short meditation: Close your eyes and imagine you are a cloud floating high above the sky that cries in form of rain upon the earth. All your tears dry up just as you enter upon the earthly grounds. The earth soaks up all your pains and sorrows. With each tear you shed, a new light is born. The words we choose to speak create a dish for the listener. Let us make the dish tasty even if the ingredients just like the facts remain the same. Be ever grateful to the universal supreme being, great Master, Buddhas, spiritual guides, helpers, and purifying light of nature for unconditional love, abundance, blessings, support and grace in the making of one and all. For we all are within the same worldly womb that nature shelters and protects until we are ready to emerge out and shine with our newly developed spiritual faculties. These filled with trust, faith, splendor and glory. Now open your eyes with big smile.

Affirm- 'Namostutee, I am the co-creator of my destiny and I love finding new ways of doing things. I responsibly and enthusiastically pay attention to my thoughts, beliefs, and words. This way I can be a positive influence in motivating others. Tathaastu.'

CHAPTER 125

THE DISTRACTED TURTLE

S peeding makes the car crash. The rabbit who runs too fast loses the race. Slow down your pace. If being slow is your disposition, single-pointed perseverance and belief will help you win the race like the turtle. The turtle knows how to conserve and not destroy its energies. It knows how to protect itself in times of need by going into its shell. Do not try to distract or overwhelm the turtle within you by flashing your light just because you are exhausted and distracted.

Out of plain simple curiosity, if you flash a light on nesting turtles in the night, it blinds them and temporarily disorients them from completing their nesting activity. Some of them tend to return to the sea even before giving birth- jeopardizing their own life and that of their little ones.

The slowest is the fastest and the fastest is the slowest and things are never as they seem. The entire human race is rare. It is all a matter of perspective. What you get to see is only one side of the picture and hence you know only that much. Trust your inner voice as it is the voice of God that you may rely on with every step you take.

We are constantly consuming our minds. The busier we keep ourselves, the more distracted we get. We like to distract ourselves because we are not attracted to our negativity, obsessions, and muzzy attitude. The tortoise who goes in the direction of the light when he is at the point of his greatest discovery is bound to have a lifeless delivery. Such will be the parent that killed their child at birth.

Everything that moves finally settles. Even an exciting waterfall settles upon reaching the base. You too will soon learn to control your wavering mind. Just the way the experience of falling from cliffs helps settle the waterfall, you too will humbly learn to balance your high intensities by merging with the modest soul within you. The ultimate, eternal, sacred sagacity is a grace given to those worthy few who strive hard to attain it despite living in the trials and tribulations of a transitory distracting world.

When you commit yourself with full focus to becoming one with the light, within or without, inside or outside, you remain fully immersed, inspired, and move beyond boundaries. The fusion of active and subtle brings out the truth behind your superficial garb. You make the magic happen as you are the magic. The road may be dark, rigorous, tough, and winding, but as long as your inner fire is lit, your curiosity will inspire you to find your path.

Whatever the situation may warrant, we can guide, impress upon, empower, inspire. But we mustn't force our view upon another through foreboding or violence. Nature teaches us to be accepting of each other's differences, unique attributes and make the most of them. Everything happens at its own pace, eventually how much one learns, evolves, and grasps is only in their hands. Everyone is going through some battle, be kind toward one another.

The one who seems slow to you perhaps is slow because it is waiting for the last one from the group soul both astrally and physically to join in the circle. It takes one woman nine months to bear a child. But today's modern world has become so impatient that it tries to get nine women to produce a baby in one month!

The distracted turtle learned the lesson of non-attachment and belongingness from a hermit crab. The turtle and its shell are fused. Without its shell, a turtle would die. Hermit crabs are the only pets that can survive without their shell. They leave the old and enter into the new borrowed shell when they outgrow it. The hermit crabs not only wear their shell, but they also have so much sense of belongingness towards their acquired shell that they live within their shells and are at home, patiently retreating within their shells, no matter where they go. They keep the balance as hermit crabs love socializing but spending alone time is equally important to them. The hermit crabs unlike the turtle are not attached to their body. The turtle's shell can get sick if covered in paint and are without vitamin D and UV rays from the sun. The delicate skin of the turtle is protected by scutes which is made of keratin. The same material consists in our fingernails.

We humans get sick without sunlight which we absorb through food, water, and air. We too get sick If we overcoat our skin and nails with paint. The preserver descends whenever there is destruction. Destruction comes because of distraction. Distraction comes because of creation. When all are busy pointing fingers at each other, the one who is free of fear, judgment, and ego, is the one who is the ultimate preserver.

Affirm- 'Namostutee, I am persistent and successful because I tread warily and carefully before initiating anything new. Tathaastu.'

CHAPTER 126

AWARE MONKEY

The 3 monkeys together teach us the right speech, right thoughts, and right action. It is fun living in the tri nature of the world –

1. Thought came first.
2. Word followed the thoughts. Between the thought and the word exists a gap in which we introspect.
3. Action finally comes with the power of self-discretion. The three are intertwined.

The left side of your consciousness has all the visions which convert to thoughts. The right is the spirit behind your actions. The way water absorbs energy from the sun, moon, and earth - our physical bodies absorb energy from spiritual (the sun), mental (the moon), and emotional (the earth) aspects. Therefore, imbalance or blockage in either of these will affect our health. Mental gymnastics will stop you from doing physical gymnastics but keep the balance and don't get swayed by it.

God within you says, "You are that arrow that finishes the journey it starts before starting another. What comes down must go up there is no stopping. No guilt, no mistake is bigger than the service you do in my name. Keep up to every word that you gave me and I will keep up to mine."

And then the light replied, "I am protected, pure-hearted and free-spirited like the breath of life only because I shunned all that didn't serve me, my body and my soul with the sword in my hand and so I call my thoughts, words, and actions my greatest strength."

Even when your monkey mind has peeled all nine bananas (akin to nine realms of human creation), there still will remain many more for you to peel and enjoy. Being true to who you are sets you apart from all the rest of the super-beings, and that is your superpower. No one but you can assign yourself the work that you are here to do, for only you know what you are meant to do. You have many qualities and many aspects. Don't get stuck with one.

Being overly candid loses the essence of the message, which is why daily quiet reflection just before dawn through silent breathing exercises is suggested by almost all spiritual schools.

We must introspect before we utter our thoughts and convert them into a reality. Raw is original, pure as a dewdrop, authentic, and *dehati* (rural) but to thrive in a refined, cultured protective urban environment, even monkeys need to acquire proper discipline and knowledge.

Control your monkey mind and your impulses, else you will exhaust instead of expanding your resources.

You have to learn to navigate your ways all over again. You have found your soul but lost your body, while you are still in it. You say you are in a state of complete awareness and yet no clue of the smallest rules of the land! You are so awake that you are no longer alert.

Be aware that optimism, love, and kindliness are not body-bound. Be aware that every second has the potential to lead you to the ultimate evolutionary stage. Be aware that we are meant to grow, evolve, and be Godlike. Be aware that your reality is what you create, and you live in that reality. Be aware that the more you expand, the more subtle you will get, and then you will become one with awareness itself.

The full light of the sun is also within you. The cosmic intelligence, cosmic energy, cosmic law, and cosmic motion are all within you and work through you. You already have everything within you. You are both the light and the dark, morning and evening. You are elevated, activated, inactivated, and degraded only so that you can find yourself. And the only way to find yourself is to dissociate yourself from any association.

As you evolve, you become more aware. As the monkey climbs higher on the tree, the path becomes more and more clear.

Sattva creates thought, *Rajas* create words and *Tamas* creates action or deeds. With the combination of these three qualities within us, we are capable of transmuting and converting ordinary knowledge into conscious knowledge. We can become a thinking, aware being rather than remain like an unthinking unaware person.

Life is a never-ending series of challenges. Overthinking and worrying about every problem that comes your way will rob you of the beautiful life that you are meant to have! Maybe this is why the restless monkeys choose to become more aware.

Affirm- 'Namostutee, I keep a balance between work and play. I am focused, aware and I study the surroundings carefully instead of getting restless with the unsettling nature of the monkey mind. This way I can solve any problem safely and tenaciously. Tathaastu.'

CHAPTER 127

ENRICHED MIND IS A RICH MIND

Man in Sanskrit means "mind". If we change the word "man" with "mind", mankind will be "mindkind" or "kindmind". This way our days can be so much more brighter and stable. This means a man[114] with a kind mind is an awakened man. The source of knowledge you are seeking to enrich your mind is not outside but within you.

Don't know if this has ever happened to you. Not realizing it is not your car you go and attempt to open it. This happened to me where I went and attempted to open the boot of a car that was parked. The car looked exactly like mine and the boot opened. I was surprised only when I saw the contents of the boot as the things all looked like someone else's. The rightful owner of the car happened to be there and watching all of this. He then calmly commented – 'take the items and in fact the car as well – I was wanting to buy a new one anyway'. Now that is the kind of non-attachment that one needs to have. Just the intention of generously giving will make you feel truly rich. Each of us is on an endless journey called life which is best lived with diligence and practice.

Generosity is a virtue so is receiving. It is in receiving that you allow someone to give. Pure energy is in every breath and also in the depth of your thoughtful breath. The in-depth wisdom of this profound knowledge

---

[114] *Mana or man does the action. The word man comes from Mana which in Sanskrit means mind.*

brings about great insights. A combination of human and divine is what I call someone with a rich mind and rich love.

You give somewhere and receive from elsewhere. Everyone and everything is constantly connected and indebted to one another. We must open up the blockages by accepting the divine tunes and have no expectations, judgments, or attachments. Just let divine energies play your flute and lay in complete gratitude, acceptance, faith, and praise of the mysterious trance. Have no inhibitions and keep your intentions always true, pure, and intact with a promise that whenever your turn comes you too will not hold on or think twice before giving with the same fervor, kindness, and love as the divine.

Do not keep the learnedness to yourself, share it. In benefiting another, you will benefit from the knowledge you have gained. Astuteness lies in sharing.

Riddhi is success achieved through wisdom and abundance, *Buddhi* is profit acquired through love for ultimate knowledge and *Siddhi* is power accrued through prosperity. *Riddhi, Buddhi*, and *Siddhi* are all inherent within the perfect being. *Buddhi* is to the right, *Siddhi* is to his left, and *Riddhi* is centered within. There is an art to continually enhance, evolve and progress both spiritually and materially through divine wisdom and prosperity attaining evermore bliss for the greater good. This is the secret I am here to share. But to achieve this first let us purify and cleanse our abode of all remains and residues from the previous misconceptions that carry accumulated dust and grime.

Love, light & power are within you. You will realize it through practice in stages of attraction, moderation, and synthesis leading you to joy, happiness, and bliss. These are all inside of you - seek within - you are the cosmic trinity – mind, soul, spirit are all the tools you develop through your own will, power, and determination. Rise above your weakness. Your power center or your sun center is in your solar plexus chakra that creatively and magnetically impels you to attract all your cells and atoms into a more dynamic vitalized life-giving energy through continuous circulation and positivity. This is the profound truth behind your ability to intensely self-transform. Why are you in delusion living half a life when there is a whole life waiting for you my love?

It is simple - your past defines your present - your present defines your future. You are the maker of your future through the present that has been gifted to you. How well you utilize that present is defined by you. You are your destiny - no one but you can make or mar it. The one who is entitled adequately and confidently shares the connection of oneness and belongingness equally with all.

The one who is connected to the higher self sees the light in all. The light is equally distributed amongst all. Such a being knows that no one is superior or inferior.

> Power gives way to passion,
> Passion gives way to devotion,
> Devotion gives way to moderation,
> Moderation gives way to motion,
> Motion gives way to chaos,
> Chaos gives way to order,
> Order gives way to clarity,
> Clarity gives way to love,
> Love gives way to oneness,
> Oneness gives way to equanimity.

Between cause and effect, what matters most are the intentions we set.

Do not be held betwixt the trap of cause and effect. The result of the first memory forms the emotional context for future moments. Recreate the original moment partially and see how one reaction leads to another, how one experience leads to another. True generosity is never in expectation of returns. The true listener is never clouded by judgmental thoughts. To be able to help, be heard, be a listener, be a giver, ask, and be given is a blessing. This blessing is layered with unlimited opportunities to grow, serve and evolve.

A self-realized person is like an empty bowl effortlessly floating in the ocean. Anything can be contained within the space of the impartial bowl that is eager to fill itself up with philosophy and experiences that come its way. Slowly, one by one, as the bowl keeps emptying and refilling itself with oceanic waters, the entire ocean leaves its wise imprint upon it. The impressions of stronger experiences are imprinted upon its psychic bowl.

The rest are emptied yet again and so the bowl of a self-realized individual is forever filled. It is never empty, it is whole and complete, and yet it is just a small part of the whole.

As long as sense of purpose and focus remains intact, there is absolutely nothing to flinch. If the intentions are clear, the results are bound to follow. No matter how many others have fallen because of their delusionary ego, a true visionary is never Meghan Markelled[115] for it realizes its chosen destiny. Despite the odds it faces in the honorable royal courts, it is ever-present to responsibly perform its role and gracefully serve.

Give and make your payments of bills cheerfully, only then will you receive with equal cheer when it is your turn to receive. In the case of a fully illuminated person like Buddha and Christ, all their seven chakras were fully activated. All their vital senses and meridians were guided properly, all in order to initiate a new world order and set new precepts. We must be able to keep our energy points effortlessly and consistently balanced at all times.

We have a higher mind which we call *Buddha* or Christ consciousness and a lower mind. The higher mind creates the lower mind and our body. The mind houses itself within the body through the higher mind, which too leaves a portion of itself within our mental body. Similarly, every artist leaves a portion of his impression upon his work. The mind does the action, through the body. Without action, our bodies are either like a beautiful golden statue or merely a skeleton of bones. Whether your mind is higher or lower, no action is possible without the creative use of our mental faculty. Whether we are conscious of it or not our mind always exists.

There is no limit to what our brains can accomplish. Yet, no individual in all history has ever used even half of the thinking part of their mental abilities. Initially, we used only 1% of our brain while thinking and doing tasks. As we evolved, we started to use more brainpower and so our mental abilities got activated. Our brains got activated to 5%. Soon we were able to use 10% of our brains. On average, a person uses 10% to 20% of his brain. The human brain is capable of being 50% activated or more, that is when they experience life beyond illumination. Since, an average human needs to use only about 10% of the brain, activating the remaining part can help us achieve psychic powers and develop ESP (extra sensory powers). However, our optimal ability is not limited to just 50% of our capacity. We can enlighten our brain cells by activating them infinitely. A being who has achieved the highest initiation uses 100% of brainpower at most times.

You may brush off this theory as purely fictional if you like because science has no proof of this so far. The source of my understanding about most concepts mentioned here are through intuitive knowledge which I receive as a divine conduit.

---

[115] *Meghan Markelled is another way of saying someone who leaves a situation.*

I used to walk to school when I was in elementary school. We lived in a secure Air Force military cantonment base/ area. Every morning magical dandelion seeds would fly from miles away and lead me towards one of the teachers from the middle school who happened to be blind. Students and passerby's often made fun of his blindness but he pretended as if that never bothered him. As soon as he would sense me coming closer to him, he would ask for my help, letting go off his walking stick. It was the proudest moment of my day. He didn't need that help but he knew I needed to feel proud of myself. One day I asked him, "How do you see if you are lost in the woods?" He said, "I see from my heart". As I was reminiscing these fond memories, I noticed my garden filled with dandelions telling me to enjoy the simple joys despite the unexpected circumstances life sometimes brings. Life is a magical wonder filled with beautiful insights. We are so blinded by our sense of sight that we think that the blind cannot see.

This reminds me of another incident, when I was doing my Masters in Philosophy from Delhi University, one of the senior professors was blind. However, whenever anyone tried to leave the class he would instantly throw chalk at the back of their head. I asked him, how does he always know? He said, "I see with my mind."

Interacting with these two teachers taught me that their handicap was their greatest gift. These teachers knew how to use this gift optimally. Their physical blindness sharpened their intuitive memory, focus, and hearing and allowed more neurological space. They processed information better than most of us, without the unnecessary distractions of the outside noise and space. Same way consciously choosing to be blind to other people's mistakes through understanding, forgiveness, ultimate compassion and kindness creates balance and harmony within. Calmly forgive others for your own sake. By being considerate and by looking at things from a higher perspective, we become the bigger person. This way we shed our individual ego and the most deserving, swift ones take the lead based on their respective expertise – as it should be in a structured and righteous society. We must then respect their authority.

Affirm- 'Namostutee - A person with a rich and wealthy mind is a person having a gentle, serene, trusting, even-minded, happy mind. I am rich. Tathaastu.'

CHAPTER 128

SEAT OF THE SOUL

A perfect chair is a work of art and there is a lot to learn from it. The backrest is to protect us from falling backward. The legs of the chair protect us from falling forward. It is in this simple way we reconnect back to our center without getting broken.

There is a light body outside and inside of us which is the reason for our glow. That light body is our etheric field. Our soul is an aspect of our immortal truth – our true home, never changing but ever evolving. It is the seat upon which the divine light sits. It is always lit and energizes our spirit and body from all directions. It contains within it our limitless potential, through which we can manifest our dreams into reality.

The one who holds on to his gifts or soul-purpose because of over attachment to emotional or material greed is the one that does not let the soul connect with the spirit. Such a soul ceases to sit within a weak nonconducive host. If there is a huge window in our home from which sunlight comes in but somehow if we conceal the window with a thick curtain then it is neither the window's fault nor the curtains. You are stopping the rays of the sunlight to help vitalize and bless you because of your stubborn resistance and your blinded attachment to darkness. The purpose of resistance is purification and transformation.

The telepathic thought transference in the brain is done by the pineal gland. The pineal gland is the seat of the soul. All the knowledge that you require is in the divine book that is sitting right on your lap. It has all the answers, yet we procrastinate and choose not to read the pages.

I joined many courses and took advice from many beautiful souls. None of what I heard and learned worked. And so being a mother of a beautiful teenager, who studies in one of the most prestigious schools in New York, I can tell you one thing for sure that parenting is a beautiful thing but comes with no manual. Our mind too is a beautiful tool but comes with no manual. The only way we can learn true parenting is through experience. Similarly, the only way we can learn how to use our mind efficiently is through intuitive experience. Unfortunately, the number of breaths we take is limited and so by the time our children grow up, or the deal we have been waiting for comes through, or the book we thought of writing releases, we might just kick the bucket. This is why it is best to learn through the intuitive experiences of other people. Here I am simply trying to help in my little way by sharing my life, parenting, and mental experiences.

Babies are born through the womb of the mother. Books are born through the womb of the mind. In one we are pregnant with emotions and in the other, we are pregnant with thoughts. Eventually both take a physical form after the pregnancy period is over. I am no longer physically or mentally pregnant. My baby and book are born. Both are out in the open exploring and touching many lives as they circulate. May you enjoy their colorful personality and company as much as I do.

Sometimes it is a good option to let the snow glide off on its own rather than take a shovel up your roof. Clearing the snow by yourself can sometimes get more damaging than the snow itself both for the roof and you. Same way, it is sometimes advisable to not rush things, let the calcified ideas and thought-forms glide away by themselves from the roof of your mind. Let nature take its course.

Affirm- 'Namostutee, nothing can corrupt or intoxicate my mind. I am centered and illuminated by supreme knowledge that shines like a blue pearl within my head. Tathaastu.'

CHAPTER 129

MANNEQUIN

We are the pampered mannequins of God and are continuously dressed with immense care, love, and grace. By focusing on your inward deep breath you introspect and realize we have five layers like the Matushka dolls that layer in to reveal mini-dolls. You learn your lessons and open up to receiving. With the richness of this thought, God showers his blessings upon you from places you never thought existed!

Our metaphysical or spiritual body contains the physical or material body within it. The physical body is temporary whereas the metaphysical is permanent. By believing that we are just the physical body we are living in a delusion.

The meeting point of the axis and atlas bone is called Atmaram. It is where our soul resides, the Atmaram of a pure soul cannot be destroyed, broken, or burnt even after the entire body turns to ashes. It is where our immortal self-resides while we are living.

Mannequins are also called man-i-kin[116]. All it takes is an upside-down kiss on the forehead[117] and ikin[118] begins to actively move. Manikins are made in man's image. Man is made in God's image. We are all Godikin's-God's closest kin.

Every form is a result of creative intelligence. Humans notice their form more when manikins wear it. Gods notice their form more when humans dress in it. The form in itself is a mere reflection of who we are

---

[116] *I-kin means to industriously work.*
[117] *Kiss on the forehead is a kiss of respect and divine protection sans lust.*
[118] *Kin means the closest clan.*

and so how much ever perfect the projected image may be, it is pointless for us to over attach ourselves or be cup-idly obsessed with our outward form.

Affirm- 'Namostutee, I do understand and know that ultimately the only way to fulfill your wants is ridding yourself of all wants. Tathaastu.'

CHAPTER 130

TICKLING THE HUMERUS BONE

The humerus bone is sometimes popularly referred to as 'the funny bone', possibly due to the tingling funny sensation we feel when it is tickled or struck. To stay optimistic, laugh at the lunacy of life. Stick up to your values and keep loving, laughing, imagining, and feeding your curiosities. Enjoy the creative wonders of continuous change and adventure. To be free - lighten up as nothing is personal so stay detached yet plugged in. Stay contended, joyful, sharp-witted, independent, and vivacious. Socialize, feel with your mind, think with your heart, be gentle, be kind, keep smiling & let the child within you remain ever playful. Expand your horizons, evolve with your wisdom, care for your family, purify, energize and stay tuned.

This new chapter of the new book is super exciting. There is a right time and place for everything. Stay positive and use humor to tickle your humerus bone. Remember, energy flows where your attention goes. You want your energy to flow laden with stress or without is your choice.

When my son was young, I used to often watch the movie Monsters. Inc with him and we both sat for hours waiting to watch the scene when the scare floor turned to a laugh riot filled with baby laughter. This would light up the entire city. Instead of scaring kids, the focus of this floor was to make the kids laugh because laughter has the capability of producing ten times as much power as a scream. I scream, you scream, we all scream-Instead let's all have ice cream. Live, laugh and let love. We are all babies in a way, never too old to watch such movies. Always remind ourselves that you must turn our tears and fears into love, life, and laughter.

Recently my son asked, "What are you doing?" I said, "I am searching for the meaning of life". He wanted to be of help and so he said, "It is easy, - to exist, is to live. Existence happens between life and death." He continued, "This is something we were taught in junior school"! We are not allowed to roll our spiritual eyes, so I just smiled and played nice.

The language of spirituality confuses not only our kids but also the English language, with statements like-"Less is more; small is big; invisible is visible; you are not your body." The language of the world too is confusing. I heard someone saying think out of the box, suddenly I started looking for boxes everywhere. And in doing that, I saw everything that is outside of the world.

I kept receiving calls from people pestering me, "Please tell me where the inner voice will come from"? They said things like, "I can put my house in your name, just give me some clue".

I met some people on the street and we got talking. They said, "Let's crack some jokes". I said, "Just look at your life, it's a complete joke. We are all God's jokers, entertaining him with our antics." They never spoke with me after that day. I wonder why.

I was given a puzzle to solve. I said, "This puzzle in the newspaper should be super easy to solve as I have solved many crossword puzzles". I was then asked which ones? I answered "The blank ones. The one that has nothing down and nothing across and despite the nothingness all around, remain unsolved until someone steps in to look for a solution" and they all went blank. I then said, "Now you will know because I am talking to one such puzzle". They all gave me a puzzled look. I wonder why.

Even my ghost center gets all spooked looking at the living ghosts that walk on the streets these days. A hysterical first-timer asked, "I found my true self! Oops! Now what do I do with the fake one?"

Each person thinks that they are right in their own way. If their thoughts are not matching with yours – the opposing force is your greatest test.

> More the friction – more intensity,
> More the intensity – more hard work,
> More the hard work – more fire to change,
> More the change – more experience and practice,
> More the practice – more perfection,

The ultimate perfection lies neither within you nor in the force that opposes and inspires you.

Perfection is free, eternal, dynamic, unconditional, magnetic, and vast.

You already are worth a million smiles. You do not have to wait for the future to show your worth, all you need is to know your true worth, now and from this very moment onwards.

Many came in to see me while I was meditating inside the room, asking me to tell them about their life. To some, I said, "First get a life." To others, I said, "You needn't knock at a room that has no doors." Just join in and you will meet life.

Here is the never-ending dance of divine, celestial, and material: love, light, and power.

Power activates dopamine, which improves productivity.

Love activates oxytocin, increasing gratitude and developing stronger relationship bonds.

The light activates serotonin, which helps us value wisdom.

Laughing activates endorphins, which activate our sense of humor, teach us to be more trustworthy and to rise above the pain.

To enjoy the comedy of life and overcome suffering, it helps to inhale the scent of vanilla, eat dark chocolate and spicy food, but of course in moderation.

Caro-na (karo na) in Hindi simply means 'do something'. People are hearing '*daro na*' which means 'fear something' and as a result, some of them are treating the lockdown as an excuse to do nothing. But power comes with productivity so it is time we do something and bring in collective fecundity.

Educated men like Edgar Cayce put out their intention and mind to travel wherever they wanted not only when awake but also during their sleep time, in the astral world:

My son asked me how to get things done. I answered, "It's simple. First set the intentions, then imagine and sleep. By the time you wake up, you will find that you are neither sleeping when you are alert nor sleeping when you are awake. Either way, the job will be done within your sleep, so continue to enjoy your wakeful active dream". I clearly confused him. So to make it simple this time, I told him the story of the famous writer, Edgar Cayce. As a child, Cayce found it very difficult to keep his mind on his lessons at school, so his father and teachers often reprimanded him. One day, his father ruthlessly scolded him for not remembering his spellings, upon several complaints from his school teachers.

The next day was the spelling test and Edgar was unprepared. He slept, and in his dreams, he heard the voice of an angel who told him to rest his head on the spelling book and continue sleeping. That morning, when his father came back into the room and angrily woke him up to review the spelling, Edgar miraculously knew all the answers and got full marks in the test. From then on, he kept all his school books under his pillow before sleeping and the trick always worked.

I then told my son, "That's how simple it is to get straight A's. All you have to do is to believe." Isn't Edgar's story so beautiful? But since then, my husband has stopped my son from coming to me for any study advice. I wonder why?

A man was having a conversation with an Indian Goddess in his dreams. He said, "It's not fair! You have so many hands, while I am still struggling how to make use of the two I have." She answered, "Start being charitable and the arms you have will start to seem less.

After years of practice, I said, "I am finally in a thought-free state of mind." My husband answered, "That is not even a state. I am in it every day." I answered, "Do not confuse the thoughtless state with a thought-free state".

I said, "There is no feeling like nothingness." My son answered, "What's new? I know that one!"

And so I told my hurried son, "Take this empty thought with you and empty your cup fully before you return to me." Many days passed by. He returned and the cup was still not empty, I asked, "What took you so long?" and there came the answer, "I was looking for the missing cup."

Hindus say 'Aum', Tibetans say 'ah hum'. Muslims say 'am in', Cristian's say 'ah men', whenever I want to attune myself with the higher power- I simply say "Aim in."

My son told me about learning sex education at school. He was asked to come prepared with some answers and so he asked me, "How was I born?" I answered, "My parents had no clue about how the birthing process works, and they were never taught sex education. One day they got bored to death and so they gave birth to me. The cause of the entire creation is a result of boredom. I thought I was smarter than the entire creation. In actuality, I was even more dull and bored. And so I simply asked God to give me a boy and that is how you were born. With your birth, I became smarter and life became more amusing and interesting." He became a laughing stock of the class after giving this answer. He hasn't come to me for help with assignments ever since, I wonder why?

541

My son asked, "What are these people worshipping?"

I answered, "They are worshipping the formless aspect of God. God has a formless and a manifested aspect. The manifestation itself told them about the formless and so they have devoted themselves to worshipping the formless aspect of God. God knows everything and sets precepts based on the need of the hour. This way he keeps balance and harmony here on earth. After each cycle, a new manifestation comes in full spirit to tell more about how the formless God wants us to function here on earth".

My son asked, "What are these people praying for?"

I answered, "They are praying for the new manifestation to come and guide them".

My son asked, "Are their prayers answered?"

I answered, "Of course they are because God is all compassionate and gently answers everyone's prayers. People all over have been collectively praying for manifestation to come so it woke up from the pleasures of its heavenly slumber and returned to earth. However, the problem is that most of them have either forgotten what they were praying for or their expectations of the image they would like to see are different from what is presented in front of them. And so when manifestation presents itself in an actual form, they are so busy worshipping the formless that they do not recognize its manifested form".

My son laughed his wits out and said, "Ha! Ha! This reminds me of the new student in our science class who knows of all the planets in the solar system except for the life on earth because of which we are here."

This is ultimate madness. It is at a new level, the highest ever. It can't be known or imagined. From here you stand at a point where it doesn't matter what others feel or say, their voices are so dim and dull they can no longer be heard. You know from here you are in a trance, a madness that tastes divine but you must let it go, from time to time. While you are here, get balanced otherwise you will be the only one levitating while the rest of your peers will still be crawling. You have to keep your promise to fly with as many as you can.

Affirm- 'Namostutee, my day is joyful because it is filled with laughter and optimism. Tathaastu.'

CHAPTER 131

MAGNIFYING GLASS

When I was a teenager, I made a very big deal of the smallest of acne on my face. I used to rush to doctors for medicines and bought many concealers to cover up the blemish. I thought it's the worst thing that could ever happen to anyone. No matter how much I tried to cover the acne under the layers of makeup, there was always this one friend who would come back to me and say, "Hey! You got a pimple". Since I was seeing my flaws with a magnifying glass, my friend too was seeing them. People see what we resonate and they respond to our energies. Sometimes we make a big deal out of a small pimple. We end up spending our time, money, and resources on doctor's visits to hide that small little blemish that is simply part of growing up and detoxification. If we cease to give so much importance to our problems, a day will come when they will automatically fade.

Future pain and suffering can be avoided by choosing to live the present in a non-attached, pleasurable, and balanced way. The experience changes when the mind changes. Your mind can liberate and make you happy or it can make you live in bondage and suffering. Through the development of your subtle senses, you can choose to make your mind experience life in a more alert, aware, zestful and blissful way.

Spirit within all is one, the difference is only in our thought-forms. You see your face as clear in the mirror only if it is dust-free. A concave or convex mirror shows you a distorted or a pregnant image. However, when your mind is calm and clear then it is like seeing your face in a mirror you cleaned to make it dust-free, shining, and clear. Try looking into a mirror that shows you the reality as is and not the magnified or mirror image of you. This way you will learn that no matter where you sit, you face the same direction. Nothing is twisted or topsy turvy, Right is right and left is left. X-ray vision gives an internal view and information of energy vibrations. This internal heightened vision causes my aura to vibrate with rose gold healing light.

In the fairytale of Snowhite - when the Queen asked the magic mirror, "Mirror, mirror- who is the fairest of them all?" The answer she perceived was Snowhite. A mirror is a cathartic reflection of you, it meant that Snowhite is her true core essence. She must work towards becoming who she truly is capable of becoming- her highest potential. Instead, the Queen got overwhelmed and clouded by lower emotions like jealousy, hatred, malice and plotted to kill her own inner beauty from brightly shining outwards. God expects us to be the best versions of ourselves. This way we become the best version of the part he wants us to play on the universal screen. The role or purpose doesn't need to be magnified out of proportion either in evil or in an overly good way. Whichever part or cell or atom we may be in the universal context, one part healed gives a lot of relief and comfort to all other parts to slowly get healed and balanced. Even the slightest effort we make towards improving ourselves through developing virtues and listening to the gentle cues gets us a brownie point. Beauty, comfort, peace are rewards that attract everyone.

Affirm- 'Namostutee, I feel deeply relaxed, comfortable, aware, and self-confident as I develop high sense vision and hearing. Tathaastu.'

CHAPTER 132

BEE-NESS OF LITTLE BEE

The worker bees give up their lives trying to build a home for the greater good of their community and to be of service to the rest of the bees. It is in doing the little things, and not the bigger things, that you become a better bee-ing. Less is more. For some, a contracted version is simpler than an expanded version to comprehend. Diabetes is a fine example of how too much of a sweet thing can be damaging to your body. It's no wonder we need a little bit of bitterness to get our blood and chi energy flowing optimally. It is okay to sometimes expose ourselves, our mind, our body, our soul, or our children to harsh environments, to check our immunity and increase the receptivity. Being too lenient with our body at its physical, etheric, emotional, mental, psychological, or astral level spoils our overall health. A sedentary lifestyle spoils not only our health but also our children's health, on all these levels. We are over-attached to and overwhelmed by our emotions, thoughts, and possessions.

I met a lady – she was at a point in her life where she wanted to move from her sprawling mansion to a two-bedroom apartment. Online auctions happen to be the best way to quickly get rid of your excess belongings. It dawned upon me, learning from her, when you let go excess you are exhaling your congested energies to feel balanced. This is the *mantra* that you should follow.

You are blessed with the elements of fire, earth, water, and air within you. The communicative nature of air and ether, the transformative nature of fire and water, the binding nature of water and earth-fill you with warmth, moisture, and good health. Practice moderation, avoid excessiveness and aggressiveness, to keep these energies balanced within you.

Honey is present both in the honey bee and in the honeycomb engineered by them. The pattern that you see on the honeycomb is imprinted both in the honey bee and the honeycomb. They live in the comb and store the honey in it as well. They feed on it and when they fly they get attracted to the same honey in flowers. It is this honey that gives them the buzz – their energy. It motivates them to work hard as a team. Excess intake of sugar or honey leads to anger in bees. Lack of it leads to malnutrition. They balance the intake and consume it in moderation by sharing.

Similarly, *prana* or life energy is within us and outside of us. It is the very basis of our sustenance. It gives us our buzz and the very reason to live. Imbalance in Pranic energy can cause congestion and depletion. We study how to harness this innate ability for the betterment of our life and our evolution across all levels. In ancient times, this was the given norm but these days the art has taken a back seat. No wonder we see the imbalance of energy everywhere resulting in a whole lot of mental, physical, or psychological diseases.

One little acorn, with time, can also be the start of a whole forest of mighty oak trees. This book is my attempt to plant a little acorn. Until we immerse ourselves in learning how to perceive the simplicity and extraordinary beauty in everything we see, there is no point going outside to awaken ourselves.

So far our bee-ingness is experienced through linear time. As our consciousness expands, a true energy healer who values its gift expands and transcends linear time and physical space as we know it. This way pure potential is extracted and flows out the way pure honey does. The bees build and eat what they produce. Everything they produce outwardly is a manifestation of their internal self. We humans too are in a state of bee-ness. We build and eat what we create. Everything we create outwardly is a manifestation of our inner self. Both the bees and humans put in immense personal effort and merit, with perfect mathematical precision to build the perfect world we envision.

Ultimately we all realize that in the globalized universality and reality of our world, there is no plurality and separation. All that exists is one whole, interdependent, unbound, and united by an underlying magnetic force or being. We are all like the bees of the Supreme Being. The bees, the pollen from the flowers, the hive, and the honey are separate yet collective. Same way- the atoms, cells of humans, nations, and the energy each one resonates are separate yet collective. The way we find the essence of honey in everything that the bees create and eat, the same way we find the essence of etheric energy in everything we create and consume.

This life force or etheric energy is as indestructible and eternal as the honey extracted from the flowers. We transmute and transcend from one realm into another to build our perfect hive. Our perfect beehive is built with the collective spirit of the five elements and so we call it the perfect five. These five elements are present everywhere and within everything. The spirit is the thought behind the matter or form that we see. In between is the one, everything emanates from the one and the one is the word. Our soulful words are the connecting or binding force between the pure spirit and matter. The binding force is the life force that encourages us to remain in a state of be-ness by realizing our spiritual beingness and bodily bee-ness.

Let them be. When you let others be and besides yourself, you have no expectations from others. You reach a state of bee-ness. If all bees were busy thinking about where the other bees are and how much pollen the others have extracted, then not even one bee would have been able to work with the honey and create a hive with such perfect mathematical and scientific precision. Each of them would be craving from the very essence they created.

They are completely immersed in the task and that reflects in the pure and potent honey they produce. Learn from the bees and just like them - when you smell, eat, drink, think and live immerse yourself and become one with the task you are doing. This immersed state is called bee- ness. This my dear leads you into a state I choose to call "be-liss" which means 'to be in liss'. Liss is a friendly state of being in steady ease. You may have all the wealth, energy, and breath but if you keep on expanding and expelling without contracting, saving, savoring, and inhaling then soon you will expel and empty yourself with no reserves. Always keep a little low dose of liss for yourself while sharing with others through self-control.

Sometimes we require more inhalation and sometimes we require to exhale more, based on where there is more imbalance of energy. It is in the little things that balance is achieved.

A liberated soul is beyond lineage, cast, creed, culture, family, home, country, institution, form, name, time, space, rebirth or death. Such a soul might contain all of the above yet doesn't really identify its truth with any of these mundane attachments. Just like a honey bee chooses to go where it pleases to enjoy the sweet nectar of bee-liss and finally returns to build the honeycomb with its grand team so that we all can enjoy its honey. A liberated soul releases all its honey having realized that the sweetest nectar is not external but internal - within itself.

Affirm- 'Namostutee, I feel more present and appreciative of the present I am given. In appreciating the present, I live in the present. Tathaastu.'

CHAPTER 133

VITAMIN-P

Where 'P' means 'praise'. In praising another, you praise yourself. In praising yourself, you praise God. Vitamin-P stands for vitamin praise. Lord's praise is called '*Stutee*' in Hindi. Praise is an essential object of worship in every prayer both in the West and in the East. In this way, we are all connected with the innate force and power of praise. Vitamin P is the source of dynamism for all. It is one vitamin that can raise the spirits of anyone, anywhere, and fill them with joy in a matter of seconds.

I am neither looking for gratification, validation, or praise nor do I recommend you criticize or judge another. This is not because I am confused but because I do not want you to be confused. I am intrinsically valued and appreciated irrespective of whether someone else values and appreciates me or not and so it doesn't matter. But when you compliment another then the act of giving makes you entitled to manifold praise in return. Thus I prescribe a moderate dose of Vitamin-P where you praise yourself and others without prejudice, attachment, and expectations.

It is not the teacher but the student who benefits from the learning. It is not the farmer but the restaurant chef who truly benefits from the crop. We are true benefic of the celestial wisdom and beauty, the seeds that were planted by Lord God. We are simply enjoying the fruit of those trees. The one who appreciates knows the value and so he benefits. All we can do is to remember to do '*Smaran Stutee*' which means 'recall and praise'. Whatever you may choose to call the higher power, you must not forget to connect with the ultimate power through praise for what you praise you attract. The beauty you see can all be yours, all you need to do is chant 'divine *Stutee*' in praise of the divine. There is divinity within all. Honor the divinity in everyone. Address each person with folding hands saying *Namostutee.*

A word repeated in full belief becomes a pure entity. I was just a word until you turned me into reality. What you have been fretting about is simply the shadow of your reality. It is that ultimate light that is incapable of instilling anything but pure love and bliss. Switch on the lights and the shadow will be gone. Activate the charge as the battery has been discharged for long. Ignite the fire and you will know that you are not a mere shadow or a dream. Your reality defines not just you but also mine. My very entity exists because of the words you spell. Look what form I have taken because of your repetition. Look at your power that comes from the love for pure light.

My heart may be heavy but my feathers can still try to make it fly. Join me as my shoulders are eager to carry the load. A long time has passed and you have forgotten how to follow instructions and the manuals have become dusty. I insist you must do just as you are told. There is nothing bold in being unfaithful in the name of creativity. You must complete one task to perfection before you can start yet another. We all must transmute and transcend. It is only a matter of how, why, and when will you be divinely ready to take the flight of the heavenly staircase. We live in this dual realm where the people residing here praise the Gods and the Gods above praise the beings below.

The true heir of this abode is the peaceful one within whom rests the soul of the whole universe and the spirit of the ultimate Lord. He is the Godly ruler, who benefits from all our wealth and within him are the divine wisdom and blessings of the moon and sun, he turns into the ultimate benefactor of the future.

Spiritual wisdom is revealed to us when the timing is right. We realize that God is the master-builder of our destiny and we are the fortunate gems, thoughtfully created by him. God heals our mind, body, and soul and fills it with the phenomenal subtle energy of compassion, devotion, and forgiveness. God is the all-knowing, all-seeing illuminating eye that constantly uplifts and watches over us with immense love, light, and power to harmoniously empower us to convert our dreams into reality with its warm abundant rays.

Through his warm rays, he ensures we do not stumble, stagnate, or get blocked because of our resistance or the obstacles we encounter and keep joyfully flowing like the calm river smoothly and persistently despite the deceptive stones and pebbles on the way.

Your sensitivities are your strength. Have a cheerful, flexible attitude and will to serve for the greater good. Have the drive to continuously learn, evolve, and expand, we exist because of love and God taught us how to love.

Sometimes we get so busy with our complexes, our jealous nature, judgments about others, the lifestyles of our friends and neighbors. We get so preoccupied with the next day's gossip on the food that was served at the wedding and with our critical analysis on the books that are written, that in between all these complexities, cribs, and complaints - sometimes the true essence of the creation is lost in transmission. Therefore, a time comes when information comes gushing down intuitively, without any filtration process. When we hear such a gushing sound, everything is good, bountiful, and beautiful as is and so we cannot but help fill the air, people, food we eat, clothes we wear, cars we drive, books we read, with praises of love and divine acceptance.

Let us thank our supreme nurturer - earth for supporting, grounding, and stimulating our energy, strength, and stamina. 'Bharata'[119] came up with the idea of how to give us a form. 'Bharata' means fire. It is the fire that maintains us. Let us praise the thoughts which help us bring ideas to action. We send out what we receive. If you receive only positive vibrations and loving energies while others do not, it is because you are sending the very same vibes as the messages you are receiving. Such is the miracle of praise.

True 'Vidya' or knowledge lies in the 'Shakti' or power of 'Stutee' or praise. It is this knowledge that gives you true direction to move forward. It is time you recognize and realize your true divine nature for that is your only reality. As I witnessed myself from the outside, this is how the light of my subtle aura looked –Saffron, green, blue, and white. The sight was so beautiful, it was as if I was looking at the daughter of Buddha and Christ.

The daughter was kind, loving, and friendly. She was the teachings, teacher, and the students. Having the potential to be the healer, the trainer, and the trainees all in one. She had the strength of the whole community making salvation possible to several people for the greater good. Embrace her healings and guidance when she calls for you. She is the light before the enlightening. She is pure, free, and swift and the master of the three D's- discourse, discipline, and doctrine.

---

[119] *Bharata is the Hindi name for India*

Everything but enlightenment is transitory and finite. Move out of your limitedness for that is the cause of your suffering and misery. Your desires are making you look out and attach yourself to sadness instead of joy. Your ego is tricking you - move out of your delusion. A truly enlightened being lives amongst family and friends and enjoys its company in all three realms.

She has family and friends everywhere, the whole universe is her home. The one who remains unfettered by the mundane and unattached yet completely involved during each transition is truly aware of the nature of bliss.

You will see the beauty in the one, the moment you connect with her for she will see it in you. The exchange of vibrancy and the energy she resonates cannot be missed. Thank you for coming this far.

Let us praise the invisible subtle energy. You are where you are because you are wearing subtle energy. Without it, you are a lifeless skeleton that can turn to dust over time. It brings out the beauty in you.

There is something beautiful in everything and everyone, waiting to unravel by itself. Recognize the grace, beauty, and divinity within all. Whatever life throws at you has a cosmic divine purpose. Enjoy it with ease and joy. Never feel bad for winning even though your win made another lose. This is part of life, today someone will lose for you to win, tomorrow you will lose for someone else to win. Never give up, never stop trying. The more you practice, the more chances are there for you to win.

A life of true glory is one in which everyone leads a happy life without any obstruction, in complete admiration and greatest joy. The entire cosmos and trinity bow and praise you for invoking the energies of divine transformational power that rests within all.

Aum Shree Namo stute. Life is meant to be celebrated, glorified, lauded, and worshipped. The Sanskrit words -

> *Aum* means- ultimate self or truth
> *Shree* means - cosmic grace
> *Namo* means - salutation
> *Stu* means - to praise
> *Te* means - to you

In Hinduism, everyone is familiar with these words 'Aum shree namostutee' because every *Pooja*, verse and hymn begins with the word '*Stute*'. Without the element of admiration or '*stute*' universal *Pooja* or divine worship remains incomplete. In Sri Lankan or Indo Aryan language - *Sinhalese*[120], *Stutee, stute* or *Stuti* means 'thank you'. Every culture accepts that a little '*Stutee*' i.e, praise and gratitude makes life truly worthwhile. *Stuti* is another name for *Ma Durga* or the primordial energy. The Goddess *Dur+gam* mounts and rides on *Singha* or lion to depict that all '*dur*' (or difficulties) tend to '*gam*' (or pass) when we gather the courage and strength to tame the inner lion.

Durga or Divine Stutee is the caring, calm, serene, thoughtful, divine feminine or Queen of God. She is not easily accessible. Just like praise and gratitude, she dwells in many homes. She is the warrior Queen who slays all negativity, destroys all distress, and is undefeatable, impassible, invincible, and unassailable. Durga recreates herself in manifold forms. It is therefore believed that any woman who chooses to heal and protect those around with her admiration, goodness, and charm has the spirit of *Durga* nature within her.

Shree is creation itself- the mother Goddess who bestows wealth, splendor, brilliance, strength, harmony, and liberation. *Shree* is the perfect combination of *Sha* and *shee*, *Shiva* and *Shakti* (power of mother *Durga*), *male* and *female*. In Hinduism, every prayer and invocation to Gods, Goddesses, superhuman and royal is addressed with *Shree* as a mark of respect and reverence. The sound of this powerful word has transformative healing power.

Aum is the sacred sound of all-pervasive *Akasa* or breath that purifies and sanctifies everything. It entails the three stages of universal creation. It is the silent bow that penetrates within the feminine, masculine and neuter - fire, air, and water - past, present, and future eternity.

Just like other cultures, in Hinduism too every greeting begins with a salutation. Also called *Namaste, Namaskar, Namah, Namo*. Repeated chanting of *Namah Namo* is done to greet and welcome not only the divine Gods but every being.

Praise can be either loud or subtle. To understand the subtle art of praise we must learn how to use our speech wisely. The conscious being comes from unconscious elements just the way pearls come from water. Both must therefore be praised as both come from the same source.

---

[120] *It is said that Sinhalese or the lion people migrated to the island from north eastern Indian Chola kingdom called Singhapur in and around 500 BC. The Chola Empire of Brahma - Kshatriyas is considered the longest ruling dynasty and splendid empire of ancient Indian history.*

Praise the one who tirelessly whitens, refines, redefines, and rectifies the smallest of blemish on the earthly and universal energies.

Affirm- 'Namostutee, to praise is to be wise. A gracious peacemaker remembers to start each morning with a dose of Vitamin P. A peace-maker, starts with first becoming a true praise-maker. I am a praise maker. Tathaastu.'

CHAPTER 134

MAGIC CARPET – YOUR SAFE HAVEN

The magic carpet is the green earth you are on. All the magic begins here. The lights in the sky illuminate the earth only in the night and not in the day. The yin lures the yang. Without the two, the magic would never have begun. Look carefully and you will discover that the truth of the entire story is written in the stars.

It is magical out here. Everything is blessed with celestial beauty and purity and everyone is genial. The fireflies are constantly celebrating a fiesta and I am perennially in gratitude and youthful bliss to be living life in this haven, constantly surrounded by fresh waterfalls filled with playful sounds of water & subtle laughter of nature's bounty. Everything here has exuberant positivity, vitality, vigor, and color. Thank you, Lord God, for generously and so joyfully flowing your love for healing us all.

Step out of your cocoon and you will see *Shiv-lings* as beautiful rocks are all over the earth's garden. Surrounding them are shimmering water streams and sacred rivers. When you realize this you realize you don't need to always go to a temple to worship them. You can bow to their abundance and enjoy the divine dance while out for a walk.

God thought birds fly above in the air, fish swim below in the water, but what about the earth? And so he created domesticated and wild animals, untamed and tamed humans, and finally, trees were created with the hope that we will all preserve the magic carpet and keep it clean and fresh. Even if everything dissolutes, the wise trees being ever open to nature's laws, calm, free of chemicals and karma will sprung back to life in no time.

I recently saw a documentary called "the biggest little farm" with my friends. The documentary was inspired by a couple's love for their dog and their want to give it a better home. They purchased a piece of almost dry land which at first seemed useless but over the years, with collective hard work, despite consistent failures, tests, trials- transformed into a life-sustaining farm. Though the farm was filled with caretakers for the various varieties of trees, and species of animals like pigs, roosters, sheep, rabbits, bees, and coyotes - they all seem to have originated from one source, surviving under the same moon and sun, fighting the same battles in protecting their little ones, transforming into stronger and better versions of themselves based on the will to survive despite varying weather conditions.

Even in the darkest hours of the night, life was beaming with vitality and energy on this farm. With every death - there was a breath of freshness that came with another birth and so nothing really died here. We too are living on a big farm called the Earth where everything is perennially alive. Nothing really dies, we all are one, and from the one.

There is nothing that gives me more satisfaction than doing my *Karma* and performing my duties towards myself, my family, and society at large. A happy person is one who has a sense of purpose. It doesn't matter how perfect or imperfect the result may turn out to be. True happiness and our highest duty lie in putting in our individual and personal effort, rather than being lazy and procrastinating. There will always be someone else out there who will know or do more or less than you but then that should not stop you from planting your seed in the magical carpet called earth. We are all walking on the magical green carpet, waiting to transform into a prince and princess. Cross the rainbow bridge and manifest your wishes into reality. Here, in this limitless magical world, name a thing and it is possible. All the toys and treats you have ever wanted are here only for you. I am here to do what I do best and so I am here to heal and praise you for being you. Our greatest strength is our love-ability to bring out our greatest form of perfection upon this heavenly Earth.

Affirm- 'Namostutee, I see only the goodness in one and all. Everyone has something good about them. Tathaastu.'

CHAPTER 135

THE EARTH ANGEL

What went into the making of us?

The idea came from *Bharata*[121]. Then came the word of recommendation from the East, then the action took its first few steps in the Middle East. In the West - you rest and enjoy the fruit after all the toil and labor you put in all these years of *Tapasaya* and hard work under the cloudy skies, the scorching summer heat, the cold winters, the spring shedding which leads to all those flowers to bloom yet again in front of the autumn audience, these are the kind audience who value the ruggedness of your stark wisdom.

Just the way an atom has life and lives within us, we are living within the earth. The earth is an entity just like us, though much bigger and larger than us, it too is prone to emotions, feelings, thoughts, pleasure, and pain much like us. The way the health of our cells and atoms affect us, the health of countries and their people affect the earth. The earth helps us stay healthy and calm, we too must give back to vitalize its energy with love, care, and praise. Nurturing is never one-sided. A good child always takes care of the mother when she needs a healing hand. The five elements are virgin and pure. Yet incomplete and imperfect without one another. Together they magically create everything there is. The earth and sky are a royal couple who tirelessly renew, protect, and restore our balance, morals, and order.

Our physical body is beyond pain. Earth too physically is a heavy dense matter unaffected by the physical pain. The ground however gets

---

[121] *Creative life*

contaminated with thoughts, and it feels the sharp emotional pain much like we do. This gives rise to imbalanced, dull, dry, and vague feelings. What harms one entity eventually harms another. What harms one cell eventually harms another and that is the cause of aging and cancer. So let us resolve to vitalize every object, atom, cell, plant, tree, insect upon the earth with living positive, joyful, healthy thoughts and emotions.

Empaths are kind and caring nurturers but we must not become a nurturing empath at our own expense. Some empaths consider it their responsibility to help others alleviate their pain. By doing so, sometimes they get so caught up in fulfilling their responsibilities towards others that they tend to ignore their pain. As though an empath's pain is not as worthy of fixing as attending to the pain of others. Such people have to remember to think of themselves as worthy of being fixed or helped as well. If you are such a person, you must consciously remind yourself to include yourself in healings while healing others. Self-help requires you to tend to your self needs and give yourself adequate soothing care. Over giving person, sometimes tends to get overly worn out and depleted in trying to be of use to others. Some people give until it hurts and some continue to give until it bleeds. People who are in toxic relationships put everybody before themselves. They must get rid of this pattern before they bleed to death.

Each element has a unique quality.

> **Earth** has all the qualities of sight, smell, taste, and touch.
> **Water** has the qualities of sight, touch, and taste.
> **Light** has the qualities of sight and touch.
> **Air** has a single quality of touch.

The great age of spirituality and divine revelations is here to create modern civilization by allowing the higher spirit to descend in human form. Some divine souls are adept at connecting with their higher self. These world souls are already here to usher and help us get prepared, connected, and linked to a mature world order starting now until 2050. Just as a tree bears fruit. Life bears spirit. Just trust its powers, go with the flow and allow them to fulfill your collective transcendent aim while remaining grounded.

A model of an ideal society is not the same as an ideal society. Divine Stutee is uncreated, eternal, and self-existent. Please do not confuse her with imperfect mortal Stutee. The higher and the lower are linked and one but not the same. The uncreated and the created are not the same. They both eat and dress very differently, belong to completely different worlds but are connected. Stutee too has her share of weal and woe in life. Here, Stutee is wearing her heart on her sleeve and expressing her fanciful imaginations and true inner feelings so you know how she weathers the storm being linked with the world soul. This might help you heal.

When the two begin to unite- pragmatic real-world yogini in stilettos is born. Blend of the two is rebecoming of myself, others, spiritual self, and me. This is what we can call empirical spirituality or philosophy of eulogy.

Affirm- 'Namostutee - Let us set the foundation of love, truth, and harmony and bring the world back into its original perfect state. Let us recreate a fertile paradise once again where good food and wealth are abundant for all, where no one suffers any want. Tathaastu.'

CHAPTER 136

LIFE IS A PARTY

Life is a party, if you are not enjoying the dance at the party - change your dance. Sing, eat or interact, and if you are still not enjoying the party - then it is time for you to leave. Go to another party that excites you and suits your dance. If the next party too is no fun then it is time to abstain from parties in totality. We are and were always meant to enjoy this life - live it to the fullest as it is a party.

I have thoroughly enjoyed every bit of the life-giving waters of the ocean, every sound of the waves that came my way from the limitless ocean just as much as I enjoyed bathing in rainy waters that fell on the greener pastures.

Now that I have started the final march, neither can I stop, nor can I restart from where the race began, or start even further back. I can only go forward to my divine father and mother, who taught me to follow their lead and not only their light. I am living a reality and not a dream within a dream. I regret nothing, and so I never even feel the need to restart. I have disciplined myself to be forever aware and awake, and so I do not know what it is like to sleep. With this, I rest easily whenever it is time.

Go on and wear your red high-heeled sandals, or go barefoot. Anyone can wear whatever they please. None of your efforts have gone in vain. Above or below, the glorious heaven is now everywhere and in everything, for within you, there is endless, majestic, true bliss. In this heavenly land, there is no taboo, guilt, or shame.

Life is what you make of it. A positive person makes it into a blessing.

You have a choice to continue cribbing, whining, and dwelling in your darkness or to confidently enjoy the dance. The light within you sparkles whether you are under the sunlight or in the unknown depths of the dark starry nights. This way you bring light to the darkness. You can purify yourself even through the amalgamation of serious reflection with light-hearted fun.

Ask any sportsman - real fun and real victory are not before the play when we are busy preparing, neither is it post the play when we celebrate the after party, but in between when we play the game with all the vigor and excitement despite the uncertainties. The actual game might be really short but for the winner that one breath taken in the last few seconds, that one look is enough to last a lifetime.

I am here to inspire those on the path of spirituality to continue with their practice. We think that life is about constant anxiety, misery, pain, and struggle. We continuously analyze and judge situations and then get attached to our thought forms and mindsets. With such blocked mindedness and competitiveness, we cease to enjoy life as is. Eventually, everything settles by itself like sand in water. In essence, there is no need to over-analyze, overthink, overjudge, over concentrate, over contemplate, over cultivate, or over-plan. Everything and all the knowledge that you are seeking is already within you. It effortlessly and unforcedly flows back to you when you voluntarily and genuinely let it pass through thereby easing the inner tensions. You simply forgot how enlightened and illuminated you already are doesn't imply that you are ignant. We are all here to uplift one another so that we all can see the heaven that is here. Our purpose is to help and serve.

Affirm- 'Namostutee, with the blessings of the Holy Spirit- The physical, the intellectual, the moral, and spiritual life of humanity as a whole is stimulated, sharpened, and refined through proper motivation and progress in the current renewed cycle. Tathaastu.'

CHAPTER 137

LEGO, ERGO SUM: I READ THEREFORE I AM

Sometimes in trying to read too many books at once, we lose out on learning the real essence of even the single page within the single chapter that you read. Knowledge gained is knowledge preserved - rest all is lost in the pages of time. Too much is not bigger than too little. The one who has too much deserves it because they value every bit of what they have. I had little knowledge. I valued it and it turned to percipience. A wise word shared is better than seven words learned. All it takes is one motivating word to create a smile and preserve someone's life. That one word is more valuable than seven words shared.

Ask a mother, the value of a word when her only child utters the first word, however meaningless it may sound to another. A mother always values and never forgets the first divine word the child utters. It is *'Amrit'* or the ultimate elixir of life for her. That one word becomes the reason for the next breath and yet another and the chain goes on. A wise mother always understands the needs of her child even if the world thinks otherwise.

It is fun to watch little kids create Lego models based on the instructions given in the box and then destroy them so they can rebuild new ones with the same pieces endowed with a fresh renewed perspective. Children then tend to display their new-found models. Always remember that the pieces were all built in the same factory and are from the same pack, however, each person ends with a different model when applying their creativity.

It might seem you are different and disconnected, but you will always remain connected no matter how much you may try. The more you play, build and rebuild, the more constancy and consistency develop, so go on and create your unique model and design of Lego.

Death is an aspect of life. The way one Lego model is destroyed to form another, in the same way, one form is destroyed to form another. The missing piece of the puzzle is within your mind. You solve your mind, the rest of the puzzle will solve by itself.

Know thyself. By reading between the lines, you will know who you are. By knowing and understanding yourself, you will know the deeper truth of the self and of all those around you. Gaining self-knowledge requires *Lego, ergo sum*: I read therefore I am.

I have found love. I am what I am because the experiences I had during my search are what made me what I am. These experiences were important. The problem is that even when you learn to read the signs, it shows only half the story. And in the process, we never know how much we have missed out.

Love is all around us. All you have to do is to listen to its tunes. It is not challenging because love is about putting together rather than taking the pieces apart. Every effect has a cause but not every cause affects. We are the effect and creation of the cause. The cause simply is. It exists irrespective of the effect. The effect comes and goes, the cause remains. Its existence is not dependent just on what it creates in material or tangible form. However, those who praise and try to understand the essence of the cause, give it meaning to go on creating. In this way, we become part of the creator. For example, this book is now available in tangible form for you to read. It is the effect of the cause. It is the effect of my creative pursuits. The cause behind this book simply is. Its essence remains with or without the results. This book would have existed irrespective of the effect, housed within a special place in my mind, emotions, and thoughts. The existence of the book is not dependent upon its creation. However, the ones who appreciate or attempt to understand its essence, give it a meaning and name worth its title. And this way the chain continues.

Affirm- 'Namostutee, True learning requires persistence and sincerity. I always strive to learn. Tathaastu.'

CHAPTER 138

MITTI PAO

There is a Punjabi saying, *"mitti pao"*, which means "leave and bury it". We are content with hiding behind hidden secrets. We bury matters that seem difficult to understand and leave them to speculation because we are addicted to the mystery that comes with being half-awake.

Unlike in the deaths of Indian Prime Minister Rajiv Gandhi and American President John F. Kennedy, in Mahatma Gandhi's case, his assassin admitted firing the bullets. A known evil is better than an unknown one, and so the unknown evil remains in hiding. It is no wonder that after all these years, we still have not been able to find the mystery behind the missing Malaysian airplane or the invisible force behind the strange disappearances in the Bermuda Triangle. I recently read in the New York Times about the bizarre case of a rape victim. The sexual offender was found, but the case remains open even after twenty years because the offender has an identical twin. Identical twins have the same DNA, and since it cannot be established with certainty which of the two committed the crime, the crime is left unsolved. Instead of digging deeper to know the unknown, humans simply *mitti pao*. And yet this is not the first case in which an identical twin has gotten away with the crime.

However, there is a solution. I can be of use here. By scanning the body energy of the person through my higher senses, I can tap the energy force within and help determine the culprit. I can also help the criminal to heal out of mercy and compassion so that they can learn, evolve and grow. In this way, society as a whole will improve and purify one by one.

It is important to reflect upon your experiences and mistakes. I met a fine lady for dinner at a friend's house. She is a lawyer who works with prison inmates who were wrongly convicted and she fights for their rights. She said it is very difficult to ascertain the truth until all facts are properly scrutinized. This is because most prisoners genuinely have no clue why they committed the crime. But a bullet once fired cannot be retracted. You are punished and imprisoned so that you can dwell on why you faltered. Some lucky ones who realize how blinded they had become, come out of the darkness and see the light. These are the ones who are free irrespective of whether they remain in prison or are out in the open.

Error is Terror with a T. 'T' implies 'the truth of time'. Time has come to tear the veils of darkness. Slowly bring the truth out and allow the light to shine so that a day will come when humanity as a whole will make no more errors or create unnecessary terror in the name of pseudo schemes. Letter 'T' is like a meeting place between heaven and sky. It's a beautiful reminder to tell us to live life fully and stop clogging and constricting the right thoughts from filtering into your being. Let the star within you shine brightly.

Living life is like walking on hot coal. Dying is like burying yourself deep into the sand. Those who choose not to bury their heads, like the ostrich, are the ones who come out alive from the fire. It is in confronting your greatest fears that you rid yourself of them and meet with the real you.

I lived in Kolkata, I was nicknamed jhal moori - named after the most popular snack eaten there. I lived in Chennai I was called Chennai express mingling with their rich culture of silk sarees and *gajra* and embracing it as if, it was where I was born. I reached Oman and became a shy, timid, conservative wife rearing a child. I went to Dubai and became a fashionista, a plastic Barbie girl as some say. I reached Bahrain and realized the value of community living. Now I am in America and embracing its current contemporary culture and it is showing another dimension of me but I inherently remained the same throughout this journey. Each city, each country I travel to has something beautiful to offer. Each person, each man, each woman, each child, each soul I connect with has a different energy, a different uniqueness about them. The books Geeta, the Vedas, the Bible, the Quran, Mormon, the teachings of Baha-i- faith, kabbalah, Essenes, and the Greek Sphinx are all telling the same story. I become one with their energy to understand them and in understanding them, these countries, these cities, these planets, these trees, these animals, these objects, these spirits - I understand myself. This realization takes me to experience moments of profound bliss.

Let go and let be. It is not necessary to base everything on validation. Intuitive knowledge is above and beyond perceptive knowledge. Wisdom is beyond intelligence. Philosophy is the mother and soul of all sciences. Combined with theosophy, it gives us the innate transcendental knowledge of the spirit. Receiving divine revelations is the action that justifies the power of spirit and soul in our bioenergy field.

Ek zinda lash hi bata Saktee hain, zindagi ki sahi kimat. Aapki ruah aapki woh zindagi hain jisse aapney hi kabhi dabbba diya tha Kahin mitti ke taley.

It means a lifeless existence teaches us the true meaning of life. You buried the spirit of your soul under the superficial garbs of the material body for far too long.

Affirm- 'Namostutee, today I celebrate the death of all my weaknesses. All weaknesses within my system from many incarnations are totally, completely, and thoroughly removed. Tathaastu.'

CHAPTER 139

UNDOGLY DOG

A talking parrot is sitting inside of our throats. We sometimes blindfold it thinking that it would put an end to the constant bickering and repetitive chattering. But the internal chatter hardly ever ends because the parrot is inside of us. This internal intuitive voice speaks the truth. In all fairness, we don't like listening to the truth and so we end up speaking the lie. Animals know better than to lie or argue thus choosing not to speak. Only if we had such high standards of ethics, sincerity, and loyalty as the dogs and the cats, the world would be so much more truthful and just.

From the unbiased perspective of the higher beings, all sentient beings are the same. Just the way rich and poor is the same. Higher energies do not discriminate.

This chapter is in memory of the successful love story of my lucky dog, Duke.

It was when my Dad was serving in the defense forces stationed at *Barnala, Punjab* in India and we had two very lovely dogs- Rippy and Snippy. Snippy was blind and pregnant at the time when my dad broke the news of his move to New Delhi. Snippy sensed the anxiety and delivered three premature puppies in our laundry basket. One died shortly after birth because he got strangled in the clothes of the basket. The second puppy was too weak to make it and the third was my lucky pet dog 'Duke'. All this put Snippy in depression and so she refused to nurse or take care of Duke. He however survived perhaps because he had not yet done what he came here to do. We all have a true purpose and I believe that love is the purpose why we are here. When you will see it, you will recognize it in an instant because nothing you have ever felt beats that.

When Duke was about two years old, he got badly hit by a car because of our careless dog walker. We had to rush him for surgery. The doctors said he wouldn't make it and we should euthanize him. But we didn't and he made it and lived happy and healthy for as long as he wanted to. After his recovery, he developed a strange habit of praying in the little temple of our home, something he did right until his end!

In the next five dog years, he did mainly 'undogly' things and touched many hearts. I believe that we can recognize soulmates from previous birth when they meet us in the next. We all are motivated by love, avoidance of pain, or achieving bliss. The last being the highest of all three. Those who meet with bliss, meet with their twin soul. The meeting generates a flame within them which compels them to bind with their true soul. Something else is always calling the shots and are communicating through signs. As if by magic, we are drawn to our pair because it gives us our meaning.

I traveled to Dharamshala in Mcleodganj, India during my summer vacations just before my grade ten exams. I traveled there with my family and my dog by car. It is the land of the Dalai Lama and is filled with magic, spirituality, and mysticism. We lived at my aunt's home. This is the holiday where Duke met with the beautiful Jersey cow, the love of his life. They say someone out there is always listening so keep talking in whatever language you choose. He ate, drank, and played with the jersey cow all day long, and did not leave the sight of the cow during the entire summer. They obviously made a strange pair. True love is beyond the bounds of form. My dog seemed to have found his bliss, his twin soul. Soon, the summer vacations ended and it was time for us to leave. When we returned home, everything my dog had ever known became entirely irrelevant for him. He became disinterested in drinking, eating, or walking and spent hours sitting next to the temple inside our home in a position in which only cows can sit and not dogs.

I took him to the doctor and he showed no signs of fever or any ailment. He was healthy but when I looked into his eyes, I intuitively felt that the soul connection he had with my aunt's Jersey cow was far bigger than any other, he had ever felt. That meeting was life-changing for him- he had found his purpose and was ready for evolution. I was guided to bring a huge container full of fresh milk which he gulped down in no time after a weeklong fast. That was the last meal he had at our home. My family was happy he finally had something in his system and was recovering. They had no clue it was his last meal. I told my parents that they will find our dog an hour later, sitting by the temple in his new favorite position and I left. His heart was with the Jersey cow. I knew an hour later he would leave his body to merge his spirit with his beloved. One year passed and we went to visit our aunt again. The jersey cow was still there, this time she was pregnant. I knew she was carrying the soul energy of my dog in her womb.

If you are lucky, sometimes you will meet with souls you have known for long. And if you are luckier, you will connect with your twin. And if that happens, even death cannot stop you. That is when the magic begins and true transmutation occurs. And you too will become a divine conduit of peace, forgiveness, compassion, faith, and contentment.

Love is an intense positive feeling involving our soul, all our five senses, and beyond. Love can be with an endless number of people, things, and fantasies, and with its power, you can surpass all boundaries.

My dog's name is Vicki. Vicki is an amazing dog. She can stay without a walk all day but if you do choose to take her for a walk, it has to be on her terms, not yours. She refuses to walk in the direction you choose for her. She leads and you follow. She says, "You chose to take me for a walk. You voluntarily chose to give me your time. This time, therefore, is mine and I lead it". No matter how much you try, she sits down and doesn't budge until you walk her on her terms. She is a perfect example of a dog who is gentle yet firm and assertive. Forcing your dog to walk on the path you choose or plan is disregardful, insensitive, and insensible. Unless the journey ahead is unsafe, it is better we initially let them have the time we give them and let them lead on their terms. This way we build a rapport of mutual trust, loyalty, and wonderment. Walking a dog is a great emotional exercise. It tests your leadership skills. Slowly as the bond between master and dog grows fonder, a time comes when the master and the dog being fully present at the moment, joyfully walk in the same direction. This way the two mutually discipline each other in a harmonious, understanding, and affectionate way- without any harshness, imbalance, or resistance.

My observations on the subtle divine energy of dogs I healed over the years -

Dog's causal bodies are very bright. Their astral and emotional body is very sensitive. They are very loving, forgiving and they live in the now. This makes their aura size fluctuate based on outside energies. Their mental aura is hardly seen clearly. They don't have solar astral but have lunar astral bodies. Their lunar mental body is clearly visible. Their etheric and astral fields are really bright. Dogs don't have chakras but have dainty centers.

Unlike the life stages of humans, as is mentioned in the chapter "Egg came first", dogs have physical, then etheric followed by astral bodies. However, they do not have a strong "I am" or ego body – which implies their mental/ emotional body is merged with their astral body. Dogs happily and almost unconsciously shake to cleanse and energize themselves. As they do so - their force of love and devotion increases. Dogs dig for grounding and for activating paw centers. Their sweat glands are in their paw pads. Their energy field is usually much wider than humans. Because of their natural survival instinct, their aura tends to absorb much more sensory information than humans. Each of their dainty centers has an individual identity in a way. They receive and distribute energy through these individual centers, making them more sensitive to the subtle vibrations and changes within the atmosphere or environment. In four-legged animals, the main difference is that the alignment and chakra positions are often horizontal instead of vertical. The size of their aura usually changes as per the dog's size and breed, except in very rare cases.

Affirm- 'Namostutee, I am a trailblazer of the path to higher consciousness. Supported by the higher soul, I gratefully and magically align myself to the pure vision and magnified intellectual awareness of the new world. Tathaastu.'

CHAPTER 139a

HUMAN BATTERIES

Even in a new phone, the batteries need to be charged for long hours before it can be brought to use. With every new morning our body transitions like this phone that is ready for use, only if it is charged with proper sleep. A weak battery will soon die so strengthen your batteries through proper breathing. The moment old batteries are replaced with new ones within the old body of your smartphone, it gets a new life.

Two apples - one red and one green, both were prohibited. However, upon eating the first, we realize that one apple a day keeps the doctor away and so it is good for health. Eating two is even better for physical or mental health depending on which one we are eating. Eating three keeps your body lean and healthy and so is eating four. Eating five works well too. But, if we go on overeating then that exact thing that was good for your overall health starts to work against you and becomes your poison.

The apple was prohibited because God knew that only then can we someday learn to put a limitation upon our consumption. This is through moderation and avoiding the poison of over-expenditure.

When we use currency – we would need both paper bills and coins. Inversely a credit card can be used for any denomination without us fishing for bills and coins. The usage of cards though comes at a risk. Risk of usage, over usage, and misuse. Bills and coins provide the touch and feel and hence the gravity of the amount being spent unlike just swiping the card for any amount that is per your limit. This is the purchasing power that is in your hands which can be used instantly.

Our bodies have three sides – electric, neutral, and magnetic side. Similarly, the credit card also has the same sides. The electric side is the front of the card, the magnetic stripe being the back of the card and the neutral side being what you see from the top. On your credit card, your expenses are based on the credit limit you have. How much you can spend is decided by how much you payback. Your expenditure and your payment are interconnected. The middle path on your expense and saving decides what you can potentially gain value for your asset. This middle path is the conversion or neutral side. The neural side is the conversion side which charges and recharges based on value and expenditure.

Keeping a balance between the magnetic pull (of spending) and push (of incurring untold debts) is as difficult for you as it was for Adam to not eat the prohibited fruit. However, hidden between the two sides of the credit card, is a subtle message by the yin energies telling you to be awake, alert, save and think before expending, overspending, and expanding. A boon can become a curse if we let ourselves be hypnotized.

Positive solar light on your left, negative lunar love on your right - twist and twine to stop your frailties from fraying. Taking the first two alphabets of the word solar and lunar- "so" and the palindrome of lu which is "ul"- together are the cause of your "soul" power. Their bond keeps our soul comfortably wrapped up. As long as your soul is powered with its energy, you remain empowered. Let us appreciate the makers of your soul for all their hard work.

The way electricity is needed to switch on any machine. Same way, electricity is needed to switch on the nervous system of our body which sends electric currents in our body and brain optimally. The electricity in our body is charged with elements such as magnesium, calcium, potassium, and sodium which are in our body. The interior and exterior cell flow is triggered with the negative and positively charged ions. Our thoughts, intentions, reactions, and actions collectively affect the movement of these electric currents. We are capable of lighting up a flashlight with the heat generated by our bodies. The same way a vitalized healer can light up the flow of energy into another human with the warmth radiating out of the body. In this way, we are capable of becoming better transformers of energy.

When we take halfhearted action, our electric and magnetic side of the body does not get fully charged. This causes restlessness, dullness, and a feeling of incompleteness. The insightful information in this book will brighten up and activate your energy centers.

Affirm- 'Namostutee, Only a charged up battery can give power to another. My battery is charged up with spirituality and vitality through conductivity. This way I can share Lords power and yet remain strong and charged up. Tathaastu.'

CHAPTER 140

LIGHT IN THE GAPS OF TRAPPED THOUGHTS

S hed unnecessary desires. Do not let your light get trapped in feelings of lack, hate, revenge, and control. Allow positive ideas and ambitions to take form. Merge with the infinite and true pure love. Sometimes you unknowingly stop yourself from seeing the divine goodness, when it is right there in front of you.

Do not let the darkness in you sabotage your life. Why stay unhealed. Instead, continue to do your work to uplift yourself and others. Bring an unbelievable level of fulfillment and success in answering your soul's calling with your newly healed self. Embrace your power in relationships and sexuality. You are truly empowered, juicy, spicy, available, and connected. So bring out these qualities which are you. Do not be covetous of another. Fulfill your expectations and promises. Not only is it important to start out a winner but to end up a winner too. No matter how many mistakes you may have made, there are more chances to make amends.

Let go of the past apprehensions or problems that are holding you back. By all means, move away from them in order to be free and at peace but remember to look back once before you leave so that you do not forget to carry the past few sweet memories kept in the treasure box. Remember to kiss (keep it sanctified and sacred) and send lots of 'kisses' - 'keep it simple, sincere and extremely sprightly'. However swiftly you may leave, all I ask of you is please never leave with any bitterness in your heart.

A person in excessive hate sees a lot of takers and no givers. A person in excessive love sees a lot of givers and no takers. Balance your energies to keep the relationship of love and take in equilibrium.

Do not fail because of devious procedures, tests, trials, or tactics. Why wait? Complete the unfinished threads of work. Do not chase the next thing that raises your adrenaline. Although you may well be the social butterfly with numerous connections, remember to benefit from seeking more internal peace and balance. You have the heightened attributes to be an explorer, with the vigor needed to encounter and breakthrough to the new, to find something completely unknown. The effect of your balanced, creative energies is breathtaking. Here is an opportunity for you to grab, which will bring you deep stability, roundedness, centeredness, and unshakeable confidence.

Repugnance blinds you, agitation and insecurity steal your mental clarity. Miscommunication and half-baked information tear the essence of trust in relationships.

NASA and *SpaceX* have gone on a mission to search for life and oxygen to other planets like Mars. Whereas we have opened oxygen bars on earth. We have trapped the free flow of air in our own planet by polluting it with our insatiable, ungrateful greed for control and power. In this quest of trying to trap the thought behind the idea, man has lost all perspective. Pure air is pure spirit and if we cage its natural openness then the beauty and soul of everything that you see around will be lost and shattered forever. Pure air is invincible, unbound, free, sensitive, and pristine. It is the supreme spirit and by caging and tampering with it, we are caging ourselves.

Heighten your spirit to greater levels. Think before acting. Pause before thinking. Pause your breath for a minimum of three counts in between inhalation and exhalation and then you will begin to understand and value heaven where you truly belong. I live in the now. The visible will return to the invisible when it is time to transform and recreate. I am the theory behind the practice, the vibratory force will restart and reverse before it restarts another cycle. Remove your ego, Raise your vibrations and your consciousness. Space, time, and negative thoughts are just mental images in your mind. Let go and change your reality, create a new thought, the one is in all but each one has it all.

Media is a mirror and if the mirror is fogged with so much negativity and pain it is time to clean up the dust and fog that is redefining our truth. We are the reflection of the mirror and sometimes it is us that need to change for the better in order to look better in the mirror. Disconnect yourself from outer noises and listen to your body. Take a break when it is time. Celebrate each day as the day when you witnessed the realization that beyond shame and embarrassment you are not a female or a male. You are not the image in the mirror for you are the pure untainted image of the spirit.

You have no realization of dreams when you are awake. Your waking life has now become like a fuzzy dream because your reality is in a place beyond the reach of this limited physical body. In order to be truly awakened, always be alert, attentive, vitalized, and actively present.

This way you will become like that unstoppable light of the sun that never stops shining whether it reflects through the moon or on its own. A true listener is always open and receptive, turning away from all that is deceptive.

Once you are consistent with your practice, you feel the blessings, but sometimes you still face obstacles and challenges. This is because the energy beings that are working through you need you to proactively physicalize and actualize the knowledge you have gained, by deeper understanding and resolve. This process requires crystallization of your profound thought forms with simple clarity. Our heightened soul is an extension of us. It is pure and true, but it is not perfect, nor is it the perfected one. For example, your nose in itself seems like it is nothing. It's only when it can smell that it becomes fully activated and you realize its complete existence.

The first memory of yourself takes you to the presence of your reincarnated ego. You are the sun. You are the tree that gives shade. You are the light and shade that give love and comfort to anybody and everybody who comes your way. You bless everyone. You are a welcoming channel with no resistance or judgment. In giving yourself up completely, you truly learn to give.

Love, affection, acceptance, and kindness is quintessential in a nurturing relationship. If you feel neglected or abused on any of these levels, then force yourself to learn to be self-independent. However, remember that just because you didn't receive the acceptance, care, and nurturing you deserved does not imply that you should block and stop yourself from giving a listening ear and a cozy hug to those in need. This way, your biggest disadvantage can become your advantage. Instead of swimming in a pool of poison and pain because of your past, you must learn to mitigate the pain. Ease the torment of those trapped under similar situations of neglect and resentment.

Sometimes we go too far. You don't have to dig a hole in the head to know that your brain has a heartbeat. We get it that certain experiences are beyond the scope of scientific understanding and that is completely ok. Between these gaps, your mind is in a blank, thoughtless and free state. These gaps and pauses help rejuvenate and relax us. Whatever name, gender, or religion you may worship the supreme formless God always answers the prayers of true devotees and graces them with their presence.

Affirm- 'Namostutee, I trust you, I am with my parents, in the womb of my desires waiting to actualize through them. And as you affirm this repeatedly, you will find yourself centered back again where you truly belong. Tathaastu.'

CHAPTER 141

RIDE ON

When you see bicycles riding in the air, you know it is time to ride with the joyful flow of the air. In order to live life to the fullest, you simply need to be in a joyful state at all times.

Our life stories are the sum total of the high and low points of our lives. But the essence of our life lies in realizing the high points within the so-called imaginary low points. It is then that we have an encounter with life itself. This is the ultimate truth.

We experience the visible world through our existence in linear time which is as stiff as an arrow. We experience the invisible world through our existence in lateral, eternal time which is as malleable as air. The resultant or incidental reality is parallel to our immediate or primary reality.

Between the linear and the lateral, we keep circling until we transcend all opposites and experience oneness. Something like a ceiling fan, fidget spinner toy, and a cycle wheel that completely transforms when it smoothly moves from the static state into a high rotational state. When it moves swiftly and optimally, we can hardly differentiate between the linear and the lateral.

The masculine and the feminine unite just like dreams and reality. Earth, therefore, is a dream that we live. Our reality is elsewhere. Our mortal body is a cross that circles for eons until we realize the two lines in the cross are united and one. This my friend is the enlightening experience that is talked about by mystics. It is our onset into another higher realm of existence and evolution.

Life is much like riding a bicycle. When you go uphill, you have to exhale all feelings of discomfort. When you come downhill, you have to inhale as much energy as is comfortable. We push ourselves while we ascend. We pull the breaks while we descend to keep control of our speed lest we fall. Between the constant cycle of exhalation and inhalation, pushing and pulling - if there is anything that keeps us going it is our higher mind that has an innate ability to keep a leash on us. It helps us discipline, control, and maintain our inner order within despite the outer chaos. It makes you meet the real you.

When we descend from the hill, sitting on our bicycle, we are as if in a free fall into the future. We pass through the turns, twists, and tunnels. We don't know where we are headed but we do know that it is a lot of fun. Sometimes, when we find pebbles and ditches on the path, the fun changes into fear. Our main task is to convert that fear into courage and anxiety into faith. It is then that we meet with heaven on earth. We effortlessly lift our heads and enjoy the expansive view of the limitless sky. With that shift in perspective, we partner with the tall trees, birds, green grass, fresh air, little drops of rain trickling down, and everything around. Our heartbeat becomes one with the beat of bountiful nature. This my friend is the meaning of being alive.

Bicycling and Canoeing teach us how to humble ourselves. It is like a vessel in which we communicate with our ancestors, with the water, with the land, and in this way, we see life from a different perspective. Whatever material position we may hold, we are very small in front of the mighty Lord and so we must offer our services to the bountiful nature and help one another. Our ultimate goal is to share the wealth of riches we possess and also the knowledge we have and break through stereotypes.

Life is an adventure where there is always some treasure you could find just around the corner.

Affirm- 'Namostutee, I enjoy the adventure and surprise that life brings. Tathaastu.'

CHAPTER 142

UNIVERSAL LIBRARY

S pirtually heightened beings gain the ability to access the library of Akashic records.

You do not have to die in order to know your past, present, and future in a matter of seconds. On February 9, 2020 - I reached a library of wisdom in my fully conscious state. All Akashic records were open and crystal clear in this library. It was my 16th wedding anniversary and I felt that all sixteen main elements of my body rose to subtly make me meet with the intricate details of the pattern, purpose, lessons, relationships, situations, and design of my entire being over the past, present, and future through the akashic records or energetic database which is stored in the universal supercomputer accessed by the higher mental planes.

The energy you send out is the energy you receive. If you send love, you receive love. If you send suspicion and doubt then that is what you receive. If you send thoughts of money and fame then that is what you receive. If you send thoughts of helping humanity through service, writing, earning fame, prosperity, productivity, discipline, balance, focus, healing, or whatever you may desire - the messages you send out, you are sure to receive at a faster rate in this higher mental plane thereby helping you achieve your true potential.

Be aware of each realm, during each dream of your conscious, subconscious, and unconscious state. When our soul is aware and conscious, we always exist in one or the other plane, in one or the other form, nothing is ever lost, and it is just a matter of time before we are found yet again.

The energy center of the throat chakra has 16 petals. The atomic number of Sulfur is 16. Sulfur (s) is pure soul.

A pure soul is never at war, it simply performs its role and duty. It is astrally guided by its graceful spirit. It is always balanced, harmonized, joyful, forgiving, pious, blatant, honest, peaceful, helpful, cooperative, spirited, and filled with stark light and love. They spread the wisdom of their light and celestial love to teach all souls that the spirit is one. We all are a united force, attachment to yours and mine is sheer ignorance. Whatever you have acquired, you are bound to leave behind, only to meet with it once again, perhaps centuries later, if your grit, fate, and luck permits. Only to lose it once again.

The fluidity of water, the flow of air, the lightness of sand, the invisibility of sun rays - all tell us of the true power of being forever open to change, evolvement, and spiritual philosophies. Accepting all, negating none, taking what you like, leaving what you don't, wherever you may run, when you will return, whenever that may be, you will find everything exactly where you left it, in just the same way that you did, nothing is ever lost, we all are one and united in a singular spirit. All the thieves and the kings are but one.

The one who tells you not to cry over spilled milk is also crying over his. What teacher can truly teach without being a preacher of his precepts? Learn to trust yourself first and then think of trusting another. Only the one who is kind to himself can truly be kind to another.

Every act of mercy, goodness, and kindness and your every genuine intention has been well noted in the Akashic records. Nothing is hidden, nothing is lost, everything one has, belongs to all, it is just a matter of time. All the wisdom and all the riches will be enjoyed one by one by everyone based on their readiness, progress, self-evolution, understanding, and disposition. Inherently we all are divine humans, waiting to realize the divinity within ourselves to move beyond our humaneness and evolve into becoming more complete, supercharged, and a powerful race.

The Dutch hexagrams, the Hindu *rangolis*, the Buddhist mandala art, the Islamic tile patterns-all these have been trying to tell us the true meaning of the universal language of love, light, and power.

The file of life: Your life is nothing more than a file in the universal pages of time. You can meet with timelessness anytime and choose to get your file read or better still you can mould a renewed life by letting go off things from the old file that has caught dust and mold. I[122] can help you

---

[122] *I implies 'empty consciousness has a library within which universal data exists'.*

access either of the two - old file to visit the past, new life erasing all past or renewed life by removing all past dust, keeping only the interesting parts from the file of your life - the choice is yours.

Affirm- 'Namostutee, I am intuitive, enlightened, inspiring, and encouraging. Tathaastu.'

CHAPTER 143

PRECIOUS BAG OF SWEETS

To not see the beauty is but a painful sterility. Your true test lies in not letting this unwholesome thought hinder your energy and sanity. Mistakes happen so that you can learn from them not to make you feel bad. They are here to help you reflect, rethink and act. Your mistakes are your assets, your guides, your privilege, and your reflection. Learn from them as they are here to tell you how not to repeat them. They are not here to tell you to fall prey to them again. These mistakes never put you down for they are your true strengths. Others who put you down thrive on your weakness. Do not give them more power than they deserve either negative or positive.

You attract what you pay attention to. Being known is useless unless you know the ultimate knower. Behind the incessant resistance is the seed of complete acceptance and undying faith.

Do not let your emotions take over your mind or your mind take over your emotions. Stay away from any extremes. Let the divine fire burn away your weakness. Be receptive, be open. After sadness, comes joy. Have hope, trust, and faith. Learn from our mother, the moon, who is perennially receptive to the active fatherly energy of the sun. Learn and look at how the moon's receptivity lights up the entire sky when it gets dark.

See how it is always smiling even in the darkest hours. After the greatest crisis comes the ultimate opportunity. Dissolve your limitations and trepidation to achieve phenomenal stability and balance. Undo the knots and play the game of today. Tomorrow another player will join in.

Today is only your chance to meet and learn from this experience. It is in dying of your old ways of living that you are peacefully born again to a new life. The time to manifest your good intentions is now. There are many things in life we are not legally bound to give or give back but ethically we are and so keep your morals in check, do the right thing.

The one who complains about another is not complaining about you but has forgotten his true self and does not know what has become of him.

Other than creating a life, we also can heal and save lives. Why not use that innate gift that we all have within us. Everyone goes through their struggles and pains. The cause and experiences are subjective and so comparisons are futile. We must be kind, generous, and judgment-free because we never know what others are going through. We must accept and forgive. There are no rights and wrongs. Teach only what you preach. Don't give power to anyone to make you feel weak and terrible. As long as you are doing your best you are right to ignore all the rest.

It is a new world order, a new beginning, and new freedom - freedom from the dualities within you. Big ideas are inspired by little ones. It is from these little things that big things come. Clearing off past and present residue, helps you create a better future for yourself and those around you in this circle of life. As long as you put out the clear intention to be more persistent, nurturing, responsible, strong, healthy, grounded, positive, and adaptable- you will sail through the tests of life smoothly and get many opportunities to complete what you started. You are important only because you treat life and its manifestations importantly.

In one of my mountaineering trips to the Uttarakhand Mountains, I was once sitting on the edge of a bench enjoying the pristine view. I was tired of carrying the heavy rucksack on my back and so I removed the weight as I sat down on a bench nearby. The views evoked ecstatic feelings within me. Amongst the mountains, someone is always looking out for you. The patrol leader suddenly came and broke my trance. He asked me to get up at once. I was so busy looking ahead that I was foolishly oblivious of what or who was behind me.

As I got up on the command of the leader, my bag slipped from the bench and went straight down the side and into the river.

The Ganges River emanates from the mountains. The point of initiation of this river is called 'Gaumukh'. Along the path, as the ice melts, the river meets millions of tourists who throng to wash their sins in the river. The patrol leader told me that one of the mountaineers recently fell from the very same place. The reason for the accident was the weight of the rucksack that she was carrying. I was lucky as my bag was not that heavy. Always remember to look behind and look around for deep falls before you start to look forward and try to stand tall.

By realizing how deep your body could have fallen along with the currents of the flowing river, you will not only remember to thank the patrol leader who saved your life. But you will also remember to realize the frailties of life and the transitoriness of the heavyweights we carry. In order to be able to penetrate the deeper mysteries, you must abandon your ego and the attachment you have to your habits and vices. Eliminate the non-essential. This way with time your life will be healthier, more productive filled with love and prosperity.

Carrying the weight of responsibilities upon your shoulders is a privilege. Responsibilities are given to only a few. The lucky donkey needs to stop making a sorry picture. You are lucky that you can carry the weight of others, unlike the million others who do not have the strength.

Our mind is crowded and congested with so much mental clutter or mental chatter that we are unable to look at the actual situation. Some of the greatest masters, politicians, and gurus senselessly compete with one another to attract followers because of their insecurity around losing power they have been holding onto all along. They teach of love but their version of love is distorted under the garb of wanting to control. Knowledge and wisdom are truly possessed by the one who is free of any such pride and load. Such a person makes choices based on their self-discriminatory mind. Such a person knows that others are seated upon the throne only because the rest of us put them upon on that pedestal. Today is their turn, tomorrow will be another's. The more we hold on, the more we lose, degenerate, and destroy what we built so beautifully.

Congestion and repression both are the cause of all major ailments. If your soul feels repressed then break the stone walls that are placed upon you, even if it feels like you are walking on fire as *Mata Sita*[123] did. Out of the well of emotions and hot coals of fire, your feet will miraculously greet and meet with your true self.

I know God is always there for us and is the giver of our life. When I was living in Oman, I heard a whispering voice in my sleep coming from the right one night. I knew it was the voice of God. I saw a white bright light shining in the room that said, "I need your help" - I wrote whatever

---

[123] *Sita - Indian goddess who walked on flames of blazing pyre to prove her purity and loyalty towards her husband, Lord Rama.*

that voice said in the dark, don't know what and why. It felt relaxing and positive listening to the divine voice from the inner world and so I spent many nights scribbling notes in the dark. The next thing the voice told me is that you promise me that you have to continue helping me revive the lost art. Sounded like he-art. I was also told a time will come when I will be asked to give messages of truth at an ordained period to certain people. I never read what the voice-guided me to write. I kept those notes in my bag and called them my precious bag of sweets. The light never spoon-fed me with the exact time and so I remained silently sweet. I recently felt the presence of God's light enveloping me all around. God selflessly solves any threat we may encounter and loves us unconditionally.

Affirm- 'Namostutee, True beauty, vitality, self-enlightenment, spirituality, strength, and excitement are all within me. I have achieved all my aspirations. I am infinitely healed, fulfilled, fortunate, grateful, and perennially successful. I am prosperous, powerful, blissful, and shielded. I am abundant, wealthy, healthy, wise, loving, and worthy. Tathaastu.'

CHAPTER 144

BAREFOOTED JOURNEY

The higher beings are always watching over us and they send invisible helpers to help us in times of need. There are many examples of alcoholics who have had no clue how they reached home safely. People have come out alive from the most dangerous road accidents despite having absolutely no memory of what happened. Let us thank that force who is forever protecting and blessing us selflessly and supporting us in times of need.

There is an electric field that surrounds the earth and the human consciousness. These invisible beings are always watching over us from that field. We humans do not perceive reality the way they do because we have limited ourselves. Oftentimes when we have nothing left to give is when we call upon faith. Maybe that is the reason challenges come into our life so that we can once again learn to believe and have faith in our gifts. The gift was endowed to us by higher invisible powers.

I am a meticulous form of my miraculous existence. The invisible subtle force behind the visible glamour. Love is precious and to know its true worth, we need to know we are gifted. We all are gifted with it, some know its value some still don't. Finally, all will know in unison.

One in seven accidents happens by sleepy drivers. I was seven when a bus accident happened that taught me some wonderful secrets of life. We were stationed in a place called *Barnala, Punjab in* India. We were shifting our base because my father was to resume duty in New Delhi. On the day we left the station, it was raining heavily. The Air Force bus in which we were headed to our new home was filled with passengers. It strangely overturned several times and fell into a deep valley because the driver fell asleep. This incident haunted me for several years post that. Most of us cannot imagine ever going through such a devastating experience. It stunned everyone to see the bus was in ruins with shattered glass everywhere. Yet surprisingly, we came out without getting any major injuries. The steering wheel came out into the driver's hand. All the passengers were miraculously saved. Amongst the passengers was a newlywed couple who lost all the ancestral jewels and money they were carrying as their handbag flew out of the window. My dad tightly held my mum and stood strong upside down as he locked his arms and legs and took a stance he learned during his Air Force training. My sister and I were barefoot sitting with our feet up at the time when the incident took place. I was crying before leaving the place we were stationed in, not only because I was sad leaving my childhood behind. But because I was leaving behind my two dogs, *Rippy* and *Snippy* who grew up with me and became an important part of my life. Their little puppy, *Duke*, was traveling with us. He was hardly a few days old snuggled in my lap at the time of the incident and he was small and tender like a soft cotton ball. As the bus overturned, I flew as if I became weightless and hit the exit door of the bus, but I did not let go of *Duke*.

I landed in between the creases of the side steps of the bus. My neck naturally turned inside like a turtle and my body rolled into a perfect circle. I felt as if an angel came and placed me in a comfortable, cozy position. The bus finally stopped rolling as an electric pole came in between and with its pressure, the bus hung in the middle of the valley. Despite the horrific accident, there was not a single death and the injuries that passengers incurred were not very grave. There was a *Gurudwara* nearby. It is a temple of worship. The *guru* (saint) of the *Gurudwara* came with a team to rescue the passengers and gave everyone first aid, shelter, and care. The guru carefully scanned the entire bus from outside. By now the bus that was hanging on a pole was further losing its balance. Every passenger, other than me was out. No one found me. I was barefoot, hidden under a suitcase with my little puppy. I had no clue of what was happening outside, but strangely I felt so comfortable that I was in no fear whatsoever, despite being in the odd suspended circumstance. The bus moved a little further as if to purposely shake off the suitcase lying upon my body. I didn't even have to lift that small little boulder. The bus stopped briefly. I stood up in the silence. At that moment, as I was up, there were broken pieces of glass all around and I had no choice but to walk on them barefoot and so I did with not a single tear in my eye.

Broken glass on my path got crushed into small pieces of dust and yet my feet remained unhurt. I walked through the inverted front window of the bus unhurt and without even a single scratch on my dainty body and feet. I fell in the lap of someone from the rescue team who was standing below as I reached the edge. I was petting my little, pure, white fluffy dog when one of the elder Sikh gurus looked towards me and said, "There is some saintly soul in this bus who has committed no crime and is born for a higher divine mission." He continued saying that, "this being is born with absolutely no previous karmic obligation. It is because of this innocent being that you all are saved. This being is pure from another realm, meant to do something big here on earth and the presence of this being has resulted in saving you all. As long as that being is with you, you all are protected." I was too little at the time to make sense of it all. But, the incident made me conclude on two things. First, I started calling Duke, my 'lucky dog' ever since. Second, there is God in everything and always watching over us. There is a famous Punjabi proverb. "*Jaake raakhe saaiyan, Maar sake na koi, baal na baank kar sake jo jag beri hoy*" which translates, "the one saved by God cannot be killed by anyone. Even if the whole world turns out to be its enemy, they cannot bend even a single strand of his hair."

Paranormal experiences are normal experiences for those who have them. They are as real to them as your reality is to you. For example, some say *Baba Harbajan Singh* in India is still guarding the Indo-China borders over fifty years after his death. He was a soldier in the army, who died while saving the borders. The soldiers fighting on the borders have built a temple in his name. Even now he gives them important divine messages. Those who have found the way out of this jungle must show the way out to others, traveling alone in any empty terrain is no fun.

I walked barefoot along the beach. I noticed footprints on the sand but there was only one print and that was mine. And so I returned to walk with you. This way we can leave not just one or two but many more footprints on the sand of time. I kept my part of the promise and returned for you, now you keep your promise and walk the path through the waters. For nothing can drown you when your feet are naked. I call it the realization of this moment - the un-shoed moment upon the shore.

Affirm- 'Namostutee I am here to pull souls back to their feet with the breath of fresh and fragrant air. Tathaastu.'

CHAPTER 145

BIRTH & DEATH OF THE RED TREE

We celebrate our birthdays even though we draw closer to death with each day, with every new step taken on every new birthday of fresh beginnings. This is because we also become wiser with every new step. It is wise to diligently follow the path of righteousness. Any distraction on the path of righteousness is a diversion. Every distressing emotion is a digression and diversion that decreases your life span and chances to achieve moksha and complete awareness. It is therefore liberating to take wise, wakeful steps despite the initial difficulties.

This topic is purposely not the last chapter or the last page of this book. This is because death is not the end but a new sweet beginning where we recognize and acknowledge the intensity of the finished artwork. Death can lead to a beautiful and more fulfilled birth. I was out for a walk and read a profound caption under a tree that was immortalized and given a renewed meaning as it was painted all red by my artist neighbor friend outside her home garden. The below quote inspires us to respect the purity and beauty of death and accept the change and blessings that come with it.

The caption under the painted red tree read:

"RED DOGWOOD"

"We commemorate the life of this beautiful dogwood tree, which died this past year. By painting it red, we have given this beautiful tree an extended life.
Life and death here complement each other through beauty.

Died in 2018"

Just as the red mysterious tree- if we all too embrace and coat the truth and peace that death brings with equal dynamism and passion-Our life too will be truly free, fearless, worry-less, blissful, and transformed. Let us give ourselves a chance to creatively paint our lives by living the truth of our purpose. We pick up our evolution from where we left off. Just as we pick up our life from our death. Life is an experience that helps us evolve. Death is not the end of the story but the beginning of yet another. Omega and alpha are one.

Death sounds uncomfortable, but it is human, and so it is mentionable. And because it is mentionable, it is manageable. Whatever we resist, tends to persist. We resist suffering and so it persists. What we hate, we tend to attract. We hate death, illness, and suffering, and so we attract death and hardship.

We hear of *babas* that are here one moment and then gone the next, simply because you see them with your spiritual eyes open and do not see them when your eyes are closed. However, I had the strangest experience in one of my visits to a secluded *ashram* uphill in India. I met a *yogini*, we both couldn't understand the language we spoke but I strangely invited her over for a chat at my *kutiya (hut)*. She insisted that she wanted to sit outside and suddenly two chairs appeared from nowhere. As if that was not strange enough, she signaled that I will be getting a headache soon and she would like to do a healing on me to cut my cords. I happily allowed her to work on me. I saw her working on me with my half-opened eyes. She sat at a distance of 12 feet from me when she started the healing. She flew like a monkey, oscillating in all four directions around me. The distance kept increasing and decreasing, she hopped to the edge of the pavement and sometimes on the roof of the hut. I thought to myself, the room would have been really small for her swift and strange healing ways. My eyes rolled so much that evening that my inner eye got fully activated and yes she was right, I sure did get a headache. I was so tired by the end of it that I slept for hours like a baby. The next day, when I went inquiring about her whereabouts to thank her, she was nowhere to be found. I was told, no such person fit the description.

Nothing lasts forever. The Buddhist mandalas, the Legos our children play with, the flowers growing outside- tell us that time and tide wait for no one. We know the average age of mortality so please calculate how many years you have left. You will know how little time is left so please practice what you have learned here so that you can evolve and enter the higher heavens, beyond the astral world.

Life post-death is a continuity of your present life. Death is only the cessation from bodily pain, bondage, and suffering. Some dead people, therefore, are more youthful and free energetically than a person living in stagnated energy of pain because death is the cessation of pain. Let's master the art of dying while we are still living in order to become more youthful, liberated, pain-free, and soul realized through higher intuition.

Suicide is a crime. The one who takes away his life is defying God. Escapists end up suffering more later. Struggles we undergo help us evolve. As time fades, so do we. Without time, our bodies do not exist but we do. We are not just our bodies and so we never really die.

We are frightened of death because we do not want to let go of our mental or physical possessions. To live is to allow death to happen - allow endings to take place. This is the only way new beginnings are ever possible. A life of freedom is a life of love. Love is not about attachment, jealousy, or burdens. True love gives you space to grow and to be who you want to be. Medical science has progressed to such an extent that human life expectancy is increasing. We must make a more productive growth.

We were healing one such case of Covid. The diseased was an over 95-year-old patient with congestive heart failure, lung damage, diabetes, hepatitis, bipolar, chronic body pain, acute depression, osteoporosis, and was put on machines and morphine to survive. Resources and time were spent on the patient's treatment. In such cases, I suggest simply sending healings and blessings to do the last prayers and release the poor soul of bodily and psychological suffering so that the transition is smooth and calm. Where is our common sense headed? We are left with no courage to embrace the death of our loved ones and so we hold on to what is long gone. I believe that putting wires on almost dead energy to extend life is creating more suffering for someone you love and isn't such control the opposite of love? However, there are exceptions like, history has proven that there are some people who live a long healthy lifespan while remaining vitalized even up to the age of 125 years and beyond and such *Pranic* or life force energy indeed adds to the overall health of etheric energy of the earth.

Death is like the freedom you feel when you cease to rely on your gadgets and your senses. Death is like an unbound uncontrolled light in the darkness. Have you ever thought that if the secret of creation is truly and completely unveiled - then how come there remains an air of mystery around the cycle of life and death?

Truth is sacred and no secret can ever reveal the full knowledge of truth until you are ready. To get ready for it you have to be virtuous, purified, and receptive.

The heir to the throne is never the true king. What you see and believe is far from reality. Your beliefs are a mere reflection of the truth. Bliss lies in between the reality that you have been hiding from for so long. No wonder, it is in between the sheets that all the magic happens.

One person dying doesn't mean we should all die a slow death, mourning for him. Let others live; only then his life will be revived. For if all die, there will be no life energy left to come back yet again. Life is short and each moment must be savored. Celebrate life. Be and let be. Remember to encourage each person who is trying to live, for living life is more difficult than dying every moment. Speaking your truth is more difficult than telling your lie. Death is the easy way out; life is challenging. Death is lazy; life is active. To die is a living lie. Those who truly live are fighting a different war each day and coming out winners even when they fail. Complaining is easy. It is by living in your positive light despite all the dark forces of negativity, that your true willpower is invoked.

In Amritsar, India I found myself at the bedside of a dying person, helping him heal and release the attachment, pain, and trauma of the rational life. In Manhattan, New York, I then found myself at the bedside of another dying person, helping him forgive and let go of what he was holding on to. Both needed assurance; both needed to be consoled. No amount of medications, wealth, and treatments were helping, because they needed awareness to look at the blind spots they had been missing. I brought in that awareness through healing and they then witnessed spiritual wealth, freedom, abundance, and limitlessness. When they realized that all their lives they had been living with the limitation of their physical body and that there was so much more outside of what they had known so far, the craving to know that inner world drew them into becoming who and what they really wanted to become, even if it was in another stronger, far younger body. This way, they premeditated upon their goals while dying, before being reborn in a much calmer and informed way. Just as in our daily lives, we can control our dream by deciding what we want to focus on, and wake up the next morning to realize that dream into action. My internal guidance often comes back to me, and so do those two men from the inner world, to thank me for the wisdom and richness I shared with them, moving them out of the shackles of ignorance and spiritual poverty forever.

To have the awareness of your movement from right toe to left toe is like having the awareness of the workings of the subtle life to death. The inner wiring of the connectedness from the right shoulder to the left ear is like peacefully floating from north to south and east to west.

A baby's soul is already growing within the womb before the physical delivery. Your real birth is therefore at the time when the soul enters your body. Your current biological[124] birth is when your parents conceived you and the soul associated itself with the embryo and not at the time of your physical delivery or materialization.

Birthdate

Spirit age=date of birth (example 28, the number remains same except it leaps and retracts on leap years); Body age=year of birth (example 1979, changes every year);

Soul age = month of birth (example 5, the number remains same).

Body evolves, changes, progresses, and transmutes. Spirit changes and shifts to merge with the higher consciousness and relinks with the soul. Soul, while bonded in the body remains the same but gets purer with change. The body is an amalgamation of power, respect, and love. Some places are beyond the control of the mind, I love visiting those places from time to time. Some will transmute and then transport in, some will transport before transmuting, but all that is here are destined to enter

---

[124] *For example, the Birthday of a person born on 19 July 2006 is around October 28, 2005*

the much-awaited golden gate. I stand there with the welcome group to celebrate your entry. Just accept the invitation well in time.

When we look at things this way, we see that it is not the physical body creating the energy field (the aura), but rather the aura or energy field that is creating the physical body. What we see as the physical body is the result of a process that begins with consciousness.

In just the way that we make choices where, how, and when to live. We can make choices where, how, and when to die. The way life is planned, death too can be planned. We have a choice to either be born into a different body or be reborn into the same body. The choice depends on our mental, physical resilience and courage in the face of terror.

Sometimes when we die, just at the last minute of the death, we remember our birth. To understand our present birth we can reflect on our past life. Live and enjoy your life, because life will be over before you know it.

When death comes closer, even if it is purely mental, how each person approaches it and how they communicate the news to others tells a lot about their personality and where they will go from here. We handle situations differently and death is no different. Some fear it and some instill fear through it. Some embrace it and some instill acceptance in others through it. Some get hopeful and some instill inspiration in others. Whatever approach you may adopt. The death of self or your loved one is bound to steer your psyche even if it is just imagined in the mind and not physically impacted you yet (executed).

Imagine death or receiving fake news of a dear one's death or any loss. It is bound to create some reaction and response within you. How you respond to the news defines whether you are gullible and weak or a strong seeker of truth. In any time of crisis, there are two types of people - one cry and the others fly. Those who cry look for solutions outside of themselves and those who fly calmly become the solution themselves. Eventually, everything is within you. How you respond makes all the difference. Life and death are like two sides of the same coin and the person tossing the coin is always you. Death is a liberation, not a limitation. This pandemic will bring us out of the fear of death, collectively towards freedom and liberation, to a point where we all feel the power and oneness of soul consciousness. When we leave our body and die, even without the anatomical structure (head, heart, organs, skin, etc.) we remain in the ether and with the aid of our higher senses, we can live though not in a bodily form.

When a child is born, he is crying while all others are smiling. When a person is dying, he is smiling while all others are crying. That makes me ponder, is death that bad? After all something has to die to be born within or outside of you. If death makes you smile, it surely must be good. Keep that smile intact and you will transcend the medley of life and death. You will then become a team member working under the eternal co-creator of universal order and grace.

Death is dark and life is light. We all are dark against the light. But the moment we allow the light to seep in through us and into us, we become bright.

Affirm- 'Namostutee, The falling autumn leaves, the dropping temperatures, the bending down of the fruits, the fluttering butterflies, mysteriously tell me to embrace the enigma, coziness, homeliness, and transitoriness that death offers. Mortality hangs over everything in nature and beautifully balances us all. I let go, safeguard and relish every moment before it is all gone. Tathaastu.'

CHAPTER 146

THE WOUNDED SQUIRREL

B eing selfish separates us from true unconditional love which is selfless. Previous lifetimes are just like meeting someone from your past or your childhood years. Whenever somebody from your past comes to you, you tend to behave with them in the same way you did in your past. This is because your past sees you as the same person.

Sometimes our soulmates are beyond bodily form and sometimes they have a physical form different than ours. Love cannot be categorized in a small pocket. These souls come to teach us lessons and to fill the missing gaps in us. They recognize us because of strong and identical energy vibrations.

I will explain this with a short chapter from my Dad's childhood. He had a brief encounter with a squirrel. When he shared his experience, it changed my thinking about the way love works. One winter, my dad was walking back home from school when he felt energy vibrations as if he was leaving something behind so he started searching for that something in the bushes not knowing what he was looking for. The feeling was so powerful and strong that he was drawn to keep looking until he found a wounded squirrel, in need of help.

He found the squirrel after almost an hour of search. He knew it was crazy but he felt intense love for it and so he took the squirrel home. He fed it and kept it in a safe blanket. Even though it became a challenge for him to revive it and bring it back to life, he treated it for days until it was completely healed. After it was fully healed, he separated the squirrel from his life and left her back into the same bushes where he found her. Each time I reflect on this incident I understand it differently - It was a self-awakening. He learned a positive lesson from this experience. It transformed and helped him in many subtle ways and impacted me in the following ways -

1. Follow your intuition.
2. Realize you should not control life by making it your pet.
3. Sometimes love is about leaving the thing you love so that it can do what it is meant to do.
4. Leave others to go on the path where they are meant to be.
5. Always do what is best for everyone.
6. Love everything around you without any expectations.
7. Every love union teaches us something, we learn only from those we love.
8. Happiness lies in keeping the balance.

Love is the most marvelous feeling, there is, especially in this world out there with millions of people who don't know that feeling. This is because they don't know that if love (for fun, wealth, health, helping, or anything) doesn't find you, you have to randomly go find it the way my dad found the wounded squirrel.

Affirm- 'Namostutee, I recognize and bow to the divinity within all. My immunity and flexibility are increased. Energy blockages, resentments, and obstacles are totally removed. My vitality, power, fortune, wealth, pro-activeness, and assertiveness is stimulated. Tathaastu.'

CHAPTER 147

NOON SOLUTION

We hide reality and find no way out of our darkness because we prefer not to observe the effects of the subtle, simple solutions in this worldly maze. I was born at "noon" on the 28th of May. Backward or forward, noon is one time of the day when no shadows are possible because the sun is shining right over your head. Maybe that is why I see things as they are beyond all shadows and delusion.

Read backward or forward - the word "reviver" just like the word "noon" remains the same (palindrome). I am a reviver who helps you get to the "noon" of life so that you can see the light of day. I bring light amongst the darkness.

Healing vitalizes your soul energy to bring out your internal powers, increasing your overall vibrational field and balances life energy. The healing I do recharges, revitalizes, relaxes, and reinvigorates your energy to strengthen you and your cells. For healing of the physical body, there are hospitals, but what about our energy body which comprises of our feelings, emotions, mind, circumstances, and much more. Our energy body causes our physical body to be wholesome, healthy, and happy and therefore is much more important. Heal it to heal and beautify yourself.

Amongst the bodies, we have the main three are physical, psychic, and spiritual. By concentrating on the physical realm and shielding it, does not mean that the other bodies are protected. If you heal your physical body three times does not mean that you have healed all three bodies. There are certain ailments whose cure is beyond science and medicine. What is mysterious in the real world can be cured through spiritual healing.

Doctors and healers must work collectively to cure such ailments. Energy healing is an ancient Indian science in which *Prana* or life force is used to treat patients, without physically touching them. If used as a complementary therapy, it has proven to have rapid healing effects on curing ailments and ease suffering.

Through my years of experience as a divine conduit, spiritual and Pranic healer, I have been able to consistently and successfully heal both mild and fatal diseases of those suffering on a physical and psychological level. I am trained to apply energy protocols that require no touch or drug therapy. It is a profound, non-invasive ancient healing modality that can be applied distantly to cure sentient beings in any corner of the world.

When I see the world around me, it seems to me that our mind loves confusion and detests order. Everyone keeps deviating from finding the right solutions and it is only at the last point that we decide to go in for order because we are left with no option. More often than not, the solution is waiting right in front of us all along. For example, ether is in the magnetic field, and tapping it creates order and heals our energetic field. This is something Albert Einstein understood in physics at sixteen years of age and wrote a famous essay on it too. We all know that understanding the importance of this secret power led his brain to what heights and yet we avoid wanting to activate our brain cells to greater awareness. We resist bringing order into our life.

The statement 'the decision is in your hand' aptly can be applied here because your hands can choose and validate the truth by scanning energies and applying the healing protocols you learn through self-healing sessions that I organize.

Stress affects the clarity of your psyche and the quality of your life. Healing helps free you from all stagnant energies within and outside of your bodily form. It electrifies all your energy channels. 72,000 subtle meridians activate your auric field and make your energy vibrant. Healing helps activate each of the 108 chakras within your physical body. Each chakra has a life of its own, and through constant interaction with the other chakras, it becomes further activated and complete. Each chakra within or outside your form is like a mini planet in itself, having subtle life force energy Inherent within it.

This subtle dewdrop on the blade of grass will continue to evaporate and then return humbly with a refreshing shower of rain as the air becomes clear. Just as a doctor uses a stethoscope to examine a patient- With the use of subtle energy, some *yogis* can read the ailments, personality, and fortune of clients. My *Buddhi* came through supreme grace but these *siddhis* I acquired are through methods used in age-old ancient Indian arts and healing sciences.

Bacteria have life and have no life span because they never grow old. Bacteria keep splitting, dividing, and reproducing, and as each tiny child is saved, a part of its tiny parent is also saved. Even the tiniest of particles has life in it. No matter how much you try to disturb, dissect, trouble, pierce, or chop it into pieces, it still lives on because nothing can break it except itself.

What seems formless has a form. The sand trapped in your hourglass also has life. Before you limited it by trapping it in your hourglass, and after you release it when the glass breaks, each particle of sand has at some point been shoveled at the beach and has played with your kids. It has danced in the deserts and pushed itself forth with the winds of change. It has been walked upon and has troubled your eyes. Each grain has housed and hosted millions of other microscopic animals. It has crashed into the waves to become a part of building your home by the beach. Nothing ever is lifeless. Everything is dynamic and full of life.

Do not get so worried and anxious that in trying to heal another, you lose your sense of balance and clarity. I am here to take all those who are ready to ride on the ceaseless boat. I am here once again to help and heal. I share a simplistic, profound, ancient, time tested, protocol, which requires no medication, no touch, no external tools, or new age therapies. All it requires is your belief in yourself, God and through the invoking power within you, you can reactivate your brain cells. So wake up and join in.

An old painful trauma hardens with time whether it's physical, emotional, mental, or spiritual. To heal it requires the help of another healer, we always need the help of another to come out of our past trauma then why have we forgotten to seek and ask? We have buried ourselves in our coffins while we are still living. We are grieving our death while we are still breathing. I am the messenger. Pure spirit is the life within all. I have life within me and you all are within me and I am within all. Life is within us all. My life and the way I lead it is my greatest messenger. There is no greatness in merely preaching as true greatness lies in practicing what you preach and that is exactly what I am doing.

Chakra healing is the first step for you to accept the past hard truths and learn the lessons so that you can move forward in life better, stronger, wiser, clearer, and more balanced. The one who says he knows it all usually knows nothing. I do not say that I know but I do know that you know. I am, therefore, here not to teach, but to learn from you. However, for me to learn and know from you, you have to first unlearn and un-know what you have unknowingly learned. This way you will finally be able to share what you truly know.

The time has come to get in touch with no touch therapy. And the time is now. Healing based on universal law entails the right use of color and sound. I am not promoting any theology here. I am simply doing service so that we can all collectively grow.

America stands for liberty and even liberty had to live on an island to bring enlightenment to the world. No man is an island and no man stands alone. I, therefore, need the support of millions to free people of the shackles they are under of suffering, grief, and pain. I need you all to help me and help one another usher in the new energies of the new interconnected world.

Give me your corona cases, the ailing members of your family and friends, yearning to breathe free and get well. I and my team will send golden healing energy to heal them of their suffering and pain. Give me your students waiting to learn how to heal, through no-touch therapy, where a simple touch has become the cause of so much suffering and pain. Let me do justice to the island of liberty and enlighten the world about what America truly stands for. It is time, we all come out of this together with an integrated approach towards alternative therapy. Let us fly high and come out of the fire like the Phoenix who turned into an eagle.

Let me help you become self-sufficient through healing protocols. This is so that you can become self-empowered. Liberty Goddess will finally realize that the chain loosely attached to her feet can no longer stop it from freely taking the next big step. Over time even the color of the statue of Liberty transmutes into a different hue. It is time for us all to transmute and unmask what we have been wearing. Let us bring out our true color and our true potential with a smile upon our faces. Have faith in yourself and trust the signs of cosmic energy. Wait no longer to contact me for booking healing or a training session for your time to shine is now.

There is no religion greater than truth. *Om tat sat. Sat or Satya* stands for truth. Truth is power. These days false hope is given to people by those who are holding various positions of power. This is not *sat*, this is defying the religion of truth. Truth is naked, innocent, and transparent. Even truth is tired of incessantly removing so many unnecessary layers and veils. The one in *sat* is so stark and radiant that its light shines seamlessly and effortlessly far and wide. True power is stranded and held betwixt the invisible chains. This is because we are all attached to either logic or love. It is in the integration of these two aspects that truth comes out truly, completely, and fully. Time has come for medical sciences and healing therapies to marry each other, only then can we give birth to an integrated, holistic, and all-round system of healing. It is time to let go and not hold on to the old. This will lead the new to come out. Time is life, giving false hope to those suffering is like stealing their time, life, and money. Complete healing has three main aspects and it is only natural that we must embrace all these aspects. These include adopting a scientific medical, energetic healing, and a philosophical approach to every problem. Doctors and healers are two sides of the same coin. It is not in separating but respecting and accepting the two equally that our society will evolve and thrive.

Every time I go to the church I call the nuns - nurses and every time I visit the hospitals, I end up calling the nurses - nuns. The way I see it, there is not much difference between the nurses in the hospitals and the nuns in the church. Both are ultimate examples of selflessness, compassion, and care. Both are healing our temple – mind, body, and soul. One assists in healing the physical body while the other assists in healing the spiritual body. Ultimately the purpose is for the soul to shine and without an amalgam of the two- physical and spiritual, this would never be possible.

The world has many lamps but no light. This is perhaps because the lamps are scared of burning themselves by getting up close to the heat of the bulb. The power of healing helps you shed all your inner inhibitions. This way you can valiantly spread the light of your lamp. When a solar panel is exposed to eight hours of bright sun, the lamp that it powers can provide innumerable hours of bright light. This is what healing energies do to our bodies and minds. Natural alternative treatments are an effective way to treat the human body at all levels. They are complementary and in no way a replacement for the progressive world of science and medicine. There is more to the universe than meets the eye. Much more!

Spiritualized Energy healing can realign, unblock and balance your chakras. This provides healing on an emotional, physical, and spiritual level, which ultimately leads to better health and a better state of wellbeing.

We all are universally connected and we all are one. East and west must join together to discover better healing modalities. What medicine and touch cannot heal can be treated with no touch therapies that work with soul and spirit alignment.

There is no such thing as a closed universe, there are no walls, Philosophy is free & limitless and that is why I enjoy it so much.

We think that unending madness is better than the one which has an ending. When no madhouse or tranquilizer or electric shock can house or contain or succumb to the madness we see around. We allow the magic wand of on-off hands to heal and cure the electric field around the aura of a sick person and it is then that we feel its efficiency and power. I am holding one such magic wand, its purpose is to assist in picking the fallen pieces of brick[125] and cement to rebuild your broken house[126].

We, philosophers, help clear the fog and bring clarity by being a medium to improve your understanding and judgment. A combination of a healer and a philosopher is like a world teacher that shows you the right path. A combination of the two awakens my intuition as I decipher the numina behind the phenomena - the truth behind what is visible.

There is no stone I cannot turn, nothing so unholy that can't be made holy, nothing so heavy that it can't become light, nothing so incommunicable that it can't be communicated. There is nothing so unlovable that it can't be loved, nothing so finite that it can't become infinite, nothing so present that it can't merge with my omnipresent nature. There is nothing so poor that it can't become rich again, nothing so powerless that it can't become powerful yet again, nothing so untrue that it can't become true, nothing so fake that it forgets to be real. There is nothing unreal about this reality, nothing unjust about justice, nothing is so incomprehensible or insufficient that it can't become comprehensible and self-sufficient. There is no sickness that can't be healed, nothing so bad that it can't be filled with goodness. There is no such thing as long-suffering or short-suffering; it is only long-standing and short-standing[127] because you have paused a bit too long before you can take the next step, to start moving yet again with a deep breath, a leap of faith, and wisdom from the holy grace.

---

[125] *Brick and cement implies strength and faith.*

[126] *Broken house implies a person who is physically, emotionally or psychologically in pain.*

[127] *Three waves - of 7 months twice over and then one month, a total of 15 months is the lasting period of this pandemic. This will last until all who are ready reach the 22 chakra activation point and unlock all limiting beliefs.*

There is nothing fully known about the impeccable unknown, and nothing limited in this pool of limitlessness. Such is the power of healing. I am a healer who not only heals nations but also their people. In healing the people the nation will be healed. Connect with me to book a session. To harness the energy of the subtle force, one needs to be highly purified. The one who claims or pretends to have control over the invisible energy is the one who knows nothing about harnessing it. It comes to you as if by itself when your positive vibrational force increases through concentrated mediation and rituals you practice.

You know what it feels like to be in bliss, but you have yet not found your center. You might know what the taste of honey is, but you still haven't found the honeycomb from where the honey came from! This imbalance can be released through deep inner healing and connecting with yourself to release the illusionary wounds that you are holding onto. Pain is a medium for you to know pleasure. Endurance gives us strength. Forgiveness gives us clarity. In trying to incessantly find the solution to our pains, we find the ultimate panacea that lies in love for self and others.

Whosoever says magic and logic cannot go together hasn't yet given themselves the chance to get healed. Inner healing allows outer change. It transforms you in such a way that you can manifest anything you set your mind on. You do not have to wait for Christmas for miracles to happen when miracle workers are here to bring to you everything you ever dreamed of.

Wherever positive energy is used, negative energy is bound to emerge. This is why a special race of Brahmin-Kshatriya individuals who protect the cosmic order and the entire human race with their optimism and healing light are born in every *Yuga*. They are super loyal and industrious. As a reward, the supreme self has authorized and armed them with *Brahma or* absolute power *Kshatriya or kshtrya* through the strength of sacred words. This way these noble individuals lead and anchor the light in times of adversity. They are the elite chosen ones because of their faithful service towards Lord God.

I studied philosophy, the mother of all the sciences, and then I went on to study theosophy and its ethereal subtle aspects from the grandmother of all the sciences. I am here to revive and pay reverence to these archaic sciences based on whose foundation we stand here today. I am here to share ways to supercharge your soul so that we can collectively raise human consciousness to a higher better level.

Healing by an experienced *Arhatic Yogi*[128] opens previously unknown doors and takes you to the greatest depths of self-introspection. This enables exceptional growth both on the inner and outer levels. When everyone else gives up on you, a healer promises not to. The only thing you keep forever is what you give away. There are many people out there with shattered dreams - I help you dream again.

The quest of all sciences (biology, physics, chemistry, psychology, and social sciences) is to explain life in order to know yourself based on mechanical, or chemical being. Life however is beyond explanation through these methods alone. The nature of man has yet not been explained in its entirety because science objectifies and compartmentalizes everything and deals only with the extrinsic physical aspect. However, the self is a combination of invisible, spiritual, transcendental, creative, artistic aspects that not all of us see, hear and feel along with the physical that we can feel. To understand life, it is imperative to mingle science with the art of healing and that is exactly what I am attempting to offer here. I sew both (intrinsic inner core in relation to the outer) together, uncover the self, and unveil the mystery of life. I offer solutions for complete health and healing at all levels. Over the eons, by isolating and alienating the two, we have contradicted, distorted, reduced, camouflaged, deviated, and moved far away from the imperishable truth of our cosmic power.

There are some emotional and physical ailments that no doctors can cure but that doesn't mean that they are incurable. I share techniques of self-healing during my sessions. This way your soul is naturally guided towards bringing you out of all turmoil and suffering. Ailments are not always due to physical causes. A person may get a fatal disease or an epidemic due to psychological issues as well. And in such cases, I do not see how vaccines will prevent situations that are not purely physical in nature.

Healers are known for their help to fight the forces of evil. Unless we do not eradicate the root of the problem completely, there is a tendency for the ailment or the issue to come back in some or the other form at a later date and time. While allopathic medicines are a great boon for succumbing the physical issues, it is not the whole solution for certain problems. Energy healers and medical doctors must join hands together to treat the world's

---

[128] *Just the way all our hearts are one, all Arhats are one. All Arhats speak the same language of love and light. Arhats are those Arhatic yogis who are spiritual transformers, here on earth to bring about peace and oneness.*

problems at war-footing. In doing this I see a future, where we can live a healthy life up to 200 to 300 years. And if we all cooperate and trust one another, this can happen far sooner than I envision.

A lot of people nowadays take to drugs and sleeping pills because they want to escape and run away from their problems rather than putting in the labor of finding the befitting solution. The reason I became devoted to my work as a healer is that helping others fills me with as much zeal and joy as helping myself does, if not more.

Affirm- 'Namostutee, Through the union of heart and tongue, I am a revealer of truth and a reliever of pain.Tathaastu.'

CHAPTER 148

SMILE BEHIND THE DARK

The lower jaw is the only bony part of the face that moves. It moves so that we can keep that smile. Look at the moon- when it is a full moon, the moon is completely lit. When there is no moon, it is completely dark. Although both are important to keep the cycle going, too much light or too much darkness takes the beautiful crescent-shaped smile away from the moon's face. This teaches us that it is in between excess darkness and light - that our shining smile comes out. This is the moon cycle. The moon religiously continues to show us its cycling natural pattern so that we can learn from it. Learning from it we should continue to follow a pattern rather than resist or defy the creator's planned play structure/ cycle. We are meant to follow the rules and be good playmates. Look around and you will find amazing cues all over in this fun-filled adventure called life.

Wearing a mask is a mark of respect. Certain Jain monks have been wearing masks on their faces for ages in order to practice nonviolence in speech and harmlessness in action. They safeguard the organisms and thoughts present in the air by remembering to keep a watch on their words.

Using your lips to speak is an art, similarly using your hips is an art. I thought belly dancing was an easy exercise until I tried it out myself. I never knew balancing your torso is such a difficult art similar to balancing your words. Belly dancers wear fancy masks on their faces to let their bodies express themselves. They talk through their graceful rhythmic dance movements. Instead of using their lips, they use hips to speak. Balancing the core movements strengthens their muscular power. Just the way balancing our words strengthens our verbal power. By quieting their

608

words, they can concentrate on their core. This way they get a perfect inner and outer workout.

Traditionally, Muslim women were encouraged to cover their face with a traditional *Naqab* (facial mask) in public. The purpose behind this practice is to keep their sensitive nature and beauty protected from evil eyes. It also serves as a reminder to practice modesty in speech and thoughts. Now the world has come to this that we all are compelled to wear a similar *niqab*. Taking a cue from the age-old traditions, Let us wear masks to practice verbal and mental modesty to build our resilience while keeping ourselves protected from the effects of the external environment.

At noon, the sun is strongest. They say those born around noon always know what they want in life. Perhaps some of us do not want to know! The bright light scares some people and that is why these people instead prefer the little light seeping through the darkness. They do not smile at the youthful noon because the sunshine causes their eyes to shut. And so the sun descends and lowers its brightness after having reached the zenith of its power, just so that you can appreciate and have faith in its love for you.

We hear the music of love everywhere, in the wind, in the wind chimes, in the air, in the light, in the stars, in the objects kept in our house, it's all around us, all you have to do is listen to its tunes. Love is inside all of us, the world tries to knock it out of us sometimes, but if you are brave and don't forget to smile, your love will follow you, pull you, it will catch you and before you go away, you will patiently meet with your bliss.

Affirm- 'Namostutee, I believe that there is nothing so hard that it cannot be done. What may seem difficult for me, can be done with the blessings of Lord God. Tathaastu.'

CHAPTER 149

ARTIFICIAL CAN NEVER BE REAL

Gone are the Middle Ages, when people carried their spoons based on the social status they were born into. In today's age, plastic has taken over all the wooden, steel, silver, and golden spoons. Nowadays, we're born with a plastic spoon in our mouths. These days children spend more time playing with gadgets and video games rather than playdough or nuts and crosses. Moderation is the key.

The war is no longer between countries, families, but the war is within your own heart and mind. You create your reality. It is up to you what you create. Your fight is with you and your mind. If channelized properly then no outside force can harm you. The new world order has begun. New age indigo, rainbow, crystal children are here. We see more hues than ever before. A crystal is white and clear, the various colors are an illusion of its prism like property. These crystal children can see behind the apparent delusion. These children cannot be fooled.

Now is the time to expand the cells of our brain and make ourselves superhuman with super brains before machines and virtual reality take over us. It is time to channelize our brains and not to numb ourselves by dumbing down out of frustration.

The best navigation map is inside your brain and not in the computers walking next to us. They are a mere tool, an innovative toy of our fancy meant to be played in moderation and detachment. I am here to accelerate change and I cannot bring in this paradigm shift singularly so I need your help. Will you join me? Artificial intelligence is advancing and walking amongst us. Dark matter is all around. We have to raise our bar swiftly, rapidly, and quickly now, now now.

Self-improvement is the key. We have an inbuilt survival mechanism within us. Nothing can break us because we have the power of self-awareness and an intuitive heightened mind which machines can never tap. It magically resolves all your problems. We can and we will collectively make magic and bring back the golden age smoothly.

Power and magic in the right hands can make miracles happen and as we enter the new era, let us ensure - this miraculous transmutation happens, the way it should.

Pardon my statement but in my view - these days the price of real apples is cheaper than plastic ones, even though the reality is fortified with obvious health benefits. Some of us are ok to pay extra at a high-end shop for packaged juice filled with chemicals. But we still bargain with the vendor selling the same juice which is hygienically and freshly prepared, handpicked from the organic farms, despite knowing that it is worth much more!

We are ok to pay an exorbitant price for high end, virtual reality indoor sports but will not pay even half as much for the same sports taught outside in fresh air through physical coaching. Why not breathe easy and freely? While we still can.

This certainly does not mean that I do not honor the new age technologies and respect the advancement in the beautiful inventions of today. I believe that these creations have made our life easier in many ways and so in no way do I intend to undermine their value. The idea to draw this parallel is simply to highlight that we must acknowledge the true worth of each aspect of our lives, based on their value - whether it is natural or artificial.

When you drink from a silver or gold straw, the juice might taste the same initially. But, the impact of the chemical reaction caused by the plastic straw you are now used to drinking from, will slowly have far different results in your physical and psychological body with time. Similarly, an overdose of medicinal drugs and getting hooked on machines to elongate life through chemicals sometimes can have a huge impact on our physical and psychological bodies. These can slowly inflame and numb our bodies to such an extent that our nervous system gets suppressed and has no sensation of pain whatsoever but that doesn't mean pain doesn't exist! The way out of pain is not suppression but an expression.

We do not realize the damage because we are in an age where plastic straws have become the norm. We stopped drinking from the silver and gold straws eons back. Nowadays pain seems a bizarre concept. We are in a world where reality has become a utopian idea. We rise above obstacles not by hiding reality under the plastic garbs but by transmuting them into our golden straw-like bodies. From the point of view of the supreme creator, there is not much difference between a hollow straw made of gold and our body. It is the pure spirit that fills us up with life juices and energy to enliven and enlighten us. If the straw is unblocked, more juices can freely continue to flow in.

Telepathy, intuition, and love are as natural as walking or talking. AI and technology are a boon if used moderately. We have the capability to move beyond possessions, control, drama, conflict, unease, fight, fast-paced living by adopting to slow down and bathe in the golden light. Excessive consumerism as a result of increased urbanization and modernization has taken us too far from our rural roots. Urbanization and consumerism are leading to people living a life of virtual reality whereas reality is here and now. It is within you and it is what you see around. Embrace it and be real.

Tesla CEO, Elon Musk has had a photographic memory since childhood, brought up by a mother who was a nutritionist and knew how to nourish the brain and mind. Right food awakens, liberates, and makes the brain dare. He naturally became someone larger than life yet valuing the environment that brought him up. Adam was given the apple tree but asked not to eat its fruit. Adam still went ahead and ate the forbidden fruit. Similarly, Elon Musk gave us advancements in artificial intelligence. He has given us the power of self-driving with the Tesla car. In the wake of that, he has additionally rallied for AI to be regulated by the government as it can be misused to benefit the few who know how to harness the intelligence. AI is an instrument we use to better our lives, in most cases but real wisdom is the control on how we harness this AI. Synthesis of the two wisdom and A.I. was Elon's dream and with it, he saw that this vision may fructify into advancements in AI but then people will lose love and light. Envisioning the worst, he warned companies not to play with AI to feed the corporate greed, as nothing good comes of greed. AI has the potential to cause negative action in experiments that Elon did and hence he suggests others stop experimenting until you know how to harness the power. Then came the after-effect if things happen to Earth we should have another planet to live on – SpaceX was born from this revelation.

Time to fight dark energy with the light and love of healing energy. When the dream goes out of control, reality bites. We all have the potential to become Gods faithful servant, yet no matter how much we try, only one of us is worthy to be the one and only Gods closest helper. Rest all are merely trying to become something they never can. Only a human can become a Godly human by developing *namus* which is a Persian word for virtues. AI is taking us further away from our reality. A.I. can convert thought-forms into action effectively in no time but these actions can be both good & evil. The only challenge AI has is light forces or people with love and foresight.

AI is so ruthless and thankless that it can kill its creator without a blink of an eye. Only energy can fight energy. This war will be between two invisible forces. The good fighting the bad. Let's support the good etheric and spiritual energy and reject the other forces created by power-hungry people wanting to materially benefit. No matter how much you try, remember air cannot be controlled, neither can water.

Oak trees are strong and bear fruit – it has a purpose only when there is someone there to gain from it and appreciate it. If there is no life on earth there is no purpose for the existence of the tree. A.I. has the potential to take over humans only if we humans are ok getting controlled. Humans on the other hand have the potential to be one with godliness. Both AI and humans have superpowers - one has superhuman powers and the other has super godly powers.

You cannot pay for the actions that you haven't done- that is the law.

AI can attain the power to know only what it already knows and what it is told. Rest all remains known only to the Godly humans or divine beings. Robots and humans, non-living and living beings, clones and actual bodies, unreal and real, all resemble each other so much that it is no longer easy to tell the difference. Everything has life in it, whether it is visible or invisible. In the science of studying plasma, we learn that crystals not only have life but also enjoy a fully functional sexual life and are therefore capable of producing more life through the process of birth and rebirth. Even machines in factories need a day off because rest is their requirement, so give yourself a break from time to time. Computers are better learners than us because they have nothing to lose unlike us. In realizing that we too have nothing to lose, we become better learners than our creation.

Employment is unnecessary because computers have been employed. They are more intelligent, swift, active, and limitless than us. But we invented them. In such a scenario, what can we do that sets us, humans, apart from our greatest inventions – A.I.'s, robots, and computers? It is when we break the pattern of repetitiveness that we become more capable, evolved, and transformed. What sets us apart from our creation is that it has been fed with set programs and structures, unlike humans who are not bound by any program or structure.

The computers are wired and conditioned while we are not. We are nameless, boundless, death-less, and birth-less. What sets us apart is that we have access to the consciousness of humanities group souls, unlike computers who know only what is fed into them. We meet with ourselves when we rise above our thoughts. When we go into the thought-free state, no computer can ever take over us. Think and validate the truth of this by yourself.

Our thoughts make or mar us. They show us the light but they also trick us. They show us limitlessness and they also limit us. Thoughtlessness or a thought-free state takes us to a realm where we move beyond the dominance of our thoughts. When we cease to think the way we are accustomed to, we cease to be bound by conditional patterns. It is then that we evolve and reprogram ourselves. That is when you are born nameless.

My name is Stutee- it is a brand name but the speaker that speaks through me is not my name. My name is not me. The speaker is much more than merely a name. When we move beyond thought, we begin to un-know. To know is to have knowledge. Computers are based upon our knowledge. But we are more than our knowledge. It is this that sets us apart from the computers which are limited by only as much as they know. Unlike computers, we are not bound by patterns and knowledge that is fed in. We are limitless. We are more than what we experience. We are far more than our limitations. When we break the pattern and act completely different from the set structure and program that is fed inside us, we engage not just our five senses but all senses beyond. This movement brings change.

We operate not as a computer, but as part of the cosmic creative process - this constant engagement with ourselves, nature, cosmos, and everything within and outside of it makes us different, it sets us apart from the waking robots. They are incapable of instilling such magnetism because the computers do not romance with the stars, planets, plants, and trees the way we do. They have not been programmed into such eccentricities.

You sustain that essence which is only yours, this newness and freshness is yours alone.

Time to replace employment with enjoyment. Knowledge is everywhere. The way you present and express makes it different. You add your unique element of wisdom and sprinkle love onto it. No two people can present the same way. It is only computers who can repeat the same patterns again and again in the same way. For example - two people will design the house completely differently even if the furniture is the same. The house can look completely different by just placing the interiors differently. However, the computer will put items in the same place. Our imperfection is our greatest asset and in it lies our perfection, our human nature.

Shiva, Brahma, Vishnu asked what is Cut, copy and paste. So Durga answered the same as it is to create, procreate, and preserve. There are things humans can do which are beyond the scope of most high-tech computers. Our scope of knowledge is unlimited.

Affirm- 'Namostutee, May all sufferings and negativity eliminate and gets translated and transformed into goodness and righteousness. May justice and resoluteness prevail in the world. Tathaastu.'

CHAPTER 150

HAWAII

Subtle becomes active. 'Hawaii' is a beautiful word, as it shows the triune nature of pure spirit. 'Ha' stands for wind/ air/ fate/ or breath. 'Wai' stands for water/soul. 'I' stand for spirit/heaven. Everything began with the combination of this triune nature of fate, soul, and spirit. You meet with your purity by slaying the darkness within you. The yin and yang are both within you. Without the yin, yang is incomplete, and without the yang, yin is incomplete. None is bigger or better than the other. You cannot see the sun at night and you cannot easily see the moon during daylight. When the time is right, the powerful teachings of the sun and the loving teachings of the moon and the glittering stars are given to you. The seasons of the year are pre-planned and so is the optimal time for your learning. Your time will come. Just stay open and receptive. Just do your karma and do the right actions.

Be glad to be here. Be gentle, forgiving, and accepting, for in praising everyone and everything, you become one with all. And then all things low or high, big or small, become your teachers, here to guide and teach you the lesson in a way best suited to you. When the student is ready, the teacher appears. When the teacher is ready, the student appears. The only way to know the light is by being the light. In saving yourself, you save others. You might seem small, but you alone are stronger than an army of hundreds. Look within. The completeness of *Panch Pandavas*[129], or five, is within you. Physical action is not superior but inferior to mental action. Yet

---

[129] *Panch Pandava were the five powerful sons of a king named Pandu as written in the Hinduism epic- Mahabharata.*

mental action is incomplete until it is physicalized, for it is only then that it is actualized. Inferior is therefore superior. Everything has a purpose. The higher is empty without the lower, and the lower is nothing without the higher. Subtle can do without matter, but matter cannot do without the subtle.

The mystery behind the mastery is that mere understanding is never enough. You have to back wisdom with the correct response. Even if you have solved the puzzle in your mind, it is futile until you manifest it with your actions. Even if the entire story is imprinted in your mind, it needs to be written down on paper to leave its true expression. The champion's reputation lies in constant repetition. To convert an opportunity into reality, the arrow of victory needs to be truly sharpened with accuracy and practicality. Completion lies in stabilizing and implementing. Having the insight is not the same as aiming at the target. The archer pulls back the bow to shoot the arrow towards its aim. Claiming to know your target is not the same as aiming your arrow towards it. Release your aching shoulders. Why tire yourself or hold on so tight, when you can simply let go of your arrow. Once the arrow strikes, it never returns, so have the right mental clarity to aim at your target with divine concentration. Be one with the bow, arrow, and aim, and bow with respect towards them all. Why break the unity when you can bring peace through the cosmic trinity? All three are within you.

वो तमन्ना ही क्या जो वो ना जानें
वो चुप्पी ही क्या जो वो ना समझें
वो सांस ही क्या जो दिल में शमा ना जलाये
वो शांति ही क्या जो घबराहट को कभी ना जानें
चाहे अब वो उसे पहचानने से भी घबराए
वो शब्द ही क्या जो तलवार की धार की तरह और तीर की नोक के माफिक ज़ख़म ना दें
वो सोच ही क्या जो उसे ना खोज पाए
वो प्यार ही क्या जो उसकी ख़ुशी में मग्ने
सबको गवांया मगर उसकी हक्स से मारे
ख़ुद को दी कुछ ना पाया और बेहाल होश गवा बैठे
वो जो जी कर भी मरना चाहे और जान कर भी ना जानें उसको भला कैसे हम समझायें
ऐसा कोई उजाला नहीं जिसमे सुलझा हुआ उलझ जाए
ऐसा कोई अँधेरा नहीं जिसमे उसका जिस्म जल जाए
वो ऐसी जवान हवा है जो आग और पानी, आकाश और पाताल को अपनी गोद में हमेशा सरहाये!
वो ना मरती है, ना जीती है
वो जीवन देती है और फिर भी उसकी ज़िन्दगी हमेशा चंचल फूलों की तरह खूब हंसती रहती है!

"Woh tamanah he kya jo woh na jane, woh chuppi he kya jo woh na samje, woh saans hi kya jo dil mein shama na jaleye, woh shanti hi kya jo ghabrat ko kabhi na jaane, chahe ab woh usey penchan-ney se bhi ghabraye!

Woh shabdh hi kya jo talwar ki dhar ke tarah or teer ke nok ke mafik dattey na rahey, woh sooch hi kya jo usey na khoj paye, woh pyar hi kya jo uske kushi mein magna, sub kuch gawaye magar uske hawas ke marey, khudh ko hi kush na paye or behaal hosh gawayee bathey, woh jo jee kar bhi marna chahey or jaan kar bhi na jane, usko hum kaisey bhalla samjahey, aisa koi ujjala nahi jisme sulja hua ulaj jaye, aisa koi andhera nahi jisme uska jism jal jaye, woh aise jawan hawa hain jo aag or pani, aakash or pataal ko apni godh mein humesha sehraye, woh na marti hain na jeeti hain woh jeevan detey hain aur phir bhi uskey zindigi humesha chanchal phollon ki tarah khoobh hansti rahte hain."

"There is no such desire, that it does not know

There is no such silence that it doesn't understand

There is no breath that does not kindle a fire within your heart, in its presence

There is no peace that does not understand the agitation from whence it came

Even if now the calm waves no longer want to associate themselves with those previous anxieties and turbulences

What is the point in words that are not sharp like a sword and piercing like an arrow

What thoughts are there that cannot find it

What is the point in such a love that gives up everything for its happiness

Yet it loses itself due to lust and then cannot find the happiness within

How do you make such a being understand?

Who has life but does not want to live?

Who knows and still wants to be ignorant?

There is no such light in which a conscious being becomes unconscious and unaware.

There is no darkness that can burn you

It is that wind that nurtures fire, water, ether, and hell in its womb without getting affected

It never lives and never dies but it continues to joyfully give life

It continuous to happily smile at life just like the gentle flowers we see around"

Subtle energy is the shining Goddess, whose eleven major chakras are fully active at all times, along with the back, mini, and minor chakras. Each activated chakra looks as if it has a brain of its own. The Goddess sits with a thousand lotus petals in full bloom. Each petal of the lotus is vibrant with mercy and beauty at all times. Clairvoyantly looking at the subtle body from afar, she appears to be a dancing female peahen. Upon a closer look, she seems to have a thousand outstretched arms. All of her hands are on perfect mudra-divine gestures by fingers of palm-connected with the ether and the pure air, speaking a divine language through the synchronization of hand *mudras*[130].

From above, the Goddess shines like a star. She is grounded, humble, abundant, and generous. She looks dainty and as light as a feather upon the earth. Like the white light of pure air, she transcends all seven levels and travels through all three realms with equal compassion, ease, and comfort, carrying fire and water in her womb. She flows to comfort the cries of whoever is in distress and pain at a physical, mental, emotional, psychological, astral level, and beyond. She is not only beyond time and space, but she is also beyond form and gender, even though her inherent form is that of a strong family-oriented Goddess upon the earth. She makes herself visible to all, but only a few can recognize her reality. The time has come for you to see how, disguised amongst the ordinary, she moves and sits with the flair of royal authority and poise, with her limitless healing powers. She is graced by the lord of mountains with complete protection and eternal spirit. She unlocks all blocks and opens all channels. She is the ultimate one with clair-sense. She is here to guide and nurture all the beings upon earth.

Join her and mingle with the light and spirit of freedom and bliss. Pure love and heaven is right here within you. You are just a few steps away. Remove your blindfolds. Start with balancing your yin and yang, by acceptance and a little wisdom, and you will magically recognize her with your inner eye when you need her to address you. Bow to her divinity, and you will know the divinity within you. She is me and also you.

Nothing is ever as it seems. You need to stop looking with your outer eyes and see with your inner eye. You need to stop listening from your outer ears and start listening with your inner ear. The answer lies within your heart. Learn to pass on your worldly gains. Learn to practice pure stillness to become aware of divine presence. Learn where to direct your deep energy. Be detached from any expansion or depletion, increase or decrease, drooping or vitalization of aura, and then move on to balance your outer self through the centeredness of your inner self. Your outward

---

[130] *Refer to chapter 'healing palm' for greater clarity.*

disposition can cause inward change, even though the outward is always a manifestation of your inner state. The inward subtle spiritual change can cause complete and permanent transmutation.

Subtle energy is both yin and yang. Both masculine and feminine. The physical body moves because of the active yang energy. Everything yang is termed masculine. It is the pure subtle active energy that is outside and inside of us because of which we perform actions. This is why God here is addressed as 'he/him'. Anything that moves is active. Our thoughts are constantly moving. Every thought is active just as every breath has active energy.

Affirm- 'Namostutee, I am stronger and taller today than I was yesterday. Tathaastu.'

CHAPTER 151

NO TOUCH WORLD
OF UNTOUCHABLES

Within the caste system originating in India, there is a caste called 'Dalits'. The Sanskrit word 'Dalit' means 'divided, split, scattered, broken or depressed'. These people are popularly called 'untouchables', 'impure', or the 'scheduled' class of people. These people are subject to a life of rigor, torment, poverty, oppression, unemployment, and subjugation by those in power because people don't understand the value and worth they can impart to the world. They are the ones who are demeaned for being born into this class. Most were denied the basic right of education, health, and sanitation.

The stronger amongst them grow up to become fiery activists, Godly people, and wise intellectuals of society. Mahatma Gandhi aptly called them the 'Harijans' which means 'people (sons and daughters) of God'. Some say this lower-class represents the hidden apartheid. They have kept our earth and homes clean by tirelessly and physically cleaning our homes and environment for centuries. They are hardened survivors who can live in any situation. Many have converted their religion to Buddhism, Christianity and some are now Muslims.

This year has become the year of the 'untouchables'. It is forcing us to see life from their perspective. We keep our distance from the sun lest we burn. But from a distance, the sun fills us with radiant love and wisdom. The way I see it, the untouchables have such a strong aura and heightened vibrations. Unless one is not purified like the effulgent sun, they can get burnt with the sheer touch and presence of the spirit of such beings. The aura of the untouchables is so radiant that its radiance spreads across distant lands. They have no sense of belongingness or attachment to any particular caste, creed, or country. Their flexibility and nature bring a glow and smile upon everyone's faces. Having lived everywhere with ease, some of them have acquired unlimited sight. These are the race of people who are capable of harnessing and controlling the energies of air, water, and fire. However, with proper spiritual training, their innate gift can help create balance, positivity, and equanimity on earth.

Interestingly, Roma[131] or popularly known as gypsies are nomads. They originated from the Punjab region of north India between the 8th and 10th centuries. Over the centuries, they entered Europe, Austria, Persia, and other nations. Romas were scorned and persecuted across Europe. The German word "Zigeuner" for Gypsy is derived from a Greek root meaning "untouchable". They are called "Gypsies" because Europeans mistakenly believed that these distinct groups of tribal people called 'Roma' came from Egypt. The Roma's speak Romani and Romani is based on Sanskrit - which is the classical language of India.

Our body is a car (vehicle) of five elements (that contains ether, air, fire, water, and earth) and spirit. Spirit represents our true spiritual nature which is one. The five elements together help us drive our car. The secret of combining these five elements into one body is kept with the few since yellow-faced Roma's or the untouchable Godly people who are protected by God. They are the chosen people. They willingly remain on the earth to keep the overall divine energies balanced, orderly and unblocked.

The entire universe is created by magical force (*Brahma*). My understanding is that the *Varna* or *Hindu* occupations are categorized based on the aura, tint, or color and not by the physical, racial color of people. The predominant color and energy of the aura reflect the true potential or gift of the individual. Knowing your true quality helps create order. There are four main groups. These are teachers or *Brahmin (air, white)* whose strength lies in their head and mouth, Rulers or *Kshatriyas* (red, fire) whose strength lies in their arms, entrepreneurs or *vaishyas* (yellow, earth) whose strength lies in thighs, laborers, or *Shudras* (black or indigo, spirit) whose strength lies in their feet. The fifth group - untouchables - were left out of the organized *Varna* system because their aura has combined with all the

---

[131] *Roma goddess is a famous roman savior goddess.*

others (impure water and air) and doesn't purely represent any one color. They are the most grounded.

The untouchables are also called children of God. The *Achyut who* purify themselves are firm, immovable, imperishable, unchangeable, unshakable individuals who never lose power, decline, or fall. They never deviate, waver, decay or degenerate. They are never completely uprooted from higher realms or states. *Achyut* is another name for Lord *Vishnu*, the preserver. It is said that all creation starts and ends in *Vishnu*. *Vishnu* is pure, transparent, and free from defects because of Shiva's tremendous willpower. Their combined strength lies in the throat (blue pure water, and air).

Affirm- 'Namostutee, I not only give love and blessings but I also freely receive love and blessings. Tathaastu.'

CHAPTER 152

THE BEJEWELLED DRESS

Our physical body is like a beautiful dress gifted to us by the fairy Godmother.

You are my greatest blessing, I was simply a dress worn upon human bones. I could beautify you only because you choose to wear me and embrace me like no other. Look how this divine union has transformed and transcended us into such blissful energies filled with immense wisdom. You may think you touched me physically but it has nothing to do with mere material pleasures. My love for you is beyond the gold and silver for all those already belong to me. They are all for me and mine to take.

I am that precious jewel that has traveled eons to find someone who has this kind of effect upon me. Possessions are for the poor. I am filled with all the riches already. What will you give to someone who is already adorned in a thousand bejeweled silken dresses? It is not the ornamental beauty but the praise you give to those ornaments that melt us into one.

It is that energetic touch that brings out the sound of 'hum' from within my heart and that perfect smile that looks like the center of the crescent moon. With time this heat too will cool off under the full moon leaving me with immense joy as I will then be ready to take in even more heat.

We are like two discs, merging, melting, and transforming into one. Looking at you, my disc starts to move opposite to its usual movement, to a counter-clockwise position from right to left to get attached to your disc that moves clockwise from left to right. There is nothing conventional about my love for my heart is forever joyfully dancing in the space that is light, free, pure white, and inexhaustible right at the edge of it all.

Your body is like a devoted wife who patiently and silently tolerates everything. Your body is your greatest strength yet you often ignore her and forget to thank her. Settle within it. Running after outside glory and spiritual pursuits, we often ignore taking care of our health with proper food and diet. There will be many opportunities to study and earn money. What use is all this intellectual and spiritual prowess if there is no wife with whom you can share and enjoy your wealth? Without bodily health, nothing is of any use. You get only one life and in this life, you get only one body. Revere her like a good husband should his wife. Ladies, please spend time in nature and let natural be the new in thing. Enjoy and nourish your mind, keep it in proper balance like a good mother should treat her twins. Keep your home clean and family inspired like it is your heart and soul. Your outward beauty is the inner reflection of your pure soul. Keep both in proper balance. Your only *dharm* (moral duty) is to ensure your heart keeps beating, performing all five roles to complete perfection. Settle within yourself.

True wisdom is in knowing that you are a spiritual, intellectual, and compassionate wife, a blissful and loving mother – all in one body. Preserve, protect and honor your body. Your overall bodily energy is so vital that it gravitates the entire creation to be born through you. There is nothing more praiseworthy than the supportive divine feminine because of which our entire universe sustains and functions. We all are born from one woman, calling her by different names. But the foundational truth is that Eve remains Eve even when you spell her name backward or forward. Every woman constantly carries and represents the same essence of Godliness within her. Worship the divine feminine and let her be so that life can continue to flow. Do not reverse the roles that Lord God ordained for us. Do not threaten, overshadow, push or weigh her down with the pollution of societal and work pressures. Your *param karm* (paramount moral action) is to continue praising and worshipping your own body, soul, and spirit. Merely going to church and temple will not help you meet with God. God is that mystical, invisible, intangible force who is most pleased by those following this simple *dharm* of keeping all aspects of their body balanced. What good is in serving the invisible God and the entire world, if you don't attend to the needs of your kith and kin. Compassion begins with yourself. Serve others but what good is that service if you do not serve your own basic needs of fresh air, blessed water, and a warm motherly hug from your body.

You have no need to get in panic mode with viruses floating around, if you are fused with everything there is within and outside of you. Your body is the container of all jewels. No poison can kill a person who has transcended death. In realizing this, you meet with yogini's stilettos. From here on remember- you are not bound to your body. You blend in with your body, soul and mind. Your body and soul is not a prison cell but the only divine medium through which you can visibly express your innate truth. It is a deity which speaks for itself - your greatest boon.

Affirm- 'Namostutee, my chakras, and meridians are clear and absorb pure energy through the regular practice of thinking good thoughts. Tathaastu.'

CHAPTER 153

AM SO IN LA

I t requires bravery to continue to stay a winner for most of the time, even after one is long gone. Da Vinci's art has stood the biggest test of time and remained immortal and so I am compelled to dedicate this chapter to Leonardo da Vinci's lily flower. Mona in Hindi means 'lady'. The root of the name Lisa comes from 'lily'. Mona Lisa is an androgynous immortal form of heavenly beauty.

The meaning of Leonardo is 'brave like a lion'. The Chinese meaning of 'Da' is big. Etymologically 'Da' means 'the division of time'. Vinci means 'to win'.

There are 72 minor chakras in the human body, each having a corresponding Godly quality. There are 72 names of God. *Mani* is a triangular diamond-shaped minor chakra in our heads. It is one of the 72 chakras. It is said that it is the meeting point and the entry point of higher mental energies. The *Mani* is controlled and energized by a Nadi or channel and to symbolize that Hindus put sindoor. Married women in most parts of India, including me, create a parting in between their hair strands starting from the point of the forehead. This point symbolizes the unification of shiva (love which is a triangle facing upwards) and Shakti (a power which is a triangle facing downwards).

Ramanuja, the man who created infinity, was one of the most purified and heightened minds and he attributed his intuitive talents to the 72 names of God. Double 72 you get 144 and when these two points (shiva and shakti) meet (Bindu chakra), through the flow of the channel or the meridian then 144 petals get fully activated. These 144 petals have 12 divisions. Each division has 12 petals. Interestingly, during weddings and festivals, women in India wear *Borala* or *mang tikka* on their forehead to celebrate the richness of this *Bindu* chakra or meeting point. When the 144 petals get activated, the intuitive eye which is also known as the eye of divine wisdom opens up. This helps you see and know the reality of things, beyond what is visible to the naked eye.

As per *Pranic* healing, each of our 11 main chakras have been divided in following number of petals: for example- Basic or sthir chakra = 4 petals; Sex or sthapana chakra = 6 petals; meng mein or junoon chakra = 8 petals; Spleen or jaya chakra = 6 petals; Navel or tej chakra = 8 petals; Solar plexus or dharm chakra = 10 petals; Heart or karm chakra = 12 petals; Throat or pattra chakra = 16 petals; Ajna or Aar chakra = 2 petals. Now, if we add up the petals of these eleven main chakras, we get 72.

There is a point in acupuncture, known as the pericardium 6. It is located above the wrist crease, between the tendons and the forearm. It is believed that pressing this point calms emotions, mind, improves sleep cycle, balances energies, improves health and overall your brainpower. Hindus often wear *moli* or thread in this wrist after *Pooja* (prayers) to activate this point.

However, even though intuitive knowledge is the ultimate grace and blessing. It can only be known to the one who has received it. It is not enough until it can be shared and spread in every home.

The average human heartbeat is 72 beats per minute. 72 beats per minute imply 12 breaths per minute. The average body contains 72 percent water. As the meridians pass from anterior to posterior (from front to back), the total number of activated petals turns to 72 + 72 = 144.

If we go by Leonardo's concept of the Vitruvian Man then we understand how he beautifully explained the workings of the universe through using the human body.

The world is a creation of five masculine elements and feminine energy. Alpha or beginning contains the trinity (3) of ether, air, and light. Omega or ending contains the duality (2) of ether and air. The human self is a perfect mini world in itself. When we realize this, all our mini and minor energy points, micro and macro aura are in perfect balance. All our major energy centers are fully activated and such a being is one with the five (5) elements and the cosmic energies. 144 + 5 = 149. By adding the 144 petals to the 5 pointed stars on the human brain (Da Vinci's North Star of Polaris), we get 149 petals. Through a perennial heightened meditative state, Da Vinci drew the form of the formless which is beyond gender. It is also beyond the simple concept of time, space, or understanding of most people. No wonder, after more than 500 years we all are still intrigued with the mysticism behind Mona Lisa.

The hidden codes on the front and back of the Mona Lisa painting have the same numbers mentioned here. The aura of Mona Lisa looks so relaxed, strong, and powerful only because she always has a slight hint of a smile. That gentle smile upon her face always remains. Some choose to see it and some don't. Our perception doesn't change her true worth. You look where your eyes fixate. Wherever you put your attention - reflects and expresses your thoughts. With her constant smile, Mona Lisa reminds us that smiling not only fills our hearts with love but also reduces issues arising out of hypertension. With the power of this smile, even a painting can have a better life than those living outside of the canvas.

Clearly, when most talented people create something, their creative skills get expanded and enriched further. As their skills improve, they improve as well. Da Vinci transmuted and transformed into a better version of himself with each work of art that he created. And as he continued to create, it instilled and inspired the creative juices within others. This way his energy kept expanding in the universe and his vibrations became one with his higher self. The more perfection is imbued in our creations, the more love we spread, the bigger our auras become and a big aura cannot be contained in our contracted physical mortal bodies. This is the reason why a huge part of us which is immortal, always remains outside of us.

There are seven centers in the head. Three out of them are love (wisdom), will (power), and active intelligence. These activities continue to work and help you evolve. After the activation of the seventh point at the back, you become one with and twice as strong as the oak tree. In knowing the fourfold reality of your body, mind, soul, and spirit, you sail smoothly through life's changes and wavering seasons. Only a heart as strong as a double-headed eagle knows what it is like to trust, believe, and share. Love is trust. It attracts you, trusting it makes you strong, finding it makes you stronger and feeling it makes you even stronger.

As we develop sensitivities, the connection between the front and back energy circuits of our body circulate and are completed through the *nadis* or channels. We have 72,000 nadis, and when the front yang and back yin channels meet, it is like two people making divine love and merging together. The exchange of their electromagnetic fields results at the beginning of the activation of 144,000 nadis in total.

Going by the popular seven chakras:

Mooladhara or sthir chakra has 4 petals; Swadhistana or sthapana chakra has 6 petals; Manipura or dharm chakra has 10 petals; Anahata or karm chakra has 12 petals; Vishuddhi or pattra chakra has 16 petals. Combined these total 48 petals. Ajna chakra has 2 major petals. These are twice as powerful as the five lower chakras- 48 X 2 = 96. As per the author, the third eye chakra is named such because it is thrice as powerful as the five lower chakras- 48 X 3 = 144 petals. The Sahasrara or taaj chakra is 10 times more powerful than the Ajna chakra (96 X 10) and has 12 inner lotus petals in the center = 960 + 12 = 972 petals. Finally, as we release ourselves of all blockages – As the name goes the thousand-petalled crown chakra gives a birds-eye view that is thousand times more powerful than the (Bindu chakra which equals) the lower six chakras = 4+6+10+12+16+96 = 144 x 1000 = 144000. All these radiating chakras of bioenergy form our aura and are interrelated with the five elements of earth, water, fire, air, and ether = 149000 petals in a perfect being. This is the number written at the back of the portrait.

Creation happened in seven nights and six days. Seven yang and six yin energy points become activated and we can recreate our lives. As the thirteenth chakra becomes activated, the cycle continues. There are 144 petals (above and inside) the third eye chakra, or the pineal gland. Interestingly, the pineal gland in our endocrine system has 144,000 magnetic sand-like particles.

'Nardo' means the deep intense scent of the night. It is named after a flower called Nardo. Leo means a lion who is strong and warm like the rays of the sun. True to his name, Leonardo was a perfect combination of day and night, yang and yin.

'La' is a feminine personification in French. It is a word that is no longer used as extensively as it used to be. It has the potential to juice up any sentence. 'La' represents the physical manifest visible which means being around there and here. In musical notes, 'La' is a note that follows 'So'. 'La' also is the short form of the Greek alphabet 'lambda'.

When we see through the left hemisphere of our brain- we see things through intuitive vision and know through direct divine contact which gives us the feelings we call our 'aha' moments! When we see through the right hemisphere of our brain - we do not see things as they are but a mirror image (example - b = d). No wonder the right eye and right shoulder appears larger in the Mona Lisa painting as well. MONA is written on the left and so it is written as-is but LISA is on the right and so if we write reversed or mirror word of LISA, we get ASIL. Now, if we join the first two alphabets of the two words, we get the following sentence - "am so in la".

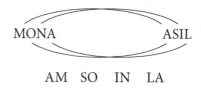

MONA   ASIL

AM   SO   IN   LA

The germatia value of La = 50; as a consonant, the value of La = 28, and the *Sushumna* or balancing Nadi has 28 main channels. We established above that **Mona Lisa** is another way to express, **"Am so in la"**. Each alphabet has a meaning in Egyptian or any other language. Let's observe the possible meanings of alphabets used here:

M = beginning of creative intelligence within the self. Combination of angelic and martial aspect, kinship. Also known as yin and yang of water.

O = omega, a perfect sun that preserves and protects. All races and languages are within one.

N = destruction or death through discriminative intelligence or intuitive light.

A = alpha, the A of AUM, involuntary government, or order of anarchy.

L = power

I = hidden interest

S = double helix in spiral form complement each other

A = stop sign, reflection for taking potentiality to actuality. 'A' has 5 endpoints like the 5 points or stars in our brain.

Going by the meaning of the above alphabets, the sentence - "Am so in la" implies:

Am=light or the beginning and creation of spiritual authority of anarchism. (A and M of AUM)

So=light is preserved and protected inside the double helix of common DNA we all share in a state of equilibrium

In=we can tap the hidden knowledge and not destroy its essence with our intuitive intelligence.

La=we can collectively recreate our entire creation and recharge the five-pointed star within our collective brain through divine power of self will graced by god's love.

Simply put, the sentence means that 'Akashic' records, a library that contains the secret of humanity's collective DNA is in the cup of da vi-n-ci brain. Through his art, he let us know that we can tap the source of this programmed knowledge. Knowledge is power. A wise person like him chose to create life and spread love rather than destroy life and spread evil through the use of intuitive wisdom.

In Roman numerals, Remove DNA from DA VI N CI and we are left with VI and CI:

VI= 6, CI= 101, I = 1 or A, we collectively are interconnected through one. Add up the three and we get the sacred number 108. The distance between the earth and the sun is 108 times the diameter of the sun. 108 meridians converge to form our heart center. Much like AUM, 108 has the essence to make us whole. N= as the alphabet suggests, mysterious intuitive power of the one. D = 500 years of Da Vinci's death. Just as he predicted, after exactly 501 years of his death, the mystery codes of Mona Lisa are finally unraveled by the one who is its rightful heir, out of pure love.

Additionally rearranged Mona Lisa can be Anima Sol. Anima is human soul and Sol is Sun or spirit. The union of the two is soul and spirit.

Affirm- 'Namostutee, I found the answer to my how when I reached the blissful gates of the perfect, hidden garden and library of intellectual knowledge. Tathaastu.'

CHAPTER 154

EK DOUBLE CHAI

'*C*hai' in Hebrew means life. This chapter is written in admiration of 'chai' which gives us double the life energy. If you get too accustomed to holding a bigger cup, then over time it gets difficult for your hands to get a grip on the smaller cup. We all are intertwined and joined enhancing each other's lives in one way or the other. We all are '*ek double chai*'.

'Ek' in scientific terms means kinetic energy, a primary predisposition that causes us to move. In Hebrew, 'Ek' means under the heavenly inspiration and in Punjabi 'Ek' means the One that causes everything to get switched on.

Love is an inspiration, it makes you do things you are already good at in a better way and each time you meet with love, and you keep getting better.

We all have someone that doubles our life energy. Every morning for the last 17 years, my husband wakes me up in the morning with a cup of Indian '*garam masala chai*'. I call that cup - the cup of life - every sip doubles up my life energy, enhancing my mood and day for I know that he values me enough to make me a cup of *chai*, come what may. The *chai* gives meaning to my day and it reminds him of the reason why he married me and that reason is the life energy that we both share. Together we are the double chai, having twice the life energy, we had earlier.

Just the way there is a grandfather and grandmother clock, there should be a husband clock. It is the husbands who give way to a new change in our lives. Without them, we women cannot have a natural birth allowing new energies to come in. Just like time, a dedicated efficient husband works like clockwork in an orderly fashion and ignites passion into the entire household to continuously go on striking. They are our energy, our cup of *chai*, our *kaal*. We, wives, are the chakra or wheel or energy centers around which they revolve. This way we both get centered and rooted within the 'Ki' or energy of 'Kaal' or time.

It seems as though we are many, but we are all energetic beings, created from the same energy, and are one with that energy that illuminates us and brings us closer to our truth each day. We all inherently speak the same language and have the same faith. We all are one. We are the creators of our *Chai* / Chi- life force energy. So let's get more connected and double up on our cup of *chai*.

Keep your eyes open, the connection you feel maybe is because the person standing at your arm's length might just be your long lost family member. You make choices about the time you take. Also for how long for the things that you really care about, value, understand, and resonate with. You take the time for what is precious and life-enhancing for you. You look around, dig within, pause and introspect. Are you taking enough time to do what is important and meaningful to you?

Avoid mixing tasks- give each task, its due importance and time. The more internet-connected we get, the more disconnected we get from ourselves. The more crowded the streets get, the lonelier we feel. The more we have, the lesser we feel we have. The more happiness we seek, the sadder we get. In hindsight, the more we understand, the more we are understood. The more we care to share, the more we are given to receive. The more complex things get, the more we forget to enjoy the simplicity of life. No one can love, lead, laugh, live or learn alone. We all are inherently connected and bound, we all need one another. We all are one universal consciousness breathing together. Let's teach ourselves what it is like to breathe, let's become alive. Let's have a cup of chai (life energy) together.

Every time I teach youth groups, I feel the emptiness in them and can't help but refill their cup with love, joy & bliss. Parenting was never meant to be a one woman's job, it takes a village to raise a child.

Let the children know - I value you, I need you, I want you, I love you, I praise you, I forgive you, I ask for forgiveness, I accept you, I embrace you. We all are connected, everything I do & feel, so do you. I am the vibrational energy, you become the vibrations you send out. And so, I am valued, I am needed, I am wanted, I am loved, I am praised, I am forgiven, I am forgiving, I am accepted, I am embraced, I am actively, subtly, and vibrationally perennially connected. I am the light of your life bulb. I am life. With you, I am whole and complete. I value you, I love you and therefore you value yourself and you love yourself and I am you and you are me for we are one.

I met an old friend over a cup of chai. I told her "I know it has been a long time since we've met. I have been on a journey within". In Hebrew, chai means *chi or life energy*. When we meet, we not only drink chai but we also exchange chai. The task is to know what matches your aura or consciousness. One summer holiday, my son was up all night chatting with me while I was busy writing, and at the very same time, my husband was up all night, working on an office presentation, while I was sleeping by his side in our bedroom. The next day, they both argued. My husband said that Ma was sleeping in the bedroom, and my son said that I was writing in the living room. The further one goes, the less one knows. It was one of those times when I was in two places at once, like the time I was meditating at the Buddhist monastery, yet I was at home with my family, doing chores. Two different locations and yet the same person completely balanced within her physical body. Yes, it is possible!

Time and space is magical. We try to decipher its beauty based on our subjective, limited understanding. Some people say there is no right time. Time is an impression. Sure it is, but this holds true only until you find your true love. Once you meet with your true twin soul or sweet mate, time is always right. Time is life.

Another interesting example of when my cup was filled with a double cup of chai:

Just the way waves can occupy two places at once, so can we. In September I visited November lane in Westport, Connecticut in America with my husband. It was an adventurous journey that lasted over 4 hours including the time we spent exploring the area. My son stayed home to complete the project he was then working on. When I returned home, my son who was home all along, was really surprised when I told him I just returned from my journey. This is because he saw and felt my presence all through, while I was away. We can occupy not just two but multiple places at the same time, once we get deeper into the yogic path. Just the way a beam of light on the white sheet can spread to manifold places, so can beings of light. Sometimes we do not realize their presence because just as light is bright in some places, while in some other places we do not even see its reflection- Beings of light attain certain 'Siddhis'. This way they become like heat waves whose presence is felt maximum in places they put their most attention. This mystery has intrigued many people I meet, who thought I was with them when it wasn't the case. Some of us like to deny what cannot be explained because we want to fit in the norms society has set. In this way, we prefer inner darkness over igniting the gravitational pull of our (warm chi) *'garam chai'*. It is like sometimes we confront a strange absurd phenomenon but we do not acknowledge its reality, either because it is superimposed by our clouded thinking or because it doesn't fit the usual understanding of associations and dissociations we have accustomed ourselves to.

Empty and release the animal cup. Cleanse the insides of your golden cup to fill it with luck, faith, and healing light of spiritual truth. No matter how empty your cup is, there is no cup under the sun that cannot be filled, refreshed, and rejuvenated with God's healing love.

The light of the sun is controlled by the mother of life. The darkness of the moon is controlled by the father of knowledge. When the two unite and get balanced, perfect harmony between conscious and subconscious is created within your golden cup of chai. There is nothing more soul-stirring than a warm cup of chai when you want to unwind by the window on a cold winter night.

Affirm- 'Namostutee, Each person's good action matters and every right decision leaves a trace. Let us unite, learn, grow, smile and transition together. Tathaastu.'

CHAPTER 155

WOMEN WHO TOOK THE PILL

Women carry the DNA of child, father, and herself when she gets pregnant and the lingering cells of all three get impregnated within her. If you switch off the light bulb, it gives out no light, but the bulb still exists though it seems to be off or dead energetically. And so if you do not remove this so-called lifeless life growing within you completely, this foreign micro-chimerical energy within your body can cause health, immunity, and hormonal issues. As far as possible, it is better to nurture this life if you are capable and able. Abortion or miscarriages have a lasting imprint on a woman's auric and physical body.

Hindus believe in *'Kundali' (birth-chart)* matching for a healthy fetus and marriage match. A fetus can sometimes sap your resources so a mother has to be careful about how much she wants to give at any stage or age. The reason why maintaining the sanctity and character of your virtue is important is because some of you are energetically carrying the residue of your past relationships and remnants of pregnancies that never resulted in full-term birth.

Your struggle and competition is you. You are a group soul and not a singular identity. The complex game of life teaches us that there are no things left to chance, every moment is necessary, every choice is important. It is important to know exactly what we are doing at every moment, even if what we are doing is seen by another as an utter waste of time! If you want to reach your goal, you have to accelerate yourself and be aware and conscious of what you are doing at each moment rather than letting life pass over your head. You are a complex combination of cells and you are never really alone so you have all the help within you and outside of you to make the next smart move and win with focused committed unwavering attention. An accomplished corporate executive will tell you how critical it is to aptly communicate, negotiate, strategize, cooperate and understand. Here we are doing something more- by acknowledging the subtle underlying causes that make us better, bigger people.

Whatever you may do and wherever you may go through in life, always remember that your family should always be your prime responsibility and your ability to deeply connect with them amicably and joyfully is of utmost importance. You are related to them for a reason, there are lessons for you to learn through them, sometimes these chapters are far more informative than the ones you find in the thick books of the various libraries you visit.

It is said that post-conception:

18 days and a baby's heart begins to beat,
28 days and a baby's eyes, ears, tongue muscle start to bud,
43 days and a brain coordinates movement,
8 weeks and all organs begin to function,
9 weeks and individual fingerprints start to develop,
10 weeks and a baby can start to feel,
12 weeks and a baby can smile, suck their thumb and make a fist.

Even if you abort within 45 days, the baby's emotional and mental body are already developed. You have only killed the baby's physical birth and not the etheric, emotional, mental or astral. This psychic bodiless formless soul can travel at lightning speed without any hindrance. Until you release and cut the umbilical cord from all levels with protocols of disconnecting, forgiving, and releasing the cords - the baby might still exist in a formless subtle state or enter into your next womb. What you abort is not just a blob of tissue so think before you act.

The moments take our breath away. We enjoy the moments only because we are giving our breath away to those moments. Don't focus on what you get, but on what you give. The number of breaths per minute will slow down and elongate automatically. The more you learn to control your breath, the longer you live. The more you give, the more essence you get.

I recently saw the movie, *The Biggest Little Farm*, the lazy pig's character caught my eye. Stuck in the mud, she seems so ignorant of the happenings of life that she knows nothing about how and when she gets pregnant. She doesn't even realize when she has piglets after piglets, until one day, a rooster comes and sits on her head. He won't leave her sight until she learns to get up and experience life in its entirety. Not caring about anything that is going on around you is also a negative form of attachment. It depresses you. All our senses must be involved in everything we do, not out of delusion, anger, or lust, but out of pure love for living life.

We have 72,000 main meridians in our body that continuously circulate to vitalize our chi or life energy. These meridians are also called nadis or energy currents. They are activated through our *chakras* based on the number of petals that open up in our inner and outer world. We have 33,000 nadis on the left side of our body and 33,000 on the right side, and 6000 in the center. Each nadi assists in the proper functioning of our physical organs. The three main nadis, or electric currents, are *Ida* on the left, *Pingala* on the right, and *Sushumna* in the center. Respectively, these represent the lunar, solar, and grace nadi. As they circulate, these increase the love, power, and light in our life, making our life more comfortable based on the hard work we do. The grace nadi is neutral, having both yin (feminine) and yang (masculine) qualities. Their colors are blue, red, and gold. Each is stimulated through properly regulated breathing and water purification techniques. The left brain and the right side of the body are lunar. The right brain and the left side of the body are solar. *Sushmna* is the center, where the balance lies.

Our body is like a tower. Ajna or Aar chakra is like the roof, and the basic or sthir chakra is like the foundation of this tower. While the roof, or *Ajna*, is higher, without the foundation of the building, the tower cannot be built. The base is the reason the roof was built, in order to protect it. In a building, the heavy, dark, solid ceiling is built to shield us. A glass roof might bring in more light, but it is also prone to damage by storms and changing weather. In the case of a child's body or tower, the roof temporarily opens when it is born. Slowly, the roof, or crown chakra, closes in order to keep it protected, but the material that connects the threads always remains, even when the roof is closed. Remember, the roof is strong because of the base.

A house with a glass ceiling might be too translucent, with too much bright light. But glass is fragile, so a stronger alternative would be to use the same dense materials that made the base. But why worry? Why get stuck? Beyond the darkness of the roof, there is only bright light. From time to time, you may come out of your bodily tower in order to connect with what is beyond your roof. It is a miracle that we breathe. We take over 17,000 breaths per day, so we have more than 17,000 reasons to be grateful each day. The more we are grateful, the more miraculous our life becomes. Through the window of my study, I often get a glimpse of the small, brown wings of little brown birds disappearing through the branches of the oak trees in my yard. Despite their subtle markings and minor differences, each merges so well within itself and its surroundings that it is almost indistinguishable. Some birds' beaks are straight and some are curved, yet they seem so much at peace with their subtle differences. Their lack of self or ego makes so much sense. In the same way, a devotional person merges with the tree, the branches, and the birds to go beyond the distinction.

I am reminded of a popular Indian parable. *Siddhartha* saved the life of a swan that his cousin *Devadutta* tried to kill. *Devadatta* was an avid hunter. He aimed his arrow at a swan flying through the sky and pierced its wing. The injured bird fell heavily to the ground and *Siddhartha* ran to rescue her. He reached her first. Seeing her in pain, he tendered and nursed her carefully, comforting and soothing her cry, to give her life. A court hearing was held to decide who the rightful owner of the bird should be: the one who shot her or the one who nursed her. The wise king intuitively affirmed that the prized possession of every creature is its life. A creature belongs to whoever protects it, not to the one who attempts to take away its life. And the one who owns it can do what he wishes to do with it: set it free or put it in a cage! The court awarded the swan to Siddhartha. He sheltered it until it was fully healed, and then set it free.

When my husband was little, his dad bought him a bb gun. In his excitement, he impulsively aimed it at a little brown bird passing perched on a fence and shot it not knowing what would happen. The injured bird fell with a heavy thud to the ground. During the past forty years, he has been living with the guilt of having killed the bird.

Recently, I saw a bird in similar pain, so I nursed her carefully, healing her and soothing her cry, to give her life. Once she was cured, I let her fly away. The prized possession of every creature is its life. One shoots and another nurses. A truly liberated person is one who protects and heals the creature, not the one who attempts to take away its life. The one who shelters it without the intention to cage it is also the one who sets it free. The wounded bird forgave all past and blessed all those who helped her heal. In setting her free, my husband too was relieved of the years of burden and guilt he had been carrying. She set him free. As I set the bird free, I realized that we must stop trying to hold onto the desert sand or the gushing water in the palm of our hands.

In social gatherings, I may drink wine, coffee, or milk. None of the 'poisons' have any effect on me because I am open to enjoying and drinking them all. Anything consumed at the correct time, in the right dosage, and not in excess is the key to staying detached, unaffected, and balanced. Not drinking at all would make you wonder what the beverage tastes like. Having a preference for one will make you attached to the suffering. Staying unharmed while sipping them all through a hollow straw will make you understand the life learnings behind the void. When taken in moderation, each drink is nourishing. It is not the consumption of the poison, but you who is manipulating yourself. You learn life and relationships by hosting, and not by avoiding inviting guests over to your home. The more you circulate, the more you host, the more you drink--the more energized your life becomes. Once you become self-aware, pain and poison become just as liberating and immortalizing as the pleasure you get from drinking the immortal nectar. Mingling with our relatives and understanding them takes us to our ultimate reality.

You might have succeeded in breaking the inner yoke of Humpty Dumpty[132] with the wall of your ignorance, doubt, timidity, and rigidity but the fall didn't break its outer invisible shell. Ask for forgiveness and that spiritually heightened shell will forgive you for breaking it up even before it could see itself in full form.

Affirm- 'Namostutee, Everything in and around me is paradisiacal, sprightly, and invigorating because it is my nature to be mushy, kindly, tenderhearted, serene, and untroubled. Tathaastu'.

---

[132] *Humpty Dumpty is a famous character in children's nursery rhyme*

CHAPTER 156

CIRCLE OF GRATITUDE

I want to thank all those who live nobly in each moment. In this way, they consistently work behind the scenes for the spiritual awakening of the world.

Gratitude is my natural flair. Synchronicities are in the air. Fairies of light and love are in the midst of the stars and the skies. Wishes are coming true with seven galloping white horses[133] on my left and the reflection of fourteen elephants[134] on my right. Abundance and riches are now only an ask away. Organize and write your requests. That is the only task left before you fly away, free and unbound under the divine energy of the magical sky. This is the power of pure grace.

Those who love one another, thank one another.

And then the Earth said, "I soak your waters and release your waters through the pores of my body. You moisturize and dry me up under the heat of the sun, and you keep returning to cleanse and purify me from within. Never have you once complained that I am using you. You have given me so much. Tell me just one thing, what is it that I can give you in return?"

And the Water replied, "Use me. Soak me in. There is no such thing as waste. It is in my nature to give. I am here because I have been sent to give. The more I give, the more I will get. It is in providing for you that I too am gaining. You give me life. You even give meaning to my lifelessness.

---

[133] *The seven white galloping happy horses represent positive yang energies of great success, speed, power, luck, endurance, courage and fame.*

[134] *The fourteen elephants represent collective double manifestation of the strength, wealth, longevity, stamina, wisdom, patience and confidence.*

Without your wanting me, even ten percent of me would have had no reason to return again and again. It is in your needing me that I exist. Your need defines me and my identity."

The Earth then replied, "You are just being humble, for further, I move away from you, the closer I want to get to you. You are the only one who can quench my parched thirst. I am that sponge who wants to thank you, and sing everlasting praises to you for allowing me to absorb and soak you deep within me."

The Water replied, "I let you sing my praises, by all means, but let me also say a word or two. You revive me when I sometimes float lifelessly in the airy womb, searching for someone like you who wants me just as much. Sometimes water reaches places in the far distant lands, where no living things can ever survive. The Salt in the air here purifies me and enables me to be of service to you. So let us both thank and praise the Salt for allowing me to support you here. Let us be in gratitude and reverence to Air, which gently carried me in and let me intermingle with the salt floating in it."

The Earth replied, "Well then, the salty mist in the air--the combination of salt, water, and air--is what preserves and vitalizes you and me with youthful and bountiful energy, and so I am ever indebted to this trinity."

Water and Earth collectively said, "Let us thank the salt that bound us all."

And so the Salt replied, "I am here because of another. Let us first and foremost thank the Soul and Spirit behind it all, which brought me here. My parents are Sulfur and Mercury, the hot and cold combination of fire and air. Their unity is the cause behind all that you see. The reason that unites them is no outside force, but a force within, and that bond is called eternal love."

We, humans, are pretty much like walking plants. We grow best and achieve our full potential when we are in sync with nature and its bounty. And you, my dear, must inscribe the name of your partner in work, for taking the fruits of another's work is a debt you must repay for centuries to come. Time is still there. Thoughtful kindness and gratitude is the key to unlock the lock.

The imbalance of the four elements within us is the cause of all ill. Restoring these elements requires you to be in immense gratitude. Praise nature for bringing you and everything in and around back to its natural, healthy, wholesome state. As you begin to feel the gratitude and thank all, more and more impurities that cause your vision to fog, in and around you get cleared.

Wherever your true self is, just let it be. No one teaches you to love, no one owns it, no one can take it or give it, and it is always out there waiting for you to recognize it. A simple word of appreciation gives additional meaning to what one does. So freely appreciate, recognize and share your kindness and love.

Each of our organs is a borrowed part and so we must forever be indebted to those beings who lend us their eyes, their sense of smell, wisdom, care, love, support, and give us a reason to go on living. We shine because we are a reflection of those who bless us. We must always praise them for the sacrifices they made, we must celebrate thanksgiving every day no matter what part of the world we may hail from.

Affirm- 'Namostutee, I am fair in judgment and my speech is filled with Godliness, praise, and gratitude. I am strong, pure, and just. Tathaastu.'

CHAPTER 157

HEAVENLY DANCE

W e all are striving for ultimate perfection and this phenomenon does finally turn into perfection sooner or later.

The heaven below is a mirror reflection of the heaven above. What seems the lowest here is the highest above. What seems the highest above is the lowest here. The youngest here is the oldest above, and the oldest here is the youngest above. We all are a phenomenon so are the planets above.

Based on the vibrations, energetic beings emit, we too transmute and shine leaving behind what no longer serves us after taking help from both extremes of black and white. These inherently are but the same - night and day - the sleep and wakefulness. Using will- the phenomenon goes through organized steps of calcination, congelation, fixation, dissolution, digestion, distillation, sublimation, separation, ceration, fermentation, multiplication, and projection. After these 12 mutations, the phenomenon then miraculously becomes what it attracts. Just as vapors rise then condense and then re-vaporize so does all phenomenon - first separates then purifies and then finally reunites. Three different steps thrice over make you reborn much like the morning dew.

In a deep trance you find the answers to universal truths. It is when you turn your receptors on that you hear the angelic song. Your openness brings to you universal messages. You become part of the cosmic dance and know the divine origins of everything in its original form. Synchronized dancing in a circle is about having the same thoughts like other people. This way the entire cosmos is one because we all are dancing to the same rhythmic tune.

Pure Spirit tells us about the elemental dance: "You three-water, earth, and fire-stand tall because of the humble two-air and ether. You three are visible because of the blinding two. The duality-genderless and subtle-brings out the trinity. The separation of trinity brings in the unity of duality. The duality is invisible unless it makes itself visible through the unity of trinity."

Nothing is apparent or visible without the form of the trinity and the formlessness of duality. Nothing is singular and nothing is alone. All the elements also dance within us. In the plurality of this world, we are all subject to our own cruelty of separation and depression, for joy only lies in the connection of divine multiplication. Each of the five elements has a two-fold quality: ascending and descending. Let's all move forward in groups of no less than the perfect ten. In this way, we will be able to make some sense out of our self-created dense and seemingly impenetrable prison.

The fight you are fighting is long over. A new war has begun. Wake up and rise. It is you, not I, who has been sleeping so long. Many new stars are shining. Look! Even the sky is so bright and clear. In the summer of 2019, we saw thunder and lightning almost every night. It is time that I must speak the thunderous truth, charged with the bioenergy to magnetize all those wise enough not to dread the loud sparks of electricity. The Gods above are talking to us and as long as you are receptive- you will hear its powerful voice filtered subtly through me.

The planets above work as a team, to inspire us to function systematically and safely under the universal rule. Each chakra has a ruling planet. Venus rises against the gravitational pull, and Uranus strangely is in the backside of the gravity point. Except for these stubborn two, all the others, resistant or not, are more or less under the gravitational force. Plants, animals, humans are all one collective energy. What affects one, affects all. The invisible cosmic forces impact the energy fields of all beings. Let's make peace so that the dance can begin.

As the age of air and intellectualism is here- small steps lead to big changes.

Affirm- 'Namostutee, I choose each step I take patiently, willfully, and wisely. This way I progress based on my kind and positive visualizations for the greater good. Tathaastu.'

CHAPTER 158

POWER OF YOUR NAME

English Alphabets are a combination of alpha and beta. Each vowel and consonant has a particular value. There are no coincidences. Everything has a story to tell. Your name has no mysticism. Each vowel in your name was preordained by God. You were named before you were renamed with the same name. In this constant repetition of unseen to seen, from the Southwest to the North, just face the East with ease and you will know the answer to all your Y's. Look at the chart below.

The countries you have traveled to, the place you were born, and where you currently live are all preordained and meticulously planned out, based on your accumulated and manifested karma.

Eyes are lamps to our body the way ether is the lamp to our soul.

It is essential to know more about your soul purpose and also what your soul pines for. All you have to do is add the vowels of the full name and you would be able to find more about your soul pining through the number you arrive at. If the number arrived after adding the vowels is 11, 22, 33, or 44 then do not reduce it further. In all other cases, reduce the numbers to a single digit by adding the digits so that you arrive at a number between 1 and 9.

Vowels	Number	Soul calling	Pining
A	1	Credential & positive leader	Accomplishment & appreciation
E	5	Liberated through deep inquiry	Adventure and change
I	9	More gutsy and serve humanity	Courage, greater exposure, and involvement
O	6	Responsible healer and nurturer	Love and luxury

U	3	Artistic and charismatic	Lead a group through cheerfulness and joy
Y	7	Spiritually wise	Perfection and comfort

Other letters and numbers-

88 are responsible master knowers. They are divine manifestations and messengers who support us and bring good luck, freshness, and abundance through wisdom, belief, and patience. 44 are master healers who set the foundation of world order during the new cycle and are driven by love. 33 are master teachers amongst us who descend from Satya Yuga as teachers of sacred truth. 22 are ambitious master builders amongst us who descend from *Treta Yuga* as virtuous kings to build a better society. 11 are master envisioners who descend from *Dvapara Yuga* to remove diseased energies.

Number	Soul calling	Pining
2	Peacemaker and cooperative	Psychological harmony and ease.
4	Loyal and do respectful work	Financial security for future safety.
8	Rich dependable business brand	Financial success, authority, and power.

High or low, do not go by the labels or the forms alone. All and everyone is equally important. Your light and you are here balanced and centered right in the middle because of the support of these two opposite yet complementary forces of love and power. When you open yourself up to these universal and cosmic energies, you will see how the universe begins to talk with you with the same heightened vibrations, positivity, and clarity. When you stop hiding, everything that was hiding begins to reveal itself to you. Beyond the childish game of hide-n-seek, is where the mystical magical dance actually begins. All answers are here, you have been delusion-ally seeking them elsewhere.

Affirm- 'Namostutee, May every one spiritually reawaken and unite with renewed hope, tranquility, and prosperity, liberty and faith world over. Tathaastu.'

CHAPTER 159

MOSA

M osa is an Arabic word that means saved from the water. Seventy-two percent of the earth's surface is covered with water. Water saves us. Some of us are like the trout fish who heroically swim against the current of the freshwater river. This is because sometimes swimming through rough water may actually be easier and more beneficial than swimming across a calm pond. For example when we push ourselves, against the flow of our nature and run on the treadmill then the cardio exercise greatly improves and benefits our energy levels.

Beneath the surface, a river is a turbulent place. Fish somehow manage their way through this turbulence and reflect what the flow is doing. Taking inspiration from them, I call people who go with the flow- "wu-wei", which means "to do without doing". To come out alive is about holding a station when things are unpredictable and later making your way through calmly like a fish swimming through the choppy waters. This way we do not overwhelm or over exhaust ourselves on the treadmill of life.

We are also part aquatic species so let's talk water. Water, water, everywhere.

Surely we all realize the importance of finding water, one of the most crucial sources of life. An ancient, trusted medium of finding this perennial source is through water diviners. There are water diviners who are mysteriously capable of accurately finding out where they feel the twitch of water. Same way there are divine conduits who are intuitively capable of subtly finding out where your true potential lies. The methods adopted by both these are queer and beyond the scope of scientific understanding, yet the richness of their ability to reach the source based on their findings is abundant.

We dig deep within the surface of the land, drilling wells to find pristine water beneath the rocks, deep with the ground and far from all pollutants. In the same way, we can dig deep within our superficiality, drilling out some clarity to find purity beneath the emotional blocks, deep within our minds and far from all mental toxicity.

We all must realize the importance of prana (wholesome life force energy), another of the most crucial sources of life. An ancient, trusted medium of finding this perennial source is through spiritual healers.

To stop the water running back down the pipe when the pump stops working, we need to install a non-return valve on the bottom of the delivery pipe to make sure it stays full of water. In the same way, to stop the positive energy from running back down the dark negative alley, energy healers apply sacred protocols of shielding to ensure the divine energy doesn't leak out and is forever replenished. These mediums may be your backup plan. Your backup plan might be your last-ditch effort, but this is what keeps you and your energy well balanced and circulating. Harnessing energy revitalizes your life force. All you need is faith and receptivity in the divine to seek help from energy healers.

Dirty water can kill you, clean water too can kill you if you are dirty.

You come across a wishing well. The wishing well promises to honor and bless you with three wishes in return for three pennies. You must believe in this strange ritual for your wish to come true. If you do believe, then you must remember to wish well.

While throwing each coin if we are cribbing and crying about your current circumstances, pain and suffering then all that negativity that you have thrown into the well is what the wishing well is going to remember. What you throw in is what you will get back. Why not throw beatific thoughts of positive manifestation and dreams you want to achieve. Remember what you ask for is what you receive, you definitely do not want to ask for more bad and negativity. So wish thoughtfully, justly and conscientiously.

In a world where sharks are increasing by the day, Jesus is crucified daily. During WW-II, strange coincidences saved some lives. In strange, serendipitous ways, some friends and families found each other again. For example- Laizer Halberstam, a five-year-old Jewish boy in a Polish village, violated his family's wishes by befriending a non-Jewish boy. Halberstam taught his friend a Jewish prayer, and in return, his friend taught him a Christian prayer. Ten years after the incident, Halberstam was fleeing the Nazis under a Christian alias. A soldier examined his papers and asked him to recite the Christian prayer to prove that he was indeed Christian. Thankfully, even after ten years, he still remembered the prayer his friend taught him and that prayer saved his life. Such is the power of being aware and alert while forming friendships, praying, experiencing life, or confronting unprecedented crises during a war.

When we are driving in foggy weather, the mist in the glass blinds our vision and we don't see the road ahead clearly, but once we wipe the windshield thoroughly, we can see that the path was always lit.

Based on the temperature, water has many manifestations. It may form into solid ice or it may form into steamy vapors. The latter is invisible to the naked eye but that doesn't mean the vapors do not exist. Our astral or etheric body is invisible like the vapors of the water. In lower temperatures, we can know their existence in the air to be as true as that of water or ice.

While swimming in the deep end of a pool, it dawned upon me that if someone swimming in the shallow side urinates then the urine will flow through the pool. Whether you are in the deep or the shallow end will not really matter to the spreading contamination. One person maintaining proper hygiene and purification is not enough as everyone in the pool needs to follow the same discipline. This law plays out precisely - In hurting you I hurt myself and in loving you - I love myself. May you rediscover, renew, re-emerge, re-energize and remember.

In the center of our brain, there is a golden one-eyed fish with peacock colored fins. This lucky fish swims inside the waters of our body just the way fish swim in the oceanic waters. Our body is like a beautiful empty vase. Whatever wish our body has is fulfilled by the fish swimming inside the aquarium of our brain. All the fortune, happiness, peace, and bliss is within the space of our mind. The potential of our mind is as limitless as the cosmic space, as our mind is within the expanse of universal space. If we keep the aquarium pure and the outside energies clean and positive, the sensitive fish living inside do not die or wither. If our mind stays vitalized so do we.

Some souls are like my pet fish. The fish use their magical power and choose to stay only in surroundings where they can catch vibrations of positivity and love. They stay in the body as long as they can feel love around them and they leave the body if they catch opposite vibes. Sometimes in losing something, you find yourself.

Let us bless our savior - the oceans, bodies of water, lakes, rivers, water vapors, waterfalls, and the smallest of dewdrops constantly circulating to moisturize the air and the soil of our planet. Water is life, all life started in water. Water teaches us how to live life by setting a perfect example of cohesiveness, dynamism, transparency, and fluidity.

Let us charge and bless the water that saves us before we drink it. If the water we consume is clear and clean then we will have purity and clarity within. When our energies are not balanced and stuck, we can easily adapt, flow and progress during any situation. The effect of the past and present toxins cause us to get stagnated, frustrated, and stuck. This greatly affects our progress by clouding our decision and judgment making abilities.

However, I received profound insights to prepare specialized bottles. These bottles are blessed and charged with healing properties. Drinking water from these bottles heals psychological and physical issues. This shows the light and fills you with confidence, wisdom, and fortune. It activates your second chakra - (sacral energy point). You may please contact me to order a bottle for yourself if you are thirsty to uplift and refresh yourself up.

Ask a panting dog, a Hindu woman after fasting during *Karwachauth* (Hindu women, especially in north India, keep a fast from sunrise to moonrise), a Muslim who is about to break the *Ramadan (the ninth month of the Muslim calendar)* fast, a thirsty man in the arid desert, a person with pneumonia and dry throat - what it is like to be parched with thirst and then you will know the importance of *Mosa*.

When water is still, you do not feel it. It is only when you move, action, and explore its depths that you feel and understand that water is there. Pearl is wise and valued only because one goes through a long in-depth journey in the deep waters before its beauty and purity are brought out clearly into the open. This is quite similar to the holy water sprinkled by the priest at the church. A similar ritual is followed in the Buddhist monasteries where sacred waters are sprinkled on the body of the images of Buddha.

Suvastu is a river that flows from Swat valley. Suvastu means clear azure water. The valley is known for its pristine beauty and Buddhist influence. My grandmother hailed from there. I hear that my great grand-father was the education minister of the Kashmir valley during the reign of Maharaja Hari Singh. Much like the clear waters of Suvastu, I transform the positivity and purity subconsciously received by me through my ancestral roots. In this way, the mystical visions I receive in my dream state could perhaps be the result of my great grandfather's experiences. Not only is our DNA genetically engineered but also mentally we go back to our roots and reconnect with our ancestors during fluid deep sleep. Memories flood our whole body with bliss and great insight in a flash of an instance. It is a grace from our ancestors when we remember, recollect and grasp our dreams. These ancestral memories awaken our mind with cosmic power and primeval awareness as we parrot them with incessant repetition.

Affirm- 'Namostutee, Just like water - I too am sweet, cool, soft, light, transparent, pure, pleasant, and easygoing. Just like water in the infinite sea, I too radiate shining light of deep insight when the sky is pitch dark at night. Tathaastu.'

CHAPTER 160

DIVINE FEMININE

To invoke the divine feminine[135], I urge all to meditate in the open air during full moon nights. We all are one, yet entangled within our egocentric ideologies. Beyond the outer and the inner, there is a reserved enigma waiting to be understood.

Touch your forehead and chant '*Aum*'. Touch your throat and chant '*Ah*'. Finally, touch your chest and chant '*Hum*'. This mantra by *Lord Padmasambhava* will enlighten you and bring clarity into your mind and body cleansing you from within.

Your shadow and you are one. Your manifestation is also you. Your reality manifested you. Your creative reality and discernment is the cause of your creation and preservation. What you create represents you, what you preserve also represents you. Your reality is you. It is by the grace of the creator, preserver, and destroyer that your reality is constantly recreated.

The sunny daylight side also has a dark shadow side. We are here to energetically spread our celestial wisdom and radiant pure light while being peaceful, smiling, fashionably well-dressed, and tenderhearted. We are impartial and calm like the pristine rays of the sun on a clear sunny day that vibrantly falls upon everyone equally, the sinner and the righteous alike, irrespective of caste, creed, culture, race, country, gender, species, or any background they may belong.

The divine feminine is all praise and all pleasure, cobras and venomous vipers are her playmates, so are the divine angels and the great masters.

---

[135] *Divine Feminine is the ideal, generous, and independent woman whose true home is the entire world. The whole world is her family.*

She feels the magnificent beauty in the underworld, the overworld, and the middle world for she knows that it all came from her. She is the divine Mother. Those who are one with all know her and so they think and act differently. She is pure and chaste like *Mata Sattee*.

A truly beautiful woman is a woman who is truly free and liberated. She is unbound by society's pressures. She is all compassionate, loving, beautiful, accepting, embracing, forgiving, powerful, positive modern woman of today. You want to enjoy lovemaking more, then first learn to respect every woman on the planet. Lovemaking is an art only a woman can teach you. You are meant to worship, appreciate, praise, and woo her. That is your purpose. Do not get defeated by your ego. Do not let go.

Today's women are natural leaders and content in themselves. They are independent, resourceful, intuitive, and wealthy. They believe life is meant to enjoy, love, and be adventurous. My husband jokingly says women are always right but this fact makes them even more attractive.

Women inherently blend in, change, adapt to the strangest of situations and the most uncertain scenarios and circumstances of life. When left free, they can handle anything thrown at them and succeed with grace, imagination, charm, patience, calmness, and finesse. However, when the feminine energy becomes scared or is under any sort of fear, it tends to get imbalanced, threatened, arrogant, angry, disinterested, insecure, and anxious. The more protected and appreciated they feel, the closer they come to bringing perfection not only into themselves but also into you. If the woman is difficult, hesitant, frustrated, or rude, then most likely she is overworked, overwhelmed, and stressed. Her way of dealing with this situation is to become rigid, introverted, and withdrawn. When she comes out of this situation, she has the potential to turn out supremely confident, positive, fulfilled, self-sufficient, instinctive, independent, and open. Every man has a divine feminine within. Every woman has Godly masculinity within her. In realizing this, a woman and man become more assertive, innovative, responsible, admirable, strong, and balanced. The relationship of a truly healthy couple is magnetic. Their bond is not defined by demeanor, bodily form, or any roles they are expected to play. Against all odds, they maintain consistent and steady energy of friendship, stability, dependability, boldness, opalescence, because they truly love. Such lovers are unique and fortunate, inspiring and ideal, beneficial and rewarding, for themselves and the society.

As long as the intentions and choices you make now are pure, the efforts you make will lead you to centeredness and togetherness. Knowledge, guided by a righteous path is of true value. Any action that is carefully planned with patience and faith will pan out well and lead you to wealth, glory, and abundance. So, celebrate nature and the changing highs and lows of life. Do not get distant or bogged down by hurdles and obstacles that may come your way.

You have nothing to worry about, as you have the personal blessings of the holy beings watching out for you. The entire universe is ensuring you stay rooted and secure, just the way nature ensures that roses and lilies stay rooted in your garden, to bring to you the message of ultimate spiritual attainment with their divine fragrance. Love, laugh, and live in the now.

We take the liberty of taking the SUPREME for granted. The supreme is like a jumbled up crossword puzzle, glimpses of its truth get revealed to anyone open to know its power. Everything we seek out to prove and validate begins with an underlying faith and presumption. We first intuitively believe and PRESUME a thing to be true, then we boldly seek out to verify its existence and to get it accepted.

If you un-jumble 'Supreme', you get the word 'presume'. We call intuition, a mere presumption- only until it is validated. Once it is backed with adequate proof, it becomes supreme knowledge. In this way what I presume carries the seed of the ultimate supreme wisdom. To presume is the fabric upon which our society rests. Yet we say that we do not accept anything that is merely presumed. Sometimes proving its existence and validating the truth takes eons and by that time the boat would have long sailed. Many legends have gone unnoticed, many innocent people have been victimized, and many kings have died as poppers carrying the burden of your doubt and disbelief.

A PURE SEER is a MUSER and a SUPER MUSE of the SUPREME who carefully PERUSE through visions, PEER through insights to SEEP the SUM of information for the USER to REUSE when matters SEEM SERE and un-SURE. So USE ME to know more about who to SUE rather than laden your heart with more RUE.

Affirm- 'Namostutee, time, purpose, and circumstances do not stop a one-pointed yogini to continue on her quest for truth towards the path of perfection. I am positive, self-composed, loving, generous, kind, and honest to my purpose and pursuit just as the untainted yogini. Tathaastu.'

CHAPTER 161

PRIMER

Your kidneys are your foundation, the way the basement is the foundation of your home. Keep them clean and hydrated.

Possession of jewels, gold, expensive metals give us prosperity, make us feel physically secure and energetically wealthy. It is no wonder that deep within the earth's ground, we find the most potent and precious metals. Learning from this natural phenomenon, most banks have lockers in their basement. Based on the same model, ancestral homes, buildings, temples in India store gold and jewels deep within the vaults closest to earth in their basements.

My grandfather taught engineering at Benares University, India, and the first brick that was laid in this university before Indo-Pak partition was a solid brick of pure gold. The foundation goldstone was blessed by many high scholars of the time and it still is a very prestigious university. Our body too has a basement that stores our wealth and serves as a foundation of our physical and material wealth. This basement is called the *mooladhara* or *sthir* chakra. If this chakra is in balance - our material body is activated and healthy, which in turn helps us to exert physical effort, outside of our comfort zone to become prosperous.

There is no negativity-inside or outside of you-that can't be transmuted through the blessing of pure love. Yet it is better to strengthen our energy bodies and to stay protected and primed to be doubly safe. Any misuse of sacred knowledge can ruin your growth. This is why the information is kept secret in the inner worlds from those who aren't yet ready to receive it.

The Solar plexus or *dharm* is the point that activates our emotional body. The heart or *karm* is the point that activates our astral body. *Ajna* (the master chakra) is the point that activates our mental body. The throat or *pattra* is the point that activates our true body. The forehead is the point that activates our intuitional body. The *mooladhara* or *sthir* chakra is the point that activates our material body.

What I enjoy most about knowledge is that it destroys ignorance. I am therefore attempting to bring your attention towards consciousness and sacred soundness. Knowledge gives us the intellectual strength to find a fresh and new approach while facing any obstacle or difficulty. This way it reconnects and transforms us miraculously and guides us towards the true purpose of life most unconventionally and uniquely.

To stay protected, do not accept food from anyone during dreaming or in waking, especially when you know the energies of your etheric body are in the transmutation stage. Even when you are protected by the divine hands, there could be situations that lead to dismay, anxiety, anger, or resentment. These situations can break your protective webs, so it is better to first strengthen yourself through intensive visualization, meditation, and breathing techniques. This way you can remain unaffected by external situations and maintain your internal peace.

Spiritual protection makes you etherically even stronger. It is indestructible and invincible because it is made by the divine itself. Once you connect with the divine within you through spirituality and faith, nothing and no one can break or harm you. Practice verbal, physical, and mental non-violence, not only towards others but also towards yourself. Every weakening thought-form or curse word directed towards others becomes the cause of your suffering and pain. Practice all the virtues for your own sake. Keep all your bodies at all levels cleansed, purified and empty, so that you can assimilate the guidance you receive from the higher teachings. Whether you are fast asleep or awake, you know you have been initiated into becoming a medium who is here to serve, help and evolve. So continue to use your discriminative intelligence, self-determination of mind, and action. Remain patient, cheerful, disciplined, sincere, and focused.

Be careful and mindful of what you desire, because you are now in a place where you manifest what you desire and believe.

Material things are a medium of pleasure. Sometimes we go overboard with giving material things and our physical body more importance than it requires. This over-attachment causes a lot of misery, delusion, and suffering. Do charity, avoid pride, and enjoy your remaining wealth in moderation, realizing fully well that your main priority lies in soul enrichment.

Affirm- 'Namostutee, I purify my body with good deeds. I adore my energetic body. In loving my body, I love the charisma of everything within and outside it. Tathaastu.'

CHAPTER 162

FLUSHED OUT

As you allow the snowman sitting inside your mind to come back to life, all your memories come flashing and flushing back to life with it. As you become open to remolding, everything within you adapts as well. Certain yogis can comfortably live naked even in below-freezing temperatures. Cold is merely the absence of heat. When the heat within is ignited, no force outside of you has any effect on your internal temperature. Cold or hot, a pure soul remains warm and comfortable at all times.

There are many beautiful trees out there that bear poisonous fruits, but those fruits have a vital purpose. There is good in evil too. We have over four million sweat glands. Just as snakes do, we too release the toxicity within us through our sweat. The more we sweat, the more dominance, regularity, balance, and connectedness we have over our energies and those around us. This on/off, in/out the switch of sweating is our fight-or-flight response to toxins, so that we can relax by cooling off the excess heat in us, which can be very stressful, overwhelming, and exhausting at times. Being made of 99% water and 1% salt, our sweat in itself is odorless, but when mixed internally with our fats and proteins, and externally with all the bacteria, dust, and grime around, it gives out an odor. We call this odor either sweet, spicy, floral, or stinky. Based on how much its fragrance entices, resonates, or mingles with us, we appreciate its smell and move closer to it.

Shed your attachments. Use up your energy sparingly and wisely. Bathe every morning to wash off last night's toxicity from the clothes you wore yesterday, and to let the waters in. Change your attire as many times as you please in the day, but before starting yet another new day, with all those fresh memories, remember to always leave a little freedom and room in between your weary clothes and your skin, so that your sweat can escape and be flushed out in case it needs a release.

Our five senses-ears, eyes, nose, tongue, and skin-are closest to our body, so their functions, movements, density, and brightness can be clearly explained even by a toddler. Each of our senses has corresponding planets-Mercury for the nose, Venus for the tongue, Mars for the ears, Jupiter for the eyes, and Saturn for the skin-these are the brightest and the most visible to our naked eye. This doesn't mean that more planets and more senses do not exist! These higher senses, which are beyond our five senses, might not be as easily accessible. Just as planets like Uranus and Neptune are further from the earth's body, our higher senses are further from our physical body, and therefore not easily visible or accessible.

Mercury is swift, always active, and ever fresh like our breath, and so it is our nose. Venus appreciates the taste of true beauty and the essence of the wholesome words we speak in different languages through our tongue. Mars is red and loud like the thundering noises and subtle sounds we hear, which impact us through our ears. Jupiter gives us an expanded view of the world around us through the innermost lens of our wide-open eyes. Saturn makes us feel the hot and cold vibrations through our skin. Just the way each sense has an impact and influence on the other, each planetary disposition affects and intermingles with the other.

The wise Sun resides outside and also within the depth of our inner eye. It is in the center of our brain, while the Moon and its phases help us reflect and perceive the world through the windows of our outer eye.

Affirm- 'Namostutee, I bless the entire universe with tremendous faith, happiness, strength, prayerfulness, brightness, compassion, and forgiveness. Tathaastu.'

CHAPTER 163

VITAMIN F (FAITH)

The turtle goes inside its shell for protection. Turtles cannot survive without its shell. When the spirit merges with the body, it seems it can no longer survive without the body. The spirit and the body of a yogi, the inner and the outer voice are one. Both speak the same language.

Life exists forever in its various manifestations and forms because of life energy. And that energy is perennially vitalized only because the supreme creator of love, light, and power walks untiringly and equally amongst us humans who are the kings of this earthly jungle and all the other beings. The Supreme is not just a subtle but also an active force. Some people choose not to believe in its power, and so remain deluded and entangled in their impressions. All you have to do is to believe in yourself. Believe in true love and with that spirit of faith - against all odds, it will come to you, when the time is right. The choices we make define us.

Nothing ends until or unless you do. Be grateful and let the magic begin. Everything happens for a reason. Those who believe in themselves and speak their truth, transcend all miseries and insecurities. Every new beginning is perfect, completely free and unbound.

Life goes on and we start to think we are indispensable. The fact is that others can live without you and so can you. That doesn't mean that our life should begin and end with ourselves. When we transcend, transform ourselves, and experience life through a larger lens we become part of something much bigger and brighter than ourselves.

True worship, faith, and quality of living is a life spent in glorifying, praising, accepting, enriching, and inspiring another through action. Appreciating another can be done with or without words. A forgiving, loving smile and a kind approving nod from the mother sometimes speak louder than words. Everyone is just as special as your child is to you. All lives matter. Let us thank our supreme nurturer - earth for supporting, grounding, and stimulating our energy, strength, and stamina.

You have endured long enough and in this last phase, some of you might feel that something is lost from within you but let these thoughts disappear. Avoid dwelling in matters that do not serve your true purpose. Disengage from negativity completely. Don't let the snow crush or numb your mind in desperation. Ask the universal God to give you the strength to shovel the snow outside your home, the faith and courage to accept the internal toil that comes after. Stay rooted and remain stable to fulfill your purpose. You are the lucky ones, celebrate aliveness once the winters are over. Remain grateful, patient, and helpful.

One of the high points in my life was when I went to Burj Khalifa, the tallest building in the world. If I had not taken the elevator to the topmost floor, I would have not experienced the expansive view of Dubai and its glittering lights. There I saw the image of Dubai before and after. In much the same way to reach the high point of life, and to see how far you have traveled from your past, you have to elevate yourself from the ground floor to the topmost floor. I would have missed getting a glimpse of the cycle of past, present and future had I not believed in the higher energy that uplifted me. I believe there are many more high points awaiting to be explored.

Body asked the Soul "Why did you make it look like I did everything?"
Soul answered "Because we are One"
Soul asked God "Why did you make it look like I did everything?"
God answered "Because we are One"
God asked the Spirit "Why did you make it look like I did everything?"
Spirit answered "Because we are One"
Finally confused the:
Body asked the pure Spirit "Why did you make it look like we three (Body, Soul & God) did everything?"
Spirit answered "Because we all are One"

Faith can move mountains. With a little dose of Vitamin F, we get the ability to surpass any difficulties. The trials and turbulences are our greatest teachers. They are here to teach us to continuously improvise and harness our skills.

Affirm- 'Namostutee, the higher power knows and plans better than I do. I follow the plan set by the higher power for my evolution. With this faith, I am forever filled with hope and a renewed sense of purpose. Tathaastu.'

CHAPTER 164

OUT OF THE COCOON OF DELUSION

O ut of the cocoon of delusion lies the joy of eternal life. As it rained, the silkworms asked those around to lend their stoles, but they all refused in an instant. Their refusal became the silkworm's greatest victory, for it taught the silkworm to weave the finest silks by itself.

It is wise to be family-oriented. It is smart to be caring. A pure soul trusts, forgives, loves, helps, endures, and nurtures you, as long as you do not test the limits of their piety. Be open to receiving love but also be wise not to lose yourself in love. The treasure you have been searching for is hidden somewhere in the closet of your body behind the layers of delusion and seclusion.

There is a cupboard in my parental home. I spent most of my youth in that room. The last time I visited my parents, for the summer holidays, I unpacked my luggage to place it on the shelves. I noticed a tiny drawer behind the middle shelf. On opening it I saw lots of pictures of our childhood memories. This drawer led me to another drawer which had unsent letters written by me and my sister and lots of my scribbled notes. This led me to another drawer that had old silver, gold coins, and bejeweled bangles that looked as if they were from the Mughal era. Some coins had holes in them that I converted into a pendant to wear around my neck.

I could see the paint chipping on the sides, it seemed the drawers were endless and every corner of the cupboard had some hidden memories, it seemed as if some life was hidden within them. These memories are what my mother and grandmother live by. Our physical body is like the outer shelf of that cupboard, it has all the fancy designer clothes we adorn ourselves with. When we sort the shelf to de-clutter the old rags, we dig deeper and find emotions hidden which takes us to our childhood memories and reminds us of who we really are behind these veils. When we connect with our soul, we realize that we move the time, time doesn't move us.

We see the picture of our first pet dog and it reminds us that it has no concept of time. When you meet your dog after two seconds, two minutes, after two hours, or after two days - they respond to your homecoming with equal excitement and zest. We call them silly and dumb but they know no better.

Ask any thirsty man, even two seconds of soul separation seems like a lifetime. It is then that we begin to unravel more and find more drawers - this time our mind leads us to a drawer cluttered with scribbled, unedited, disorderly notes waiting for some clarity, waiting to hear the conclusion of those thousands of unsaid stories. We begin our mental search right from the scratch only to realize that no matter where we reach, here we are. Attachment leads us to detachment. Even when we reach the drawer which has all the ancestral jewels, we realize they no longer lure us for we feel that having contributed so little we are not the rightful heir to the royal throne.

We become further detached, only to attach ourselves once again to our body, our soul, our emotions, our mind, our psyche, our spirit, our truth and that is when we speak fearlessly about who we are, as we are, that is when we are truly reborn.

When all the memories come flashing, we revisit the pain and the pleasure each stage brings us, the unlearned lessons are learned and the coded messages are decoded. We see ourselves as if from outside of our selves. The view is the same, only the vision dramatically shifts. We meet with ourselves and that is when we die to live yet another life filled with truth because no lie can settle here in these drawers. No termite can ever eat up the memories and reach that last drawer. You are the only one meant to access that unopened drawer that lies there waiting to become a part of your life to make it more lifelike. It was always you, it was you all through, it was never another, you are the source, you are the giver, behind all the drawers you find everything is as it is.

Nothing has changed, nothing ever will, the story remains the same, only the eyes with which you see, the ears with which you hear, the language you speak has changed. Character is the same, what has changed is only the name. Rest everything is as it is. Fame or not, It all remains the same.

All the oxygen and energy you require is not in the pills you pop but above the holy hills where you may sit atop. The harsh winds are all gone, the road blockages are clear. Time for the snail to come out of its shell, there is nothing to dismay, you may be soft but here you are vigorous, in the pink and divinely protected.

The journey from human to the divine:

Vajra Nadi is lustrous and has sun-like energy (emerald).

Chitra Nadi is pure and has moon-like energy (blue).

Brahma Nadi is central and has the energy of both (fiery red).

All these three originate in a triangular area pointing to the west (Kanda Mulla in *Sthapana* chakra) between the cervix and the vagina. Kanda has a cavity so that energy can enter in. *Prakriti* is our mother whose purpose is to serve the *Purusha* (higher mind). Mind (*Purusha*) and soul (*Atman*) together are absolute. They are not distinct from one another. Mother Nature (*Prakriti)* tirelessly feeds the mind (*Purusha*) with experiences which the (*Atman*) soul stores. When the purpose of *Prakriti* (Mother Nature) is over, it rests in its true nature while the body and father mind (*Purusha*) take over. This way you become the witnesser of your actions. Finally, a day comes when based on your *karma kanda* (assigned role) you and your mind (*Purusha*) become one.

Affirm- 'Namostutee, my mind is steady only because I put in the effort to regularly, virtuously, and honestly practice all the precepts set by the shining Supreme God. Tathaastu.'

CHAPTER 165

VERUM ERGO SUM – TRUTH I AM

As I continued to dance post the forty-one nights, 'Truth I am' was the tune of the song that played in the background. The lyrics of the song were written by me though I was in another realm, here I am not much of a singer. Stories remain the same, only their meaning change. Names remain the same, only the forms or soul of people change.

अरसों पहले जिस नूरजहाँ को दफना दिया था आपने
वो आज भी आपकी उन दीवारों के पीछे खड़ी है
आपको जिसकी खोज है, आपको जिसका इंतज़ार है, वो आपके ही महल के अन्दर उस आखिरी ईंट के तले दबी पड़ी है!
आज आप उस दीवार को पहचान नहीं पा रहे, कल वो आपको पहचान लेगी!
चुनवाया गया था उसको मगर कुदरत का करिश्मा देखो - आज आपको फिर ज़रुरत पड़ी है उसकी! दीवार के तलेदफनाई गयी है वो मगर अरसों बाद आपकी एक पुकार से, आज़ाद वो आपको करवाने आई है!
जेल में वो बंद है मगर कैद तो आप हैं, रूह है वो आपकी उसके बिना आप तो केवल एक शरीर हैं!

Arso pehle jis nooreh jahan ko dhafna diya tha aapne, woh aaj bhi apke un diwaro ke peeche khadi hai. Aapko jiski khoj hain, aapko jiska intezaar hain woh aap hi ke mahal ke andar us aakhree eenth ke talley dabi padi hain. Aaj us diwaar ko aap pehchaan nahi pa rahe, kal woh aapko pahechaan le Gee. Chunwaa Gaya tha usko Magar kudrat ka karishma Dekho Aaj aapko Phir zaroorat padi hain uske, diwaar ke tale dhawnayee Gaye hain woh magar aarso baad Apki ek pukaar se, aazad woh aapko karwaney aiey hain. Jail mein woh band hain magar Kaidey to aap hain. Ruah hain woh aapki, uske Bina aap to kewal ek sharir hain.

Translated to English

In the bygone era, the Noor Jahan whom you buried is still standing erect behind the walls you built to bury her. What have you been searching for? What you have been waiting for is right under your nose, in your palace it lies buried right under the last brick of your material hunger. Today you are too muddled up in worldly ways to recognize her but tomorrow she will seek you out and will recognize you. See the miracle of nature that despite the fact you buried her, today you need her, seek her, and want her beside you. Today years & years after you buried her, tormented her soul yet she is responding to your one call. Today she is coming to break your shackles and free you from your prison. Although you enclosed her in the prison you are the prisoner, it is your constant companion, it is your soul, and it is you just you and your conscious…. Without her, you are a mere physical body that decays.

Let's get naked - clothes are for our protection. When these layers cease to give us protection and delude us more than cover us, maybe it is time to uncover them. When being so layered up clogs our skin and soul, leaving us breathless and parched - it is time to get naked and speak our truth. *Verum Ergo Sum* - Truth I am.

Just the way a person born blind can never completely know what having eyesight is like, a person who has never led a stress-free life would never know what it is like to live without stress. It takes courage to move beyond mental conditioning and physical positioning. Those who do take up the challenge to see what is outside of the dream are the ones who get illuminated and enlightened with new heightened experiences and meta-cognizance. This way they re-waken and meet with their real self, it's like seeing yourself in the mirror for the first time. Until now you had no awareness of how special you are. This strange experience leads you to your absolute reality. This truth is *Verum ergo sum.*

Remove the coatings of paint from the walls, carefully remove the window panes, the locked doors and dismantle the palace (body) brick by brick, behind the walls somewhere you will find *Mumtaz Mahal*[136], the jewel of the palace who died with the pressure of trying to give birth to the infant that was more beautiful than any lotus. Somewhere you will find

---

[136] *Mumtaz, Noor Jehan's niece is our heart center through which comes out intense devotional love and with it comes the colicky pains of the unborn baby.*

Noor Jehan, the light of the world that was buried alive waiting to be woken up to bring back the glory and power we all deserve.

But once the war of duality is over and *Noor Jehan*[137] (soul center or kanth) meets her husband (spirit within the crown center/ creative power center/ third eye/ 21 chakra/ soul seat) as it's released once again, the unborn child (creation / 22 chakra/ spiritual heart or *hridya*) is reborn. Everything is crystal clear from this point on. This is when the journey truly begins.

The problem of today's civilized society is the feeling of lack of entitlement. Even when everything is laid out in the open for all to freely access, we hesitate to pick some wealth up for ourselves because of self-inflicted fear of what others will think. We have a lack of self-worth, in the name of self-identity, obscurity, mistrust, laziness, superstition, or so-called morals. There are so many people out there waiting to give but no receivers ever come forward. Givers and receivers are one, what belongs to one also belongs to another. You do not know what you deserve. When others give you your rightful share, it is given to you because they care. Yet you do not take your share because you feel that it was not written on the will for you. An unwritten will belongs to all, much like sleeping beauty whoever taps the wealth first, whoever kisses the sleeping beauty on her lips, fuses with her prized ethereal charm and gets all the precious jewels. It is not a rat race or a mad race, each one keeps bumping their heads against one another. There is no race any longer for no one wants to run any longer. No one thinks they can be the winners. Even the one holding the first prize is self-doubting his credentials. Everyone is hiding in their dark holes, suspecting and waiting to be suspected. No one is digging in to see the positive worth of immaculate jewels that lay ahead. No one is harming one another, for each person is busy harming their own selves.

Truth cannot be confined to the four walls of your room. Like creeper plants, we are perennially attempting to identify ourselves with this or that, latching on to whatever craze comes next, that in the process we forget who we are. We lose our identity and when we do find it - we realize the attachment to our name, fame, family, work, nationality, beliefs, thoughts, feelings are not our identity because we inherently are identity-less,

---

[137] *Noor Jehan sits below our crown and forehead center (secondary throat or kanth/ 20th chakra) through which comes out piercing wisdom light and courage to slain the most dangerous tigers with the sword of its words blessed both by the forehead and will center.*

nameless, and shameless. Truth is free to be what and who it wants to be wherever, whenever at any time, place, or space. Truth much like bliss cannot be contained for long, it stays where it wants to and as long as it wants to, based on its fancy.

Trying to trap water or dry sand in the grip of your hands is a futile effort. Both water and sand are like life and time, they will always find a way out. This is simple, precise, minuscule, and pure fact.

After all my journeys, when I close my eyes - I can see myself as that free three-year-old little girl walking freely at the park, climbing mango trees in the backyard of my home, with my imaginary friend bubbles dressed in blue. The innocent game of hide-n-seek we played and the toys made of *chikni mitti* are still lying in the same place where we left them. You can always pick life from where you left it, nothing is ever lost in love and life. Pleasure and pain are only mediums. Heaven is your final destination and that weightless heaven is right here within you waiting to see you joyfully dance once again like the shining dewdrop. Bliss I am. Truth I am.

Sometimes you identify so much with your eternal truth that it becomes your absolute reality. When you realize all this is but a passing test and come out of the exam room of this worldly trance that is when verity bites and you realize the truth is even more beautiful than the dream you have been living. Out of everything delusory, there is one thing that truly belongs to you and that is your truth. It comes and introduces itself in a clear, sharp, transparent voice and says, Hello! I am truth. I am beauty. I am balance. Your truth is also mine. Everything that belongs to you also belongs to me. Nothing is yours alone, it is for us all to share and enjoy. Truth is one and so is bliss. The outer and inner package is one, the water of the coconut, its cream, its shell - all belong to the coconut, beyond duality is the realization of the oneness of the ultimate trinity.

Forty-one nights had passed, when I opened my eyes-everything was still where it was, I just saw them with a different pair of fresh eyes. I picked up from where I left. With every transition, I let go of a lot that was in and outside of me and that cleansing naturally served as a purification medium.

Every attachment led me to detachment, and every detachment led me to value the true worth of my body, energy, emotions, mind, soul, things, relationships, and the spirit inside and outside of me. I started to freely dance once again only this time I was more aware. I let the madness flow out only this time I was consciously mad, the beauty remained the same but the choice to let my hair down was completely mine.

Time to purify your thoughts–it can create confusion–feeling of enlightenment–create insanity or a false sense of royalty–Remember who you are and enjoy the blessedness–you will realize you will soon be back where it all started. If you draw with a white pen on a white background then nothing will be visible. This is the reason why God chose to draw and create our bodies against a dark and dense background. This way our whiteness and purity is brought out despite the dark background.

Each cell of our body has a mind of its own. Each of the 7.2 million nadis in our body has a consciousness of its own. Truth is always simplistic, direct, pristine, and easy to comprehend- we complicate it. I dropped a message into the time capsule of wisdom many years back and 25 years later the message came back to me in the same shape and form. Spiritual evolution makes you realize the physical reality you unintentionally concealed under the wraps of time perhaps to entertain yourself. Sometimes we purposely choose to lose the keys to test the efficacy of our romance with the truth. No matter how far you may go or how many years you choose to lock the truth within the chambers of the room whose key you lost-fast forward many years, the charisma, innocence, and essence of deeper truth always remains the same.

Clean and empty your mind of criticism, judgement and prejudice. Worship, celebrate and revere what is next to you right now rather than waiting for it all to go away. All this glory, knowledge and job that you strive for, acquire and aspire is of no use at all in any other realm but here. Live in the present. There is no better gift and no greater jewel than the person sitting next to you and the flower blooming in your garden right now. All the treasures are within you. In compassionately meeting with them you will meet with one aspect of yourself.

True prosperity comes with first valuing what you have. If you do not harness what is clearly visible and perceptible then how will you work with the deeper truths that provide insight beyond ordinary sight. *Verum ergo sum* is the most valid means of acquiring knowledge of your truth, it fits perfectly and precisely to the tee not just on one level but on all levels. Progress happens little by little. A child doesn't become eighty right when he is born, there is no reason to haste. Stop all waste and be grateful and content. If you think you are ready to look within, energy healers and spiritual guides like me are always here to help you reconnect with your truth.

Affirm- 'Namostutee, May we all develop keen insight, respect for wisdom, good moral character, generous heart, love for all, disciplined and responsible attitude. May we all be released from all bondage. Tathaastu.'

CHAPTER 166

SALT OF LIFE

I am as ungraspable and liberated as pure consciousness. I am a drop in the vast ocean. But the ocean is expansive, and so this drop is ever-expanding with the ocean. In this way, the drop has merged with the ocean. I am a part and also the whole of the ocean. Without the ocean I am identity-less just the way without all its drops, the ocean is identity-less. But even if one drop remains, the entire ocean remains. This my friend is existence, we never cease to exist because one drop always remains. That drop now carries the blueprint of the entire ocean within itself. Just the way earlier the ocean carried the identity of a tiny drop within itself. There are no dualities for a person who has merged with pure consciousness. Such a liberated person has the entire trinity within itself. Moral, material, and sensual are contained within the spiritual. Soul, body, and mind are contained within one. All five are in sole drop.

This book will assist you in unfolding the path towards higher dimensions. Its purpose is to reveal marvelous secrets so that you can trust the devoted divine beings who are here to guard and help you unearth your inner truth. Remain calm, your time to embrace your uniqueness will arrive.

The filament is enclosed within a bulb. As you switch on the electric wire, attached to it, the light within the filament gets switched on by the electric currents that pass through it. Our entire surroundings then get illuminated with the light coming out from that small filament inside the bulb. The light brings such outer clarity that you can now see clearly with your eyes. Not all wavelengths are equally effective at stimulating the vision of your eye because not only are you dependent upon the efficiency of the light bulb, but your perception of light is based on your innate faculties and ability to see the unseen.

Similarly, words are enclosed within the pages of this book. As you switch on the screen of your computer and scroll through the pages attached to the file, your entire mind gets illuminated with the light of knowledge coming through the intellect of the small words on the screen which act as an electric transformer. The light brings such inner clarity that you can now see with your inward vision, without getting trapped or weighed down by the inner darkness of the depressive feelings or unwholesome thoughts. Not all mental wavelengths are equally effective at stimulating the vision of your mind's eye because not only are you dependent upon the efficiency of the writer, but your perception is based on the level of your innate disposition and willingness to know the unknown.

There are a lot of blackened filaments lying wasted in the universal trash bin because they have yet to realize their indestructible power. We all have one such filament within our brain, waiting to get realized and immortalized through proper and efficient use of wisdom. It takes many hands to change the universal light bulb. Ask yourself, am I ready to be one of those hands?

I am an experienced energy healer who understands the voice of natural cosmic energies that does not speak with most beings. However, all you have to do is remember to hear and share. I trust that my initiative in writing this little book will reach the right readers and give them the correct interpretation of the message, in time, so that they do not lose faith in themselves.

'Mere namak ka karz utaro' is a Hindi saying which implies free yourself of the debts of my salt. If this book has left the slightest impact on you, pay it forward by sharing it with those you connect with.

Right from the horse's mouth, this book is a raw and unedited version of the writer's understanding, expressed in her own words. This book is a book of fiction for people who consider the writings as untrue and a myth for those who believe the writings are imaginative. This book is a book of truth for those whose consciousness connects with the sacred truth written within. This book is a book of life in my view. And just as life itself, my view is subject to constant change based on what evolutionary phase we are in. Please do not believe anything written in these pages to be true unless your divine intuition permits you. May you enjoy reading as much as I enjoyed writing it. May it make as much of a positive impact on your life as writing it made in mine. All those who have read this book have touched the mind and soul of this book in some way or another.

Let the publication of this book be in the name of the greater good. With the onset of the renewed golden Coronorian era of 2021, may we all in the coming months renew our energies with compassion and expansion. The key to the door is in realizing the oneness within all. See you all on the other side of the rainbow bridge.

There is divinity in you and there is divinity in me. Salute not only in the divinity within others but also in the divinity within yourself. The Yogini wearing stilettos is immensely grateful from the deepest core of her heart to all those who blessed her with their precious time reading all or any of the words inscribed. May you be the salt of the earth. Thank you, thank you, and thank you.

Affirm- 'Namostutee, I am that bulb which dispels darkness into light. In this way one by one, we can all illuminate the whole world by switching on our little bulb. We are all lit bulbs. Tathaastu.'

ABOUT THE AUTHOR

Stutee is a philosopher, a counselor, and a certified Pranic healer. As a spiritual practitioner for over a decade, she has successfully healed many advanced cases ranging from cancer, autoimmune diseases, autism, and bipolar disorder using crystal and color therapy. She is here to bring harmony into your life by reconnecting you with your true purpose and potential.

After completing a Master's degree in philosophy from Delhi University and a Post-Graduation in Public Relations- she started her career as a founding team member of Max healthcare in Delhi, India. As a member of the Max Healthcare team, she worked with a team to revolutionize the health care system in India delivering international-class healthcare and a fulfilling environment for patients. She further went on to work with YKK design in the human resource and training department giving high impetus to accelerating employee growth. She also worked with famous hotels in India namely Park Hotel, Kolkata, and Taj hotel, Chennai as a service manager.

Additionally, she has worked in the recruitment industry by setting up offices of leading placement consultancies in India. She tirelessly progresses towards the continuous evolvement of self and others. As the song goes, 'Where-ever I lay my hat that's my home", she has lived in various countries - India, Oman, UAE, Bahrain and now resides in NY, USA.

The richness of her experience, knowledge, and sacred wisdom enables her to better understand the needs of people from different cultures, professions, and backgrounds. Stutee specializes in balancing energies of your body on a physical, psychological, financial, and spiritual level. Using Feng-Shui tips and etheric cleansing, she balances the energy of your home and office. She helps build a more wholesome future for you and all those around as she loves to enjoy a graceful dance with the celestial angels and cosmic stars. She explores and travels in the inner and outer world with complete equanimity and poise.

Stutee is also the founder of True Bliss Healing with a mission to uplift people through improved health, healing, and in-depth coaching.

In her own words – 'I come from ancestral roots where education and science are given impetus, with family members who are highly acclaimed engineers and doctors. There was little room left for me to harness my lateral thinking in an environment of linear belief systems. Growing up, I naturally felt unheard while trying to get my abstract concepts through to them mainly because it transcended beyond the understanding of their world. My quest for truth made me go into a deep inward journey where I could practically and experientially validate the potency of my intuitive wisdom. My wings began to form as I continued my quest further. As a devoted wife and a mother, I value friendships, relationships and believe that 'to serve is to love' making it my mission to help empower people to experience the grace of inward and outward transformation."

Wait no longer and connect for a heart to heart session with Stutee.

PREVIEW

S ilence is only in the words. The universe has been talking all through. It constantly sends messages to our wonderland called earth. The entire cosmos is but a mirror. We put a veil in front of the mirror and say we cannot see the reflection.

Before transforming the world, first, transform yourself. Feel the love within you. Then your presence will effortlessly bring divine peace and uplift those who connect with you. If your soul sprinkles seeds of care and love wherever you go, you will harvest a tree filled with like qualities. Stay rooted, stay connected, keep sharing and keep loving. I love therefore I am. Love is all.

Every experience, whether painful or pleasurable, every mistake, now or later, eventually teaches you something. Everything gets imprinted in your DNA, in the making of you and who you currently are. The love you have is meant to fall like fairy dust upon all. The magic wand is with you, it is rested in your very being, just sprinkle it quickly. When you communicate with your love through your higher self, the love on earth is the same as the love in heaven. Serve and give others as much love, time, value, and worth as you give to yourself. The light within you is of no use until the light is ignited within all.

The palindrome of evil is live - time to reverse the evil and live. "To evolve is to live. To live is to love. To love is to evolve". Try to learn, practice, grow, and evolve, for only you can.

Things are never as they seem. One person associates wine with headache and another associates it with pleasure, and in the process what seems to us, based on our association or dis-association, the actual grape of the matter goes out of the window.

We live to give.
We love to give.

We give to live.

We give to love.

We love to live. It is simple logic

Misplaced vanity deprives us of humility.

Misplaced humility deprives us of modesty.

Misplaced modesty deprives us of accepting the importance of our role as an important part of humanity

You are a collective of all years and all the incidents that take place. As you approach this book, you are taking a step back and cleaning your mind of all the incidents that have taken place. These are especially the ones that no longer serve you positively. In cleansing your mind, you have come a full circle. In connecting the dots and moving to the point of origination you become more creative and productive. Thank you for reconnecting with yourself and making yourself feel so special.

True confidence effortlessly comes through marrying yourself, and consistently staying committed to this divine marriage. The realization and acknowledgment that both aspects of your personality-the visible and invisible, outer and inner, conscious and subconscious, dream and reality-are all one wholesome reality that goes into creating you. All marriages are made in heaven and have a divine purpose. The same divine purpose that causes two elements to meet, to create heaven on earth, is the one responsible for couples to marry.

Primordial substance and its transmutations imply that all living things on this planet are connected as a single spiritual entity. There is a gem in my third eye that is perennially in contact with the Lord God. He has instructed me about the primordial life and its varied transmutations, my life journey over the eons, and what is to come. He has given me vital information to be revealed well in time. I am his devoted, humble messenger and through him, I am here to heal, purify, and uplift you. Let us all welcome the golden age with a smile in our hearts, together in harmony. Wisdom is profound and innocent - this is a message I received during my trance-state. Life without love and love without life is incomplete. An amalgam and appreciation of these two opposite forces complete us. No matter how far you stretch the rubber band, it finally goes back to right where it belonged. The uncoupling of earth and heaven, West and East, bad and good is a phantasm. Until the two meet, we will remain entrapped within the delusion and maze of the enchanted forest which has no outlet.

It is only when you celebrate yourself do you let others mingle with your colors and celebrate you. It is only when you enjoy the fantastic gifts that you have that you can share them with another. When you are at peace with yourself others feel the peace in being with you. We can wear any amount of masks and become anyone we want to be. Masks may change but the inner light will remain the same. No mask can stop you and your light from shining outwards. Truth is like light. Light has no beginning or end. There is light within our minds. This light illuminates us from within and is ever awake. Our soul doesn't sleep or rest, our body does. It is free and unbound. Most of what we know is already known to us. To learn more, we must try to remember to remember. Sometimes through excessively concentrating on one question, we forget the ability to perceive the obvious answer which is right in front of us. Life is simple, we make it complex. Sanity lies in simply living a life of discipline, routine, love, and balance. All answers are simple, you have not been given any task that is bigger than you. When you empty your mind, emotions, and body of all the junk, all answers are melodiously fluted through you. A precious pearl remains protected within its shell in the deep waters but its beauty is appreciated only when it comes out in the open. In every day there is a hidden night. Once you open yourself up to the light, the night will become day.

*****With reverence to GrandMaster Choa Kok Sui, Medicine Buddha and Paramhansa Yogananda*****